POETRY
for Students

Advisors

Jayne M. Burton is a teacher of English, a member of the Delta Kappa Gamma International Society for Key Women Educators, and currently a master's degree candidate in the Interdisciplinary Study of Curriculum and Instruction and English at Angelo State University.

Mary Beth Maggio teaches seventh grade language arts in Schaumburg, Illinois.

Tom Shilts is the youth librarian at the Okemos branch of Capital Area District Library in Okemos, Michigan. He holds an MSLS degree from Clarion University of Pennsylvania and an MA in U.S. History from the University of North Dakota.

Amy Spade Silverman has taught at independent schools in California, Texas, Michigan, and New York. She holds a bachelor of arts degree from the University of Michigan and a master of fine arts degree from the University of Houston. She is a member of the National Council of Teachers of English and Teachers and Writers. She is an exam reader for Advanced Placement Literature and Composition. She is also a poet, published in *North American Review*, *Nimrod*, and *Michigan Quarterly Review*, among others.

Mary Turner holds a BS in Secondary Education from East Texas State University and a Master of Education from Western Kentucky University. She teaches English 7 and AP English 12 literature and composition at SBEC in Southaven, Mississippi.

Brian Woerner teaches English at Troy High School in Troy, Ohio. He is also a Program Associate of the Ohio Writing Project at Miami University.

POETRY
for Students

Presenting Analysis, Context, and Criticism
on Commonly Studied Poetry

VOLUME 39

Sara Constantakis, Project Editor

Foreword by David J. Kelly

 GALE
CENGAGE Learning·

Detroit · New York · San Francisco · New Haven, Conn · Waterville, Maine · London

Poetry for Students, Volume 39

Project Editor: Sara Constantakis

Rights Acquisition and Management:
Margaret Chamberlain-Gaston

Composition: Evi Abou-El-Seoud

Manufacturing: Rhonda Dover

Imaging: John Watkins

Product Design: Pamela A. E. Galbreath,
Jennifer Wahi

Content Conversion: Katrina Coach

Product Manager: Meggin Condino

For product information and technology assistance, contact us at
Gale Customer Support, 1-800-877-4253.
For permission to use material from this text or product,
submit all requests online at **www.cengage.com/permissions.**
Further permissions questions can be emailed to
permissionrequest@cengage.com

While every effort has been made to ensure the reliability of the information presented in this publication, Gale, a part of Cengage Learning, does not guarantee the accuracy of the data contained herein. Gale accepts no payment for listing; and inclusion in the publication of any organization, agency, institution, publication, service, or individual does not imply endorsement of the editors or publisher. Errors brought to the attention of the publisher and verified to the satisfaction of the publisher will be corrected in future editions.

Gale
27500 Drake Rd.
Farmington Hills, MI, 48331-3535

ISBN-13: 978-1-4144-6706-1
ISBN-10: 1-4144-6706-0

ISSN 1094-7019

This title is also available as an e-book.
ISBN-13: 978-1-4144-7390-1
ISBN-10: 1-4144-7390-7
Contact your Gale, a part of Cengage Learning sales representative for ordering information.

Printed in Mexico
1 2 3 4 5 6 7 15 14 13 12 11

Table of Contents

Just a Few Lines on a Page

I have often thought that poets have the easiest job in the world. A poem, after all, is just a few lines on a page, usually not even extending margin to margin—how long would that take to write, about five minutes? Maybe ten at the most, if you wanted it to rhyme or have a repeating meter. Why, I could start in the morning and produce a book of poetry by dinnertime. But we all know that it isn't that easy. Anyone can come up with enough words, but the poet's job is about writing the *right* ones. The right words will change lives, making people see the world somewhat differently than they saw it just a few minutes earlier. The right words can make a reader who relies on the dictionary for meanings take a greater responsibility for his or her own personal understanding. A poem that is put on the page correctly can bear any amount of analysis, probing, defining, explaining, and interrogating, and something about it will still feel new the next time you read it.

It would be fine with me if I could talk about poetry without using the word "magical," because that word is overused these days to imply "a really good time," often with a certain sweetness about it, and a lot of poetry is neither of these. But if you stop and think about magic—whether it brings to mind sorcery, witchcraft, or bunnies pulled from top hats—it always seems to involve stretching reality to produce a result greater than the sum of its parts and pulling unexpected results out of thin air. This book provides ample cases where a few simple words conjure up whole worlds. We do not actually travel to different times and different cultures, but the poems get into our minds, they find what little we know about the places they are talking about, and then they make that little bit blossom into a bouquet of someone else's life. Poets make us think we are following simple, specific events, but then they leave ideas in our heads that cannot be found on the printed page. Abracadabra.

Sometimes when you finish a poem it doesn't feel as if it has left any supernatural effect on you, like it did not have any more to say beyond the actual words that it used. This happens to everybody, but most often to inexperienced readers: regardless of what is often said about young people's infinite capacity to be amazed, you have to understand what usually does happen, and what could have happened instead, if you are going to be moved by what someone has accomplished. In those cases in which you finish a poem with a "So what?" attitude, the information provided in *Poetry for Students* comes in handy. Readers can feel assured that the poems included here actually are potent magic, not just because a few (or a hundred or ten thousand) professors of literature say they are: they're significant because they can withstand close inspection and still amaze the very same people who have just finished taking them apart and seeing how they work. Turn them inside out, and they will still be able to come alive, again and again. *Poetry for Students* gives readers of any age good practice in feeling the ways poems relate to both the reality of the time and place the poet lived in and the reality of our emotions. Practice is just another word for being a student. The information given here helps you understand the way to read poetry; what to look for, what to expect.

With all of this in mind, I really don't think I would actually like to have a poet's job at all. There are too many skills involved, including precision, honesty, taste, courage, linguistics, passion, compassion, and the ability to keep all sorts of people entertained at once. And that is just what they do with one hand, while the other hand pulls some sort of trick that most of us will never fully understand. I can't even pack all that I need for a weekend into one suitcase, so what would be my chances of stuffing so much life into a few lines? With all that *Poetry for Students* tells us about each poem, I am impressed that any poet can finish three or four poems a year. Read the inside stories of these poems, and you won't be able to approach any poem in the same way you did before.

David J. Kelly
College of Lake County

Introduction

Purpose of the Book

The purpose of *Poetry for Students* (*PfS*) is to provide readers with a guide to understanding, enjoying, and studying poems by giving them easy access to information about the work. Part of Gale's "For Students" Literature line, *PfS* is specifically designed to meet the curricular needs of high school and undergraduate college students and their teachers, as well as the interests of general readers and researchers considering specific poems. While each volume contains entries on "classic" poems frequently studied in classrooms, there are also entries containing hard-to-find information on contemporary poems, including works by multicultural, international, and women poets.

The information covered in each entry includes an introduction to the poem and the poem's author; the actual poem text (if possible); a poem summary, to help readers unravel and understand the meaning of the poem; analysis of important themes in the poem; and an explanation of important literary techniques and movements as they are demonstrated in the poem.

In addition to this material, which helps the readers analyze the poem itself, students are also provided with important information on the literary and historical background informing each work. This includes a historical context essay, a box comparing the time or place the poem was written to modern Western culture, a critical overview essay, and excerpts from critical essays on the poem. A unique feature of *PfS* is a specially commissioned critical essay on each poem, targeted toward the student reader.

To further help today's student in studying and enjoying each poem, information on audio recordings and other media adaptations is provided (if available), as well as reading suggestions for works of fiction and nonfiction on similar themes and topics. Classroom aids include ideas for research papers and lists of critical and reference sources that provide additional material on the poem.

Selection Criteria

The titles for each volume of *PfS* are selected by surveying numerous sources on notable literary works and analyzing course curricula for various schools, school districts, and states. Some of the sources surveyed include: high school and undergraduate literature anthologies and textbooks; lists of award-winners, and recommended titles, including the Young Adult Library Services Association (YALSA) list of best books for young adults.

Input solicited from our expert advisory board—consisting of educators and librarians—guides us to maintain a mix of "classic" and contemporary literary works, a mix of challenging and engaging works (including genre titles that are commonly studied) appropriate for different age levels, and a mix of international, multicultural and women authors. These advisors also consult on each volume's entry list, advising on which titles are most studied, most appropriate, and meet the broadest interests across secondary (grades 7–12) curricula and undergraduate literature studies.

How Each Entry Is Organized

Each entry, or chapter, in *PfS* focuses on one poem. Each entry heading lists the full name of the poem, the author's name, and the date of the poem's publication. The following elements are contained in each entry:

Introduction: a brief overview of the poem which provides information about its first appearance, its literary standing, any controversies surrounding the work, and major conflicts or themes within the work.

Author Biography: this section includes basic facts about the poet's life, and focuses on events and times in the author's life that inspired the poem in question.

Poem Text: when permission has been granted, the poem is reprinted, allowing for quick reference when reading the explication of the following section.

Poem Summary: a description of the major events in the poem. Summaries are broken down with subheads that indicate the lines being discussed.

Themes: a thorough overview of how the major topics, themes, and issues are addressed within the poem. Each theme discussed appears in a separate subhead.

Style: this section addresses important style elements of the poem, such as form, meter, and rhyme scheme; important literary devices used, such as imagery, foreshadowing, and symbolism; and, if applicable, genres to which the work might have belonged, such as Gothicism or Romanticism. Literary terms are explained within the entry, but can also be found in the Glossary.

Historical Context: this section outlines the social, political, and cultural climate in which the author lived and the poem was created. This section may include descriptions of related historical events, pertinent aspects of daily life in the culture, and the artistic and literary sensibilities of the time in which the work was written. If the poem is a historical work,

information regarding the time in which the poem is set is also included. Each section is broken down with helpful subheads.

Critical Overview: this section provides background on the critical reputation of the poem, including bannings or any other public controversies surrounding the work. For older works, this section includes a history of how the poem was first received and how perceptions of it may have changed over the years; for more recent poems, direct quotes from early reviews may also be included.

Criticism: an essay commissioned by *PfS* which specifically deals with the poem and is written specifically for the student audience, as well as excerpts from previously published criticism on the work (if available).

Sources: an alphabetical list of critical material quoted in the entry, with full bibliographical information.

Further Reading: an alphabetical list of other critical sources which may prove useful for the student. Includes full bibliographical information and a brief annotation.

Suggested Search Terms: a list of search terms and phrases to jumpstart students' further information seeking. Terms include not just titles and author names but also terms and topics related to the historical and literary context of the works.

In addition, each entry contains the following highlighted sections, set apart from the main text as sidebars:

Media Adaptations: if available, a list of audio recordings as well as any film or television adaptations of the poem, including source information.

Topics for Further Study: a list of potential study questions or research topics dealing with the poem. This section includes questions related to other disciplines the student may be studying, such as American history, world history, science, math, government, business, geography, economics, psychology, etc.

Compare & Contrast: an "at-a-glance" comparison of the cultural and historical differences between the author's time and culture and late twentieth century or early twenty-first century Western culture. This box includes pertinent parallels between the major scientific, political, and cultural movements of the time or place the poem was written, the time or place the poem was set (if a historical work), and modern Western culture. Works written after 1990 may not have this box.

What Do I Read Next?: a list of works that might give a reader points of entry into a classic work (e.g., YA or multicultural titles) and/ or complement the featured poem or serve as a contrast to it. This includes works by the same author and others, works from various genres, YA works, and works from various cultures and eras.

Other Features

PfS includes "Just a Few Lines on a Page," a foreword by David J. Kelly, an adjunct professor of English, College of Lake County, Illinois. This essay provides a straightforward, unpretentious explanation of why poetry should be marveled at and how *PfS* can help teachers show students how to enrich their own reading experiences.

A Cumulative Author/Title Index lists the authors and titles covered in each volume of the *PfS* series.

A Cumulative Nationality/Ethnicity Index breaks down the authors and titles covered in each volume of the *PfS* series by nationality and ethnicity.

A Subject/Theme Index, specific to each volume, provides easy reference for users who may be studying a particular subject or theme rather than a single work. Significant subjects from events to broad themes are included.

A Cumulative Index of First Lines (beginning in Vol. 10) provides easy reference for users who may be familiar with the first line of a poem but may not remember the actual title.

A Cumulative Index of Last Lines (beginning in Vol. 10) provides easy reference for users who may be familiar with the last line of a poem but may not remember the actual title.

Each entry may include illustrations, including photo of the author and other graphics related to the poem.

Citing Poetry for Students

When writing papers, students who quote directly from any volume of *PfS* may use the following general forms. These examples are based on MLA style; teachers may request that students adhere to a different style, so the following examples may be adapted as needed.

When citing text from *PfS* that is not attributed to a particular author (i.e., the Themes, Style, Historical Context sections, etc.), the following format should be used in the bibliography section:

"Angle of Geese." *Poetry for Students*. Ed. Marie Napierkowski and Mary Ruby. Vol. 2. Detroit: Gale, 1998. 8–9.

When quoting the specially commissioned essay from *PfS* (usually the first piece under the "Criticism" subhead), the following format should be used:

Velie, Alan. Critical Essay on "Angle of Geese." *Poetry for Students*. Ed. Marie Napierkowski and Mary Ruby. Vol. 2. Detroit: Gale, 1998. 7–10.

When quoting a journal or newspaper essay that is reprinted in a volume of *PfS*, the following form may be used:

Luscher, Robert M. "An Emersonian Context of Dickinson's 'The Soul Selects Her Own Society'." *ESQ: A Journal of American Renaissance* 30.2 (1984): 111–16. Excerpted and reprinted in *Poetry for Students*. Ed. Marie Napierkowski and Mary Ruby. Vol. 1. Detroit: Gale, 1998. 266–69.

When quoting material reprinted from a book that appears in a volume of *PfS*, the following form may be used:

Mootry, Maria K. "'Tell It Slant': Disguise and Discovery as Revisionist Poetic Discourse in 'The Bean Eaters'." *A Life Distilled: Gwendolyn Brooks, Her Poetry and Fiction*. Ed. Maria K. Mootry and Gary Smith. Urbana: University of Illinois Press, 1987. 177–80, 191. Excerpted and reprinted in *Poetry for Students*. Ed. Marie Napierkowski and Mary Ruby. Vol. 2. Detroit: Gale, 1998. 22–24.

We Welcome Your Suggestions

The editorial staff of *Poetry for Students* welcomes your comments and ideas. Readers who wish to suggest poems to appear in future volumes, or who have other suggestions, are cordially invited to contact the editor. You may contact the editor via E-mail at: **ForStudentsEditors@cengage.com.** Or write to the editor at:

Editor, *Poetry for Students*
Gale
27500 Drake Road
Farmington Hills, MI 48331-3535

Literary Chronology

1591: Robert Herrick is born in London, England.

1648: Robert Herrick's poem "Corinna's Going A-Maying" is published in *Hesperides: Or, The Works Both Humane & Divine of Robert Herrick.*

1674: Robert Herrick dies in Devonshire, England.

1772: Samuel Taylor Coleridge is born on October 21 in Ottery, St Mary, England.

1798: Samuel Taylor Coleridge's poem "Frost at Midnight" is published in *Fears in Solitude.*

1807: Henry Wadsworth Longfellow is born on February 27 in Portland, Maine.

1819: Walt Whitman is born on May 31 in West Hills, Long Island, New York.

1834: Samuel Taylor Coleridge dies of heart failure on July 25 in London, England.

1856: Walt Whitman's poem "Miracles" is published in the second edition of *Leaves of Grass.* A revised, shorter version of the poem is published in 1881.

1873: Walter de la Mare is born on April 25 in Charlton, England.

1880: Henry Wadsworth Longfellow's "The Tide Rises, the Tide Falls" is published in *Ultima Thule.*

1882: Henry Wadsworth Longfellow dies of complications of peritonitis on March 24 in Cambridge, Massachusetts.

1892: Walt Whitman dies on March 26 in Camden, New Jersey.

1897: Louise Bogan is born on August 11 in Livermore Falls, Maine.

1912: Walter de la Mare's poem "The Listeners" is published in *The Listeners, and Other Poems.*

1920: Amy Clampitt is born on June 15 in New Providence, Iowa.

1924: Nguyen Thi Vinh is born in French Indochina.

1924: Yehuda Amichai is born on May 3 in Wuerzburg, Germany.

1929: Adrienne Rich is born on May 16 in Baltimore, Maryland.

1930: Derek Walcott is born on January 23 in Castries, Saint Lucia, West Indies.

1944: Eavan Boland is born on September 24 in Dublin, Ireland.

1947: Jane Kenyon is born on May 23, 1947 in Ann Arbor, Michigan.

1950: Julia Alvarez is born on March 27 in New York, New York.

1956: Walter de la Mare dies of age-related illness on June 22 in Twickenham, England.

1963: Adrienne Rich's poem "Ghost of a Chance" is published in the collection *Snapshots of a Daughter-in-Law.*

1966: Natasha Trethewey is born in Gulfport, Mississippi.

1966: Sherman Alexie is born on October 7 in Spokane, Washington.

1968: Louise Bogan's poem "Song for the Last Act" is published in *The Blue Estuaries: Poems 1923–1968.*

1970: Louise Bogan dies of heart failure on February 4 in New York, New York.

1973: Nguyen Thi Vinh's poem "Thoughts of Hanoi" is published in English in *Voices of Modern Asia: An Anthology of Twentieth-Century Asian Literature.*

1976: Derek Walcott's poem "Sea Canes" is published in *Sea Grapes.*

1977: Yehuda Amichai's poem "Seven Laments for the War-Dead" is published in English in *Amen.*

1990: Jane Kenyon's poem "Let Evening Come" is published in *Harvard Magazine* and later collected in *Let Evening Come.*

1992: Derek Walcott is awarded the Nobel Prize for Literature.

1993: Natasha Trethewey's poem "Flounder" is published in *Callaloo.* In 2000, it was published in *Domestic Work.*

1994: Amy Clampitt's poem "Syrinx" is published in *A Silence Opens.*

1994: Amy Clampitt dies of cancer on September 10 in Lenox, Massachusetts.

1995: Jane Kenyon dies of leukemia on April 22 at Eagle Pond Farm in Wilmot, New Hampshire.

1995: Julia Alvarez's poem "Exile" is published in *The Other Side/El Otro Lado.*

1996: Sherman Alexie's poem "The Powwow at the End of the World" is published in *The Summer of Black Widows.*

2000: Yehuda Amichai dies of cancer on September 25 in Jerusalem, Israel.

2007: Eavan Boland's poem "Domestic Violence" is published in *Domestic Violence.*

2007: Natasha Trethewey receives a Pulitzer Prize for poetry for her collection *Native Guard.*

Acknowledgements

The editors wish to thank the copyright holders of the excerpted criticism included in this volume and the permissions managers of many book and magazine publishing companies for assisting us in securing reproduction rights. We are also grateful to the staffs of the Detroit Public Library, the Library of Congress, the University of Detroit Mercy Library, Wayne State University Purdy/Kresge Library Complex, and the University of Michigan Libraries for making their resources available to us. Following is a list of the copyright holders who have granted us permission to reproduce material in this volume of PFS. Every effort has been made to trace copyright, but if omissions have been made, please let us know.

COPYRIGHTED EXCERPTS IN *PfS*, VOLUME 39, WERE REPRODUCED FROM THE FOLLOWING PERIODICALS:

Americas, v. 59, March/April, 2007; v. 59, May/June, 2007. © 2007 Organization of American States. Reproduced by permission of *Americas*, a bimonthly magazine published by the General Secretariat of the Organization of American States in English and Spanish.—*Houston Chronicle*, May 16, 2004. Copyright 2004 Houston Chronicle Publishing Company. Reprinted with permission. All rights reserved.—*Irish Times*, March 15, 2007 for "Violence Amid the Verses" by Belinda McKeon; March 24, 2007 for "Pre-eminent Poet of Experience" by Fiona Sampson. Reproduced by permission of the author.—*Kenyon Review*, v. 10, winter, 1988 for "Toward a Tragic Wisdom and Beyond" by Mark Irwin. Reproduced by permission of the author.—*Nation*, v. 240, February 23, 1985; v. 265, November 3, 1997. Reproduced by permission.—*New England Review*, v. 17, summer, 1995. Copyright © 1995 Middlebury College. Reproduced by permission.—*Papers on Language & Literature*, v. 4, spring, 1968. Reproduced by permission.—*Poetry*, v. 165, December, 1994 for "High Reachers" by Robert B. Shaw; v. 172, July, 1998 for "Review of 'The Collected Poems of Amy Clampitt'" by John Taylor. Reproduced by permission of the author.—*Poetry and the Foundation of Light: Observations on the Conflict between Christian and Classical Traditions in Seventeenth-Century Poetry*, v. 158, June, 1991 for "Culture, Inclusion, Craft" by David Baker. Reproduced by permission of the author.—*Publishers Weekly*, v. 243, September 16, 1996; v. 247, August 14, 2000. Reproduced from *Publishers Weekly*, published by the PWxyz, LLC, by permission.—*TriQuarterly*, v. 120, winter, 2005 for "Rooms by the City: Three Undated Poems by Louise Bogan (1897-1970)" by Mary Kinzie. Reproduced by permission of the author.—*Tulsa Studies in Women's Literature*, v. 12, fall, 1993 for "Contradictions: Tracking Adrienne Rich's Poetry" by Alice Templeton. Reproduced by permission of the publisher and the author.—*Women's Review of Books*, v. 10, May, 2001. © 2001 Women's Review, Inc. Reproduced by permission.—*Women's Review of Books*, v. 23, September/October, 2006. Reproduced by permission.—*World Literature Today*, v. 56, winter, 1982; v. 71, spring, 1997; v. 84, July/August, 2010. Reproduced by permission of the publisher.

COPYRIGHTED EXCERPTS IN *PfS*, VOLUME 39, WERE REPRODUCED FROM THE FOLLOWING BOOKS:

Harris, Judith. From *Bright Unequivocal Eye: Poems, Papers, and Remembrances from the First Jane Kenyon Conference*. Peter Lang, 2000. Reproduced by permission.—Kenyon, Jane. From *Otherwise: New & Selected Poems*. Graywolf Press, 1996. © 1996 by the Estate of Jane Keyon. Reproduced with the permission of the publisher, Saint Paul, Minnesota.—James E. Miller, Jr. From *A Critical Guide to "Leaves of Grass"*. University of Chicago Press, 1957. Reproduced by permission.—Swardson, H.R. From *Poetry and the Foundation of Light: Observations on the Conflict between Christian and Classical Traditions in Seventeenth-Century Poetry*. University of Missouri Press, 1962. Reproduced by permission.—Trethewey, Natasha. From *Domestic Work*. Graywolf Press, 2000. © 2000 Natasha Trethewey. Reproduced with the permission of the publisher, Saint Paul, Minnesota.—Williams, Cecil B. From *Henry Wadsworth Longfellow*. Twayne Publishers, 1964. Copyright 2000 Gale Group, Copyright 2007 Gale, Cengage Learning.

Contributors

Susan K. Andersen: Andersen holds a Ph.D. in literature. Entry on "The Powwow at the End of the World." Original essay on "The Powwow at the End of the World."

Bryan Aubrey: Aubrey holds a Ph.D. in English. Entries on "Domestic Violence" and "Seven Laments for the War-Dead." Original essays on "Domestic Violence" and "Seven Laments for the War-Dead."

Laura Bussey: Bussey is an independent writer specializing in literature. Entry on "Exile." Original essay on "Exile."

Catherine C. Dominic: Dominic is a novelist and a freelance writer and editor. Entries on "Corinna's Going A-Maying," and "The Tide Rises, the Tide Falls." Original essays on "Corinna's Going A-Maying," "The Tide Rises, the Tide Falls," and "Thoughts of Hanoi."

Charlotte M. Freeman: Freeman is a writer, editor and former academic living in small-town Montana. Entry on "Ghost of a Chance." Original essay on "Ghost of a Chance."

Diane Andrews Henningfeld: Henningfeld is an emerita professor of English at Adrian College who writes widely for many educational publications. Entry on "Let Evening Come." Original essay on "Let Evening Come."

Michael Allen Holmes: Holmes is a writer and editor. Entries on "The Listeners" and "Thoughts of Hanoi." Original essays on "The Listeners" and "Thoughts of Hanoi."

David Kelly: Kelly is a writer and instructor of literature and creative writing. Entries on "Sea Canes" and "Song for the Last Act." Original essays on "Sea Canes" and "Song for the Last Act."

Michael J. O'Neal: O'Neal holds a Ph.D. in English. Entry on "Frost at Midnight." Original essay on "Frost at Midnight."

Rachel Porter: Porter is a freelance writer and editor who holds a bachelor of arts degree in English literature. Entry on "Flounder." Original essay on "Flounder."

Laura Beth Pryor: Pryor has been writing professionally for over twenty-five years, and holds a degree from the University of Michigan. Entry on "Miracles." Original essay on "Miracles."

Bradley A. Skeen: Skeen is a classicist. Entry on "Syrinx." Original essay on "Syrinx."

Corinna's Going A-Maying

ROBERT HERRICK

1648

Robert Herrick's seventeenth-century poetry is known for its craftsmanship, lyricism, and blending of both spiritual and sensual elements. His poem "Corinna's Going A-Maying" is no exception. In this poem, the speaker alludes to his love affair with the subject of the poem, Corinna, and he beckons her to join in the springtime rituals traditionally celebrated in the month of May. In the course of describing the rites of spring enjoyed at this time through festivals held on May Day, the first of May, the speaker makes reference to Greek and Roman mythology, pagan rituals, and Christian beliefs. Although the tone of the poem connotes an air of celebration and joy, the final stanza of the work underscores the finite nature of youth and ultimately of life. The end of the poem is colored with implications of decay and death. On the surface, it is a rousing poem extolling the pleasures of love and lust, but in the course of the poem a darker, fuller picture of life is drawn, one in which the dangers of sin are hinted at and the certainty of death is detailed. The way the poem both has religious overtones and apparently endorses worldly pleasures has been the focus of much critical analysis, as has the poem's formal structure.

"Corinna's Going A-Maying" was originally published in the 1648 collection *Hesperides: Or, The Works Both Humane & Divine of Robert Herrick*. This large collection is available in *The Complete Poetry of Robert Herrick*, edited, introduced,

Robert Herrick

and annotated by J. Max Patrick, published by New York University Press in 1963.

AUTHOR BIOGRAPHY

Although his exact birth date is unknown, records indicate that Herrick was baptized on August 24, 1591. He was the seventh child of Nicholas Herrick, a goldsmith, and Julian Stone Herrick, whose name has also been rendered as Juliana or Julia. When Herrick was about fourteen months old, his father fell or jumped from an upper-story window in the Herrick home. Initially, the fall was believed to be intentional, and had the suicide charge stuck, the Herrick property would have reverted to the English monarchy, as was the law at the time. The charge, however, was dropped. Herrick's mother never remarried. Little else is known about his childhood.

When Herrick was sixteen years old, he was apprenticed to his uncle, also a goldsmith, but the ten-year agreement was terminated before Herrick had completed his apprenticeship. At the age of twenty-two, Herrick enrolled at St. John's College at the University of Cambridge, although because of financial difficulties Herrick later transferred to Trinity Hall, a less expensive college at the same university. Herrick graduated in 1617, and he left few traces of his activities for the next several years. After becoming an ordained Anglican minister in 1623, Herrick apparently gained some recognition as a poet, for scholar and poet Richard James praised Herrick in his 1625 work *The Muses Dirge* (as noted by Roger B. Rollin in the 1993 *Dictionary of Literary Biography*, Volume 126, *Seventeenth-Century British Nondramatic Poets*). Herrick participated as one of several chaplains in a 1627 crusade, led by the Duke of Buckingham, to free the French Protestants on the Isle of Rhé. Many members of the expedition were lost in a storm as the ships retreated to England. Retiring to a quieter life in 1629, Herrick became the minister of the parish of Dean Prior in Devonshire.

During the Civil War in England (a war that was waged largely between supporters of the absolute authority of the monarchy and supporters of Parliament), Herrick remained loyal to King Charles I. The war was also fraught with religious tensions, as the Parliamentarians were primarily Puritans—Protestants who wished to remove all traces of Roman Catholicism from the Anglican Church (the Church of England). When parliamentary supporters and Puritans gained power, Herrick was expelled from his parish in 1647, along with many other clergymen. It is believed that Herrick then moved to London for a time.

In 1648, he published a collection of more than a thousand poems. Included in the volume, *Hesperides*, is the lyric poem "Corinna's Going A-Maying," along with a collection of religious poems titled *His Noble Numbers*, dated the previous year. Herrick returned to his clerical post at Dean Prior in 1660, at the beginning of the Restoration, when the monarchy was restored with the return of King Charles II (the son of Charles I) to England. Herrick served as a clergyman until his death in 1674.

POEM TEXT

> Get up, get up for shame, the Blooming Morne
> Upon her wings presents the god unshorne.
>   See how *Aurora* throwes her faire
>   Fresh-quilted colours through the aire:
>   Get up, sweet-Slug-a-bed, and see   5
>   The Dew-bespangling Herbe and Tree.

Each Flower has wept, and bow'd toward the
   East,
Above an houre since; yet you not drest,
      Nay! not so much as out of bed?
      When all the Birds have Mattens seyd,   10
      And sung their thankfull Hymnes: 'tis sin,
      ay, profanation to keep in,
When as a thousand Virgins on this day,
Spring, sooner then the Lark, to fetch in May.

Rise; and put on your Foliage, and be seene   15
To come forth, like the Spring-time, fresh and
   greene;
      And sweet as *Flora*. Take no care
      For Jewels for your Gowne, or Haire:
      Feare not; the leaves will strew
      Gemms in abundance upon you: 20

Besides, the childhood of the Day has kept,
Against you come, some *Orient Pearls* unwept:
      Come, and receive them while the light
      Hangs on the Dew-locks of the night:
      And *Titan* on the Eastern hill   25
      Retires himselfe, or else stands still
Till you come forth. Wash, dresse, be briefe in
   praying:
Few Beads are best, when once we goe a
   Maying.

Come, my *Corinna*, come; and comming, marke
How each field turns a strcct; each street a Parke   30
      Made green, and trimm'd with trees: see how
      Devotion gives each House a Bough,
      Or Branch: Each Porch, each doore, ere
      this,
      An Arke a Tabernacle is
Made up of white-thorn neatly enterwove;   35
As if here were those cooler shades of love.
      Can such delights be in the street,
      And open fields, and we not see't?
      Come, we'll abroad; and let's obay
      The Proclamation made for May: 40
And sin no more, as we have done, by staying;
But my *Corinna*, come, let's goe a Maying.

There's not a budding Boy, or Girle, this day,
But is got up, and gone to bring in May.
      A deale of Youth, ere this, is come   45
      Back, and with *White-thorn* laden home.
      Some have dispatcht their Cakes and
      Creame,
      Before that we have left to dreame:
And some have wept, and woo'd, and plighted
   Troth,
And chose their Priest, ere we can cast off sloth: 50
      Many a green-gown has been given;
      Many a kisse, both odde and even:
      Many a glance too has been sent
      From out the eye, Loves Firmament:
Many a jest told of the Keyes betraying   55
This night, and Locks pickt, yet w'are not a
   Maying.

Come, let us goe, while we are in our prime;
And take the harmlesse follie of the time.

We shall grow old apace, and die
Before we know our liberty.   60
Our life is short; and our dayes run
As fast away as do's the Sunne:

And as a vapour, or a drop of raine
Once lost, can ne'r be found againe:
      So when or you or I are made   65
      A fable, song, or fleeting shade;
      All love, all liking, all delight
      Lies drown'd with us in endlesse night.
Then while time serves, and we are but
   decaying;
Come, my *Corinna*, come, let's goe a Maying.   70

POEM SUMMARY

The text used for this summary is from *The Complete Poetry of Robert Herrick*, edited by J. Max Patrick, New York University Press, 1963, pp. 98–100. Versions of the poem can be found on the following Web pages: http://www.poetryfounda tion.org/poem/176696 and http://www.bartleby.com/101/247.html.

Stanza 1

"Corinna's Going A-Maying" is a five-stanza poem. A stanza is a division of poetry that groups the lines of the poem into related sections; stanzas divide poetry in the same way that paragraphs divide prose. In the first stanza, the speaker addresses the as-yet-unnamed young woman who lies in bed. In the first line of the poem, she is urged to rise. The next thirteen lines of the stanza proceed to make plain the lateness of the morning, and the speaker begins to delineate the reasons why the young woman should be getting up. This is done first through a reference in the second line to a god whose hair is uncut and who rides on morning's wings. As J. Max Patrick observes in his notes to "Corinna's Going A-Maying" in the 1963 *The Complete Poetry of Robert Herrick*, Herrick refers here to the sun god Apollo, from Greek and Roman mythology. The poet, establishing that the sun has risen, turns his attention to morning's colors, using the Roman goddess of the dawn, Aurora, to illustrate the array of colors that are now visible and the way dew sparkles on plants and trees. Flowers have opened and turned toward the sun rising in the east. The sun, the speaker states, has been up an hour, and still the young woman is in bed. The birds have said their morning prayers and sung their hymns. It is sinful, the speaker informs her, to remain inside, when May Day celebrations are about to begin. May

MEDIA ADAPTATIONS

- "Corinna's Going A-Maying" is available as an MP3 download from Saland Publishing's 2007 collection *Poetry Readings*, read by Dame Peggy Ashcroft.

Day, the first of May, in Herrick's time was a springtime celebration that merged pre-Christian springtime traditions focused on fertility and renewal with a veneration of the Christian figure of the Virgin Mary, the mother of Jesus. The title's use of the term Maying, or going a-Maying, refers to participation in May Day celebrations.

Stanza 2

In the second stanza, the speaker encourages the young woman to rise and adorn herself like spring, with boughs and flowers. Reference is made to the Italian goddess of flowers, Flora. The woman is reminded to not bother embellishing her appearance with such things as jewels, for the ornaments that nature provides are more appropriate for the occasion. She is beckoned forth while the morning is still young, and the dew reflects the rising sun like rosy pearls. Another reference is made to Greek mythology, when the speaker refers to the sun as Titan, resting in the east, waiting for the young woman to arise. The Titans were the gods and goddesses descended from the god Uranus and the goddess Gaia, and the Titan Helios was a sun god, according to Greek mythology. The young woman in question is asked once again to rise, wash, get dressed, and not be long in saying her morning prayers.

Stanza 3

As the third stanza opens, the young woman is identified as Corinna. The speaker asks her to come with him and to notice as she does so the way the natural world is incorporated with the artificial world of the village. Fields become streets, streets becomes parks, he says, as people festoon their homes with boughs and branches in order to celebrate May and the coming of spring. In decorating in this manner, the speaker observes,

people make their homes into holy places of worship. In particular, the speaker comments on the use of whitethorn branches. (In an explanatory note provided by the editor of *The Complete Poetry of Robert Herrick*, whitethorn is called a traditional symbol of both joy and pain.) The speaker goes on to wonder where the amusements of the May celebration may be found, and he calls to Corinna to join him in the search. Beckoning her, he insists that they obey the decrees of the day, that they have been sinning by staying inside and should do so no longer. Rather, he states, they should at last go a-Maying.

Stanza 4

Every young man and woman has already risen to welcome in May, the speaker states as the fourth stanza opens. Some have already returned to their decorated homes and have eaten the festive cakes of the season, before Corinna and the speaker have even departed. The speaker goes on to describe the ways in which these other individuals participated in the spring celebration. They have already romantically pursued one another, become engaged, and found priests to marry them. They have already romped together in the green grass, played kissing games, shared longing looks and lusty jokes, the speaker insists, but he and Corinna have not yet left for the celebration.

Stanza 5

In this stanza, the speaker urges Corinna to go with him to celebrate while they are in the prime of their lives and to enjoy the benign customs of the season. For soon, he warns, they will age and die. He urges Corinna to enjoy the freedom and pleasures of youth with him before their short days run their course. He compares life to a raindrop quickly dried by the sun, suggesting that their youth will soon disappear. All the love and joy they share now will die with them for all eternity, the speaker proclaims. Even as they are living, they are dying, he notes, and he uses this argument to urge Corinna to enjoy with him the time they have together during this May celebration.

THEMES

Youth

In "Corinna's Going A-Maying," the speaker is extremely focused on the passage of time. Throughout the poem, he emphasizes the joys

TOPICS FOR FURTHER STUDY

- In "Corinna's Going A-Maying," Herrick refers to ancient Greek and Roman gods and goddesses. Research these mythological figures and write a report about them. Discuss the period when belief in these figures flourished and why the religious practices surrounding the gods and goddesses ceased. Cite all of your sources and present your paper as a written document or as a Web page you create for this assignment.

- "Corinna's Going A-Maying" offers lush descriptions of the countryside in spring. With a small group, read *Ordinary Things: Poems from a Walk in Early Spring*, a slim volume of young-adult poems about spring by Ralph Fletcher, published in 1997 by Atheneum. Select several of the poems to analyze, and compare the images, language, structure, and themes of the poems with those of "Corinna's Going A-Maying." Are there similarities between the works? Or, in your opinion, do the differences in time (the seventeenth century versus the twentieth) and location (England versus America) make comparisons more challenging? Create a blog in which members of the group post their views and discuss these poems.

- Zeb-un-Nissa (1637–1702) was a Persian princess who lived in India during Herrick's time. (The area once known as Persia is modern-day Iran.) Zeb-un-Nissa wrote a series of poems using the *ghazal*, a poetic form traditionally used in Arabic to express human love. In her collection *The Diwan of Zeb-un-Nissa*, unpublished during her lifetime, the Muslim poet explores human and divine love, particularly in the poems numbered fifteen through twenty. Using the translation by Magan Lal and Jessie Duncan Westbrook in the 1913 edition of the work published by E. P. Dutton, study the poetry of Zeb-un-Nissa. How do the poems incorporate references to both human relationships and spiritual feelings? Considering this, do you find Zeb-un-Nissa's poems similar to Herrick's "Corinna's Going A-Maying?" Write an essay in which you explore these ideas.

- Herrick published his poetry during the English Civil War. Research this period in history. What issues inspired the violence? Who were the leaders during this conflict, and how was it resolved? Compile your findings and a detailed chronology of the war. Present this information as a research paper, a visual presentation (such as a PowerPoint presentation), or a series of storyboards or posters.

- Herrick's poetical structure in "Corinna's Going A-Maying" is calculated to suit his thematic aims. Study the meter and rhyme patterns in his poem and attempt to mimic them to some degree in a poem of your own creation. Experiment, for example, with the iambic rhythm (a pattern of one unaccented syllable followed by one accented syllable), and divide your poem into fourteen-line stanzas. Choose a theme relevant to Herrick's poem, such as spring, young love, or mortality. Share your poem with the class through either a live reading or a recording that your classmates can view online.

- Like "Corinna's Going A-Maying," Herrick's "To Blossoms" and "To Daffodils" are often referred to as *carpe diem* (seize the day) poems. Compare these three poems and examine the way Herrick uses symbolism from the natural world to convey his themes. What do these poems reveal about Herrick's views on youth, experience, aging, and death? Write a comparative essay in which you analyze these topics. Note to teachers: Herrick's "To the Virgins, to Make Much of Time" also invites comparison with "Corinna's Going A-Maying" but may not be appropriate for younger students. These poems are all available in *The Complete Poetry of Robert Herrick*, edited, introduced, and annotated by J. Max Patrick, published by New York University Press in 1963.

of youth, particularly those to be experienced during the May Day celebrations. In the final stanza, he depicts in stark terms the contrast between youth and old age, and he makes a passionate argument for enjoying youth before it disappears forever. In fact, the May Day the poem centers on may be regarded not only as a particular day but, in a larger sense, as the speaker's youth in general. The speaker repeatedly describes the dawning of the day, emphasizing the beauty and glory of the morning, as well as the fact that the morning will not last. While others are out enjoying May Day, Corinna is still in bed. The speaker implores her, throughout most of the poem, not to waste the morning but rather to celebrate as enthusiastically as the other young men and women have already begun to do.

In the poem's final stanza, the ages of the young lovers (Corinna and the speaker) are linked both to the morning and to the season of spring, when the speaker states that they should begin enjoying the day while they are in the prime of their lives. Before them lies the fullness of the day, of the season, and of their young lives, but the speaker reminds Corinna of the transient nature of this state. Just as morning progresses to afternoon and evening, and spring to summer, autumn, and winter, so will their youth gradually transform itself to adulthood and eventually old age. While youth is associated with morning, spring, vitality, beauty, and romantic love, old age is associated with desiccation and decay, and it is followed shortly by the eternal night of death.

Romantic Love

The idealism and physicality of the love and romance associated with youth is a central feature of "Corinna's Going A-Maying." Initially, in the first two stanzas, the speaker sets the stage by describing the morning of the May celebration; he requests that his love rise to greet the day. As the poem progresses, his desire for Corinna to get up and join the May Day celebration will become increasingly urgent. In the second stanza, Corinna is again begged to rise. She is told to get up and to allow herself to be seen, but not adorned with the usual trimmings. The speaker urges Corinna to be brief in her morning rituals and to even shorten her prayers that day. After insisting yet again in the third stanza that Corinna delay no longer, the speaker becomes frustrated with her, noting that other young lovers are already enjoying the each other's company, while he and Corinna have not

The first stanza of the poem references the morning dew. (zhuda / Shutterstock.com)

yet left the house to join the morning's festivities. In some detail, the speaker describes an array of activities in which he and his Corinna could be partaking. In a final plea to Corinna, the speaker reminds her of the fleeting nature of their youth, of how little time they actually possess to enjoy one another. In this regard, "Corinna's Going A-Maying" is often described as a "carpe diem" poem. *Carpe diem* is a Latin term meaning "seize the day," and it is associated with the notion of living life to the fullest.

Nature

In "Corinna's Going A-Maying," Herrick uses vivid details and references to Greek and Roman mythology to describe the natural world. The sun is described as a god, the morning as a goddess. The morning dew adorns the branches upon which it hangs like jewels, and the flowers themselves worship the rising sun. The world of nature Herrick depicts is lush, green, and fertile. In every stanza, Herrick elevates the natural world to a divine status, and the lavishly described elements of nature serve as a backdrop for the speaker's eager pursuit of his love, Corinna. In some ways, Herrick's depiction of nature seems to overshadow the romantic substance of the poem. This apparent imbalance suggests the permanence of the natural world. While the morning, the season of spring, the month of May, and the youth of the lovers are all finite in their own ways, the natural world that Herrick embellishes with mythological elements is presented as eternal; it is ever changing with the seasons but nonetheless permanent. Although time steals beauty and vibrancy from the young lovers, in Herrick's view it makes little lasting impact in the world of nature, where breathtaking vitality is renewed with each dawn.

STYLE

Linked Sonnets

Herrick structures "Corinna's Going A-Maying" into five stanzas of fourteen lines each. Although these fourteen-line stanzas do not completely match the traditional English sonnet form, as developed by poets who preceded Herrick (such as Sir Philip Sidney and William Shakespeare), there are a number of resemblances. Each stanza is further linked to the other stanzas in the work by theme and the repetition, particularly in the final couplet (a rhymed pair of lines). In this way, Herrick links the sonnets to form a longer, more complex work.

In terms of subject matter, Herrick's poem is typical of many English sonnets written with the express purpose of wooing a lover or otherwise conveying romantic notions. The speaker in "Corinna's Going A-Maying," for example, repeatedly calls for Corinna to rise from bed and enjoy the Maying celebrations, which, as he outlines in the fourth stanza, include a few romantic activities. In the final stanza, his wooing becomes more urgent, as he impresses upon Corinna the fact that they will not be young forever and should enjoy their youth while they have it.

Sonnets have several possible structures. In most sonnets, the poem ends in a rhymed couplet that in some way comments on the preceding lines or serves as a conclusion. Herrick makes use of this summary couplet in "Corinna's Going A-Maying." In each stanza, a reference is made to the May celebrations. In the first stanza, the speaker references the young women who have already risen to welcome May. In the second, he stresses to Corinna to make haste and to be brief in her prayers so that they may go Maying. In the third, the same sentiment is underscored, as the speaker urges Corinna to not delay. The concluding couplet of the fourth stanza presses home the fact that other young lovers have enjoyed the May

celebration to its fullest, in many ways, and still the speaker and Corinna have not yet gone a-Maying. The final couplet of the poem, in the fifth stanza, has a graver tone, and in it the speaker insists they enjoy themselves while they are still young. This repetition serves as the link by which Herrick ties together the sonnets in which Corinna is wooed by her lover.

Another hallmark of the English sonnet is its meter. Meter is a pattern of accented and unaccented (sometimes called stressed and unstressed, or short and long) syllables in the lines of a poem. This pattern gives the poem its rhythm. One unit of this rhythm is called a foot. The number and type of feet in a line determine the poem meter. Sonnets are typically written in iambic pentameter. An iamb is a foot of poetry consisting of one unaccented syllable followed by one accented syllable. If five of these units occur in one line of poetry, it is said that the line is written in iambic pentameter. Iambic pentameter reflects, in general, the natural speech patterns of the English language. In "Corinna's Going A-Maying," Herrick loosely employs the rhythm of iambic pentameter, used in the poem's couplets, as well as iambic tetrameter (in which there are four accented syllables rather than five in the line of poetry), used in the poem's quatrains. (A couplet is a pair of rhymed lines. A quatrain is a grouping of four rhymed lines.) The poem is structured, then, as a series of sonnets, and each sonnet is constructed of a series of couplets and quatrains. By using this formal structure, Herrick establishes an elegance and a fluidity of rhythm that serves the subject matter of the poem, in both its eloquent wooing of Corinna and its vivid descriptions of the natural world.

Lyric Poetry

A lyric poem is simply a brief poem in which the poet expresses emotion, rather than telling a story. A lyric poem can take a variety of forms, including the sonnet. Herrick is highly regarded as a lyric poet. As Jonathan F. S. Post states in the 1999 *English Lyric Poetry: The Early Seventeenth Century*, "Few poets in English have seemed to be so triumphantly and naturally lyrical as Herrick." Although the structural analysis of "Corinna's Going A-Maying" reveals a certain complexity, the effect achieved through such a structure is to produce, through the use of the iambic rhythm and rhymed couplets and quatrains, a tone that is at once playfully informal, emotionally sincere, and graceful. Until the final stanza, the tenor of the poem is urgent but teasing. Laced with references to gods and goddesses of mythology and breathtakingly detailed descriptions of the natural world, the poem reveals the speaker's simple intentions. He seeks to entreat his lover to join him and participate with him in the lusty rites of spring. In the final stanza, his anxiety about the briefness of youth lends a serious note to his urgings, but his argument remains the same.

HISTORICAL CONTEXT

The English Civil War

Herrick wrote during the turbulent years leading up to and during the English Civil War. Charles I ascended the throne in 1625. A gradual resentment built up in Parliament during the course of his reign. Reputed to be deeply religious, Charles favored an Anglican Church that was highly embellished with ritual. To many who passionately opposed anything having the appearance of Roman Catholicism, Charles's tendencies, along with his marriage to the Roman Catholic Henrietta Maria of France, intensified suspicions that Charles would reintroduce Roman Catholic practices, hierarchies, and ceremonies to the Anglican Church.

The conflict between the Roman Catholic Church and the Anglican Church (also known as the Church of England) dates back to the 1530s, during the reign of King Henry VIII. England grew resistant to the increasing amount of power Rome wielded in England through the Church. In addition, King Henry VIII sought an annulment from his wife Catherine of Aragon, dissolution of the marriage that the Church refused to allow. Official ties with the Roman Catholic Church were dissolved, and Parliament decided that the King of England would serve as the head of the Church of England. At this point in history, the Anglican Church emerged as a Christian sect rooted in both Protestant and Catholic traditions.

During the reign of Charles I, his Catholic troubles were rivaled by opposition to his policies in the English Parliament. By 1629, Charles had dismissed Parliament four times. At the time, dismissing Parliament was still legally within the king's powers. After a Scottish rebellion prompted by the king's imposition of new religious reforms, in 1640, Charles recalled, or reinstated, Parliament. This Parliament was quickly dissolved as well, but a new Parliament was called later that year. His conflicts with this Parliament escalated until 1642, when Charles called for all subjects loyal to him to support him. Open warfare between parliamentary supporters and those who supported the monarchy ensued. Parliament was dominated during these years by a religious sect that came to be known as the Puritans. This was a conservative group that sought to strip the Anglican Church of open displays of Roman Catholicism in prayers, church services, and the structure of the Church. The struggle between Charles and his Parliament was fueled as much by these religious differences as by the conflict over the monarch's powers.

In 1646, Charles handed himself over to the Scottish Army, who in turn delivered him to parliamentary forces. Refusing to surrender, Charles then attempted to negotiate with the Scots and the parliamentarians. He convinced the Scottish army to fight for him, leading to a renewal of hostilities in the second Civil War of 1648. Later that year, Charles was defeated. The army, formerly loyal to Charles, decided that peace could not be achieved while Charles I lived. King Charles I was subsequently tried, found guilty of high treason, and beheaded in January 1649. The position of king was then abolished.

England entered a new phase in its history, in which, without a monarch, it became a republic. This period became known as the Interregnum. During this time, the military leader Oliver Cromwell rose in prominence, having fought Charles's forces during the Civil War and having successfully quelled Irish uprisings. In 1651, after Charles I's son negotiated an agreement with the Scots and was crowned Charles II of Scotland, Cromwell defeated Charles II's efforts to invade England. After Parliament was dissolved in 1653, Cromwell became the Lord Protector of England. He was offered the role of king but refused, and he died in 1658. After a brief period in which Cromwell's son Richard unsuccessfully took the helm of the Protectorate, the Army asked Charles II to return to England as king. Charles II returned to assume the throne in 1660, and the period that would become known as the Restoration began.

The Cavalier, or Carolinian, Poets

A number of poets who wrote during the reign of Charles I supported him during the events leading to the civil war; they became known as the

COMPARE
&
CONTRAST

- **1640s:** The Puritans become an increasingly powerful religious sect. They oppose Roman Catholic influences in the Anglican Church (the Church of England), seeking to strip out prayers, ceremonies, and traditions that date back to the days when the Roman Catholic Church dominated England's religious and political spheres.

  Today: Anglicanism is the dominant faith practiced in the United Kingdom. Recent figures indicate that 1.7 million people attend Church of England services monthly, and 1.1 million people attend weekly. After the seventeenth century, the term *Puritan*, as applied to a group of religious believers, is no longer prevalent, but early Puritans shaped the evolution of the Protestant Church in both the United Kingdom and the United States.

- **1640s:** The English Parliament seeks to curtail King Charles's powers. In particular, Parliament's members oppose certain religious reforms, as well as the king's legal right to dismiss Parliament and maintain absolute authority. Warfare breaks out in England in 1642, when parliamentary supporters take up arms against King Charles I and those loyal to him. The ensuing English Civil War rages for years, until Charles is captured, found guilty of treason, and beheaded in 1649.

  Today: In the United Kingdom, the monarch (Queen Elizabeth II) wields only ceremonial powers, rather than political ones. The Parliament of the United Kingdom is made up of an elected body (the House of Commons, consisting of 650 members) and an appointed body (the House of Lords). The number of Lords is not fixed; the House of Lords currently has 792 voting members.

- **1640s:** Poets who remain loyal to King Charles I later become known as the Cavalier, or Carolinian, poets. These include Herrick, Thomas Carew, and Richard Lovelace. They write about their society and their daily lives and romances, using traditional poetic structures. Many of these poets are influenced by the poet Ben Jonson, who wrote a generation before the Cavalier poets published their own works. Jonson's classicism (that is, his reverence for Greek and Roman principles of craftsmanship and harmony in the arts) and his elegance of style are mirrored in the work of the Cavalier poets.

  Today: Twenty-first-century British poetry embraces both traditional, formal poetry that is structured through meter and rhyme and experimental poetry that is opposed to the restrictions posed by such forms. Themes reflect the contemporary world; some poets write about their personal lives, romances, tragedies, or everyday experiences, while other poets focus on the dramatic and often violent changes in the modern world. Some twenty-first-century poets who are popular and widely anthologized are Jay Bernard, Amy Blakemore, Siddhartha Bose, Colm O'Shea, and James Womack.

Cavalier poets or the Carolinian poets. (The adjective *Carolinian* describes the time period during which King Charles reigned.) Their poetry was not overtly political, but in some cases it did demonstrate an intimate knowledge of King Charles's court. These poets, the most prominent of whom were Herrick, Thomas Carew, Sir John Suckling, and Richard Lovelace, often wrote poetry about Carolinian society. Such poetry focused on the conventions (typical, accepted social behaviors) of this society and daily social lives of members of this social class. According to critics such as Roy Bennett Pace, in his 1918 work *English Literature*, the primary criticism leveled against the poetry of the Cavalier group was that the subject matter, even in a complex work, was essentially trivial. The poetry of the Cavalier poets, Pace states, "is charged with a lack of

The third stanza describes a tree-lined park and street. (*Dudarev Mikhail / Shutterstock.com*)

seriousness, and we declare it guilty." Of this group of poets, Herrick is often singled out as being superior to his fellows in terms of the range of his subject matter. He deals more heavily than the other Cavalier poets with the subjects of nature and religion, and he treats them in a way that balances out the charge of the triviality of his other verses.

CRITICAL OVERVIEW

Herrick is often regarded as competent but not one of the great English poets. There is not much evidence regarding the contemporary critical or popular reception of Herrick's collection *Hesperides*. As Roger B. Rollin claims in his 1993 essay on Herrick for the *Dictionary of Literary Biography*: "What is certain is that his book did not explode upon the literary scene nor did it, during his lifetime, bring him the literary fame he so avidly desired."

Hesperides, the collection in which "Corinna's Going A-Maying" was published, often receives mixed assessments by critics of the twentieth and twenty-first centuries. In his 1918 survey of English poetry and prose, *English Literature*, Pace states that "with all his merits Herrick cannot be a called a poet of the first rank." Pace claims that what Herrick's poetry lacks is a sense of vitality, "something that touches deep chords in human experience." Cleanth Brooks writes, in a much cited 1947 analysis of the poem included in *The Well Wrought Urn: Studies in the Structure of Poetry*, that Herrick attempts to reconcile "conflicting claims of paganism and Christianity" in the poem.

In the 1999 *English Lyric Poetry: The Early Seventeenth Century*, Post describes Herrick's collection as both "beautiful" and "baffling." After praising Herrick's lyricism, Post goes on to assert that "despite Herrick's profound concern with ceremony in its many forms, it is still nearly impossible to determine how 'seriously' we are meant to take him as a poet." In his assessment of "Corinna's Going A-Maying," Post states that Herrick's "casual assimilation of the classical and the colloquial, the majestic and the immediate . . . is surely Herrick at his best." Post concludes that Herrick's "seductive invitation runs counter to the spirit" of the poem's scriptural references.

Other critics evaluate *Hesperides* as a whole. Stephen B. Dobranski, in the 2005 book *Readers and Authorship in Early Modern England*, argues that the collection contains numerous self-reflexive and self-conscious references. By examining these, Dobranski explores the relationship between Herrick and his readers. Other recent approaches to *Hesperides* in general and "Corinna's Going A-Maying" in particular focus on Herrick's use of Greek and Roman allusions. Syrithe Pugh, in the 2010 *Herrick, Fanshawe, and the Politics of Intertextuality: Classic Literature and Seventeenth-Century Royalism*, studies Herrick's references to the works of the Roman poet Ovid and draws a connection to the elements of sexuality in "Corinna's Going A-Maying."

CRITICISM

Catherine Dominic

Dominic is a novelist and a freelance writer and editor. In the following essay, she explores Robert Herrick's inclusion of Christian and pagan elements in "Corinna's Going A-Maying," maintaining that despite the apparent coexistence or reconciliation of these distinct philosophies within the poem, Herrick subtly insists upon their opposition, rather than their synthesis.

"Corinna's Going A-Maying" is a poem in which the divergence and convergence of various forms of ritual and spirituality are explored. Robert Herrick takes up two distinct threads and toys with the ways in which they intersect. Herrick describes May Day celebrations as lusty springtime rites that call to mind pagan fertility celebrations, and at the same time, he weaves Christian undertones into the fabric of the poem. Herrick juxtaposes references to Greek and Roman mythology, along with allusions to and descriptions of physical, romantic relationships, with references to Christian beliefs, symbols, and traditions. The inclusion of the pagan and the Christian elements, of the sensual and the spiritual, in "Corinna's Going A-Maying" creates an illusion of the unity within the poem. Some critics have suggested that these different elements are even reconciled. In a much-cited analysis of the poem, published in 1947 in *The Well Wrought Urn: Studies in the Structure of Poetry*, Cleanth Brooks suggests that such a reconciliation is underscored in the poem's fourth

> THE INCLUSION OF THE PAGAN AND THE CHRISTIAN ELEMENTS, OF THE SENSUAL AND THE SPIRITUAL, IN 'CORINNA'S GOING A-MAYING' CREATES AN ILLUSION OF THE UNITY WITHIN THE POEM. SOME CRITICS HAVE SUGGESTED THAT THESE DIFFERENT ELEMENTS ARE EVEN RECONCILED."

stanza, when the young lovers who have enjoyed the romance of the May celebrations come before their priest and seek the blessings of the Church through marriage. Yet other features of Herrick's poem suggest rather that it is the tension between the sensuality of the May Day festivities and the Christian traditions that Herrick seeks to explore and emphasize.

In the first stanza of the poem, Herrick spends a number of lines discussing the morning and the rising sun in terms of the Roman goddess Aurora and the Greek and Roman god Apollo. Herrick's images are lavish, as when the morning opens her wings and presents the glorious god of the sun. The spectacular colors of dawn are complemented by the foliage dripping with sparkling dew. Intermingled in this stanza are also Christian religious references. In the opening line of the poem, Corinna is immediately chastised, however playfully, being told by the speaker that she should be ashamed to still be in bed. This notion of shame is linked to the corresponding idea of sin later in the stanza. After making references to both morning prayers (matins) and hymns, the speaker insists that it is not just sinful but blasphemous for Corinna to have not yet risen. He then mentions the virgins who celebrate May Day. While the reference may simply be intended to suggest the young women who are already out of doors enjoying the celebrations, the reference also calls to mind the Virgin Mary and highlights the Christian overtones of May Day celebrations, as the month of May became associated with the Christian veneration of the mother of Jesus Christ.

The second stanza of "Corinna's Going A-Maying," like the first, references goddesses and gods. Flora, an Italian goddess of flowers, is used as a means of exploring a wealth of details

WHAT DO I READ NEXT?

- Herrick's collection *Hesperides*, which contains "Corinna's Going A-Maying," displays the range of the poet's themes, styles, and techniques. Originally published in 1648, the work is also available in *The Complete Poetry of Robert Herrick*, edited, introduced, and annotated by J. Max Patrick, published by New York University Press in 1963.

- Richard Lovelace was one of Herrick's fellow Cavalier poets. Some of his poetry is collected in the 1987 *Richard Lovelace: Selected Poems*, edited by Gerald Hammond and published by Carcanet Press.

- *The Cavalier Poets: Their Lives, Their Day, and Their Poetry*, by Carl Holliday, originally published in 1911 and reprinted in 2010 by General Books, details the society and culture that were the background for the work of the Cavalier poets.

- Writing during Herrick's age, Chinese poet Liu Yuan created a wood-block printed book, *Lingyan ge* (1669), in which images of members of the Tang dynastic court are accompanied by poetic couplets. The work also includes images of religious icons and suggests the relationships between the court, religion, and the poetry of the time. Analyzing the work, Anne Buruks-Chasson reproduces Liu Yuan's poetry in the 2010 *Through a Forest of Chancellors: Fugitive Histories in Liu Yuan's "Lingyan ge," an Illustrated Book from Seventeenth-Century Suzhou*, published by Harvard University Asia Center.

- Acclaimed Hispanic American poet Pat Mora's collection of poetry about young love, *Dizzy in Your Eyes*, is geared toward a young-adult audience. In each of the poems, the poet employs a different narrative voice. The collection was published in 2010 by Knopf Books for Young Readers.

- *Anglicanism: A Very Short Introduction*, by Mark Chapman, provides a summary of Anglican history and beliefs, providing students of Herrick's work with a basis for understanding the beliefs of the poet and the religious controversies that divided his time. Chapman's book was published by Oxford University Press in 2006.

---

regarding the flowers and foliage glistening like jewels in the morning sun. Another sun god appears in this stanza as well, as Herrick refers to Titan approaching from the east. In Greek mythology, the sun god Helios, because of his parentage, falls into the powerful class of gods and goddesses known as the Titans. Again, Herrick draws the reader's attention to not just the pagan deities of ancient mythology but to Christian rites as well, when he refers to prayers and beads. As an Anglican priest, Herrick would have been familiar with the rosary, a string of beads corresponding to prayers said in succession. The use of the term *beads* here refers to such a series of prayers. However, despite this reference, Herrick's speaker encourages Corinna to pray quickly, to say fewer prayers that morning. She is admonished to rush through her morning religious rituals so that she can enjoy with the speaker the playful celebrations of May Day.

In the third stanza, the Christian elements of the poem are emphasized in the speaker's references to the decoration of homes so that they resemble an ark or tabernacle (ornamented cabinets in which religious items of sacred significance are stored). Such decorations, are, as the speaker points out, traditionally made from whitethorn branches or blossoms. The whitethorn tree, also known as the hawthorn tree, blossoms in May and features prominently in May Day celebrations. The May Pole itself, around which celebrants dance, is believed to have traditionally been made from hawthorn branches. As scholars such as Charles Hardwick, in the 1872 *Traditions, Superstitions, and Folk-Lore: Chiefly Lancashire, and the North of England,* point out, the May Pole is a phallic symbol. The tradition of dancing around the May Pole with ribbons celebrates union and fertility. Herrick weaves Christian notions of devotion and sacrament into a May Day celebration frowned upon by the conservative Puritans and widely recognized as a celebration of love, romance, and fertility. In the couplet that concludes this stanza, the speaker once again urges Corinna to come with him and join the May Day festivities. Whatever his intentions are for celebrating this festival with Corinna, the speaker implies in the next-to-last line of the stanza that he and Corinna have already enjoyed a physical relationship. He states that they should refrain from sinning any longer, as they have already done, by lingering together. Although he does not specify where they have lingered, up to this point the speaker has made it plain that Corinna is still in bed. Now, he seems to reveal that he has not simply arrived at her door and asked her to join him but rather that he has been with her all along. It appears, then, that Corinna and the speaker have already been together, and furthermore, that the speaker wishes to celebrate the May Day festivities in a similarly physical fashion. The speaker's desires are persistent and clear.

The speaker's view of May Day and his intentions regarding how he wishes to spend his time with Corinna are made even plainer in the next stanza. After noting that many young men and women have already enjoyed the celebrations and have even become engaged to be married in the process, the speaker then delineates the May Day activities that others have enjoyed and that he clearly wishes to partake in. He notes that many gowns have been stained green, suggesting that many young women have already enjoyed a romp in the grass with their lovers. He also makes reference to kisses exchanged between young couples. In the final couplet of the poem, the speaker alludes to the telling of jokes rife with sexual innuendo. Although Brooks has maintained that the pagan and Christian elements of the poem are reconciled in this stanza, when the frolicking lovers seek their priests and vow to marry, the presence of so many references to sexual relationships throughout the poem undercuts the religious intentions that Brooks emphasizes. While some of the lovers may eventually seek to marry, the speaker's focus throughout the poem has been on physical pleasure, rather than Christian piety. Every religious reference has been countered by examples

The last stanza mentions growing old together.
(DNF-Style Photography / Shutterstock.com)

of pagan rituals and beliefs or to allusions to the "sins" the young couples are committing in the name of the May Day celebrations.

In the final stanza of the poem, the speaker's emphasis on enjoying the physical pleasures of romantic relationships is further emphasized. After pointing to the harmlessness of such enjoyments, the speaker then draws attention to the rapidity with which he and his lover Corinna will age and die. He beckons Corinna to share with him love, passion, and delight. In this final stanza, as the speaker observes how quickly time passes, he does not beg Corinna to repent her sins, or to marry him, or to pray. All references to spirituality and Christian tradition have been abandoned. The focus is exclusively on enjoying youth and love while such things last. There is no mediation, or balance, between the spiritual and the sensual in this final stanza of the poem. All emphasis is on the sensual. Throughout the rest of the poem, Herrick mingles the notions of religion and romance, presenting a Christian reference or view and countering it almost immediately with an allusion to paganism, mythology, or sexuality. He pays lip service to Christian rites and traditions, he nods respectfully toward priests, prayers, and piety, but in the end, Herrick's attitude seems to be one of appeasement rather than sincerity. In considering the realities and desires of youthful love, Herrick in the end does not marry the spiritual with the sensual. There is no synthesis of the two as the references to religion fade away. Rather, Herrick, through his speaker, advocates the full enjoyment of one's youth and the romances of this period of life.

Source: Catherine Dominic, Critical Essay on "Corinna's Going A-Maying," in *Poetry for Students*, Gale, Cengage Learning, 2012.

H.R. Swardson

In the following excerpt, Swardson discusses the effectiveness of sensuous natural imagery and classical elements in Herrick's poetry.

...The ceremony of mirth receives its fullest expression, however, in one poem, "Corinna's going a-maying." It is not necessary to dwell in great detail on its mingling of Christian and pagan elements; the poem has, for this, caught the attention of many critics and has been expertly analysed by Cleanth Brooks [in *The Well Wrought Urn*, 1947]. Brooks points out, in the flowers bowing to the East, in the birds saying matins and singing hymns, in the village houses becoming 'arks' and 'tabernacles,' that the May Day rites are conceived 'as religious rites, though, of course, those of a pagan religion.' It is a 'sin' and 'profanation' to abstain from these rites of nature. Use of the word 'sin' in this way, a near reversal of common Christian application, points up a 'clash between the Christian and pagan world views.' Man's relation to nature is significant in this. 'Corinna,' says Brooks, 'is actually being reproached for being late to church—the church of nature. The village itself has become a grove, subject to the laws of nature. One remembers that the original sense of "pagan" was "country-dweller" because the worship of the old gods and goddesses persisted longest there. On this May morning, the country has come into the village to claim it, at least on this one day, for its own. Symbolically, the town has disappeared and its mores are superseded.' These elements qualify the theme in that 'the poem is obviously not a brief for the acceptance of the pagan ethic so much as it is a statement that the claims of the pagan ethic—however much they may be overlaid—exist, and on occasion emerge, as on this day.' Corinna, who is told to 'Rise; and put on your Foliage' along with the other 'budding' boys and girls 'is subject to nature, and to the claims of nature.... Not to respond is to "sin" against nature itself.' Brooks points out, finally, a 'reconcilement of the conflicting claims of paganism and Christianity' in 'the village boys and girls with their grass-stained gowns, coming to the priest to receive the blessing of the church':

> IN 'CORINNA,' HOWEVER, WHICH IS THE BEST OF THE CEREMONY POEMS, THE TENDENCY IS VERY MUCH TOWARD *INCLUSION* IN A CHRISTIAN CONCEPTION—WITHOUT A SACRIFICE OF ANY OF THE VITAL QUALITIES OF THE PAGAN WORLD."

And some have wept, and woo'd, and plighted Troth,
And chose their priest, ere we can cast off sloth.

All this amounts to a most mature and compelling expression of the *carpe diem* theme.

It is, withal, necessary to emphasize one point about the use of religious terms in this poem, for their effect may be misunderstood. We have seen in some preceding poems that the claims of Herrick's natural world are often made compelling as a kind of parallel or counter religion. In this kind of poem the claims are, in a sense, made *against* a Christian conception of experience. In "Corinna," however, which is the best of the ceremony poems, the tendency is very much toward *inclusion* in a Christian conception—without a sacrifice of any of the vital qualities of the pagan world. Certainly the pagan attitude gets its due. At first glance the poem may seem like a love poet's parody of a religious poem, sensual love receiving an ironic sort of sanction by a witty reversal of sin and virtue wherein the terms of worship are applied to this pagan activity. But the poem is not a parody. The 'sin' is not religious piety; if we take the literal interpretation, sloth, if anything, is the sin. The matins that the birds say and the hymns they sing are not just rites of nature; we have no reason to believe they are not sincerely Christian too. 'Few beads are best,' but the beads are still said. They are not the alternative to this activity. Finally, the wooing ends with the choice of a priest for marriage.

Such mirth is thus not licence, as the typical *carpe diem* poem would have it, nor is it to be abjured, as strict Christian moralism might have it. At the same time that the poem works against the narrowly pious attitude in Christianity, it makes some use of the undeniable wisdom in the Christian order of life, including its action within some lawful boundary and recognizing considerations that are entirely foreign to the classical *carpe diem* statement. So we have 'harmless folly,' 'cleanly wantonness,' and fun that ends in marriage. The classical *carpe diem* argument which abounds in Elizabethan and Cavalier lyrics makes an illuminating contrast when set alongside Herrick's treatment of the theme. Consider first Ben Jonson's "Song to Celia":

> Come my Celia, let us prove
> While we may, the sports of love;
> Time will not be ours, for ever:
> He, at length, our good will sever.
> Spend not then his guifts in vaine.
> Sunnes, that set, may rise againe:
> But if once we loose this light,
> 'Tis, with us, perpetual night.
> Why should we deferre our joyes?
> Fame, and rumor are but toyes.
> Cannot we delude the eyes
> Of a few poore houshold spyes?
> Or his easier eares beguile,
> So removed by our wile?
> 'Tis no sinne, loves fruit to steale,
> But the sweet theft to reveale:
> To be taken, to be seene,
> These have crimes accounted beene.

The customary end of the argument is adulterous seduction, a goal unchanged from Catullus to Jonson. With this we may compare Herrick's famous "To the Virgins, to make much of Time." The first three stanzas proceed in the normal way:

> Gather ye Rose-buds while ye may,
> Old Time is still a flying:
> And this same flower that smiles to day,
> To morrow will be dying.
>
> The glorious Lamp of Heaven, the Sun,
> The higher he's a getting;
> The sooner will his Race be run,
> And neerer he's to Setting.
>
> That Age is best, which is the first,
> When Youth and Blood are warmer;
> But being spent, the worse, and worst
> Times still succeed the former.

But the fourth stanza puts in place of the usual enticement a word quite foreign to the classical *carpe diem* poem: 'marry.'

> Then be not coy, but use your time;
> And while ye may, goe marry:
> For having lost but once your prime,
> You may for ever tarry.

The end in marriage, the sound advice against becoming an old maid, corresponds to the choosing of a priest after the frolic in "Corinna." Herrick is able to make the *carpe diem* argument, and do some justice to it, yet end within the Christian fold.

In conclusion it must be remembered that this effort either to compete on even terms or to reconcile the 'pagan spirit' with religious attitudes is not anything like a consistent programme in Herrick's poetry. The proportion of poems in which it appears is small. A great many of the poems in *Hesperides* may be mere erotic 'indulgence' as they have been called. But we need not require a conscious and consistent formulation on the part of the poet. What gives these occasional poems their special interest and, I think, excellence, is that in them we do not have purely erotic or voluptuous effects but we have the various manifestations of the 'pagan spirit'—nature, love, fairy lore, verse, wine, mirth—conceived as an order of experience, an order deserving ritual, ceremony, and art. It is this ceremonial quality, a ritual elevation, that helps give this experience a value beyond that of immediate pleasure. The worth of this kind of experience is most frequently realized or defined against the opposition or resistance, often implicit, of common Christian attitudes. The opposition stands against both the 'pagan ethic' and the classical literary tradition. This is what we mean when we speak of a tension between Christian and classical traditions. It is not present in the mass of purely erotic poems, such as "The Vine" or the various anatomies of woman. Nor is it really present in the many recantations Herrick makes in the *Noble Numbers*, at least not as a fruitful source of definition and understanding of complex and paradoxical values. It is most fruitful in those poems which are neither complete renunciations nor simple paeans of joy, but in which some effort is made to assert the claims of one order of experience without denying the certain and recognized value of another order. This, I take it, is what occurs in "Corinna."

Source: H. R. Swardson, "Herrick and the Ceremony of Mirth," in *Poetry and the Foundation of Light: Observations on the Conflict between Christian and Classical Traditions in Seventeenth-Century Poetry*, University of Missouri Press, 1962, pp. 40–63.

Nathan Drake

In the following excerpt, Drake offers an overview of Herrick's literary career and reputation.

It is only within a short period, that due attention has been paid to the minor poets of the seventeenth century; round the names of Shakespeare, Johnson, Cowley, Milton, Waller, Denham and Dryden, a lustre so brilliant had been diffused, that the reputation of numerous poets of

> ONE CHIEF CAUSE OF THE NEGLECT
> INTO WHICH THE POETRY OF HERRICK HAS
> FALLEN, IS ITS EXTREME INEQUALITY."

the same age was nearly lost in their splendour. In the course of the last thirty years, however, a spirit of literary research, and a warm partiality for the whole body of our elder poetry, have been strongly awakened; the works of Davies and of Hall, of Phineas and Giles Fletcher, of Browne and Carew, of Suckling and Marvel, have been republished; various and well-selected extracts, from a multitude of authors contemporary with these, have likewise made their appearance in the Collections of Percy, of Headley, and of Ellis; and Anderson, in his edition of the British Poets, has, with great propriety, introduced many a neglected though highly poetic writer of this period.

Notwithstanding these exertions, however, there still remain involved in partial obscurity some votaries of the Muse, who deserve a better fate. I would particularly mention, as entitled to rank foremost in the list, the names of George Wither, James Shirley, and Robert Herrick. Of the two former, some beautiful portions have been given to the world, by Percy, Gilchrist and Ellis, yet much is left highly worthy of preservation. Wither was a most versatile and voluminous writer, extremely unequal, and, for the most part, very coarse and colloquial in his language, yet are there dispersed, through his bulky tomes, and especially through his *Juvenilia*, many passages admirably picturesque, and many amatory songs of great elegance.... Shirley, having been principally known as a dramatic poet, his smaller pieces, which were printed in 1646, were comparatively little noticed....

If Wither and Shirley, however, may be said to have been unjustly neglected, the charge will apply, with much greater truth, to the productions of Robert Herrick, a poet scarce even known by name, and of whom, until very lately, the brief notices of Phillips, Anthony Wood, and Grainger, were all that preserved his existence from oblivion. It was in the *Gentleman's Magazine* for 1796 and 1797, that the greater part of the lovers of poetry of the present age first learnt,

that our bard had even written; here are given some additional events and anecdotes of his life, and in the *Specimens of the Early English Poets*, are four extracts from his volume of poems....

One chief cause of the neglect into which the poetry of Herrick has fallen, is its extreme inequality. It would appear he thought it necessary to publish every thing he composed, however trivial, however ridiculous or indecorous. The consequence has been, that productions, which Marlowe or Milton might have owned with pleasure, have been concealed, and nearly buried, in a crude and undigested mass. Had he shewn any taste in selection, I have no doubt the fate of his volume, though reduced two thirds of its present size, had been widely different. Perhaps there is no collection of poetry in our language, which, in some respects, more nearly resembles the *Carmina* of Catullus. It abounds in Epigrams disgusting and indecent, in satirical delineations of personal defects, in frequent apologies for the levity of his Muse, and repeated declarations of the chastity of his life; it is interspersed, also, with several exquisite pieces of the amatory and descriptive kind, and with numerous addresses to his friends and relations, by whom he appears to have been greatly beloved. The variety of metre he has used in this work is truly astonishing; he has almost exhausted every form of rhymed versification, and in many he moves with singular ease and felicity.

It has been observed by Mr. Headley, that "Waller is too exclusively considered as the first man, who brought versification to any thing like its present standard. Carew's pretensions to the same merit, are seldom sufficiently either considered or allowed. I may venture, I think, to introduce Herrick to my reader, as having greatly contributed toward this mechanical perfection. Many of his best effusions have the sweetness, the melody and elegance of modern compositions. He was nearly, if not altogether, contemporary with Carew, for, if the account of Clarendon, who had been intimate with him, be correct, Carew lived fifty years, and as we know that he died in 1639, he must have been born only a year or two anterior to Herrick. It is true Carew's Poems were published earlier, being given to the world shortly after his death, probably in the year 1640 or 1641, for the second edition of his Works bears date 1642; but as Herrick's productions were all written before 1648, and many of them twenty, or, perhaps, thirty years previous to this period, it is obvious he could have been no imitator of the friend of Clarendon, but must have been indebted merely to his own exertions and genius, for the grace and polish of his versification. I consider likewise, the two little Poems, entitled the "Primrose" and the "Inquiry," which were first published in Carew's Works, and afterwards appeared among the Poems of Herrick, to have certainly belonged to the latter, and to have been attributed to Carew by the Editor's mistake. In the first place it is not probable that Herrick, who certainly superintended and arranged his own productions, and who must have been familiar with the volume of his ingenious rival, would have republished these pieces as his own, if he had not possessed a prior claim to them; and, secondly, the Poem termed the "Enquiry," by the Editor of Carew, is, in Herrick, addressed to a beloved Mistress, to "Mrs. Eliz. Wheeler," under the name of the lost Shepherdesse, and by the nature of its variations from the copy in Carew, bears indubitable marks of being the original, from whence those lines were taken, and which, being probably written early, and circulated in Manuscript by Herrick's friends, might easily, from a general resemblance of style and manner, be mistaken, by the Editor, for a genuine production of Carew.

If, in point of versification, Herrick may enter into competition with either Carew or Waller, he will be found still more competent to contend with them as to sentiment and imagery. It has been justly observed, that "Carew has the ease, without the pedantry of Waller"; the remark will apply with equal propriety to Herrick. His amatory poems unite the playful gaiety of Anacreon with the tender sweetness of Catullus, and are altogether devoid of that mythological allusion and cold conceit, which, in the pages of Waller, so frequently disgust the reader. There is a vein also of rich description in the poetry of Herrick, undiscoverable in the productions of the two other poets, and which resembles the best manner of Milton's Minora and Marlowe's Passionate Shepherd. Nor has he been unsuccessful in imitating the Horatian style and imagery . . . , while, at the same time, the morality of another portion of his lyrics, breathes an air of the most pleasing melancholy. I hesitate not, therefore, to consider him in the same degree superior to Carew, as Carew most assuredly is to Waller, whose versification, as I have elsewhere observed, has alone embalmed his memory. . . .

[Herrick] has attempted, it is true, no production of any considerable length, nor has he ventured into the lofty regions of the epic or dramatic Muse. The joys of Love and Wine, pictures of country life and manners, or playful incursions into the world of ideal forms, where

> Trip the light fairies and the dapper elves,

form the chief subjects of his poetry. Of these, some are written in a style and metre, which display no inferior command of language and versification, whilst their elegance, their tenderness or imagery is such, as to excite a well-founded admiration.

Unfortunately, like most authors of the age in which he lived, he has been totally inattentive to selection, and has thrown into his book such a number of worthless pieces, that those which possess decided merit, and which are few, if compared with the multitude which have none, are overlooked and forgotten in the crowd. Out of better than *fourteen hundred* poems, included in his *Hesperides* and *Noble Numbers*, not more than one hundred could be chosen by the hand of Taste. These, however, would form an elegant little volume, and would perpetuate the memory and the genius of HERRICK.

Source: Nathan Drake, "On the Life, Writings and Genius of Robert Herrick," in *Literary Hours: or, Sketches, Critical, Narrative, and Poetical, Vol. III*, T. Cadel and W. Davies, 1804, pp. 25–88.

SOURCES

Brooks, Cleanth, *The Well Wrought Urn: Studies in the Structure of Poetry*, Harcourt Brace, 1947, pp. 67–79.

"Charles I," in *History of the Monarchy: The Official Website of the British Monarchy*, http://www.royal.gov.uk/HistoryoftheMonarchy/KingsandQueensoftheUnited Kingdom/TheStuar ts/CharlesI.aspx (accessed April 21, 2011).

"Charles II," in *History of the Monarchy: The Official Website of the British Monarchy*, http://www.royal.gov.uk/HistoryoftheMonarchy/KingsandQueensoftheUnited Kingdom/TheStuar ts/CharlesII.aspx (accessed April 21, 2011).

"Church of England Provisional Attendance Figures for 2009," in *Thinking Anglicanism*, http://www.thinkingang licans.org.uk/archives/004854.html (accessed April 21, 2011).

Dobranski, Stephen B., *Readers and Authorship in Early Modern England*, Cambridge University Press, 2005, pp. 150–82.

Hardwick, Charles, *Traditions, Superstitions, and Folklore, Chiefly Lancashire and the North of England*, A. Ireland, 1872, pp. 83–95.

Herrick, Robert, "Corinna's Going A-Maying," in *The Complete Poetry of Robert Herrick*, edited by J. Max Patrick, New York University Press, 1963, pp. 98–100.

"How MPs Are Elected," in *UK Parliament*, http://www.parliament.uk/about/mps-and-lords/members/electing-mps/ (accessed April 21, 2011).

"Interregnum," in *History of the Monarchy: The Official Website of the British Monarchy*, http://www.royal.gov.uk/HistoryoftheMonarchy/KingsandQueensoftheUnited Kingdom/TheStuarts/Interregnum.aspx (accessed April 21, 2011).

Kurtz, Johann Heinrich, "Anglicanism and Puritanism," in *Church History*, Funk & Wagnalls, 1890, pp. 14–19.

Mulholland, Helene, "Rapid Influx of New Peers Has Made House of Lords Too Full, Report Warns," in *Guardian* (London, England), April 20, 2011, http://www.guardian.co.uk/politics/2011/apr/20/house-of-lords-too-full-report-warns (accessed April 21, 2011).

Pace, Roy Bennett, *English Literature*, Allyn and Bacon, 1931, pp. 86–117.

Patrick, J. Max, ed., Notes to "Corinna's Going A-Maying," in *The Complete Poetry of Robert Herrick*, New York University Press, 1963, p. 100.

Post, Jonathan F. S., *English Lyric Poetry*, Routledge, 1999, pp. 91–134.

Pugh, Syrithe, *Herrick, Fanshawe and the Politics of Intertextuality: Classical Literature and Seventeenth-Century Royalism*, Ashgate Publishing, 2010, pp. 39–56.

Rollin, Roger B., "Robert Herrick," in *Dictionary of Literary Biography*, Vol. 126, *Seventeenth-Century British Nondramatic Poets, Second Series*, edited by M. Thomas Hester, Gale Research, 1993, pp. 168–81.

Schroedel, John, and Jenny Schroedel, *The Everything Mary Book: The Life and Legacy of the Blessed Mother*, F & W Publishing, 2006, pp. 107–20.

FURTHER READING

Cross, Claire, *Church and People: England 1450-1660*, Wiley-Blackwell, 1999.

> In this volume, Cross provides a detailed study of the conflict within England between the church and the government, delineating the way the people of England were subject to the authorities

of both systems. The conflicts between church and state and between groups competing for power within each realm are analyzed.

McDowell, Nicholas, *Poetry and Allegiance in the English Civil Wars: Marvell and the Cause of Wit*, Oxford University Press, 2009.

> McDowell explores the time period of the English Civil War from the perspective of Andrew Marvell, Herrick's contemporary. Marvell, unlike the Cavalier poets, remained ambivalent about his allegiances, and he associated with both monarchists and parliamentarians.

Rollin, Roger B., *Robert Herrick*, Twayne Publishers, 1992.

> Rollin's account of Herrick's life and work is one of the few biographical accounts available.

Wiseman, Susan, *Conspiracy and Virtue: Women, Writing, and Politics in Seventeenth-Century England*, Oxford University Press, 2007.

> Focusing on the years 1620 through 1688, Wiseman explores the official exclusion of women from the political world and demonstrates the ways in which they nevertheless became involved in this sphere through their writings and through other means. Wiseman includes writings by both men and women on this topic, and she studies the works of such writers as Elizabeth Avery, Aphra Behn, Anne Bradstreet, Margaret Cavendish, Queen Christina of Sweden, Lucy Hutchinson, John Milton, Elizabeth Poole, and Henry Jessey, among others.

SUGGESTED SEARCH TERMS

Herrick AND Corinna's Going A-Maying

Herrick AND carpe diem

Herrick AND Cavalier poetry

Herrick AND Anglicanism

Herrick AND English Civil War

Herrick AND nature poetry

Herrick AND Hesperides

Herrick AND Charles I

Herrick AND love poetry

Herrick and Carolinian poetry

Domestic Violence

EAVAN BOLAND

2007

"Domestic Violence" is a poem by the distinguished Irish poet Eavan Boland. Published as the title poem in Boland's collection *Domestic Violence* in 2007, it is one of many poems in the collection that combine personal reflections with observations and questions about the sectarian violence that began in the British province of Northern Ireland in 1969 and continued for thirty years.

In this poem, the poet looks back on the beginning of the Troubles, as the conflict was known in Northern Ireland, and considers the question of the relationship between public and private worlds. She was living near Dublin, Ireland, at the time, which was not directly affected by the violence, so she witnessed the Troubles not as a participant but on the television news. She had just married and was raising two daughters during the 1970s. Was she then unconnected to the violence that broke out in the northern part of the island? Or is everyone somehow involved in what happens in or near their country, even though their own personal lives seem to have no connection to it? As a reflective poem that considers the interwoven fabric of domestic life and Irish history, "Domestic Violence" serves as an introduction to some of the themes that have repeatedly occupied Boland during her career.

AUTHOR BIOGRAPHY

Boland was born on September 24, 1944, in Dublin, Ireland. Her father, Frederick Boland, was a diplomat who held posts in London and New York City, and her mother, Frances, was a painter. Boland attended a convent school in London from 1950 to 1956 and a school in New York City from 1956 to 1959. She then returned to Ireland and attended a convent school in Killiney, County Durham. Already a lover of poetry with a talent for writing it, she self-published her pamphlet *23 Poems* in 1962. That same year she enrolled at Trinity College, Dublin, from which she graduated with a degree in English in 1966. She became a junior lecturer at Trinity in 1967 but soon decided that she was not suited to a full-time academic career because it would not nourish her creative writing. Her first full-length book of poems was *New Territory* (1967). This was followed by *The War Horse* (1975) and *In Her Own Image* (1980). During this period Boland also worked as a journalist, publishing book reviews and other pieces on culture in the *Irish Times* and other publications.

In the meantime Boland had married Kevin Casey, a novelist, in 1969, and they had two daughters. More poetry collections followed: *Night Feed* (1982), *The Journey* (1983), *Outside History: Selected Poems, 1980–1990* (1990), *In a Time of Violence* (1994), *A Christmas Chalice* (1994), and *Collected Poems (1995)*, published in the United States as *An Origin Like Water: Collected Poems, 1967–1987* (1996).

Boland then published *Code* (2001), which appeared in the United States as *Against Love Poetry (2001)*. It was selected by the *New York Times* as a notable book in 2001, and also was awarded the Smartt Family Prize by the *Yale Review*. *New Collected Poems* appeared in 2005, and *Domestic Violence,* which contains the poem, "Domestic Violence," in 2007. The book was short-listed for the Forward Prize.

Boland has won many literary awards, including the Irish American Cultural Award, 1983; the Lannan Award for Poetry, 1994; the Irish American Literary Award, 1994; and the Bucknell Medal of Merit, 2000. She has taught at academic institutions, including Bowdoin College, Brunswick, ME; University of Utah, Salt Lake City, UT; and as Hurst Professor at Washington University, St. Louis, MO, in 1993. She holds honorary degrees from University College,

Dublin, 1997; Strathclyde University, 1997; Colby College, 1998; and Holy Cross College, 2000.

Since 1995, Boland has been Bella Mabury and Eloise Mabury Knapp Professor in Humanities and director of the creative writing program at Stanford University in California.

POEM SUMMARY

The text used for this summary is from *Domestic Violence*, W. W. Norton, 2007, pp. 13-15. A version of the poem can be found on the following Web page: http://www.poetryfoundation.org/archive/poem.html?id = 180326.

Section 1
The poem is divided into four sections. The first section consists of three stanzas. In the first stanza, the poet describes a quiet natural scene in a village in Ireland in the winter at night. The moon is visible. She sees some seedlings, but in the dark they seem divorced from their surroundings, as if they are standing alone. She recalls a clever slogan she has seen in the window of the butcher's shop in the village. It is a friendly sign and its presence here suggests the poet's familiarity with the life of the village.

In the second stanza the poet looks back at her own life. She refers to the many changes in her life the year she got married. One of those changes was that the young couple moved to the suburbs. Lines 3 and 4 emphasizes that they were very young (although it is probably only in retrospect that the poet, many years later, realizes how young she then was). They did not know much about things and were very wrapped up in themselves, as if their lives and relationship were all that mattered and all that existed.

The third stanza recalls how the young married couple would hear another couple, presumably their neighbors, quarreling at night. Their voices sounded angry. In lines 3 and 4, the poet uses this recollection from the past to make an observation about life, in which she states that there is always some problem or other in a close relationship, even when the people involved love each other.

Section 2
In this section, which has four stanzas, the personal references of the first section expand to

MEDIA ADAPTATIONS

- In a 2008 interview with Elizabeth Austen on a Puget Sound, Washington, radio station, Boland read "Domestic Violence." The recording is hosted at the Public Radio Exchange (http://www.prx.org/pieces/24834-interview-with-irish-poet-eavan-boland).

include references to what was happening in the wider world at the time. Lines 1 and 2 refer to the civil disturbances in modern Ireland that began in 1969 but also had a long history going back hundreds of years. The country is referred to as a diseased body exhibiting its symptoms for everyone to see, including the poet and her husband. They wondered what had happened to their land, which they knew to be beautiful. In the second stanza the poet mentions some aspects of the country they obviously had a deep affection for, including its rivers, hills, and mountains. She mentions the area around Dublin, the Republic of Ireland's capital city. She adds an ominous note when she says that this was the country they thought they knew—implying that there was something else going on that they were not aware of. This becomes clearer in the next stanza when the poet describes what they used to watch on their old and small television set. On the television they saw the Ireland they loved transformed into a grim place. Because of the violence that had broken out, they would see accounts of killings, many of them, and funerals. The country seemed to have become a place full of grief. The larger, public world has impinged, via television, on their smaller, private world.

In stanza 4 the poet reflects on how they did not understand what caused the violence. They did not understand it at the time and they did not understand it any better later. They knew that some people hated other people, but what the root cause of that hatred was, and in what sense people were living their lives in the wrong way, they did not know.

Section 3

The entire section consists of one sentence, spread over two stanzas, and formed into a question. The poet reflects about the situation she has described in the previous stanza. She asks herself: If the purpose or function of memory is simply to remember and not to understand or make amends or do anything other than simply remember, and if the poet in her kitchen is safe from the turbulent events she watches on television, why does one persistent question arise? She describes this question as one a nameless woman asks a man, but it may also be thought of as one she herself asked her husband, or which any woman in Ireland at the time might have asked her man. The question is, what else might they have done, either to prevent the violence or to produce a different outcome? The question may also refer to their personal relationship. The question has urgency about it and is repeated many times. It emphasizes that the private, personal world of couples and families is not cut off from the public world of society as a whole.

Section 4

The final section of the poem has three stanzas. The first stanza begins with a blunt statement that "we," meaning perhaps the people of Ireland at the time of what they called the Troubles, failed. They failed to prevent violence and solve the problems that caused it. Line 2 states that the times were important and called for great people and great actions, but the people at the time failed to rise to the occasion. But in line 3 the poet reverses course. She asks directly why she wrote the previous two lines when she does not believe what they say.

In the second stanza the poet proceeds on the assumption that her words in lines 1 and 2 of the previous stanza were not true. In contrast to the sentiments in those earlier lines that said she and others had failed, she says that "we," meaning she and her husband and their children as well as many similar families, stayed together and were happy. The children grew up there and have now left home. Whereas the first two lines of the first stanza posited a connection between the personal and public world, in which everyone must take some responsibility, this stanza emphasizes how individual families went about their daily lives, unconnected to the Troubles.

In the final stanza the poet returns to the quarreling couple she mentioned in section 1. It as if she is anticipating the reader's question about who that couple was and whether the poet and her husband ever wanted to know who they were. The final line answers the question in a cryptic manner. The poet says she thinks she knows who that couple was, and that she always knew. The implication is that the quarreling couple were, in a sense, everyone. Everyone was involved in what was going on in Ireland at the time.

THEMES

Past

"Domestic Violence" looks back on events of more than thirty years ago, some of which were themselves rooted in past events in Irish history. The poet looks back to a specific time, beginning in 1969. This date is not explicitly stated in the poem, but the poem is clearly autobiographical. Boland married in 1969, and the speaker refers to her marriage in stanza 2 of the first section. She and her husband then moved to the Dublin suburbs, which she also refers to in the poem. The poem refers to her youth at the time; she was in fact twenty-five years old. She recalls how the Troubles in Northern Ireland began in that year, and it came as a shock to her and her husband. They had grown up in the 1950s and early 1960s, a time of relative peace in Ireland's long history of sectarian strife and conflict with the British, so they were unable to understand the conflict fully, either at the time or later.

The poem emphasizes how the past impinges on the present, an appropriate theme for a poem about Irish history, in which conflicts going back hundreds of years still influence the present. The poet looks back on these events with questions not only about what happened and why, but how those public events they witnessed on television impinged upon the private world of their personal lives. Those personal lives had previously seemed so separate, so unconnected to the horrible world of murder and mayhem that was taking place elsewhere on the island.

Boland seems to try out different approaches to the question, suggesting at one point (the beginning of section 4) that the people of Ireland—including herself, one presumes—failed to rise to the occasion when difficulties sprang up. However, she quickly rejects that conclusion and focuses on the smaller, personal details of her own life with her family, which was a happy one. How could that be considered a failure, in the same sense that Irish society failed during that period by lapsing into sectarian violence?

The conclusion she reaches seems to be that the quarreling couple she refers to are more deeply connected than she had then realized (or had been willing to acknowledge) to the public violence she witnessed on the television screen. Everyone, it seems, is connected to that violence, in some way or another, even people who do not at the time see the connection. As she now considers the past, she sees how the public and the private worlds are connected; they seep into each other and cannot remain separate.

Conflict

Conflict at many different levels is central to the poem. Personal conflict is apparent in the third stanza of section 1, when the poet mentions the quarreling couple who lived, it would seem, next door. The poet and her husband listen to them quarreling in the night. The poet seems to universalize the conflict immediately after that when she comments that there is always something not quite right, even in the best of relationships.

There is also severe conflict at the societal level. This is the sectarian violence between Protestants and Catholics in Northern Ireland that broke out in 1969 and continued into the 1970s and beyond. Northern Ireland was ruled by Britain, and the majority of Catholics in the province, who were discriminated against by the Protestants, wanted Northern Ireland to sever its link to Britain and unite with the overwhelmingly Catholic Republic of Ireland. With its capital in Dublin, the Republic of Ireland had, at the time, been an independent nation for nearly fifty years. The poet lived in a Dublin suburb and watched the reports of the violence in Northern Ireland on television. For the most part, Dublin escaped the sectarian violence. However, on one notorious day in May 1974, a series of car bombings in the city killed twenty-six people and wounded nearly three hundred.

The Catholics in Northern Ireland were supported by the Irish Republican Army, a terrorist organization that carried out attacks against British troops in Northern Ireland and against Protestant civilians. The Protestants created

TOPICS FOR FURTHER STUDY

- *Mairead Corrigan and Betty Williams: Making Peace in Northern Ireland* (1998) by Bettina Ling is a biography for young readers about two women who started a peace movement in Northern Ireland and were awarded the Nobel Peace Prize in 1976. After reading the book, write a short essay in which you summarize how their movement started and what it achieved.

- After doing research in the library and online, prepare a digital interactive timeline for the Northern Ireland Troubles with at least twelve dates on it, showing the main events of the Troubles from 1968 to 1998. Give a class presentation in which you outline the course of the Troubles and explain why the Good Friday agreement in 1998 provided the framework for the ending of the violence.

- Go to UMapper.com and create a map of Ireland. Locate and name the border between the Republic of Ireland and Northern Ireland, the major cities (Dublin, Belfast, Derry), and the six counties that make up Northern Ireland. Explain the role of each of those cities in the Troubles. Distribute your map and notes to other students through your blog.

- Using Internet and library research, describe the role played by the United States in the resolution of the Troubles in Northern Ireland. What was the role of the U.S. Special Envoy for Northern Ireland in the 1990s? Would peace have been achieved without the assistance of the Special Envoy? Write a short essay or a poem about U.S. involvement in the peace process in Northern Ireland.

- Millions of Americans trace their ancestry to Ireland. Research the history of immigration from Ireland in the eighteenth and nineteenth centuries. Why did so many Irish people immigrate to the United States? Were the Irish immigrants welcomed in the United States? How many Americans today claim Irish roots? Give a class presentation in which you describe the main events that led to Irish immigration and describe the effect that it has had on the United States.

---

paramilitary groups of their own that carried out attacks against Catholics. This produced a seemingly endless cycle of violence—as the third stanza of the section 2 of the poem makes very clear.

STYLE

Metaphor

The central metaphor in the poem is the equation of the quarreling couple with the troubles of Ireland at the time. The metaphor makes the point that the personal is also the social and the political. At the macro level, the quarreling couple might be thought of as the Protestants and the Catholics, Ireland's two warring factions. The parallel between the personal and the societal levels is made clear by the way the last line of section 2 repeats, with the substitution of the words "wrong" for "right" and "love" for "hate," the last line of section 1. Section 1 is about the personal; section 2 is about the societal dimension of life. The metaphor is also implied in the title of the poem. Domestic violence is usually used to describe violence within a family; the poem applies the term to a wider sphere of violence—domestic in that sense means within a nation, not foreign.

Imagery

The imagery of the poem presents a contrast between an idyllic and a nightmare setting. The

The setting of the poem is in Ireland. *(Patryk Kosmider | Shutterstock.com)*

first stanza suggests a friendly village in which nothing untoward takes place, but the second stanza announces a change, without specifying what that change was, and the third stanza introduces the notion of conflict for the first time. Section 2, stanza 2 creates a picture of an ancient, familiar Ireland that has long endured and is loved by the speaker, but this is followed in the third stanza by images of death and sorrow as transmitted by news reports on television. The transition is foreshadowed in section 1, stanza 1, by the use of the word "orphans" to describe the way the seedlings appear by moonlight. The word "moonlight" is repeated in section 2, stanza 3, in the context of funerals, which gives another, more somber meaning to the earlier reference.

HISTORICAL CONTEXT

Irish History

The Troubles, as they were known, that began in Northern Ireland in 1969 can only be understood in the context of hundreds of years of Irish history. For centuries Ireland was dominated by England, its larger neighbor across the Irish Sea. In 1171, England's Henry II invaded Ireland and declared himself king of Ireland as well as England. From that point on Ireland struggled against English domination. During the reign of Elizabeth I (1558–1603), there was a full-scale attempt by Protestant England to subdue Catholic Ireland. By the early seventeenth century English rule over Ireland had been established. Many members of the Catholic aristocracy fled to Europe. England's King James I (1603–1625) seized Catholic lands, mainly in the north of Ireland, and gave them to Protestant settlers from England and Scotland. By about 1640, 100,000 Protestants loyal to the English crown had settled in the north. This planted the seeds of a conflict that would continue for centuries and break out again in 1969, since the Irish Protestants of the twentieth century were, for the most part, descended from those early English and Scottish settlers and remained loyal to the British crown.

During the seventeenth century the Irish continued to resist English rule, and a crucial

COMPARE & CONTRAST

- **1960s–70s:** Northern Ireland has its own parliament and the province is self-governing. However, as a result of the Troubles, the British government first suspends and then, in 1973, abolishes the Northern Ireland parliament. The province is then ruled directly from London.

  Today: Self-rule is restored to Northern Ireland by means of the Northern Ireland Executive and the Northern Ireland Assembly. The assembly consists of 108 members and ensures that all groups in Northern Ireland are adequately represented and have a share of power.

- **1960s–70s:** Annual parades are a source of tension in Northern Ireland, especially the Orange Order's July 12 parades, which commemorate the Protestant victory at the Battle of the Boyne in 1690. In Belfast the parade takes a traditional route through largely Catholic, nationalist areas. The nationalists, who want independence from Britain, object to what they see as triumph-

  alism on the part of the Protestant Unionists, who are in favor of British rule. Security forces must turn out in large numbers to prevent violence.

  Today: The July 12 Orange Order parade in Belfast remains a source of tension and violence. In 2010, nationalists attempting to block the parade throw petrol bombs at riot police, and the march is delayed by ninety minutes.

- **1960s–70s:** The Irish Republican Army begins a terrorist campaign to drive the British out of Northern Ireland. Many people are killed. In one incident in Belfast on July 21, 1972, IRA bombs kill nine and injure 130.

  Today: In 2006, the Independent Monitoring Commission in Northern Ireland reports that the Irish Republican Army has ceased all paramilitary activities. In 2007, the Ulster Volunteer Force, a Protestant paramilitary group, promises that it will not use violence against Catholics.

---

battle took place in 1690. This was the Battle of the Boyne, which took place just outside Drogheda, on the eastern Irish coast. In the battle, the forces of the England's Protestant King William of Orange (1689–1702) defeated those of the Catholic James II, who had been deposed by William and was seeking to reclaim the English throne. The battle was won decisively by William of Orange, whose victory solidified the Protestant domination of the north of Ireland (the area known as Ulster) that would continue for hundreds of years. Indeed, the battle took on great symbolic importance for Protestants in Ulster who continued to celebrate their victory even into the modern era. In the 1960s, Protestants in Northern Ireland celebrated the Battle of the Boyne with an annual parade in Belfast,

Northern Ireland's capital city, and other cities. During the Troubles, the Belfast parade, organized by the anti-Catholic Orange Order, was a source of tension because it passed through some areas of the city that were predominantly Catholic, and this was seen as provocation by Catholics.

In the eighteenth century, English laws banned Catholics from holding political office and owning land. This discrimination began to ease in the nineteenth century, particularly as a result of the Emancipation Act of 1829, under which Catholics were allowed to hold political office. Irish nationalism was on the rise at this time, and a movement calling for home rule for Ireland developed. British Prime Minister William Ewart Gladstone supported home rule, but

The second stanza references the bloody violence in Ireland. (Dirk Ercken | Shutterstock.com)

his efforts to pass a bill in the British Parliament that would establish it failed in 1886 and 1893. In 1914, the Third Home Rule Act passed, providing self-government for Ireland within the United Kingdom, but enactment of it was postponed until after World War I (1914–18).

In Dublin in 1916, the Easter Rising of Irish nationalists was suppressed by the British. In 1919, the Irish parliament declared Ireland to be an independent republic. This led to a war between the Irish nationalists and the British. In 1921, Irish leaders signed a treaty with Britain that created the Irish Free State, in which the large majority of people were Catholics. The new state did not include the six northern counties in Ireland that made up Ulster: Antrim, Armagh, Down, Fermanagh, Londonderry, and Tyrone. In these counties Protestants formed the majority and they continued to be part of the United Kingdom, although they were granted self-rule. In this way, Ireland was partitioned into two: twenty-six southern counties made up the Irish Free State and six northern counties constituted Northern Ireland.

The Troubles

The modern Troubles in Ireland began in late 1968. Catholics in Northern Ireland, who made up about one-third of the population, had long suffered from discrimination in housing, jobs, and political representation. In part inspired by the U.S. civil rights movement, Catholics began to air their grievances in street demonstrations. The demonstrations led to violent clashes between Catholics and Protestants, and in 1969, British troops were sent to Ulster to keep the peace. The troops were initially welcomed by the Catholic population but were soon seen to be defenders of the status quo, simply reinforcing the strength of the Protestants who were determined to maintain their privileged status. The situation deteriorated further when the Catholic cause was taken up by a resurgent Irish Republican Army (IRA), a nationalist group that had fought against the British in the 1920s. The IRA began a campaign of terrorism designed to end British rule in Northern Ireland and create a united Ireland. However, the Protestant Unionists also believed passionately in their cause and abhorred the idea of becoming a minority in a

Catholic-majority Republic of Ireland. They formed various paramilitary groups of their own that also carried out terrorist attacks. The sectarian warfare claimed many lives.

In 1971, the British government began detaining suspected IRA members without trial. By 1975, when internment without trial was ended, over two thousand men had been imprisoned. The number of British troops stationed in Northern Ireland increased to 22,000 in 1972. This year proved to be one of the most violent. In January, British troops fired on peaceful Catholic demonstrators in Londonderry (which the Catholics called Derry), killing thirteen people. The incident became known as "Bloody Sunday" and fueled bitter resentment in the Catholic population, and the violence worsened. In a twenty-one-month period in 1971 and 1972, 589 people died in Northern Ireland as a result of the Troubles, and 8,223 people were injured. The Irish nationalists were determined to drive the British out, but the British insisted that because the majority of the population in Northern Ireland wanted to remain part of the United Kingdom, the government would not entertain the idea of ceding sovereignty over the province to the Republic of Ireland. In 1985, after the political wing of the IRA, Sinn Fein, gained in political power in Northern Ireland's government, the Anglo-Irish Agreement was reached, acknowledging that Northern Ireland would remain free of the Republic as long as the majority of citizens wanted to be independent, but gave the Republic legitimate input into how Northern Ireland was ruled. The agreement did not end the violence, but it paved the way for the Good Friday Agreement in 1998, which created an assembly to govern Northern Ireland and helped drastically decrease the violence of the Troubles.

CRITICAL OVERVIEW

As the title poem in a collection by one of Ireland's leading poets, "Domestic Violence" has attracted some comment by reviewers. In *Booklist*, Patricia Monaghan calls the poem "stunning" and suggests that it is likely to be reprinted many times in poetry anthologies. According to Monaghan, the poem makes a "tight connection between an ordinary neighborhood's refusal to acknowledge the battery

of a wife and the nation's inability to come to terms with sectarian violence."

For Jennifer Keating-Miller in the *Irish Literary Supplement*, the poet's emphasis on how young she was at the time "refers not only to a newly-wed couple but a fledgling nation, emerging from years of colonial rule with fervent efforts to assert political and cultural sovereignty." Keating-Miller concludes that "Boland's reflections betray both regret and whispers of wisdom from lessons learned.... The haunting answer binds the individual and national strands at play throughout with the admittance of personal accountability."

In the *Southern Review*, Jay Rogoff notes an allusion in "Domestic Violence" to the poetry of W. B. Yeats about the ignorance of youth. He writes: "Like Yeats, [Boland] interweaves personal and political history, but unlike him, she watches from a distance, on her...television screen." In the poem, "Irish history keeps hovering like a failed marriage.... Ireland, not the marriage, suffers the 'domestic violence' of Boland's title." Rogoff's comment about the other poems in the book show that the themes elaborated in "Domestic Violence" are central to Boland's purpose. The poems "explore these interrelationships among self, memory, family, and country. With few exceptions, their diction, their syntax, and their figurative language all skillfully reinforce the personal and political themes Boland has so unobtrusively introduced."

CRITICISM

Bryan Aubrey
Aubrey holds a Ph.D. in English. In the following essay, he discusses "Domestic Violence" in terms of the contrast between the poet's younger self and the more mature perspective she attains in later life.

The Troubles in Northern Ireland have long faded from the newspaper headlines, replaced by news of sectarian conflict in other parts of the world. In the second decade of the twenty-first century, Northern Ireland is on a new chapter in its history. Few who recall the Troubles can have been unmoved by the sight of the Reverend Ian Paisley, a fire-breathing Protestant Unionist minister throughout the conflict, shaking hands with his once arch-enemy, Martin McGuinness of Sinn Fein (the political wing of the Irish Republican Army), at the swearing-in of a

WHAT DO I READ NEXT?

- Boland's collection *The War Horse*, published in 1975, contains many poems that reflect on the Troubles in Ireland. "Child of Our Time," for example, commemorates a child who was killed by a car bomb in Dublin in 1974. *The War Horse* is out of print but many of the poems in it can be found in Boland's *Collected Poems* (1995).

- Born in 1948, Ciaran Carson is an Irish poet who was raised as a Catholic in Belfast, Northern Ireland. He has written many poems about the Troubles, some of them marked by humor and satire. His *Collected Poems* was published in 2009. Many of the poems from his earlier collections, including *The Irish for No* (1987), *Belfast Confetti* (1993), and *Breaking News* (2003), which examine the Troubles, are contained in this volume.

- Seamus Heaney is considered by many to be the greatest living Irish poet. He won the Nobel Prize in Literature in 1995. Heaney was born in Northern Ireland and was living in Belfast in 1969 when the Troubles broke out. Like many Irish poets, he has written about those times in collections including *Wintering Out* (1973) and *North* (1975). His *Opening Ground: Selected Poems, 1966–96* (1999) contains a representative selection of his works.

- The 2002 nonfiction title *Making Sense of the Troubles: The Story of the Conflict in Northern Ireland* by David McKittrick and David McVea is a thorough and unbiased account of what happened in Northern Ireland during the Troubles and why it happened. The book covers the period from 1921, when Ireland was partitioned into two, to the historic agreements reached by 2000 that led to an end of the conflict.

- "The Distant Past" is a short story by distinguished Irish novelist and short story writer William Trevor. First published in 1975, it can be found in Trevor's later collections, *The Collected Stories* (1992) and *Ireland: Stories* (1995). The story is set in Ireland over a period of about fifty years, from about 1920 to the early 1970s, and deals with the conflicts between the British and the Irish, and the Protestants and Catholics.

- *Voices of Northern Ireland: Growing Up in a Troubled Land* by Carolyn Meyer is a book for young adults published in 2002. The author spent six weeks in Northern Ireland, interviewing young people in schools and other community organizations. She found that many of the young people were unwilling to break out of the traditional ways of thinking that prevail in their religion, whether Protestant or Catholic. In addition to the interviews, the author includes useful historical information about the Troubles.

- The long-standing conflict between the Palestinians and the Israelis has some parallels to the conflicts in Ireland. In *Palestinian: Teenage Refugees and Immigrants Speak Out (In Their Own Voices)*, edited by Nabil Marshood (1997), six Palestinian teenagers living in the United States discuss their views on the Arab-Israeli conflict.

- John Montague is a prominent Irish poet. His collection *The Rough Field* (originally published in 1972 and available in a 2005 reprint) is an epic poem that, like the work of Boland, intermingles the personal and the political, the past and the present. In Montague's case this covers several hundred years of Ulster history. There are many memorable poems in this collection, including "A Grafted Tongue," which is about the way a colonizing power can control the colonized people by imposing on them a language not their own.

power-sharing government in Northern Ireland in 2007. Paisley and McGuinness were about to become first minister and deputy first minister, respectively, in the Northern Ireland Assembly. It was a day that many thought they would never see, testimony to a community's willingness to heal itself after several decades of violence in which 3,600 people lost their lives, and 36,000 were injured.

Turn the clock back and it is not difficult to visualize the hatred, fear, and violence that blighted Northern Ireland, an area no larger than the state of Connecticut, just one and two generations ago. In addition to the people directly affected by the violence, millions of others throughout the United Kingdom and United States would, like the speaker in Eavan Boland's poem "Domestic Violence," watched nightly news stories on television about the succession of bombings, shootings, assassinations, and funerals that began in 1969 and intensified during the 1970s. It was a difficult time when two cultures with a deep-rooted antipathy toward each other found themselves unable to live peaceably together any more, and two governments, the British and the Irish, were unable to use their power to find a solution to the problem.

It is not surprising that so many Irish poets who lived through the Troubles, either near or far away, have felt compelled to offer in their poetry reflections on a period in Irish history that will perhaps always be remembered with sadness, regret, and sometimes anger. Boland is no exception. The fact that in *Domestic Violence*, which was published the same year that the Northern Ireland Assembly was embarking on a new era of peace and cooperation, Boland revisited the Troubles in a way that is reminiscent of her 1974 book *The War Horse* is testimony to the depth at which the memory of those times is seared into the Irish memory.

"Domestic Violence" is the reflection of a person who was on the surface uninvolved in the Troubles, except that she was an Irish citizen living near Dublin at the time. She was involved simply because, although she was neither a direct participant nor later historian, she was living on the island at the time that the Troubles broke out. Her life, on the face of it, had little to do with the Troubles. She was raising her young family and was happy. But the poem achieves its effect by contrasting her self-described

ignorance at the time, wrapped up in her own personal life, with the questions she asks herself, from a more mature perspective, after the passage of many years. That past still casts its shadows, as the reference to the light in the kitchen that is too weak to stop the encroachment of darkness (section 3) makes clear. The poem suggests the passage from the blithe ignorance of youth to the greater wisdom bestowed by age.

The poet's later self is more questioning than her earlier self, for whom the day-to-day life of the family seemed to be sufficient. In her deliberations about the past, she asks three direct questions. The first (section 3), regarding what people might have attempted to do avoid the violence, is asked by a woman—the poet perhaps or any woman in Ireland at the time—of a man. The question has a resigned air to it, as if the woman believes there was no alternative for them, in those past days, to have acted differently. The second question comes in section 4, after the poet has offered a straightforward judgment about herself and the people of Ireland, stating that they failed to rise to the occasion when it was demanded of them. She then immediately retracts the statement, wondering why she said it when she knows it is untrue. It is as if her mind is still troubled, uncertain; she seizes on an easy explanation that involves a judgment against herself but then realizes that the truth may be otherwise, and perhaps more subtle. The third question comes in the final stanza, in a reference to the quarreling couple mentioned early in the poem. The question refers to the poet's knowledge and level of curiosity about that couple, and the reader will understand the possible symbolic identity of the couple as the two quarreling factions in Ireland at the time. The way the question is posed suggests that the poet's younger self lacked the will to inquire; the desire to know was not yet embedded deeply enough in her. And yet, as the last line emphatically if cryptically states, she knew more than she was willing to acknowledge.

The affirmation with which the poem ends may puzzle some readers because it merely hints at something, without giving any clear idea about how the theme the poet has been developing about the connection between the personal and the public sphere of life is to be resolved. It is of course the prerogative of any poet to speak gnomically, to merely allude to a truth that cannot be expressed in a discursive manner as might

The couple questions their decisions in stanza three. (Kurhan | Shutterstock.com)

be done in prose. For further illumination, it might be pertinent to point out that "Domestic Violence" is the name given not only to this poem but also to the first section of the book, encompassing nine poems, which allude in some way to violence done to Ireland, to the way the present is still colored by a bitter past. "Irish Interior," for example, reflects on Ireland's tragic nineteenth century history through a drawing made in 1890 of a man and woman with loom and spinning wheel. When people look at the drawing they do not really see all that it represents of loss and oppression because they do not care to—like the speaker of "Domestic Violence" in her youth who does not want to face uncomfortable realities—even though the opportunity is there, as the poet is keenly aware. "Histories" seems to allude to the Troubles in the first stanza, and then presents in the second stanza an image of the poet's mother standing in an outside shed. There is no apparent connection between the Troubles reported on the radio and the simple picture of the woman

in the apron in the shed, but again, as with "Domestic Violence" the point seems to be that these two unrelated worlds do touch, in ways that may not be apparent on the surface but are nonetheless real. Another poem, "Silenced," alludes through mythology to the brutal silencing of a female voice and the way that voice still finds a way of conveying what was done to it. A reference to the contemporary Ireland of the poet makes the relevance of such a story apparent; it also might remind the reader that the speaker of "Domestic Violence" is female, and she speaks not in bold tones but in whispers and conveys not only a sense of powerlessness to alter what was happening but also an unwillingness at the time even to bring to consciousness what she knew about it. Speaking out the truth, it seems, has not been an easy thing for a woman in Ireland to do.

Source: Bryan Aubrey, Critical Essay on "Domestic Violence," in *Poetry for Students*, Gale, Cengage Learning, 2012.

Fiona Sampson

In the following review, Sampson opines that Boland's work continues to deepen in both humanity and complexity as Boland continues to claim the subject of domestic interiors as her own.

Forty years after her first book, *New Territory*, was published, Eavan Boland's work continues to deepen in both humanity and complexity. This is the more remarkable since her highly-articulated ars poetica has already remapped the territory of contemporary poetry. But *Domestic Violence* does just what its title implies; breaking apart the certainties of those very domestic interiors which Boland has famously made her own.

In part this is because her "Domestic Violence" is as much the bitterness of 20th-century Irish history as it is the intimate failures of a couple: "nothing is ever entirely/ right in the lives of those who love each other." A sophisticated semantic enjambment (the Irish nation, Boland suggests, is characterised by such bloody love) creates collective resonance. That resonance is explicit in the book's closing section, Becoming the Hand of John Speed, named for "the agile mapping hand of John Speed/ making The Kingdome of Ireland, 1612." Ten poems— all but one in Boland's characteristic first person—situate the poet, or rather her poetic attention, in specific historical spaces from which to "map" the country.

In the first of these, Atlantis, a 14-line poem—punningly subtitled A Lost Sonnet— suggests a culture of drowning one's sorrows might be a remedy for that ancient longing the Welsh call hiraeth. Yet the piece is also a lament for a personal lost youth: "I miss our old city - // white pepper, white pudding, you and I meeting / under fanlights and low skies to go home in it." Fine characterisation aside, the sheer poetic delight of these lines is that wilful category error—one cannot be "under" fanlights and skies in the same way, since fanlights are not horizontal—which snags the attention. Boland is a knowing, witty poet, whose every allusion is advertent. Formation, for example—"In the distance I can hear the Kish lighthouse— / a phrase from the coast, saying salt water, saying danger"—echoes TS Eliot's "Fear death by drowning," from his own urban lament, *The Wasteland*; and Boland makes her understanding of the power of literary tradition explicit in *The Nineteenth-Century Irish Poets*, whom she

sees as "poisoned," and poisoning, by repression: "Now I see what they left us. The toxic lyric. // The poem for which there is no antidote."

Still, as the sheer pragmatism of such an image of poison and antidote suggests, the in-every-sense interior world we associate with Eavan Boland is never far away. The title poem of the book's third section, Indoors, owns: "I have always wanted a world that is cured of the outdoors." Yet that "pastoral of inland elements" is subtly disrupted here. If the Boland of 1990's key collection, *Outside History*, adopted a poetics of naming, in which a piece of antique jewellery, a linen cupboard, work as touchstones, *Domestic Violence* emerges—beautifully—into a poetics of seeing. The book is coloured from its first lines by all that is "winter, lunar, wet. At dusk / pewter seedlings became moonlit orphans."

This single finely observed line introduces us to Boland the colourist. Elsewhere, there are "rooms where skirts appear steeped in tea;" spring air "tinged with a colour close to vinegar, / sure sign of rain;" "slate-blue moonlight;" silk "showing / the gloomy colour pewter becomes / by candlelight;" "bronze-green perch in a mute river." Everything is subtle, muted as "an Irish sky"—or as the claustrophobic chiaroscuro in which history appears. As Irish Interior says, "There is always this: a background, a foreground."

And, while these images are vividly sensed, they are also, and in every sense, haunting. For the young Heaney, poetry was "Digging;" for the mature Boland it is archaeology: "not a science but / an art of memory." In Wisdom, the buried past is resurrected: "pushing its surface back into the world, / lifting it clear of its first funeral." Characteristically, this imagery stuns with intellectual as well as sensory clarity; its evocation of physical revelation is underpinned by religious comprehension. The world Boland here explores still further is not only palpable, but structured by a deep understanding of its own mysteriousness. She is our pre-eminent poet of experience, evoking that strange nexus where thought, feeling and sense all struggle to contain both the everyday and its extraordinary connotations. In *Domestic Violence*, she shows us once again the rare contingency of our world and all that we invest in it.

Source: Fiona Sampson, "Pre-eminent Poet of Experience," in *Irish Times*, March 24, 2007.

"

WHEN IT COMES TO POETIC FORM, BOLAND HAS LONG BEEN SOMETHING OF A BOAT-ROCKER."

Belinda McKeon

In the following review and interview, McKeon and Boland discuss what being an Irish poet means to Boland.

"It was winter, lunar, wet," begins the title poem of Eavan Boland's new collection, *Domestic Violence*. It seems an instantly recognisable opening to a Boland poem.

It was "winter, lunar, wet;" it was also almost 40 years ago, and a terrible time in Ireland, and a strange, raw time in the life of a young couple in a new house in the Dublin suburbs. Boland, the master of the lyric poem which is at once intensely thrilling and quietly devastating, which always seems to root its reader to the spot, returns in her new collection to the trials and tensions that have long haunted her poetry. They have consistently been at her poetry's centre, but they have never—because they are so deep, so fiercely scored into the complicated sense of Irish identity she explores in her work—worn out their welcome, never exhausted their worth.

History and responsibility, myth and meaning, the privacies of motherhood and womanhood, the pressures of the world pressing up against the kitchen window, and the seeming chasms between those things; it is familiar ground for Boland, but in her 10th collection this ground is freshly, unflinchingly disturbed.

"I think that you always do have a central preoccupation in writing poetry," Boland says. She is 63, with soft, dark hair and eyes that flash with reaction and knowledge. "Writing poems, for me, is a bit like mining a seam of rock. One day you get some silver, and the next day you get just rock. But it's your piece of rock and it doesn't much change. You just get better at mining it, that's all. And so I do think of myself as having those preoccupations and going back to them, over and over."

For more than a decade, Boland's time has been spent mostly in the United States. At Stanford, she is professor in Humanities and director of the Creative Writing programme, and director of that programme's highly prestigious Stegner Fellowship. Despite living abroad for such a long time, she says she is still fundamentally an Irish poet. "I never will be anything else," she says. "I lived away when I was a child, I lived in America for three years [her father, an ambassador, was posted to the UN General Assembly in 1956]. I divide my time between Stanford and Dublin, and I come back to Dublin every 10 weeks, so I don't lose contact that way."

However, she's deeply interested, at the same time, in life in today's United States, she says. She's interested in the "conversations" which she sees to be happening there. And not just in poetry, of course—although being in the US, she says, gives her a through-line to "broader conversations" about poetry, to the exchange over "borders and boundaries," between different coasts—but also in politics, for Boland has been, from the beginning, a markedly political poet. And if the title poem of *Domestic Violence* addresses the guilt and the difficulty of building a private life, of building a family in a country which had just "broke[n] out its sores for all to see," in a house whose little television gave out "grey and greyer tears / and killings, killings, killings, / and moonlight-coloured funerals," then a poet who lives in the US today, who grapples every day with questions of the poetic and the political, must have things, indeed, to say about the relationship of domesticity to violence, about the tension between home ground and the distant echo of a terrible war.

And Boland does have things to say—but through her poetry, as the new volume shows, and never with a loudspeaker, never in a preaching or overt way. "When people came here in the 1970s and spoke about Ireland and about what Ireland needed to do, I was often offended," she says. "And I made up my mind that I would never go to another country, any other country, and tell them what to think or do or say about their own lives." She listens "very sympathetically" to American conversations, she says, and is "often enlightened" by them.

"It's not a stretch for me. I love America. I was a child there. And I wish it well. There is nothing that outsiders can do but listen to this conversation of change in America, which is much more rigorous than a lot of outsiders in

Europe see it as being, much more heartfelt, anguished and self-challenging than it is given credit for."

The "anguish" of being a poet in America now is one with which Boland certainly must see her students struggling. She clearly adores teaching—"I have always been a teaching poet. I always want to go into a classroom"—and talks of her undergraduates and her Stegner fellows with genuine respect and pride. She loves the moment, when teaching a poem, "when the poem ceases to be yours and becomes theirs." That is what happened to her with poetry in her early life, and with great teachers, she says, and it is satisfying to watch it make a difference in the lives of her students.

Teaching, essay-writing and editing are endeavours which quicken her "archaeological interest in poetry," she says; she is fascinated by "the origins of things." She has edited, with Ed Hirsch, a new anthology on the sonnet, which will be published later this year, but she smiles at the suggestion that the long immersion in the sonnet form which the book must have required might influence her own poetry in any formal way. "No, I'm not a sonneteer at all. I'm not a closed-form person. There will be no theory leading to practice on this one."

When it comes to poetic form, Boland has long been something of a boat-rocker. She has "intellectual questions" about most established forms, she says—about a "hierarchical" form such as elegy, for example. "I have been a poet who has been in some kind of dissident relationship since I was very young to the tradition and the structures of poetry," she admits. "I mean, if there's any difference, it's just that in getting older, I've felt freer to question it than I did when I was younger. When you're a young poet, you simply don't know what right you have to question things. When you're an old poet, you feel that it's your duty to question them."

And question she does. She questions WB Yeats, and the "shibboleths" of the revival poetry he created, and his patronising treatment of rural Ireland and of the rural poet. This is despite the fact that Yeats is, "without a shadow," the most important of poets for her: "The bringing of a really high lyric agenda to an increasing sense of powerlessness is one of the great artistic models of this or any time," she says.

She questions Patrick Kavanagh, and the exclusionary nature of the literary scene over which he presided, even though Kavanagh was her hero for his intelligent understanding of the parochial (as opposed to the provincial), and for his "mighty leap" out of Yeats's shibboleth, which showed her, "as a woman and as a poet," that she was "not bound by the pre-existing patterns, however set in stone they were."

She questions poetic form and the publishing business—whereas she was lucky enough to make her heroes from "the durable, the dissident, the powerful presences like Kavanagh and Clarke," young writers now are smothered by "this toxic environment of celebrity writing." And she questions the nature of critique in and about literature today; to be vigilant, to be mindful of who and what is being excluded by a literary movement or a literary tradition, she says, a literature cannot work off the critique which applied to a previous situation.

"You can't be nostalgic for the grandeur of a previous moment. You really need to look at the moment and fashion the critique for the moment you're in. Otherwise you'll get a time lag; you'll end up not understanding the moment you're in." It's writers themselves who must make this critique, she says.

Boland herself created her critique, with her 1995 prose narrative *Object Lessons*, in which she reflects deeply and memorably on the relationship, for the poet, between womanhood and nationhood. "A lot of writers will say to you, well, I just want to write, and I respect that," Boland says, "but I think the danger of that is that their writing will be located in someone else's critique. I want to hear the process by which they're thinking." That process can come across, she says, through interview, through articles, through readings, through comments. "I want to know how to find their work in that process, and how they find their work in it."

The process through which Boland has found *Domestic Violence* is one in which she has been engaged for decades. The book comes from her suspicion of the cult of the sublime as the only fit subject for poetry, from her belief in the crucial importance and validity for poetry of the domestic, of the interior, of the apparently mundane, and from her anger at the way the "domestic poem" has been disparaged by the tradition as trivial, as "womanly," as a second-class citizen. In this month's *American Poetry*

Review, Boland writes about how three poems—Charlotte Mew's *Rooms*, Thomas Kinsella's *Another September*, and Else Lasker-Schüler's *My Blue Piano*—gave her encouragement as a young poet, gave her, with their unembarrassed concentration on the interior, grist for her own poetic and critical mill. They taught her, she says, "to speak the vernacular of an ordinary life . . . to say the words love and vision in plain speech."

In a palpable way, the new collection comes from a process that has been going on, not just since the beginning of Boland's career, but since her childhood. Her mother was a painter, and painters, says Boland, "got there long before poets" where the vitality and the power of the domestic interior is concerned. "You will look at many interiors by painters, and they are studies in disquiet. Studies in the malaise of what is not there, what's missing, what echoes in spaces. I'm interested in that."

She knew she had a new collection, she says, when she wrote a poem about the artist Michael Harnett, a still-life painter who left Clonakilty for Philadelphia during the famine, and whose image is on the cover of the US edition of *Domestic Violence*. Harnett painted simple objects, but "very eerie objects—violins, fruit, tin whistles, letters, notes." And in them all was an echo of the place from which he had come. "It so struck me that this man came from the cauldron of history," says Boland, "and wanted to paint an enclosed meaning into these surfaces. He was a noted realist painter, but there is this sense, in those objects, of everything that had been lost. And somehow, for me, that's where the book was going. The way that the object, the interior, is this cipher for all that goes into it and all that can be hidden by it."

Source: Belinda McKeon, "Violence Amid the Verses," in *Irish Times*, March 15, 2007.

SOURCES

Boland, Eavan, "Domestic Violence," in *Domestic Violence*, W. W. Norton, 2007, pp. 13–15.

Browne, Joseph, "Eavan Boland," in *Dictionary of Literary Biography*, Vol. 40, *Poets of Great Britain and Ireland since 1960*, edited by Vincent B. Sherry, Jr., Gale Research, 1985, pp. 36–41.

Keating-Miller, Jennifer, "An Accomplished Collection from Eavan Boland," in *Irish Literary Supplement*, Vol. 27, No. 2, Spring 2008, p. 21.

Kee, Robert, *Ireland: A History*, Little, Brown, 1982, pp. 191–248.

Monaghan, Patricia, Review of *Domestic Violence*, in *Booklist*, February 15, 2007, p. 25.

"Northern Ireland Begins 'New Era,'" in *CNN.com*, May 9, 2007, http://www.cnn.com/2007/WORLD/europe/05/08/northern.ireland/ (accessed March 24, 2011).

Ogden, Chris, *Maggie: An Intimate Portrait of a Woman in Power*, Simon and Schuster, 1990, pp. 211–28.

"Police Attacked at Orange March Protest in Belfast," in *BBC News*, July 12, 2010, http://www.bbc.co.uk/news/10605617 (accessed March 24, 2011).

Rogoff, Jay, "Musings: History, Memory, Myth," in *Southern Review*, Vol. 44, No. 1, Winter 2008, pp. 181–94.

"The Work of the Assembly," in *Northern Ireland Assembly*, http://www.niassembly.gov.uk/the_work.htm (accessed June 27, 2011).

FURTHER READING

Foster, R. F., ed., *The Oxford Illustrated History of Ireland*, Oxford University Press, 1989.
> In six essays by Irish scholars, this book examines Irish history from the earliest times up to the late 1980s. One of the essays is about the relationship between Irish literature and history. There are over two hundred illustrations and twenty-four full-color plates.

Gelpi, Albert, "'Hazard and Death': The Poetry of Eavan Boland," in *Colby Quarterly*, Vol. 35, No. 4, December 1999, pp. 210–28.
> Gelpi examines the influence of the American poet Adrienne Rich on Boland's work.

Klauke, Amy, "An Interview with Eavan Boland," in *Northwest Review*, Vol. 25, No. 1, 1987, pp. 54–61.
> In this interview, Boland speaks about the difficulties confronting any Irish woman poet who wants to develop her own voice, as well as other topics.

Villar-Argaiz, Pilar, *Eavan Boland's Evolution as an Irish Woman Poet: An Outsider within an Outsider's Culture*, Edwin Mellen Press, 2007.
> This is a feminist reading of Boland's poetry seen in the context of postcolonial theory and modern Irish literature. Villar-Argaiz shows the importance of Boland's nationality and gender and how her work has evolved in an attempt to avoid marginalization.

SUGGESTED SEARCH TERMS

Eavan Boland AND domestic violence

Irish AND woman AND poet

History of Ireland

Troubles AND Northern Ireland

Protestant ascendancy

Bloody Sunday AND Northern Ireland

Irish Republican Army

Republic of Ireland

Partition of Ireland

Battle of the Boyne

Eavan Boland AND Irish poetry

Exile

JULIA ALVAREZ

1995

Although best known as a novelist, Julia Alvarez has also earned a reputation as a gifted poet. Her third collection of poetry was 1995's *The Other Side/El Otro Lado*, in which "Exile" appears. The poem tells the autobiographical story of the night Alvarez and her family fled the Dominican Republic to the safety of America. The poem tells nothing of the political reasons for the exile, instead focusing on what the experience looked and felt like to the ten-year-old narrator.

The central event of *Exile* has been described by Alvarez as the most traumatic experience of her life, but the poem has a calm, measured feel. The poet captures the voice of a young girl who is confused, finding comfort in her naïve assumptions that being with her parents ensures her security. The family makes it safely to New York City to begin a new life, and the end of the poem points strongly to the struggles of identity and assimilation to come. Written in free verse and employing occasional wordplay, the poem relies heavily on a swim motif as it conveys themes of security and escape.

AUTHOR BIOGRAPHY

Alvarez was born on March 27, 1950, in New York City. When she was only a few months old, her parents decided to return to their native Dominican Republic to raise their family. The

Julia Alvarez (AP Images)

Alvarez family remained there for ten years before fleeing back to America. Alvarez's father, a physician, was active in an underground political group, and for years, he and his family had been spared by leveraging the influence and prestige of his wife's prominent family. All of that came to an end when his role in a planned assassination against dictator Rafael Trujillo was discovered. To save himself and his family, Dr. Alvarez took his family and fled to the safety of America. Four months later, the Mirabel sisters, who had established the rebel group, were killed. Alvarez wrote about them in her book *In the Time of Butterflies*. Settling back into life in America, Dr. Alvarez recited poetry at home and supported his wife and four girls with his medical practice in Brooklyn.

Alvarez's dual identity, having roots both in the Dominican Republic and America, has profoundly shaped her life and writing. In *Latina Self-Portraits: Interviews with Contemporary Women Writers*, Alvarez admits,

> I don't think I would have become a writer if I had not come to the United States at the age of ten. I did not have a literary childhood. Seeing people read was a rare thing.

She adds, however, "At the same time, though, I think I was in a very storytelling culture." Even today, she visits the Dominican Republic and maintains ties through a coffee farm she and her husband own. The land is not just a sustainable coffee farm; it is also home to a school established to promote literacy.

Alvarez recalls feeling disconnected from most of her reading schoolwork until high school. The stories and illustrations depicted people and experiences to which she could not relate. In high school, she learned about Walt Whitman and Emily Dickinson, both of whom she points to as being role models and inspirations for her from a young age. Her higher education began at Connecticut College, where she attended from 1967 to 1969; she completed her undergraduate degree at Middlebury College in 1971. She completed her master of fine arts degree at Syracuse University in 1975 and then attended the Middlebury Bread Loaf School of English from 1979 to 1980. In 1989, Alvarez married physician Bill Eichner.

A collection of poetry, *The Housekeeping Book* (1984), was Alvarez's first published book. Because this collection presents a merging of everyday domesticity and the rigors of traditional poetic forms, Alvarez is sometimes labeled a feminist writer. It was 1991's *How the Garcia Girls Lost Their Accents*, however, that brought her widespread recognition. While regarded as a novel, the book is technically a collection of fifteen interwoven, but separate, stories. When her publisher agreed to release *The Other Side/El Otro Lado* in 1995 to keep her happy with the work relationship, Alvarez also revised her first book of poetry for a second release. In all, she has had almost twenty books published, including poetry, novels, young-adult fiction, and essays.

Alvarez's work has captured the attention of critics and peers. Her many achievements include a Robert Frost poetry fellowship, a National Endowment for the Arts grant, a PEN/Oakland Award, a Yaddo residency, and a National Book Critics Circle Award finalist designation for *In the Time of Butterflies*. Privileged to teach and encourage young writers, Alvarez has been a professor or writer-in-residence at many universities, including George Washington University, University of Vermont, and her alma mater, Middlebury College.

POEM SUMMARY

The text used for this summary is from *The Other Side/La Otro Lado*, Plume, 1996, pp. 25–28. Versions of the poem can be found on the following Web pages: http://www.burgin.kyschools.us/HS/jdouglas/EXAIL/the%20poem.htm and http://www.sjsu.edu/faculty/mary.warner/StudentLinks/2009_Fall/Frances_McClellan.htm.

The subtitle of "Exile" reads "Ciudad Trujillo, New York City, 1960." This gives the reader the setting, letting him know that the poem takes place both in the city of Trujillo in the Dominican Republic and in New York City. The poem is told in the first person by a ten-year-old girl who is ostensibly addressing her father in real time. Although Alvarez wrote the poem more than thirty years later, she adopts the voice of herself as a child, describing events and feelings as they happen.

Stanza 1–4

She describes her father (Papi) telling her that he was taking the family to the beach that night, so she needed to hurry and get dressed. He keeps watch out the window, making sure that everything stays quiet. The city is past curfew, so there is no activity in the streets. The narrator heard her father talking to his brothers in tense whispers, making plans. When they notice that the little girl is listening, they try to cover their true plans by acting like they are planning a beach trip. Even though she is only ten, the narrator realizes that their laughing is an act.

In another room, Mami is getting the other children packed, allowing them to bring only one toy each. Just as the narrator could see through her uncles' phony laughing, she sees that her mother's eyes are red as she lies about going to the beach so Papi can rest. Line 16 brings the disconnect of the scene into sharper focus as the narrator explains that they were all dressed in their best clothes and shoes. Not only are the adults' words disconnected with their true intentions, but the plan to go to the beach is disconnected with the party clothes Mami puts on the children.

Stanza 5–7

Stanza 5 brings the first admission by the narrator that she knows something is wrong. She quickly adds, however, that her naïveté led her to believe that nothing could go wrong with the adults in charge, so she returns to feeling secure. They quietly leave the house, and the narrator adds a retrospective note that they were leaving the house they would not see for a decade.

Stanza 6 introduces the poem's predominant motif of swimming. The narrator recalls letting herself relax in deep water with her arms outstretched, not sinking as she usually did when she went swimming.

Stanza 7 reveals that the narrator is not literally swimming as she describes floating away from their neighborhood, through gates, down winding roads, and to the highway. She also depicts her Papi driving with a grim expression. Part of the narrator still holds onto the belief that they might actually be going to the beach, as she concludes the stanza with the fact that they are on the highway headed toward the coast.

Stanza 8–11

In stanza 8, the narrator tells about driving past a checkpoint and making a dash toward the airport. When the younger sisters realize they have missed the turn to the beach, they begin to cry. All the while, Mami tries to comfort them with promises of an even greater surprise that would have to be a secret until they all got there. The narrator has already begun to understand that what they are doing that night is going to be a major turning point and bring it with it great loss. Once they arrive at the airport, they wait all night until a plane comes early in the morning for them. Before boarding the plane, Papi turns to take in one last look at his homeland. Once on the plane, the narrator says, both she and her father lose part of themselves.

Stanza 12–14

Stanza 12 picks up weeks later, after the family has settled into their new life in the United States. The narrator and Papi are walking together as he explains things that are new to the girl, such as escalators and blue eyes. They stop to look at a Macy's window, where a scene is set up showing a father and a daughter at the beach. She notices how different the mannequin father looks from her father; where the mannequin is trim and confident in his beachwear, her father has a moustache, a suit, and an accent. Then she notices how different she is from the mannequin girl. The mannequin looks like Heidi, but Alvarez does not tell the reader how the narrator sees herself.

Stanza 15–17

In stanza 15, the emotional implications of the scene are brought forward. The narrator reveals that she and Papi stand there amidst the wonders of the new country but struggle to feel as lucky as maybe they should. Instead of talking about that, they talk about the objects in the window scene. When they step back from the window, they can see their own images reflected in the glass. Where the mannequins are casual and confident, she and her Papi look like visitors who are overdressed and out of place.

In the final stanza, the narrator likens herself and Papi to swimmers about to plunge into the waters around the island of their homeland. The swimmers see their reflections in the water before they dive in and see themselves as enthusiastic, yet fearful and uncertain.

THEMES

Escape

The central event of the poem is the family's escape from the Dominican Republic to the United States. The poem's subtitle alerts the reader to the fact that this single poem will have two very different settings within a short period of time. Alvarez skillfully launches her story in the first two lines by telling the truth in the first line (that they fled the country) and the cover story in the second line (that they were going to the beach). This is how Papi and his brothers orchestrate the escape, by telling the children that they are all going for a trip to the beach. However, the tense whispering among the men and Mami's red eyes indicate that something much more heart-wrenching and dangerous is happening.

The escape scene takes place at night, after curfew, and the family leaves the house very quietly. There is an air of secrecy that even the ten-year-old narrator can sense. Although she allows herself to go along with the beach story, she knows something bigger is happening. Rather than worry, she has the luxury of being a trusting child who believes that whatever the grown-ups are doing, everything will be okay. There is a sense of urgency that seems unimportant to the young narrator, but the reader understands it is a by-product of the danger they are all in. The whispering, the darkness of night, the back roads, and the waiting at the airport for a mysterious plane to arrive and take them all away: all of these elements of the poem indicate that as dangerous as the escape itself is, staying would be even more dangerous. This poem is autobiographical; Alvarez's family really did flee the Dominican Republic in 1960 when she was only ten. What the poem does not explain is why it was so critical that they all get out of the

country. Papi was a member of a rebel group planning to assassinate the dictator Rafael Trujillo. The situation became more serious, and the only chance of surviving was to take the whole family and leave in secret. Although the poem does not give these details, it does capture the atmosphere of the urgency to escape.

When they arrive in New York City and settle into their new lives, they are left asking what a successful escape really means to a family. They are safely out of the Dominican Republic, but they are transplants in a strange, foreign culture where they feel more like visitors than citizens. Escape, it seems, is not so simple. They are safe, but their safety costs them comfort and belonging. As the poem ends, the narrator reveals that her heart is still with her homeland. She has physically escaped but is emotionally still there.

Security

As a ten-year-old girl, the narrator conveys the importance of security in her personal world. Children are not concerned with political coups or where the family will live; like the narrator, they are only concerned with the family being together and a trusted adult being in charge. That is all she needs to allay her fears and uncertainty about what is clearly a tense situation. The adults recognize the children's need for security, so they tell them they are all going for a trip to the beach. Papi, Mami, and the uncles all pretend (although not well) that a family trip is all they are getting ready to do.

Because the narrator is more savvy than the adults realize, she understands that the scene is not what it appears to be. She notices the way the men talk to one another, that their laughter is fake, that her father watches out the window, and that her mother's eyes are red from crying. In stanza 5, she states outright that she knows everything does not make sense, but because adults are in charge, it never occurs to her to worry that anything might go wrong. Consequently, in the next stanza, she allows herself to relax as she imagines herself floating in water.

In stanza 9, the narrator admits that she has figured out that they are doing something major and life-changing. Unlike her sisters, however, she is not crying. Her sisters are upset because they are not going to go to the beach after all. Even though the narrator understands that there is far more at stake than a fun outing, she remains

TOPICS FOR FURTHER STUDY

- Read the section of the poem that is about Rafael Trujillo. Choose four other dictators in world history to research, and see what comparisons you can draw among the five. Look at factors such as personality, culture, economy, politics, structure of rule, and so on. Create a map of the world with at least twenty countries labeled, and make a key to go with it, assigning different colors to different susceptibilities of dictatorship. Finally, color in your map according to your key, so that your final product is a map showing which countries are more susceptible to dictator rule and which are less. Print a pamphlet or create a Web site that explains the factors your research yielded, with a short description of the five dictators you studied.

- Using whatever materials you have on hand, put together a store window display (probably a miniature) of the story told in "Exile." Consider which people you will include, what they should wear, what background or props support the story, and how you will convey the essence of the poem. You may focus on one particular scene or put together a mix of elements; be as artistic as you like in design and materials.

- Christina Gonzalez's young-adult novel *The Red Umbrella* is about a teenage girl living in Cuba in 1961. When the revolution heats up, her parents send her and her little brother to Nebraska until they can safely join them. Read the book and notice how similar the stories are in terms of culture, time period, and political exile. What is intriguing, however, are the differences. Choose an angle (such as plot, themes, or character studies of the protagonists), and write an essay for a literary journal. In addition to explaining the differences in terms of your angle, you should also come to some general conclusions about literary expression. You and your teacher can decide whether to submit it to actual journals for consideration.

- Using a social-networking site such as Facebook, create a genealogy-themed page or survey to find out reasons families and individuals originally came to the United States and from where they came. Actively pursue respondents, trying to get at least a few hundred. Collect as many responses as possible to get an idea of what reasons, dreams, or fears are so compelling that they move people to start a new life in a new country. If you are not using a survey format, put your results in an easy-to-understand chart or graph. Be sure to include your own family.

---

calm. In fact, given the subject of the poem, the narrator maintains a composed, matter-of-fact tone throughout. This suggests a very deep sense of security, even in the midst of great danger. It is a message about children and their faith in the adults in their lives.

In New York City, the narrator recalls walking around with her father as he explains the sights and sounds of a new country. They walk hand in hand, a visual reminder of the security the father gives his daughter. The only moment in the poem in which the narrator's security

seems to form a crack is in the fifteenth stanza, where she confesses that she and her father are making a great effort to feel luckier than they actually felt. It is a moment of doubt, but they continue talking as if everything is fine.

As the poem ends, the narrator shows the reader how out-of-place she and Papi felt, wondering if they would ever find their places in this new culture. Even with an uncertain future, she describes herself with Papi. He was there in the events of the first stanza, and he is there in the last. That is the source of security for the narrator,

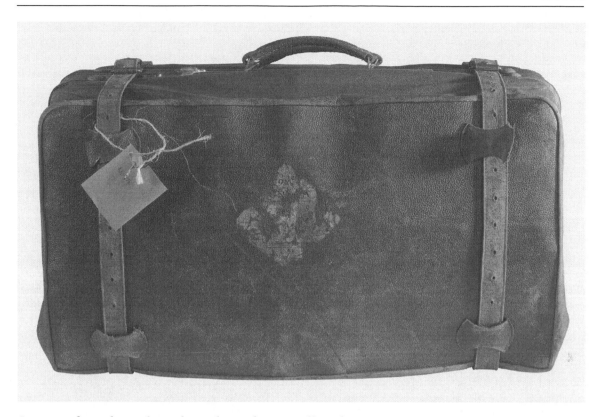

In stanza four, she explains that only one bag was allowed. (*Karam Miri | Shutterstock.com*)

whether she is fleeing the country under cover of night or struggling to settle into a foreign culture.

STYLE

Motif

Related to the idea that the family in "Exile" is preparing for a family trip to the beach, Alvarez uses a swimming motif throughout the poem. Of course, the family is not going to the beach at all, but that is the story the adults tell the children as they pack to flee the country. Even though the ten-year-old narrator knows there is more going on than a trip to the beach, she thinks in terms of swimming, floating, and diving as her family drives through the night and then boards a plane headed to America.

The motif is introduced in stanza 6, where the narrator expresses her feelings of security by describing herself as relaxing back in deep water with outstretched arms. She does not sink as she usually does, so she is able to float out of the

neighborhood, down the back roads, and onto the highway that takes them to the airport. The narrator's imagination produces this light-hearted swimming imagery despite the reality that she is in a car racing toward safety and freedom and away from danger. The motif reflects her emotional state.

In stanza 9, the motif returns, this time reflecting the narrator's thoughts. When she tells the reader that Mami admitted that they were not going to the beach, but to an even bigger surprise that she could not tell them yet, the narrator says that she has already swum ahead. Her understanding of the gravity of the situation is growing intuitively, and she compares it with being more threatening than the deep end of a swimming pool. This explains why, in the next stanza, she explains that they waited in their car at the airport, and she swam all night in a restless sleep.

As they board the plane, Papi takes a last long look at his homeland. The narrator notices it and thinks he looks like he is searching for a swimmer who is far away, trying to wave her back to shore. Entering the cabin, the narrator thinks that she and her father both know that something within them is now drifting away. Here, the swimming motif is less direct but serves to reflect the narrator's loss.

In New York City, she and Papi stop to admire a store window depicting a scene of a father and daughter at the beach. The motif here is a reminder of what they are not. They were supposed to go on a beach trip, but they did not. The mannequin father and daughter are all-American, which she and Papi are not. The scene is relaxed and self-assured, which they are not. Therefore, the poem ends with the narrator telling her father that they are like swimmers diving into the waters surrounding their homeland. They see their own reflections in the water before they take the plunge, and they see their own anticipation and fear. With this, Alvarez uses the motif to reflect the family's awkwardness and uncertainty in their new home.

Figurative Language

"Exile" is written in free verse, and Alvarez uses figurative language in a natural way that does not disrupt the flow of the poem. Because the narrator addresses Papi throughout and it is unlikely the speaker is actually talking to her father, the poem is in the form of apostrophe (a statement, question, or request addressed to an inanimate object or concept or to a nonexistent or absent person).

The second line of the second stanza contains alliteration (the repetition of initial sounds), and when the two words are spoken together, the result is an example of onomatopoeia (use of words whose sounds express or suggest their meaning) that sounds like the whispering of the men. The last line of the fourth stanza is very repetitive, even to the point of internal rhyme. It draws the reader's attention to the detail the narrator gives about the children being dressed in their very best clothes usually reserved for parties. It is a telling detail, but easy to overlook because it comes on the heels of Mami's emotional strain. Alvarez skillfully uses sound to bring the reader's attention to the line.

The motif necessarily incorporates symbolism and metaphor, but Alvarez also introduces a simile in the sixth stanza. She compares her outstretched arms to those of Jesus on the cross. In the next stanza, Alvarez uses repetition to convey the distance and the carefully planned route

they are driving. Simile also describes the way Papi gazes at the horizon before boarding the plane (line 41), and the fact the little girl in the window display looks like Heidi (line 55).

Alvarez introduces a strong element of imagery in the sixteenth stanza. As the narrator and Papi back up from the window display, they see their own reflections superimposed on the carefree beach scene. The narrator sees in a clear, visual way just how different they are than the all-American family in the display. They look the way they feel, like visitors.

HISTORICAL CONTEXT

Rafael Trujillo

Rafael Leonidas Trujillo Molina (1891–1961) was born and reared in the Dominican Republic. Coming from a humble background, he chose the military as his career field, and by 1925, he was the general overseeing the country's military. A political crisis led to an election in 1930, which Trujillo won by beating, killing, and threatening anyone who backed his opponent. This was a sign of things to come.

After a hurricane devastated the Dominican capital of Santo Domingo, he went to work establishing martial law and showing himself to be a man of action. Once the city was restored, he renamed it after himself and continued his tight grip on the country. Even during years when he seemed to be stepping down as president, he put someone in his place that he could control and maintained personal control of the military, intelligence, and other organizations. Rebel groups formed to fight back against Trujillo and try to overthrow or assassinate him. Julia Alvarez's father was a member of one of these groups, but it is obvious that such groups and activities were extremely dangerous.

Trujillo's reign was three decades of censorship, limited civil liberties, rule by intimidation (torture, murder, exile), and spies to tell Trujillo anything he wanted to know. His cruelty extended to other people besides Dominicans. During the 1930s, he felt his people's racial purity and beliefs could only be harmed by the Haitians coming in search of work. He ordered a massacre in 1937 that resulted in at least ten thousand deaths.

COMPARE
&
CONTRAST

- **1960s:** During the 1960s, the Dominican Republic experiences a time of extreme political unrest. Rafael Trujillo, who ruled as a dictator for thirty years, is assassinated in 1961. This leads to a time of civil war as some Dominicans support the elected president Juan Bosch, while others favor military rule. American President Lyndon Johnson sends troops in 1965 to end the war and help the election that brings about the presidency of Joaquin Balaguer.

  1990s: The economic unrest that arises as the result of the political upheaval of the 1960s is still a major problem. The combined problems of few jobs for wage laborers and agricultural hardships result in a 30 percent unemployment rate. Just as during Trujillo's rule, a small percentage of the people own a large percent of the businesses, creating a huge gap between the elite few in the upper class and the struggling working class.

  Today: The turn of the century does not bring economic or political stability to the Dominican Republic. The devaluing of the peso, mass government job cuts, blatant political favoritism (such as that shown by President Hipolito Mejia), and rising costs of utilities lead to riots, strikes, and unrest. Overpopulation and economic inequality cannot be easily overcome by the more democratic system in place because the problems are so overwhelming.

- **1960s:** After the arrival of American troops in the Dominican Republic in 1965, a significant number of Dominicans migrate to the United States. Many of those who emigrate are Bosch supporters or hold similar political views.

  1990s: After the rise in Dominican immigration to the United States in the 1960s, the numbers remain steady through the end of the twentieth century. In fact, during the 1980s and 1990s, more Dominicans arrive in the United States than Cubans. Census data show that even into the 1990s, most Dominican Americans are Dominican born. The areas with the highest concentrations of Dominican communities include New York, New Jersey, Massachusetts, and Florida.

  Today: As of the 2000 census, there are 765,000 Dominican Americans. They are the fourth-largest Hispanic group in the United States population. With the exception of Santo Domingo (the capital of the Dominican Republic), New York City is home to the largest population of Dominicans in the world.

- **1960s:** There are no major works published in English by Dominican writers.

  1990s: A few Dominican Americans rise to prominence in letters. The strongest literary voice is poet and author Julia Alvarez. In addition, Tony Marcano is a prominent journalist who works as a reporter and editor for nationally known newspapers.

  Today: Dominican-born American writer and creative writing professor Junot Diaz wins the 2008 Pulitzer Prize for Fiction for *The Brief Wondrous Life of Oscar Wao*. Annecy Baez garners critical acclaim for *My Daughter's Eyes and Other Stories*.

Trujillo and his family and friends kept a tight rein on the economy by owning most of the businesses and land in the country. By ending migration out of the Dominican Republic and offering better health services, Trujillo succeeded in growing the population. During his rule, the population doubled to three million people.

Trujillo was assassinated in 1961, and his family went into exile. Unfortunately for the Dominican Republic, political stability would remain elusive.

In stanza seven, papa drove the old Ford to the airport at night. (SNEHIT / Shutterstock.com)

Dominican Culture and Family

The family structure among Dominican Americans has changed as Dominicans have become more assimilated into American culture. Traditionally, Dominican families are large and share their homes and lives with each other, as opposed to the more nuclear family common in America. Security comes from the family, and loyalty to the family comes before everything else. The negative side of this is evident when rulers such as Trujillo allow nepotism to overshadow what is best for the nation.

Dominican households are traditionally patriarchal, where the man oversees the family's finances and has the final say on major decisions affecting the family. Because several generations often form their own community, the oldest man is given the highest level of respect and authority. The female head of the household has authority over the household itself, including housekeeping, child rearing, and nurturing. As with the men, the oldest woman is given greater respect

and authority. Considering that several generations may be living together, she has a significant responsibility overseeing her children, daughters-in-law, and household matters.

CRITICAL OVERVIEW

Many critics and readers who approach Alvarez's poetry collection *The Other Side/El Otro Lado* are intrigued. While she has written poetry before, she is best known for her fiction. Typical of her writing, these poems reveal a thoughtful and introspective writer giving a voice to her personal experiences. In *The Other Side/El Otro Lado*, Alvarez shares with the reader the challenges and triumphs of being a woman with a foot in two cultures. In "Exile," she relates the night she and her family fled the Dominican Republic at night to the safety of America.

A *Publishers Weekly* contributor writes that Alvarez "claims her authority as a poet with this collection," adding that the collection offers "direct, reflective and often sensuous poems." Sandra M. Gilbert echoes this assessment in *Poetry* as she writes, "Alvarez produces memoristic narratives in a range of sometimes quite complex forms along with prose poems, love poems, and elegiac lyrics."

Other critics are taken with Alvarez's diversity in the collection, as she explores her own multifaceted identity and experiences. In the *Dictionary of Literary Biography*, Kathrine Varnes observes that in *The Other Side/El Otro Lado*, as in other collections, Alvarez "uses the pleasure of poetic form as a way of understanding, perhaps fixing for a moment, the identities of immigrant, daughter, author, divorcée, woman, sister, lover, friend, and character." Varnes specifically commends the section titled "Making Up the Past" (in which "Exile" appears) for doing "just what it promises, filling in the gaps of memory and knowledge with stories from her girlhood in New York."

Other critics have made special mention of how specific *The Other Side/El Otro Lado* is in terms of Alvarez's immigrant past. In *Americas*, Ben Jacques deems the collection "poignant," noting about the family's escape in "Exile," "Freed from Trujillo, they were also free from everything they loved." Jacques adds, "In *The Other Side/El Otro Lado*, she establishes her identity as a Dominican American poet, returning to island muses and themes." Another contributor to *Americas*, Elizabeth Coonrod Martinez observes:

> These poems are sensitive and introspective, touching on the plight of field workers and household maids, many of whom are transitioning from life on the island to life in New York and are struggling to acquire a new language. The immigrant voice is primary.

CRITICISM

Jennifer Bussey

Bussey is an independent writer specializing in literature. In the following essay, she examines the commonalities of the narrator in Julia Alvarez's "Exile," Anne Frank in Anne Frank: The Diary of a Young Girl, *and Sophie Caco in Edwidge Danticat's* Breath, Eyes, Memory.

Julia Alvarez is one of the best-known Dominican writers in America. Her fiction, poetry, and essays have enabled American readers to understand the Dominican American experience and the struggles of a people whose homeland has been ravaged by troubled politics and economics. So, how did this sensitive and expressive writer wind up in America in the first place? When she was only ten, her family fled the Dominican Republic in fear of retribution from the oppressive regime Alvarez's father actively opposed. Not only did that chapter in her life forever change her course, but it gave her entrance into a group of writers making a platform for their immigrant stories. Beneath the stories of immigrant families tied to two cultures are often deeper stories of displacement and adaptation. It only stands to reason that such a traumatic experience would impact a young girl in a unique way; therefore this essay will look at three displaced young women.

The unlikely common thread among Alvarez's "Exile," *Anne Frank: The Diary of a Young Girl*, and Edwidge Danticat's *Breath, Eyes, Memory* is their protagonists. All three girls are exiles moving through the experience at a critical point in their maturation. The narrator in "Exile," Anne Frank, and Sophie are forced to adjust to changes that will transform these impressionable years. In each story, a young girl is picked up from a familiar and comfortable life and moved to a different life in a completely new setting.

ALL THREE GIRLS ARE EXILES MOVING THROUGH THE EXPERIENCE AT A CRITICAL POINT IN THEIR MATURATION. THE NARRATOR IN 'EXILE,' ANNE FRANK, AND SOPHIE ARE FORCED TO ADJUST TO CHANGES THAT WILL TRANSFORM THESE IMPRESSIONABLE YEARS."

In "Exile," the narrator is only ten when she is told to pack for a trip to the beach with the family. Because the speaker is telling the story many years after it happened, she has the advantage of having a perspective that she did not have at the time. However, Alvarez carefully separates what she knew then from what she knows now. She tells the reader specifically what things she realized and how she responded. For instance, she sensed that something was not quite right about the way they were preparing for a family trip to the beach, but she was assured by the naive belief that as long as the adults were in charge, everything would be okay.

The young narrator is also very insightful, as children often are. Adults sometimes underestimate how much a child can understand, and Alvarez honors that about her young self by telling the reader how she stayed calm in the midst of uncertainty, sensed a loss she could not quite put her finger on, and understood as they all boarded the plane that she and her father were somehow leaving something behind that would drift away.

Once in America, she and her father walk together as he explains things like escalators to her. They stop at a Macy's window to admire a beach scene in a window display. It depicts an all-American father and his all-American daughter enjoying fun in the sun. Although the scene is cheerful, the narrator and her father respond to it with doubt. They are not sure how or if they can fit into their new culture and what it might cost them. It is a difficult thing to make sense of, especially at the age of ten, when issues of identity, self-esteem, and womanhood are emerging. The narrator enjoys a feeling of security throughout the poem; what is missing is angst and resentment.

WHAT DO I READ NEXT?

- In 2002, Alvarez's young-adult novel *Before We Were Free* was published, telling the stories the author heard from friends and cousins who had lived as teenagers during Trujillo's rule. She preserves the experience of living everyday life while juggling growing up and the constant awareness of an oppressive political regime.

- Alvarez's *In the Time of Butterflies* (1994) tells the heart-breaking story of the Mirabel sisters, three women who founded a rebel group against the dictator Trujillo in the Dominican Republic. This was the group of which Alvarez's father was a member, so the murder of the sisters just after the Alvarez family fled in 1960 came as a personal tragedy.

- Sandra Cisneros's classic *A House on Mango Street* (1984) tells the coming-of-age story of a young girl growing up in the barrio in Chicago. The book tells her story, which ranges from tragic to hopeful, through a series of vignettes.

- *The Farming of Bones* (1999) by Edwidge Danticat tells the harrowing story of her native Haiti and the genocide that took place under Trujillo's reign when the Haitian people went to the Dominican Republic. Based on actual historical events, the story is a terrifying reminder of the possible extremes of a cruel dictator.

- The mass migration in the mid-twentieth century from the Dominican Republic to the United States is explored in *A Tale of Two Cities: Santo Domingo and New York after 1950* by Jesse Hoffnung-Garskof (2010). The author goes beyond the historical facts regarding the growth of the Dominican population in New York to demonstrate how the influx of Dominicans has impacted New York and how having such a large population of Dominicans in New York affects the communities in the homeland.

- Katherine Min's *Secondhand World* (2008) tells the story of Isa and her Korean American family as they deal with the aftermath of a family tragedy and confront the confusion and awkwardness of finding identity and place in two cultures.

Because she is telling the story as an adult and these things are not present, the reader can safely conclude that there was no seething anger then, nor is there any now.

In *Anne Frank: The Diary of a Young Girl*, thirteen-year-old Anne records her thoughts and experiences in a journal she received as a birthday present shortly before she and her family went into hiding in 1942. They were a Jewish family living in Nazi-occupied Amsterdam, and Anne's father, Otto, made arrangements for his family to hide with another family, the Van Daans, on the third floor of a secret apartment. Anne's diary chronicles the bits of news they receive about the war and their responses to it. It also reveals the dreams of a young girl's heart—dreams of being famous, writing a romance, finding love, and growing up like everyone else. Like any teenager, she records her frustrations with her sister and her growing and sometimes conflicted feelings for Peter Van Daan. She is extremely introspective and likes to write about her views of the world. Given the situation she and her family were in, her idealism and optimism continue to inspire readers today.

Anne's displacement actually began before she and her family went into hiding. The family had lived in Germany, but life there under Nazi rule had become increasingly difficult for Jewish families. The Franks were no exception. They were subjected to wearing the Star of David to identify them as Jews, and Anne was transferred to a different school. These were the early signs of separation and persecution. Anne had already experienced displacement on government orders and felt what it was like to be treated differently and, in effect, rejected from aspects of her life that had been normal. The Franks left Germany to live in Amsterdam, hoping to escape the restrictions, but went into hiding when they found themselves no safer there. Their secret hiding place was raided by the Germans in 1944, and the group was separated from each other and sent to concentration camps.

While in hiding, Anne is as separated from the life she knew as normal, as is the narrator in "Exile." Without the freedom to leave the apartment, see friends, walk down the street, go to school, and so on, Anne must adapt to a major life change. She faces it head on in her diary, but it is certainly not easy. Sometimes she describes her stubbornness, frustration, and the stress that comes with living in close quarters with the same people day after day. At other times, she expresses optimism and a forgiveness that is somewhat unfathomable. Like the narrator in "Exile," Anne is naive and finds comfort in knowing that the adults are in charge.

In *Breath, Eyes, Memory*, Danticat introduces Sophie Caco. Sophie is a twelve-year-old girl living in Haiti with her aunt. Despite the danger that comes with the political unrest in Haiti, Sophie's mother and aunt determined it was better for her to stay with her aunt than accompany her mother to America. Sophie's mother, Martine, left Haiti when Sophie was only two, and she sends money home.

What Sophie learns when she joins her mother in America is that her mother is not the wise, beautiful goddess she always imagined; she is a tormented, emotionally unhealthy woman. Sophie learns that she was the product of her mother's rape by a guerrilla soldier, and her mother has never been able to cope with the trauma. When Sophie arrives, her mother carries on traditions that emotionally scar the girl, especially the tradition of testing for virginity. Consequently, the mother damages Sophie's spirit, and Sophie marries a man much older than she in hopes of having the life she wants. The transition from life in Haiti to life in America is disastrous, and Sophie returns to Haiti for a time.

Sophie's story is tragic from the time she leaves Haiti to join her mother. Although she had been separated from her mother in Haiti, she led a sheltered, happy life with her aunt whom she loved deeply. Once in America, she is forced to deal with the reality of her mother's personality and history, her own struggles with her body and sexuality, the mistakes she makes, her mother's eventual suicide, and a deep unrest that follows her wherever she goes. Sophie is displaced in every sense of the world, and unlike the narrator in "Exile" and Anne Frank, she never really finds the security and belonging she so desperately needs. That is an awful lot for a girl to manage at the age of twelve.

What these three very different stories reveal is the absolute need for the security of family in a time of displacement. In "Exile," the narrator is uprooted and moved to a place where she feels more like a visitor to a foreign land than a citizen. However, from the time she is packing to leave for the "beach trip" all the way to the Macy's window where she stands hand-in-hand with her father, she has her family to carry the burden for her. That is where she gets her reassurance and her optimism that things will turn out fine. Even when she does not see how they will turn out, she has the confidence of knowing that she is going to be okay. Her father is a major source of security for her, and her emotional connection to him is evident throughout the poem. It is what saves her from becoming lost in her displacement.

For Anne, the time in the "secret annexe" is made bearable by the fact that her entire family is there. Although it is an extremely trying time, she has the emotional luxury of knowing she can write happily (or unhappily) in her diary because the adults have made arrangements for food, water, and safety. She has people she can talk to who care about her, and she is in no way alone. It is an odd thing to say she has security when she is in hiding from the Nazis, but that is how she feels. To make the point, imagine how all that security vanished when they were discovered and she was separated from her family, not knowing if she would ever see any of them again. At that point, her displacement took on a tragedy from which she would not return.

What is different about Sophie is that her displacement actually takes her away from her security with her aunt, who was the only mother she had ever known. Going to live with her mother offered no reassurance or peace because her mother had none to give. Away from real family, Sophie comes

In stanza 13, the reader knows the destination. (Steven Pepple / Shutterstock.com)

undone. She desperately seeks family by trying to have a relationship with her mother and then by marrying an older man, but nothing works. When she goes back to Haiti, it is obvious she is trying to reverse her displacement and reconnect with real family. Going back to the United States, she faces a broken marriage and the eventual violent suicide of her mother.

The story of these three girls reminds readers how fundamental family security is to preteen and teenage girls. Even in the most dramatic situations—ones most of us will only know in books—they are able to rebound and adapt as long as they have the structure and security of a family. It allows them to continue to be children still growing up because the family is taking care of the adult things, while nurturing the girls through their difficult years. Sophie's story shows what happens when that security is stripped away and a young girl has no choice but to start making adult decisions before she has the life experience, wisdom, or emotional maturity to deal with adult situations.

Source: Jennifer Bussey, Critical Essay on "Exile," in *Poetry for Students*, Gale, Cengage Learning, 2012.

Elizabeth Coonrod Martínez

In the following essay, Martínez analyzes Alvarez's role in bringing Latina literature to U.S. audiences.

History demonstrates that literary periods are launched by daring, intrepid writers or poets who appear to have suddenly sprouted from nowhere. Later these writers are acclaimed as initiators of movements, but the many years they barely subsisted while writing tomes that languished in wait for a publisher are rarely remembered.

Think of Gabriel García Márquez, now recognized as one of the "fathers" of the so-called Latin American Boom of the late 1960s, when (mostly male) writers erupted onto the international stage with their novels dubbed as magical realism. Or the two Mexicans—Laura Esquivel and Ángeles Mastretta—recognized for launching a "boom" of women writers in the 1980s, when women's novels finally began to be published in greater numbers. Just as Garcia Márquez and the writers of his generation were not the first to create a great Latin American novel, Esquivel and Mastretta are not the only significant

> " LIKE OTHER WELL-KNOWN WRITERS AT THE INCEPTION OF A LITERARY PERIOD, ÁLVAREZ WILL FOREVER BE REMEMBERED AS THE FIRST DOMINICAN-AMERICAN WRITER AND ONE OF THE FIRST LATINAS IN A DECADE OF A GREAT DEAL OF ATTENTION FOR THIS GROUP."

women writers of the 20th century. But in each case they will forever be remembered as those who launched a literary period. Julia Álvarez occupies a similar place in U.S. literature as one of the initiators of Latina literature, principally novels written in English by women of Latin American heritage. While members of the largest minority population in the U.S. had been producing novels and poetry throughout the 20th century, few who published before Sandra Cisneros' *The House on Mango Street* or before the beginning of the now-recognized Chicano/Latino era are famously remembered.

"I feel very lucky to happen to have been a writer at the watershed time when Latino literature became a literature that was not just relegated to the province of sociology," Álvarez says. "But I still feel there is a certain kind of condescension toward ethnic literature, even though it is a literature that is feeding and enriching the mainstream American literature . . . [And], definitely, still, there is a glass ceiling in terms of the female novelists. If we have a female character, she might be engaging in something monumental but she's also changing the diapers and doing the cooking, still doing things which get it called a woman's novel. You know, a man's novel is universal; a woman's novel is for women."

The content of novels written by women may be different, but Alvarez feels that all stories come from the same source: "The great lesson of storytelling is that there is this great river that we all are flowing on of being a human being and a human family. So, when the market comes up and says 'Latina writers,' and this is for this or that market, it is [simply] part of how things are broadcast out there, but really, that's not what

the writing is about. It's about interconnectedness. And sure, Faulkner is from the south, or such and such poet has an Irish background and you can hear it in the lines; that is a way to get a handle on this mysterious current of narrative that is so important to us."

In Álvarez's case, she is the ubiquitous Dominican-American writer. Her novel *In the Time of the Butterflies*, based on the heroic Mirabal sisters who lived in the time of the Trujillo dictatorship in the Dominican Republic, is now a staple of college literature classes. Her first novel, *How the García Girls Lost Their Accents*, published in 1991—along with Cisneros' *The House on Mango Street* in 1984 and Cristina García's *Dreaming in Cuban* in 1992—officially launched the new movement of Latina writers. Their "hyphen" experience, straddling borders or cultures in the U.S. as people of Latin American or Caribbean descent, foments new critical ideas. The current generation of Dominican-American New York writers (Angle Cruz, Loida Maritza Pérez, Nelly Rosario, and Junot Díaz) now hopes to achieve the success Álvarez has had.

A certain element of luck, and very precise publicity, played a role in the now easy recognition of Julia Álvarez and Sandra Cisneros. In 1990 they and two other writers—Denise Chávez and Ana Castillo—posed for a group photo arranged by their New York agent Susan Bergholz to promote their forthcoming novels. The one-page photo article ran in the magazine *Vanity Fair* under the title, "The Four Amigas," a publicity stunt that helped usher in a Latino literary generation.

"That was a shock to me," Álvarez says, "One of the things that surprised me was the publicity machine that happens around books, and that people take pictures. I only knew how to love a book and go to the library and get the next book by the writer. You don't think of all the publicity stuff.

"I was just so happy that I had this novel coming out because I was up for tenure, and my chairman basically said, 'you know if you don't have a book, it's not going to be a pretty story.' So when I heard that *García Girls* was taken and would be published, I just thought of it as the book that would get me tenure. But then it did so well that seven years later, I gave up tenure to become a full-time writer."

Her first novel was followed by *Butterflies* in 1994, a sequel to *García Girls* called ¡*Yo!* in 1997, and another historical novel, *In the Name of Salomé*, in 2000. In a period of fifteen years Álvarez has released fifteen books: four books of poetry, a collection of essays titled *Something to Declare*, four children's books, and *A Cafecito Story*, which counters global capitalism and demonstrates the need for a slow process of growing and preparing excellent coffee beans. Last April, she embarked on a multi-city book tour to promote her latest novel, *Saving the World*. It was a grueling schedule, with 24 stops in five weeks, but she appeared radiant late in the tour, sparkling with enthusiasm during her readings.

The slender woman with dark, curly hair and hazel eyes is a vegetarian, which may account for her physical stamina, but she also possesses a vibrancy of spirit that draws people in. Her ophthalmologist husband, Bill Eichner, accompanied her on the tour. At each juncture, they presented a gift of organic coffee, brewed and served to those who turned out to hear her. She explained how she was researching a new historical novel when the September 11 tragedy occurred in 2001 and that that occurrence had influenced her to create a second story, alternating a contemporary character's angst with the historical journey of a small expedition that transported the smallpox vaccine across the world. She quotes from Dante, stating that her modern character is experiencing a "dark night of the soul, which we now pathologize and call depression." Álvarez's voice is soft but her words are very clearly enunciated: "It is about being a human being. With stories we have these ways of deeply connecting as human beings."

After the reading, she takes questions, and responds candidly to each. Does her story have a moral or a message? "Sometimes things happen to us, and [since] we humans have created narrative, at times like this we bring it to bear on what has happened. I do think narratives are important and powerful, but novels don't answer questions, they're not solutions."

Someone asks whether she first writes in English or Spanish. When Álvarez responds, "I am not truly bilingual, I am English-dominant," there is silence in the room, as though the audience is surprised by that revelation. Her works, like those of many other Latino writers, are translated to Spanish by other individuals.

Despite the fact that she and her husband purchased farmland in the Dominican Republic in 1996 to help foment a cooperative of independent coffee-growers, they do not visit the island regularly. In 2004, they sold some of the tracts to others who wanted to help in the project, and Álvarez spends most of her time at her permanent residence for nearly two decades in Weybridge, Vermont. It is quite near the Canadian border, and there are many more residents of French and German heritage than Latinos; her reality is more of a snowy setting than a tropical one. She frequently states, "I live in sleepy Vermont. I live on a dirt road." The surrounding community consists mostly of farms and the nearest town is Middlebury, where Álvarez holds the position of Writer-in-Residence at Middlebury College. She describes her routine as time spent in the college library or in her home office. "I go to work every day and I do the work, the same way that my neighbor goes and takes care of his sheep, and Bill goes to the office. That's just what I do, mid what I am focused on."

It was some ten years ago that she came upon the idea for her latest novel. "I was doing research for *In the Name of Salomé*, studying the history of Hispaniola, and [saw] a little footnote that mentioned smallpox had broken out. The Eastern half [of the island] was occupied by the French, the western half was in revolution, and smallpox was raging among the troops. A smallpox expedition that was going around the world with carrier orphan boys had just arrived in the New World with the vaccine, but unfortunately it was not able to make a landfall in the Dominican Republic. And I thought, what's this? So that's how [the idea] started. I didn't say, here is my story, I just thought, oh my gosh, I have never read this before.

"First I called a friend who is a medical historian, and he had never heard of it; he thought I was making it up. So I went to the college library and took out every book on smallpox that was there. This was soon after 9/11, when Homeland Security wanted librarians to turn over everybody taking out questionable books, and here I was with 30 titles on smallpox."

The heroes in *Saving the World* are numerous real-life orphans, first 22 who travel from Spain to the Americas, then 26 who travel from Mexico to the Philippines, in each case accompanied by their teacher/caretaker (a woman), and the scientific doctor (a man) who is credited with the mission. The orphans are employed as live carriers of the vaccine, a feat that did not harm them. "One of the reasons that I wanted to write the book is that the child carriers are all but forgotten and deserve a place in human recollection. Some of the names, we know, [although] often just first names.

"We think about civilization and its great projects and the things that are cutting-edge and move us forward as a human family. [Often] we know the architect, or the great doctor that led the expedition, but really, the actual work was done by the little guy who put the stone in the cathedral, by the carriers of the vaccine, or the anonymous person on whose back rides our progress. The same could be true of the novelist: they get their name in the book, they get to be the star, but you're standing on a lot of shoulders, that's how you got to touch the sky. So I feel like we need to give credit where credit is due."

How does a writer get noticed and onto the path to published works and fame? And what inspires and guides them toward this path? Often the work is produced in anonymity for years. "I was passionate about this calling. You know, I was 41 when *García Girls* was published, so I had been writing for a while."

Álvarez's book of essays, published in 1998, explores and explains many of the occurrences behind the creation of her novels. In the first chapter, titled "Customs," she describes her grandfather, who (during her earliest years in the Dominican Republic) consistently asked his various grandchildren what they wished to become. On a first occasion, she replied, "a bullfighter," but he informed her that only men could be bullfighters. Next she said, "a cowboy," and he replied that she meant "cowgirl." The next time a trip was made to New York, relatives brought back child cowboy outfits for the boys and a cowgirl outfit for her. She was greatly disappointed because instead of the toy guns and ropes that complemented the boys' outfits, she received a strap-on purse and mirror. Later on she told her grandfather she wished to become an actress, because they got to know the world, try all modes of travel, learn other languages, and wear all sorts of costumes. Where do you get these ideas? he replied. Then her mother told her she needed to eat more, because she was too skimpy to become an actress, and that she must learn to

sing and dance. None of these things interested Álvarez. By the end of the essay, she tells her grandfather that she will become a poet, and he replies, yes, that is a very good choice. Her childhood observations reveal the curiosity for life and people that creates a great writer.

Winning awards is always a significant element in an author's success, and it helps financially as well. Álvarez received literary awards and fellowships early in her career; poetry awards in 1980, 1982, and 1984–85; and a PEN Oakland Award as well as a prize from Berkeley's Third Woman Press in 1986. That same year she was awarded a fellowship to participate in the Bread Loaf Writers Conference, where she began crafting novels, and the following year she received a grant from the National Endowment for the Arts.

Her earliest forays into creativity were as a poet. Álvarez's first small book of poetry, *The Housekeeping Book*, was published in 1984. It was a collaboration with Dominican poet Sherezada "Chiqui" Vicioso, who founded a circle of women poets in New York in 1980 to help fledgling authors get published. These poems were joined with new poems, often celebrating nature, in an edition titled *Homecoming*, published in 1991. And in 1996, Álvarez issued *Homecoming: New and Collected Poems*, including poems that are expressions of daily life and domestic chores, of finding ritual in the mundane. Her poems often explore family stories from the perspective of the woman, her search for identity, and her views on patriarchal privilege. The "homecoming" is also a return to the home of language, significant for those living in exile.

Another collection, *The Other Side/El otro lado* (1995), explores the lives of the people in the lowest economic class in the Dominican countryside. These poems are sensitive and introspective, touching on the plight of field workers and household maids, many of whom are transitioning from life on the island to life in New York and are struggling to acquire a new language. The immigrant voice is primary.

Álvarez's recent book of poems, *The Woman I Kept to Myself* (2004), is a self-reflection, where cultural practices are interwoven with images of isolation and nature, from the perspective of a woman who chooses writing over traditional roles like motherhood. This poetic voice is discernible in Álvarez's novels, which explore in greater detail the heritage of the Dominican-American.

Several of the poems are in bilingual form. In one, the speaker imagines "a literary border guard turning you back to Spanish," a likely commentary on Spanish-language critics who call for proper use of Spanish. In another, the line, "Tu tiempo ya llegó," indicates acceptance of the bilingual U.S.-Latino personage. Another poem is similar in context to an essay in *Something to Declare*, stating that the Latino is "all-American."

How the García Girls Lost Their Accents highlights the differences between Caribbean and U.S. cultures that impede assimilation as well as the contradicting gender messages immigrant girls hear from their two cultures. Racial aspects not discussed in Dominican society are broached here. When the García girls visit relatives on the island each summer, they see that light-skinned babies—especially male babies—are considered a great treasure for a family. Dominicans are said to have a café-con-leche or a "caramel" color, while those of darker complexion are called Haitians. The present generation of Dominican-American writers has continued on this theme with even more overt descriptions of racial discrimination.

Álvarez's best-known work is *In the Time of the Butterflies*, a tribute to women heroes and others who struggled against Dominican dictator Rafael Trujillo. As with each of her novels in Spanish translation, this one has garnered considerable attention on the island. It may have even inspired Peruvian novelist Mario Vargas Llosa to write his novel set in the Dominican Republic, *La fiesta del chivo* (2000). As early as 1969, however, Dominican Pedro Mir (of Puerto Rican and Cuban parents) had published a long poem, "Amén de mariposas," celebrating the Mirabal sisters of Álvarez's novel.

Now, *Saving the World* joins several of her themes: women's roles in society, how human beings interact and change societies, and the severe contrasts between life in the first and third worlds.

"Certainly, it's a novel about the huge discrepancies that exist between different parts of the world. Now that we're [so] mobile, we know and carry within us those kinds of discrepancies, unsettling differences in which people get to have what. And of course, that's very much part of the novel, in terms of what happens when the desperate rise up."

"There was always the option of just telling Isabel's story, the epidemic story, which is engaging and riveting enough. That's all I was going to do, and then 9/11 happened, and I think a lot of us writers, and a lot of Americans, suddenly started to ask ourselves: Oh my goodness, what is this world we are living in? Where are we headed? How can we turn this around, if there is so much hatred, so much division, that nobody's safe any more? And one of the things I asked myself as a writer, like my [other character] Alma, is, what are stories for? What does it matter that you read a story, and it moves you, and makes you feel the feelings that enlarge your spirit when things happen in your life? What does it mean that you are a carrier, like the boys with the vaccine, of a narrative that you know about, either historical or because you read a source?

"That's why I have Alma so obsessed and taken with Isabel's story and the epidemic, and then things start to happen to her. That was the impetus. How does she take this story? What does that do for her? I didn't have an answer. You write novels because you want to find things out. I didn't know anything. I just wanted to follow that track. So in part, *Saving the World* is also a novel [asking] what stories can do. Can they save us?"

Like other well-known writers at the inception of a literary period, Álvarez will forever be remembered as the first Dominican-American writer and one of the first Latinas in a decade of a great deal of attention for this group. What is her impression of the critical reception of her work?

"You know, you move intuitively as a writer, using craft. Then later people will see or point out, or you yourself will see a couple or more basic themes running through there, but you didn't know you were spinning it, even intentionally."

It is the reader that matters most to her. In fact, she feels that no story is "alive" until the reader has absorbed it. "What you hope for with a story is that it opens [up] some little insights, some knowledge of character and of self that wasn't there before, that it nurtures the human spirit and gets passed on, so that we're able to make different choices and be a little more aware of each other, of the human experience.

"Why does Whitman say, 'Look for me under your boot soles' at the end of *Leaves of Grass*? He doesn't mean that literally. He is dead, he is under our boot soles, or our shoes, but he is alive while we are reading this poem, he's inside us. At the end of *The Woman I Kept to Myself*, there's a poem entitled 'Did I redeem myself?' and the last two lines are: 'And you, my readers, what will you decide when all that's left of me will be these lines?'"

Source: Elizabeth Coonrod Martínez, "Progenitor of a Movement," in *Americas*, Vol. 59, No. 2, March/April 2007, pp. 6–13.

Fritz Lanham

In the following article, Lanham examines the roots of Alvarez's poetry.

Julia Alvarez, child of the sweltry Caribbean, loves winters in Vermont. Not the cold, no, but "the bareness and the quietness and the simplicity." A 10-inch blanket of snow apparently focuses the mind wonderfully.

On this spring day, the diminutive writer is swathed in a large black wrap, fending off the chill generated not by Mother Nature but by the robust air-conditioning unit of a downtown Houston hotel. Below her fine-boned face, centered on her blouse, she wears, like a breastplate, an ornate silver pin in the shape of a butterfly.

Alvarez's many admirers—some of whom heard her read earlier in the day at the Houston Public Library—would immediately recognize the allusion to *In the Time of the Butterflies*, her National Book Award-nominated 1994 novel about the three Mirabal sisters, known in their native Dominican Republic as las mariposas or "the butterflies." The sisters, who had plotted the overthrow of Dominican strongman Rafael Trujillo, were murdered in 1960. The middle sister's daughter gave Alvarez the pin.

She has lived in Vermont since 1988, longer than she's lived anywhere else, she explains in a lightly accented voice. But her fiction, though written in English, is rooted in the Dominican Republic, where she spent her girlhood, and in her experiences as a Latina immigrant to this country. Her manner is warm, and her brown eyes are cheerful. She seems delicate and lively.

She's best-known for her four adult novels. *Butterflies* and *How the Garcia Girls Lost Their Accent* (1991), about the sometimes funny, sometimes painful adjustment to life in the United States, are considered classics of contemporary Latino literature. *Yo* (1996) is a sequel to *Garcia Girls*.

> WHEN SHE BEGAN WRITING, SHE WAS RELUCTANT TO CALL HERSELF AN AMERICAN WRITER, BECAUSE SHE WAS WRITING ABOUT DOMINICAN CHARACTERS."

Her most recent novel, *In the Name of Salome* (2000), tells the story of a famous poet and her daughter who settle in the United States. Like *Butterflies*, it's rooted in fact. Alvarez's collection of autobiographical essays, *Something to Declare*, appeared in 1998; she has also written children's and young-adult books.

The critic Ilan Stavans has rightly observed: "In the current wave of Latina novelists she strikes me as among the least theatrical and vociferous, the one listening most closely to the subtleties of her own artistic call. She stands apart stylistically, a psychological novelist who uses language skillfully to depict complex inner lives for her fictional creations."

What fans of Alvarez's novels may not realize is that she's also a poet—indeed, started out as a poet, and remains passionately committed to the form. She has published four collections, the most recent of which, *The Woman I Kept to Myself* (Algonquin), came out last month and was the occasion for her mid-April reading in Houston.

Discussion of that book prompts Alvarez to extol the virtues of Vermont winters. Pulling herself erect in the voluminous hotel lobby chair, she extracts a piece of paper from her purse. On it she's written the words of the poet Josephine Jacobson, who kept a willow branch in her study.

"The Japanese have a word for the spirit that inhabited that willow: wabi," she reads. "Wabi is a way to approach life. It is the beauty found in extreme simplicity, a contentedness in bareness and in doing without. Wabi beauty possesses depth. An object imbued with wabi is believed to contain an old soul."

"That," Alvarez says, refolding the paper, "describes for me the dead of winter in Vermont."

She's tried to infuse *The Woman I Kept to Myself* with the spirit of wabi. The 75 autobiographical poems include childhood memories ("Out in the playground, kids were shouting Spic! / lifting my sister's skirt, yanking her slip") and confrontations with aging and death ("My friend said what was hardest were the signs / her mother left behind: a favorite dress / misbuttoned on a hanger; library books / covered in paper bags, way overdue").

She writes about her evolution as a Latina writer and about the interplay of English and Spanish in her life. Her husband and sisters make appearances. Growing older, the loss of parents, what it means to become the elder of the tribe, what to do with the time left us—these are some of the themes in the book.

The poems seem both carefully crafted and artlessly intimate, ordinary experiences mediated through wrought language. Each consists of three stanzas of 10 lines, in blank verse, 10 syllables per line. Despite their formal structure, the poems are neither stiff-necked nor arcane. Alvarez favors "the simplicity, the everyday spokenness" of American English, she says. She aims for "the musicality in the everyday" language. More like William Carlos Williams, less like Wallace Stevens.

"It's a later-in-life book," she says, one that uses writing as a way to know things. "For me writing is . . . a way that I experience this baffling, beautiful, painful experience of being alive."

So what does poetry do for her, to her, that fiction doesn't?

Alvarez has a metaphoric explanation at her finger's tip. This is obviously a question to which she's given thought.

"I think of poetry as the scout, going out into the unknown, into what has yet to be put into words. Poetry addresses that place where we feel our own mortal loneliness.

"And then come the novels—they're the settlers. They bring the wagons, they have kids, they have births, they have deaths, they need to build a school, they need to have a place to have a dance. There's lots of characters. It's a different kind of relationship between the reader and the narrative."

Alvarez alternates between novel-writing and poetry-writing. Having disgorged large amounts of experience into prose, she finds it rejuvenating to deal with "the atom," language at its most elemental, addressing the essential questions: "Who am I, what am I thinking about, what are the things that come into my life that I process by writing them down?" For her, that's the realm of poetry.

"I tell this to my young writers: Writers aren't people who know things. They're people who want to find things out."

. . .

Julia Alvarez was born in March 1950 in New York City, where her Dominican parents were in self-imposed exile from the brutal Trujillo dictatorship. When Julia was 3 weeks old, the family returned home, believing the political situation had improved. They remained for 10 years, until 1960, when Julia's physician-father fell under suspicion of anti-government activity. The family fled to the United States, settling in an upper-middle-class section of Queens.

In the Dominican Republic, Julia had "dressed like an American, eaten American foods and befriended American children," as she told one interviewer. "I had gone to an American school and spent most of the day speaking and reading English." She expected to fit right into her new environment.

It didn't happen. Her American classmates taunted her and her sisters for their accents. Her private-school English hadn't prepared her for the lingo of fast-talking New Yorkers. The sensitive girl, feeling marginalized and uncomfortable, retreated into the world of reading, "the table set for all," as she's fond of saying. "I would get inside a book, and it just spoke to me." She came to know the power of words and decided she wanted to conjure such magic. She's also admitted that revenge fed her choice of a vocation.

"I told myself that one day I would express myself in a way that would make those boys feel bad they had tormented me. At some point, though, revenge turned into redemption. Instead of pummeling those boys with my success, I began to want to save them. I wanted to change those looks of hate and mistrust."

She earned an undergraduate degree from Middlebury College in Vermont—her extended introduction to that state—and a master's in creative writing from Syracuse University, then embarked on a career as a "migrant writer." She taught at the University of Vermont, George Washington University and the University of Illinois, never in one place very long. "I really moved around America," she says. "The good part of it is I got to know the United States."

But it was hard. "A writer badly needs an address," she says, quoting Isaac Bashevis Singer about how a writer needs to feel attached to a place, even if it's not the place he ends up writing about. "When you're still trying to figure out where you're going to do your laundry and who your doctor is going to be—and you're doing this every couple of years—you're not settled yet into a community enough to really focus on the work."

That began to change in 1988 when she was hired at Middlebury College. She taught there full time until 1998 and now is writer-in-residence, teaching creative writing part time and counseling Latino students.

She and husband Bill Eichner, an ophthalmologist with a rural Vermont practice, visit the Dominican Republic several times a year, in part to oversee an organic-coffee-growing enterprise and literacy project they started there. Alvarez's career as part-time coffee farmer began with an article she wrote for the *Nature Conservancy*. Researching the piece, she met small farmers who were trying to cultivate coffee the traditional, ecologically friendly way but who were losing out—and losing their land—to big agribusinesses.

The farmers had banded into a cooperative. They asked Eichner (who has rural roots in Nebraska) and Alvarez for help, and in 1997 the couple began buying small plots of land and planting them with coffee. They market the coffee from their own farm as well as others, and they use the income to fund a school to teach the locals and their children how to read.

As a business enterprise, the farm has been a financial drain, Alvarez says, in part because she and her husband can't be there to run it all the time. They've turned their land holdings over to a nongovernmental organization to create a model farm to teach organic methods. They've also arranged to sell their coffee via the Internet. You can order it through their Web site— www.cafealtagracia.com ("This is coffee with a conscience, brought directly to your cup by farmers who practice conservation with a vengeance.").

. . .

Alvarez's work is about "the identity of the in-betweens," to use Stavans' words, about those in this country but not entirely of this country. When Alvarez came to the United States, the terms Latino and Latina hadn't been invented. She was called "Spanish."

"We didn't come from Spain, but we were Spanish," she says with a shrug. Later she identified herself as a "Dominican-American," the Dominican part referring to life at home, among the familia, the American part to public life in a country still wedded to the assimilationist model.

When she began writing, she was reluctant to call herself an American writer, because she was writing about Dominican characters. "There was this gulf," she says, "between the stories I had to tell and the voice that I had, and what I thought those had to be for me to become an American writer."

Reading *The Woman Warrior*, the 1989 memoir by Chinese-American writer Maxine Hong Kingston, was a transformative experience. The book taught her that stories by non-Anglos could be just as American as any others and that they could be literature and not simply a species of sociology.

Now Alvarez self-defines without the hyphen. "More and more I'm comfortable with talking about myself as an all-American," she says.

"My roots, my traditions, my stories, my rhythms are from the Latin part of the Americas, but the language I learned to master and to craft into stories or poetry is from the northern part of the Americas. So I really am an all-American girl. . . ."

. . .

"Writers aren't people who know things," says Julia Alvarez. "They're people who want to find things out." Best known for such novels as '*In the Time of the Butterflies*' and '*How the Garcia Girls Lost Their Accents*,' Alvarez says writing is her way of grappling with "this baffling, beautiful, painful experience of being alive."

Source: Fritz Lanham, "Julia Alvarez: All-American Writer: *Garcia Girls* Author Delivers Intimate yet Carefully Crafted Poems," in *Houston Chronicle*, May 16, 2004, p. 8.

SOURCES

Alvarez, Julia, "Exile," in *The Other Side/La Otro Lado*, Plume, 1996, pp. 25–28.

Danticat, Edwidge, *Breath, Eyes, Memory*, Vintage, 1998.

Donghi, Tulio Halperin, "A Decade of Decisions," in *The Contemporary History of Latin America*, edited and translated by John Charles Chasteen, Duke University Press, 1993, pp. 292–336.

Frank, Anne, *Anne Frank: The Diary of a Young Girl*, Pocket Books, 1953.

Gilbert, Sandra M., Review of *The Other Side/El Otro Lado*, in *Poetry*, August 1996, p. 285.

Gilbertson, Greta, and Douglas T. Gurak, "Household Transitions in the Migrations of Dominicans and Colombians to New York," in *International Migration Review*, Vol. 26, No. 1, Spring 1992, p. 27.

Guarnizo, Luis E., "Los Dominicanyorks: The Making of a Binational Society," in *Annals of the American Academy of Political and Social Science*, Vol. 533, May 1994, p. 71.

Heredia, Juanita, "Citizen of the World: An Interview with Julia Alvarez," in *Latina Self-Portraits: Interviews with Contemporary Women Writers*, edited by Bridget Kevane and Juanita Heredia, University of New Mexico Press, 2000, pp. 19–32.

Jacques, Ben, "Julia Alvarez: Real Flights of Imagination," in *Americas*, Vol. 53, January 2001, p. 22.

Martinez, Elizabeth Coonrod, "Julia Alvarez: Progenitor of a Movement: This Dominican-American Writer Weaves Passionate Sensibilities through Her Works with the Gift of Seeing through Others' Eyes," in *Americas*, Vol. 59, March/April 2007, pp. 6–9.

Pessar, Patricia R., "The Linkage Between the Household and Workplace of Dominican Women in the U.S.," in *Caribbean Life in New York: Sociocultural Dimensions*, edited by Elsa M. Chaney, Center for Migration Studies of New York, 1989, pp. 241–45.

Review of *The Other Side/El Otro Lado*, in *Publishers Weekly*, April 24, 1995, p. 65.

Varnes, Kathrine, "Julia Alvarez," in *Dictionary of Literary Biography*, Vol. 282, *New Formalist Poets*, Thomson Gale, 2003, pp. 16–23.

Zakrzewski Brown, Isabel, "Social Customs," in *Culture and Customs of the Dominican Republic*, Greenwood, 1999, pp. 79–104.

FURTHER READING

Alvarez, Julia, *How the Garcia Girls Lost Their Accents*, Algonquin, 1991.

> This young-adult novel about four sisters adjusting to life in America after fleeing the Dominican Republic was the breakthrough title that earned Alvarez a following among critics and readers.

Herrera, Andrea O'Reilly, ed., *A Secret Weaver's Anthology: Selections from the White Pine Press Secret Weavers Series: Writing by Latin American Women*, White Pine Press, 1998.

> The White Pine Press published a series of twelve volumes of writings by Latin American women, and this volume anthologizes selections from across the series. Forty women from thirteen countries writing in all genres are represented.

Patterson, Richard E., "Resurrecting Rafael: Fictional Incarnations of a Dominican Dictator," in *Callaloo: A Journal of African Diaspora Arts and Letters*, Vol. 29, No. 1, Winter 2006, pp. 223–37.

> The works of three authors—Julia Alvarez, Edwidge Danticat, and Mario Vargas Llosa—are compared to examine how literature has responded to the dictatorship of Rafael Trujillo.

Pons, Frank Moya, *The Dominican Republic: A National History*, Markus Wiener Publishing, 2010.

> Pons is a respected scholar on Dominican history, and this updated history informs readers about the political history, the colonization and self-rule phases, and the profound impact of socioeconomic factors in the country.

SUGGESTED SEARCH TERMS

Julia Alvarez AND Exile

Exile AND poem

The Other Side/El Otro Lado

Exile AND literature

Dominican literature

formalist poets

immigrant literature

fathers AND daughters

Rafael Trujillo

Dominican Republic AND Julia Alvarez

Flounder

NATASHA TRETHEWEY
1993

Natasha Trethewey's "Flounder" was first published in 1993 in the academic journal *Callaloo*; however, it did not receive much critical attention until its publication seven years later in Trethewey's first book of poems, *Domestic Work*. Many critics have praised the poems in *Domestic Work* for their originality and seeming effortlessness. "Flounder," like many of Trethewey's poems, portrays a figure from Trethewey's life. In this case, the figure depicted is Aunt Sugar, the sister of Trethewey's maternal grandmother. Because of the interaction between the speaker of the poem and the Aunt Sugar character, and because both Trethewey and the speaker of poem are biracial, it is reasonable to infer that the speaker in "Flounder" may represent some past incarnation of Trethewey herself.

Trethewey's being half black and half white is a situation that is directly confronted in "Flounder." Just as the half-black, half-white fish struggles to breathe above water, so too the biracial speaker of the poem struggles with her identity. In this way, the flounder in the poem symbolizes the speaker. The poem's title, "Flounder," refers not only to the fish in the poem but also to the struggles depicted in the work, as the word *flounder* means to struggle. Interestingly, Trethewey combines both traditional and more contemporary stylistic elements in "Flounder"; for example, it includes several traditional ballad stanzas written in African American vernacular English.

Natasha Trethewey (AP Images)

A copy of the poem "Flounder" can be found in Natasha Trethewey's collection *Domestic Work*, published in 2000 by Graywolf Press.

AUTHOR BIOGRAPHY

Trethewey was born in 1966 in Gulfport, Mississippi, to the poet Eric Trethewey and Gwendolyn Grimmette. Significantly, Trethewey was born to a white father and an African American mother at a time when anti-miscegenation laws, which banned interracial marriage, were still in effect in Mississippi. Race is a theme that frequently occurs in Trethewey's poetry. When Trethewey was six years old, her parents divorced, and she moved with her mother to Decatur, Georgia. During the summers, she visited her grandmother in Mississippi and her father in New Orleans, Louisiana. In 1985, when Trethewey was nineteen, her mother was brutally murdered by her ex-husband Joel Grimmette, whom she had divorced two years before. Trethewey's mother is also the subject of many of her poems.

After high school, Trethewey studied English and creative writing at the University of Georgia. She went on to earn a master's degree in English and creative writing at Hollins University, where her father is a professor of English. She eventually earned a master of fine arts degree in poetry from the University of Massachusetts.

Though Trethewey published many poems in the early 1990s, including "Flounder," which was first published in *Callaloo* in 1993, she first gained widespread recognition for her poetic talents in 1999 when her first book of poetry, *Domestic Work*, was selected by Rita Dove to receive the Cave Canem Poetry Prize for the best first book by an African American poet. Following the publication in 2000 of *Domestic Work*, which included the poem "Flounder," she was awarded the Mississippi Institute of Arts and Letters Book Prize and the Lillian Smith Award for poetry in 2001. To date, she has received countless awards, prizes, and fellowships in honor of her work, including the 2007 Pulitzer Prize for poetry for her collection *Native Guard* and the 2008 Mississippi Governor's Award for Literature.

In conjunction with her career as a poet, Trethewey has had an extensive career in the world of academia. She taught as an assistant professor of English at Auburn University in Alabama and held positions at Duke University and the University of North Carolina, Chapel Hill.

As of 2011, she held the Phyllis Wheatley Distinguished Chair and was professor of poetry in the creative writing program at Emory University. She is married to Brett Gadsden, a professor of African American history at Emory University, and lives in Georgia.

POEM TEXT

> *Here*, she said, *put this on your head.*
> She handed me a hat.
> *You 'bout as white as your dad,*
> *and you gone stay like that.*
>
> Aunt Sugar rolled her nylons down   5
> around each bony ankle,
> and I rolled down my white knee socks
> letting my thin legs dangle,
>
> circling them just above water
> and silver backs of minnows   10
> flitting here then there between
> the sun spots and the shadows.

This is how you hold the pole
to cast the line out straight.
Now put that worm on your hook,   15
throw it out and wait.

She sat spitting tobacco juice
into a coffee cup.
Hunkered down when she felt the bite,
jerked the pole straight up   20

reeling and tugging hard at the fish
that wriggled and tried to fight back.
A flounder, she said, *and you can tell*
'cause one of its sides is black.

The other side is white, she said.   25
It landed with a thump.
I stood there watching that fish flip-flop,
switch sides with every jump.

POEM SUMMARY

The text used for this summary is from *Domestic Work*, by Natasha Trethewey, Graywolf Press, 2000, pp. 35–36. Versions of the poem can be found on the following Web pages: http://www.poetryfoundation.org/poem/237548 and http://famouspoetsandpoems.com/poets/natasha_trethewey/poems/17895.

"Flounder" is a narrative poem, which means it is a poem that tells a story. It consists of seven stanzas, each of which has four lines, that describe an interaction between an older African American woman named Aunt Sugar, and her young biracial niece. The poem is told from the perspective of the young girl, who is reflecting back on her Aunt Sugar teaching her how to fish. Some of the poem's words are italicized to signify that they were spoken aloud by Aunt Sugar. The words in the poem that are not italicized are the girl's narration of the event.

Stanza 1

The first line of the poem makes it immediately clear that someone is speaking, although the reader is not yet aware of who the speaker is or to whom he or she is speaking. In lines 1 and 2, the speaker, Aunt Sugar, hands her niece a hat and instructs her to wear it. In lines 3 and 4, Aunt Sugar gives the young girl a justification for the order: she wants the girl to wear the hat to protect her light skin, which is similar to that of her (presumably) white father. Aunt Sugar compares the girl's skin to her father's, in line 3, implying that Aunt Sugar, by contrast, does not have white skin. In line 4, it becomes clear that Aunt Sugar intends to ensure that her niece's skin remain

light and untanned. The straightforward way that Aunt Sugar speaks in this stanza indicates that she is not a woman to avoid bringing up potentially delicate topics, such as skin color; she is the type of person to speak her mind.

Stanzas 2 and 3

There is a shift between the first and second stanzas, as Aunt Sugar is no longer speaking and the young girl begins narrating. The girl explains to the reader how she and her Aunt Sugar removed their socks and let their legs hang over the edge of what is probably a dock. The girl describes moving her feet around right above the water and watching the minnows swim just underneath it, quickly moving back and forth.

Stanza 4

In the fourth stanza, Aunt Sugar begins speaking again, explaining to the girl how to properly hold a fishing pole and cast a line. Because of Aunt Sugar's instructional tone, it is clear that while she is explaining she is simultaneously casting a line into the water. Aunt Sugar's words in this stanza not only inform the reader that the two characters in the poem are fishing but also suggest that this is a poem about more than just fishing. It is a poem that deals with an elder relative passing on knowledge to a younger relative. In this stanza, the reader also learns that Aunt Sugar is not concerned with being particularly lady-like; she is a skilled fisherwoman.

Stanzas 5–7

The last three stanzas are considered together because they are linked by the action of Aunt Sugar catching a fish, reeling it in, and pulling it onto the dock. Aunt Sugar is further characterized in the first two lines of stanza 5, when she spits out tobacco juice. Chewing tobacco is traditionally seen as a masculine habit. In line 19, Aunt Sugar feels a bite on her line, and in lines 20–22, she struggles with the fish, attempting to reel it in. In lines 23–25, she speaks again, identifying the fish as a flounder and explaining to the young girl how to identify a flounder: they are distinctively patterned, with one white side and one black side. In line 26, Aunt Sugar finally manages to pull the fish onto the dock, where it lands with a thud. In lines 27 and 28, the young girl, mesmerized, watches the fish flail around, landing alternately on its white and black sides.

TOPICS FOR FURTHER STUDY

- "Flounder" is a poem in which the speaker is forced to think about her identity in a way she never had before. Recall a moment that caused you to consider your identity in a new light or question something that you had always believed to be true. Write a poem in any style that conveys the impact of this moment and expresses how it made you feel.

- Trethewey is a poet who frequently bases her poems on historical events. Locate a poem, story, song, painting, or film that reinterprets a real historical event. Try to choose an event or a work of art that speaks to you and your heritage. Create a multimedia presentation for your classmates in which you explain the historical event and how it is portrayed in the artwork that you found.

- Read the young-adult novel *Black Storm Comin'* by Diane Lee Wilson. Though it is set a century before the poems in *Domestic Work*, the protagonist, Colton, deals with some of the same racial issues that appear in Trethewey's poems. After reading *Black Storm Comin'*, consider how the themes of the work compare to the themes present in "Flounder" and some of the other poems in *Domestic Work*. Are there any thematic similarities between the two books? Can you find any similarities between Colton, a biracial boy growing up in

the Civil War era, and the speaker of "Flounder," a biracial girl growing up in the civil rights era? Do you think there are aspects of being biracial or multicultural that affect people regardless of time and place? Provide your answers to these questions in an essay in which you support your opinions with evidence from the two texts.

- To better understand the historical climate in which Aunt Sugar and her niece live, use the Internet and print sources to do some research about the civil rights movement in Mississippi. Be sure to make a note of laws, speeches, marches, and hate crimes that were relevant to the civil rights movement. Using a computer program, compile the landmark events that you discover on an interactive time line that illustrates the progress of civil rights.

- "Flounder" is a poem that uses African American vernacular English, a common dialect. Dialects are an important literary device because they can help the reader gain a sense of who a character is. Read a poem or a short story in which one or more characters speaks in a dialect. If you are unsure what a dialect is, research common dialects on the Internet. Create a glossary giving definitions and word origins of terms that differ from standard American English.

THEMES

Opposites

The themes of opposition and contrast appear many times in the poem. The main opposition is the two characters themselves: Aunt Sugar is an older, knowledgeable, dark-skinned woman who instructs, while the speaker is a young, naïve, light-skinned girl who observes. Another opposition exists between Aunt Sugar's dialect and that of the narration. There is also an opposition between action and inaction, as Aunt Sugar struggles to hoist the flounder upon the dock,

while the young speaker passively observes. However, the most obvious opposition in the poem is the one revealed in the last two stanzas: one of the sides of the flounder is black, and the other side is white. The flounder flops around on the dock, struggling to get back into the water, alternately revealing its black side and its white side. That the flounder's struggle results in its switching between its black side and its white side suggests that perhaps a similar struggle is taking place within the young narrator, who is, like the flounder, half black and half white.

Aunt Sugar and the narrator dangled their feet off the pier. *(Dmitriy Shironosov / Shutterstock.com)*

Black-White Relations

Black-white relations—specifically, the implications of the young speaker's biracialism—are also present in the poem. It is evident by the third line that race is an important factor in the poem, when Aunt Sugar points out, in African American vernacular, that the speaker's skin is nearly as white as that of her father. Using context clues, the reader can infer that the speaker's father is white and her mother is black and that Aunt Sugar belongs to her mother's side of the family. When Aunt Sugar instructs the speaker to don a hat to protect the lightness of her skin, it is clear that Aunt Sugar sees value in its remaining light. The comparison with the speaker's father's skin indicates that Aunt Sugar is concerned with preventing it from darkening, not simply preventing a sunburn. As a black woman, Aunt Sugar knows that there are cultural privileges that come with having white or light skin, and she wants her niece to enjoy those privileges even though she herself has never been able to.

Struggle

The theme of struggle is manifest both in Aunt Sugar's struggle with the fish and the fish's struggle to breathe on the dock. Both the tone and the action of the poem are relatively calm until line 20, when a physical struggle begins between Aunt Sugar and the flounder. From that point on, the poem is rife with struggle. A climactic battle between the two is detailed in lines 22 and 23, but the flounder ultimately loses as it is hoisted up on the dock. Yet even then, the fish continues to struggle to breathe. It flails about, landing alternately on its right side and its left, hoping to make it back into the water. While she was reeling it in, Aunt Sugar had pointed out that it has one black side and one white side, allowing the reader to make the connection that the struggle between black and white is perhaps mirrored in the young biracial speaker, who will spend the rest of her life struggling to define herself.

Observation

The young speaker of the poem is consistently a passive observer, removed from the action of the poem. Aside from removing her socks and hanging her legs over the edge of the dock, she does not speak or act at any point in the poem. She watches as Aunt Sugar explains how to fish and catches a fish, and she watches as the fish flops around on the dock. The speaker's role as an observer is crucial, because by her recounting this moment it is apparent that in her observation she not only learned how to fish but also learned something about the nature of black and white and a creature that combines the two.

STYLE

Rhymed Quatrains

As Cynthia Hogue points out in her essay "Poets Without Borders," published in the *Women's Review of Books*, "Flounder" is composed of rhyming quatrains. A quatrain is a stanza of poetry that has exactly four lines. A quatrain is said to be rhyming if it possesses an *AABB, ABAB, ABBA,* or *ABCB* rhyme scheme, meaning that the final syllable in at least one line of the quatrain must rhyme with the final syllable in at least one of the other lines of the quatrain. Each of the seven stanzas in the poem is a rhyming quatrain with an *ABCB* rhyme scheme, meaning that the last syllables in the second and fourth lines of each of the quatrains rhyme with one another, but the last syllables in the first and third lines do not. As Hogue points out, a quatrain with an *ABCB* rhyme scheme is one of the most commonly used stanzas in the history of Anglo-American poetry, and countless iconic poems written by classic white poets have been written in this form. It is frequently referred to as the ballad stanza.

As a contemporary poet, Trethewey somewhat ironically appropriates the classic ballad stanza in "Flounder," even using this form for the stanzas that are written using African American vernacular. Rhyming quatrains typically supply a poem with an even and rhythmic pattern and a sense of finality, or closure, at the end of each stanza. The natural rhythm of the poem typically leads the reader to expect an idea or sentence to end at the end of a quatrain and a new idea to begin at the start of the next. In "Flounder," Trethewey plays with this sense of closure between the fifth and sixth stanzas and again between the sixth and the seventh stanzas. At the end of the fifth stanza, the rhythm and rhyme provide a sense of closure that is not duplicated in the plot, as the climactic action of this stanza carries over to the next without the need for a pause. Similarly, in line 24 at the end of the sixth stanza, the finality suggested by the cadence implies that Aunt Sugar is

done speaking, when in fact her speech carries on seamlessly into the next stanza.

African American Vernacular English

In "Flounder" Aunt Sugar speaks in a dialect of English commonly referred to as African American vernacular. The omission or condensing of sounds from words, as in lines 3 and 4, is typical of this dialect. African American vernacular English is particularly widespread in the southern coastal states, such as Mississippi, where Trethewey's family was based and where she spent much time as a child. Implementing a dialect in a literary work is a way to add linguistic variation to the work, as well as to tell the reader something about the character who is speaking in it, such as that character's race, geographical location, or many other things. African American vernacular English is a dialect so widely used that its presence does not tell us very much about Aunt Sugar, but in conjunction with other clues, the reader can ascertain that she is most likely an African American woman living in the rural South. This particular dialect is frequently used in Southern literature.

HISTORICAL CONTEXT

Anti-miscegenation Laws

Growing up as a biracial person in the Deep South on the heels of the civil rights movement undoubtedly forms the background for Trethewey's poetry. Trethewey was born to a white father and an African American mother in Mississippi in 1966, when anti-miscegenation laws were still in effect. Anti-miscegenation laws originated in the United States as early as the colonial era (though the term *miscegenation* was not coined until the 1800s) and were enacted to criminalize marriage and intimate relations between people of different races, most often aimed at blacks and whites. Racist readings of certain passages of the Bible were frequently used as justifications of these laws. Many states repealed these laws in the late nineteenth century, and many more repealed them following World War II, after Nazi Germany enforced similar laws banning relations between Aryans and non-Aryans.

The laws were not overturned in Trethewey's home state of Mississippi until June 12, 1967, when the Supreme Court, in the *Loving v. Virginia* case, set a precedent stating that persecuting people on the basis of participating in an interracial relationship was unconstitutional. The Supreme

COMPARE
&
CONTRAST

- **1990s:** Racist ideology is still surprisingly present in the United States. A 1993 study commissioned by the National Science Foundation that surveyed white Americans, reported by Loretta Ross in "White Supremacy in the 1990s," found that 51 percent of the respondents who identified themselves as conservatives and 45 percent of respondents who identified as liberal think African Americans are "aggressive and violent."

  Today: Racial sensitivity is still very much present in the United States. On April 23, 2010, Arizona Governor Jan Brewer signs an illegal immigration bill that sparks much controversy. The law makes it a crime for immigrants to not carry their immigration papers with them at all times and authorizes police officers to request immigration papers from anyone they suspect of being in the country illegally. Critics of this bill claim that it will promote racial profiling.

- **1990s:** In 1991, 95.5 percent of married couples surveyed by the United States Census Bureau are "same race couples." This means that nearly 4.5 percent of married couples are interracial.

  Today: A study conducted by Stanford University in 2005 finds that 7 percent of all couples married in the United States are interracial couples.

- **1990s:** African American female poets achieve landmark firsts. In 1993, Rita Dove becomes the first African American woman to serve as the poet laureate of the United States.

  Today: A great deal of African American poetry, including that of African American women, is ubiquitously respected, celebrated, anthologized, and studied. The first *Norton Anthology of African American Literature* is published in 2003, the *Oxford Anthology of African-American Poetry* in 2005, and the *Cambridge History of African American Literature* in 2011.

Court stated that the laws were designed to promote white supremacy. Even after anti-miscegenation laws were overturned, racial tensions lingered in the Deep South, and their existence is something that the characters of "Flounder" are very much aware of. It is evident that the young girl in the poem, like Trethewey, is of mixed race. Aunt Sugar instructs her to cover her light skin, which is similar to her father's, with her hat to protect it from being tanned by the sun. Aunt Sugar wants to maintain the lightness of her niece's skin because she knows that being white, or being perceived as white, means being socially privileged over other races in the 1960s and 1970s in Mississippi.

Racism in the South

Anti-miscegenation laws are not the only aspect of racism that inform the poem's subject matter and the attitudes of its characters. Trethewey was born in Mississippi, and even after moving to Georgia with her mother, she returned there in the summers to visit her maternal grandmother and her Aunt Sugar, who was her grandmother's older sister. Trethewey's grandmother and her Aunt Sugar, or at least characters based on them, appear in many of her poems. Though Trethewey was born at the end of the civil rights movement and thus was not alive to witness the most horrific years of racism in the South, her Aunt Sugar and the Aunt Sugar in "Flounder" certainly were. The notorious Ku Klux Klan murders of Mississippi civil rights workers James Chaney, Andrew Goodman, and Michael Schwerner occurred in 1964, just two years prior to Trethewey's birth. Chaney, Goodman, and Schwerner were civil rights workers who traveled to Longdale, Mississippi, to investigate the ruins of the Mount

The poem concludes with a discussion of the flounder they caught. (Undersea Discoveries | Shutterstock.com)

Zion United Methodist Church, a civil rights meeting place that had been burned down. Upon their arrival in Longdale, the men were arrested and detained on false pretenses by town deputy Cecil Price, a member of the White Knights of the Ku Klux Klan. Upon their release from the county jail, the men were trailed by Klan members and eventually beaten and murdered.

Aunt Sugar would have been completely aware of an atrocity such as this and the many others that occurred in the South during the time when Trethewey was young. Though the young girl in the poem may be oblivious to implications of her mixed-race status, her Aunt Sugar certainly is not. On the contrary, it is Aunt Sugar's awareness of racism against African Americans that motivates her to shield the young girl's light skin with a hat and prevent it from darkening.

CRITICAL OVERVIEW

Though "Flounder" did not receive much critical attention upon its original publication in the *Callaloo* journal in 1993, many critics took note

of it following its publication in Trethewey's first published book of poems, *Domestic Work*, in 2000. *Domestic Work* received widespread praise among critics, and "Flounder" was frequently noted as a standout poem.

In the Winter 2000/2001 volume of *Ploughshares*, critic Kevin Young reviewed the work. Young praises *Domestic Work* for its originality and delicate potency. He states:

> *Domestic Work* does what a first book should, and more, all while avoiding what first books often do—either borrowing themes from other poets or recycling a narrow vision of family life. Here Trethewey brilliantly discusses family, not for its extremes or its small hurts, but rather for the small intimacies that symbolize larger sufferings of history, both personal and public.

Young also praises the effortless appearance of Trethewey's poetry and says, "For a book about work, we rarely see Trethewey sweat."

In her 2001 essay "Poets Without Borders," published in the *Women's Review of Books*, Hogue gave *Domestic Work* a soaring review. She specifically comments that the language Trethewey implements in the poem reflects and reinforces the binary that the poem establishes between black and white. Hogue identifies this racial tension in the poem as a manifestation of Trethewey's own ambivalence as a person of mixed race. For the poems in which Trethewey's own life experience was clearly evident, such as "Flounder," Hogue expresses a particular affinity: "Half the volume is made up of well-turned, autobiographical poems like 'Flounder,' two for the poet's white father, 'Mythmaker' and 'Amateur,' and two for her dead mother, 'Family Portrait' and 'Saturday Drive,' are particularly poignant." Of *Domestic Work* as a whole, Hogue remarks: "Trethewey's vision, steeped as it is in a genuinely tragic sensibility culled from personal and racial history, has a depth of compassion that is hard-won. I admire the ambitious plumbing of those histories, that depth."

Like Hogue, Rafael Campo, in a 2003 review of *Domestic Work* and other works published in the journal *Prairie Schooner*, also attributes a powerful quality to Trethewey's poems of opposition:

> Trethewey also exerts interesting pressures on traditional forms; she herself identifies as a particular hybrid, an African American woman who can "pass" as white. This internal duality helps produce entirely unique sonnets shot through with bluesy inflections, and occasionally-rhymed quatrains that resonate with a kind of call-and-response undercurrent. It is poems like "Flounder," "Saturday Matinee," and "White Lies," in which she courageously places herself at the crossroads of two oft-opposing narratives, that most fully reveal her mettle as a poet.

Campo further explains that the impact of *Domestic Work* as a collection occurs not in spite of but because of Trethewey's talent for presenting everyday life. Campo observes: "This precocious book is full of quiet portraits of dignity and duty, brimming with the unobvious yet gleaming details of daily life."

In a 2002 review of *Domestic Work*, published in *Callaloo*, Jacquelyn Pope explains the characteristics that dominate each of the four sections of the book. According to Pope, the first poems in the book are marked by themes of stillness and motion, and the second section of poems revolves around Trethewey's grandmother. In the third section, to which "Flounder" belongs, Pope observes: "Trethewey turns to autobiographical subjects. Initially, these poems seem less energetic than those in the previous sections, but they have a cumulative power, particularly a group of poems about racial identification and passing." Pope concludes:

The love in this book is pure and poignant, the self-knowledge never self-congratulatory. Trethewey's respect for craft enables her to adroitly sidestep clichés and heavy-handedness. She is a poet who takes her responsibilities seriously, and *Domestic Work* is an engaging and impressive debut.

CRITICISM

Rachel Porter

Porter is a freelance writer and editor who holds a bachelor of arts degree in English literature. In the following essay, she argues that in "Flounder," Aunt Sugar not only teaches her young niece how to fish but also, by educating her, thrusts her into a world marked with racial identifiers.

The shallowest reading of Natasha Trethewey's "Flounder" reveals a poem in which an aunt teaches her young niece how to fish. Undertones of racial identity are certainly present in Aunt Sugar's comments to her niece, but upon first reading they seem casual, offhanded, and inconsequential. Upon closer examination, though, it seems undeniable that this is a poem almost exclusively about race and identity struggle, disguised as a poem about fishing. This is not because Aunt Sugar's words concerning color are particularly potent or plentiful but because of the profound impact they have on her young niece, who is also the poem's narrator. With just a few words, Aunt Sugar catapults her niece from a world of racial obliviousness into one where she will constantly struggle internally to define her external appearance as either black or white, when, like the flounder, it is simultaneously neither and both. Just as Aunt Sugar educates her niece about racial identity through the symbol of the flounder, the poem "Flounder" demonstrates to the reader how racial identity is constructed and maintained.

To understand why Aunt Sugar's words have such a great impact on the speaker of the poem, it is necessary to understand the nature of their relationship and their relative positions in the poem. Aunt Sugar is, first and foremost, a caregiver to the speaker. This is evident in the first stanza when she instructs the speaker to wear a hat to protect her skin from the sun. Additionally, when in the first stanza Aunt Sugar comments that the young girl's skin is almost as white as her father's skin, it is evident that the speaker is half white and half black, while Aunt Sugar is

WHAT
DO I READ
NEXT?

- *Native Guard*, published in 2006, is Trethewey's third collection of poems, for which she was awarded the Pulitzer Prize for poetry in 2007. In this collection, Trethewey's late mother and the history of the state of Mississippi serve as subjects for many of her poems. Trethewey also tells the story of the Louisiana's Native Guard, which was formed in 1862, a troop of men who were newly freed slaves and the Union army's first black regiment. Many of them were left for dead or shot by their white compatriots.

- *Bellocq's Ophelia*, published in 2002, was Trethewey's next collection of poems after *Domestic Work*. The poems are told from the perspective of a light-skinned mulatto woman working as a prostitute in New Orleans prior to World War I. This woman, Ophelia, is a persona created by Trethewey to represent a light-skinned woman depicted in many early-twentieth-century photographs taken by E. J. Bellocq in New Orleans's red-light district.

- *Half and Half: Writers on Growing Up Biracial and Bicultural*, edited by Claudine C. O'Hearn, was published in 1998. This work, which is aimed at young adults, is a collection of essays by authors who, like Tre- thewey, are all biracial and bicultural. Contributors including Gish Jen, Bharati Mukherjee, James McBride, and Roxane Farmanfarmaian, speak about their experiences growing up multicultural.

- *The Southern Poetry Anthology, Volume II: Mississippi* was edited by Stephen Gardner and William Wright and published in 2010. This anthology includes the work of poets who are native to Mississippi, including Trethewey, Gordon Weaver, Angela Ball, Paul Ruffin, Julia Johnson, and T. R. Hummer, among others. It provides readers with an opportunity to contextualize Trethewey's work within that of some of her peers.

- *What Are You? Voices of Mixed-Race Young People*, edited by Pearl Fuyo Gaskins in 1999, is a collection of essays, interviews, and poetry written by young adults of mixed race about their experiences growing up in America. Topics addressed in this work include discrimination, family dynamics, and self-esteem.

- *Night Clerk at the Hotel of Both Worlds* was published in 2007 by Angela Ball, who, like Trethewey, is a poet from Mississippi. Trethewey and Ball are known as two of Mississippi's most prolific contemporary poets.

---

not. It then becomes apparent exactly why Aunt Sugar wants the girl to wear the hat and maintain the lightness of her skin: in the long run, she will have an easier life if people perceive her as being white instead of black. In the second stanza, more contrasts are established between Aunt Sugar and the speaker. The two simultaneously remove their socks, but whereas Aunt Sugar is wearing nylons on her bony legs, the young girl is wearing white knee socks. This contrast indicates that Aunt Sugar is probably a much older woman, while her niece is a girl so young she still dons knee socks. The use of the adjective *white*, which typically denotes innocence, purity, and naïveté,

to describe the girl's appearance or clothing twice within the first seven lines of the poem also suggests that she must be very young. Aunt Sugar, by contrast, who speaks in a confident vernacular, chews tobacco, and knows her way around a fishing pole, is not. Aunt Sugar is more than a caregiver to the young girl, she is an educator able to pass on her worldly knowledge to her niece and warn her about the struggles that are bound to befall her as a biracial child growing up in the Deep South.

Just as the young girl is presumably ignorant of the challenges that await her in life, so too is the flounder oblivious to the fishing hook that will

> WITH JUST A FEW WORDS, AUNT SUGAR CATAPULTS HER NIECE FROM A WORLD OF RACIAL OBLIVIOUSNESS INTO ONE WHERE SHE WILL CONSTANTLY STRUGGLE INTERNALLY TO DEFINE HER EXTERNAL APPEARANCE AS EITHER BLACK OR WHITE, WHEN, LIKE THE FLOUNDER, IT IS SIMULTANEOUSLY NEITHER AND BOTH."

yank him out of his comfortable world. This is only one of the ways that the girl and the unsuspecting fish are similar. As soon as Aunt Sugar gets a good look at the fish, she identifies it as a flounder and explains that she can tell because it has one white side and one black side. Aunt Sugar pulls the fish onto the dock where she and her niece have been sitting, and the young girl silently observes as the fish hops around, alternately landing on his white side and his black side.

It seems, from the girl's speechless observation and the fact that she has chosen to recount this moment to the reader, that something about watching the fish struggle to alternate between black and white seems significant to her, being herself both black and white. Perhaps in this moment the commonalities between herself and the flounder become apparent to her. Indeed, the flounder's floundering, his flopping around switching from white to black and back again, is symbolic of the messy negotiation that awaits the young girl as she ventures into a segregated world, trying to find a place where she, as neither one thing nor the other, fits in.

Aunt Sugar does not want her to go into this world unaware of the implications of her race. Whether deliberately or not, it is Aunt Sugar who reflects the girl's race back to her, through her comments, and allows the girl to see it and recognize it the way other people will undoubtedly see it. When the girl was born years before to her black mother and white father, like any other baby she was as unaware as the flopping flounder of her outward appearance or the social significance the color of her skin might have. Physical characteristics, such as skin color, do not inherently posses meaning. They gain meaning when a

collective body of people attaches significance to them. Before this incident, the girl may have been ignorant of the social implications of being biracial, but via the flounder, Aunt Sugar helps her realize that external appearance is something that people use as a primary identifier, label, and sometimes basis for judgment. Just as Aunt Sugar was able to identify and label the flounder based on his coloring, people will constantly attempt to categorize the young girl based on the color skin as well.

Through her lesson, Aunt Sugar does more than just teach the girl that white and black will be used as labels to identify her; she also inadvertently indicates which label is more negatively consequential in the time and place she is growing up in. Aunt Sugar first hints at this in the first stanza of the poem, when she urges her niece to wear a hat to protect the whiteness of her skin. If the girl was not already aware of the inherent privileges of having light skin, this moment—when her aunt, who cares about her, attempts to protect it—surely must indicate to the girl that there is something desirable about having white skin and therefore undesirable or detrimental about having dark skin. In the South, where racism was still rampant at the time Trethewey was growing up (and presumably the time the poem is set), this was definitely true.

Aunt Sugar emphasizes this point in a different way in the last two stanzas of the poem. Because the poem is divided into rhyming quatrains, the rhythm of it creates a sense of finality at the end of each stanza. When reading the poem aloud, a reader will naturally pause at the end of each stanza, because the rhythm of the poem suggests it, almost forces it. This is the case with every stanza in "Flounder," and particularly stanza 7, in which Aunt Sugar identifies the fish as a flounder by its black side. Although in the next stanza she goes on to point out the fish's other side, it initially seems that she is going to stop speaking at the end of the stanza. In fact, when she mentions its white side in the first line of the next stanza, it almost seems like an afterthought, tacked on to the end of her description, and in a way it is. In Trethewey's home state of Mississippi, where her real Aunt Sugar lived, children of mixed race were legally categorized as the race of color, no matter how light or dark their skin was. This means that although the color of their skin may have confused or even fooled people sometimes, legally a person who was half white and half black would be regarded as black. By mentioning the flounder's white side as an afterthought, Aunt Sugar is reflecting the attitudes of many other people toward mixed-race children. Even though the young girl in the poem has one white parent and one black parent, to many people she would encounter, her blackness is what primarily defines her.

By making comments about race and by illustrating how to identify a creature based on its appearance and its color, Aunt Sugar allows the speaker to see the two sides of the flounder reflected in herself. "Flounder" is undeniably a poem that deals with instruction and the passing down of knowledge to a younger generation, but the young girl's fishing instruction is nearly irrelevant in light of the larger lessons Aunt Sugar provides.

Source: Rachel Porter, Critical Essay on "Flounder," in *Poetry for Students*, Gale, Cengage Learning, 2012.

Cynthia Hogue

In the following review, Hogue compares the voices of Trethewey and poet Matthea Harvey.

Within the vastly dissimilar aesthetic projects that characterize Matthea Harvey's and Natasha Trethewey's prizewinning debut collections, there are a few points at which the two collections resonate together. Both open avenues of dialogue between poetry and art by investigating and contemplating the issues that representation raises: how do we represent what we see? How do we accurately and respectfully represent another?

Both Harvey and Trethewey already have distinctive and mature voices. Both locate themselves in relation to one tradition or another: in Harvey's case, to the twentieth-century avant-garde; in Trethewey's, to the Harlem Renaissance. Their relationship to such formal traditions is where the two diverge: Harvey is seeking formally to write an innovative, postmodernist poetry, whereas Trethewey situates her poetry formally and linguistically in relation to African American history and Anglo-American literary tradition. But both collections reach beyond such descriptive frameworks.

Harvey wrote *Pity the Bathtub Its Forced Embrace of the Human Form* with postmodernism in mind: many of the poems are written in meaningful fragments and respond to current debates about poetry. Discussing such debates in a recent issue of the literary journal *Fence*, poet and critic Juliana Spahr suggests that emerging writers of her generation advocate a poetics of "joining," by which she means the tendency to disregard the aesthetic boundaries of various poetic schools. Harvey is a good example of this generation. One of her predominant themes is the self's perception of the world and the representation of self, and her poems strikingly negotiate this theme through style and form as well as content.

Hers may seem a difficult poetry to many readers, so let me begin by describing Harvey's use of form in more detail. Many of the poems resemble prose poems in shape and often read like "exquisite corpse" exercises (a surrealist technique of disrupting narrative: different people each write a line of a poem without knowing what the others have written). Lines are usually long and unvaried in length, there are rarely formal stanza breaks and there is often no use of punctuation.

There are some interesting exceptions. "The Illuminated Manuscript," for example, is formatted according to the illumination being described: monoscenes are comprised of single, block stanzas, while diptychs or triptychs are split into two or three parallel parts, in which case the word columns can be read both horizontally and vertically. But in most of the poems the reader is compelled forward with logical but not typographical pauses.

A section from the opening, prefatory poem, "Translation," illustrates Harvey's main method:

> They see a bird that is bright in both beak and
> feather
> And call it cardinal not thinking to import the
> human
> Kind words welcome those who stumble to shore
> With the tilt of the sea still in their step salt stains
> At their hems that seem to map out coastlines left far
> Behind the new songs are the old absurd hopes

A woman wiping the table sings bring me plans
And money or fans and honey each word more
Nothing is quite the same here a woman writes a
    letter
Near the lighthouse but the fog is so thick the words
Run as she writes them for a moment she can't tell
The sea spray from the fog one falls back the other
    stays
Suspended between two houses in the distance is a
Clothesline with a red shirt on it but she sees a bird

Who are the "they" who first see a cardinal? What is their relation to the woman wiping the table or the woman writing a letter, who observes a clothesline but "sees a bird"? Questions about the poem's narrative coherence are clearly beside the point, for the poem is up to something else. This is a poem about how we humans perceive, how we invariably (mis)represent the phenomenological world and ourselves. The poem opens with seeing a bird and closes with a woman writing (surely a figure for the poet) near a lighthouse. Words and visual images run together in the scene as if in fusion through the processes of the brain's circuitry. They run together in the poem as well: we can't always "tell" form from content (or vice versa).

Another poem that explores this fusion method is aptly titled "Lessons in Seeing," a poem in three subtitled sections. The first section, "Examination," opens with a little girl's eye exam, during which she sees an E not as a letter but as an image. In response to the doctor's instructions to read what she sees, she tells him what she perceives as an object:

.... comb coming down
Comb going up and two kinds of comb
Distracted the optometrist fusses
with different lenses
And reaches behind her to stop
the machine's
Humming he measures her head
her eyes and the space
Between her braids her white
parting looks like a chalk
Path carved out of a brown hill
in the part of England
He grew up in....

The girl is reading the letter E but seeing a comb in different positions. The doctor is analyzing her sight but in looking at the part between her braids, he is seeing in his mind's eye a path he walked as a child. The mind thinks associatively in and through images, the real thing morphing into the remembered scene. As the doctor recalls toward the end of the poem: "Clarity is for reading not for seeing a painter once sternly said."

In Part Two, "Trompe L'Oeil," an artist makes a living by painting exact replicas of oriental rugs on the floors of the affluent (her original idea had been "to transform concrete walls into airy windows"). As she defines it, trompe l'oeil "tells two stories this is what it means to fool the eye to / Fool the eye into seeing what—is there behind and beyond." Seeing accurately, as this poem ironically proposes, can be foiled by what is seen, just as the clarity needed for the act of reading can be complicated by what is read.

If there is a caveat in my high regard for Harvey's collection, it is in the nature of what is not there, not what is there, about which I have a delighted appreciation. I don't want to belabor the point, but given that it goes to the heart of the difference between these two poetic projects, let me explain by contrast.

I quoted a line from Harvey's "Lessons in Seeing"—"Between her braids her white parting looks like a chalk"—without comment. The girl's race is denoted as natural, almost unnoticeable (how many of us white readers, in fact, noticed?). Compare this line, with its casual mention of "white parting," to the opening of "Flounder" in Natasha Trethewey's *Domestic Work*:

Here, she said, put this on your head.
She handed me a hat.
You 'bout as white as your dad,
and you gone stay like that.

In Trethewey's poem, not noticing race is a luxury that neither Aunt Sugar nor her niece enjoy. White is not an unconscious norm but a conscious ideal, a precious possession that Aunt Sugar strives to teach the child of mixed-race heritage to protect in the same way as she teaches the child to fish:

This is how you hold the pole
to cast the line out straight.
Now put that worm on your hook,
throw it out and wait.

When Aunt Sugar catches a flounder, the child watches her, fascinated on a number of levels: She sat spitting tobacco juice into a coffee cup.

Hunkered down when she felt the bite,
jerked the pole straight up
reeling and tugging hard at the fish that wriggled
    and tried to fight back.
A flounder, she said, and you can tell 'cause one of
    its sides is black.
The other side is white, she said.
It landed with a thump.
I stood there watching that fish flip-flop,
switch sides with every jump.

Just as the poem's language switches effortlessly between "black" vernacular to "white" English, so we surmise that the child will find herself flip-flopping between the absolutes of white and black as she grows up: she will literally and figuratively flounder to breathe. In this poem, white and black have, by implication, everything to do with how both aunt and child are socially positioned. The aunt's handing the child a hat to protect her face suggests that the aunt foresees what the child will discover: that she will go back and forth between privilege (because she is nearly white) and prejudice (because she is not white). The rhymed quatrains are utterly apt, a traditional form in Anglo-American poetry that Trethewey has critically and semantically recontextualized.

Half the volume is made up of well turned, autobiographical poems like "Flounder"; two for the poet's white father, "Mythmaker" and "Amateur Fighter," and two for her dead mother, "Family Portrait" and "Saturday Drive," are particularly poignant. But the distinctive center of this collection, to my mind, is the title series of poems from photographs by Clifton Johnson of working class black women in New Orleans and Mississippi at the turn of the last century. In "Wash Women,"

> The eyes of eight women
> I don't know stare out from this photograph saying
>   remember.
> Hung against these white walls, their dark faces,
>   common as ones I've known,
> stand out like some distant Monday
> I've only heard about.

These women could be the speaker's grandmother and her sisters. The speaker could be observing a moment that captured the history of labor and survival in her mother's family. Beyond the photograph's frame, the speaker-observer can hear the women's laughter, imagine them taking a streetcar to the movie house, or crocheting by a window. She listens as one of the women, so like her grandmother, croon hymns. But within the photographer's framing of them,

> women do not smile,
> their lips a steady line
> connecting each quiet face.
> They walk the road toward home,
> a week's worth of take-in laundry
> balanced on their heads
> lightly as church hats. Shaded
> by their loads, they do not squint,
> their ready gaze through him,
> to me, straight ahead.

Like the photographer, Trethewey captures the women's quietly defiant pragmatism (it only

looks like resignation), while at the same time sketching in deft strokes the lived richness of their lives, however imaginary the small joys.

Likewise imagined is the inner life of a female elevator operator. She reads the moles on the hands of her passengers, the itching of her own palms and an eye twitching as signs of a change in her fortunes, for "she's tired of the elevator switch, // those closed-in spaces, white men's / sideways stares." But what she imagines as a "boon" is eloquently telling of the limits of her circumscribed world:

> What's to be gained from this New Deal?
> Something finer like beauty school
> or a milliner's shop—she loves the feel
> of marcelled hair, felt and tulle,
> not this all day standing around,
> not that elevator lurching up, then down.

Trethewey's use of form—here, another poem in rhymed quatrains (there are superb sonnets as well)—is trenchant. The honed, spare quality of the quatrain above, with its scheme of perfect and slant rhymes (Deal, school, feel, tulle) is as full of music and longing for a dream deferred as a blues lyric or a hymn. And in that resonant ending on "down," we feel the augur of the girl's fate, and the hopes and dreams that may come to naught but sustain her nonetheless.

If I am deeply moved by poem after poem in Trethewey's collection, I am not unmoved by Harvey's poetry, albeit often for a beauty of expression that is untranslatable into prose English. Yet even though I think I understand every word of Trethewey's poetry, because it seems more obviously accessible, I know that there are aspects of the lived experience of growing up as a person of color in this country to which I am blind because I grew up white. I see the word, but like Harvey's oriental carpet painter, it tells two stories.

While I nudge Harvey for her apparent universalizing color-blindness, I admire the ambitiousness of the poetry, its abstract and lyric breadth. Trethewey's vision, steeped as it is in a genuinely tragic sensibility culled from personal and racial history, has a depth of compassion that is hard-won. I admire the ambitious plumbing of those histories, that depth. These collections together demand that the traditions with which they are in dialogue move over and make room for them. As such, they constitute what I do not hesitate to call equally admirable, even stunning debuts by two serious—and seriously talented—poets.

Source: Cynthia Hogue, "Poets without Borders," in *Women's Review of Books*, Vol. 10, No. 8, May 2001, p. 15.

Publishers Weekly

In the following review, a contributor to Publishers Weekly *contends that the collection* Domestic Work *is a social commentary.*

With poems based on photographs of African-Americans at work in the pre-civil rights era 20th-century America (not included), Trethewey's fine first collection functions as near-social documentary. In tableaux like "These Photographs" and "Signs, Oakvale, Mississippi, 1941," Trethewey evenly takes up the difficult task of preserving, and sometimes speculating upon, the people and conditions of the mostly Southern, mostly black working class. The sonnets, triplets and flush-left free verse she employs give the work an understated distance, and Trethewey's relatively spare language allows the characters, from factory and dock workers to homemakers, to take on fluid, present-tense movement: "Her lips tighten speaking / of quitting time when/the colored women filed out slowly/to have their purses checked, / the insides laid open and exposed/by the boss's hand" ("Drapery Factory, Gulfport, Mississippi, 1956"). When Trethewey, a member of the Dark Room Collective (a group of young African-American writers including Thomas Sayers Ellis, Kevin Young and Janice Lowe), turns midway through the book to matters of family and autobiography, the book loses some momentum. But when the speaker comments on the actions of others, as in "At the Station," the poems correspondingly deepen: "Come back. She won't. Each / glowing light dims / the farther it moves from reach, // the train pulling clean/out of the station, The woman sits/facing where she's been. // She's chosen her place with care— / each window another eye, another / way of seeing what's back there." Trethewey's work follows in the wake of history and memory, tracing their combined effect on her speaker and subjects, and working to recover and preserve vitally local histories.

Source: Review of *Domestic Work*, in *Publishers Weekly*, Vol. 247, No. 33, August 14, 2000, p. 348.

SOURCES

"After 40 Years, Interracial Marriage Flourishing," in *MSNBC.com*, April 15, 2007, http://www.msnbc.msn.com/id/18090277/ns/us_news-life/ (accessed April 27, 2011).

Archibold, Randal C., "Arizona Enacts Stringent Law on Immigration," in *New York Times*, April 24, 2010, p. A1.

Campo, Rafael, Review of *Domestic Work*, in *Prairie Schooner*, Vol. 77, No. 4, Winter 2003, pp. 181–85.

Hamilton, Ashley C., "Natasha Trethewey: A Biography," in *Mississippi Writers and Musicians*, http://www.mswritersandmusicians.com/writers/natasha-trethewey.html (accessed April 15, 2011).

Hogue, Cynthia, "Poets without Borders," in *Women's Review of Books*, Vol. 18, No. 8, May 2001, pp. 15–16.

"Natasha Trethewey," in *Poets.org*, http://www.poets.org/poet.php/prmPID/442 (accessed April 15, 2011).

"Natasha Trethewey Biography," in *Famous Poets and Poems.com*, http://famouspoetsandpoems.com/poets/natasha_trethewey/biography8 (accessed April 15, 2011).

Petty, Jill, "An Interview with Natasha Trethewey," in *Callaloo*, Vol. 19, No. 2, Spring 1996, pp. 364–75.

Pope, Jacquelyn, Review of *Domestic Work*, in *Callaloo*, Vol. 25, No. 2, Spring 2002, pp. 695–97.

"Race of Wife by Race of Husband," in *U.S. Census Bureau*, http://www.census.gov/population/socdemo/race/interractab1.txt (accessed April 20, 2011).

Ross, Loretta, "White Supremacy in the 1990s," in *Political Research Associates*, http://www.publiceye.org/eyes/whitsup.html (accessed April 20, 2011).

Trethewey, Natasha, "Flounder," in *Domestic Work*, selected and introduced by Rita Dove, Graywolf Press, 2000, pp. 35–36.

Young, Kevin, Review of *Domestic Work*, in *Ploughshares*, Winter 2000–2001, Vol. 26, No. 4, pp. 205–07.

FURTHER READING

Dittmer, John, *Local People: The Struggle for Civil Rights in Mississippi*, University of Illinois Press, 1995.

Dittmer's study of the civil rights movement in the 1960s in Mississippi provides the reader with a portrait of violence that the older women depicted in Trethewey's poems, such as her grandmother and Aunt Sugar lived through, and the social climate into which Trethewey was born. By focusing solely on Trethewey's home state of Mississippi, Dittmer is able to provide a more detailed portrait of the civil rights movement than can be found in broader, nationwide histories.

Flora, Joseph M., and Lucinda Hardwick Mackethan, eds., *The Companion to Southern Literature: Themes, Genres, Places, People, Movements, and Motifs*, Louisiana State University Press, 2002.

Flora and Mackethan's work is an encyclopedia of everything that has to do with Southern literature. The topics covered in this work include genres, customs, locales, stereotypes, historical events and entities, and places that are particular to Southern literature. This book would be particularly helpful for a reader who is unfamiliar with the South, reading literature that draws upon Southern motifs and themes.

Henninger, Katherine Renee, *Ordering the Facade: Photography and Contemporary Southern Women's Writing*, University of North Carolina Press, 2007.

Henninger's book of criticism focuses particularly on photography and literature produced by Southern women, including Trethewey. Henninger explains how each of the authors she includes contributes to the literary motif of the Southern woman, such as Aunt Sugar in "Flounder."

Trethewey, Natasha, *Beyond Katrina: A Meditation on the Mississippi Gulf Coast*, University of Georgia Press, 2010.

This work is a reflection on the damage done to the author's hometown by Hurricane Katrina in 2005. As always in Trethewey's work, these poems address deeply personal topics, including family. Trethewey explains the effect of the devastation on her elderly grandmother, who had to permanently evacuate her home, and her brother, who began trafficking in cocaine after the properties he owned were destroyed by the storm.

Williamson, Joel, *New People: Miscegenation and Mulattoes in the United States*, Louisiana State University Press, 1995.

Williamson's book provides a social and legal history of the familial mingling of whites and blacks in the United States and the mulatto children who have resulted from mixed-race relationships. In addition to providing a thorough history, Williamson speculates about how the increasing frequency of interracial relationships will affect race relations in the United States.

SUGGESTED SEARCH TERMS

Natasha Trethewey

Natasha Trethewey AND Flounder

Natasha Trethewey AND Domestic Work

Natasha Trethewey AND poetry

Natasha Trethewey AND Aunt Sugar

Natasha Trethewey AND anti-miscegenation

Natasha Trethewey AND Mississippi Delta

Mississippi Delta AND poetry

Poetry AND African American vernacular English

Poetry AND rhymed quatrain

Frost at Midnight

SAMUEL TAYLOR COLERIDGE
1798

"Frost at Midnight" is a lyrical poem composed by the British author Samuel Taylor Coleridge. Coleridge wrote the poem in 1798, and it was published that same year in his collection *Fears in Solitude*. The year 1798 could be considered something of a high-water mark in English poetry, for that same year Coleridge and his friend and fellow poet William Wordsworth published *Lyrical Ballads*. *Lyrical Ballads* could arguably be considered one of the most important collections of poetry in the history of English literature. Not only did it launch the careers of Coleridge and Wordsworth, but it also marked a kind of official beginning of the English romantic movement in letters. For the next three decades, some of the most recognizable names in English literature—Wordsworth, Coleridge, Percy Bysshe Shelley, John Keats, George Gordon Lord Byron, Sir Walter Scott—were responsible for an outpouring of poetry (and in the case of Scott, fiction as well) that redefined poetry in English. Much of their work continues to be popular today, not only with literary scholars but with everyday readers as well.

In the twenty-first century, "Frost at Midnight" is unlikely to strike readers as in any way unconventional, daring, or experimental. It is a meditative poem in which the poet uses his observations of nature to reflect on the future of his infant son, who is sleeping nearby as the poet makes those observations. However, in 1798, many readers would have regarded this

Samuel Taylor Coleridge (The Library of Congress)

poem as something almost entirely new in English poetry. Coleridge, along with Wordsworth, was a pioneer in writing a type of poetry that was conversational and informal. The poem is written in blank verse (meaning that it has no rhyme scheme), and the reader senses that the poem records a series of reflections unified by rhythm and imagery rather than by formal poetic devices. The poem can be found in virtually any anthology of romantic poetry, including *The Penguin Book of Romantic Poetry*, edited by Jonathan Wordsworth and Jessica Wordsworth and published by Penguin Books in 2005. The poem can also be found online at the Poetry Foundation Web site.

AUTHOR BIOGRAPHY

Coleridge was born on October 21, 1772, at Ottery St. Mary in Devonshire, England. His father was a minister, and in his early years Coleridge inherited his father's scholarly interests. After his father died, Coleridge attended a school called Christ's Hospital in London, where he studied classical writers and was an avid

reader. An excellent student, he won a scholarship to Jesus College at Cambridge University, which he attended from 1791 to 1793. His personal life, however, was tumultuous. He was in debt, his health was not good, he associated at Cambridge with political radicals, and he fancied himself desperately in love with the sister of one of his earlier schoolmates. He impulsively left school and joined the army, but his brothers were able to get him discharged and take him back to Cambridge.

In the years that followed, Coleridge became acquainted with other notables in the romantic movement, including Robert Southey and Charles Lamb. He married a woman he did not love, Sara Fricker, who was the sister of Southey's fiancée. Like most of the figures associated with the romantic movement, he was intrigued by the French Revolution (which had begun in 1789), with its promise of the spread of democracy and the downfall of aristocratic, monarchical forms of government. An idealist, he planned with Southey a utopian community that was to have been set up in Pennsylvania, but the project came to nothing. He published his first collection of poetry, *Poems on Various Subjects*, in 1796. Sadly, he suffered from bouts of neuralgia (marked by acute, severe, intermittent pain that radiates along nerves). He also suffered from periods of depression. To find relief from the pain and depression, he began to use opium, and he battled an addiction to the drug for the rest of his life.

Coleridge met Wordsworth in 1795. By 1797, the two were intimate friends, and each inspired the other as poets and thinkers, leading to the publication of Coleridge's *Fears in Solitude* (which included "Frost at Midnight") in 1798 and, that same year, of their joint volume, *Lyrical Ballads*. It was during this period that Coleridge wrote many of the poems for which he is most famous, including *The Rime of the Ancient Mariner*, the first part of *Christabel*, and *Kubla Khan*—although a number of the poems he wrote during this period were not published until 1816.

Throughout the years that followed, Coleridge traveled. He spent time in Germany, where he became intrigued with new currents of thought flowing from German philosophers. He spent time on the Mediterranean island of Malta, hoping the warm climate would restore him to health. He also toured Scotland with

Wordsworth and his sister, Dorothy. He fell in love with Sarah Hutchinson, the sister of the woman who would later become Wordsworth's wife; he addressed his 1802 poem "Dejection: An Ode" to her. In 1808, he began a series of lectures on literature at England's Royal Institution, and the following year he launched a short-lived literary journal. In 1810, he quarreled with Wordsworth, and although the quarrel was smoothed over, the two men grew apart. These were dark days for Coleridge, for he continued to suffer from poor health, his marriage was a shambles, and he was in debt. He supported himself by journalism, and during the years 1813 to 1816 he lectured on Shakespeare in Bristol, England. He also began work on *Biographia Literaria*, a work of literary criticism. He continued to lecture on literature, and in 1825, he published *Aids to Reflection*, a work of theology. After embarking on another tour of Germany, he published *Constitution of Church and State* in 1830. He died of heart failure in London, England, on July 25, 1834.

POEM TEXT

The Frost performs its secret ministry,
Unhelped by any wind. The owlet's cry
Came loud—and hark, again! loud as before.
The inmates of my cottage, all at rest,
Have left me to that solitude, which suits   5
Abstruser musings: save that at my side
My cradled infant slumbers peacefully.
'Tis calm indeed! so calm, that it disturbs
And vexes meditation with its strange
And extreme silentness. Sea, hill, and wood,   10
This populous village! Sea, and hill, and wood,
With all the numberless goings-on of life,
Inaudible as dreams! the thin blue flame
Lies on my low-burnt fire, and quivers not;
Only that film, which fluttered on the grate,   15
Still flutters there, the sole unquiet thing.
Methinks, its motion in this hush of nature
Gives it dim sympathies with me who live,
Making it a companionable form,
Whose puny flaps and freaks the idling Spirit   20
By its own moods interprets, every where
Echo or mirror seeking of itself,
And makes a toy of Thought.

But O! how oft,
How oft, at school, with most believing mind,   25
Presageful have I gazed upon the bars,
To watch that fluttering *stranger!* and as oft
With unclosed lids, already had I dreamt
Of my sweet birth-place, and the old church-
tower,   30
Whose bells, the poor man's only music, rang
From morn to evening, all the hot Fair-day,
So sweetly, that they stirred and haunted me
With a wild pleasure, falling on mine ear
Most like articulate sounds of things to come!   35
So gazed I, till the soothing things, I dreamt,
Lulled me to sleep, and sleep prolonged my
dreams!
And so I brooded all the following morn,
Awed by the stern preceptor's face, mine eye   40
Fixed with mock study on my swimming book;
Save if the door half opened, and I snatched
A hasty glance, and still my heart leaped up,
For still I hoped to see the *stranger's* face,
Townsman, or aunt, or sister more beloved,   45
My play-mate when we both were clothed
alike!

Dear Babe, that sleepest cradled by my side,
Whose gentle breathings, heard in this deep
calm,
Fill up the interspersèd vacancies   50
And momentary pauses of the thought!
My babe so beautiful! it thrills my heart
With tender gladness, thus to look at thee,
And think that thou shalt learn far other lore,
And in far other scenes! For I was reared   55
In the great city, pent 'mid cloisters dim,
And saw nought lovely but the sky and stars.
But *thou*, my babe! shalt wander like a breeze
By lakes and sandy shores, beneath the crags
Of ancient mountain, and beneath the clouds.   60
Which image in their bulk both lakes and
shores
And mountain crags: so shalt thou see and hear
The lovely shapes and sounds intelligible
Of that eternal language, which thy God
Utters, who from eternity doth teach   65
Himself in all, and all things in himself,
Great universal Teacher! he shall mould
Thy spirit, and by giving make it ask.

Therefore all seasons shall be sweet to thee,
Whether the summer clothe the general earth   70
With greenness, or the redbreast sit and sing
Betwixt the tufts of snow on the bare branch
Of mossy apple-tree, while the nigh thatch
Smokes in the sun-thaw; whether the eave-
drops fall
Heard only in the trances of the blast,   75
Or if the secret ministry of frost
Shall hang them up in silent icicles,
Quietly shining to the quiet Moon.

POEM SUMMARY

The text used for this summary is from *English Romantic Poetry and Prose*, edited by Russell Noyes, Oxford University Press, 1956, pp. 408–409. Versions of the poem can be found on

MEDIA ADAPTATIONS

- An audio version of "Frost at Midnight" is contained in *English Romantic Poetry*, read by John S. Martin. The recording was made in 1962 by Folkway Records and is available as an MP3 download.
- A more recent audio version of "Frost at Midnight" is part of the collection *Poetry of Samuel Taylor Coleridge*, read by actor Sir Ralph Richardson. The recording was released in 2009 by Saland Publishing and is available as an MP3 download.
- Another audio version of "Frost at Midnight" is contained in the collection *The Richard Burton Poetry Collection*, read by the famed actor Richard Burton. The recording was released in 2010 by Saland Publishing and is available as an MP3 download.

the following Web pages: http://www.poetry foundation.org/archive/poem.html?id=173242 and http://www.eecs.harvard.edu/~keith/poems/frost.html.

Stanza 1

"Frost at Midnight," consisting of four stanzas of irregular length, is a quiet, meditative poem, ostensibly delivered as the poet sits in his cottage at midnight, his infant son sleeping nearby in his cradle. The first stanza makes clear that it is cold outside, for frost is forming on the window. The poet hears the cry of an owl outside. He emphasizes his solitude, which allows him to meditate. He also emphasizes the calmness of the scene, although he says that the moment is so calm that his thoughts are vexed. He contemplates the natural world outside the cottage, with the ocean, the forests, and the hills, as well as the nearby village, where life goes on unheard, much as dreams are unheard. He calls the reader's attention to the fire in the fireplace, which, at this late hour, is beginning to die out. The only movement in the cottage is the film, or very low

flames, fluttering on the fireplace grate; according to English folklore, these films, called strangers, were thought to foreshadow the arrival of an absent friend. The narrator then thinks that the fluttering of the flames in the quiet surroundings creates sympathy between the flames and himself, for he sees his own thoughts as fluttering and inconsistent as well.

Stanza 2

The poet reflects on his days at school, when he had gazed on the bars of a fireplace grate and seen these strangers. He had also had dreams that returned him to his place of birth and its churches. He thinks of the church bells that rang on fair days, calling the ringing of the bells music for poor men. He says that the bells haunted him and made him think of the future. He would continue to gaze at the fire until he slept, and his sleep would lengthen his dreams. The following morning he would continue to gaze at the fire, as though he were studying a book. Sometimes, he says, the door would open partway and his heart would leap, for he believed that a stranger in the form of a townsman, an aunt, or his sister had arrived.

Stanza 3

In the third stanza, the poet directly addresses the sleeping baby. He listens to the baby's gentle breathing, which fills up the vacancy of the calm as well as the gaps in the poet's thoughts. He says that the sight of the baby fills him with happiness and reflects that the baby will grow up to have experiences in other places. The poet notes that he had been brought up in the crowded and dim city, where the only things of beauty he could see were the sky and, at night, the stars. The baby, however, will lead a life in which he can experience nature in the forms of lakes, shores, and mountains, all reflected in the shapes of clouds. The baby will grow up to experience the language of God, who is part of the natural order and teaches people about himself through nature. God, then, will form the child's spirit.

Stanza 4

In the final stanza, the poet expresses the wish that all seasons of the year will be sweet to the child. He hopes that the child can experience the beauty of the green summer and of the winter, when red-breasted birds sing from the snow on the branches of an apple tree and the thatched roofs of cottages steam as the sun melts the snow on them. He continues his reflection on winter by envisioning the fall of water from the eaves and the formation of frost and icicles that shine in the moonlight.

THEMES

Nature

One of the chief features of the romantic movement was a heightened interest in the natural world. Beginning in roughly the mid-eighteenth century, poets began to turn their attention to nature. Some poets stressed the solitude and silence of nature, which allowed reflection. Others stressed the grandeur of nature, while still others emphasized nature's changeability. Nature plays a prominent role in "Frost at Midnight." The poet uses the formation of frost on the window as a jumping-off point for his reflections. The poem makes reference to the hooting of an owl, to seas, forests, mountains, and hills, to the quiet of nature, and, in the final stanza, to the passage of the seasons. The poem also contrasts nature, with its simplicity and solitude, with the noise and dirt of the city.

The poet uses these reflections on nature to express the hope that the infant son lying in his cradle nearby will be able to lead a life of simplicity, one that is in tune with nature. In the romantic imagination, the natural world was an expression of the divine, and it was only through contemplation of nature that a person could experience his or her own basic goodness. In contrast, the city, with its crowds, dirt, and artificiality, produced an inauthentic, cramped, unfulfilling life. Contemplation of nature also opened up a person's emotions, intuitive powers, and passions, much as it does in "Frost at Midnight." By tapping into emotions and intuition, according to Coleridge and his contemporaries, a person could avoid living a life limited by reason and rationality and instead lead a life enriched by passion and freedom.

Dreams

The romantic movement, at least in Great Britain, developed as a reaction against the intellectual trends of the seventeenth and eighteenth centuries. This earlier period in English literature is variously referred to as the Age of Reason, the Enlightenment, or sometimes the Augustan Age (referring to the classical writers

of ancient Rome under Caesar Augustus). At the risk of oversimplifying, the poetry of this age is best described as being marked by rational thought. It tended to be highly formal, with strict rhyme and metrical schemes (meter is the pattern of stressed and unstressed syllables). The poetry was not contemplative but rather analytical, not enthusiastic but rather cool and measured. Much of the poetry was satiric, as writers used poetry to attack evils or absurdities that they perceived. In these ways, the poetry bore many of the characteristics of the classical poetry of the Augustan Age in ancient Rome (roughly the first century BCE into the first century CE). It was a poetry that appealed more to the mind than to the heart, more to thought than to emotion.

The romantics, in contrast, were more interested in exploring nonrational, emotional states. One way in which they did this was through emphasis on dreams and dreamlike states, for they believed that these states of mind were more human and authentic. Thus, in "Frost at Midnight," the poet enters into a state of contemplation that is almost dreamlike. Clearly, the setting of the poem is the darkness of midnight. He is in a cottage where the only light is provided by the flickering of flames in the fireplace. The surroundings induce in him a trancelike state that allows his mind to wander. He sees in the flames of the fireplace a "stranger" that touches on his romantic longings. In the second stanza, Coleridge refers explicitly to dreams when he reflects on his earlier life at school and how he would dream. He talks about the gaps between thought. Thought is rational, but it is in the gaps between thinking that genuine, authentic experience is to be had. Very often for the romantics, these gaps were dreams, trances, and moments of undisciplined contemplation, where truth and insight could be achieved.

Father-Child Relationships

"Frost at Midnight" is in some sense an autobiographical poem. The voice of the poem is that of Coleridge himself, and although he does not name his infant son in the poem, that infant was in fact his son, Hartley. Throughout the poem, Coleridge expresses his wish that his son will lead a life that will allow him to contemplate the wonders of the natural world. His reflections on his son induce him to think about his own childhood, particularly his time at school.

TOPICS FOR FURTHER STUDY

- Research the history of the French Revolution, which began with the storming of the Bastille prison in Paris in 1789. Think about why there were so many writers, artists, and philosophers in England (and elsewhere) buoyed by the revolution. Why did it tend to fuel their sense of optimism? Present your findings in a report or presentation.

- The names of both Coleridge and his friend Wordsworth are often associated with the Lake District, a region in northwest England. In fact, the two are sometimes referred to as the "Lake poets." Conduct Internet and traditional research on the Lake District. Find images of the Lake District, particularly those of spots in the region that the poets frequented (for example, Grasmere and Rydal Mount), and share them with your classmates in a digital format using PowerPoint or SlideShare. Explain to your classmates how the Lake District might have inspired the romantic poets.

- What was the romantic movement in English literature? Conduct research on the history of the romantic movement. Prepare an interactive digital timeline or a traditional poster board timeline that includes the movement's major authors and works. Supplement your time line with works written by non-English authors. (Germany was a source of inspiration for the romantic writers.)

- A prominent poet in the American Harlem Renaissance (a flowering of literature, art, and music in New York City's Harlem neighborhood in the 1910s and 1920s and beyond) was Countee Cullen, who often looked to the romantics for his inspiration. Locate a copy of Cullen's poem "Saturday's Child" (available online at http://www.poetryfoundation.org/archive/poem.html?id=171340), a lyric poem suitable for young-adult readers that touches on the relationship between a father and his child, born into the poverty of an African American community. Write an essay that contrasts the vision and aspirations for the next generation contained in this poem and "Frost at Midnight." Post your essay to the class blog and invite your classmates to comment on your opinions.

- Conduct Internet and traditional research on Coleridge's proposed utopian community, which he planned to create with fellow writer Robert Southey. What was the name of the proposed community? Where was it to be located? On what principles was it to be run? Why did the project never come to fruition? Most importantly, what was the appeal of such a community to a romantic poet like Coleridge? Share your findings with your classmates in a multimedia presentation.

After his father's death in 1781, Coleridge, still just a boy, was sent to a London school called Christ's Hospital, a charity school founded in the sixteenth century. He was rarely allowed to return home, and he spent his time reading—everything from classical writers such as Virgil (a Roman writer) to the tales of the Arabian Nights. In London, he would rarely have had opportunity to experience the beauties of nature, particularly since London at that time tended to be crowded, noisy, smelly, crime-ridden, and dirty, with ramshackle housing (with few windows, because windows were taxed), lack of clean water, and an appalling lack of sanitation. (For example, dead animals were often left to rot in the streets, and most people disposed of their human waste by simply emptying chamber pots out onto the streets.)

Coleridge touches on his sense of loneliness and isolation at school in London and his wish for something better. He transfers this wish to

In the first stanza, the frost is described. *(Andrew Roland / Shutterstock.com)*

his infant son, hoping that his son will be able to experience the beauties of nature, with its hills, forests, streams, lakes, mountains, and the like. In this way, his son will be able to understand the language of God and allow God to mold his spirit. Coleridge's views are characteristic of the views of the romantics, who tended to see themselves as living at the dawn of a new age of freedom, artistic endeavor, and the fulfillment of utopian dreams.

STYLE

Blank verse

The term *blank verse* is used loosely to refer to any poetry that does not rhyme. Strictly speaking, though, blank verse refers to unrhymed poetry using the metrical form called iambic pentameter. Iambic pentameter lines are composed of metrical units consisting of five two-syllable feet with the first syllable unaccented, the second accented. This is the metrical form used in "Frost at Midnight."

An examination of the lines shows that most of them consist of ten syllables, or five metrical feet, although there are exceptions, with some lines containing eleven syllables. Further, the general pattern is for an unaccented syllable to be followed by an accented syllable, although again, there are variations. Blank verse was a metrical form favored by the romantics (and in fact widely used since the sixteenth century by poets, including Shakespeare) because it mirrors the rhythms of natural English speech, particularly because it was flexible. It accommodated, for example, an extra syllable or variations in the pattern of accented and unaccented syllables. It also gave the poet freedom to allow the grammar of a sentence to spill over from one line into the next: lines did not have to end with periods or commas that mark a break in the sentence structure.

In this way, romantic poetry in general differed from the poetry of the Enlightenment, which tended to adhere strictly to a metrical form, one in which units of lines corresponded strictly with the grammatical units of a sentence. "Frost at Midnight" is often referred to as a conversational poem, and the romantics often wrote poetry that was conversational in tone. Although Coleridge was hardly original in his use of blank verse, he used its flexibly to create poems that were organized not by form but by the play of his mind as he contemplated experience.

Imagery

An image is a concrete representation of an object or sensory experience. Typically, imagery refers to visual sensory experience, but imagery can also be used to represent sounds and smells. Sometimes, imagery is literal; that is, the images have no particular meaning beyond their obvious denotation. Sometimes, imagery is figurative, meaning that it extends the obvious meaning of the words. The romantic poets, including Coleridge, placed great emphasis on precise observation in their delineations of the natural world, and therefore their poetry is filled with visual and other forms of imagery. In "Frost at Midnight," Coleridge relies primarily on literal imagery. He wants to recreate for the reader the physical details surrounding him and that he recalls from his earlier days. Much of this imagery is visual: he takes note of the frost, the moon, icicles, and other natural phenomena, as well as the fluttering of the flames in the fireplace and the steam rising from snow melting on a thatched rooftop. Some of the imagery is aural, including the hoot of an owl and the tolling of church bells that he remembers from his school days. All of this imagery comes together to create a portrait of a poet who allows himself to observe in detail his surroundings and use those surroundings as fuel for contemplation.

Interior monologue

Interior monologue is a narrative technique in which a character's thoughts are revealed in a way that appears to be uncontrolled by the author. The interior monologue typically aims to reveal the inner self of a character. It portrays emotional experiences as they occur at both conscious and unconscious levels. Images are often used to represent sensations or emotions. Typically, the term is used in discussions of fiction, where authors use the technique to reveal the state of mind of a character. The term, however, can also be applied to a poem that is written to accomplish the same end. The reader is invited to imagine the speaker of the poem as a character, set in a certain situation, who reveals his thoughts and emotions through the lines of the poem.

In this sense, "Frost at Midnight" bears many of the characteristics of an interior monologue. The "character" is seated in his cottage. The time is midnight or thereabouts. It is cold outside, so a fire burns in the fireplace. Near the speaker is his infant son, asleep. The scene, with its quiet and isolation, prompts musing on the part of the poet. He observes the frost forming on the window and the flickering of the fire in the fireplace. He meditates about the natural surroundings and the nearby village. These musings prompt him then to think about his own childhood and the role of dreams in his life when he was at school. This in turn prompts him to think about his upbringing and to draw a contrast between life in the crowded city and life surrounded by the beauties of the natural world. These reflections then forge in him the hope that his son will be able to grow up surrounded by these beauties and that God, as reflected in nature and conceived of as a teacher, will mold the son's spirit.

HISTORICAL CONTEXT

Age of Revolution

"Frost at Midnight" makes no reference to historical events. However, historical events in the late 1700s played a major role in influencing the thinking of the romantic poets in England and throughout Europe. British writers such as Coleridge would have followed events on the European continent closely, and those events had a profound impact on the romantics.

During the late eighteenth century, powerful intellectual trends were at work in Europe. These trends would sweep away tradition and give rise to revolutionary sentiments. The first of these revolutions took place against Great Britain in what would become the birth of the United States in 1775. The second was the revolution in France which erupted when Parisians stormed the Bastille prison in 1789. What followed was years of turmoil in France as the nation attempted to install a revolutionary government that ended the monarchy, curbed aristocratic privilege, broke the monopoly of the Catholic Church, and provided citizens with a greater measure of political equality.

COMPARE
&
CONTRAST

- **1790s:** Education often takes place in the homes of the upper classes or the homes of members of such professions as the law or the ministry. Many students are sent away from home to boarding schools for varying lengths of time. Typically, only boys receive formal schooling.

  Today: Although boarding schools continue to operate, most students attend public or private schools in their community while living at home, and formal schooling is available equally to boys and girls.

- **1790s:** Opium, much of it imported from China, is legal and often self-administered by people with illnesses, pain, or depression; many women take opium to relieve menstrual discomfort, and opium in the form of laudanum is often given to teething infants and irritable children. A significant number of people are addicted to opium, which they usually ingest in the form of a tincture (liquid medicine), but this type of drug addiction, while discouraged, is not highly stigmatized.

  Today: Medicines made with opiates (morphine, for example) are highly regulated and legally available only through prescription from a doctor—and then only to alleviate the most serious pain. The most common illegally used opiate is heroin, and addiction to this type of drug is highly stigmatized.

- **1790s:** The population of London is just under one million. The city has no sanitary facilities, and waste is dumped into the river Thames, which is the source of the city's drinking water. Many people die or become seriously ill with infectious diseases caused by impure water and lack of sanitation.

  Today: The population of London is about 7.8 million people. Like any modern city in a developed nation, London provides clean water and sewage treatment, sharply diminishing the incidence of infectious disease.

Artists and philosophers called for a return to nature and promoted the belief in the inherent goodness of people, providing intellectual support for revolutionary fervor. In France, one of the most influential writers was Jean-Jacques Rousseau, who began the body of his 1762 essay *Du contrat social* (On the Social Contract) with the words: "Man is born free, and everywhere he is in chains." He began his 1762 novel *Émile* with the words: "God makes all things good; man meddles with them and they become evil." The subtitle of *Émile* is *ou, De l'éducation* (Or, On Education), and the novel goes on to depict a child of nature who lives a simple country life, his senses attuned to the natural world. While these and other books by Rousseau and other writers did not call for revolution, they planted in people's minds the seeds of revolt against a repressive, artificial, established order.

In a very real sense, Coleridge's musings in "Frost at Midnight" and his longing that his son, too, be a child of nature can be traced back to the viewpoints Rousseau made popular in France and that provided, in part, the intellectual underpinnings for the French Revolution.

In England, attitudes toward the French Revolution were mixed. Writers such as Coleridge and Wordsworth were excited by the lofty goals of the revolution. They believed that the revolution represented the liberation of mankind. However, like many people in England, they were revolted by the violent turn the revolution took. Political radicals in France attempted to impose a stifling uniformity on French revolutionary society, and during the Reign of Terror, numerous aristocrats—and people who supported the aristocracy (or were thought to)—were executed.

As stanza one ends, the fire is burning down. *(CoolR | Shutterstock.com)*

In the wake of the revolution, Napoleon Bonaparte seized control of the nation. From the 1790s until his death in 1821, he led armies in an effort to sweep away monarchies in Europe and spread the ideals of the revolution. Although revolution dominated events on the continent during these years, England escaped revolution—although many Britons feared a Napoleonic invasion. Despite the political turmoil, warfare, and violence that attended the French Revolution, the revolution fired the idealism of English romantics. In his poem "France: An Ode," written in 1798, Coleridge expressed a common view when he stated that France fervently desired to be free and that he felt both hope and fear as a result of the French Revolution.

CRITICAL OVERVIEW

While "Frost at Midnight" is not one of Coleridge's major poems, it generally has been held in high regard by critics and scholars. Among his contemporaries, the opinion expressed by a reviewer for the *British Critic* in 1799 is typical. The reviewer writes that the poem "is entitled to much praise. A few affectations of phraseology, are atoned for by much expressive tenderness, and will be avoided by the author's more mature judgment."

More recent critics and scholars have expressed similar admiration for the poem. Arden Reed, in his essay "Frost at Midnight," writes:

> Recent criticism has generally presented the poem as one of Coleridge's rare imaginative successes, pointing out the speaker's increasing awareness and the poem's growth in "organic unity" as it rounds back upon itself to form a perfect circle.

Similarly, Stephen Prickett, in *Coleridge and Wordsworth: The Poetry of Growth*, calls "Frost at Midnight" "one of his finest poems." Prickett continues by pointing out that

> the associative drift of his mind reveals itself in a series of contrasts. The cold calm of the present night is juxtaposed with the bells of Ottery St Mary on a hot summer fair-day in

his childhood. His own childhood is seen, in turn, through the bored nostalgia of the schoolboy at Christ's Hospital.

In his essay "Coleridge and Wordsworth: Collaboration and Criticism from *Salisbury Plain* to *Aids to Reflection*," Richard Gravil calls "Frost at Midnight" one of "the very greatest poems of 1798" and praises the poem for its "perfected ruminative tone." Michael O'Neill, in his essay "Coleridge's Genres," writes that the poem "delights by offering itself as a process, a reverie, that with miraculous delicacy ends up as an artistically organized product."

Paul Magnuson, in his essay "The 'Conversation' Poems," writes: "In the 'Conversation' poems, Coleridge adopts a natural symbolism in which the perceiving, remembering, imagining mind searches for images of itself and God in nature." Also, in contrast to some earlier nature poets, Coleridge can "deepen the psychological insight and the philosophical meditations on the relation of the mind to nature."

Finally, in *Samuel Taylor Coleridge*, Virginia L. Radley discusses "Frost at Midnight" in conjunction with "This Lime-Tree Bower My Prison." She writes:

> Although no conversation poem can rightly be said to stand equally with the poems of high imagination [including *Kubla Khan* and *The Rime of the Ancient Mariner*], ... certainly "Frost at Midnight" and "This Lime-Tree Bower . . ." both have within them that quality of heart so essential to these latter poems. Because of this quality, and because of the striking effectiveness of their imagery, these poems can be said to be the true harbingers of Coleridge's greatest poems.

CRITICISM

Michael J. O'Neal

O'Neal holds a Ph.D. in English. In the following essay, he examines the conception of nature implicit in Coleridge's "Frost at Midnight."

The romantic poets, including Coleridge, were children of eighteenth-century rationalism. This was a view of life that reduced the physical world to the laws of physics and thereby tended to reduce the human spirit to inconsequence. The romantic revival tried to formulate a way of looking at the world that could restore

FOR COLERIDGE, MEMORY AND IMAGINATION BECAME THE KEY PEOPLE COULD USE TO ESCAPE THE LIMITATIONS OF AN ARTIFICIAL WORLD, AS REPRESENTED BY THE CITY, TO ACHIEVE A MORE LINKED, INTERTWINED UNITY WITH THE NATURAL WORLD."

significance to the human spirit by examining the place of humankind in the physical universe.

Different poets in the romantic movement accomplished this end in different ways. Percy Bysshe Shelley, for example, emphasized in his poetry the transcendence of nature. Nature was something that existed above and beyond individuals, and it was something that was in a constant state of flux and transformation. As a result, his depictions of nature tended to be symbolic of change and, eventually, mortality. In simple terms, the depictions of nature in his poetry were noisy and full of movement: rivers rage through ravines, cloud formations are in constant flux, and the physical world is in perpetual motion. Through it all, nature remains inaccessible, but contemplation of nature gives people a sense of power, vitality, and life.

Coleridge, in contrast, viewed nature as something more permanent and stable. Like his friend Wordsworth, he believed that within the limits of reality, the individual had the power to change in his mind the conditions of his experience. Unlike Shelley, Coleridge was not troubled by mortality. Rather, what troubled him was man's isolation from nature. For Coleridge, memory and imagination became the key people could use to escape the limitations of an artificial world, as represented by the city, to achieve a more linked, intertwined unity with the natural world.

Thus, while the reader senses that the nature imagery in Shelley (and some other romantic poets) is symbolic, the nature imagery in poems such as "Frost at Midnight" is more literal and real. The frost that forms on the window is real frost, and the cold night air surrounding the poet's cottage is genuine cold air. When the

WHAT DO I READ NEXT?

- Coleridge's "This Lime-Tree Bower My Prison," written in 1797, bears many similarities to "Frost at Midnight." Because of an injury, the speaker is unable to join his companions in a walking tour, but while sitting in a bower of lime trees is able to reflect vicariously on the beauty and divinity of nature through their experience. The poem can be found in *The Penguin Book of Romantic Poetry*, edited by Jonathan Wordsworth and Jessica Wordsworth and published by Penguin Books in 2005.

- William Wordsworth's "The World Is Too Much with Us," written in about 1802, is a sonnet that expresses themes common to the romantic poets, including the belief that modern city life is corrupting and that a life surrounded by nature is superior. The poem can be found in *The Penguin Book of Romantic Poetry*, edited by Jonathan Wordsworth and Jessica Wordsworth and published by Penguin Books in 2005.

- Students interested in fictional treatments of the French Revolution would enjoy Kimberly Brubaker Bradley's *The Lacemaker and the Princess* (2007), a young-adult novel that narrates the events of the French Revolution both from the aristocratic side (the princess) and from the viewpoint of a common person (the lacemaker).

- Students interested in historical treatments of the French Revolution might begin with Laura K. Egendorg's *The French Revolution* (2003), a volume in the Greenhaven Press's "Opposing Viewpoints in World History" series suitable for young adults. The book presents both primary and secondary sources that offer different perspectives on the event that permanently altered Europe.

- Another major English romantic poet was Percy Bysshe Shelley, whose poem "Mont Blanc," written in 1816, is a reflection on the power and majesty of nature as represented by Mont Blanc, located between France and Italy and the highest mountain peak in the Alps. The poem can be found in *The Penguin Book of Romantic Poetry*, edited by Jonathan Wordsworth and Jessica Wordsworth and published by Penguin Books in 2005.

- After the romantic movement spread to Spain, Gustavo Adolfo Bécquer emerged as one of the leading Spanish romantic poets. He was the author of two collections, *Rimas* (Poems) and *Leyendas* (Legends). The works are available in Spanish in a 2007 collection, *Rimas y Leyendas*, published by Edimat Libros, and selections from the works can be found in a 2006 dual Spanish-English edition by the same title; the pieces are translated into English by Stanley Appelbaum, and the book is published by Dover Publications. Each of the poems and legends is quite brief.

- Readers interested in contemporary poetry for young adults about nature could begin with *Poems for a Small Planet: Contemporary American Nature Poetry* (1993), edited by Robert Pack and Jay Parini. Readers can compare and contrast attitudes toward nature in modern life with those of the eighteenth- and nineteenth-century romantic writers such as Coleridge.

---

poet refers to the surroundings of his cottage and the village, the forests, hills, and streams are real and literal—they have no symbolic significance beyond their existence. As the poet contemplates his youth, the natural world he longed for was real, and when he expresses hope that his son will become a child of nature, the natural world of icicles, the moon, and the passage of the seasons again is real rather than symbolic. In his view, a person can achieve meaning by living in the real world of nature, for nature is something that can be grasped with the hand and hung onto for security.

Coleridge places considerable emphasis on the quiet and solitude of the scene. In the first line the frost is said to perform a ministry that is secret, and that comparison is repeated in the poem's final stanza. The poet says that everything in the scene is at rest, including his infant son, who is sleeping peacefully nearby. The first stanza emphasizes quietness, silence, and calm. Nature is said to be hushed. The fire in the fireplace has burned low so that there is only a quiet fluttering; the reader pictures not leaping flames but a soft, gentle, blue glow.

Coleridge, however, is interested in much more than simply depicting a scene. The romantic poets were generally "nature poets," but they were interested in creating far more than just pleasant scenes. The natural world historically had been something that humans were to conquer and use. Developments in science and technology—the very beginnings of the Industrial Revolution were taking place at around this time—giving humankind a sense of mastery of nature. The natural order was often abused; during his time in London, Coleridge would have witnessed the terrible pollution of the river Thames, which was an open sewer. Particularly on warm days, the city stank from the pollution, and during colder weather, the air would frequently have been dense and acrid with fumes from the burning of coal in thousands of fireplaces and cook stoves.

The romantics were not "environmentalists" in the modern sense of the word. They did, however, envision a purer, more wholesome natural world, and they were able to experience such a world in the country's more rural settings, such as the Lake District in northwest England, where Coleridge spent much time with Wordsworth and their friends. Nature, then, was the source of quiet and calm. It provoked contemplation. It provided a means by which the poets could forge an imaginative unity with their surroundings and overcome human limitations.

Thus, the quiet scene in "Frost at Midnight" prompts musings and contemplation. Nature becomes a force that enables Coleridge to find some kind of meaning, stability, and permanence in his life. The images of nature return

him in his imagination to his school days, when he would similarly gaze at the fire and dream about his earlier life, an activity that soothed him and caused him to dream. In both scenes—the one in the present of the poem and the one in the poet's past—the film in the fireplace brings to mind the folk belief in "strangers," which foreshadow the arrival of an absent relative or friend. In turn, these recollections remind him of his days in London, when he felt pent up by the city's dimness. Thus, the poem establishes a clear contrast between city life, with its artificiality, and the rural setting of the poem, which can provide Coleridge and, more importantly, his son with a more authentic life.

In the third stanza, "Frost at Midnight" takes a slightly religious or theological turn. The shapes and sounds of nature are said to be intelligible, for they are part of an eternal language—note the emphasis again on permanence—spoken by God. God is conceived as a being who teaches humans about himself through the natural order. He is thus described as a great universal teacher, one who will be able to form the spirit of the son. Again, this type of religious view was in contrast with some of the religious views prevailing during the eighteenth century. On the one hand, many people adhered firmly to religious dogma and particularly to a literal interpretation of the Judeo-Christian Bible.

This type of religious belief was one that the romantics tended to reject outright, for they saw it as limiting human freedom and imagination. They did not believe that meaning could be constructed through religious dogma, which was one reason they supported the French Revolution, for the revolution broke the power of the church and the church hierarchy in France. On the other hand, many of the rationalist thinkers of the eighteenth century adopted a religious philosophy called deism. They believed in God, but they regarded God as absent from human affairs. An image often used was that of God as a great watchmaker or clockmaker, who constructed the world, set it going, and then withdrew. Thus, the deists did not believe that God continued to reveal himself in the natural world or in human affairs.

The romantics adopted a third view. While rejecting religious dogma, they saw God as imminent in the world. God not only created the world but continued to reveal divine truths through the agency of nature. This type of view is often called "pantheism," a belief that God and nature are one and that nature is in effect God. Using this term to describe Coleridge's religious views would be a vast oversimplification, but the notion of an essential unity of spirit and matter would come close to describing Coleridge's religious views during this period of his life. Put simply, the natural world was not simply a mechanism but rather a vital, ongoing manifestation of the divine.

Critics and literary historians have sometimes relied on two slightly odd Latin phrases that capture the idea. The first of these phrases is *natura naturata*, which can be translated as "nature natured." This means that nature is something fixed, static, and created, with emphasis on the past tense; nature is "done." The other phrase is *natura naturans*, which can be translated as "nature naturing." This phrase suggests that nature is an ongoing process—rather like the seasons to which Coleridge calls attention in the final stanza of "Frost at Midnight." According to this view of nature, people live in a realm of becoming. Nature, then, is a way to return to one's origins in the ongoing creativity of God.

Coleridge is often thought of as the romantic poet who placed the most emphasis on the supernatural. "Supernatural" in this context refers not to religious belief but to a realm beyond the material world. He has gained this reputation primarily because of some of his other, more well-known poems, including *Kubla Khan* and *The Rime of the Ancient Mariner*. "Frost at Midnight" places considerably less emphasis on the supernatural, but it does make reference to "strangers." This was the folk belief that the filmy, low flames of a fire in the fireplace could portend the arrival of an absent friend or relative. A key component of the romantic revival was the return to a more primitive, authentic existence. For this reason, many of the romantics were intrigued with the medieval period, and poets such as Robert Burns and novelists such as Sir Walter Scott sparked a revival in folk tales, folk beliefs, and legends, many of which had a supernatural component. Gathering all these threads together—the emphasis on nature, the role of memory and the imagination, the contrast between the city and the countryside, the romantic conception of God, the folk beliefs of a more "primitive"

Stanza five reflects on the change of seasons.
(giangrande alessia | Shutterstock.com)

(and hence more authentic) time—the reader finds in "Frost at Midnight" a kind of compendium of the chief features of the romantic spirit.

Source: Michael J. O'Neal, Critical Essay on "Frost at Midnight," in *Poetry for Students*, Gale, Cengage Learning, 2012.

Robert Lynd

In the following excerpt, Lynd explores the unique character of Coleridge's brilliance and discusses some of the poet's notable idiosyncrasies.

(2) COLERIDGE AS A TALKER

. . . Coleridge's talk resembles the movements of one of the heavenly bodies. It moves luminously on its way without impediment, without conflict. When Dr. Johnson talks, half our pleasure is due to our sense of conflict. His sentences are knobby sticks. We love him as a good man playing the bully even more than as a wise man talking common sense. He is one of the comic characters in literature. He belongs, in his eloquence, to the same company as Falstaff and Micawber. He was, to some extent, the invention of a Scottish humourist named Boswell. "Burke," we read in Coleridge's *Table Talk*, "said and wrote more than once that he thought Johnson greater in talking than writing, and greater in Boswell than in real life." Coleridge's conversation is not to the same extent a coloured expression of personality. He speaks out of the

> ONE CANNOT READ MUCH OF HIS TALK
> ABOUT POLITICS WITHOUT AMAZEMENT THAT SO
> WISE A MAN SHOULD HAVE BEEN SO FREQUENTLY A
> FOOL. AT THE SAME TIME, HE GENERALLY REMAINED
> AN ORIGINAL FOOL. HE NEVER DEGENERATED INTO A
> MERE PARTISAN."

solitude of an oracle rather than struts upon the stage of good company, a master of repartees. At his best, he becomes the mouthpiece of universal wisdom, as when he says: "To most men experience is like the stern lights of a ship, which illuminate only the track it has passed." He can give us in a sentence the central truth of politics, reconciling what is good in Individualism with what is good in Socialism in a score or so of words:

> That is the most excellent state of society in which the patriotism of the citizen ennobles, but does not merge, the individual energy of the man.

And he can give common sense as well as wisdom imaginative form, as in the sentence:

> Truth is a good dog; but beware of barking too close to the heels of Error, lest you get your brains knocked out.

"I am, by the law of my nature, a reasoner," said Coleridge, and he explained that he did not mean by this "an arguer." He was a discoverer of order, of laws, of causes, not a controversialist. He sought after principles, whether in politics or literature. He quarrelled with Gibbon because his *Decline and Fall* was "little else but a disguised collection of . . . splendid anecdotes" instead of a philosophic search for the ultimate causes of the ruin of the Roman Empire. Coleridge himself formulated these causes in sentences that are worth remembering at a time when we are debating whether the world of the future is to be a vast boxing ring of empires or a community of independent nations. He said:

> The true key to the declension of the Roman Empire—which is not to be found in all Gibbon's immense work—may be stated in two words: the imperial character overlaying, and

finally destroying, the *national* character. Rome under Trajan was an empire without a nation.

One must not claim too much for Coleridge, however. He was a seer with his head among the stars, but he was also a human being with uneven gait, stumbling amid infirmities, prejudices, and unhappinesses. He himself boasted in a delightful sentence:

> For one mercy I owe thanks beyond all utterance—that, with all my gastric and bowel distempers, my head hath ever been like the head of a mountain in blue air and sunshine.

It is to be feared that Coleridge's "gastric and bowel distempers" had more effect on his head than he was aware of. Like other men, he often spoke out of a heart full of grievances. He uttered the bitterness of an unhappily married dyspeptic when he said: "The most happy marriage I can picture or image to myself would be the union of a deaf man to a blind woman." It is amusing to recall that one of the many books which he wished to write was "a book on the duties of women, more especially to their husbands." One feels, again, that in his defence of the egoism of the great reformers, he was apologizing for a vice of his own rather than making an impersonal statement of truth. "How can a tall man help thinking of his size," he asked, "when dwarfs are constantly standing on tiptoe beside him?" The personal note that occasionally breaks in upon the oracular rhythm of the *Table Talk*, however, is a virtue in literature, even if a lapse in philosophy. The crumbs of a great man's autobiography are no less precious than the crumbs of his wisdom. There are moods in which one prefers his egotism to his great thoughts. It is pleasant to hear Coleridge boasting: "*The Ancient Mariner* cannot be imitated, nor the poem *Love. They may be excelled; they are not imitable.*" One is amused to know that he succeeded in offending Lamb on one occasion by illustrating "the cases of vast genius in proportion to talent and the predominance of talent in conjunction with genius in the persons of Lamb and himself." It is amusing, too, to find that, while Wordsworth regarded *The Ancient Mariner* as a dangerous drag on the popularity of *Lyrical Ballads*, Coleridge looked on his poem as the feature that had sold the greatest number of the copies of the book. It is only fair to add that in taking this view he spoke not self-complacently, but humorously:

I was told by Longmans that the greater part of the *Lyrical Ballads* had been sold to seafaring men, who, having heard of the *Ancient Mariner*, concluded that it was a naval song-book, or, at all events, that it had some relation to nautical matters.

Of autobiographical confessions there are not so many in *Table Talk* as one would like. At the same time, there are one or two which throw light on the nature of Coleridge's imagination. We get an idea of one of the chief differences between the poetry of Coleridge and the poetry of Wordsworth when we read the confession:

> I have the perception of individual images very strong, but a dim one of the relation of place. I remember the man or the tree, but where I saw them I mostly forget.

The nephew who collected Coleridge's talk declared that there was no man whom he would more readily have chosen as a guide in morals, but "I would not take him as a guide through streets or fields or earthly roads." The author of "Kubla Khan" asserted still more strongly on another occasion his indifference to locality:

> Dear Sir Walter Scott and myself were exact but harmonious opposites in this—that every old ruin, hill, river, or tree called up in his mind a host of historical or biographical associations, just as a bright pan of brass, when beaten, is said to attract the swarming bees; whereas, for myself, notwithstanding Dr. Johnson, I believe I should walk over the plain of Marathon without taking more interest in it than in any other plain of similar features. Yet I receive as much pleasure in reading the account of the battle, in Herodotus, as anyone can. Charles Lamb wrote an essay on a man who lived in past time: I thought of adding another to it on one who lived not *in time* at all, past, present, or future—but beside or collaterally.

Some of Coleridge's other memories are of a more trifling and amusing sort. He recalls, for instance, the occasion of his only flogging at school. He had gone to a shoemaker and asked to be taken on as an apprentice. The shoemaker, "being an honest man," had at once told the boy's master:

> Bowyer asked me why I had made myself such a fool? to which I answered, that I had a great desire to be a shoemaker, and that I hated the thought of being a clergyman. "Why so?" said he. "Because, to tell you the truth, sir," said I, "I am an infidel!" For this, without more ado, Bowyer flogged me—wisely, as I think—soundly, as I know. Any whining or sermonizing would have gratified my vanity, and con-

firmed me in my absurdity; as it was, I laughed at, and got heartily ashamed of, my folly.

Among the reminiscences of Coleridge no passage is more famous than that in which he relates how, as he was walking in a lane near Highgate one day, a "loose, slack, not well-dressed youth" was introduced to him:

> It was Keats. He was introduced to me, and stayed a minute or so. After he had [left] us a little way, he came back, and said: "Let me carry away the memory, Coleridge, of having pressed your hand!" "There is death in that hand," I said to——, when Keats was gone; yet this was, I believe, before the consumption showed itself distinctly.

Another famous anecdote relates to the time at which Coleridge, like Wordsworth, carried the fires of the French Revolution about him into the peace of the West Country. Speaking of a fellow-disciple of the liberty of those days, Coleridge afterwards said:

> John Thelwall had something very good about him. We were once sitting in a beautiful recess in the Quantocks, when I said to him: "Citizen John, this is a fine place to talk treason in!" "Nay! Citizen Samuel," replied he, "it is rather a place to make a man forget that there is any necessity for treason!"

Is there any prettier anecdote in literary history?

Besides the impersonal wisdom and the personal anecdotes of the *Table Talk*, however, there are a great number of opinions which show us Coleridge not as a seer, but as a "character"—a crusty gentleman, every whit as ready to express an antipathy as a principle. He shared Dr. Johnson's quarrel with the Scots, and said of them:

> I have generally found a Scotchman with a little literature very disagreeable. He is a superficial German or a dull Frenchman. The Scotch will attribute merit to people of any nation rather than the English.

He had no love for Jews, or Dissenters, or Catholics, and anticipated Carlyle's hostility to the emancipation of the negroes. He raged against the Reform Bill, Catholic Emancipation, and the education of the poor in schools. He was indignant with Belgium for claiming national independence. One cannot read much of his talk about politics without amazement that so wise a man should have been so frequently a fool. At the same time, he generally remained an original fool. He never degenerated into a mere partisan. He might be deceived by reactionary ideals, but he was not taken in by reactionary leaders. He was no more capable than Shelley of mistaking Castlereagh for a great man, and he did not join in the glorification of Pitt. Like Dr. Johnson, he could be a Tory without feeling that it was necessary at all costs to bully Ireland. Coleridge, indeed, went so far as to wish to cut the last link with Ireland as the only means of saving England. Discussing the Irish question, he said:

> I am quite sure that no dangers are to be feared by England from the disannexing and independence of Ireland at all comparable with the evils which have been, and will yet be, caused to England by the Union. We have never received one particle of advantage from our association with Ireland.... Mr. Pitt has received great credit for effecting the Union; but I believe it will sooner or later be discovered that the manner in which, and the terms upon which, he effected it made it the most fatal blow that ever was levelled against the peace and prosperity of England. From it came the Catholic Bill. From the Catholic Bill has come this Reform Bill! And what next?

When one thinks of the injury that the subjection or Ireland has done the English name in America, in Russia, in Australia, and elsewhere in quite recent times, one can hardly deny that Coleridge was a sound prophet, though for other reasons than he thought.

It is the literary rather than the political opinions, however, that will bring every generation of readers afresh to Coleridge's *Table Talk*. No man ever talked better in a few sentences on Shakespeare, Sterne, and the tribe of authors. One may not agree with Coleridge in regarding Jeremy Taylor as one of the four chief glories of English literature, or in thinking Southey's style "next door to faultless." But one listens to his *obiter dicta* eagerly as the sayings of one of the greatest minds that have interested themselves in the criticism of literature. There are tedious pages in *Table Talk*, but these are, for the most part, concerned with theology. On the whole, the speech of Coleridge was golden. Even the leaden parts are interesting because they are Coleridge's lead. One wishes the theology was balanced, however, by a few more glimpses of his lighter interests, such as we find in the passage: "Never take an iambus for a Christian name. A trochee, or tribrach, will do very well. Edith and Rotha are my favourite names for women." What we want most of all in table talk is to get an author into the confession album. Coleridge's *Table*

WHAT THE POETS OF THE LAKE SCHOOL EXTOLLED WAS A DEFINITE, ACTUALLY EXISTING *SUM OF LIBERTIES*—NOT LIBERTY."

Talk would have stood a worse chance of immortality were it not for the fact that he occasionally came down out of the pulpit and babbled.

Source: Robert Lynd, "The Wisdom of Coleridge," in *The Art of Letters*, T. Fisher Unwin, 1920, pp. 122–33.

George Brandes

In the following essay, originally published in 1875, Brandes compares the view of liberty of the Lake Poets with those of the later romantic poets Lord Byron and Percy Shelley.

Coleridge and the other members of the Lake School would never have dreamt of calling themselves anything but warm friends of liberty; the days were past when the reactionaries called themselves by another name. Coleridge wrote one of his most beautiful poems, the *Ode to France*, in the form of a hymn to liberty, to his constant love for whch he calls clouds, waves, and forests to testify; and Wordsworth, who dedicated two long series of his poems to liberty, regarded himself as her acknowledged champion. A cursory glance at the works of these poets might well leave us with the impression that they were as true lovers of liberty as Moore, or Shelley, or Byron. But the word liberty in their mouths meant something different from what it did in Moore's, or Shelley's, or Byron's. To understand this we must dissect the word by means of two simple questions: freedom, from what?—liberty, to do what?

To these conservative poets freedom is a perfectly definite thing, a right which England has and the other countries of Europe have not—the right of a country to govern itself, untyrannised over by an autocratic ruler of foreign extraction. The country which has this privilege is free. By liberty, then, the men in question understood freedom from foreign political tyranny; there is no thought of liberty of action in their conception at all. Look through Wordsworth's *Sonnets*

Dedicated to Liberty, and see what it is they celebrate. It is the struggle of the different nations against Napoleon, who is described as a species of Antichrist. (Scott calls him "the Devil on his burning throne.")

The poet mourns the conquest of Spain, Switzerland, Venice, the Tyrol, by the French; he chants the praises of Hofer, the undaunted, of brave Schill, and daring Toussaint L'Ouverture, the men who ventured to face the fierce conquerors; and he sings with quite as great admiration of the King of Sweden, who with romantically chivalrous folly threw down the gauntlet to Napoleon, and proclaimed his longing for the restoration of the Bourbons. (Ere long Victor Hugo and Lamartine, in their character of supporters of the Legitimist monarchy, followed suit in singing the praises of the Swedish king and his son, Prince Gustavus Vasa.) Hatred of Napoleon becomes aversion for France. In one of the sonnets ("Inland, within a hollow vale, I stood") Wordsworth tells how the "barrier flood" between England and France for a moment seemed to him to have dwindled to the dimensions of a river, and how he shrank from the thought of "the frightful neighbourhood"; in another he rejoices in the remembrance of the great men and great books England has produced, and remarks that France has brought forth "no single volume paramount...no master spirit," that with her there is "equally a want of books and men."

He always comes back to England. His sonnets are one long declaration of love to the country for which he feels "as a lover or a child," the country of which he writes: "Earth's best hopes are all with thee." He follows her through her long war, celebrating, like Southey, each of her victories; and it is significant of his attitude that, appended to the *Sonnets Dedicated to Liberty*, we find the great, pompous thanksgiving ode for the battle of Waterloo. We of to-day ask what kind of liberty it was that Waterloo gained; but we know full well that the group of poets whose heroes were the national heroes—Pitt, Nelson, and Wellington, and who sang the praises of the English constitution as being in itself liberty, and lauded England as the model nation, won a degree of favour with the majority of their countrymen to which their great poetic antagonists have not even yet attained. Wordsworth and his school considered the nation ideal as it was, whereas the others tried to compel it to turn its

eyes towards an ideal, not only unattained, but as yet unrecognised; the former flattered it, and were rewarded with laurels; the latter educated and castigated it, and were spurned by it. Scott was offered the post of Poet Laureate, and Southey and Wordsworth in turn occupied it; but to this day the English nation has shown no public recognition of what it owes to Shelley and Byron. And the reason is, that these men's conception of liberty was utterly different from that of the Lake School. To them it was not realised in a nation or a constitution—for it was no accomplished, finished thing; neither was their idea of the struggle for liberty realised in a highly egoistic war against a revolutionary conqueror. They felt strongly what an absence of liberty, political as well as intellectual, religious as well as social, there might be under a so-called *free* constitution. They had no inclination to write poems in honour of the glorious attainments of the human race, and more especially of their own countrymen; for in the so-called land of freedom they felt a terrible, oppressive want of freedom—of liberty to think without consideration of recognised dogmas, to write without paying homage to public opinion, to act as it was natural to men to their character to act, without injury from the verdict of those who, because they had no particular character of their own, were the most clamorous and unmerciful condemners of the faults which accompanied independence, originality, and genius. They saw that in this "free" country the ruling caste canted and lied, extorted and plundered, curbed and constrained quite as much as did the one great autocrat with his absolute power—and without his excuse, the authority of intellect and of genius.

To the poets of the Lake School, coercion was not coercion when it was *English*, tyranny was not tyranny when it was practised under a *constitutional monarchy*, hostility to enlightenment was not hostility to enlightenment when it was displayed by a *Protestant* church. The Radical poets called coercion coercion, even when it proceeded to action with the English flag flying and the arms of England as its policemen's badge; they cherished towards monarchs generally, the objection of the Lake School poets to absolute monarchs; they desired to free the world not only from the dominion of the Roman Catholic priesthood, but from priestly tutelage of every description. When they heard poets of the other school, who in the ardour of youth had been as progressive as themselves, extolling the Tory Government of England with the fervour which distinguishes renegades, they could not but regard them as enemies of liberty. Therefore it is that Shelley, in his sonnet to Wordsworth, writes:

> In honoured poverty thy voice did weave
> Songs consecrate to truth and liberty.
> Deserting these, thou leavest me to grieve,
> Thus having been, that thou shouldst cease to be.

Therefore it is that Byron is tempted again and again "to cut up Southey like a gourd." And therefore it is that the love of liberty of the Radical poets is a divine frenzy, a sacred fire, of which not a spark is to be found in the Platonic love of the Lake School. When Shelley sings to liberty:

> But keener thy gaze than the lightning's glare,
> And swifter thy step than the earthquake's tramp;
> Thou deafenest the rage of the ocean; thy stare
> Makes blind the volcanoes; the sun's bright lamp
>
> To thine is a fen-fire damp;

we feel that this liberty is not a thing which we can grasp with our hands, or confer as a gift in a constitution, or inscribe among the articles of a state-church. It is the eternal cry of the human spirit, its neverending requirement of itself; it is the spark of heavenly fire which Prometheus placed in the human heart when he formed it, and which it has been the work of the greatest among men to fan into the flame that is the source of all light and all warmth in those who feel that life would be dark as the grave and cold as stone without it. This liberty makes its appearance in each new century with a new name. In the Middle Ages it was persecuted and stamped out under the name of heresy; in the sixteenth century it was championed and opposed under the name of the Reformation; in the seventeenth it was sentenced to the stake as witchcraft and atheism; in the eighteenth it became first a philosophical gospel, and then, through the Revolution, a political power; in the nineteenth it receives from the champions of the past the new nickname of Radicalism.

What the poets of the Lake School extolled was a definite, actually existing *sum of liberties*—not liberty. What the revolutionary poets extolled was undoubtedly true liberty, but their conception was so extremely ideal, that in practical matters they too often shot beyond the mark. In the weakening of all established government they saw only the weakening of bad government; in the half-barbaric revolts of oppressed races they saw the dawn of perfect liberty. Shelley had so little knowledge of his fellow-men that he thought the great victory would be won if he could exterminate kings and priests at a blow; and Byron's life was almost over before he learned by experience how few republican virtues the European revolutionists leagued together in the name of liberty possessed. The poets of the Lake School were safeguarded against the generous delusions and overhastiness of the Radical poets; but posterity has derived more pleasure and profit from the aberrations due to the love of liberty in the latter than from the carefully hedged in and limited Liberalism of the former.

Source: George Brandes, "The Lake School's Conception of Liberty," in *Main Currents in Nineteenth Century Literature: Naturalism in England*, translated by Mary Morison, William Heinemann, 1905, pp. 85–159.

SOURCES

Coleridge, Samuel Taylor, "France: An Ode," in *English Romantic Poetry and Prose*, edited by Russell Noyes, Oxford University Press, 1956, p. 410.

———, "Frost at Midnight," in *English Romantic Poetry and Prose*, edited by Russell Noyes, Oxford University Press, 1956, pp. 408–409.

Gravil, Richard, "Coleridge and Wordsworth: Collaboration and Criticism from *Salisbury Plain* to *Aids to Reflection*," in *The Oxford Handbook of Samuel Taylor Coleridge*, edited by Frederick Burwick, Oxford University Press, 2009, pp. 24, 26.

"London, 1800–1913," in *The Proceedings of the Old Bailey*, http://www.oldbaileyonline.org/static/London-life19th.jsp (accessed April 6, 2011).

Magnuson, Paul, "The 'Conversation' Poems," in *The Cambridge Companion to Coleridge*, edited by Lucy Newlyn, Cambridge University Press, 2002, p. 34.

Noyes, Russell, ed., *English Romantic Poetry and Prose*, Oxford University Press, 1956, pp. xix–xxxiii, 373–79, 408–410.

O'Neill, Michael, "Coleridge's Genres," in *The Oxford Handbook of Samuel Taylor Coleridge*, edited by Frederick Burwick, Oxford University Press, 2009, p. 381.

Prickett, Stephen, *Coleridge and Wordsworth: The Poetry of Growth*, Cambridge University Press, 1970, pp. 47, 49.

Radley, Virginia L., *Samuel Taylor Coleridge*, Twayne Publishers, 1966, p. 56.

Reed, Arden, "Frost at Midnight," in *Samuel Taylor Coleridge*, edited by Harold Bloom, Chelsea House Publishers, 1986, pp. 191–92.

Review of "Frost at Midnight" in *Samuel Taylor Coleridge: The Critical Heritage*, edited by J. R. de J. Jackson, Barnes & Noble, 1970, p. 49; originally published in *British Critic*, June 1799, pp. 662–63.

Rousseau, Jean-Jacques, *Émile*, in *Literature Network*, http://www.online-literature.com/rousseau/emile/1/ (accessed April 6, 2011).

———, *The Social Contract*, in *Literature Network*, http://www.online-literature.com/rousseau/social-contract-or-principles-/2/ (accessed April 6, 2011).

"2009 Round Demographic Projections for the London Plan (Revised)," in *Greater London Authority Intelligence Update*, http://www.london.gov.uk/sites/default/files/dmag/Update%2016-2010%202009%20Round%20 Demographic%20Projections%20for%20the%20London%20Plan%20(rev).pdf (accessed April 6, 2011).

FURTHER READING

Arnold, James R., *The Aftermath of the French Revolution*, Twenty-First Century Books, 2008.

As the title suggests, this volume focuses on the effects of the French Revolution. It traces how the revolution created the expectation that countries could be ruled by democratic governments, without hereditary kings and queens who exercised arbitrary power. The book demonstrates how the revolution gave rise to the middle class, diminished the power of the church, ended feudalism, and created a new, more modern sense of national identity.

Ashton, Rosemary, *The Life of Samuel Taylor Coleridge: A Critical Biography*, Wiley-Blackwell, 1998.

This volume not only provides details about the author's life, but as a critical biography, it links that life to his works. Readers interested in such facets of the author's life as his opium addiction, his literary criticism, and his marital relationship will find a wealth of information here.

Cranston, Maurice, *The Romantic Movement*, Wiley-Blackwell, 1994.

This relatively brief book discusses the romantic movement not just as a British phenomenon but as a European one. The author focuses on how romanticism manifested itself in England, Italy, Spain, and Germany and locates the characteristics that romanticism in these countries had in common despite their national differences: an emphasis on liberty, introspection, and the exotic.

Plantinga, Leon, *Romantic Music: A History of Musical Style in Nineteenth-Century Europe*, Norton, 1984.

The romantic movement extended to other artistic forms, including painting and music. Readers interested in the romantic era of music, which included such composers as Beethoven, Schubert, Liszt, and others, will find in this volume discussion of how romanticism and the intellectual trends that supported it found expression in music.

SUGGESTED SEARCH TERMS

Coleridge AND religion

eighteenth-century London

English romantic movement

French Revolution

Frost at Midnight

Jean-Jacques Rousseau

Lyrical Ballads AND Coleridge AND Wordsworth

romantic movement

romanticism AND nature

Samuel Taylor Coleridge

William Wordsworth

Frost at Midnight AND Coleridge

romanticism AND Coleridge

Coleridge AND Wordsworth

Ghost of a Chance

ADRIENNE RICH
1962

"Ghost of a Chance" was first published by Adrienne Rich in her 1963 collection *Snapshots of a Daughter-in-Law* and can also be found in the Norton Critical Edition *Adrienne Rich's Poetry and Prose* (1993). Like the collection in which it appears, "Ghost of a Chance" represents that moment when Rich's poetic subject turned from the masculine universal that she had been taught was the ideal subject to the specific experiences of living as an intelligent, artistic, politically engaged woman. It is one of her last poems to feature a male persona, and the imagery of the poem in which a person striving for intellectual life is dragged back into the undertow of expectation mirrors the subjects Rich was wrestling with during that time. Having won major awards for her first two books of poetry, Rich described the shock with which she realized that after her marriage she was expected to abandon her career and to devote herself to her children and to her husband's career. *Snapshots of a Daughter-in-Law* and "Ghost of a Chance" represent the moment when she began to interrogate the definitions of masculine and feminine and how those archetypes functioned in society.

This is the central question of all of her subsequent work, and this poem and indeed much of the collection demonstrate the work of a poet at the cusp of discovering the true subject of her life's work. Adrienne Rich has had one of the longest careers in American literary history. She published her first book in 1951 and continues to

Adrienne Rich (Getty Images)

publish into her eighties. She is equally as well known for her political activism in the cause of peace and social justice as she is for her pioneering writings, in both poetry and prose, in modern feminism.

AUTHOR BIOGRAPHY

Rich was born in Baltimore, Maryland, on May 16, 1929, to Helen and Arnold Rice Rich. Her mother had been a concert pianist, and her father was a doctor and pathologist at Johns Hopkins Medical Center. Her parents were ambitious about Rich's future, and she excelled at school, eventually enrolling at Radcliffe College in Boston, Massachusetts. In 1951, the year she graduated from Radcliffe, W. H. Auden awarded Rich the prestigious Yale Younger Poets Prize for her first collection, *A Change of World*. His citation that the poems were "neatly and modestly dressed, speak quietly but do not mumble, respect their elders but are not cowed by them" has become an infamous example of the patronizing attitude of most male poets toward female poets at the time.

In 1953, Rich married Alfred Conrad, a Harvard economist, and they had three sons: David in 1955, Paul in 1957, and Jacob in 1959. "I married in part because I knew no better way to disconnect from my first family," Rich said in an interview with John O'Mahoney in the London *Guardian*. "I

wanted what I saw as a full woman's life, whatever was possible."

Although she published a second volume, *The Diamond Cutters*, in 1955, it was not until the 1963 publication of her third book, *Snapshots of a Daughter-in-Law* (in which "Ghost of a Chance" appears), that the true subject matter of her life's work began to appear: describing actual female experience versus the social expectations levied against women, issues of political representation and repression, and the means by which formal poetic choices serve to critique or uphold the repressive forces of society. Unlike her earlier books, *Snapshots of a Daughter-in-Law* uses free verse to examine deeply personal topics, in particular the difficulties of being a thinking woman who struggles with the physical and emotional experience of motherhood and who chafes at the social expectations inherent in the identities of wife and mother.

Throughout the 1960s, Rich became involved in the anti-war movement, the civil rights movement, and most deeply in the nascent women's movement. In 1970, shortly after they separated, Alfred Conrad committed suicide, leaving Rich to raise their three sons alone. She retreated into her political work and her poetry and came out as a lesbian during this time. In 1976, she moved in with the Jamaican writer Michelle Cliff. They have been together ever since.

Although this was a painful period in her personal life, it coincided with some of her most powerful poetry. The 1970s saw the publication of *The Will to Change* (1971); *Diving into the Wreck* (1973), for which she won the National Book Award; and *Twenty-one Love Poems* (1976). As the scholar and poet Deborah Pope noted in the *Oxford Companion to Women's Writing in the United States*, it was during this time that Rich

> began to draw on contemporary rhythms and images, especially those derived from the cinematic techniques of jump cuts and collage. [Her work at this time] demonstrate[s] a progressive coming to power as Rich contends against the desolation patriarchy enacts on literal and psychic landscape. Intimately connected with this struggle for empowerment and action is the deepening of her determination "to write directly and overtly as a woman, out of a woman's body and experience."

Rich has published twenty-five volumes of poetry and seven collections of prose, including the groundbreaking *Of Woman Born: Motherhood as Experience and Institution* (1976). Her work has garnered continuous praise throughout her career, and she has been awarded countless prizes, from the Yale Younger Poets Award while she was still in college to the Medal for Distinguished Contribution to American Letters: National Book Foundation in 2006 and a Lifetime Recognition Award from the Griffin Poetry Prize in 2010. In 1997, Rich was awarded but turned down the National Medal of the Arts; in an essay written that same year, she explains why: "[T]he very meaning of art, as I understand it, is incompatible with the cynical politics of this administration.... [Art] means nothing if it simply decorates the dinner table of the power which holds it hostage."

POEM SUMMARY

The text used for this summary is from *Adrienne Rich's Poetry and Prose*, W. W. Norton, 1993, p. 1617. A version of the poem can be found on the following Web page: http://writersalmanac. publicradio.org/index.php?date = 1999/02/01.

The title of this poem, "Ghost of a Chance," refers to a colloquial phrase that means a chance that is no chance at all, a chance with the least likelihood of happening. If a ghost is insubstantial by its nature, something that no longer exists, something that, like our lost loved ones, we wish still existed, then it is this figment of a chance that serves as the nominal image for Rich's poem.

Lines 1–2

The first two lines tell us that the speaker sees a man and that the man is attempting to do intellectual work, to think. That these two lines are set off from the rest of the poem by a break isolates them. The man is alone; he is an object of observation on the part of the narrator of the poem. These two lines also introduce the second-person point of view of the poem. Addressed to an unnamed "you," the poem thus brings the reader directly into the action of the poem.

Lines 3–5

After the break, the next three lines once again address the reader, telling the reader that what he or she wants is to warn off everything that might distract the man from his task. The sight of the isolated man, trying to step out of the welter of ordinary life for a moment in order to

MEDIA ADAPTATIONS

- There is an Adrienne Rich audiobook in the Voice of the Poet series (http://www.amazon. com/Adrienne-Rich-Voice-Poet/dp/05537148 99). Published by Random House in 2002, the audiobook contains historical recordings of Rich reading poems from her long career. The readings are arranged chronologically, and the audiobook comes with a printed volume that contains the poems along with an introduction by the poet J. D. McClatchy.

- Starting in 1988, the Lannan Foundation (http://www.lannan.org/lf/bios/detail/adrienne-rich/) produced a series of video programs on poets and writers that were distributed free to public libraries. In 1999, the foundation awarded Rich their Lifetime Achievement award and produced a three-volume series on her life and work. These videos contain footage of Rich reading from her work, as well as in conversation with the Irish poet Eavan Boland.

- PennSound, the Web site of the Center for Programs in Contemporary Writing at the University of Pennsylvania (http://writing. upenn.edu/pennsound/x/Rich.html), has an extensive series of podcasts of, by, and about Rich. Many of these were recorded during Rich's 2005 visit as a Kelly Writer's House fellow. Both audio and video podcasts are available at this site.

- Ohio University's Wired for Books Web site (http://www.wiredforbooks.org/adriennerich/) has made Rich's 1987 interview with Don Swaim available for free download as a Ram or MP3 file.

formulate deliberate thoughts, is one that the narrator of the poem seems desperate to protect.

Lines 6–9

The next fourteen lines are formed from a single sentence, the beginning of which signals a turn in the action of the poem. The first two central images are of figures in isolation: the man who is trying to think and the person who is watching him. Now the gaze shifts to take in a force larger than the man that threatens to engulf him. This force is described as a source of terror to the poem's narrator and is described as comprising familiar comforts. Since to think is to engage in intellectual work that usually requires that one questions the comfortable assumptions under which one lives, Rich posits this onslaught of familiarity as being in opposition to thought, as endangering it.

Lines 10–14

In line 10, the man who is trying to think, the man who is trying to evade the onslaught of comfort and familiarity, is compared to a fish washed up on the beach. The effort to think, to escape comfort, has left the man stranded in inhospitable territory where he is out of his depth and where he struggles to survive. At line 13, the fish imagery begins to incorporate the popular imagery of evolution. The fish is close to crawling as aquatic creatures were presumed to do as they evolved into land-dwelling animals. In traditional evolutionary thought, the terrestrial animals, like humans, were thought to be more highly evolved than aquatic animals, so this becomes an image of growth and evolution. The thinking man is portrayed in this poem as superior to others who simply go along with what is expected.

Lines 15–16

However, in line 15, Rich's imagery becomes more explicit about the toll that attempting to escape the comforts of familiarity can take. The fish-man finds he cannot breathe in this new atmosphere, he has not entirely evolved the ability to breathe air instead of water, and so the attempt is painful and comes close to killing him.

In line 16, a wave arrives and the fish-man is pulled back into the sea where his ability to breathe is restored. However, being pulled back into the sea renders him blind and signals the end of his evolutionary attempt to grow beyond the familiar consolations into something more deliberate and intellectual. Not only that, but the sea, a force we usually think of as impersonal, is triumphant at recapturing the fish-man, indicating that the sea, like the fish, is not a literal image, but a metaphoric one. The actual sea does not have emotions and therefore cannot

feel triumph, but in this poem the sea is a metaphor for the all-engulfing force of social convention and comfort against which one who thinks, or writes, or creates must struggle.

THEMES

Individualism

While Rich's first two books of poetry were praised for their facility with accepted poetic forms, for their modesty, and for what Richard Howard described as a sort of coziness, the majority of her work, starting with *Snapshots of a Daughter-in-Law*, the collection in which "Ghost of a Chance" appears, has often been criticized for being excessively political or stridently feminist. Beginning with *Snapshots*, Rich has defended not just her own poetry but all poetry that seeks to truly express the inner imagination of the individual and to rescue language from those forces that seek to drain it of its meaning. In her 1997 essay "Why I Refused the National Medal for the Arts," Rich put forth her vision:

> Art is our human birthright, our most powerful means of access to our own and another's experience and imaginative life. In continually rediscovering and recovering the humanity of human beings, art is crucial to the democratic vision.

"Ghost of a Chance" dramatizes the emotional difficulty of claiming a space for individual meaning. The person who is the subject of the poem is trying to think, not trying to learn or to understand, which would imply that the person is attempting to take in knowledge from an external source. Instead, the person is trying to come up with new thoughts of his very own. This is hard work. The narrator wants to clear a space in which the subject can do his work but can only watch as the man's efforts are swamped, engulfed by an enormous wave of received experience. Even if the individual wants to engage in independent thought, it is so painful, he is left gasping, trying to breathe air that is painful to his lungs; when the wave of what he already knows washes over him, it is a relief to return to the sea. Rich's poem is a pessimistic one, one that dramatizes the quest for individualism as doomed, yet it is the desire to emerge from the undifferentiated sea and to evolve into a fully functioning individual that forms the core image of this poem. The life of the individual remains the goal toward which the poem strives.

TOPICS FOR FURTHER STUDY

- Although "Ghost of a Chance" seems like a fairly simple lyric poem, it contains a series of very specific images, some of which are deliberately set off by line breaks. Team up with a partner and match each line with an illustration that you feel visually represents that line. Then use an online photo program like iPhoto to first create a slideshow in which there is at least one image for each line. Using a program like GarageBand, create a podcast of your slideshow in which you narrate each slide with the line of poetry it represents. Present to your class, and explain why you chose the images you did.

- Rich's central image in "Ghost of a Chance" is that of a fish attempting to escape from the sea. Research the theory of evolution, especially as it involves the evolution of aquatic organisms to terrestrial life. Create a PowerPoint presentation, complete with illustrations and historical evidence tracing the history of this theory, and compare and contrast the ways that Rich's imagery both conforms to the popular understanding of evolutionary theory and diverges from it.

- Find a picture of a child in a natural setting that appeals to you: this can be a family photo of yourself, a sibling, or a parent as a child or an illustration from a magazine or that you find online. First, list as many physical details of the setting as you can see in the picture. Then list as many physical details of the setting as you can imagine from the picture. Make a list of how the child feels in this place, among these items. Where are the parents? Does the child want the parents there, or not? What conflict does the child feel in this natural set-

ting? Cut up the lists, and arrange them on a blank piece of paper to form the outline of a poem. Use this outline to write a poem describing the child's experience in the setting.

- Read Marjane Satrapi's young-adult graphic novel *Persepolis*. While Satrapi's book is set in a different place and time than "Ghost of a Chance," her protagonist struggles to find a place in her culture where her gender and her creative and intellectual drives are not at war with one another. Compare the lives of both writers, and write an illustrated story or poem in which Satrapi and Rich encounter one another. Rich is old enough to be Satrapi's grandmother, and yet her life history is one of rebelling against external constraints in a similar manner. Imagine what these two women might have to say to one another.

- Adrienne Rich was born in 1929, a time when discrimination against women was commonplace and pervasive: for instance, when she went to university, it was to Radcliffe College, which was the women's college associated with Harvard University. Women were not admitted to Harvard as undergraduates until 1973. Take video interviews of women in your family tree about what opportunities were open to them as girls. Were they encouraged to do well in school? Were they expected to have a career or to focus only on their family life? Are there stories or photographs of women in your family tree who achieved unexpected things? Using iMovie, cut and paste the interviews together into a coherent tale of how women in your family have negotiated social expectations over the generations.

Consciousness

Rich's career has been dedicated to documenting the difficulty of coming to full human consciousness and the obstacles that impede that quest.

This is the difficulty dramatized in "Ghost of a Chance." There is a person struggling to emerge into deliberate thought. The narrator of the poem recognizes that this is a difficult task and attempts to clear a space in which the man can do this difficult work. However, the narrator can only watch as the man struggles. He appears to be drowning in the foreign air of a world that is unfamiliar to him, the world of full human consciousness. As the narrator watches, the protagonist is swept back into the metaphoric sea of conventional thought. That the subject of the poem fails in his quest only serves to underscore the difficulty of the struggle to achieve full consciousness as a human being.

This struggle not only plays out in this specific poem but is a thread across the sixty years during which Rich has been a working poet. While she is primarily known as a feminist poet, that is, someone whose concern is with the struggle to escape the false expectations of womanhood imposed by traditional patriarchy, Rich's political concern for the expression of full humanity extends beyond feminism. In both poetry and prose, she has explored the many ways in which social, political, and economic forces conspire to make extremely difficult this work, which she would argue is not only the work of making art but the work of becoming fully human.

Entrapment

The 1950s were one of the most socially conformist periods in American life, and women were told that domestic life as a wife and mother would make them complete, whole, and happy. Rich was a successful poet and academic before she married, and her shock that she was expected to give up her career, as well as her discovery that it was nearly impossible to think with three small children underfoot, led to the eight-year gap between *Snapshots of a Daughter-in-Law* and the book that preceded it.

Rich has written extensively of the pressure she felt to marry and have children in her twenties. She told John O'Mahoney, in a 2002 interview in the London *Guardian*: "I married in part because I knew no better way to disconnect from my first family.... I wanted what I saw as a full woman's life, whatever was possible." Throughout this period, however, Rich found herself feeling increasingly trapped by her circumstances. In a 1960 journal entry, also quoted by O'Mahoney in the London *Guardian*, she wrote that motherhood left her wrestling with "the suffering of ambivalence: the murderous alternation between bitter resentment and raw-edged nerves, and blissful gratification

The poem begins with a reference to a man thinking. (Rafael Ramirez Lee / Shutterstock.com)

and tenderness. Sometimes I seem to myself...a monster of selfishness and intolerance."

One sees this fear of entrapment dramatized in "Ghost of a Chance." The force that the protagonist is trying to escape is the engulfing sea of consolatory familiarities, the ease with which life flows for those who find contentment in the status quo. The images of escape in this poem are also images of great pain, a beached fish who cannot breathe outside of the water, the struggle to survive in the unfamiliar territory of land and air that threatens to kill the protagonist. Even the one image of rescue, that of the wave sweeping the half dead fish back out into the waters where it can live, is also an image of death, for to be swept back into the sea of consolation is the result of one's failure to evolve into life on land. The thinking man fails in this poem. He fails to succeed in his quest to think independently of the undertow of social convention and expectation, and the force that defeats him is triumphant that the solitary thinking man has been defeated in his attempt at individuality and has been subsumed back into the larger group of social convention.

STYLE

Free Verse

Free verse is defined by the absence of the specified metrical structures that define formal verse formats like the sonnet, villanelle, and ghazal. In her first two books of poetry, Adrienne Rich had been particularly praised for her facility with formal verse, so her decision to write free verse in *Snapshots of a Daughter-in-Law* is one of the signals of her determination to move toward a poetry that expressed her particular experience. "Ghost of a Chance" consists of three sentences, arranged over eighteen lines of varying length. It is written in free verse, and the line breaks vary throughout the poem.

One key to reading poetry written in free verse is to examine the line breaks, those places where the poet chooses to end the line. Sometimes they coincide with the end of a sentence or a grammatical break such as a comma or semicolon, but in free verse, line breaks also often serve as points of emphasis. Poets using free verse may also decide to isolate a single word on a line, as Rich does twice in this poem, both times with short three-letter words that describe elemental forces: air and sea.

Another advantage of free verse is that a poet can manipulate the lines to imitate the thing that they describe. The poem moves from short, declarative and descriptive statements to the single long sentence that stretches across fourteen lines and that describes the movement of the sea. The penultimate line of the poem, for instance, which is a long rushing line, imitates the rush of the wave it describes as it moves up the beach.

Point of view

Point of view is the position from which a work of art is narrated. In "Ghost of a Chance," Rich uses the pronoun *you*. This stance is known as second-person point of view and is often used when an author wants to bring a sense of immediacy to a work. By addressing the reader as *you*, the author implies that he or she is addressing the reader directly. It implies a relationship between narrator and reader and also implies that the reader is in some fundamental way like the narrator.

Snapshots of a Daughter-in-Law, the collection in which "Ghost of a Chance" appears, marks the transition point in Rich's career between her earlier poetry, which was very successful in pleasing an audience of older male poets whom she viewed as authorities, and her later work, in which her goal was to express the experience of a thinking woman in contemporary society. As such, we see a shift in pronouns in this collection.

In her 1971 essay "When We Dead Awaken," Rich admitted that moving away from the universalized masculine persona and pronoun was difficult for her. "I hadn't found the courage yet to do without authorities," she writes in that essay, "or even to use the pronoun 'I'—the woman in the poem is always 'she.'" Although here Rich is referring to the title poem of the collection, one can see her struggling with gender and pronouns in "Ghost of a Chance."

This is one of the last poems in Rich's long career in which she will use the figure of a man as a universal figure, that is, instead of writing about a specific man, or a specific woman, the figure of the thinking man here is meant to stand in for a thinking person. In the same vein, because Rich does not yet feel confident enough to use the first person (I), which would situate this poem specifically in a female sensibility, she resorts to the second-person pronoun (you), which can apply to either gender.

Metaphor

Metaphor is one of the central stylistic hallmarks of poetry. Most poems seek to use figurative language in order to evoke new ways of thinking, whether that shift is in the way we think about a particular subject or about the nature of language itself. The work of the poet is to expand the ordinary meaning of words and expressions to illuminate new ways of thinking or feeling. There are two primary forms of metaphor: comparative metaphors, which rely on the formula *A is B*, and substitution metaphors, in which the poet uses term *A* in place of term *B*.

The second type of metaphor is the one that Adrienne Rich is using in "Ghost of a Chance" when she uses imagery of the sea and waves to represent the old familiar comforts and when she uses images of a fish gasping on the beach to represent the man who is trying to think. While she is not saying that the man is a fish, she is pointing out how moving beyond the boundaries of what one has always known can be painful, can leave one feeling as though the very air has become difficult to breathe.

Although readers often misunderstand metaphor as a sort of a puzzle, as an author saying something other than what he or she meant, it is important to remember that by creating metaphors, the poet is expanding our understanding beyond the boundaries of ordinary thought. That is, by working with language in a metaphoric manner, the poet creates new ways of imagining language and the world. Because much of Adrienne Rich's work involves exposing the ways that traditional thinking about language upholds gender and power structures that are inherently oppressive, it is safe to claim that her work subscribes to this expansionist approach to language and metaphor.

HISTORICAL CONTEXT

The period in which Adrienne Rich's poetry came to artistic fruition was an era of enormous social change in American society, a time in which the long work of erasing distinctions of class, race, gender, and sexual orientation began; work that goes on to this day. Beginning in the 1960s, Adrienne Rich has been identified as both a poet and a political activist, and she was active in the three major liberation movements that have effected so much change in American life. Shortly before *Snapshots of a Daughter-in-Law*, the collection in which "Ghost of a Chance" appears, was published, Rich was a rather conventional person. She was the mother of three sons, the wife of a prominent academic scholar, and a lauded poet whose work reflected the academic standards of the day by aspiring to impersonality and universality. Rich's life became entwined with these political movements and mirrors their growth in many ways. She became a dedicated activist seeking civil and political rights for the disenfranchised, as a feminist and as a lesbian.

Civil Rights Movement

Although legal slavery ended during the Civil War, the intervening century had seen the imposition of many laws segregating African Americans from the mainstream of American educational, political, and economic opportunity. By the early 1960s, the civil rights movement, as it came to be known, was picking up steam, and many white intellectuals and artists like Rich were joining the effort to end segregation. The cornerstone of the civil rights movement was nonviolent political protest, and those working to end segregation did so by

deliberately breaking the segregation laws using confrontational but nonviolent tools like sit-ins and large public marches. Those seeking to retain segregation often used violence against the protesters, and these images broadcast on television and in newspapers were so shocking to mainstream white Americans that little by little, segregation laws were dismantled. The culmination of the movement was the passage of two important pieces of legislation: the Civil Rights Act of 1964 and the Voting Rights Act of 1965.

Women's Rights Movement

While women involved in the segregation movement found empowerment in political action, many began to chafe at the expectation that they were less important than the men and that only men were fit to run the movement. Women were expected to provide support but never to lead, and it was not long before many began to question whether the division of labor between the genders was as inherently unnatural as the division of labor between the races.

At the same time, feminist theorists like Betty Friedan, Gloria Steinem, and Adrienne Rich were analyzing social expectations of men and women and critiquing the strict segregation of the genders that had characterized the decade after World War II ended. Why, they asked, was it only the work of women to raise children? Would children not benefit from equal involvement by both of their parents? Why was the social expectation that women, especially those with college educations, would be most satisfied by running a home? Why would running a business or school or government not be just as satisfying, if not more so?

Women used many of the tactics of the civil rights movement to work for the repeal of laws that denied women rights to financial independence from their fathers and husbands, as well as to rewrite the legal codes surrounding divorce and the custody of children to be more equitable. Passage of federal anti-discrimination legislation like Title IX in 1972 opened the world of competitive sports to girls who had never before been allowed to play at the high school and college levels (which led in turn to stronger women's Olympic team representation). Women such as Geraldine Ferraro and Shirley Chisholm ran for president, and although gender representation is hardly equitable, Hillary Clinton's primary campaign for the presidency in 2008 put to rest the idea that a woman cannot be a viable candidate.

COMPARE & CONTRAST

- **1960s:** In 1963, Betty Friedan publishes *The Feminine Mystique*, an important early text in what has come to be known as second-wave feminism. After World War II, society insists that the truly feminine woman will find her life's purpose in being a wife and mother. Friedan describes an emptiness and discontent that she observes among housewives and names it the "feminine mystique." The book sets off a nationwide discussion about the role of women in families and in society at large.

  Today: Women run for President of the United States as Hillary Clinton did and serve as Secretary of State as she, Condoleezza Rice, and Madeleine Albright all have. Women compete in sports at the highest levels, they make up more than half of most college populations, and they serve on the boards of major corporations. However, there is still an element of society that believes the only proper role for a woman is to serve as a wife and mother, and despite decades of discussion and activism to advance women's rights, the role of women in society continues to be hotly debated.

- **1960s:** On a sweltering night in 1969, the police raid the Stonewall Inn, a gay bar in New York's Greenwich Village neighborhood, causing a riot that sets off a national movement to extend civil rights to homosexuals. Many states still have laws against homosexual behavior, and it is very unusual for homosexual people to "come out" publicly. Discrimination against gays and lesbians in the workplace, in housing, and in many other aspects of everyday life is common.

  Today: While discrimination still exists against gay and lesbians, most legal strictures against homosexuality have been repealed or overturned by the courts. Openly gay actors and musicians appear in major movies and on television. The military repeals the ban on gay service members, and states increasingly grant same-sex couples the same marriage rights and responsibilities as straight couples. Although gay rights remains a staple of some political opposition, poll numbers show increasing percentages of the population no longer object to homosexuality.

- **1960s:** The struggle for civil rights for African Americans is the central political battle of the decade, one that claims the lives of leaders like Martin Luther King, Jr., Malcolm X, and Robert Kennedy. Despite these terrible losses, as the decade closes, discriminatory laws are dismantled across the country, schools are desegregated, and federal equal-opportunity laws open to African Americans many economic, academic, and political opportunities that were previously impossible to imagine.

  Today: While the election of Barack Obama as president of the United States demonstrates that the last barrier to political power is definitively broken for African Americans, the persistence of racist objections to his presidency demonstrate that many white citizens still have difficulty accepting equality of the races. Nonetheless, African Americans continue to achieve at all levels of society and are even reversing the Great Migration to the north that took place in the decades before the civil rights movement.

Gay and Lesbian Rights Movement

The Stonewall riots of 1969 are generally considered the beginning of the modern gay rights movement in American history, and gay activists also have adopted the civil rights movement as a template. Adrienne Rich spent much of the 1970s interrogating how feminism and lesbianism are related, and her 1980 essay "Compulsory Heterosexuality and Lesbian Existence" became a foundational document in the new field of queer studies.

Rich and other lesbian feminists felt that lesbians were shut out equally by the male-dominated

Rich implies that thinking exhausts men. *(Alexandre Nunes / Shutterstock.com)*

gay rights movement and by a feminist movement that was blind to the ways in which it prioritized heterosexual relations. The lesbian wing of the feminist movement sought to challenge the very definitions of feminism: was feminism merely a negotiation of the relationships between men and women, or was it also fundamentally about defining womanhood in relation to itself, by examining the relationships between women, independent of men? For several years, Rich was associated with a separatist tradition of lesbian feminism, one that chose to restrict itself to a woman-centric view of the world and to avoid all relations with men where possible.

Politically, the decades after Stonewall saw a gradual and uneven acceptance of homosexuality as a natural state of humanity, and slowly discriminatory laws were repealed or overturned by court statutes. Although discrimination and hate crimes against gay people still occur, over the course of Rich's career, and specifically in the four decades since the publication of "Ghost of a Chance," gay rights have advanced to the point where several states have legalized marriage between same-sex partners and the military has repealed its ban on gay service members.

CRITICAL OVERVIEW

"Ghost of a Chance" was published in *Snapshots of a Daughter-in-Law*, Adrienne Rich's third collection of published poetry, the one that marks the turning point in her career from a sort of prodigy to a poet beginning to find her true artistic calling. Rich's first two books, *A Change of World* (1951) and *The Diamond Cutters and Other Poems*(1955), had been highly praised for their conformation to traditional poetic forms and meter.

Although there is nothing shoddy in *Snapshots of a Daughter-in-Law*, it was in this book that Rich both began to shed the strictures of what she had been taught to believe poetry should be and to experiment with what she truly wanted her own poetry to be. She began writing longer, looser lines, experimenting with fragmented stanzas, and for the first time, introducing a female persona into the poems. Rich explains this change in her 1971 essay "When We Dead Awaken":

> In the late fifties I was able to write, for the first time, directly about experiencing myself as a woman.... I began to feel that my fragments and scraps had a common consciousness and a common theme, one which I would have been very unwilling to put on paper at an earlier time because I had been taught that poetry should be "universal," which meant, of course, non-female. Until then I had tried very much *not* to identify myself as a female poet.

Snapshots of a Daughter-in-Law received very few reviews at the time. Edgar Robinson reviewed "Four Lady Poets" for the *Chicago Review* in 1969, and he says of the collection: "Miss Rich is modern, her psyche is sandpapered the way mine is, and I feel her. And the line is modern too." However, Richard Howard, writing for *Poetry* magazine in 1963, while admitting that he mourns the technical brilliance of Rich's earlier work, notes:

> I can see that in the later pieces she is doing something new, generating a tenser tone, beyond cosiness, and the energy of this reaching style must stand surrogate for the knowingness of her past poems that seemed to be possessed of an effortless control.

Rich felt that the book was written off for being "too bitter and personal." However, as the decades have passed, it has become clear that *Snapshots of a Daughter-in-Law* is the book that forms a clear pivot from the derivative yet accomplished poetry of her early collections to the passion and formal experimentation that are to characterize her mature poetry for the next four decades. Albert Gelpi notes in his essay "Adrienne Rich: The Poetics of Change":

> *Snapshots of a Daughter-in-Law* (1963) is the transitional book in Adrienne Rich's development.... What happens is the crucial event in the career of any artist: a penetration into experience which makes for a distinguishing style.

In *Snapshots of a Daughter-in-Law*, we see a woman struggling with both form and language to find a way to express the reality of her lived experience.

Judith McDaniel, in her essay "'Reconstituting the World': The Poetry and Vision of Adrienne Rich," describes the struggle to determine whether the problem is

> a woman writing in a man's voice and poetic form—or simply the problem of a formal style which made writing difficult with infants to care for. But both are connected to the use of a language which the poet is finding increasingly awkward.

Rich's struggle was amplified by the fact that, as McDaniel points out,

> In the fifties and sixties it was difficult for a woman to escape the fact that poet was a masculine noun.... in *Snapshots of a Daughter-in-Law* the standard of beauty and achievement is still male.

Although Rich struggles against this notion, McDaniel concludes by pointing out that in *Snapshots of a Daughter-in-Law*, the woman of the future, Rich tells us, will be "at least as beautiful as any boy." In later work, of course, Rich will fully break free of the notion that poetry is inherently masculine.

CRITICISM

Charlotte M. Freeman

Freeman is a writer, editor and former academic living in small-town Montana. In the following essay, she examines how the protagonist's struggle to evolve in "Ghost of a Chance" mirrors Adrienne Rich's struggle at the time of its writing to reinvent poetry and to open a poetic space in the form for a woman's experience.

Adrienne Rich published "Ghost of a Chance" in 1963 in *Snapshots of a Daughter-in-Law*, the collection that represents a turning point in her career. In her earlier two books, as she explained in her opening remarks for a 1964 poetry reading reprinted as "Poetry and Experience," she felt "that a poem was an arrangement of ideas and feelings, predetermined, and it said what I had already decided it should say." Whereas by the time she had worked her way to the end of the series of poems, including "Ghost of a Chance," that comprise *Snapshots of a Daughter-in-Law*, she had come to feel that in the production of such poetry she had "suppressed, omitted, falsified even, certain disturbing elements, to gain that perfection of order."

In "Poetry and Experience," Rich described how it was while writing this important transitional collection that she moved from writing "poems *about* experiences" to writing "poems that *are* experiences, that contribute to my knowledge and my emotional life even while they reflect and assimilate it." While it is the production of this second kind of poetry that has fueled Rich's career over its remarkable sixty-year span, the terror of making the leap from the formally controlled

WHAT DO I READ NEXT?

- Although the title of Carol Ann Duffy's anthology *I Wouldn't Thank You for a Valentine: Poems for Young Feminists* (1997) implies a dreary collection of message poems, this volume collects the voices of female poets old and young, who speak on topics as diverse as race, gender, class, sex, politics, and shopping. There are poems about mothers and daughters, about women at work, and about the always-fraught process of learning to find one's own voice.

- *Girl Walking Backwards* by Bett Williams (1998) is the story of Skye, a sixteen-year-old navigating a change to a new high school, relationships with her mother and mostly-absent father, and her attraction to her friend Jessica, whose sullen affect, all-black clothing, and moodiness initially strike Skye as signs that they are soul mates. Jessica leads Skye into the troubled world of raves and drugs, and when Jessica suffers a breakdown, Skye must come to terms with their relationship, as well as her relationships with her family, her other friends, and her fellow members of the volleyball team.

- Jeanette Winterson won the Whitbread Prize for first novel for *Oranges Are Not the Only Fruit* (1987). This coming-of-age novel is narrated by a character also named Jeanette, who struggles to escape her overbearing and repressive evangelical mother. Convinced from an early age that she is indeed one of God's chosen, Jeanette must come to terms with her growing realization that she is not attracted to men or boys. Written with the same astonishing attention to image and sentence that characterizes Winterson's later work, this is a stunning and poetic novel.

- In *Abeng* (1984), Michelle Cliff, Adrienne Rich's longtime partner, tells the story of Clare Savage, a mixed-race twelve-year-old growing up in Jamaica in the 1950s. As she comes of age she struggles to find a way to reconcile her mixed heritage, descended from both Maroon slaves and an English slaveholder (who burned one hundred slaves alive on the eve of emancipation). Cliff's novel dramatizes the multigenerational damage inflicted on both the colonizers and the colonized.

- *Arts of the Possible*, Adrienne Rich's 2001 collection of essays and conversations, is a rich introduction to Rich's nonfiction work. The first section of the book reprints three of her essays from earlier in her career: "When We Dead Awaken: Writing as Re-Vision," "Women and Honor: Some Notes on Lying," and "Blood Bread and Poetry: The Location of the Poet," while the second half of the book contains her more recent thinking on the role of art and poetry in a society she considers deeply driven by political and economic inequalities.

- *The Fact of a Doorframe: Poems, 1950–2001* (2001) is an update to the 1984 title of the same name and takes on the difficult task of compiling Rich's poetry across what has been a long and storied career. As such, it serves as an excellent entry point for those readers who would like both to read more of her work and to see how it has changed and evolved over time.

- When Audre Lorde died from cancer in 1992, Rich organized a group of poets to go on tour with her final collection, *The Marvelous Arithmetics of Distance: Poems 1987–1992*. Rich felt it was important that despite her friend's death, the poems were spoken aloud, as they were meant to be, so that they resonated through the individual voices of Lorde's friends who survived her.

poetry for which she had garnered much acclaim to the more open and experiential poetry can be seen dramatized in "Ghost of a Chance."

"Ghost of a Chance" examines the plight of a person caught between two worlds. This intermediate space is uncomfortable and even life-threatening

> WE CAN ONLY BE GRATEFUL THAT UNLIKE
> THE FIGURE IN 'GHOST OF A CHANCE,' ADRIENNE
> RICH DID EVOLVE AND THAT SHE HAD THE COURAGE
> TO BREATHE THE RAW AND AGONIZING AIR IN HER
> QUEST TO REINVENT POETRY."

to the man who is trying to evolve from one state to another, for in order to evolve, the old form must die and be replaced with a new self. The poem concerns a solitary figure, a man, who is observed in the act of attempting to think. This act is terrifying to the narrator of the poem, who tries to clear a space in which the man can complete his labors.

The imagery in the poem then shifts to the beach, where the man is now compared to a fish who has been stranded on the shore by an errant wave. The labor of thinking is compared to the agony of the fish trying to breathe air when it has not yet evolved the lungs to do so. At the poem's end, the sea sweeps in and saves the fish, and yet this image of salvation is complicated by the parallel the narrator has drawn between the sea and the social forces of comfort that erode the will to do the hard work of thinking.

This poem was written at a time in Rich's career when she too was forced to allow one artistic identity to die in order to reinvent herself, and when she had not quite completed the transformation from the rather conventional, if extraordinarily skilled poetry with which she began her career, to the more experimental and ultimately more successful poetry that she has written for the subsequent forty years. While the protagonist in "Ghost of a Chance" fails to make this transition and is subsumed back into the sea of convention, Rich, in writing "Ghost of a Chance" and the other poems in *Snapshots of a Daughter-in-Law*, succeeded in her quest to kill off a poetic identity that had become confining and to reinvent herself as the prolific artist who has continued to publish vigorous and exciting work over a period of more than sixty years.

The first two lines of "Ghost of a Chance" identify and isolate the figure of a person trying to think. The narrator of the poem uses the second-person voice to point out this figure to the reader. By directly addressing the reader using the pronoun *you*, the poet invokes the imperative voice. This imperative opening demands that the reader direct his or her attention to the object of the narrator's interest, it brings the reader into a direct relationship with the narrator and makes him or her complicit in examination of the figure of the man. It brings the reader into the suspense the narrator describes watching the man's attempt and her terror that he will fail and fall back into the comforts of the familiar. Using this voice also allows the poet to insert herself into the poem without having to specify the gender from which she does so, and this elision of gender in "Ghost of a Chance" is one of the hallmarks of this transitional period in Rich's career.

That the central figure of the poem is explicitly described as a man is another sign of the transitional nature of this poem in Rich's career. There are very few men in her later poems and almost none who occupy this indeterminate gender position: is he meant to be read as an actual man, or is she using the word "man" to signify "human being?" Rich scholar Judith McDaniel notes in "Reconstituting the World: The Poetry and Vision of Adrienne Rich": "In the fifties and sixties it was difficult for a woman to escape the fact that poet was a masculine noun." Rich herself has written about her own struggle with gender during this time in her essay "When We Dead Awaken." She explicitly states that the work she was doing on the poems that became *Snapshots of a Daughter-in-Law*

> had a common consciousness and a common theme, one which I would have been very unwilling to put on paper at an earlier time because I had been taught that poetry should be 'universal,' which meant, of course, nonfemale.

She goes on to add that even as she was experimenting with writing explicitly gendered poetry, one that reflected the experiences and frustrations and joys of her life as a wife and mother, she found: "I had not found the courage yet to do without authorities, or even to use the pronoun 'I.'"

This admission leaves us with several options when interpreting the use of the figure of the man in this poem. Rich could have meant for us to think of this figure as specifically masculine. Considering her reputation as a feminist who for a considerable period of time believed in a radical separatist ideology, one might be tempted to interpret the man as a figure of sarcastic ridicule. Reading the poem this way, one could conclude that she is displaying a figure of a man to point out that men as a gender do not think particularly well or often. Tempting though this might be as a subject of inquiry, it would be a historically inaccurate interpretation. In 1962, when this poem was published, Rich was still living, in ostensible happiness, as a wife and mother of three. Rich also tends not to be a poet who often uses ridicule as a rhetorical device; while she often expresses great anger at social injustice in her work, she rarely exhibits ridicule.

What seems more likely, considering Rich's own statements about her struggle to redefine her relationship to poetry and gender at that time, is that she used the word man in the old-fashioned gender-neutral sense to indicate a person or a human being. This was quite a common usage, especially in the early 1960s, which would make this a more historically appropriate interpretation, especially in light of Rich's own statements about the difficulties she was having with gender-specific writing. In order to write from a gendered position as a woman, Rich had to overcome centuries of social construction declaring that to be a woman poet was somehow to be a lesser poet. In this poem, the fact that she chose to use the male gender for the person engaging in the struggle to move beyond the boundaries of what he already knows underscores the difficulties she was having at this time in moving beyond the idea that the male gender equals the universal, while the female gender can always only refer to a woman, someone who is, by definition then, not universal.

Albert Gelpi, in his essay "Adrienne Rich: The Poetics of Change," suggests that the figure of the man represents "the power of mind and will and judgment" and that "Ghost of a Chance" "pits a man's discriminating intellect against the backward suck of the female sea, undifferentiated and undifferentiating." If we stick to our earlier interpretation that the figure of the man stands as an emblem of any person, then we can see how "Ghost of a Chance" expresses the artistic challenge that faced Rich as an artist at that time. Rich had been taught that to be a poet was to tap into the masculine, intellectual side of one's being and that the proper goals of poetry were, as she said in "Poetry and Experience," "control, technical mastery and intellectual clarity." However, for the nearly ten years between her second and third books, Rich's life had been lived in the "backward suck of the female sea" in a world defined by the physical demands of a woman's body, a body that had carried three pregnancies, nursed three infants, and been given over nearly entirely to the tasks of motherhood.

If we read the man trying to think as an analogue for Rich trying to write poems during this time, then the poem can be seen as a vision of how difficult a challenge that had been. Coming into the unfamiliar air, daring to write a new kind of poem, a poem that to quote "Poetry and Experience" once again, was "willing to let the unconscious offer its materials, to listen to more than the one voice of a single idea," was to risk losing everything. Rich's entire career had been built upon a reputation for clarity, for single-pointed formal brilliance. To let the voice of the unconscious in is to risk not being taken seriously, but not to take that risk is to be like the person in the poem, the person who is returned blind to the sea.

We can only be grateful that unlike the figure in "Ghost of a Chance," Adrienne Rich did evolve and that she had the courage to breathe the raw and agonizing air in her quest to reinvent poetry. She is largely responsible for breaking down the old ideals that formal control was the ultimate value in poetics and for legitimizing a woman's experience as one of many subjects of poetry.

Source: Charlotte M. Freeman, Critical Essay on "Ghost of a Chance," in *Poetry for Students*, Gale, Cengage Learning, 2012.

Alice Templeton

In the following essay, Templeton provides an overview of the major trends and themes of criticism in Rich's poetry.

Adrienne Rich's poetry has always raised important, difficult questions about the cultural uses of poetry and the ideology of poetic and critical tradition. For over forty years her work has provided the occasion for critics to comment on the art of poetry, its political significance, the character of poetic tradition, and the value of poetry as a critical and creative cultural activity. Ranging in tone from eulogistic to condemnatory, prescriptive to paternal, these critical statements comprise a narrative that divulges part of the use to which Rich's poetry has been put; and like an exemplary exercise in dialogical discourse, the narrative implied by Rich criticism contains contradictory claims whose meanings modulate as new contexts and statements arise.

Rich implies that for men, thinking can be compared to a fish out of water. (*Rafael Ramirez Lee*)

In 1951 W. H. Auden praised Rich for the craftsmanship and modesty in the poems in her first volume, *A Change of World*, published in the Yale Series of Younger Poets. Though Auden greatly underestimated Rich's role in reshaping the modernist tradition, the two issues raised in his introduction continue to interest critics of Rich's work: the question of whether Rich manages the "detachment from the self and its emotions without which no art is possible," and Rich's place in poetic tradition, especially her development from a "modest" participant in modernism to a radical critic of the solipsism and sexism often implied in a modernist aesthetic. The artistic standing of Rich's poetry and its resistant relation to the dominant poetic tradition preoccupy critics throughout every stage of Rich's work, from the early formalist poetry in her first two volumes, through the woman-centered, feminist writings culminating in the seventies with *The Dream of a Common Language* (1978), to Rich's postmodern feminist critique of a range of subjects, including her personal heritage, the legacies of historical and national location, and

ideologies of time and aging in the volumes since *A Wild Patience Has Taken Me This Far* (1981).

Seven books of criticism published in English in the last twenty years express contradictory evaluations of Rich's work as they illustrate the challenges that her poetry presents to academic criticism. In 1975 Norton issued a critical edition [*Adrienne Rich's Poetry*], edited by Barbara Charlesworth Gelpi and Albert Gelpi, which includes selected poems, excerpts from Rich's prose and interviews, critical articles, and reviews. Published on the heels of Rich's first overtly feminist volume of poetry, *Diving Into the Wreck* (1973), the Norton critical edition collects pieces that reveal the tension and contradiction characteristic of Rich criticism in the sixties and seventies. While Robert Boyers condemns Rich's work for having become "charged...with the nauseous propaganda of the advance-guard cultural radicals" and urges the poet to abandon the "will to be contemporary" for higher, aesthetic ground, Wendy Martin praises the poetry for organizing "an intricate and complex cluster of perceptions which comprise the reality of the modern

> AS RICH CONTINUES TO SEARCH FOR
> 'A READER BY WHOM I COULD NOT BE MISTAKEN,'
> THE CRITIC OF RICH'S WORK WILL ASPIRE TO
> BE THAT READER."

woman." Certainly Rich's enfranchisement of the female reader partly accounts for the threat some critics perceive to aesthetic excellence: Boyers even charges that Rich appeals to readers who "are nothing but contemporary and who therefore can have little sense of the proper gravity of the poetic art." Two apparently contrary critical impulses emerge in the Gelpis' edition, sometimes manifested, as with Helen Vendler, in the same critic: the defense of poetry as a nonpolitical, universal, aesthetic enterprise and the appreciation of Rich's oppositional stance, particularly her articulation of the complications of contemporary feminist thinking. The criticism in the Gelpis' first collection portrays a poet who has been admitted into the academic canon but on probationary terms.

Nearly ten years after the Norton critical edition appeared, Jane Roberta Cooper edited an anthology of criticism entitled *Reading Adrienne Rich* (1984), which includes articles on the poetry (all written by women), reviews from 1951–1981, and studies of Rich's prose. As Cooper puts it, the critical essays "interpret Adrienne Rich's work on the terms she has chosen in the last decade," while the reviews are included "for their historical value." Among the reviews Cooper finds a "decisive split" between "feminist and patriarchal understandings of poetry, criticism, and gender"; those written before *Diving Into the Wreck* "betray the blind spots of masculine literary culture" by failing to acknowledge the poetry's specific focus on women's experience, while those written after 1973 are more likely to read Rich's work from a feminist perspective. The themes discussed in the essays remain constant concerns in Rich's poetry and in the criticism: the connection between poetry and political change, Rich's reading and writing of women's history in her poetry, language as both a liberating and constraining cultural legacy, the poet's engagement in a radical feminist discourse, Rich's feminist ethics, her place in

American poetic tradition, and the poetry's intertextual resonances with the work of other poets. What is most apparent about these essays now is their determination to apply Rich's own feminist terminology and way of reading, as gleaned from her prose, lectures, and the poems themselves, without introducing extrinsic or nonfeminist critical paradigms. The essays are both valuable for their sympathetic hermeneutic, especially as we gain historical distance from that time, and limited to the level of expository analysis because of it.

Also in 1984, Myriam Diaz-Diocaretz, Chilean poet and translator of Rich's work, published three essays as a book under the title *The Transforming Power of Language*. To explain Rich's development of a feminist poetic discourse that emphasizes the communicative function of poetry over its expressive value, Diaz-Diocaretz analyzes Rich's unique author-position, the centrality of the reader in the poetry, and the constant inclusion within Rich's poems of "alien texts" that clarify and complicate the poet's stance. For example, the allusions to canonic English poetry in "Snapshots of a Daughter-in-Law" reveal the speaker's sense of cultural betrayal even as they express her knowledge of high culture; and the lines from Susan B. Anthony's diaries and the echo of Matthew Arnold in "Culture and Anarchy" establish a complex historical context for contemporary women's activism that is at once nurturing and conflictual. For Diaz-Diocaretz, as for Adrian Oktenberg in Cooper's book, Rich's radical feminist discourse is epitomized in *Twenty-One Love Poems*, the cycle of lesbian lyric poems that reinvents as it subverts the tradition of heterosexual love sonnets. Though the book lacks careful editing, Diaz-Diocaretz's use of continental critical concepts, specifically Michel Foucault's "author-function" and Julia Kristeva's "intertextuality," makes her feminist analysis more suggestive for the present reader than much of the criticism that depends solely on close readings and critical paradigms intrinsic to Rich's writing.

In *Translating Poetic Discourse* (1985), Diaz-Diocaretz expands her analysis of Rich's radical poetic discourse by discussing the particular ideological and linguistic difficulties of translating Rich's poems into Spanish. In the case of Rich's poetry, translating worlds is as crucial as translating words: the translator must not only communicate with the reader steeped in the norms of the Spanish world but also find equivalents in that world for the cultural icons and texts that

Rich constantly incorporates as a means of defining her iconoclastic, "homosocial" stance in relation to dominant culture. The book continually offers examples of the ways in which Rich's use of language, not just her themes, challenge heterosexual cultural assumptions. It provides not only a systematic semiotic reading of Rich's work, but also insight into the ideological, creative work of translation and its importance in shaping literary history. Diaz-Diocaretz is one of the few critics of Rich's work who, without qualifications, embraces Rich's radicalism, locating it in her use of language rather than in themes alone.

In *The Aesthetics of Power* (1986), Claire Keyes frames her chronological reading of Rich's poetry through *A Wild Patience Has Taken Me This Far* (1981) with American feminist concepts, including Elaine Showalter's "wild zone," Judith Kegan Gardiner's definition of female identity as a process, and Tillie Olsen's insistence on the usefulness of art. Keyes traces Rich's development of a specifically "female" aesthetics as the poet attempts to resolve the "dilemma of power" that her identity as both poet and woman raises: the "artist's ability to shape her forms does not necessarily translate to her ability to shape her environment or gain control over her life." According to Keyes, Rich eventually conceptualizes a "beneficent female power—both personal and political—predicated upon her own experience as woman and poet." Yet Keyes concludes that in *A Wild Patience* Rich's beliefs take precedence over poetry, so that "truth" is not discovered in the process of making the poem, but is preordained. Like many critics of Rich's work, even sympathetic ones, Keyes finally abandons the crucial question raised by her own analysis and by Rich's poetry— i.e., the connection between poetic and literal power—and retreats in her conclusion to the comfort of rather standard aesthetic criteria. Keyes worries that Rich too often strays outside the boundaries of the poetic enterprise to write documentary disguised as poetry. The present reader might value the book more if Keyes had examined in theoretical terms the assumptions behind her aesthetic judgments and the antagonism she finds between the aesthetic and pragmatic powers of poetry.

The most recently published full-length study of Rich's work, Craig Werner's *Adrienne Rich: The Poet and Her Critics* (1988), offers readings of Rich's poems in the context of her entire poetic project while it examines other critics' approaches, many of which ignore the process-oriented poetics Rich espouses. Even as he defends Rich's own process as the primary context for evaluating individual poems, Werner offers very close, formalist readings and analyses of prosody of single poems. In this way he not only argues for the organic integrity of Rich's canon, but also answers those critics, including Helen Vendler and Cary Nelson, who find aesthetic flaws in much of Rich's politically engaged work. Werner describes the contradictions within Rich criticism as a "clash" between academic critics who, rather than actually engaging in Rich's process, dismiss her feminism as mere orthodoxy and Rich's feminist aesthetics, which works against the "cultural solipsism" and isolated subjectivity that literary study has traditionally privileged. Unlike most criticism that analyzes Rich's poetic career as a self-conscious process of personal and communal transformation, Werner's study is organized primarily by themes, and only secondarily by chronology.

Werner closes his book with a chapter that places Rich in the context of American poetry, a task that compels critics of all leanings. Several critical books that attempt to define poetic tradition devote a section or chapter to Rich's work. Suzanne Juhasz's *Naked and Fiery Forms* (1978), Deborah Pope's *A Separate Vision* (1984), Wendy Martin's *An American Triptych* (1984), Alicia Ostriker's *Stealing the Language* (1986), and Paula Bennett's *My Life a Loaded Gun* (1986) all place Rich's work in a continuum of American women's writing. David Kalstone's *Five Temperaments* (1977), Cary Nelson's *Our Last First Poets: Vision and History in Contemporary American Poetry* (1981), Charles Altieri's *Self and Sensibility in Contemporary American Poetry* (1984), and Walter Kalaidjian's *Languages of Liberation: The Social Text in Contemporary American Poetry* (1989) evaluate Rich's unique contribution to American poetry by comparing her vision and poetics to those of male contemporaries. Rich's formal training and self-conscious participation in poetic tradition demand that her work be understood in the context of mainstream American poetry; yet her position since the early seventies as a radical political poet who challenges the very terms of academic literary debate makes her a resistant, uncooperative figure in conventional discussions of poetic tradition. As Anne Herzog has commented, it is impossible to assimilate Rich's political poetry fully into "a tradition which exonerates instead the formally-interested, politically 'disinterested,' 'complete' and controlled personal lyric." Certainly, though, in the present climate of politicized criticism, it is now impossible for critics either to take the claims of such a tradition at face value or to ignore the political implications of the personal lyric, no matter what disclaimers come with it.

The emphasis in Rich's feminist writing on the communicative value of poetry also places her work within the American poetic tradition but sets it against the American formalist critical tradition. Helen Vendler notes that like mainstream, "plain-style" American poets who resist elitist aestheticizing in favor of engaging an "ordinary" audience, Rich "asks to be judged on effectiveness, rather than on conventional ideas of 'beauty.'" Cary Nelson explains, with some regret, that Rich's poetics, which values poems more as a means to effect change rather than as aesthetic ends in themselves, disrupts the authority of externally imposed aesthetic standards: "The criterion for value becomes the degree to which the poem participates in the developing poetic. A particular poem may be of interest . . . even when it is not very good." As Oktenberg has said, unlike most contemporary poets who produce "an accumulation of poems," Rich has created a self-contextualizing, self-referential "body of work" that alternately satisfies and disappoints formalist critical strategies. Perhaps no American poet is as convinced as Rich is of the liberating potential of literary experience yet at the same time as systematically skeptical of the ideological machinery on which literary study rides.

That fact makes the Gelpis' latest version of the Norton critical edition [*Adrienne Rich's Poetry and Prose* (1993)] a welcome but somewhat disquieting newcomer to the party of Rich criticism. It is long overdue, since the original edition (1975) has been outdated as a textbook for some time. The new edition represents Rich's writing more fully by reprinting selected poetry through *An Atlas of the Difficult World* (1992) and selected prose published since the earlier edition. It retains three of the critical essays from the earlier version (by W. H. Auden, Albert Gelpi, and Helen Vendler), includes some feminist essays from Cooper's book (by Judith McDaniel, Adrian Oktenberg, Olga Broumas, and Margaret Atwood), and also adds more recent critical pieces by Charles Altieri, Terrence des Pres, and Willard Spiegelman that valuably analyze Rich's distinct poetic strategies, especially in the context of American poetry and of "political" poetry. A

timeline of critical poses unfolds: the early formalist criticisms and reviews with their reserved praise of Rich's promise, the feminist essays that appreciate the poetry for its focus on social and personal transformation, and the newer brand of essentially formalist essays that grant rather than resist the political coloring of Rich's lyric pose as they discuss primarily aesthetic issues. The political awareness in the recent essays especially reveals the difference that work like Rich's has made in critical standards, yet alongside the tones of formalist caution and feminist commitment, they also suggest a new, subtle level of tension between the poet and the critical establishment. Now, instead of displacing the antagonistic or overly accommodating critical attitude, perhaps the challenge for Rich's writing as it seeks to invite the reader into cultural participation will be overriding the current nonchalance about poetry's political value, an attitude that can easily trivialize the costs and rewards of Rich's poetic project even as it acknowledges them.

The Gelpis' book stands as a reminder that even as the poet lives and writes, the historical grit that irritated her into writing poetry is already being ground to a smooth textual surface (by history? by critical overdetermination? by changes in cultural values?), whose rough geology will have to be composed by the reader's historical imagination. Rich's poetry demands the jagged, painful terrain of engaged memory, not just the soothing continuity of order. Like most retrospective collections of selected works and critical essays, the new Norton edition by its nature implies a continuum in the poetry and the criticism that obscures the risks involved in each of Rich's own writings and the turbulence her work caused among critics—difficulties that the collision of different kinds of texts, not just academic essays and reviews, might convey. If it were not for the poetry itself, the new Norton critical edition would make it easy to forget that Rich was ever, and ever is, on probation, if no longer obviously with the critical establishment, then with her own creative and political conscience.

Because Rich's poetry constantly puts the practice and use of literary art under suspicion, almost no critic of Rich's work can avoid discussing the paradoxes and politics within the criticism itself; however, along with weaving its own self-reflexive narrative, criticism also needs to account for the cultural currency of Rich's work outside the academy. Feminist-informed cultural critics are likely to focus more on the participatory role of the reader in Rich's writing, noted by Diaz-Diocaretz, Patrocinio Schweickart, and others, to determine the pragmatic effects of Rich's poetry as it works to transform the reader from a passive cultural receptor into an active cultural participant.

Future criticism promises to be more eclectic in its uses of theory both to reflect the insights of postmodern feminism and to address Rich's extension, in her latest three volumes, of feminist analysis to ideological systems other than sexual difference. Rich's most recent volume *An Atlas of the Difficult World*, which concerns individual and communal uses of monuments and icons of all kinds, clearly calls for more acute discussions of the relations between aesthetic value and existential effect, and demands further critical examination of our ways of reading and using cultural icons, including poems and poetic tradition. As Rich continues to search for "a reader by whom I could not be mistaken," the critic of Rich's work will aspire to be that reader. Both will find qualified fulfillment because, fortunately, like the constantly changing narrative composed by Rich's critics, the poetry will not keep still for either the writer or the reader.

Source: Alice Templeton, "Contradictions: Tracking Adrienne Rich's Poetry," in *Tulsa Studies in Women's Literature*, Vol. 12, No. 2, Fall 1993, pp. 333–40.

SOURCES

"Adrienne Rich," in *Poetry Foundation*, http://www.poetryfoundation.org/bio/adrienne-rich (accessed March 21, 2011).

"Adrienne Rich," in *Poets.org*, Academy of American Poets, http://www.poets.org/poet.php/prmPID/49 (accessed March 21, 2011).

Friedan, Betty, "The Feminine Mystique," in *History of Ideas on Woman: A Sourcebook*, Perigree Books, 1977.

Gelpi, Albert, "Adrienne Rich: The Poetics of Change," in *Adrienne Rich's Poetry and Prose*, W. W. Norton, 1993, pp. 285, 288.

Howard, Richard, "Poetry Chronicle," in *Poetry*, Vol. 102, No. 4, July 1963, p. 258.

McDaniel, Judith, "Reconstituting the World: The Poetry and Vision of Adrienne Rich," in *Adrienne Rich's Poetry and Prose*, W. W. Norton, 1993, p. 314.

O'Mahoney, John, "The Profile: Adrienne Rich," in *Guardian* (London, England), June 15, 2002, http://www.guardian.co.uk/books/2002/jun/15/featuresreviews.guardianreview6 (accessed April 15, 2011).

Pope, Deborah, "Rich's Life and Career," in *Modern American Poetry*, http://www.english.illinois.edu/maps/poets/m_r/rich/bio.htm (accessed March 21, 2011); originally published in *The Oxford Companion to Women's Writing in the United States*, Oxford University Press, 1995.

Rich, Adrienne, "Ghost of a Chance," in *Adrienne Rich's Poetry and Prose*, W. W. Norton, 1993, pp. 16–17.

———, "Poetry and Experience," in *Adrienne Rich's Poetry and Prose*, W. W. Norton, 1993, p. 165.

———, "When We Dead Awaken," in *Adrienne Rich's Poetry and Prose*, W. W. Norton, 1993, pp. 175.

———, "Why I Refused the National Medal for the Arts," in *Steven Barclay Agency: Lectures and Readings*, http://www.barclayagency.com/uploads/pdf/richwhy.pdf (accessed April 25, 2011); originally published in *Los Angeles Times*, August 3, 1997.

Robinson, Edgar, "Four Lady Poets," in *Chicago Review*, Vol. 21, No. 3, December 1969, p. 115.

"Stonewall Rebellion," in *New York Times*, April 10, 2009, http://topics.nytimes.com/top/reference/timestopics/subjects/s/stonewall_rebellion/index.html?scp=1-spot&sq=stonewall%20rebellion&st=cse (accessed April 15, 2011).

FURTHER READING

Lessing, Doris, *The Golden Notebook*, Simon and Schuster, 1962.

> Also published in 1962 was Doris Lessing's groundbreaking novel, *The Golden Notebook*. It tells the story of Anna Wulf, a female writer who has split her writing into four different notebooks: the black, in which she chronicles her biographical experience in Africa; the red, in which she chronicles her experience in the Communist party; the yellow, in which she writes the story of the painful love affair in which she is mired; and the blue: in which she describes her dreams. There is also the Golden notebook of the title, in which she struggles to integrate these experiences into a coherent narrative. The novel deals with many of the same themes that concerned Rich at the time: how to be politically and artistically engaged, how to be free of gender politics, and how to be a parent.

Montefiore, Jan, and Claire Buck, *Feminism and Poetry: Language, Experience, Identity in Women's Writing*, rev. ed., Pandora, 2004.

> Originally released in 1987, this collection was one of the first to rethink feminism and its relationship to poetry in theoretical terms instead of in the essentialist mode that dominated the 1970s and early 1980s. Montefiore incorporates the post-structuralist theories of Luce Irigaray, Roland Barthes, and Jacques Lacan and begins the work of investigating the ways that language itself is a

gendered structure. Montefiore is particularly good on the history of how the male gender came to be seen as universal and neutral and the difficulties of building a tradition of women's poetry.

Plath, Sylvia, *Ariel: The Restored Edition*, Harper Perennial, 2005.

Sylvia Plath was a contemporary of Rich's, and the poems in this volume, written during the terrible winter of 1962–63 that ended with Plath's suicide, struggle with many of the issues that Rich wrestled with: love, passion, sex, children, and the problems of being a woman artist. The original version was edited by Plath's estranged husband, the poet Ted Hughes, who rearranged the order of Plath's manuscript, added poems she had not included, and dropped some that she had. This volume, edited by Plath's daughter Freida Hughes, seeks to restore the manuscript Plath left behind to its original form.

Rich, Adrienne, *The Fact of a Doorframe: Poems, 1950–2001*, Norton, 2001.

A revised version of an anthology originally released in 1984, this volume not only contains a new introduction but brings the survey of Rich's poetry into the twenty-first century. The book contains selections from each of Rich's collections to that point, including her most famous poems, "Diving into the Wreck" and "Planetarium." This book is the best opportunity for someone new to Rich's work to get a sense of its duration and breadth.

Rich, Adrienne, *What Is Found There: Expanded Edition*, Holt, 2003.

This expanded edition of a collection of Rich's essays from 1993 continues the long conversation she has been having with the American people about the role of the artist in society, the mechanisms of power, and their effect on all people, especially on women. Although Rich long ago left separatist feminism behind in favor of a critique of how power oppresses across the spectrum, her writings are still relevant and powerful, and her description of the inner life of a working artist is one that no aspiring writer should miss.

SUGGESTED SEARCH TERMS

Adrienne Rich

Adrienne Rich AND feminism

Adrienne Rich AND motherhood

Adrienne Rich AND poetry

Adrienne Rich AND politics

Adrienne Rich AND lesbian

Adrienne Rich AND art

Adrienne Rich AND *Snapshots of a Daughter-in-Law*

Adrienne Rich AND Ghost of a Chance

Let Evening Come

JANE KENYON

1990

"Let Evening Come" is a short lyric poem by Jane Kenyon, written in a traditional American form known as plain style. The poem portrays the closing of the day on a farm. Kenyon simply and beautifully describes the fading light across the homely objects of the yard. The sounds and rhythms of the poem are calming and hymn-like. By the end of the poem, the reader understands that thematically "Let Evening Come" is a poem about accepting death and finding comfort in faith.

Kenyon wrote this poem while her husband, poet Donald Hall, some nineteen years her senior, was battling liver cancer. Neither Hall nor Kenyon fully expected him to live. Ironically, it was Kenyon herself who died just five years after the composition of "Let Evening Come" from an aggressive form of leukemia. She was just forty-seven years old.

First published in *Harvard Magazine* in 1990, "Let Evening Come" is available in *Let Evening Come*, published in 1990 by Graywolf Press, and in *Otherwise: New and Selected Poems*, published in 1996, also by Graywolf Press. It can also be found online at Poets.org and on the Poetry Foundation's Web site.

AUTHOR BIOGRAPHY

Kenyon was born in Ann Arbor, Michigan, on May 23, 1947, the daughter of Reuel and Polly Kenyon. She grew up in a rural area just outside

the city and attended a one-room schoolhouse through the fourth grade, according to her husband, Hall, writing in an afterword to Kenyon's book *Otherwise*. Her father was a jazz musician who played at local clubs and taught music privately. Her mother was also a vocal musician who gave up her career after her children were born. Laban Hill, in *American Writers*, notes that Reuel Kenyon suffered from clinical depression and that Polly Kenyon was manic-depressive, making "home life difficult."

Kenyon began writing poems while still a junior high school student. After graduation from high school, Kenyon attended the University of Michigan, earning a bachelor of arts degree in 1970, and continuing on to earn her master of arts degree in 1972. Kenyon met Hall as an undergraduate student in one of his large classes in 1969. The following fall, she took a small workshop with Hall and the two became friends, although not romantically involved. They began their courtship in 1971, while Kenyon was a graduate student. Hall, nineteen years older than Kenyon, was in his forties, recently divorced, and already a well-established poet, according to Hill and John H. Timmerman in *Jane Kenyon: A Literary Life*. The couple married in April 1972.

In 1975, Kenyon urged Hall to give up his position at the University of Michigan and move to Eagle Pond, Hall's family farm in Wilmot, New Hampshire. The move was formative for both of them. Timmerman notes that Kenyon began writing in a disciplined fashion as well as reading deeply into the works of John Keats, Anna Akhmatova, Elizabeth Bishop, and Anton Chekhov.

Kenyon published her first book of poetry, *From Room to Room*, in 1978. Robin M. Latimer, writing in the *Dictionary of Literary Study: American Poets since World War II*, describes the book as "the poetic diary of a honeymoon, in which a young wife explores the spaces between her and her husband, and her new and former homes."

A visit to Eagle Pond by poet Robert Bly led to Kenyon's intensive, eight-year-long study of Russian poet Anna Akhmatova. In 1977, Kenyon began working with Vera Sandomirsky Dunham, a professor of Russian Literature at the State University of New York, to translate the poems. In 1985, Kenyon published a small volume of these translations, *Twenty Poems of Anna Akhmatova*. The poems were later collected in the 1999 posthumous collection *A Hundred White Daffodils: Essays, Newspaper Columns, Notes, Interviews, and One Poem*.

Kenyon continued working on her own poetry as well, despite her ongoing problems with depression. In an interview with Bill Moyers conducted in 1993, Kenyon told him:

> Depression is something I suffered from all my life. I'm manic-depressive, actually, and I was not properly diagnosed until I was thirty-eight years old. . . . Mine behaves almost like a serious depression only and I rarely become manic.

In 1986, Kenyon published *The Boat of Quiet Hours*, another collection of poems, and followed this publication with *Let Evening Come* in 1990, a collection that included "Let Evening Come." (The poem was first published in *Harvard Magazine* and was included in *The Best American Poetry* in *1991*.) Kenyon came into her own with the publication of this volume; as Hill writes, "*Let Evening Come* is clearly a work of a mature poet and exhibits this maturity in the cohesiveness of the collection." In 1993, Kenyon published *Constance*, her last book of poetry published while she was alive. Perhaps the most notable poem in the volume is "Having It Out with Melancholy." Sharon J. O'Brien, writing in *Notable American Women*, argues that this poem is "perhaps the most powerful description of depression in American literature."

In 1989, Hall was diagnosed with colon cancer, which became liver cancer by 1993. It was not expected that he would live. Ironically, Kenyon succumbed to cancer at age forty-seven. Diagnosed in January 1994 with aggressive leukemia, Kenyon traveled to Seattle for a bone marrow transplant later than year. The treatment was not effective, however, and by April 1995, after twenty-three years of marriage, Kenyon and Hall learned her cancer had returned. She died on April 22, 1995, in their home at Eagle Pond. In her last weeks, Kenyon and Hall finished planning the volume and selecting the poems for *Otherwise: New and Selected Poems*, published in 1996.

In the years since her death, Kenyon's stature has grown among readers and critics alike. As Keith Taylor notes in "The Presence of Jane Kenyon," Kenyon's poetry has "quickly and deeply . . . penetrated the cultural landscape."

POEM TEXT

Let the light of late afternoon
shine through chinks in the barn, moving
up the bales as the sun moves down.

Let the cricket take up chafing
as a woman takes up her needles   5
and her yarn. Let evening come.

Let dew collect on the hoe abandoned
in long grass. Let the stars appear
and the moon disclose her silver horn.

Let the fox go back to its sandy den.   10
Let the wind die down. Let the shed
go black inside. Let evening come.

To the bottle in the ditch, to the scoop
in the oats, to air in the lung
let evening come.   15

Let it come, as it will, and don't
be afraid. God does not leave us
comfortless, so let evening come.

POEM SUMMARY

The text used for this summary is from *Otherwise: New and Selected Poems*, Graywolf Press, 1996, p. 176. Versions of the poem can be found on the following Web pages: http://www.poetry foundation.org/poem/175711, http://www.poets. org/viewmedia.php/prmMID/16019, and http://www.poetryoutloud.org/poems/poem.html?id = 175711.

"Let Evening Come" is an eighteen-line pocm containing six stanzas of three lines each. Kenyon uses the words of the title as a sort of refrain that repeats itself throughout the poem, specifically as the closing phrase in stanzas 2, 4, and 6. In addition, stanzas 1, 2, 3, 4, and 6 begin with the word "let," the first word of the title. These artistic decisions unify the poem, as well as creating a soothing pattern of sound. Her use of this word also sets the pace of the poem.

Stanzas 1–2
Stanza 1 contains one sentence that extends over the three lines. The poet describes a moment late in the day, just as the sun is beginning its journey toward sunset. She speaks of the way the interior of a farm building is illuminated by the sinking sun. There is a contrast between the way the sunlight moves toward the top of the interior and the sun itself sinking in the horizon. Even in the fading day, light shines through small holes in the building's siding.

The first word of the poem, "let," casts the poem in the imperative mood used for direct commands. In imperative sentences, the subject is understood, not stated. For example, in the sentence "Don't touch my book," there is an unstated "you." The command is directed by the speaker to "you," whoever he or she is. As a result, the reader of "Let Evening Come" must determine who it is that Kenyon addresses. If it is God, then the poem is a kind of prayer, asking God to let the nighttime come peacefully and quietly and in its own time. If it is the reader, however, it is more instructive, containing the gentle reminder that all must let go at the close of day or at the close of life.

In stanza 2, Kenyon invokes the sounds of summer insects in the twilight, as well as the sound of a woman knitting. She closes the stanza with a repetition of the poem's title, a phrase that functions as a refrain throughout the poem. By connecting the woman's knitting to the insect's singing, Kenyon tells readers that all creatures are part of the cycle of the day, and by extension, the cycle of life.

Stanzas 3–4
In stanza 3, Kenyon continues cataloging objects at the end of the day. She mentions a gardening tool left forgotten in the yard, with moisture condensing on its surface. In the second line, she signals that the sun has set as the planets and the moon begin to shine in the growing darkness. Again, Kenyon connects the large and the small, the high and the low. The farm implement is the most homely and earthly of items, meant for digging in the soil. The planets, stars, and moons in the sky are large, beautiful, and far away. Yet all must acquiesce to the cycles of time.

In stanza 4, all four sentences begin with the word "let." Kenyon describes a small creature returning to its home for the night. She also asks that the summer breezes quiet, as they do in the early evening, and that the farm outbuilding darkens. The stanza once again closes with the words of the title. By shortening her sentence length and starting each sentence with the same word, Kenyon speeds up the pace of the poem. Although this stanza seems choppier because of the internal stops formed by the periods at the

MEDIA ADAPTATIONS

- "Let Evening Come" has been adapted for song in *Briefly It Enters: A Cycle of Songs from the Poems of Jane Kenyon for Voice and Piano, 1994–1996*, William Bolcom, E.B. Marks Music, 1996, and in *Let Evening Come: For Soprano, Viola, and Piano*, E. B. Marks Music, 2003.

- "Let Evening Come" was recorded by the Brisbane Chamber Choir on their 2006 album *Time and Eternity*. The recording is available as an MP3 download.

- In 1993, Kenyon and Hall were featured in an hour-long documentary that aired on Public Broadcasting Service. *Donald Hall and Jane Kenyon: A Life Together* features Hall and Kenyon reading their poetry and speaking with interviewer Bill Moyers about poetry and their lives. The film was produced by Films for the Humanities and Sciences and is available through Films Media Group.

end of each sentence, its rhythm mirrors the increasing speed with which night is falling.

Stanzas 5–6

Stanza 5 marks a change in the poem. The stanza is one sentence of four phrases, a direct contrast to the previous stanza that is composed of four complete sentences. The first two phrases list objects on the farm, while the third phrase refers to the human breath. The final phrase is again "let evening come." This long sentence wants to be read with one breath, without end stops. The reference to breathing at the end of the second line reinforces this sense. At the same time, by introducing the act of breathing into the poem, Kenyon also introduces the opposite, the act of not breathing, synonymous with death. At this point, the reader begins to realize that the poem is more than a simple cataloging of the farm at sunset.

In the final stanza, Kenyon once again begins with the word "let." This use, however, problematizes just whom Kenyon is addressing: until this point, the poem reads like a prayer with the understood "you" being God. However, in this stanza, Kenyon instructs the reader to not be frightened. She ends this thought with a period, implying a breath, and then begins the final sentence of the poem, a sentence that assures the reader that because the Lord provides solace even in the gathering darkness, the reader should allow the night to fall. Although Kenyon never directly identifies her subject or theme as death, by the last stanza it is clear that this is a poem about letting go, about bowing to the inevitability of death.

THEMES

Death

"Let Evening Come" is a poem about the close of day observed by the poet in a farmyard. She details the light in a shed, the bales of hay, a garden hoe, the settling of evening dew, the moon and stars, and finally the act of breathing. She writes of the animate and the inanimate, all part of the natural world. As the light fades, Kenyon describes the gentle quieting of the landscape: insects begin to hum, a woman sits down after a long day to do needlework, a wild animal returns to its home, the breeze stops. In each line, there is movement toward the end of day. And as the day ends, movement and daily business ceases. Although unspoken, night is the time for sleep, for a retreat from the things of this world.

In the fifth stanza, Kenyon departs from external objects such as shovels and containers to an internal process, the act of breathing. She writes that evening comes even to the breath in the body, shifting the poem away from evening toward the life-sustaining practice of breathing. During the night, breath slows.

In the final stanza, she repeats her title, followed by a phrase that points to the inevitability of evening coming as part of a natural cycle. Although Kenyon has not mentioned the word "death" at any place in her poem, it is clear that the fading light is a metaphor for the fading of life. A metaphor is a figure of speech that compares two items or ideas by suggesting similar qualities held by each. For example, a poet might

TOPICS FOR FURTHER STUDY

- With a small group of your classmates, collect photographs and illustrations from books, magazines, and online that remind you of the poem "Let Evening Come." Scan or add the photos into a computer program such as iPhoto. Find the MP3 downloadable file of "Let Evening Come" by William Bolcom. Using your illustrations and music, create a slide show to present to your classmates.

- Using your creativity, write a play depicting the composition of "Let Evening Come." To do so, you will need to thoroughly research Kenyon's life, as well as her marriage to the poet Donald Hall, using books, journal articles, interviews, and biographies. With a small group, perform your play for your classmates. Record the play and upload the file to YouTube so that others can view your work.

- Read Dylan Thomas's poem "Death Be Not Proud." What were the circumstances of Thomas's composition? How does "Death Be Not Proud" reflect some of the same themes as "Let Evening Come"? Write an essay comparing and contrasting the two poems.

- Several critics have discussed poets whose work inspired Kenyon, including John Keats, Emily Dickinson, Elizabeth Bishop, Anna Akhmatova, and Robert Bly. With a group of your classmates, find and read a selection of poems by these poets. Select the poems that seem to your group to resonate most fully with "Let Evening Come" and present a poetry reading to your class. To manage the work, break down tasks into smaller parts and create a schedule of deadlines.

- Kenyon suffered from debilitating depression as a result of her bipolar disorder, also known as manic depression. What is bipolar disorder? What are the symptoms? How can the disease be managed? Find answers by reading books such as Russ Federman's young-adult nonfiction volume *Facing Bi-Polar: The Young Adult's Guide to Dealing with Bi-Polar Disorder* (2010). Additionally, read what Kenyon had to say about her disorder in interviews and in poems such as "Having It Out with Melancholy." Draw connections between what you have learned about bipolar disorder and Kenyon's writing process. Create a Power Point presentation to inform your classmates about what you have learned.

---

say that his lover's eyes are gems, meaning that both sparkle and are of great value.

In "Let Evening Come," Kenyon is drawing a metaphoric comparison between evening and impending death. In the evening, people and creatures slow down and stop what they are doing to prepare for rest and sleep. In the poem, rather than literally meaning that the objects and creatures of the farmyard are settling in for a night's sleep, Kenyon is writing about the long sleep of death.

Despite death's participation in the natural cycle of life, it is a frightening proposition. No human has returned from the dead to share the experience, so death remains the largest mystery of human existence. Kenyon soothes herself and her readers in the final stanza, urging herself and her readers to let go and allow the natural course of life and death to occur.

Acceptance

Dylan Thomas, in his famous poem "Do Not Go Gentle into that Good Night," written on the occasion of his father's death, urges readers to fight against the fading light and to never give up. His position on death is far different from Kenyon's in "Let Evening Come."

In stanza two, a woman knits while crickets chirp. (*Phillip Hobbs-Andresen | Shutterstock.com*)

In this poem, Kenyon moves herself and her readers toward acceptance of the inevitability of death. It is not simple resignation, but rather a conscious choice, an acknowledgement that all things in creation must end. In many ways, the poem brings to mind the message of Ecclesiastes 3:1–2: "For everything there is a season, and a time for every matter under heaven. A time to be born, and a time to die."

Only by understanding oneself as a part of a larger natural cycle can an individual come to an acceptance of death as part of life. Just as each sunrise brings with it a sunset, each birth brings with it an inevitable death. Accepting that frees the individual to live life fully, appreciative of all of God's creation.

Comfort

"Let Evening Come" is not only a poem about the acceptance of death, it is also a poem that offers comfort and solace. The images Kenyon creates throughout the poem point readers to a place of letting go. Just as a restful evening provides comfort after a day spent in activity, the ending of life can provide a rest after a life well

lived. It is true that most people fear death, in spite of their faith or belief system. Most people also fear that death will be accompanied by pain. In this short poem, Kenyon's prayer is that evening (or death) will come quietly and swiftly. In the end, she tells the reader, and herself, to have no fear.

The poem offers comfort in two ways to the person who is dying: in the first place, the dying person is reassured and told not to fear. Kenyon believes that God will be with the person as she or he dies. Secondly, the dying person does not need to worry about his or her survivors, since God will support them. Likewise, those who must suffer the loss of a loved one can be comforted by their own faith and the faith of the loved one as he or she meets his or her death.

STYLE

Sound

"Let Evening Come" is a poem filled with alliteration and assonance. Alliteration is the repetition of consonant sounds; assonance is the repetition of internal vowel sounds. The use of these repeated sounds results in a poem that is unified in its sound, its structure, and its theme.

The most-used alliteration in the poem is the consonant sound *l*. Kenyon uses this sound twenty-five times in the poem; given that there are only 124 words in the entire poem, the *l* sound is clearly predominant. There is a long tradition in English for songs used to comfort children and babies to employ the *l* sound. The name given to such songs is lullaby. The point of the songs is to lull a child to sleep. Songs such as the well-known Christmas song "Coventry Carol," which features the phrase "Lully, lullay, thou little tiny child," and features the refrain "by by lully lullay," demonstrate this kind of alliteration. This song is sung to comfort the baby Christ child.

While "Let Evening Come" is not a lullaby per se, it draws on the conventions of the lullaby by its use of alliteration and repetition of words. Further, the poem functions similarly to a lullaby by asking for peace and comfort at the end of the day, and by extension, at the end of one's life.

Kenyon also uses alliteration within each stanza. In stanza 2, for example, she repeats the *k* sound. Because the images in this stanza are of the chirping of a small insect and a lady who begins to knit at the close of the day, the *k* sounds reinforce these images by imitating the sounds that both the insect and the click of the woman's knitting instruments make. The *k* sound also repeats in the first lines of stanza 3, 4, 5, and 6, joining the stanzas.

In stanza 3, Kenyon repeats the sound of the letter *s*. This sound is one associated with quiet, and gentle breezes. In the poem, Kenyon associates the sound with celestial objects as well as with the green ground. In stanza 4, the *s* sounds continue into the first line, joined by *d* sounds that repeat four times in the stanza.

In the final two stanzas, the *l* sounds, the *k* sounds, the *s* sounds and the *d* sounds echo throughout, recalling the sounds that have built throughout the poem, and adding a soft, musical quality that is comforting. Kenyon's use of alliteration is essential for both the aesthetic enjoyment of the poem as well as for thematic unity.

Rhythm

While "Let Evening Come" does not employ a regular meter, such as iambic pentameter (a ten-syllable line comprised of five pairs of unstressed-stressed syllables), the poem is filled with soothing rhythms. Kenyon accomplishes this by using repeating combinations of poetic feet. A poetic foot is an arrangement of two or three syllables with various stressed and unstressed syllable. For example, when broken into syllables and stresses, the word "constantly" could be written CON-stant-ly, and serve as an example of a poetic foot called a dactyl.

Kenyon most commonly uses the anapest, a foot of two unstressed syllables followed by a stressed syllable. A phrase such as "in the late morning sun" is comprised of two anapests: in the LATE morn-ing SUN. Kenyon also commonly uses the iamb, a foot of one unstressed syllable followed by a stressed syllable. For example, Shakespeare's famous line, "But soft, what light through yonder window breaks?" is comprised of five iambs: but SOFT, what LIGHT through YON-der WIN-dow BREAKS? The words "Let Evening Come" could be written thusly: let EVE-ning COME, an example of two iambs.

Kenyon's pattern is not as regular as that used by Shakespeare in the above example, but a pattern *does* emerge when the reader examines the entire poem. Using "DAH" to represent a stressed syllable and "dah" to represent an unstressed syllable, the first stanza of "Let Evening Come" sounds like this:

dah dah DAH dah DAH dah dah DAH

dah dah DAH dah dah DAH dah dah

DAH dah DAH dah dah DAH dah DAH

In this stanza, Kenyon uses six anapests and three iambs. (The end of line 2 carries over to line three to complete the foot.) While Kenyon varies this pattern slightly throughout the poem, she always returns to the anapest, breaking its monotony with an occasional iamb in a rhythmic dance.

In the final stanza, in order to draw attention to the most important phrases in the poem, Kenyon's rhythm shifts:

dah dah DAH dah dah DAH dah DAH

dah dah DAH dah DAH dah DAH dah

DAH dah dah dah DAH DAH dah DAH

Again, there is the anapestic-iambic dance; the last line, however, is the first and only time when a stressed syllable is immediately followed by another stressed syllable. By inserting a small, unstressed word before the final repetition of the title of the poem, Kenyon forces the stress on to the word "let," a word that has not been stressed throughout the poem. She also inserts a slight pause before the word "evening" begins. This, along with the period in the second line, serves to slow the reader down in the last lines of the poem, just as sunset slows down the pace of the day.

HISTORICAL CONTEXT

The United Church of Christ

Kenyon and Hall belonged to the South Danbury Christian Church near their farm in New Hampshire, and this community became an important part of their lives. The South Danbury Christian Church belongs to the United Church of Christ (UCC) denomination, a denomination whose roots go back to the very beginning of American history, particularly in New England. Indeed, churches such as the South Danbury Christian Church can trace their lineage back to Reformation England.

The Protestant Reformation began in 1517 when Martin Luther famously nailed his 95 theses to the door of the Wittenberg Cathedral, protesting a number of Roman Catholic practices. Luther did not intend to start a new church; rather, he wanted to reform the Roman Catholic Church and rid it of practices he saw as ungodly. However, Luther's action started a wave of protests across Europe. Ulrich Zwingli (1484–1531) and John Calvin (1509–1564) joined the call for reform in Switzerland.

Meanwhile, in 1538, Henry VIII of England broke with Rome, establishing the Church of England under the leadership of the Archbishop of Canterbury. This Church, however, was not truly Protestant; it maintained most of the rituals and doctrines associated with the Roman Church. Consequently, reformers in England (who became known as Puritans or Separatists) continued to agitate for a complete reform of the church. The Puritans were often persecuted for their beliefs.

One such group left England for the Netherlands, and they eventually returned to England in preparation for sailing to North America to build their own colony, a place where they could practice their religion without persecution. These were the Pilgrims, who founded the Plymouth Colony in present-day Massachusetts. Some of the churches formed by New England settlers were called Congregationalist Churches in that the government of the church was located within the local congregation, not within some central authority. Congregationalists believed that the leader of each individual congregation was Jesus Christ.

During the early eighteenth and nineteenth centuries, additional denominations grew out of the Protestant roots of the United States. The Christian Church, according to the UCC Web site, opposed denominationalism, calling for the unity of all Christians. Hall's ancestors were founders of the South Danbury Christian Church.

By 1931, the Congregational Church and the Christian Church united to form the Congregational Christian Church, a union that lasted until 1957. In 1957, the Evangelical and Reformed Church joined with the Congregational Christian Church to form the United Church of Christ. The South Danbury Christian Church was part of this merger.

The United Church of Christ, according to the UCC Web site,

> has roots in the 'covenantal' tradition—meaning there is no centralized authority or hierarchy that can impose any doctrine or form of worship on its members. Christ alone is Head of the church. We seek a balance between freedom of conscience and accountability to the apostolic faith. The UCC therefore receives the historic creeds and confessions of our ancestors as testimonies, but not tests of the faith.

In other words, the UCC does not require statements of faith from its members, or adherence to specific creeds, such as required by many denominations. Rather, members and congregations are free to choose their form of worship, and are not held to doctrinal requirements. For Kenyon and Hall, the South Danbury Christian Church offered a place to practice their faith in an inclusive, accepting community.

Puritan Plain Style

From their earliest days on the North American continent, Puritans put pen to paper. The New England colonies in particular developed a strong intellectual life. At the core of Reformation

COMPARE
&
CONTRAST

- **1990s:** Kenyon's various treatments for bipolar disorder include such drugs as Elavil, Ludiomil, Doxepin, Norpramin, Prozac, Lithium, Xanax, Wellbutrin, Parnate, Nardil, and Zoloft, according to her biographer John Timmerman and Kenyon's poem "Having It Out with Melancholy."

  Today: A new range of treatment options exists for bipolar disease. However, a National Institute of Mental Health study in the *New England Journal of Medicine* in 2007 demonstrates that mood stabilizers such as lithium or valproate are more effective when given alone than when paired with antidepressants such as those used by Kenyon.

- **1990s:** According to Roberta McKean-Cowdin, reporting in the *Journal of Clinical Oncology* in 2000, liver cancer increases in mortality and incidence among men and women, increasing 12.3 percent in men and 12.9 percent in women between 1990 and 1995.

  Today: Liver cancer rates continue to increase, according to the Centers for Disease Control. The National Cancer Institute estimates that 24,120 new cases and 18,910 deaths take place in 2010.

- **1990s:** According to McKean-Cowdin, from 1973 through 1991, cancer mortality increases. Beginning in 1991, of the twenty leading cancers, incidence and mortality rates decrease in eleven types of cancer in men, and twelve types of cancer in women, and mortality rates for all cancers decline 2.8 percent in men and 0.4 percent in women.

  Today: The Centers for Disease Control reports that while incidence rates for many cancers decline between 2003 and 2007, leukemia, kidney, pancreas and thyroid cancers, and melanomas of the skin increase during the same period.

- **1990s:** According to the Association of Religion Data Archives, the United Church of Christ has a membership of 1,599,212 in 1990. By 1999, that number drops to 1,401,682.

  Today: Like other mainline Protestant denominations, the United Church of Christ membership continues to decline. In 2008, the Association of Religion Data Archives reports a membership for the United Church of 1,111,691. The 2009 Annual Report of the United Church of Christ notes that the denomination now has 1,080,199 members.

---

theology was the belief that the scriptures held the key to each individual's salvation. Each person must be able to read the scriptures in order to find his or her own way to salvation. This led to translations of the Bible into English. In addition, the advent of the printing press put Bibles into the hands of middle-class people. It is not surprising, then, that literacy was both highly valued and widespread.

Of course, many of the texts produced during the early colonial period in New England were sermons; in addition, however, writers such William Bradford produced history, and Anne Bradstreet and Phyllis Wheatley composed poems.

Edward Taylor and Jonathan Edwards are two other well-known early American writers.

Many of these writers developed a way of writing known as "plain style." In contrast to the ornate and flowery writing popular in England at the time, the Puritan writers produced writing that was plain, intelligent, logically consistent, and natural. Writers chose simple words over complicated ones, Anglo-Saxon over Latinate terms, and straightforward grammar, according to Norman Foerster and his colleagues, the editors of *American Poetry and Prose: Part One: From the Beginnings to 1865.* They also note that the early New England writers looked outward

Stanza three brings nightfall. (*Bill Fehr | Shutterstock.com*)

at the natural world at the same time that they delved inward to explore the inner life of the individual. They were highly self-reflective writers who were also keenly aware of the details of life around them.

Kenyon, living and writing in New England for twenty years, and worshiping in a Congregational setting, absorbed the nuance of the plain style. Her writing reflects both the historical and cultural roots of the Puritan forebears.

CRITICAL OVERVIEW

From her earliest work, Kenyon has enjoyed favorable critical reception. Frequently it has been difficult to separate her reputation from that of her husband, Donald Hall, who is regarded as one of the most distinguished American poets to have emerged during the twentieth century. Since her death, however, Kenyon's stature has continued to grow, and although

her life was entwined with Hall's, she has achieved her own place as an important American poet, enjoying both critical and popular success. Liam Rector notes in the *American Poetry Review* that as of 2004, her volume *Otherwise: New and Selected Poems* (including "Let Evening Come") had sold over 50,000 copies; by 2006, Taylor records in "The Presence of Jane Kenyon" that over 70,000 copies of the volume were in print. Taylor writes that "the posthumous success of her *Otherwise: New and Selected Poems* has few parallels in contemporary poetry."

"Let Evening Come" first appeared in *Harvard Magazine* in 1990, and then in the collection *Let Evening Come* (1990). In reviewing this volume for *Publishers Weekly*, Penny Kaganoff writes that the poems are underscored by "subtle tension masterfully created by Kenyon's exacting language and alternating images of light and ever-encroaching darkness." Kaganoff is not wholly positive in her evaluation, however; she also writes that Kenyon's language occasionally "falls flat." Likewise, David Baker, reviewing the same volume for *Poetry* in 1991, finds the poems of *Let Evening Come*, with few exceptions, to be disappointing in their plainness and brevity.

On the other hand, later reviewers found Kenyon's poetry moving and important. David Barber, writing in the June 1994 edition of *Poetry*, holds that "her planed-downed honesty and clarity are not just virtues, but powers." By 1996, the year after her death, Robert Richman wrote an article in *New Criterion* in which he praises Kenyon as a poet belonging "in the first rank of the poets of her generation." In the same year, Adrian Oktenberg wrote a review of *Otherwise* in the *Women's Review of Books*, in which he proclaims that "Jane Kenyon's achievement is to write powerfully of beauty and sorrow, and at the same time to make both entirely convincing to the skeptical modern reading, who already knows so much."

Moreover, while earlier reviewers found Kenyon's work too brief and too plain spoken, later reviewers such as Sarah Crown, writing in 2005 for the London *Guardian* about the publication of the British edition of *Let Evening Come*, identifies an "undertow of bleakness" in Kenyon's poetry, giving "her work a darker, more complex mood." Constance Merritt, writing in *Prairie Schooner* in 1998, suggests that Kenyon's poems in *Otherwise* are reminiscent of Emily Dickinson, arguing that theme, subject matter and an "intricate equilibrium between evanescence and durability, gravity and grace . . . weds the work of these two poets into a singular tradition." Judith Harris, in her 2000 critical article "Vision, Voice, and Soul-Making in 'Let Evening Come,'" however, finds in the poem an affinity to John Keats, particularly to his poem "To Autumn."

Of all Kenyon's poems, "Let Evening Come" is among her most popular and the most critically acclaimed. As John Felstiner writes in a 2007 article appearing in the *Iowa Review*, "Let Evening Come" is "as fine as it gets in our time." In an article appearing in *Perspectives Journal*, Timmerman offered similar praise:

> Such qualities as these—her earnest searching and at least tenuous answers, her joy in nature and keen eye for every detail that constitutes it, and her polished poetic forms, so condensed and crystalline, that lie luminous on the page like a well-lit entryway for the writer—mark

Jane Kenyon as one of the most significant Christian artists of the latter 20th century.

Perhaps the best way to close a critical appraisal of Kenyon's poetry is through her own words. In an interview with David Bradt appearing in the Winter 1995 edition of *Plum Review*, Kenyon told Bradt:

> The poet's job is to tell the whole truth and nothing but the truth, in such a beautiful way that people cannot live without it; to put into words those feelings we all have that are so deep, so important, and yet so difficult to name. . . . The other job the poet has is to console in the face of the inevitable disintegration of loss and death.

CRITICISM

Diane Andrews Henningfeld

Henningfeld is an emerita professor of English at Adrian College who writes widely for many educational publications. In the following essay, she examines Kenyon's religious background, her love of the natural world, and her creation of prayer in "Let Evening Come."

Many readers approaching "Let Evening Come" for the first time jump to the conclusion that Kenyon wrote the poem with the knowledge of her own impending death from leukemia. Such is not the case; the poem was written during the days when Kenyon and her husband Donald Hall were engaged in a fierce battle against Hall's liver cancer. Kenyon rarely wrote about her own leukemia; as Wesley McNair notes in the *Iowa Review*, "only one poem, 'The Sick Wife,' was written in the months of her fatal illness." Removing "Let Evening Come" from the context of Kenyon's final illness allows readers to ponder it as a poem with a broader purpose, a poem in which Kenyon uses the language of prayer and litany to both ask for and promise peace in the face of growing darkness. In doing so, as Emily Gordon writes in the *Nation*, "Kenyon stretches the limits of her faith—religious, personal and natural."

Kenyon's early religious background, however, was not conducive to her growth in the Christian faith. She often had to stay with her fraternal grandmother at her grandmother's large boardinghouse in Ann Arbor, Michigan. Her grandmother, Dora Baldwin Kenyon, was a devout Methodist. Laban Hill, writing in

> THE POEM IS FAR MORE THAN A SWEET-SOUNDING LULLABY, HOWEVER. 'LET EVENING COME' IS A PRAYER TO GOD, SELF, AND READER, A PRAYER FOR PEACE, HOPE, AND COMFORT AT THE END OF THE DAY AND AT THE END OF LIFE."

American Writers: A Collection of Literary Biographies, notes that Dora Baldwin Kenyon had "dark obsessions with Christ's Second Coming and the end of the world as we know it." Such beliefs instilled fear and dread into the sensitive girl.

In response, Kenyon rejected the religious beliefs of her family. According to John H. Timmerman in his article "In Search of the Great Goodness: The Poetry of Jane Kenyon," "Partly rebellious by nature, and partly aware of her own capacity for wrongdoing, young Jane simply went home and announced that she was done with religion forever."

At the same time, Kenyon developed a love of nature at an early age. She grew up in a rural area outside the city of Ann Arbor, and she felt most at home in the country, attending a one-room schoolhouse and spending much of her time out of doors. Speaking about her childhood in an interview with David Bradt published in the *Plum Review*, Kenyon said, "That's when I fell under the thrall of nature....I fell in love with the natural world when I was a kid, so my poems are full of the natural world." In the natural world, and in her poetry, Kenyon found solace.

When Kenyon moved to Eagle Pond Farm, her husband's ancestral home in New Hampshire, in 1975, she began to rethink her religious beliefs, brought about by their attendance at the South Danbury Christian Church, affiliated with the United Church of Christ. Timmerman relates that Kenyon found herself deeply moved by the minister's sermons, and soon found herself studying the early Christian mystics and the Bible. Thus, the two threads of Kenyon's early life were renewed and reformed through living in the rural New England countryside and growing in community with the South Danbury Church. During her years at Eagle Pond, as Sharon J.

WHAT DO I READ NEXT?

- *Kira-Kira* (2004) by Cynthia Katahoda is a young-adult novel about a Japanese American family struggling through prejudice, terrible working conditions, and the death of the oldest daughter, Lynn, from lymphoma. Told by younger sister Katie, who must care for her sister, the story is set in 1950 in Georgia.

- Roberta Reeder's edition of *The Complete Poems of Anna Akhmatova* (2000) is a respected translation and collection of the Russian poet's work. Kenyon greatly admired Akhmatova and translated twenty-six of her poems.

- *The Best Day, the Worst Day* (2006) by the poet Donald Hall is his memoir of life with his wife, Jane Kenyon, and the impact her illness and death had on him.

- *A Hundred White Daffodils: Essays, the Akhmatova Translations, Newspaper Columns, Notes, Interviews, and One Poem* (1999) is a posthumous collection of Kenyon's miscellaneous writings.

- Mary Oliver's poetry collections *Thirst* (2006) and *Red Bird* (2009) touch on themes of life, death, grief, and consolation. Like Kenyon, Oliver focuses spiritual connection to the natural world.

- *The Invisible Ladder: An Anthology of Contemporary Poetry for Young Readers* (1996), edited by Liz Rosenberg, offers a young-adult introduction to poetry, complete with photographs of the poets and commentary from selected poets about how they became poets. Kenyon's mentor Robert Bly is one of many poets included.

O'Brien writes, "Her poetry reveal[ed] her deepening awareness of the divine, which she continued to find incarnated in the things of this world."

In "Let Evening Come," Kenyon finds the divine incarnated in the everyday objects of a farmyard, and in the cycles of nature. When asked by Bill Moyers in a 1993 interview how she came to write "Let Evening Come," Kenyon responded, "That poem was given to me." When Moyers asked who gave it to her, Kenyon answered, "The muse, the Holy Ghost.... I went upstairs one day with the purpose of writing something redeeming, which is not the way to write, but this just fell out." What "fell out" was a "poem of unusual reverence," notes Judith Harris in "Vision, Voice and Soul-Making in 'Let Evening Come.'"

At the same time, the poem was not only divine in inspiration, it was also a product of human effort, a product of the natural world. Both Keith Taylor, in the *Michigan Quarterly Review*, and Timmerman, in his book *Jane Kenyon: A Literary Life*, reveal the many versions the poem went through before Kenyon arrived at her elegant, luminous, and tightly controlled final draft.

Kenyon's crafting of her words results in an eighteen-line poem, carefully divided into three-line stanzas. In each stanza, she details the mystery of the fading sunlight as it crosses over bales of hay, a garden hoe, and a shed. The voice is calming, lulling, created through the abundance of the *l* sound and through the repetition of the title. The poem is far more than a sweet-sounding lullaby, however. "Let Evening Come" is a prayer to God, self, and reader, a prayer for peace, hope, and comfort at the end of the day and at the end of life.

Harris argues that the poem "is formed by the language of the imperative." Harris here attends to the grammatical structure of the poem. The word "let" that begins the title and is repeated throughout is an example of the imperative mood, the grammatical form one uses in English to make a command. It echoes the words of creation, the words God spoke in the beginning of all time, as recorded in Genesis 1:3: "Let there be light." In addition, Harris asserts, "One of the marked features of [Kenyon's] work is the ordering power of incantation, or repetition, in which details are perfectly noticed."

There are two problems, however, with Harris's reading. In the first place, the use of the imperative suggests that the speaker has the power to create whatever it is that he or she commands. Kenyon has no such power; she can command

neither nature nor God. Evening will come, as it will.

In the second place, although the title phrase is repeated, calling attention to detail as Harris suggests, her use of the word "incantation" seems amiss. Incantation derives from the Latin "incantare," meaning to bewitch, or enchant. Incantation in contemporary English is most commonly used to denote a series of words used in a magical spell. For Kenyon, there is nothing magical about the coming of evening. Evening comes as a part of the natural cycle of the natural world.

Moreover, God does not perform magic and interrupt the natural cycles of God's creation. Nor can one try to conjure up God through magical spells. Rather, the relationship between humans and God is one of covenant, a promise of faithfulness made by God to God's people, and a promise of faithfulness made by God's people to God. That Kenyon would have this understanding of the relationship between God and God's people is underscored by her acceptance of the theology of the United Church of Christ, a denomination with Puritan roots, founded on the notion of covenant.

Thus, while the title phrase can be read neither as command nor incantation, it can be read as a litany. The word "litany" has special meaning in a religious sense, etymologically deriving from the Greek word for entreaty. Rather than a command, a litany is a form of prayer, spoken by clergy and congregation, in supplication, as a petition to God. The ceremonial repetitions in the litany confirm and renew the promises between God and people.

The first five stanzas of the poem serve to remind readers of the loveliness of the natural world, the mystery of space, the cycles of life. The natural rhythms of the world have been set in motion by God, and the litany acknowledges God's power over light and darkness, life and death. The prayer asks not that the natural rhythm of creation be disrupted in order to prolong a single human life, but rather that the human eye, heart, and mind take in the rightness of the natural order.

In her article in *World Literature Today*, Sandra Cookson writes, "Many of the best poems in [*Otherwise*] are lighted by or open out into a surprising and fully earned moment of revelation." The final stanza of "Let Evening

The fox returns to his den at night in stanza four. (*Yanik Chauvin | Shutterstock.com*)

Come" holds just such a revelatory surprise. If the reader has assumed that the preceding five stanzas are in the form of a prayerful petition to God, the final stanza is an abrupt shift. In the final stanza, Kenyon no longer addresses God, but the reader and herself, signaled by the use of the first-person plural pronoun at the end of the second line.

In so doing, Kenyon asks the reader, and herself, to accept the growing darkness as part of a natural cycle, a cycle created by God as a part of a grand plan that includes all of nature: day and night, light and dark, the animate and inanimate, life and death. As John Felstiner writes in the *Iowa Review,* "'Let Evening Come' turns closest to prayer in turning closest to nature." In the mystery of the final moment, Kenyon offers, and takes, solace in nature and in God's presence. As Kenyon eloquently shared with Moyers:

> There are things in this life that we must endure which are all but unendurable, and yet I feel there is a great goodness. Why, when there could have been nothing, is there something?

> This is a great mystery. How, when, there could have been nothing, does it happen that there is love, kindness, beauty?

Source: Diane Andrews Henningfeld, Critical Essay on "Let Evening Come," in *Poetry for Students*, Gale, Cengage Learning, 2012.

Todd F. Davis and Kenneth Womack
In the following excerpt, Davis and Womack contend that Kenyon gracefully blends the theme of mortality with a gratitude for life in her poetry.

...Jane Kenyon's poetry documents what Donald Hall refers to as the "ordinary pleasures" of life in rural New Hampshire—a calf born in November, a trip to the town dump, the wash hanging on the line, a walk with the dog at sunrise, a hay wagon left in a newly mown August field. Yet an ever-present sense of mortality, of finitude, marks this sense of tranquillity. As with the Russian poet Anna Akhmatova—whose verse Kenyon adored, and, with the encouragement of Robert Bly, skillfully translated—Kenyon's poetry insists that we can never escape the truth of our condition: that human existence

" FOR KENYON, THE GRACE THAT REVEALS
ITSELF IN ORDINARY EXPERIENCE OFFERS MOMENTS
OF FORTUNATE RESPITE FROM THE LARGER
TRIBULATIONS OF OUR CONDITION."

consists of change, and, ultimately, that all spiritual and aesthetic experiences, no matter how transcendent, must come to an end. Kenyon discovers in our mortality a form of grace, a kind of redemption inherent in the inescapable movement toward death that may lead into the light, away from the darkness. In "Sick at Summer's End," Kenyon metaphorically depicts this notion as a release from the physical laws of the earth—brought on by an illness that has affected her equilibrium—into a new spiritual realm: "I'm falling upward, nothing to hold me down." In her verse, Kenyon recognizes that the search for an understanding of death does not come easily; such wisdom arrives with a price. By using the "things" of everyday existence, Kenyon achieves some insight into what Galway Kinnell calls, in his poem "Lastness," "the brightness / gathered up of all that went before."

Similar to the poetic achievements of such Deep Image poets as Bly or Kinnell but unique in her conception of the world, Kenyon also struggles with the loss of those whom she loves, as well as with the inevitable prospect of her own death. In the title poem of her posthumously published volume, *Otherwise* (1996), Kenyon employs a rather understated and flat diction in order to illustrate the richness of daily routine. By repeating four times the simple phrase, "It might have been otherwise," in a relatively short, twenty-six line poem, Kenyon transforms the cataloging of such banal activities as eating cereal and walking the dog into moments rife with images of grace. She savors the "sweet milk, ripe, flawless peach"; she reminds herself and the reader that to lay down with one's mate for a nap or to sleep in a bed in a "room with paintings on the walls" is a gift, not an experience to be counted upon or taken for granted. As the poem concludes its meditation on the simple, blessed acts of daily existence, Kenyon draws the reader away from the notion of expecting "another day / just like this day" toward the fact, painful and disturbing as it may be for some, that one day "it will be otherwise." Yet the poem does not lament this certainty. Rather than questioning this aspect of our existence, "Otherwise" urges us toward an ethics of grace, an embrace of the ordinary, blessed activity of life through its insistence that we acknowledge that one day the aesthetic and spiritual trappings of our existence will all come to an end.

In *Love's Knowledge: Essays on Philosophy and Literature* (1990), Martha C. Nussbaum reminds us that such an ethics of grace lies in our acceptance of uncertainty, in our belief in the inevitable risk that faith demands. "You can't aim for grace really," she writes. "It has so little connection, if any, with your efforts and actions. Yet what else can you do?...Faith is never beyond doubt [and] grace can never be assured." Recent insights in contemporary moral philosophy and ethical criticism provide a myriad of valuable insights into this mysterious and intriguing aspect of Kenyon's verse. Comprehending such an ethics of grace requires that we recognize our own mortality and its impact upon the often mundane, yet no less affecting, experiences that mark our workaday lives. An inherent indefinability characterizes the sense of goodness that we glean from such moments. In her important work of moral philosophy, *The Sovereignty of Good* (1970), Iris Murdoch elaborates upon the concept of goodness and the ways in which our personal configurations of it govern human perceptions regarding the relationship between the self and the world. For Murdoch, our mortality allows us to achieve grace and to recognize the goodness in our daily existence. "There is a special link between the concept of Good and the ideas of Death and Chance," Murdoch writes. "A genuine sense of mortality enables us to see virtue as the only thing of worth; and it is impossible to limit and foresee the ways in which it will be required of us." In short, our capacity for experiencing grace requires that we resign ourselves to the uncertainty of our existence; an ethics of grace also demands that we exploit our very mortality as the lens through which we perceive the goodness and beauty that surrounds us, and that may, on some fortunate day, become known to us.

A reading of Kenyon's verse in the context of an ethics of grace reveals her wide-ranging analysis of this phenomenon in her poetry. In addition to providing her with a means for establishing meaningful relationships with thematically similar works by Keats and Akhmatova, the ethical construct of grace affords Kenyon with a mechanism for commenting in her poetry upon both grace's fleeting impact upon our lives and its interconnections with such issues as the nature of faith, the concept of ethical gifts and the act of giving, and the necessary existential boundaries of our own mortality. As Kenyon's verse demonstrates, such instances of grace in the course of our lives provide us with significant moments of moral vision, with opportunities for what Cora Diamond refers to in *The Realistic Spirit: Wittgenstein, Philosophy, and the Mind* (1991) as "moral improvisation." According to Diamond, the moral life—or a "sense of life as lived in a world of wonderful possibilities"—can offer a venue for "adventure and improvisation," for perceiving those chance instances of beauty and reflection with which life occasionally confronts us (313, 316). As Kenyon reveals in her poetry, the value of these moments of "adventure and improvisation" depends entirely upon how completely we avail ourselves of their occurrence. To enjoy their splendor and simplicity, we must engage in the phenomenon that Nussbaum describes as the "active sense of life," the human capacity for participating fully—emotionally, spiritually, and aesthetically—in all that life entails. Viewed from this perspective, life offers the possibility of a "moral achievement, and the well-lived life" becomes itself "a work of literary art" (148).

. . . Kenyon's experiences with grace often manifest themselves as moments of epiphany in her verse. In *Let Evening Come* (1990), Kenyon employs the following lines from William Maxwell as an epigraph: "So strange, life is. Why people do not go around in a continual state of surprise is beyond me." Kenyon's work abounds with epiphanies triggered by the most conventional of acts. "Finding a Long Gray Hair"— included in her first volume, *From Room to Room* (1978)—offers a superb example of Kenyon's capacity for discovering the grace of mortality in the mundane. In this instance, the poet scrubs the wooden floors of the centuries-old farmhouse only to find "a long gray hair / floating in the pail." Easily overlooked, the hair becomes a symbol of the poet's own mortality. If this were all the poet observed, it would serve well enough to remind us of time's encroachment,

the irrevocability of age; yet it would suggest nothing of the potential grace which is part of growing older. Consequently, Kenyon witnesses her life's redemption in this poem through the community of women who also once cleaned this kitchen; in the simple act of scrubbing the floor, she finds herself interconnected with women from other eras who lived in this house, who went through these same motions:

> I scrub the long floorboards
> in the kitchen, repeating
> the motions of other women
> who have lived in this house.

While in other poems Kenyon finds the grace of mortality in her connection to God and her hope for heaven, in "Finding a Long Gray Hair" she displays the ways in which our patterns of living and our shared prospect of dying bring us into human community. The chores of daily living, if nothing else, connect us, and Kenyon concludes the poem by observing in a gray hair floating in a wash bucket her "life added to theirs."

By speaking of the timeless human community that Kenyon embraces in "Finding a Long Gray Hair," we do not wish to suggest that she effects some radical separation between the communion found with others and the communion found with God. To state this issue more precisely, Kenyon actually senses the presence of the Holy Spirit as a life force that binds us all together. Hers is a God of love and comfort, one quite different from her grandmother's. In several collections, Kenyon includes poems of theological debate, mostly with her grandmother. In *Constance*, "The Argument" describes a speaker whose memory is triggered by the woodsmoke of a neighbor's chimney and makes her question whether she is a "Judas" made for some "unquenchable fire." Such a notion comes from her "Grandmother's / vengeful God, the one who disapproves of jeans and shorts for girls, / dancing, strong waters, and adultery." What the poet remembers most, however, are her grandmother's words at the funeral of her Uncle Hazen: "'All things work together for the good / for those who love God.'" As a child, she cannot accept that death might be construed as good, and cries at her grandmother, "'No! NO! How is it good to be dead?'" Again, Kenyon cannot reconcile her understanding of God with her grandmother's; it disturbs her that her grandmother believes in a God who "would come out of the clouds / when they were least expecting him, / choose one to be with him in heaven / and leave the other there alone."

Kenyon's conception of God differs dramatically from her grandmother's, yet, ultimately, God must be seen as the source of the grace that she finds in mortality. As she explains in several poems in *The Boat of Quiet Hours*, the mystery of the Trinity, especially the third person identified with the Holy Ghost, may evade us but it still astounds us, as it did Mary, "by suddenly coming near" ("The Bat"). Kenyon struggles with those who would scoff at her belief. Such a commitment to belief, however, leads her toward an acceptance—fraught with grief and anger at times—of mortality. In "Briefly It Enters, and Briefly Speaks," God becomes "the maker, the lover, and the keeper"; the "food on the prisoner's plate"; the "water rushing to the well-head / filling the pitcher until it spills"; "the longest hair, white / before the rest"; and "the one whose love / overcomes you, already with you / when you think to call my name." It is this God—despite the ever-present fact that "the day comes at last, / and the men struggle with the casket / just clearing the pews" ("The Pond at Dusk")—who offers Kenyon comfort, who brings her grace so that she may say,

> Let it come, as it will, and don't
> be afraid. God does not leave us
> comfortless, so let evening come.
> ("Let Evening Come")

In this way, Kenyon's triumphant words remind us of the ethics of grace and the comfort and meaning that it brings to our lives.

For Kenyon, the grace that reveals itself in ordinary experience offers moments of fortunate respite from the larger tribulations of our condition. Such instances also provide us with a means for enjoying grace and for recognizing the revitalizing power of the human spirit. In *Metaphysics as a Guide to Morals* (1993), Murdoch laments "the loss of the particular, the loss of the contingent, [and] the loss of the individual" so vital to our conceptions of the self and the ways in which we approach the world. Murdoch comprehends the uncertainty and mystery inherent in human experience: "The life of morality and truth exists," she writes, "within an irreducible incompleteness" (490). In her poetry, Kenyon affords us with a glimpse into the moments of grace and simplicity that characterize

> "'LET EVENING COME' IS FORMED BY THE LANGUAGE OF IMPERATIVE, A POEM THAT URGES THE READER TO PAY ATTENTION."

the most profound aspects of our experience. Whether musing about faith, the act of giving, or her own mortality, Kenyon challenges us to observe the ethics of grace that exists in our own lives.

Source: Todd F. Davis and Kenneth Womack, excerpt from *Bright Unequivocal Eye: Poems, Papers, and Remembrances from the First Jane Kenyon Conference*, edited by Bert G. Hornback, Peter Lang, 2000, pp. 87–97.

Judith Harris

In the following essay, Harris lauds the serenity in the face of an inevitable death, and the calm assurances of solace in Kenyon's poem "Let Evening Come."

... In "Let Evening Come," Kenyon begins with the motion of sunlight, suggesting a balance of upward and downward, rising and falling:

> Let the light of late afternoon
> shine through chinks in the barn, moving
> up the bales as the sun moves down.

Sunlight is seen so indirectly, as a belated influence on what has already been nourished by it. From the poet's point of view, the bales no longer initiate sunlight, yet sunlight is so resplendent in the barn it pleases the poet's eye, her pre-existing need for beauty. Sunlight is therefore worthy of praise. We should bear in mind that in this beginning stanza, we, as readers are situated very close up, although the agency of light is as distant as it could be. In the next stanza, there is activity, work, labor that consumes time in the day, as the poet writes:

> Let the cricket take up chafing
> as a woman takes up her needles
> and her yarn. Let evening come.

The cricket chafes as the woman scrapes the needles of her yarn. *All* is process, and all is interrelated. The poet is compelled by the last remnants of time before its darkening, when it is transfigured into something else, something yet to be named. Accepting the evening's coming, Kenyon warns us against exhausting ourselves trying to save what can't be saved because it is already subject to mutability. Although darkness will come, and the poet's vision will be eclipsed, the objects themselves remain. There is always something of this world left in any other. Here is an axis of faith:

> Let the dew collect on the hoe abandoned
> in the long grass. Let the stars appear
> and the moon disclose its silver horn.

Each stanza in the poem begins with the verb "let," as if to convey acceptance of the inevitable or to permit in a specified manner, or to release from confinement. But "let" also suggests the idea of leaving something unfinished or undone. The present moment demands the subsequent moment to continue or complete it. With time, Kenyon advises, things (like the juice of the apple) age and transform into a different form or taste; even the body decays and finds its way into dust. In the next two stanzas, Kenyon makes us even more aware of the lassitude of the day's ebbing energies and the need for rest. Rest is essential even if it will only contribute to more labor. "The dew collects on the hoe," and then every thing accounted for is equally at rest or emptied by loss, light, or lack. Yet in Kenyon's accounting for objects that become empty ("the sandy den," the wind that retires, the shed that goes black), she also anticipates that which would fill them:

> Let the fox go back to its sandy den.
> Let the wind die down. Let the shed
> go black inside. Let evening come.
> To the bottle in the ditch, to the scoop
> in the oats, to air in the lung
> let evening come.

Between these two stanzas there is a significant change in perspective. From the positioning of the one who yields to something forthcoming, we shift to the object which receives the allotment of some kind of sustenance. The body is filled by the soul as the soul is emptied of the body. In the absence of one, there is the presence of the other. The same is true of the word: it is simultaneously the absence and presence of the thing it signifies. Whether God exists or not, the need for comfort in approaching death makes God necessary to the poem, just as the oats are necessary to the scoop, the den to the fox, and air to the lung. The poet's vision is a synthesizer of things, an interpreter of an otherwise incoherent language that marks itself on both the world and the page.

Like the still life painter, Kenyon persists in finding the rightness of placed things by continuing to arrange and compose objects in space while rendering those objects through the mediation of an art-language. Each object defined and sanctified in nature appears to be the manifestation of the poet's thought, and this thought unifies human thought with God's intention. There is a compositional rightness of things placed in the position in which they were intended.

What Kenyon discovers in closer scrutiny of these objects is their aesthetic quality, that which is not subject to mutability or decay. Yet the poet is ambivalent:—in pursuit of transcendent beauty which would supersede the sensual, she seems unable or unwilling to sacrifice the sensuality that includes the cost of temporal process. Imagination, as Keats maintained, is a prefiguration of the transcendent realm, and our love of *sensual* beauty in this world is (for the believer) a realm that follows and in which life originates. Evening is always another sudden afterlife, comprised of all the light and darkness that has come before and after it.

"Let Evening Come" is formed by the language of imperative, a poem that urges the reader to pay attention. The speaker is telling herself what she has to do, which is to do nothing, to give up all resistance to what one can't control in language or process. The same is true of the reader who yields to what the writer has placed before him or her. At a certain point, the poem is a fate that encloses the participant within. Indeed, we are watching and listening to Kenyon watching and listening, but to what? It is both her voice, and not her voice. It is the comfort we give ourselves in believing that there is a voice we do not yet know, which nevertheless speaks as God does, and reaches deep from within us.

Kenyon's powers of incantation were a combined achievement of poetry and prayer. One of the marked features of her work is the ordering power of incantation, or repetition, in which details are perfectly noticed. There is survival power in the ability to repeat one's self, a formal power in incantation that sets itself against enormous resistance. The poetic self becomes permeable and is able to pass into the world that might otherwise destroy it.

A poem of unusual reverence, "Let Evening Come" is written in the manner of the psalm, which praises God. In fact, the text resembles the Old Testament psalm, "Lord of the World." Both praise God's omniscience in the world as a comfort in distressful times; God is important not only to the soul but to the suffering body that, in soul-making, creates the soul: "My soul I give unto his care / Asleep, awake, for He is near, / And with my soul, my body too / God is with me, I have no fear." Compare these with the closing lines of "Let Evening Come":

> Let it come as it will, and don't
> be afraid. God does not leave us
> comfortless, so let evening come.

The adjective "so" works here to amplify the factual nature of the assertions made in previous stanzas. *Because* of the reasons given above (the ordering of apparently arbitrary or disconnected phenomena), the speaker contends there is sufficient proof that God does not leave us without a purpose supportive of our living or our dying. The evening, like the morning, has its own kind of naturalization, its own means of individuation. The same is true of the poet's language now invested in the things of which it is conscious. Attention turns to intention. Language not only acknowledges, but illuminates the mysterious object Kenyon seems to say, *let evening come*, by fully accepting what will be handed over to it. Objects of the world, first owned and then dispossessed, are sloughed off, as the body is sloughed off by the soul that has been incarnated by it.

In one of Keats' famous letters, he discusses how the poet should use the world as a means of "Soul-Making." Out of a life of pain and sorrows, one makes a soul. The soul does not so much bear one's sorrow or grief as it is born from sorrow and grief. The soul is what slips through the felt-experience of pain or anguish. It accrues value as the person who suffers begins to give up, piece by piece, attachments to temporal things.

We can assume that Kenyon was familiar with Keats' axiom. Her writing is full of references to both the letters and the poetry. According to Donald Hall, in a letter, Kenyon's study of Keats was painstaking and perennial. He recalls that Kenyon spent two years absorbed in her study of Keats—the poems, the letters, the biographies. "Let Evening Come" captures the essence of Keats' Soul-Making, a process of necessary pain and annihilation, not only informed by sorrow but actually constituted by it.

As is true of Keats' "To Autumn," Kenyon's sense of natural order in "Let Evening Come" quickens the pace of the drowsed poet who, like Keats' gleaner (the personified Autumn in the ode), reminds us we must gather what has just ripened on the vine. Sometimes, the beauty of natural process overcomes and oversaturates our senses, so much so that we embrace beauty even in the shadow of approaching death. For Kenyon, this perception of beauty sensed in the physical world was both ideal and eternal. Although the poem itself embodies natural process and growth, it also uses its praise of things in language as a means of preserving reverence and meaning.

Within the framework of "Let Evening Come," the poet's attention is drawn by the things of this world; but it is equally drawn by the nouns that name them. Words will eventually outlast things, merely in the act of the poet's saying them. For it is only the word, or the name, that survives natural process and decay. The poet's word, properly handled, is a ghostly presence that returns even after it has expired, something that mortal bodies cannot do.

Like Keats, Kenyon was well aware of the stages one goes through in leaving earthly attachments behind. In mourning, Freud reminds us that we must give up connections to lost objects and accept substitutes in their place. The only substitute available to the poet, as to the mourner, is more often than not language itself, in which the poet takes refuge. But words are always in some sense without the things they stand for. Appropriately, Hall's long elegy to Kenyon is entitled *Without*. These poems, for and to Kenyon, become a realm where what is fading is still present; and yet, at the same time, these fading presences are pieces of the evidence of what is always missing, what we are always "without."

But in the poem "Let Evening Come," poetic identity and self-division are not the issue—faith is: faith in something solidly beyond the pained self that can in fact support it. "Let Evening Come" is a companion to Keats' "To Autumn," an ode about acquiescence to and acceptance of death. Both poems bring together oppositional states of fertility and decay. Both poems are about lingering at the last "oozings" of the cider press, hours by hours. But Kenyon's voice helps her to listen to the words that console her, the words that persuade her of God's nearness even in moments of self-desertion. Keats' consolation was not part of the immediate drama of the poem, but rather underneath the scenic display of autumnal activities.

Kenyon's cyclical return to the essence of the word "evening" as something that will come not once but for eternity, enclosing within itself all of the evenings that have come and gone, at last gives her a sense of rightness and equilibrium. All things will come in time; the fruit falls propitiously, when it ripens. This is ultimately the rightness of placed things, when the poet knows there is nothing to be gained from moving them into yet another position. No one will miss the simple but profound meaning of this psalm-like poem, no one will fail to miss the message of comfort Kenyon so eloquently inspirited within it.

For consolation, Kenyon sought in the origins of language itself the possibility of God's support. This is nowhere more evident than in the poem, "Let Evening Come." In Kenyon's work, we can and do hope for something more than a physical existence in the world. "God *does* not leave us comfortless" writes Kenyon, not God *would* not or *will* not leave us comfortless. This simple verb, the "non-conditional," may well persuade us that Kenyon herself was eventually consoled by her voice and her vision. She would have to align herself, as she saw Keats did, with those powers through which she affirmed her life as part of an ongoing process of Soul-Making.

Source: Judith Harris, "Vision, Voice, and Soul-Making in 'Let Evening Come,'" in *Bright Unequivocal Eye: Poems, Papers, and Remembrances from the First Jane Kenyon Conference*, edited by Bert G. Hornback, Peter Lang, 2000, pp. 63–68.

SOURCES

Baker, David, "Culture, Inclusion, Craft," in *Poetry Criticism*, edited by Lawrence J. Trudeau, Vol. 57, Thomson Gale, 2004; originally published in *Poetry*, Vol. 158, No. 3, June 1991, pp. 161–64.

Barber, David, Review of *Constance*, in *Poetry Criticism*, edited by Janet Witalec, Vol. 56, Thomson Gale, 2004; originally published in *Poetry*, Vol. 164, No. 3, June 1994, pp. 161–64.

Bradt, David, "Jane Kenyon: An Interview," in *Poetry Criticism*, edited by Lawrence J. Trudeau, Vol. 57, Thomson Gale, 2004; originally published in *Plum Review*, Vol. 10, Winter 1995, pp. 115–28.

Cookson, Sandra, Review of *Otherwise: New and Selected Poems*, in *World Literature Today*, Vol. 71, No. 2, Spring 1997, p. 390.

Crown, Sarah, Review of *Let Evening Come*, in *Guardian* (London, England), October 8, 2005, p. 18.

Duin, Julia, "Just In: Latest Church Statistics," in *Washington Times*, February 12, 2010, http://www.washington times.com/weblogs/belief-blog/2010/feb/12/latest-church-growth-stats-in/ (accessed April 18, 2011).

Felstiner, John, "'Kicking the Leaves': Donald Hall and Jane Kenyon at Eagle Pond Farm," in *Iowa Review*, Vol. 37, No. 1, Spring 2007, pp. 54–64.

Foerster, Norman, "The Colonial Period," in *American Poetry and Prose: Part One from the Beginnings to 1865*, Houghton Mifflin, 1970, pp. 3–10.

Gordon, Emily, "Above an Abyss," in *Poetry Criticism*, edited by Lawrence J. Trudeau, Vol. 57, Thomson Gale, 2004; originally published in *Nation*, Vol. 262, No. 17, April 29, 1996, pp. 29–30.

Hall, Donald, "Afterword," in *Otherwise: New and Selected Poems*, by Jane Kenyon, Graywolf Press, 1996, pp. 217–20.

Harris, Judith, "Vision, Voice, and Soul-Making in 'Let Evening Come,'" in *Poetry Criticism*, edited by Lawrence J. Trudeau, Vol. 57, Thomson Gale, 2004; originally published in *Bright Unequivocal Eye: Poems, Papers, and Remembrances from the First Jane Kenyon Conference*, edited by Bert G. Hornback, Peter Lang, 2000, pp. 63–68.

Hill, Laban, "Jane Kenyon," in *American Writers, Supplement VII, A Collection of Literary Biographies*, edited by Jay Parini, Charles Scribner's Sons, 2001, pp. 113–44.

"Jane Kenyon," in *Poetry Foundation*, www.poetryfoundation.org/bio/jane-kenyon (accessed March 18, 2011).

Kaganoff, Peggy, Review of *Let Evening Come*, in *Publishers Weekly*, Vol. 237, No. 13, March 30, 1990, p. 56.

Kenyon, Jane, "Childhood, When You Are in It," in *A Hundred White Daffodils*, Graywolf Press, 1999, pp. 61–76.

———, "Let Evening Come," in *Otherwise: New and Selected Poems*, Graywolf Press, 1996, p. 176.

———, "Having It Out with Melancholy," in *Otherwise: New and Selected Poems*, Graywolf Press, 1996, pp. 189–93.

Latimer, Robin M., "Jane Kenyon," in *Dictionary of Literary Biography*, Vol. 120, *American Poets since World War II, Third Series*, edited by R. S. Gwynn, Gale Research, 1992, pp. 172–75.

"Liver Cancer," in *National Cancer Institute*, 2010, http://www.cancer.gov/cancertopics/types/liver (accessed April 19, 2011).

"Many Cancer Rates Continue to Decline," in *Centers for Disease Control and Prevention*, April 12, 2011, http://www.cdc.gov/Features/dsCancerAnnualReport (accessed April 18, 2011).

Merritt, Constance, Review of *Otherwise: New and Selected Poems*, in *Poetry Criticism*, edited by Lawrence J. Trudeau, Vol. 57, Thomson Gale, 2004; originally published in *Prairie Schooner*, Vol. 72, No. 1, Spring 1998, pp. 171–76.

McKean-Cowdin, Roberta, et al., "Declining Cancer Rates in the 1990s," in *Journal of Clinical Oncology*, Vol. 18, No. 11, June 2000, pp. 2258–68.

McNair, Welsey, "A Government of Two," in *Poetry Criticism*, edited by Lawrence J. Trudeau, Vol. 57, Thomson Gale, 2004; originally published in *Iowa Review*, Vol. 28, No. 1, Spring 1998, pp. 59–71.

Moyers, Bill, "An Interview with Bill Moyers," in *A Hundred White Daffodils*, Graywolf Press, 1999, pp. 145–71.

O'Brien, Sharon J., "Jane Kenyon," in *Notable American Women: A Biographical Dictionary*, edited by Susan Ware and Stacy Lorraine Braukman, Harvard University Press, 2004, pp. 341–42.

Oktenberg, Adrian, Review of *Otherwise: New and Selected Poems*, in *Women's Review of Books*, Vol. 13, No. 10–11, July 1996, p. 27.

Rector, Liam, "Remembering Jane Kenyon," in *American Poetry Review*, Vol. 33, No. 6, November/December 2004, pp. 57–58.

Richman, Robert, "Luminous Particulars," in *Poetry Criticism*, edited by Lawrence J. Trudeau, Vol. 57, Thomson Gale, 2004; originally published in *New Criterion*, Vol. 14, No. 9, May 1996, pp. 76–80.

"Short Course in the History of the United Church of Christ," in *United Church of Christ*, http://www.ucc.org/about-us/short-course/the-congregational-christian.html (accessed April 19, 2011).

Taylor, Keith, "The Presence of Jane Kenyon," in *Michigan Quarterly Review*, Vol. 45, No. 4, Fall 2006, pp. 702–712.

Thomas, Dylan, "Do Not Go Gentle into That Good Night," in *Poets.org*, www.poets.org/viewmedia.php/prmMID/15377 (accessed April 27, 2011).

Timmerman, John H., "In Search of the Great Goodness: The Poetry of Jane Kenyon," in *Perspectives Journal*, May 2003, www.rca.org/page.aspx?pid = 3204 (accessed April 15, 2011).

———, *Jane Kenyon: A Literary Life*, William B. Eerdman, 2002, pp. 1–24, 136–44, 173–78.

"U.S. Membership Report: Denomination Groups, 2000," in *Association of Religion Data Archives*, http://www.thearda.com (accessed April 18, 2011).

"What Medications Are Used to Treat Bi-Polar Disorder?" in *National Institute of Mental Health*, September 28, 2010, http://www.nimh.nih.gov/health/publications/mental-health-medications/complete-index.shtml#p ub6 (accessed April 18, 2011).

FURTHER READING

Hall, Donald, *Without*, Mariner Books, 1999.
Hall writes movingly of his grief and love for his late wife in this volume of poetry written soon after her death.

Kenyon, Jane, *Collected Poems*, Graywolf Press, 2005.
Kenyon's first four books are included in their entirety in this collection, along with the poems of *Otherwise* and four previously uncollected poems, among other items.

Peseroff, Joyce, ed., *Simply Lasting: Writers on Jane Kenyon*, Graywolf Press, 2005.
This book includes personal reminiscences of Kenyon by other writers as well as reviews of her books, critical and personal essays, and letters.

Styron, William, *Darkness Visible*, Vintage, 1992.
Novelist William Styron describes his own descent into depression in this well-written but painful memoir.

SUGGESTED SEARCH TERMS

Jane Kenyon

Donald Hall

Let Evening Come AND Jane Kenyon

Otherwise: New and Selected Poems

death AND faith

nature AND religion

bipolar disorder

Jane Kenyon AND lyric poetry

Jane Kenyon AND Eagle Pond Farm

Jane Kenyon AND Anna Akhmatova

Jane Kenyon AND plain style

United Church of Christ

Puritan AND plain style

acceptance of death

comfort AND prayer

litany

Let Evening Come

The Listeners

WALTER DE LA MARE

1912

The early-twentieth-century British author Walter de la Mare is acclaimed for stirring, mesmerizing poems—such as "The Listeners"—that seem to hurl the reader to distant, unfamiliar places, perhaps untold centuries into the past or perhaps deep into the subconscious dreamscapes of the reader's own mind. De la Mare led a contented but unexceptional life, rarely leaving the shores of Great Britain other than to lecture in the United States. Perhaps this bounded existence, though, was what allowed him to retain a childlike appreciation for the world throughout his life and inspired him to devote his poetic gifts to exploring the hidden, spiritual spaces in the human heart.

"The Listeners" is de la Mare's most famous, most widely anthologized poem, and it was a favorite recitation assignment among British schoolteachers for decades. The poem was lent a heightened degree of mortal significance when the English novelist and poet Thomas Hardy, on his deathbed in 1926, asked his wife to read him three poems before he passed away, the first being "The Listeners." In the poem, a dutiful traveler has arrived on horseback at an old castle or château that seems deserted and feels haunted by lingering specters that listen but never reply to the traveller's knocks and appeals. The poem first appeared in *The Listeners, and Other Poems* (1912) and is also included in de la Mare's *Collected Poems, 1901–1918*, Vol. 1 (1920).

Walter de la Mare (*The Library of Congress*)

AUTHOR BIOGRAPHY

De la Mare was born in the village of Charlton, Kent County, England, on April 25, 1873. His father, already sixty-two when Walter was born, died when he was four, so de la Mare was raised solely by his Scottish mother, Lucy Sophia, to whom he was deeply devoted and who read him many nursery rhymes and fairy tales. The name Lucy appears frequently in his poetry. After the father's death, the family left the idyllic village life for London, and de la Mare began his education at the choir school of St. Paul's Cathedral. The school and choir were extremely demanding, with seven days a week filled with studies, practice, and performance, leaving only an hour of free time each day. At the age of sixteen, de la Mare founded and edited St. Paul's *Choristers' Journal*, printing nine issues—with the contributions probably written mostly by himself—in 1889 and 1890. He gained employment as a bookkeeper in the London office of the Anglo-American Oil Company, where he would work for almost twenty years. Meanwhile, he wrote in his spare time, publishing his first story, "Kismet," in the *Sketch* in 1895. He also published in the *Cornhill*, the *Pall Mall Gazette*, and *Black and White*, all under the

pseudonym Walter Ramal. In 1899 he married Constance Igpen, with whom he would have four children. He published his first volume of poems, *Songs of Childhood*, in 1902. He finally used his real name in publishing his first work of prose fiction, *Henry Brocken*, in 1904.

In 1908, when a pension from the British government in the amount of one hundred pounds yearly enabled him to retire from his office job, the thirty-six-year-old de la Mare could at last devote himself full time to writing. His reputation remained minor at first, even with the publication of what would be his most famous children's story, *The Three Mulla-Mulgars* (now known as *The Three Royal Monkeys*), in 1910. But with the publication of *The Listeners, and Other Poems* in 1912 and the inviting children's verse of *Peacock Pie* in 1913, de la Mare became a household name. From then on he wrote and published regularly, contributing to magazines and journals as well as producing his own novels, children's stories, and poetry collections for all ages. Revealing many of the facets of life he found particularly fascinating, in 1939 a unique anthology—a mix of poetry and prose with an expansively contemplative hundred-page introduction, *Behold, This Dreamer! Of Reverie, Night, Sleep, Dream, Love-Dreams, Nightmare, Death, the Unconscious, the Imagination, Divination, the Artist, and Kindred Subjects*—was published. In 1946, at the age of seventy-three, reusing the label of the hero from "The Listeners," he presented the story of a man's fatal endeavor to cross a desert plain on a faithful white horse in his long poem *The Traveller*. De la Mare was inducted into the British Commonwealth's Order of the Companions of Honor in 1948 and into the Order of Merit in 1953. He died at his home in Twickenham, England, on June 22, 1956.

POEM TEXT

'Is there anybody there?' said the Traveller,
  Knocking on the moonlit door;
And his horse in the silence champed the grasses
  Of the forest's ferny floor:
And a bird flew up out of the turret,   5
  Above the Traveller's head:
And he smote upon the door again a second time;
  'Is there anybody there?' he said.
But no one descended to the Traveller;
  No head from the leaf-fringed sill   10

Leaned over and looked into his grey eyes,
    Where he stood perplexed and still.
But only a host of phantom listeners
    That dwelt in the lone house then
Stood listening in the quiet of the moonlight   15
    To that voice from the world of men:
Stood thronging the faint moonbeams on the
    dark stair,
    That goes down to the empty hall,
Hearkening in an air stirred and shaken
    By the lonely Traveller's call.   20
And he felt in his heart their strangeness,
    Their stillness answering his cry,
While his horse moved, cropping the dark turf,
    'Neath the starred and leafy sky;
For he suddenly smote on the door, even   25
    Louder, and lifted his head:—
'Tell them I came, and no one answered,
    That I kept my word,' he said.
Never the least stir made the listeners,
    Though every word he spake   30
Fell echoing through the shadowiness of the
    still house
    From the one man left awake:
Ay, they heard his foot upon the stirrup,
    And the sound of iron on stone,
And how the silence surged softly backward,   35
    When the plunging hoofs were gone.

POEM SUMMARY

The text used for this summary is from *The Listeners, and Other Poems*, Henry Holt, 1916, pp. 64–65. Versions of the poem can be found on the following Web pages: http://www.poetryoutloud.org/poems/poem.html?id = 177007 and http://www.poetry-archive.com/m/the_listeners.html.

Lines 1–8
The lines of "The Listeners," though not broken into stanzas, are arranged in couplets (sets of two) and further grouped into quatrains (sets of four). The first line of each couplet usually ends in no punctuation or a comma, while each couplet's second line, which is indented, usually ends in a colon, semicolon, or period. Odd-numbered lines do not rhyme, while even-numbered lines rhyme within each quatrain—line 2 rhymes with line 4, line 6 with line 8, and so forth.

The first line introduces the Traveller (note that the British spelling is used). The capitalization of the word gives it the status of a name or title. He is knocking on a door in the nighttime, asking if anyone is there, as the moon shines on the scene. The man's horse, perhaps tied to a tree

MEDIA ADAPTATIONS

- Anna Larson composed a musical setting of de la Mare's poem "The Listeners." It was published in 1984 by Arsis Press as *The Listeners: For Medium Low Voice and Piano*.

or waiting loyally untethered, can be heard eating the grass that grows on the fern-covered forest ground. A bird flies up from a small tower, in wording that suggests that the man is at the door of a castle-like structure or château. He knocks again and repeats his question.

Lines 9–20
Line 9 notes that nobody comes down to the door to respond to the Traveller's knocks and calls. Above him, there is a windowsill that is bordered by leaves, perhaps ivy or some other climbing plant. But no one leans over that windowsill to respond to him. If someone had, that person would have witnessed the Traveller's gray eyes and his confusion and stillness. The narrator notes in line 13 that only phantoms stand present at that isolated house to hear the human Traveller's words. They cluster in the moonlight on a stairway that descends to a deserted hall (perhaps the entryway). The long-unmoving air has been disturbed and agitated by the Traveller's voice.

Lines 21–28
Line 21 returns from the listeners' perspective to the Traveller's perspective—and the reader may note that the sections devoted to the different perspectives are contained within quatrains and thus slightly separated from each other by the rhyme scheme. Here, the Traveller gets a visceral or emotional sense of the alien nature of whoever or whatever might be there listening but not responding. The horse, moving about and eating the grass, is again heard. Overhead, the starry sky is screened by the leaves of the canopy of branches. The Traveller strikes the door a third time, louder now, and raises his head, giving his voice greater resonance. He asks whoever is

listening to tell those he came to see that he visited as promised but was given no reply.

Lines 29–36
The listeners never move in response to the Traveller's visit, despite his words' echoing around throughout the shadowy domicile. Indeed, with regard to the present scene, at least, the Traveller is the only person who remains awake. The Traveller's departure is heard rather than seen, as he mounts his horse and as the horse's iron-shod hooves strike the stone paving. When the sound of the Traveller's horse disappears into the distance, the quiet atmosphere from before their arrival eases back into place.

THEMES

Stillness and Silence
In the absence of a definitive conception of what the circumstances of "The Listeners" signify—and the details are so few as to make any notions about its meaning no more than conjecture—the aesthetic and emotional aspects of the poem are foregrounded. What de la Mare stresses above all, and thus imparts to the reader above all, is the eerie stillness that pervades the scene. The house, with its phantoms that stand waiting but never stir, is the center of the stillness, which proves so powerful or infectious that the Traveller himself is unable to speak for what seems a long time through the middle of the poem.

Lack of motion is accompanied by lack of sound. The silence is broken only by the Traveller's words and knocks, the horse's eating, and the bird flying up. These individual actions occur in distinct, separated moments, so that the sounds serve to accentuate the silence as much as they disturb it; this sense is established in lines 2 and 3, where the descriptions of the Traveller's knock and the horse's eating are separated by a mention of the quiet of the scene. Similarly, a line that describes only the ground of the forest, and no noise or motion, precedes the mention of the bird in line 5. Thereafter, nothing but the man and horse moves or makes noise.

In the end, the most disruptive sound, the clip-clop of the horse galloping away, is immediately eclipsed by a final mention of the perfect silence that returns as the horse and rider disappear. In that de la Mare so effectively evokes a profound sense of stillness and silence while the poem's content otherwise defies thematic analysis, what are essentially aspects of the tone can be regarded as primary themes.

Nothingness
While the visceral sense evoked by the poem is one of stillness, the corresponding emotional sense is one of absence or nothingness. The Traveller evidently expected to find someone at the château he is visiting, in accordance with a pledge he once made, but he receives no reply. Nonetheless, the poet, a narrator with a privileged view of the scene, assures the reader that phantoms are present, specters or ghosts whom the Traveller indeed feels to be there, not with his senses but with his heart. Now, the reader may not believe in phantoms or ghosts, perhaps favoring psychic or scientific explanations for any and all paranormal activity. From this point of view, the Traveller could be said to merely imagine these phantoms, whose existence the poet then records as true. But even the reader who does not believe in ghosts is spurred to visualize the phantoms through the descriptions first of what nobody is actually doing—coming down to the door or leaning out the window—and second of what the phantoms are said to be doing and where: they almost exclusively stand around and, of course, listen.

Frederick L. Gwynn and Ralph W. Condee pinpoint the relevance of this imagery in their 1954 *Explicator* essay, remarking, "The ghostly quality of the poem derives mainly from its capacity to personify nothingness." This notion is echoed by A. E. Dyson in an analysis of the poem in the *Critical Quarterly*: "Nothingness itself comes near to incarnation." Dyson further notes, "In de la Mare, loneliness is defined against nothing: indeed, it relates to the perennial human awareness of nothing, which underlies our particular histories often tingeing them with a sense of the unreal, and may be deeper even than a sense of the tragic." In "The Listeners," in terms of living beings, no one but the Traveller is there; the castle or château is empty. But the absence of living beings, the nothingness, is palpable as an eerie, commanding presence.

STYLE

Cryptic Dreamscape
With its vague and cryptic scenario, "The Listeners" lures the reader into positing an interpretation of the significance, both literal and symbolic,

TOPICS FOR FURTHER STUDY

- Select five poems from one of de la Mare's volumes intended specifically for children, such as *Peacock Pie* (1913). In an essay, for each poem, provide a detailed analysis of the content, tone, rhyme, and meter. Then explain what makes the poem particularly suitable for children and, drawing on your own reactions, remark upon whether and why older readers might also appreciate the poem. In concluding, discuss de la Mare's general strengths as a poet for children as shown in the selected poems.

- For several days, try to recall your dreams upon waking up in the morning, and record any that are especially interesting, strange, or deeply felt. Select one of these episodes—which may be quite brief, as the episode in "The Listeners" is—to present in the form of a poem of at least thirty lines. (If your dream memories prove elusive, you may add details later.) Your poem, like de la Mare's, should have some sort of rhyme structure and at least a loose meter—a repeating pattern of stressed and unstressed syllables. You may choose to use either a third-person (referring to yourself as "he" or "she") or a first-person (referring to yourself as "I") perspective.

- Write out the entirety of "The Listeners" using musical notation: decide on a time signature, standardize the number of measures per line, use notes of varying lengths to represent each spoken syllable, and introduce rests where appropriate. You may choose to use only two different pitches, representing stressed and unstressed syllables; three or four different pitches, to represent varying levels of stress on syllables; or as many as you like, fully rendering the poem as a piece of music. Then, either record yourself playing this composition on any instrument you choose or input the composition into a computer application that will play the tune for you. Finally, demonstrate how well your composition fits the poem by reading "The Listeners" aloud while playing back the recording, matching the syllables and notes.

- Create a comparative biographical study focusing on de la Mare and one of the following American writers: Henry David Thoreau, Robert Frost, or Walt Whitman. Compare and contrast how the men's lives were shaped by their experiences, and discuss how their worldviews are reflected in their literary output. Use excerpts from their works and present your findings as an essay or a multimedia presentation or a Web page.

---

of the Traveller's peculiar visit, and various commentators have leaned toward various interpretations. As noted by Gwynn and Condee in their *Explicator* essay, referring to correspondence appearing in that journal in the 1940s, "Readers have seen the Traveler as God, Christ, the Holy Ghost, *a* ghost, Man, *a* man, or Walter de la Mare; the listeners have been made to stand for the powers of darkness, the riddle of life, the dead, a living household, Man, or de la Mare's schoolmates." Thinking philosophically, Dyson observes, "As symbolism, the setting has all the material for an exploration of the meaning of existence itself." The question posed by the Traveller in the first line is one that almost everyone has spoken at one time or another; no matter how exotic the setting may be, the reader can undoubtedly relate to the experience of asking a question of the universe but receiving no reply. Gwynn and Condee go so far as to deny the characters any symbolism at all, in view of their vagueness, and assert that they exist purely for the poetic effect produced by the scenario: "The listeners are not an allegorical symbol but simply the poetic personification of the silence which the human being finds and leaves at the house."

The poem begins with the traveller knocking on a door. *(Felix Mizioznikov / Shutterstock.com)*

Between the extremes of choosing a particular symbolic interpretation of the poem and refuting all symbolic interpretations, there is a middle way, a view of the poem that allows for all interpretations but commits to none. Dyson prioritizes such a view in analyzing the poem's uncanny emotional pull on the reader, describing it as "like a dream, which may be diversely and plausibly interpreted after we wake, but which has its own symbolic vividness beyond any or all of the meanings it can be shown to have." That is, whether or not the reader can come to any logical conclusion about the poem's premises, the essence of its effect lies in what the reader feels, rather than what one thinks. De la Mare himself, in a piece of private correspondence presented by A. Bentinck in the *Explicator* in 1991, suggests just such an indefinite universality in explaining "The Listeners." Having often been asked about it, de la Mare reports that he has "usually suggested that the very kind enquirer should keep to any meaning he may have himself been able to find in it." He elaborates, but hesitantly:

> I am now a little vague concerning what *was* the intended meaning of those particular lines. Its

rudiments, I think, were that the Traveller is a reincarnation revisiting this world beneath the glimpses of the moon, and there asking the same old unanswerable questions of The Listeners only conceived but never embodied— who for ever frequent, it would seem, this earthly existence. But then are even these rudiments divinable—from the poem? Every poem, of course, to its last syllable is its meaning; to attempt any paraphrase of the poem is in some degree to change that meaning & its effect on the imagination,—and often disastrously.

Thus nullifying the import of the specific scenario he conceived in writing the poem, de la Mare proceeds to proclaim: "In the finest poems the meaning fairly fizzles and rays out in every direction. It is the primal cell capable of infinite subdivision & of innumerable potentialities."

Musical Meter

The fairly hypnotic experience of reading "The Listeners" is enhanced by the ornate and unique metrical scheme employed by de la Mare. Definitive analysis of the meter of the poem is complicated by the great variety in the numbers of syllables per line. Within each couplet, the first line, usually ten or eleven syllables, is consistently longer than the second, usually seven or eight syllables; but across couplets, corresponding lines often have contrasting lengths. For example, where line 5 has ten syllables, line 7 has thirteen; where line 29 has ten syllables, line 31 has fourteen. Thus, if one wishes to read the entire poem at a consistent pace, the shorter lines must be read more slowly to allow time for the longer lines to be spoken over the same interval. The scholar Henry Charles Duffin, in his volume *Walter de la Mare: A Study of His Poetry*, refers to this as a "hesitation motif," one that produces "queer, uncanny music" set to a "staccato measure." Over the course of the poem, Duffin declares, "the atmosphere grows strange, breathless, ghostly; skin creeps, hair begins to rise; the poet's mood is ours. The poet's aesthetic passion prompted this hesitating form, and form induces in us the passion of the poet." To complete the discussion, Duffin observes that many lines can be read with three stressed syllables, within feet, or sets, of three or more syllables each, making for a loose version of a pattern called anapestic trimeter (an anapest consists of two unstressed syllables followed by one stressed, and a trimeter line would contain three of these anapests). However, this meter gets crowded in the longer lines, and it fails to account for the pauses one naturally reads into the shorter lines. Duffin thus sees a sort of pentameter (a line with five feet) in which pauses must account for the syllables absent from the shorter lines. For example, he diagrams line 4 as an anapest followed by four iambs (unstressed followed by stressed), with the first beat of each iamb represented by a pause. A natural reading then collapses the line in such a way that three syllables remain stressed, while two pauses are introduced, preceding each of the last two words.

Robert M. Pierson takes a more directly musical approach in his 1964 essay in *English Studies*. Like Duffin, he observes that the lines are readily analyzed as carrying three stressed beats each but produce a peculiar rhythm, suggesting that a more nuanced metrical reading would be a better fit. He thus perceives four beats per line, with a silent beat, like a rest in music, appearing at the end of most lines. In a number of lines (especially lines 15, 17, 23, and 31), the fourth stressed beat is instead claimed by the words themselves, with the final two syllables each meriting a stress. In scanning various lines from the poem, Pierson turns to musical notation, using quarter notes for the majority of

beats, half notes (or longer) to account for pauses in the middle of lines, eighth (or sixteenth) notes for quicker beats, and rests at the ends of most lines. In concluding, the critic notes two interesting metrical subtleties. First, in general, the odd-numbered lines feature more variation in patterns of syllables, while the even-numbered lines are more consistent and steady. Thus, the reader is repeatedly cast adrift in a free-flowing line, then anchored by a steady line; this rhythmically reflects the poem's alternate depiction of the formless phantoms and the human Traveller, who is anchored in reality.

In addition, on a more specific level, the meter varies more in the passages on the listeners, less in the passages on the Traveller. The first twelve lines are quite steady, although the meter flutters a bit along with the bird in line 5, while the extra syllables in line 7 convey the Traveller's increasing anxiety. After the phantoms appear, lines 15, 17, and 19 all seem to waft around as a ghost might. Lines 21–28 read steadily. But after the phantoms return in line 29—where, with a bit of phonetic flair, the third and fourth words serve as a sort of phantom echo of the last word, the title of the poem—line 31 makes a few last ripples in the reader's ear, ripples that, along with the sounds of the horse galloping away, dissipate completely by the end of the poem.

HISTORICAL CONTEXT

From Romanticism to Georgian Poetry

In "The Listeners," as in much of de la Mare's poetry, it is impossible to identify the setting as a particular period in history. As Dyson remarks, "The Traveller might be Any Man, the episode Any Time and Any Place, as in a sense they are." This absence of historical or social context allows the humanity, or ghostliness, of his poems' characters to touch the reader all the more strongly. This aspect of his verse accords with his own historical status, in that he can be characterized as a poet who was displaced in time. His style is appreciated as profoundly romantic, but the peak of romanticism, had passed nearly a century before his time. He can be classed with the Georgian poets of the 1910s, who sought to revive the intellectual spirit of poetry after the flatness of the preceding Edwardian decade However, by 1919 de la Mare, in a letter cited by Robert H. Ross in *The Georgian Revolt: Rise and Fall of a Poetic*

COMPARE & CONTRAST

- **1910s:** With an English translation of Sigmund Freud's *Interpretation of Dreams* published in 1913, Freud's increasingly popular psychoanalytic perspective, revolving around the novel concept of the unconscious, is brought to bear on the dream lives of patients and other curious minds.

  Today: Some modern psychology departments in universities now focus on perspectives gleaned from research in neuroscience rather than Freud's psychoanalytic framework. They focus on the chemical processes that take place in the various regions of the brain. Professional psychologists increasingly prescribe medication to their patients rather than conversational counseling.

- **1910s:** With mass production of the Model T enabled by Henry Ford's assembly-line innovations in 1908, and with a Ford factory set up in England in 1911, millions of middle-class Americans and Britons exchange their horses and carriages for the exciting personal automobile.

  Today: Cars, trucks, and sport-utility vehicles are ubiquitous, enveloping cities in pollution and clogging streets with traffic jams. Cities turn to ever more drastic methods to reduce traffic volume, such as in London, where a fee must be paid to use central city roads during rush hours.

- **1910s:** With motion-picture technology still in its infancy, people rely on simple illustrations and their imaginations to bring the images of literature to life. Attention spans are long, and even a poem can provide a supernatural thrill.

  Today: High-definition television, the Internet, and multimillion-dollar movies (packed with spectacular explosions, life-or-death chases, computer-generated ghosts, aliens, fantasy creatures, and apocalypse scenarios) result in consumers who increasingly find their imaginations less active. The reading of a poem, when it happens, is likely to be followed not by a long moment of quiet introspection but by a rapid click to the next Web site or a glance at a mobile phone.

Ideal, 1910–1922, considered himself "a rather stale old bird to be chirping in the new nest" and only reluctantly assented to his inclusion in the later Georgian anthologies. In the wake of the Europe-wide trauma of World War I, the verse of the Georgians proved to lose its appeal, and the modernism of poets such as T. S. Eliot and Ezra Pound pulled poetry into a wholly new era.

The British romantic period, which was only labeled as such in retrospect, is considered to have spanned roughly the years 1789 to 1832, when major poets such as William Wordsworth, Samuel Taylor Coleridge, and John Keats flourished. These poets drew on classical and Renaissance-era works in fashioning verse that proved particularly suitable for an era when the democratic and liberating ideals behind the American and French revolutions were echoing throughout Western cultures. In his essay "Romantic Poets and Contemporary Poetry," Andrew Bennett summarizes the "powerful conglomeration of ideas" that romanticism represented, including "newly invigorated notions of imagination, inspiration, genius, and the sublime; the celebration of Nature as an antidote to the rapid industrialization and urbanization of society," and the idea "that poetry is a 'passion.'" These aspects of romanticism in particular are reflected in de la Mare's verse. His practice of poetry as sublime passion is noted by Duffin, who comments:

> De la Mare makes us aware of a life, a world, an experience, which are instantly recognized as not only different from anything the common day has to offer, but more real, partaking more of the eternal, in the same way as the mystic's knowledge of God.

The setting is an apparently empty house in the forest. *(Kimberly Palmer | Shutterstock.com)*

In the wake of romanticism came the Victorian era, defined by the long reign of Queen Victoria from 1837 to 1901. Throughout this era, poetic approaches continued along romantic lines, with emotional and spiritual experiences prioritized over intellectual ones. References to mythology and classical works were commonplace. Notable British poets from this era include Alfred Tennyson and Elizabeth Barrett Browning. Although some poets who began work in this period, such as Thomas Hardy and the Irish poet William Butler Yeats, remained active through the beginning of the twentieth century, no new poetic impetus of significance took hold until the Georgian poets announced themselves through the 1912 publication of the first anthology of *Georgian Poetry* compiled by Edward Marsh. This volume presented only new poems from the last two years, including several of de la Mare's poems from *The Listeners*, among them the title poem and the Orientalist ode "Arabia."

These poets, most of whom were only beginning to make a name for themselves, intended a stylistic revolt against the Victorian tradition, which some perceived to have run its elaborate,

sentimental course. The early Georgians, rather than producing carefully contrived, extravagant verse, advocated the poetic search for truth and sincere reflections of life. In favoring this realist approach, some abandoned the sort of archaic or strictly poetic language that one would never have heard spoken in real life. Still, describing the anthology in an essay in the *Edinburgh Review*, de la Mare points out that some essential aspects of poetry are eternal: new generations of poets must inevitably both stray from and follow the continuous tradition. He declares that among the Georgian poets, "a wholesome independence is manifest, together with as wholesome an exuberance and bravado. Their faults are the faults of youth.... But there is no anarchic challenge of old ideals, no obvious tendency towards any particular *ism*." He observes that "the general trend of the work is lyrical—with a dramatic undercurrent," with the qualities of lyrical poetry said to be "intensity of vision, imagination,... metrical craft, economy of means, music and finish." De la Mare sums up the nature of Georgian poetry thus: "In a word, unquestionable *seriousness*, as distinguished from what another generation rather solemnly and chillingly called 'high seriousness,' is the sincere mark and claim of this anthology."

Marsh would compile four more *Georgian Poetry* anthologies by 1922, by which time his particular brand of poetic excellence had lost much of its appeal. World War I had a devastating effect on many of the Georgian poets, whose sincere optimism was negated by harsh reality and whose youthful spirit abruptly receded into an unrecoverable past. Rupert Brooke, one of the Georgian poets, was among those whose lives where claimed by the war; he wrote until the end, and his war sonnets and heroism would both be solemnly celebrated. But the fourth and fifth Georgian anthologies were critically lamented to be unprovocative, lacking in vigor, and narrow in range. De la Mare even advised Marsh to remove some of the poets, including himself, who had graced the previous anthologies, but to no avail. In the wake of the war, neo-Georgian poets withdrew from the realist ideals of their predecessors and retreated into simpler, idealized forms, but the emotional thrust needed for such poetry was lacking. As Ross relates in his history, the moon was duly glanced up at so many times that readers came to not actively imagine that lustrous wonder of the night sky but rather simply to see the word *moon* again and again. Moreover, Marsh had somewhat conservative tastes, and while the vagueness of emerging modernists—which they considered an appropriate way of representing the social and psychological confusion of the postwar world—was coming to the fore, Marsh demanded a poetic clearness that left too little to the reader's imagination. Georgian poetry, seen by the 1920s as formal, bland, and mechanical, was thus doomed to be an anachronism; it was not merely unmodern but thoroughly antimodern. De la Mare, at least, never lost his poetic inspiration. Although he did not adopt the modernist style of Eliot and Pound and the Americans Gertrude Stein and E. E. Cummings, he nonetheless outlived the era of Georgian poetry in popular terms. Most appreciators consider de la Mare's verse to be timeless.

CRITICAL OVERVIEW

Few critics approach de la Mare without mentioning the ineffable appeal of "The Listeners." Most cannot resist chiming in with thoughts about the most essential aspects of the poem and possible symbolic meanings. In a 1960 essay on the poem, Dyson points out that it is emblematic of de la Mare's work as a whole: "The loneliness of the soul in itself, somewhere between waking and sleeping, between midnight and dawn. This is de la Mare's territory, and inside it there are few to equal him." Noting that specific symbolism is not needed to lend this poem meaning, he observes, "What de la Mare does is to dramatise, with exquisite precision, the moment of challenge and doubt when the isolated soul questions the unanswering universe." Dyson concludes that de la Mare's "odd, but impressive achievement has been to make the strange, the non-existent even, almost tangible, with the tangibility that language and poetry can confer"—an achievement the critic identifies as being "at the very end of one of the roads of romanticism." Situating de la Mare among the other Georgian poets of the 1910s, Dyson affirms that while his contemporaries used words like "lone," "empty," "phantom," and "strangeness" so lavishly as to "turn them into routine gestures," de la Mare used them in such fundamental, genuine ways that in his poems, the words never lost their power.

In *British Poetry in the Age of Modernism*, Peter Howarth likewise ties "The Listeners" to de la Mare's overall themes: "Fascination with the *experience* of absence and vacancy is central to de la Mare's outlook, with its abiding interest in ghosts, graves and silences." The inquiry repeated by the Traveller in "de la Mare's most well-loved poem" is considered the poet's "most famous question." In her lecture on de la Mare's long poem *The Traveller*, published in the *Proceedings of the British Academy* of 1953, Victoria Sackville-West gives "The Listeners" its due attention: "In that flawless poem—too familiar to read to you here—the sense of fear and mystery is pervading: a shiver of apprehension goes through us from the very first lines." Leonard Clark, in his monograph *Walter de la Mare*, in general terms that easily apply to "The Listeners" declares, "The secrets of Walter de la Mare's craftsmanship are quaint fancy, vowel melody, and cunning rhythm, all combining to give haunting overtones, strangeness, and spellbinding dreams."

Acknowledging that de la Mare receives relatively little critical or popular attention in the twenty-first century in his 2008 essay "The Kingdom of Never-to-Be," Eric Ormsby comments, "Nowadays, we think of Walter de la Mare—if we think of him at all—as an unusually skilful musician of words, a fastidious but dated versifier." But if de la Mare is considered dated, it is perhaps largely because modern audiences' imaginations have lost the ability to delve into, and be delved into, by a poem. As Ormsby states, "Enchantment was what he was after," and "The Listeners," with its "exquisite craft," "seamless weave of narrative and lyric," and "ineffably spooky atmosphere," is as entrancing as poetry can be. Ormsby relates that after Thomas Hardy—one of de la Mare's poetic inspirations—had this poem read to him on his deathbed, he is said to have remarked, "That is possibly the finest poem of the century."

CRITICISM

Michael Allen Holmes

Holmes is a writer and editor. In the following essay, he considers "The Listeners" as a waking dream of de la Mare's that merits interpretation from a universal perspective.

The significance of the scene described in "The Listeners" is so tantalizingly obscure that the reader must inevitably search for possible symbolic meanings and perhaps further, for a driving thematic force. That such a force is so difficult to identify contributes greatly to the poem's appeal, as well as its stylistic excellence, with the spectral qualities of the poem itself matching those of the listeners therein. The first waves of commentators posited allegorical identities for the poem's characters, but later critics responded to this chaotic assemblage of clashing notions by trying to wipe the slate clean. Frederick L. Gwynn and Ralph W. Condee, in the *Explicator* in 1954, somewhat wryly insist that in the absence of more detail, all the Traveller "can stand for is Keeping One's (Unspecified) Word." They do allow that "it remains to see whether or not these figures are allegorical," but in their own analysis, they deny all symbolism in reducing the listeners to an impeccable, but otherwise unprofound, instance of poetic personification of silence. From a contrasting perspective, A. E. Dyson, in the *Critical Quarterly* in 1960, proposes that, with the poem being so dreamlike, various interpretations—perhaps even all—could be considered legitimate. De la Mare himself supported this perspective, telling those who asked about "The Listeners" that they should stick to whatever meaning they happen to find

> THIS POEM ABOVE ALL THE POET'S OTHERS MAY REPRESENT A SORT OF UNIVERSAL DREAM— ONE WHOSE SYMBOLS AND MEANING, BEYOND ANY CONSCIOUS CONCEPTIONS OF DE LA MARE'S, MUST HOLD SOME SIGNIFICANCE ON THE SCALE OF MODERN WESTERN CIVILIZATION."

in the poem. Helpfully in this regard, when writing to a friend in 1944—some thirty-two years after the poem's publication—de la Mare could only sketchily recall the scenario he originally envisioned. In the letter (cited by A. Bentinck in the *Explicator* in 1991), he calls the Traveller "a reincarnation revisiting this world," characterizes his inquiries as "the same old unanswerable questions," and states that the listeners "for ever frequent, it would seem, this earthly existence." Yet regardless of these dimly recollected notions, de la Mare's comments elsewhere suggest that, for any given poem he has written, his conscious framework for the verse may not be as significant as the unconscious foundation that supports it. Thus, perhaps the profoundest inherent meaning of the poem is to be found in an interpretation of it as a dream of de la Mare's.

In the long introduction of de la Mare's 1939 anthology *Behold, This Dreamer! Of Reverie, Night, Sleep, Dream, Love-Dreams, Nightmare, Death, the Unconscious, the Imagination, Divination, the Artist, and Kindred Subjects*, the poet provides a splendid unified, autobiographical exploration of every concept in the volume's title. The high point of the essay comes with his discussion of a perceived foundation of poetry in the poet's unconscious mind. First, considering the relationship between dream and poetry, he writes, "When any particular poem has for theme either an actual or a fictitious dream we associate it with all that we think and feel in regard to dreaming." And in this regard, "Anything dream-like may happen in a dream; everything that happens in a dream is dream-like." Thus, any dreamy sort of poem "appeals at once to the dream-self of its reader, and, that done, *like* dream, it may indulge his credulity in respect to any wonder, marvel, mystery, fantasy or extravagance appropriate

WHAT DO I READ NEXT?

- One of de la Mare's most curious and critically acclaimed publications is the novel *Memoirs of a Midget* (1921), in which a man named Walter presents the purported memoirs of a smaller-than-average person, whose experiences are representative of those of any sensitive soul.

- De la Mare demonstrates the leanings of his spiritual poet's mind in the collection of essays *Pleasures and Speculations* (1940), which includes his lecture "Rupert Brooke and the Intellectual Imagination," extolling the visionary perspective of children.

- A biography of de la Mare, *Imagination of the Heart: The Life of Walter de la Mare* (1993), was written by a close acquaintance of the poet's, Theresa Whistler.

- De la Mare's musicality and spookiness merit comparison with the American author Edgar Allan Poe, whose most famous poem, a dark lyrical tale, is the title work of *The Raven, and Other Poems* (1845).

- Robert Frost met and developed a friendship with de la Mare, and his poem "The Census-Taker" (1921), in which a census official confronts a deserted house, is reminiscent of "The Listeners." The former poem is available in the *Complete Poems of Robert Frost* (1949).

- De la Mare has been described as a disciple of Thomas Hardy, who was at first a novelist but shifted to poetry later in life. Hardy's first poetry volume is *Wessex Poems and Other Verses* (1898). In "A Meeting with Despair," a man visits a dismal moor and is confronted by a strange and shadowy figure.

- The English author Kenneth Grahame, like de la Mare, found himself stuck in an office job and responded by delving into his imagination to produce works like *The Wind in the Willows* (1908), a pastoral classic of children's literature that is suitable for adults as well.

- In the story collection *The Jungle Book* (1894), the British author Rudyard Kipling, who was raised in India, provides fables populated by jungle animals and one human boy named Mowgli. The stories, which are appropriate for young adults, serve to highlight the division between the wilderness and human-centered civilization.

- The Gambian poet Tijan M. Sallah published *Dream Kingdom: New and Selected Poems* in 2007. This collection constitutes an exploration of the mystical and mythical foundations of poetry.

---

to the region of sleep." With "The Listeners," then, the reader may experience the Traveller's visit as surreal, like a dream, and also record the episode as profoundly, and perhaps decipherably, significant in the way that dreams are.

De la Mare goes on to assert that poetry is not, like functions of the intellect alone, a strictly logical, rational process: "Since language is acquired and is not innate, the intellect must supervise its use as a medium; but it cannot of itself originate poetry—any more than a craftsman originates the material in which he works. The mind is in the service of the imagination, not vice versa." And the best poetry,

de la Mare indicates, may be produced when the imagination is let loose. He asserts that in great imaginative verse, "it was a dream-self that kept the poet company in the conception and in the actual composition of his poem." De la Mare turns to quoting his fellow English poet Herbert Read's *Collected Essays* to express the epitome of this connection with one's dream-self: Read avers "that all the poetry I have written which I continue to regard as authentic poetry was written immediately, instantaneously, in a condition of trance." De la Mare then concludes, "In widely differing degree this is true of all poetic experience," and the reader senses that he feels very much as Read does. Henry Charles Duffin, in *Walter de la Mare: A Study of His Poetry*, confirms this impression. In his opening section, Duffin follows the spiritual tracks of the poetic unconscious directly to a divine source: "Lyric poetry is the voice of God. But the voice speaks, in different poets, with varying degrees of authenticity." This authenticity depends on the poet's degree of contact with beauty and truth, and "de la Mare belongs to a very small band of poets whose contact is peculiarly close and vital because it partakes of the directness, the immediacy, of mysticism." Indeed, de la Mare is recognized as something of a poetic mystic—a distant relative of American transcendentalists like Henry David Thoreau and Walt Whitman—and, it may be noted here, in some traditional societies, the dreams of the mystic or shaman are essentially sacred, constituting messages from the divine. In Duffin's words, de la Mare "found reality . . . in dream—the dream of wake or sleep, intuitive understanding, contemplative union with the eternal."

All of these notions contribute to suggest that "The Listeners" has proven itself to be de la Mare's most popular poem and thus can be said to have most fully resonated with the English-speaking world's collective mind. This poem above all the poet's others may represent a sort of universal dream—one whose symbols and meaning, beyond any conscious conceptions of de la Mare's, must hold some significance on the scale of modern Western civilization. In other words, the poem may represent a sort of waking dream experienced and recorded by de la Mare on behalf, as it turns out, of all of society, or at least of Western society. (While the poem may or may not have similar appeal in translation, the modern English-speaking centers of Great Britain and the United States can be largely considered representative of the psychological experiences of other European/Westernized nations.) The poem's images and symbols, then, may be best considered not in a directly allegorical fashion, as one might approach deliberately constructed prose fiction or even a lyrical poem with a discernible plot, but in a loose, impressionistic fashion, specifically as a dream of Walter de la Mare's and generally as one experienced by the collective Western mind of the last hundred years.

Given that the psychoanalytic pioneer Sigmund Freud was a contemporary of de la Mare's and that an English translation of Freud's *The Interpretation of Dreams* (1899) was first published in 1913, one might be tempted to hazard

a Freudian interpretation of "The Listeners." However, de la Mare expressly distances himself in *Behold, This Dreamer!* from Freudian dream interpretation, which he considered disproportionately focused on innate sexual drive at the expense of the romantic and spiritual aspects of life. With respect to reading dreams symbolically, de la Mare points out that various symbolic schemes might be legitimate: "There is scarcely an object around us that cannot be conceived of as a symbol figurative of anything with which the waking mind is deeply concerned." As read by critics, de la Mare is deemed most especially concerned with loneliness, the isolation of the human soul, and at the end of that road, death—notions that culminate in his long poem *The Traveller* (1946). While the protagonist of that poem should not be identified as one with the Traveller in "The Listeners," it seems likely that de la Mare's concept of his famous original character was echoing through his mind when, thirty years later, he wrote his poignant story of a man riding his horse across a strange land in a journey, both physical and spiritual, that ends in death. One critic, Victoria Sackville-West, notes that the horse in that poem suggests itself as symbolic of the Traveller's soul.

While it might be instructive to delve as deeply as possible into the psychology and personal experience of de la Mare, such an investigation would be beyond the scope of this essay. Regardless, in attempting to universalize de la Mare's dream-poem, the barest facts of his life may suffice to establish a symbolic framework that could apply to others' outlooks as well. He was about thirty-eight years old when he wrote "The Listeners," meaning that it been only two years since he was finally able to leave the employment at the London office of the Anglo-American Oil Company that he had held for nearly twenty years. His family's limited financial circumstances had originally forced him to accept the job, in which he worked some fifty-seven hours a week adding up statistical figures and copying documents. His sensitive poet's mind was veritably imprisoned in the rote intellectual demands of his work. And so after his release, one might expect to find in his unconscious a blend of lingering anxiety over such a claustrophobic environment and profound relief at having finally escaped it. As Alison Lurie notes in her essay "Is There Anybody There? Walter de la Mare's Solitary Child," the poet's early years, spent "at the edge of the countryside he loved," were idyllic, making the urbanized, regimented aspects of his teenage years and young adulthood comparatively difficult to bear. In Lurie's words—employing imagery especially relevant to "The Listeners"—when de la Mare finally received the grant that allowed him to focus solely on writing, "he was out of the woods—though in his case this seems the wrong metaphor, since nothing delighted and fascinated him more than an ancient and shadowy forest."

"The Listeners" famously opens with the Traveller's inquiry as to whether anyone is present, spoken at a door lit by the moon. Three direct mentions of the moon are made in the poem, and all are associated not with the forest but with the castle or château. After the moonlight's first appearance at the door, it figuratively enters the house to shine on the floors and stairwell and give the phantoms a place to linger—an image so essential that it is repeated in surprisingly similar language in lines 15 and 17; the image thus anchors the poem's second quatrain and provides the foundation for the third. The moon is indirectly referred to once more in line 31, which describes the moon-cast shadows inside the house. In *Behold, This Dreamer!* de la Mare proclaims of the moon that while "she pacifies the peaceful," on the other hand, "she can intensify darkness; give magic to the bewitched; terror to vacancy; horror to the haunted; an edge to the spectral. Her presence in sky or room deepens solitude; prepares for the ghostly." Thus, here, the moon literally highlights the isolated, unstirring, incommunicable semi-existence inhabited in perpetuity by the phantoms. On the other hand, the forest—that timeless poetic repository of romantic sentiment—is described in line 24 as lit not only by the fickle, ever-waxing-and-waning moon but by the vast, unbounded, inextinguishable canopy of stars.

Once one perceives the associations of finite moonlight with the château and the infinite starlight with the forest, it becomes clear that a striking dichotomy, or division, is reinforced throughout the poem. The Traveller stands on a threshold between two vastly different worlds: that of the structure before him, which is enclosed, limited, darkened, and essentially a place of death, and that of the starlit, leafy forest, where his living horse repeatedly stirs, nourishing itself with the earth's simple bounty of grass. Nature has taken small steps to reclaim the château; but the bird only roosts atop the turret, and some leaves only fringe the windowsill; the inside of the building remains a realm devoid of life. The Traveller casts his gaze, or at least the narrator suggests that his gaze or attention is cast, from the château to the forest and back again several times in the course of the poem—as though he is meditating on a choice between them. The detail of the Traveller's gray eyes is a curious one. This might suggest that the Traveller's mind is clouded or overcast with uncertainty, but the detail seems specific to the perspective of someone leaning out the window of the building, which itself is likely gray. In other words, perhaps in imagining his Traveller from the window view, de la Mare conceived the gray of the building reflected in the Traveller's eyes. Perhaps if the poem had provided the perspective of the horse, the man's eyes would have appeared green, like the grass.

From a universal perspective, this dichotomy between forest and château is readily conceived to represent the contrast between wilderness and civilization—between the world in which everything is alive, where humans must establish equality and symbiosis with the surroundings, and the world in which natural life and the land itself are defiled and obliterated to allow for the concentrated habitation of human beings. The road of civilization, as the twenty-first-century reader realizes far more clearly than de la Mare possibly could have, leads to ever-grayer worlds—with pavement and concrete separating humankind from the soil, steel buildings rising ever higher to blot out the sight of the sky, exhaust spewing from cars, fumes bellowing from industrial plants, smog hovering over cities—and to ever lonelier, unhappier people, who in the modern era increasingly turn to vast arrays of digital stimulation, disembodied interactions, fantasy indulgence, psychotropic drugs, chemical-enhanced foods, and other manufactured contrivances to cope with the mind-numbing circumstances they must endure simply to be cogs in the wheel of civilization. With their intellects taken over by society, people try to recuperate through artificial stimulation of mind and body alike—and the human spirit recedes, even vanishes. In the poem, the phantoms, viewed from the Traveller's perspective, may represent ghostly echoes of all those humans whose souls have been assimilated by the motive-warping forces of institutionalized education, a society governed by the tenets of capitalism, material definitions of success, and untold other aspects of "civilized" life.

This Traveller seems to be visiting the château, or the great gray construct of civilization, out of an obligation. Indeed, the obligation to be a productive member of society is one intended to be instilled in every child who passes through the modern educational system; the fulfillment of this aim is the primary social function of schooling. Thus, many a Western person has faced this psychological dilemma: an instilled sense of obligation brings one to the door of civilization, but one senses that civilization is in certain ways a house of death, especially in spiritual terms. In this poem-dream, the Traveller confronts this dilemma in a vivid, surreal scenario that can leave little doubt in the reader's mind as to what choice he should make. The Traveller was obliged to visit this place, presumably to make contact with someone; perhaps he was even expected to simply enter regardless of his reception or lack thereof. With this man, however, the sense of death lurking inside is overwhelming. He stands on the threshold for some time, but feeling the strange presence of the phantoms, he makes no effort to gain entrance. He does not pull at the door, which may not even be locked; he does not walk along the wall or circle the structure, looking for another door. No, the Traveller knocks a fair three times, just enough to satisfy his sense of duty, and no more, and then declares aloud the fulfillment of that duty—as if, in the absence of any evident living listeners, to convince himself, rather, that he has indeed done so. De la Mare was luckily, blissfully able to escape civilization's house of spiritual death—how else to describe the statistical department of an oil company?—to pursue the charmed life of the self-sufficient writer at the enviable age of thirty-six. Many a Western soul since then has never found such escape, condemned to a spectral existence in civilization's gray embrace. But through "The Listeners," every reader, however trapped in reality, gets to cast a mystic, all-perceiving gaze at the castle of civilization; recognize the hollow desolation of the purgatory of compromised souls therein; and turn, skip over the grass, mount the waiting steed, and gallop off into the eternal pagan paradise of the sacred wilderness.

Source: Michael Allen Holmes, Critical Essay on "The Listeners," in *Poetry for Students*, Gale, Cengage Learning, 2012.

Glen A. Love

In the following essay, Love considers de la Mare's "The Listeners" as a source for Robert Frost's "The Census-Takers."

Walter de la Mare's "The Listeners" (1912), a poem which Robert Frost consistently praised in the highest terms, bears so close a resemblance to

The traveller arrives and leaves on horseback.
(Vaclav Volrab)

Frost's "The Census-Taker" (1921) that it strongly suggests itself as a source for the Frost poem.

According to Sidney Cox, Frost's admiration for "The Listeners" arose from its affirmation of "the reality of the undefined"; it is this quality which pervades Frost's poem, in which a census-taker, who sets out to define reality in the most literal way by counting people, discovers a more cogent reality in his awareness of the human presences within a deserted house. The main points of the narrative are the same in both poems; a lone visitor comes to an isolated dwelling to fulfill some kind of responsibility to its inhabitants. He finds the place deserted, but, in its loneliness and silence, he feels an arresting sense of those whom he was to have met. He finally speaks directly to these presences, and in so doing both affirms, and at the same time breaks off, their hold upon him. At the center of both poems is an apprehension of the house's emptiness and stillness so intense that the place becomes peopled through this apprehension by means of a series of "negated personifications." In "The Listeners," "no one descended to the

Traveller: / No head from the leaf-fringed sill / Leaned over and looked into his grey eye"; "'... no one answered'"; "Never the least stir made the listeners...." Similarly, Frost's visitor came to the house "not dwelt in now by men or women...."; "I found no people that dared show themselves, / None not in hiding from the outward eye." "They were not on the table with their elbows. / They were not sleeping in the shelves of bunks."

Frost seems to have transformed, item by item, each romantic detail of "The Listeners" into its harshest realistic counterpoint. De la Mare's moonlit summer night becomes Frost's raw, windy autumn evening; the earlier poem's lush, leafy forest setting is reduced by Frost to a cut-over wasteland of stumps and rotting trunks, where "every tree / That could have dropped a leaf" was down itself; de la Mare's castle becomes a one-room, slab-sided, tar-paper shack. De la Mare's listeners display a certain Victorian decorum as they stand and listen quietly; on the other hand, the census-taker, hearing the door banging in the wind, feels that his conjectural presences are "rude men," rough lumberjacks who pass in, slamming the door shut, "each one behind him / For the next one to open for himself." Were they there, the visitor imagines, they would be eating with their elbows on the table, or sleeping in the board bunks. De la Mare's traveler, presented in third person, is a horseman whose actions are strong and decisive; his mission is a mysterious one. ("'Tell them I came, and no one answered, / That I kept my word,' he said.") Conversely, Frost's first person narrator is a rather timid (he arms himself against the presences with an ax-handle), introspective civil servant, carrying out some mundane and insignificant state function; his reflective tendencies (toward "dreary, unofficial counting") lead him beyond the terse final declaration of de la Mare's traveler, into his rather convoluted summary-utterance:

> "The place is desert and let whoso lurks
> In silence, if in this he is aggrieved,
> Break silence now or be forever silent.
> Let him say why it should not be declared so."

The poems close in characteristic fashion, with de la Mare's horseman galloping off and Frost's narrator reflecting quietly upon his experience.

Frost has left ample evidence of the effect of "The Listeners" upon him. Despite his belief that "you *must not* disillusion your admirers with the tale of your sources and processes," he has taken no pains to conceal his admiration for de la Mare as a lyric poet and for "The Listeners" as his finest work. Frost, who met de la Mare when in England, called him "greatest of living poets" (132), although "hardly of the fashion." (104); elsewhere he said that "the nineties produced no single poem to put beside [de la Mare's] 'The Listeners'" (139); Sidney Cox recalls Frost's estimate of it as "the greatest poem in English in recent years."

Judging from the impression which the de la Mare poem made upon him, and in view of the correspondences of "The Census-Taker" to it, "The Listeners" may be posited as an important influence upon Frost's later poem.

Source: Glen A. Love, "Frost's 'The Census-Taker' and de la Mare's 'The Listeners,'" in *Papers on Language & Literature*, Vol. 4, No. 2, Spring 1968, pp. 198–200.

SOURCES

Bennett, Andrew, "Romantic Poets and Contemporary Poetry," in *The Cambridge Companion to British Romantic Poetry*, edited by James Chandler and Maureen N. McLane, Cambridge University Press, 2008, pp. 263–65.

Bentinck, A., "De la Mare's 'The Listeners,'" in *Explicator*, Vol. 50, No. 1, Fall 1991, pp. 33–35.

Clark, Leonard, *Walter de la Mare*, Henry Z. Walck, 1961, pp. 9–30.

De la Mare, Walter, *Behold, This Dreamer! Of Reverie, Night, Sleep, Dream, Love-Dreams, Nightmare, Death, the Unconscious, the Imagination, Divination, the Artist, and Kindred Subjects*, Greenwood Press, 1969, pp. 24–25, 85, 102, 107, 110.

———, "An Elizabethan Poet and Modern Poetry," in *Georgian Poetry, 1911–22: The Critical Heritage*, edited by Timothy Rogers, Routledge, 1977, pp. 106–114; originally published in *Edinburgh Review*, April 1913, pp. 377–86.

———, "The Listeners," in *The Listeners, and Other Poems*, Henry Holt, 1916, pp. 64–65.

Duffin, Henry Charles, *Walter de la Mare: A Study of His Poetry*, Sidgwick and Jackson, 1949, pp. 3–38.

Dyson, A. E., "Walter de la Mare's 'The Listeners,'" in *Critical Quarterly*, Vol. 2, 1960, pp. 150–54.

Gwynn, Frederick L., and Ralph W. Condee, "De la Mare's 'The Listeners,'" in *Explicator*, Vol. 12, No. 4, February 1954.

Hopkins, Kenneth, *Walter de la Mare*, Longmans, Green, 1953, pp. 7–9, 31–34.

Howarth, Peter, *British Poetry in the Age of Modernism*, Cambridge University Press, 2005, pp. 108–109, 127.

Kirkham, Michael, "Walter de la Mare," in *Dictionary of Literary Biography*, Vol. 19, *British Poets, 1880–1914*, edited by Donald E. Stanford, Gale Research, 1983, pp. 109–31.

Love, Glen A., "Frost's 'The Census-Taker' and de la Mare's 'The Listeners,'" in *Papers on Language & Literature*, Vol. 4, No. 2, Spring 1968, pp. 198–200.

Lurie, Alison, "Is There Anybody There? Walter de la Mare's Solitary Child," in *Boys and Girls Forever: Children's Classics from Cinderella to Harry Potter*, Penguin, 2003, pp. 47–61.

Marsh, Edward, *Georgian Poetry: 1911–1912*, Poetry Bookshop, 1912.

McCrosson, Doris Ross, *Walter de la Mare*, Twayne, 1966, pp. 11–12, 47–59.

Ormsby, Eric, "The Kingdom of Never-to-Be," in *New Criterion*, Vol. 26, No. 8, April 2008, pp. 4–8.

Pierson, Robert M., "The Meter of 'The Listeners,'" in *English Studies*, Vol. 45, No. 5, October 1964, pp. 373–81.

Ross, Robert H., *The Georgian Revolt, 1910–1922: Rise and Fall of a Poetic Ideal*, Southern Illinois University Press, 1965, p. 206.

Sackville-West, Victoria, "Warton Lecture on English Poetry: Walter de la Mare and 'The Traveller,'" in *Proceedings of the British Academy, 1953*, Kraus, 1977, pp. 23–36.

FURTHER READING

Blake, William, *Songs of Innocence and of Experience*, Princeton University Press, 1994.

> Originally published as two separate volumes in 1789 and 1794, these poems, accompanied by the original illustrations, explore the rupture between childhood innocence and the maturation enforced by civilization.

Whicher, George Frisbie, *Poetry and Civilization: Essays*, Russell & Russell, 1968.

> In this volume, Whicher considers the various intersections of poetic inspiration and the progress of civilization.

Wilson, Colin, *Poetry and Mysticism*, City Lights Books, 1986.

> Originally published in 1969 by the company that brought fame to the Beat poet Allen Ginsberg, this volume offers an existential examination of the spiritual role fulfilled by the poet.

Wolff, Werner, *The Dream—Mirror of Conscience: A History of Dream Interpretation from 2000 B.C. and a New Theory of Dream Synthesis*, Greenwood, 1952.

> Wolff provides a comprehensive survey of perspectives on dreams from ancient times to the mid-twentieth century, combining ideas from Freud, the Swiss psychiatrist Carl Jung, and others in establishing his own framework for understanding dreams.

SUGGESTED SEARCH TERMS

Walter de la Mare AND The Listeners

Walter de la Mare AND children's poetry

Walter de la Mare AND Georgian poetry

Walter de la Mare AND dream OR mystic

romanticism AND Georgian poetry

The Listeners AND meter

Thomas Hardy AND Walter de la Mare

mysticism AND romanticism

Georgian poetry AND twentieth century

The Listeners AND Walter de la Mare AND meter

Robert Frost AND Walter de la Mare

Miracles

WALT WHITMAN
1856

Walt Whitman's poem "Miracles" first appeared as "Poem of Perfect Miracles" in the 1856 version of *Leaves of Grass,* which was the collection's second edition. Over the many editions of *Leaves of Grass*, Whitman shortened the poem from its original thirty-five lines to the twenty-three-line version analyzed here. The poem can be found in the Norton Critical Edition of *Leaves of Grass* (as well as any other edition of the collection).

"Miracles," though not one of Whitman's more celebrated poems, encompasses many of the themes common to Whitman's work: the wonders of nature, a celebration of life, and an appreciation for small moments and sensual pleasures. The style of the poem is characteristic of many of Whitman's better-known poems, including "Song of Myself" and "I Sing the Body Electric."

AUTHOR BIOGRAPHY

Whitman was born Walter Whitman, Jr., on May 31, 1819, in West Hills, Long Island, New York. He was the second of four sons born to Walter Whitman, a carpenter, and his wife, Louisa. Whitman attended school until he was eleven years old; his family lacked the means to continue his formal education, so Whitman went to work, but continued to study on his own.

Walt Whitman (*National Archives and Records Administration*)

In 1836, Whitman tried teaching, but found it a frustrating endeavor. In 1838, he started his own small Long Island newspaper; though the paper did not last long, the experience led to journalism work for other more established newspapers. In 1842, he became the editor of a well-known New York daily newspaper called the *Aurora*. In the *Aurora* he was able to publish his articles on politics, literature, and entertainment, as well as short stories and poems. He also contributed stories to other publications.

Whitman was politically active as a member of the Free Soil Party, which was devoted to blocking the spread of slavery to the western states. He frequently wrote political commentary and editorials. However, when the party's candidate lost to Zachary Taylor in 1848, Whitman was bitterly disappointed, and became less active politically. He continued to voice his opinions through stories and articles, speaking out against the Fugitive Slave Law and the Compromise of 1850, which allowed slavery to move into the west. But as he continued writing, Whitman shifted his focus away from politics and onto poetry, writing the poems that would fill the first edition of his most well-known work, *Leaves of Grass*. The first edition was published

on July 4, 1855. Whitman's father did not live to see his son's great success as a poet; he died at about the same time the volume was published.

The first edition of *Leaves of Grass* contained twelve poems, including classics such as "Song of Myself" and "I Sing the Body Electric" (though they were not titled in the original edition). The volume was not highly acclaimed by critics, but Whitman received a letter from Ralph Waldo Emerson praising the book as "the most extraordinary piece of wit & wisdom that America has yet contributed." Encouraged, Whitman went back to work, expanding the volume to thirty-two poems. This second edition was published in 1856.

Leaves of Grass continued to grow; the next edition, published in 1860, contained 178 poems. Unfortunately, shortly after the new edition was released, the Civil War began, and the publishers of the book were forced into bankruptcy.

In 1862, Whitman's brother George was injured in the Battle of Fredericksburg. Whitman traveled immediately to Virginia to see him. Though George survived, Whitman witnessed much suffering at the army camp and was inspired to become involved. He secured a government position in Washington in order to follow the war more closely, and he began regularly visiting soldiers in war hospitals. He worked so tirelessly to aid the soldiers and their families that by the end of the war, his own health had deteriorated.

Throughout the war, Whitman continued to write as well. After President Abraham Lincoln was assassinated, Whitman wrote four poems memorializing the president, whom he greatly admired. The poem "O Captain! My Captain!" became one of his most popular works, though many critics prefer the elegy "When Lilacs Last in the Dooryard Bloom'd." He collected his war poems into a book titled *Drum Taps*, first published in 1865, and later incorporated into *Leaves of Grass*.

The year 1873 delivered two significant blows to Whitman from which he never fully recovered: the death of his mother and a paralyzing stroke. He moved to New Jersey so that his brother George and his family could care for him. For the next nineteen years he remained at home, receiving numerous literary visitors, overseeing new volumes of his work, and consulting with biographers recording his life. He died on March 26, 1892.

POEM SUMMARY

The text used for this summary is from *Leaves of Grass and Other Writings: Walt Whitman*, Norton, 2002, p. 327. Versions of this poem can be found on the following Web pages: http://www.poets.org/viewmedia.php/prmMID/20162 and http://www.bartleby.com/142/226.html.

The poem is written in free verse, a poetic form in which the lines have no fixed metrical pattern, a style characteristic of Whitman's work.

Stanza 1

"Miracles," originally titled "Poem of Perfect Miracles," in the 1856 version of *Leaves of Grass*, uses the word miracle, a term normally reserved for spectacular events (a patient near death suddenly recovering, for instance, or the parting of the Red Sea), to describe everyday occurrences. To Whitman, all of life is a miracle. After asserting this claim in the first two lines of the long first stanza, he uses the next thirteen lines to list off some of these daily miracles. After the first miracle (walking in Manhattan), each of the next twelve lines begins with the word *or* (beginning several consecutive lines with the same word or words, a technique known as anaphora, is a common practice of Whitman's.) In lines 15 and 16 he restates his thesis, that all these things are miracles.

Many of Whitman's examples of miracles come from nature, but he also lists such ordinary activities as having dinner with others, observing strangers while traveling, walking through the city, and talking with loved ones. Natural miracles include wading on the beach; being still in a forest; watching animals, honeybees and other insects, and birds; and observing the sky at sunset, the stars, and the moon.

Stanza 2

In the second stanza, which is just four lines long, Whitman ceases to cite specific entities such as animals or people, and instead uses measurements to encompass a larger scope. This shift is reflected in Whitman's use of the word *every* at the beginning of each line (rather than *or*). Using these measurements emphasizes his point that everything in life is a miracle—not just walks in Manhattan, or honeybees at work, but the entirety of the universe. Every part of the

MEDIA ADAPTATIONS

- Fifteen different recorded readings of Whitman's "Miracles" are available as free downloads at www.librovox.org.

- Three different unabridged recordings of *Leaves of Grass* are available for purchase at www.audible.com. Ed Begley, Robin Field, and Mel Foster are the readers.

- Susan L. Roth created a colorful children's picture book from this poem, *Nothing but Miracles*. The book features a family of cats experiencing their own "miracles" (gazing at stars, walking through the woods). The book was published by National Geographic Children's Books in 2003.

day, measurable part of the world, and bit of the ocean is dense with miracles.

Stanza 3

In the last stanza, Whitman focuses on the ocean, citing it as a never-ending miracle; fish, rocks, the sea's movement, and boats on the water piloted by men are miracles. Whitman then states that these are the strangest miracles of all, though whether he means the elements of the sea or the men inside the ships is left to the reader to decide.

THEMES

Nature

"Miracles" lauds the wonders of nature, from the vast sea to the smallest insect. The harmony of nature and man is a theme to which Whitman often returned; he viewed man as an element of nature, and he sometimes personified the land, giving it human characteristics. In his memoir, *Specimen Days*, Whitman wrote about traveling through the Rocky Mountains:

TOPICS FOR FURTHER STUDY

- Whitman's original version of this poem (written in 1856) was twelve lines longer than the version discussed in this chapter. Read the longer version, "A Poem of Perfect Miracles," available at the Walt Whitman Archive (http://www.whitmanarchive. org/published/LG/1856/poems/24). Write a short paper on why you think Whitman chose to remove those lines. Do you think the longer or shorter poem is better? Why?

- Write your own miracles poem, using examples from your own experience (riding a bike, or visiting a favorite friend). Try to use the same structure that Whitman used in his poem.

- Set Whitman's poem (or your own, if you wrote one) to music. You may use an existing melody or write your own. If you have computer software for creating music (such as GarageBand), use this to record the song and burn a disc to play for your class or post to YouTube.

- "Miracles" is a very visual poem. Create your own movie illustrating the poem, using nature and city scenes. Record your voice reading the poem as a soundtrack, or put the words of the poem on the screen. Upload your movie to YouTube and ask your classmates to comment.

- Poets in the United States in the nineteenth century were beginning to develop their own, uniquely American voice. Compare Whitman's "Miracles" to the famous eighteenth-century English poem, Thomas Gray's "Elegy Written in a Country Churchyard." Both poems use many images of nature, including insects, birds, and the sea. How is Whitman's poem different? Write an essay explaining why Whitman's poem seems more modern than Gray's.

- Whitman was deeply affected by the tragedy of the Civil War, and he wrote many poems about it. His own brother was injured in the Battle of Fredericksburg. Create an interactive timeline of the Civil War, with links to key historical events and poems written by Whitman at approximately the same times.

- Written after Lincoln's death, "O Captain! My Captain!" is Whitman's most well-known poem; ironically, it is not typical of Whitman's usual style. Compare "O Captain! My Captain!" to "Miracles" and "Song of Myself" (poems more characteristic of Whitman's style). Write an essay explaining why "O Captain! My Captain!" is considered an unusual poem for Whitman. Now try rewriting "O Captain! My Captain!" to make it more consistent with the style of "Miracles."

- Watch the DVD of PBS's *American Experience: Walt Whitman*. Write a review of the program. Did it give you new insight into Whitman's work? Was it missing information you would have liked to know? Rate the program on a five-star scale. Now gather the ratings from other class members and make a chart of them. What is the average star rating for this DVD?

- Walt Whitman spent many hours aiding wounded soldiers during the Civil War. Read "The Wound-Dresser," a poem he wrote about his experience tending injured soldiers. Then read Rosemary Wells's young-adult Civil War novel *Red Moon at Sharpsburg* (2007). Research the battle featured in the novel, the Battle of Antietam, and make a chart showing the total number of soldiers involved and the number of casualties on each side.

'I have found the law of my own poems,' was the unspoken but more and more decided feeling that came to me as I pass'd, hour after hour, amid all this grim yet joyous elemental abandon . . . the chasm, the gorge, the crystal mountain stream.

In this poem, the human elements—strangers in a car, men in a boat, dinner companions—are given no more (and no less) importance than the insects, animals, and other aspects of nature. In fact, the observation of strangers seen on public vehicles (line 8) is followed immediately in the next line by the observation of bees in a hive (line 9). Through this impartial listing, Whitman conveys the message that humanity and nature are equally miraculous, and exist as a harmonious whole (as opposed to the idea of dominant man ruling over nature).

Sensuality

Whitman wrote often about the human form and its sensual pleasures. Whitman believed that the body was sacred, as it housed the soul. Though the physical body is not as dominant a theme in this poem as in others (such as "I Sing the Body Electric"), sensual pleasures are listed among the many miracles. Wading barefoot along the beach, sleeping in bed with a loved one, and having dinner are all listed as miracles, and Whitman's choice of words in describing the moon's curved shape gives even the skies a sensual quality. In the original, longer version of the poem, Whitman also included human limbs and organs among the miracles listed.

Celebration of the Everyday

Poets of the eighteenth century usually wrote on exalted themes: biblical episodes, great battles, or famous historical figures. Later in the century, some poets like Robert Burns began to write about the common man. In the nineteenth century, Whitman takes this a step further by celebrating the most everyday occurrences—riding in public transit, eating dinner—as miraculous. The grandeur of ordinary things, and of nature, recurs in other Whitman poems. In section 31 of "Song of Myself," Whitman describes a mouse as a miracle, and in his elegy for Abraham Lincoln, "When Lilacs Last in the Dooryard Bloom'd," he refers to a leaf as a miracle as well.

Democracy

Whitman felt a deep connection to his country and to the ideal of democracy; he believed strongly that

Whitman saw miracles in nature scenes. (Le Do / Shutterstock.com)

the common man should have the same rights as those with more money or impressive family names. Note how "Miracles" bestows the same status on all people: loved ones, strangers, acquaintances, and the men in ships on the sea are all designated miracles. Both the city and country are miracles as well, and are equally represented. This is significant when one considers the coming conflict between the states, as the South was dominantly agricultural (the country) and the North was more industrialized (the city).

STYLE

Free Verse

"Miracles" is written in free verse, meaning that the poem has no fixed metrical pattern. While this does not seem that unusual to modern readers, it was still considered a fairly new technique in Whitman's time. Most poetry of the late eighteenth and early nineteenth centuries was still following fairly strict metric patterns, and adhered to common themes and categories (odes, elegies, and pastorals, for example). While earlier poets experimented with free verse, Whitman was one of the first to adopt it as his predominant poetic style.

Though free verse does not have a fixed meter, it is not necessarily without rhythm; as noted above, the repetition of words and phrases, and the similar structure of successive lines can create rhythm within a free verse poem.

Lists

Whitman often used lists in his poems; the majority of "Miracles" is a list. Lines 2 through 16 are all one sentence, with many clauses repetitively listing the various miracles. Whitman is known as the poet of democracy, and by listing the tiniest elements of nature (honeybees, for example) in the same way as he lists loved ones, the sea, and Manhattan, he gives all these elements a democratic equality. Also, by citing strangers and acquaintances as equally miraculous as loved ones, he celebrates all people, without ranking them in importance.

Repetition

Whitman uses anaphora, the repetition of a word or phrase at the beginning of successive clauses, to establish a rhythm within the poem. The many repetitions of the word *or* give the poem the hypnotic quality of a chant. In lines 4 through 10, each *or* is followed by a verb; in the next four lines Whitman lists nouns, things he is observing.

Within the interior of the poem, Whitman repeats other words as well. He uses the word *miracle* or *miracles* seven times. He refers to how wonderful insects and sunsets are in two consecutive lines (lines 12 and 13). Whitman also repeats a phrase referring back to himself three times.

HISTORICAL CONTEXT

Conflict between the States

In 1856, when Whitman wrote the original version of "Miracles," the country was already embroiled in conflicts that would shortly lead to the Civil War. The dispute over whether new U.S. territories would allow slavery or not grew more heated with the addition of new land acquired in the Mexican War in 1848. The Compromise of 1850 allowed citizens of the new territories of New Mexico and Utah to decide for themselves whether or not they would be free or slave states once admitted to the Union, a policy that became known as popular sovereignty. This ambiguous stance disappointed Whitman, who strongly opposed slavery and its expansion into new territories. Shortly after the Compromise he expressed his bitter disapproval in a poem titled "House of Friends," which took its title from a Bible passage, Zechariah 13:6: "And one shall say unto him, what are these wounds in thy hands? Then he shall answer, Those with which I was wounded in the house of my friends."

In 1854, the Kansas-Nebraska Act further aggravated the conflict between the North and South by repealing the Missouri Compromise of 1820, which had forbidden slavery north of latitude 36°30′N (except for Missouri). Two years later, a U.S. Senator from Massachusetts named Charles Sumner delivered an impassioned speech denouncing the Kansas-Nebraska Act, in which he included personal insults against one of its authors, Andrew Butler. Butler's nephew, Preston Brooks, a representative from South Carolina, later approached Sumner at his desk and beat him severely with a cane. The altercation was symbolic of the growing antipathy between North and South; though Brooks was censured by outraged northerners, he became something of a hero in the South.

In 1857, the Dred Scott Decision brought the United States one step closer to civil war. Dred Scott was a slave whose owner had taken him to two free states, where he had lived for years before returning to the South. Dred Scott claimed that because he had lived in these free states, he was a free man. The case was in various courts for ten years, ending in the United States Supreme Court. The justices of the Supreme Court—many of whom had been appointed by pro-slavery presidents—decided that because Scott was descended from African slaves, he could not be an American citizen, and so had no right to sue. The Court also declared the Missouri Compromise unconstitutional. The decision incensed the North and paved the way for Abraham Lincoln's candidacy in the 1860 presidential election. Once Lincoln was elected, southern states began the process of secession, beginning with South Carolina in December 1860. Finally, on April 12, 1861, the first shots were fired by the Confederacy on Fort Sumter in Charleston, South Carolina, beginning the Civil War.

The Civil War had a great influence on Whitman and his poetry. He devoted himself to chronicling the horrors of the war in both poetry and prose, using his experience with soldiers in war hospitals. His deep identification with his country and the ideals upon which it was founded made America's crisis a personal one for Whitman.

COMPARE
&
CONTRAST

- **1850s:** As of 1855, over 75 percent of workers labor at a job related to the land (farming, herding, or ranching).

  Today: Less than 2 percent of Americans make their living through farm work. The majority of workers work indoors, and people spend much less time in nature than in the nineteenth century.

- **1850s:** The number-one cash crop in the United States is cotton, grown in the South using slave labor.

  Today: The top crop in America is corn, followed by soybeans; cotton is number seven on the list of U.S. cash crops. Slave labor, abolished after the Civil War, is no longer used.

- **1850s:** Riding in a car, an activity Whitman mentions in "Miracles," means riding in a public car or omnibus pulled by horses.

  Today: Personal automobiles are the main mode of American transportation; the first practical modern automobile was patented by Karl Benz in 1886.

The Industrial Revolution

The nineteenth century brought astonishing progress in transportation, communications, science and industry. From 1830 to 1850, the length of completed railroad lines increased from just twenty-three miles to over nine thousand. The steamboat, which had been invented in the late eighteenth century, was improved significantly during this time, so that it became a viable method of transporting goods. Samuel Morse invented the telegraph in 1844, and in 1846, Elias Howe invented the sewing machine, which revolutionized the textile and clothing industry. Advances in the textile industry, which began with Eli Whitney's invention of the cotton gin in the late eighteenth century, contributed to the conflict between the states. Demand for cotton increased, which increased the amount of land needed for crops and the number of slaves the South required to work this land. This made the South especially eager for new territories to allow slavery.

Many significant advances in science were made in this period as well, including the 1859 publication of Charles Darwin's *On the Origin of Species*, in which he outlined his theory of evolution. Scientific and industrial advancements caused a shift away from religion and towards science. "Miracles" reflects this shift. Though the title would seem to imply a religious theme, the poem avoids any religious imagery, and at no point does Whitman mention God. Poems in earlier periods would rarely rhapsodize about the miracles of nature without citing its creator. Whitman not only omits God, he uses scientific language to state his case.

CRITICAL OVERVIEW

Most of the criticism available from the nineteenth century focuses on *Leaves of Grass* as a whole, rather than individual poems. The most influential piece of criticism on the volume's first release in 1855 was not an official review, but a letter of praise written to Whitman by Ralph Waldo Emerson, quoted by M. Jimmie Killingsworth in *The Cambridge Introduction to Walt Whitman*. Emerson told him, "I am very happy in reading it, as great power makes us happy."

Other reviews of the first and second editions of *Leaves of Grass* were mixed. Some of the more openly sexual poems shocked and appalled Victorian-era readers, and some critics found Whitman's earthy, sensual style crude and unrefined. A reviewer of the 1860 edition in the *Springfield Daily Republican* (titled "'Leaves of

Time with family is important to Whitman in this poem. *(Losevsky Pavel | Shutterstock.com)*

Grass'—Smut in Them") rants that, "the pure in society will shun it, and . . . it will be sought out and laughed over by lewd women and prurient boys and hoary-headed old lechers." Likewise, a reviewer of the 1856 edition (in which "Miracles" first appeared) in the *Christian Examiner* characterizes the work as a "crazy outbreak of conceit and vulgarity" which "teems with abominations."

However, even some who found the work objectionable were willing to see its merits. A reviewer for the *New York Daily Times*, reviewing the 1856 volume, writes,

> With all this muck of abomination soiling the pages, there is a wondrous, unaccountable fascination about the *Leaves of Grass*. As we read it again and again, and we will confess that we have returned to it often, a singular order seems to arise out of its chaotic verses.

In a similar vein, a reviewer for the *Brooklyn Daily Times* states,

> There is a deep substratum of observant and contemplative wisdom as broad as the foundation of society, running through it all; and whatever else there is of questionable good, so much at least is a genuine pearl that we cannot afford to trample it under our feet.

Some critics felt that too much was being made of Whitman's supposed immorality. A review by Edward Everett Hale for the *North American Review* claims,

There is not a word in it meant to attract readers by its grossness, as there is in half the literature of the last century, which holds its place unchallenged on the tables of our drawing-rooms.

Those who could see past the issue of indecency often found a simplicity, freshness, and originality in Whitman's poems that held their interest. A reviewer for the *Harvard Magazine* writes, "There is something wholesome, fresh, invigorating, in this book, and we like it." This opinion is echoed by a contributor to the *Boston Banner of Light*: "The whole body of these Poems—spiritually considered—is alive with power, throbbing and beating behind and between the lines."

Like his choice of subject matter, Whitman's disregard for traditional poetic forms aggravated some critics, but delighted others. A reviewer for the *Saturday Review* writes: "Mr. Whitman has adopted a metre which . . . is calculated to make the labour of writing poetry much slighter than it has been usually considered." Charles Eliot Norton, in a largely favorable review in *Putnam's Monthly*, complains that Whitman writes "neither in rhyme nor blank verse, but in a sort of excited prose broken into lines without any attempt at measure or regularity." But Henry P. Leland, in the *New York Saturday Press*, asserts that Whitman's straightforward, free-form style is just what American poetry needs. He characterizes traditional poetry as a "vine long unpruned . . . graceful lines, spiral tendrils, flaunting leaves, but very little fruit."

Critical opinion of *Leaves of Grass* grew more and more favorable over time. Whitman's work during the Civil War, and a volume titled *Poems of Walt Whitman*, published in 1868, which omitted some of the more supposedly licentious poems from *Leaves of Grass*, brought Whitman's work to the attention of more readers.

CRITICISM

Laura Beth Pryor

Pryor has been writing professionally for over twenty-five years, and holds a degree from the University of Michigan. In the following essay, she examines the poem "Miracles" in the context of Whitman's religious beliefs and the influence of

WHAT DO I READ NEXT?

- The book *Poetry for Young People: Walt Whitman* (Sterling Publishing, 1997), edited by Jonathan Levin and illustrated by Jim Burke, offers a selection of Whitman's poetry, along with helpful information about the relation of each poem to Whitman's overall work, symbolism, and techniques used. Also included are definitions of some of the more difficult words in the poems.

- *Between Two Fires: Black Soldiers in the Civil War* by Joyce Hansen (Franklin Watts Publishing, 1993) chronicles the experience of African Americans who fought in the war, despite opposition by some. Lincoln himself was reluctant to allow black troops until a shortage of soldiers forced his hand. Written especially for a young-adult audience, the book provides many examples of significant contributions to the war effort by African American companies, and an extensive bibliography for those who wish to read more on the subject.

- Though Whitman is known primarily as a poet, he did publish a collection of his prose writings, titled *Specimen Days and Collect*, available from Dover Publications (1995). The book includes diary excerpts, essays, and most notably, a series of writings on his experiences aiding the war wounded. It also includes writings from his later years, after he was disabled by a paralytic stroke.

- African American "jazz poet" Langston Hughes cited Walt Whitman as one of his influences, and even wrote a short poem in tribute to Whitman, titled "Old Walt." *The Collected Poems of Langston Hughes*, released by Vintage Publishing in 1995 and edited by Arnold Rampersad, includes all of Hughes's poetic work, as well as a chronology of Langston's life and work and textual notes on the poems.

- Whitman was influenced by American transcendentalist Ralph Waldo Emerson, and though he did not know Emerson personally at the time, he sent him a copy of his first edition of *Leaves of Grass*. Emerson responded with an encouraging letter praising Whitman's work. Emerson's most influential works are collected in *The Essential Writings of Ralph Waldo Emerson*, published by Modern Library in 2000.

- Whitman strongly opposed slavery. His contemporary, Mark Twain, wrote one of the most famous novels featuring slavery, *The Adventures of Huckleberry Finn*, A 125th anniversary edition of the novel is available from the University of California Press (2010), including updated notes, and an assortment of advertisements, playbills and letters from Twain's first book tour. The book is edited by Victor Fischer and Lin Salamo, members of the Mark Twain Project at the University of California, Berkeley.

Ralph Waldo Emerson's philosophy on these beliefs.

A nineteenth-century reader presented with a poem titled "Miracles" would likely be expecting a poem with a religious theme. And though other poems in *Leaves of Grass* feature plenty of references to God and the soul, this poem, a poem all about miracles, does not. Despite this omission, or perhaps because of it, "Miracles"

can be seen as a manifestation of Whitman's philosophy of religion, one influenced strongly by both the transcendentalist movement and his family's Quaker beliefs.

Whitman's fierce belief in the divinity of the individual, irrespective of class, wealth, or education, informed both his politics and his religious views. As the poet of democracy, Whitman espoused a democratic view of God as well. In

---

section 48 of "Song of Myself," Whitman writes that he sees God in everything, but can't imagine a being any more wonderful than himself. This kind of statement, decried as arrogant by many nineteenth-century critics, reflects Whitman's exaltation of the individual—not merely himself, but all individuals. In "Miracles," Whitman takes this thought one step further; not only are all individuals divine, but every grain of sand, every drop of the sea, every insect or animal is equally sacred, because all are part of a divine whole. Whitman's use of nature images is, to him, religious; in "I Sing the Body Electric," he writes that he believes nature reflects his soul.

Whitman's grandmother was a Quaker, and his father was friends with the Quaker dissenter Elias Hicks, who believed that each individual should find their own personal connection with God by discovering an inner light that would lead them. According to Barbara Marinacci, author of *O Wondrous Singer! An Introduction to Walt Whitman*, Whitman believed that "God was a vast and positive force that pervaded the universe, not some petty-minded and cranky deity who fussed over human frailties and failures." As a result, Whitman was never attracted to organized religion and was not a churchgoer. Whitman believed that to feel God's influence, he had merely to look about; it was not necessary to be in a chapel or cathedral. This idea pervades "Miracles," as every miracle that Whitman lists in the poem is an everyday sight or happening that requires no special religious ritual or affiliation to appreciate.

Whitman was heavily influenced by the writings of Ralph Waldo Emerson. After finishing his first edition of *Leaves of Grass*, Whitman sent a copy to Emerson, whom he admired but had never met. In "Miracles," the influence of Emerson and his religious beliefs can be seen, especially if one examines Emerson's 1838 address to a group of Harvard Divinity School graduates. In 1832, Emerson had resigned his position as a Unitarian minister because he no longer believed in the ceremony of communion. In his address to the graduates, he espoused his belief that the "sentiment of virtue," an innate knowledge of God and his laws, lies within every man. "If a man is at heart just," said Emerson, "then in so far is he God; the safety of God, the immortality of God, the majesty of God, do enter into that man with justice." Whitman expresses the same idea in section 48, line 1284 of *Song of Myself*,

when he writes that he sees the face of God when he looks in the mirror. Emerson also told the graduates that Jesus "spoke of miracles; for he felt that man's life was a miracle, and all that man doth, and he knew that this daily miracle shines, as the character ascends. But the word Miracle, as pronounced by Christian churches, gives a false impression; it is Monster. It is not one with the blowing clover and the falling rain." Elsewhere in the speech, Emerson claimed that the mind of God "is everywhere active, in each ray of the star, in each wavelet of the pool." Here Emerson expressed the exact idea that Whitman is communicating in "Miracles": the difference between capital M Miracles (note how Emerson, in writing his lecture, did not capitalize "miracles" as defined by Jesus) and the miracles of daily life. The "blowing clover and the falling rain" and "each wavelet of the pool" could easily be added to Whitman's list of miracles; not only is Emerson's concept the same, the language is very similar to Whitman's as well.

Because man has God within him, Emerson stressed, "Man is the wonder-worker. He is seen amid miracles." Emerson felt that, rather than celebrate the soul of man, the church exploited spectacular Miracles to elevate Jesus beyond the status of man, to deny that a mere mortal could have God within him. He urged the divinity graduates, much as Elias Hicks might have, to "dare to love God without mediator or veil." This personal experience of the divine that both Whitman and Emerson valued so highly was the ultimate democracy, because it gave every man equal access to God, without the church as "mediator."

In the 1881 version of "Miracles," Whitman removed several lines that had appeared in earlier volumes. Examining the lines that were removed, one may note that some contain judgments or express preferences (for instance, he writes of being with the kind of people he most enjoys). This editing was in accordance with his goal, as he wrote in his notes, "To change the book—go over the whole with great care—to make it more intensely the poem of *Individuality . . .* ruling out, perhaps, some parts that stand in the way of this." By removing these lines, Whitman retains the equality, the democracy of the miracles he lists. In much the same way, Emerson sought to change the barriers the church was placing between individuals and God, to remove the pretense that clergymen

In the final stanza, the miracle of the sea is described. (Willyam Bradberry | Shutterstock.com)

had a greater right to approach God and have a spiritual connection with Him; God, Emerson asserted, does not offer his support and wisdom just to a certain kind of people.

Earnest as he was, Emerson was not rewarded for his democratic candor; his speech resulted in an uproar from clergymen in America, who called Emerson an atheist. The discounting of Jesus' capital M Miracles, they felt, was tantamount to blasphemy. Emerson was not deterred and continued to assert and refine his philosophy; four years later, in the essay "Self Reliance," he restated his belief in a direct connection between man and God: "The relations of the soul to the divine spirit are so pure, that it is profane to seek to interpose helps." Whitman's work was also attacked as blasphemy, and called "impious and obscene," illustrating Emerson's own assertion, "To be great is to be misunderstood." Though the poem "Miracles" is not one of the poems attacked for indecency, it still reflects Whitman's belief that the sacred can be found anywhere and everywhere, and it was this belief that freed Whitman to make poetry on topics that others found unsuitable and crude. Like Emerson, he strove to communicate the wonder and power of the individual, a being created in the likeness of God, not an inferior facsimile.

> WHITMAN'S DEPARTURE FROM CONVENTIONAL POETIC FORMS HAS LED SOME TO BELIEVE THAT HE HAD NO EAR FOR THE MUSIC OF POETRY. HE HAD, OF COURSE, A VERY KEEN EAR."

Source: Laura Beth Pryor, Critical Essay on "Miracles," in *Poetry for Students*, Gale, Cengage Learning, 2012.

James E. Miller, Jr.

In the following excerpt, Miller discusses the characteristics and merits of Whitman's short poems from Leaves of Grass.

So much critical attention has been paid to Whitman's long poems that it is frequently forgotten that much of *Leaves of Grass* is made up of short poems, some of them ranking with the best of Whitman's poetry. Although it is probably true that Whitman's expansive temperament was best fitted for poems of some length, it is equally true that his genius enabled him at times to create brilliant short lyrics. Perhaps one of the reasons for the nature of Whitman's reputation is that the longer poems are more easily "detachable" from the whole of *Leaves of Grass* and are less dependent on their context for their fulness of meaning. Whitman's short poems frequently refer and have application to the entire body of his work. But a critical treatment of *Leaves of Grass* would be incomplete without some attention to the short poems. The attention of this chapter, though inadequate (as all criticism is, ultimately, inadequate), is meant to account for a few of the flashes of brilliance the reader of *Leaves of Grass* perceives in the short lyrics as he browses through the volume.

One of the most notable elements of many of the short "leaves" is what might be termed their cryptic quality, a quality of ambiguity, even evasiveness, which suggests an abundant complexity of meaning. This quality, a deliberate technique consciously developed by the poet, perhaps reaches its maximum use and effectiveness in "Calamus," but it appears throughout *Leaves of Grass*. When Whitman asserts, somewhat defiantly, in one of his prefaces to his book, "I have not been afraid of the charge of obscurity," he not only aligns himself with the dominant tradition in twentieth-century poetry but also reveals an important element of his poetic technique. Whitman's "obscurity" was motivated by the poet's realization that there was a good deal of "obscurity" about the ultimate nature of things. One could have assurance, could be certain, but such *emotional* insight was not necessarily accompanied by *philosophical* insight. That the emotions were not confirmed by the intellectual understanding made them no less valid, particularly as subject of poetry. Perhaps it was precisely in this area that poetry found its most appropriate subject matter; for the rich language of poetry could suggest, could hint at what existed beyond man's understanding. . . .

In an "Inscriptions" poem ("Poets to Come"), Whitman asserts the philosophical inadequacy of his poetry: . . . It is clearly this attitude, acknowledging the inadequacy of language to embrace systematically the complexity of "reality," that underlies Whitman's technique of the cryptic, the ambiguous, the suggestive, in poetry. . . .

Another dominant device present in many of the fine short poems is the catalogue. Perhaps this device is more tolerable in the brief than in the long poem because it appears to be under a stricter control. In any event in the best of the short-poem catalogues, the function or purpose of the "list" of swiftly succeeding images is sharply pointed. Like the cryptic element in Whitman's poetry, the catalogue, really an ecstatic and extended engagement with—delight in—the physicality of the universe, derives from a fundamental point of view held by the poet. Whitman confesses in one of his "Inscriptions" poems—"Beginning my Studies":

> Beginning my studies the first step pleas'd me so much,
> The mere fact consciousness, these forms, the power of motion,
> The least insect or animal, the senses, eyesight, love,
> The first step I say awed me and pleas'd me so much,
> I have hardly gone and hardly wish'd to go any father,
> But stop and loiter all the time to sing it in ecstatic songs.

This confession goes far toward explaining the nature of and the cause for the catalogues in *Leaves of Grass*. But if there is a realization in this poem of the difficulty of getting beyond the physical, there is also an acute awareness that "mere fact consciousness" is only the "first step."

This awareness is elevated to the level of a cardinal principle in Whitman's poetics.

The principle was proclaimed in the 1855 Preface: "The land and sea, the animals fishes and birds, the sky of heaven and the orbs, the forests mountains and rivers, are not small themes . . . but folks expect of the poet to indicate more than the beauty and dignity which always attach to dumb real objects . . . they exact him to indicate the path between reality and their souls." Pleasant though it might be to construct poems only of images, Whitman affirms the necessity for the poet to go beyond, to perceive relationships and probe connections, to discover and convey the spiritual significance of the physical fact. In this step lies the supreme act of perception of the poetic process, as difficult as it is rewarding.

Whitman appears at his best when he allows his mind free play over a seeming multitude of "physical facts," ferreting out submerged relationships and illuminating imbedded significances. Three brilliant short poems may serve as examples of Whitman's adaptation of the catalogue technique to the brief lyric: "I Hear America Singing," "The World Below the Brine," and "I Sit and Look Out."

One of the most frequently reprinted poems in *Leaves of Grass*, "I Hear America Singing" presents an image of America that America would like to believe tree—an image of proud and healthy individualists engaged in productive and happy labor. Mechanic, carpenter, mason, boatman, deckhand, shoemaker, hatter, woodcutter, plowboy—from city to country, from sea to land, the "varied carols" reflect a genuine joy in the day's creative labor that makes up the essence of the American dream or myth. After the catalogue of the men of the various crafts and occupation the poet turns to the women: . . .

The women of the men sing at their labor too, as the poet, figuratively reversing time, places in order first a mother, then a wife, and finally a girl. These songs of one's own ("what belongs to him or her") are carols of spiritual possession—of the possessed individuality, of possessed life and potentiality for contribution to the onward stream of life. If the fused image of mother-wife-girl, following as it does the catalogue of happy craftsmen, suggests that fulfilled emotions of "Children of Adam," the closing image of the poem, an image of night rather than day, with its "party of young fellows" singing "their strong melodious songs," suggest the fulfilled emotions of "Calamus." America singing emerges as a happy, individualistic, proudly procreative, and robustly comradely America. It is surprising that in such brief poem so much of Whitman's total concept of modern man could be implied. Perhaps its "casual" inclusiveness is one of the reasons for its popularity. . . .

The same genius that enabled Whitman to assemble the items of a catalogue and discover in the total a significance greater than the sum of the parts endowed him also with keen poetic insight into the brief vignettes life seems always freely presenting to the perceptive. Some of Whitman's most brilliant short poems are hardly more than vivid descriptive accounts of such vignettes, through every phrase of which flickers forth the flame of suggestive meaning, the whole finally consumed in a flash of brilliant insight. In this technique, as in the catalogues, the operating principle is the poet's attempt, subtly but firmly, "to indicate the path between reality" and the soul. . . .

Whitman's departure from conventional poetic forms has led some to believe that he had no ear for the music of poetry. He had, of course, a very keen ear. And it is this very combination of freedom from convention with attention to subtle formal properties ("The profit of rhyme is that it drops seeds of a sweeter and more luxuriant rhyme") that gives Whitman's poetry its distinctive quality. The freedom from the usual poetic restrictions conveys the sense of wild abandonment; the subtle attention to rhythm and sound modifies this sense with the suggestion of almost magical control. The total impression, then, is one of primitive ritual—of rites of abandonment instinct with form.

This aspect of Whitman, so important to the total effect of his poetry, is elusive, almost impossible to isolate for analysis. . . .

Frequently the central poetic device in Whitman's short lyrics is musical in nature—unconventional music, perhaps, but no less musical for that. Some of the poems draw their entire sustenance from such a "device"; remove the device, and the poems have no reason for existence. Without the word "unfolded," "Unfolded Out of the Folds" would be deprived of its cause for being. The incantation permitted by the repetition of this single word constitutes the lifeblood of the poem. Quite frequently Whitman's short

lyrics employ some form of primitive, bardic chant. Some of his best brief poems are brilliant incantations that hypnotically weave a mystic magic spell. . . .

Critical neglect of Whitman's short poems has unfortunately led many to assume that his brief lyrics are not worth serious attention. In reality his poetic genius is evident in a large number of his short poems. They are, no doubt, overshadowed by the longer poems, which are more ambitious and richer in complexity of detail and structure. The characteristic devices Whitman created or discovered for the embodiment of his poetic ideas and dramas may be more subtly and more effectively interrelated and fused in the longer poems, but in isolation these techniques serve very well for the achievement of specific circumscribed poetic purposes. These devices serve particularly well for the creation of brief lyrics, which not only must stand alone but also must be integrated into a totality that has a unity and structure created by individuality of style as well as of point of view.

Source: James E. Miller, Jr., "The Smaller Leaves," in *A Critical Guide to "Leaves of Grass,"* University of Chicago Press, 1957, pp. 142–60.

Louis Untermeyer

In the following essay, Untermeyer characterizes Whitman as the single most "American" poet.

The four days in February that did triple duty by celebrating the centenary of James Russell Lowell, the birthday of George Washington and what seemed to be an Anglo-American alliance, were not without a significant humor. Held ostensibly to honor the author of "The Vision of Sir Launfal," there were not a half a dozen American poets of note at any of the various dinners, theatre-parties and public love-feasts. Among all the tributes showered upon Lowell the diplomat, Lowell the bookman and Lowell the foe of slavery, there was no word for Lowell the recorder of homely folk or Lowell the seditious "pacifist." Scraps of his academic odes were read with unction, placid stanzas on Agassiz and Longfellow were printed with polite approbation; but scarcely anyone spoke of the first three Biglow Papers, and no one dared to quote such stanzas of flat conscientious objection as:

> Ez for war, I call it murder—
> There you hev it plain an' flat;
> I don't want to go no fuder
> Than my Testyment for that . . .
> Er you take a sword an' dror it,

An' go stick a feller thru,
Guv'ment ain't no answer for it,
God'll send the bill to you.

But what was possibly the most curiously ironic feature of the celebration was the unanimity of the press in echoing the *New York Times*' estimate that "a more determined, a more thorough American than Lowell it would be hard to find." No one evidently thought of searching— or they would have found that another poet, the most truly indigenous writer we have ever produced, was born just a hundred years ago at West Hills, Long Island. Nor would the joint festivities have been any the less appropriate for, strangely enough, it was England that first discovered the authentic Americanism of Walt Whitman.

It will be interesting to observe how many of our universities and academies of arts and letters appreciate Whitman's liberating influence even to-day; May thirty-first (Whitman's birthday) will be a fresh test for those who dwelt with such emphasis on the fact that Lowell used the English language. I venture to predict that there will be no four-day chorus of lauds and magnificats. It is one thing to glorify a man who has worked industriously in the bonds of an old rhetoric and a routine romanticism; it is another thing to praise the man who struck off the bonds. And it is as a liberator, even more than as a poet, that Whitman has influenced American art. Whether we regard him as pioneer or (as Van Wyck Brooks has it [see *NCLC*, v. 4, pp. 563–64) the great precipitant, there is scarcely any strong tendency in native letters that Whitman has not somehow strengthened, clarified, impelled, democratized.

He came with a double-barreled challenge to a literary aristocracy. His was, first of all, a democracy of thought, of emotion, of theme. When the New Englanders (whose colonial poetry was not nearly as representative of New England as of old England) were going to village blacksmiths and chambered nautili for embroidered mottoes and neatly-turned maxims, he was taking his material hot from the raucous tumble of life. While most of his transatlantic contemporaries were strolling elegantly through Bulfinch's *Mythology*, hymning the minor amours of the major Greek divinities, Whitman was writing:

Come, Muse, migrate from Greece and Ionia.
Cross out, please, those immensely overpaid accounts;

That matter of Troy and Achilles' wrath, and
Æneas', Odysseus' wanderings.
Placard "Removed" and "To Let" on the rocks
of your snowy Parnassus . . .
For know a better, fresher, busier sphere; a
wider, untried domain awaits and demands you.

It was Whitman who first revealed "the glory of the commonplace"; for him ugliness was fused perfectly in a vast harmonic counterpoint. Nothing remained casual. He showed the ordinary in a blaze of color that shamed the attempted brilliance of the PreRaphaelites; his daily street-corners, ferries, bridges, were more bewildering than the lunar landscapes of Poe. His barbaric yap could be softened to express a lyric ecstasy over a blade of grass which to him was "no less than the journeywork of the stars"; his naïf wonder dwelt on the miracle of a mouse that would "stagger sextillions of infidels" and his own hairy hand, whose "narrowest hinge puts to scorn all machinery." It is this large naturalism, this affection for all that is homely and of the soil that set him apart from his fellow-craftsmen as our first American poet.

And the cow, crunching with depressed head,
surpasses any statute . . .
And the running blackberry would adorn the
parlors of heaven.

Scarcely less important than his anti-patrician thought, was his democratic speech. It was Whitman's use of the rich verbal matter that he found in the street rather than in libraries that made his influence so dominating. And, again in distinction to his scholarly compatriots, it was an American speech he was using. He even went so far as to declare that he often thought the whole of *Leaves of Grass* was only a language experiment, an effort toward a democratic (as opposed to a merely genteel) tongue. "It is," he said, "an attempt to give the spirit, the body, the man, new words, new potentialities of speech— an American, a cosmopolitan (the best of America is the best cosmopolitanism) range of self-expression. The new world, the new times, the new peoples, need a tongue according—yes, what is more, they will have such a tongue— will not be satisfied until it is evolved." He went back to this thought a score of times. One can find it amplified with a hundred suggestive phrases and variations in his *An American Primer*, a sketch for a lecture that was never delivered, a series of astonishing notes that extended over ten years. Here is an illuminating scrap:

I like limber, lasting, fierce words. I like them applied to myself—and I like them in newspapers, courts, debates, congress—Do you suppose the liberties and the brawn of These States have to do only with delicate lady-words? with gloved gentleman words?...Bad Presidents, bad judges, bad editors, owners of slaves, monopolists, infidels, castrated persons, shaved persons, supplejacks, ecclesiastics... cry down the use of strong, cutting, beautiful, rude words. To the manly instincts of the People they will forever be welcome.

And, here, in this half-musing, half-brusque fragment, the poet and propagandist join hands:

What is the fitness—what the strange charm of aboriginal names?—Monongahela—It rolls with venison richness upon the palate. Among names to be revolutionized: that of the city of "Baltimore."

American writers, he prophesied, would learn to love their own land and the language that reflected it; they would show "far more freedom in the use of words. Ten thousand native idiomatic words are growing, or are already grown...words that would be welcomed by the nation, being of the national blood." And it was Whitman, with his prodigal energy and vulgar health, that blazed the way through a forest of pedantry and clichés.

The breadth, the jubilant acceptance, a roughshod faith in life and death—these things led a regiment of writers out of sequestered gardens and worm-eaten towers, once labelled ivory. It was a new literature that followed; it flourished in the coarse sunlight and the keen air. It had strong roots in the earth; from its seeds sprang Frost, Sandburg, Dreiser, Oppenheim, Anderson, Masters, Lindsay and a score of autocthonous others. It was not so classic a thing as a renascence; it was a slow and painful birth. And thus one looks to the last of May. In the centenary of Whitman, American letters celebrates its own birthday. (pp. 245–47)

Source: Louis Untermeyer, "A Whitman Centenary," in *New Republic*, Vol. 18, No. 229, March 22, 1919, pp. 245–47.

Arthur Clive

In the following excerpt, Clive demonstrates that Whitman's character of life is reflected in his poetry.

[After] a long and close study of Whitman it is my opinion that the character of his life is reflected in his poetry as truly as that of any modern poet has been reflected in his. It is this in Whitman that is most admirable and most beneficent....

Whitman is unceasingly gay, and fresh, and racy. He speaks of common things, and men, and the common sights of everyday life, and yet he is always artistic. The things he observes are significant and such as arrest the eye and the mind, and make a deep mark in the memory. He expresses more than happiness, he expresses exultation. The two hemispheres of the soul he describes as love and dilatation, or pride....And so he often uses the word arrogant in a good sense. His poems teem with such words as superb, perfect, gigantic, divine. At his touch the dry bones of our meagre humanity are transformed, and man starts forth like a god, in body and in soul superhuman. The blurring concealing mist peels away, and we see a new heaven and a new earth. It is no longer a mean thing to be a man. From a hundred points he comes back always to this, that man is great and glorious, not little and contemptible. (p. 706)

But even exultation is not enough to satisfy the boundless ambition of this man. There is in him a suggestion of something enormous, something bursting the limits of mundane existence and pouring around on all sides, invading the supernatural world, in which, unlike most literary men, he seems fully to believe....

Thus death is more the beginning than the end. What it concludes is glorious, but what it begins is divine. Whitman is a mystic. He pours a glamour over the world. From the supernatural sphere, so natural to him, strange light is shed that transfigures the universe before his eyes and before ours. (p. 707)

Whitman, not a moment too soon, has appeared singing the body electric.

The intellectualism which has marked the century—the cultivation of sentiment and the emotions—threatened to enfeeble and emasculate the educated classes. The strong voice of Whitman, showing again and again, in metaphors and images, in startling vivid memorable language, the supreme need of sweet blood and pure flesh, the delight of vigour and activity and of mere existence where there is health, the pleasures of mere society even without clever conversation, of bathing, swimming, riding, and the inhaling of pure air, has so arrested the mind of the world that a relapse to scholasticism is no longer possible. (pp. 708–09)

[All] the simple employments and operations in which the common people are engaged; and the different aspects they present perpetually recur to him and arrest his mind at all times. It was this that at first produced the impression that he was an uneducated man. On the contrary no English poet except perhaps Shelley was so well acquainted with all that could be learned from books....

[Beyond] all others he is the poet of the day. He knows all that can be known by one person of the stored accumulations of the *savants*, and this knowledge appears in his works as poetry. (p. 710)

Certainly one cannot detect affectation in Whitman. He has at all events attained honesty. But the simplicity which would make him welcome to that class in the community which he more particularly affects he has not attained. The common people, whom he likes most, and who most like him, are not those who can comprehend or care for his poems. (pp. 711–12)

Whitman professes to contemn culture and education, yet he is a perfect representative of both. It is the cultivated classes who receive and recognise him, and it is to them that he is beneficial. He is subtle, profound, psychological, a mystic. He is nothing if not metaphysical, nothing if not erudite.... He sees everything with the eye of a cultivated poet and philosopher—with the eye of a man who knows much and can give a reason for the faith that is in him. (p. 712)

Under a mask of extravagance, of insane intensity, Whitman preserves a balance of mind and a sanity such as no poet since Shakespeare has evinced. If his sympathies were fewer he would go mad. Energy and passion so great, streaming through few and narrow channels, would burst all barriers. His universal sympathies have been his salvation, and have rendered his work in the highest degree sane and true. He is always emphatic, nay violent, but then he touches all things. Life is intense in him, and the fire of existence burns brighter and stronger than in other men. Thus he does his reader service: he seems out of the fullness of his veins to pour life into those who read him. He is electric and vitalising....

No poet since Shakespeare has written with a vocabulary so fruitful. Words the most erudite and remote, words not quite naturalised from foreign countries, words used by the lowest of the people, teem in his works, yet without

affectation. You can take away no word that he uses and substitute another without spoiling the sense and marring the melody. For where Whitman seems roughest, rudest, most prosaic, there often is his language most profoundly melodious. (p. 714)

The hardening, vulgarising influences of life have not hardened and vulgarised the spiritual sensibilities of this poet, who looks at this world with the wondering freshness of a child, and to the world beyond with the gaze of a seer. He has what Wordsworth lost, and in his old age comes trailing clouds of glory—shadows cast backward from a sphere which we have left, thrown forward from a sphere to which we are approaching.

He is the noblest literary product of modern times, and his influence is invigorating and refining beyond expression. (p. 716)

Source: Arthur Clive, "Walt Whitman: The Poet of Joy," in *Gentleman's Magazine*, Vol. 15, December 1875, pp. 704–716.

SOURCES

"Dred Scott's Fight for Freedom," in *Judgment Day*, Public Broadcasting System, http://www.pbs.org/wgbh/aia/part4/4p2932.html (accessed May 5, 2011).

Emerson, Ralph Waldo, "An Address Delivered before the Senior Class in Divinity College, Cambridge, Sunday Evening, July 15, 1838," in *History Tools,* http://www.historytools.org (accessed April 29, 2011); originally published in *The Prose Works of Ralph Waldo Emerson*, Vol. I, rev. ed., James Osgood, 1875, pp. 65–81.

———, "Self Reliance," in *Ralph Waldo Emerson Texts*, http://www.emersoncentral.com/selfreliance.htm (accessed April 29, 2011).

"Extension," in *National Institute of Food and Agriculture,* United States Department of Agriculture Web site, http://www.csrees.usda.gov/qlinks/extension.html (accessed April 29, 2011).

Gettman, Jon, "Marijuana Production in the United States (2006): Comparison with Other Cash Crops," in *DrugScience.org*, http://www.drugscience.org/Archive/bcr2/cashcrops.html (accessed April 29, 2011).

Hale, Edward Everett, Review of *Leaves of Grass* (1855), in *Walt Whitman Archive,* http://www.whitmanarchive.org/criticism/reviews/leaves1855/anc.00018.html (accessed April 29, 2011); originally published in *North American Review*, January 1856, pp. 275–77.

Kelly, Martin, "Industrial Revolution," in *About.com*, http://americanhistory.about.com/od/industrialrev/a/indrevoverview_2.htm (accessed April 29, 2011).

Killingsworth, M. Jimmie, *The Cambridge Introduction to Walt Whitman*, Cambridge University Press, 2007, pp. 1–47, 105–122.

"'Leaves of Grass'—Smut in Them," in *Walt Whitman Archive*, http://www.whitmanarchive.org/criticism/reviews/leaves1860/anc.00187.html (accessed April 29, 2011); originally published in *Springfield Daily Republican*, June 16, 1860, p. 4.

Leland, Henry P., "Walt Whitman," in *Walt Whitman Archive*, http://www.whitmanarchive.org/criticism/reviews/leaves1860/anc.00186.html (accessed April 29, 2011); originally published in *Saturday Press*, June 16, 1860, p. 1.

"Maps Showing the Progressive Development of U.S. Railroads, 1830-1950," in *Central Pacific Railroad Photographic History Museum*, http://cprr.org/Museum/RR_Development.html (accessed April 29, 2011); originally published by Association of American Railroads, January 1951.

Marinacci, Barbara, *O Wondrous Singer! An Introduction to Walt Whitman*, Dodd, Mead, 1970, pp. 6–56.

Norton, Charles Eliot, Review of *Leaves of Grass* (1855), in *Walt Whitman Archive*, http://www.whitmanarchive.org/criticism/reviews/leaves1855/anc.00011.html (accessed April 29, 2011); originally published in *Putnam's Monthly*, September 1855, pp. 321–23.

Review of *Leaves of Grass* (1860), in *Walt Whitman Archive*, http://www.whitmanarchive.org/criticism/reviews/leaves1860/anc.00037.html (accessed April 29, 2011); originally published in *Boston Banner of Light*, June 2, 1860.

Review of *Leaves of Grass* (1856), in *Walt Whitman Archive*, http://www.whitmanarchive.org/criticism/reviews/leaves1856/anc.00033.html (accessed April 29, 2011); originally published in *Brooklyn Daily Times*, December 17, 1856.

Review of *Leaves of Grass* (1855) and (1856), in *Walt Whitman Archive*, http://www.whitmanarchive.org/criticism/reviews/leaves1856/anc.00031.html (accessed April 29, 2011); originally published in *Christian Examiner*, Vol. 60, November 1856, pp. 471–73.

Review of *Leaves of Grass* (1856), in *Walt Whitman Archive*, http://www.whitmanarchive.org/criticism/reviews/leaves1856/anc.00233.html (accessed April 29, 2011); originally published in *Harvard Magazine*, January 3, 1857, pp. 40–41.

Review of *Leaves of Grass*, in *Walt Whitman Archive*, http://www.whitmanarchive.org/criticism/reviews/leaves1856/anc.00032.html (accessed April 29, 2011); originally published in *New York Daily Times*, November 13, 1856, p. 2.

Review of *Leaves of Grass*, in *Walt Whitman Archive*, http://www.whitmanarchive.org/criticism/reviews/leaves1860/anc.00044.html (accessed April 29, 2011); originally published in *Saturday Review*, July 7, 1860, pp. 19–21.

Selcer, Richard F., "Agriculture," in *Civil War America, 1850-75*, Infobase Publishing, 2006, p. 86.

Whitman, Walt, "I Sing the Body Electric," in *Leaves of Grass*, edited by Michael Moon, Norton, 2002, pp. 81–87.

———, "Miracles," in *Leaves of Grass*, edited by Michael Moon, Norton, 2002, p. 327.

———, "Song of Myself," in *Leaves of Grass*, edited by Michael Moon, Norton, 2002, pp. 26–78.

———, "Whitman on His Art," in *Leaves of Grass*, edited by Michael Moon, Norton, 2002, pp. 783–89.

———, "Wounded in the House of Friends," in *Prose Works*, David McKay, 1892, http://www.bartleby.com/229/4013.html (accessed May 6, 2011).

FURTHER READING

Bloom, Harold, ed., *Walt Whitman*, "Bloom's Classic Critical Views" series, Bloom's Literary Criticism, 2007.
> In this book, well-known literary critic Harold Bloom provides a biography of Whitman, a critical analysis of his work, and a collection of essays by various authors. The essays are arranged in chronological order to illustrate the trends in criticism of Whitman's work. Essay contributors include author D. H. Lawrence, literary theorist Kenneth Burke, literary critic and biographer R. W. B. Lewis, and several others.

Buell, Lawrence, ed., *American Transcendentalists: Essential Writings*, Modern Library, 2006.
> As the title implies, this volume includes the most well-known writings of the transcendentalist movement, such as Emerson's "Nature," "American Scholar," and "Self-Reliance," as well as Thoreau's "Walden." It also features writings by Whitman, Nathaniel Hawthorne, and even an essay on the movement by Charles Dickens. Women writers of the movement are also included, such as women's rights activist Margaret Fuller and educator Elizabeth Peabody.

Loving, Jerome, *Emerson, Whitman, and the American Muse*, University of North Carolina Press, 2011.
> Loving compares the lives and careers of Walt Whitman and Ralph Waldo Emerson, finding similarities not just in the philosophy of their writing, but also in the trajectory of their major life events. He illustrates how both authors helped to define American literature and philosophy as unique entities apart from European influence, and yet each had their own personal, idiosyncratic vision.

Reynolds, David S., *Walt Whitman: A Cultural Biography*, Vintage, 1996.
> Reynolds's biography focuses on how the cultural climate and historical events of Whitman's

time shaped his writing. He provides a comprehensive look at Whitman's era, including developments in science and industry, changing attitudes towards religion, political upheaval, and, of course, the Civil War. He also examines how Whitman's intense identification with his country influenced both his work and his personality.

Timmons, Todd, *Science and Technology in Nineteenth Century America*, Greenwood Press, 2005.

Timmons examines the sweeping changes in transportation, communications, science, and industry in the nineteenth century, and how these changes affected the everyday life of American citizens. Besides Timmons's extensive analysis of how this progress transformed American society, the book also includes a timeline of inventions and advancements, and is illustrated with a selection of nineteenth-century photographs.

SUGGESTED SEARCH TERMS

Walt Whitman

Miracles

Walt Whitman AND Miracles

Poem of Perfect Miracles

Leaves of Grass

Walt Whitman AND Ralph Waldo Emerson

Walt Whitman AND Civil War

Walt Whitman AND Abraham Lincoln

Walt Whitman AND criticism

Walt Whitman AND nature

Walt Whitman AND equality

Walt Whitman AND transcendentalism

Leaves of Grass AND Walt Whitman

The Powwow at the End of the World

SHERMAN ALEXIE
1996

Sherman Alexie is of Spokane/Coeur d'Alene heritage. He prefers being called an American Indian rather than a Native American. His prolific literary career and instant fame as a writer in his early twenties were surprising, given his childhood poverty on the Spokane reservation. He has been celebrated for his versatility in many genres: poetry, songs, short stories, novels, and screenplays. He has produced films and become a popular performer in poetry slams, on TV guest appearances, and as a stand-up comedian. His themes have dealt with racism and the crippling colonial legacy for Indians. Alexie is noted for his humor in pointing out the incongruities of white and native worlds.

His poem "The Powwow at the End of the World" is a satiric statement about the fate of his tribe in the Columbia River basin as their salmon culture was destroyed by settlers, gold and uranium miners, the Grand Coulee Dam, and nuclear reactors. Not until the end of the world, he imagines, will his tribe and their harmonious way of life on the land return. The poem can be found in the collection *The Summer of Black Widows*, published by Hanging Loose Press in 1996.

AUTHOR BIOGRAPHY

Alexie was born on October 7, 1966, in Spokane, Washington, to Lillian Agnes Cox (of the Spokane, Flathead, and Colville tribes) and Sherman

Sherman Alexie (Getty Images)

Joseph Alexie (of the Coeur d'Alene tribe), one of six children. He underwent brain surgery at six months for hydrocephalus (a condition in which cavities in the brain are expanded by excess fluid). The doctors said he would be mentally retarded, but instead, he was precocious, learning to read by the age of three. He grew up in poverty with an alcoholic father on the Spokane Indian reservation in Wellpinit, Washington, where he went to primary school. To prepare for college, Alexie transferred to Reardan High School, a primarily white school, in 1981. He excelled and flourished, becoming captain of the basketball team, class president, and a debater. He enrolled in Gonzaga University in Spokane from 1985 to 1987 to become a doctor, but, overwhelmed, he began drinking to excess.

In 1988, he transferred to Washington State University in Pullman, receiving a bachelor of arts degree in American studies in 1994. There he took creative writing under Alex Kuo, his mentor. He began publishing his poems and stopped drinking to become serious about writing. *The*

Business of Fancydancing (poems and stories) and *I Would Steal Horses* were published in 1992, and Alexie's success was immediate. Two more books of poetry, *Old Shirts and New Skins* and *First Indian on the Moon*, came out in 1993, as well as a book of short stories, *The Lone Ranger and Tonto Fistfight in Heaven.*

In 1994, Alexie married Diane Tomhave (of the Hidatsa, Ho-Chunk, and Potawatomi tribes) and moved to Seattle. *Reservation Blues*, his first novel, came out in 1995, along with *Reservation Blues: The Soundtrack*, a musical collaboration between Alexie and Jim Boyd. The novel won the Before Columbus Foundation American Book Award and a Granta Award. A second novel, *Indian Killer*, was published in 1996, along with *Water Flowing Home* (poetry chapbook) and *The Summer of Black Widows* (poetry). Alexie premiered his award-winning film *Smoke Signals* at the Sundance Film Festival in 1998. He began his career as a stand-up comedian, a poetry performer, and TV guest at this time. *The Toughest Indian in the World* (short stories) and *One Stick Song* (poetry) came out in 2000, the former book winning the PEN/Malamud Award for Short Fiction. A second film, which he wrote and directed, *The Business of Fancydancing*, was shown at the Sundance Film Festival in 2002. *Ten Little Indians* (short stories) in 2003 was the *Publishers Weekly* Book of the Year. "What You Pawn I Will Redeem," from that book, was included in *The Best American Short Stories 2004.*

In 2005, the poem "Avian Nights" from *Dangerous Astronomy*, a poetry chapbook, won the Pushcart Prize. *Flight* (a novel) and *The Absolutely True Diary of a Part-Time Indian* (young-adult book) came out in 2007. *The Absolute True Diary* won a National Book Award for young-adult literature and an American Indian Youth Literature Award. *Face* (poetry) was published in 2009, as well as *War Dances* (stories), which won a PEN/Faulkner Award. As of 2011, Alexie and his wife lived in Seattle with their two sons.

POEM SUMMARY

The text used for this summary is from *The Summer of Black Widows*, Hanging Loose Press, 1996, p. 98. A version of the poem can be found on the following Web page: http://www.poe tryoutloud.org/poems/poem.html?id=177413.

"The Powwow at the End of the World" is a twenty-seven line, free-verse poem with varying line length and no end rhyme. The strong repetition and rhythm of the lines, however, suggest the drumbeat and dance of the apocalyptic powwow, or communal dance of Indians that the speaker says will take place at the end of the world. The meaning of the poem is carried not by units of individual lines but by nine sentences embedded in the poem. Each sentence has the same repetitive beginning but develops a different point, building to the climax of the powwow at the end. The speaker is an Indian answering the demand that he forgive the past, by an audience (probably white) that seems surprised or uncomfortable with Indian anger. The audience is addressed in the second person as "you," an aggressive move to shift attention back the audience. The speaker is not defensive but authoritative, speaking in chant-like oratory, as though in a court of justice that will finally weigh the blame of the American colonizers at the end of days.

First Sentence

The first sentence runs two and a half lines and introduces the charge repeated in every sentence that the Indians should forgive. The speaker's increasing demands show that he will only forgive when the injustice of cultural domination has been completely undone. In the first sentence, he says he will forgive when an Indian woman knocks down the Grand Coulee Dam with her shoulder.

The premise of the poem is audacious and satiric: the audience is implicated as complicit in the atrocities committed on Indians, by its very request that the Indians should now forget about what was done to them by the white European colonizers for five centuries, including taking their land, killing them and their environment, culture, and religion.

Even in the first sentence a tension is established between the colonizers' Christian religion of forgiveness and the Indian demand for reparation for the crimes committed. The fact that the implied Christian audience advises forgiveness is hypocritical since the settlers hardly behaved like Christians when they were killing and robbing the Indians and then trying to convert them to Christianity, without any sense of irony or conscience. There is also the implication of white greed, another contradiction to the Christian ethic of sharing and brotherly love. The line breaks in this sentence build suspense and emphasize the irony of the speaker's response. He is angry at the hypocrisy and makes it clear that forgiveness will only come at the end of the world, when an Indian woman has the power to push down the Grand Coulee Dam, a signal that justice has returned to earth.

The paradoxical image of the massive cement dam yielding to the push of an Indian woman is, first of all, a satiric demonstration of how unlikely forgiveness will be. This task, as one might guess, is not going to happen any time soon, only at the end of the world. Until then, he cannot forgive. Alexie makes an ironic joke with this image, but he may also be using a woman as a symbol of Indian justice and law, for in native tribes, women were often the counselors and judges. When a native woman can destroy a cement dam, it will show that the world has reversed its values of a male-dominated technology, abusive of mother nature.

Having a woman as an agent of nature's vengeance restores the power balance in human relations as well, for Alexie often speaks of the cruel patriarchy and abuse of women that Indians learned from white culture. Restoring the dignity and power of the native woman restores the dignity of the tribe. With this first statement, the speaker puts the audience on the spot. In fact, he accuses the readers directly of racial and natural injustice that is essentially unforgivable.

Second Sentence

The second sentence repeats the demand for Indian forgiveness, and the speaker replies he will forgive as soon as all the other dams downriver from the Coulee Dam are burst. The image here and in the next sentences, of floodwaters released, keeps increasing the volume of water, like a tsunami that will eventually wash away civilization.

Third Sentence

The third sentence insists that Indians will forgive when the released waters of all the dams find their way to the mouth of the Columbia at the Pacific Ocean, which will raise the level of the ocean. Here the speaker conveys the power of nature, artificially restrained and enslaved by humans with their dams.

Fourth Sentence

The fourth sentence claims that the Indians will forgive when the first drop of the released Columbia River to reach the ocean is swallowed by a salmon waiting in the Pacific. The salmon will know it is time to return when it tastes that first drop of the free river. The line breaks leave the word and image of the salmon on a line alone, emphasizing its importance and sacredness to the Spokane tribe. The salmon has been denied its right to swim up the Columbia where it has spawned for thousands of years before the white man blocked the river with cement. The Spokane tribe believed the salmon to be immortal, a divine gift to them from the salmon king. In the ocean, they believed, salmon had human forms and transformed themselves into fish to be food for the Indians. The tribe had to treat the fish with respect or they would not come.

Fifth Sentence

The fifth sentence says the Indians will forgive when the salmon swims upstream past the flooded cities and destroyed dams on the Columbia and past the abandoned nuclear reactors of Hanford. These images of floods and nuclear disasters combine biblical, holocaust, and science fiction scenes of the last days of human civilization, perhaps a prophecy of doom for human arrogance.

The reference to Hanford refers to the federal site built on the Columbia River during World War II to produce plutonium for the atomic bombs, part of the Manhattan project. Without adequate safety procedures, the site released large amounts of radioactive waste into the Columbia River. Food and water all over Washington State were contaminated for decades, but the government did not admit this problem until 1986. By 1987, all the nuclear reactors at Hanford were shut down, but cleaning up the residual waste is a lengthy, ongoing process.

Sixth Sentence

The sixth sentence explains forgiveness will come when the salmon swims into the mouth of the Spokane River where it meets the Columbia River and when the fish continues swimming up the Spokane River until it reaches a bay on the reservation where the speaker waits for it alone. The solitary appearance of the speaker waiting for the salmon suggests he is the last of his tribe. The rest have been destroyed.

The solitary speaker waiting for the salmon also evokes the ancient Spokane rite of the First Salmon. Each year a single man was honored by being selected to spear the first salmon in the spring. The fish was ritually cooked and eaten by the whole tribe, and the bones were returned to the river so the fish could magically regenerate. The ritual began the fishing season when thousands of salmon were caught and preserved for the coming winter. This sentence brings the drama to a more personal and local level to the Spokane Reservation and the homeland of the speaker's tribe. He waits for the salmon in a secret spot, a sacred assignation and reconciliation. The sentences become longer towards the end of the poem, imitating the unleashed flow of the free rivers and the salmon's long swim back home to the speaker from its exile.

Seventh Sentence

The seventh sentence says forgiveness will come when the salmon leaps up in the night, throwing a lightning bolt to ignite the brush and starting a bonfire as a signal for all scattered Indians to return home. Fire is a frequent symbol in Alexie's poems, signifying destruction or cleansing. The idea of a salmon able to start a fire gives it a magical and sacred character. The return of the salmon would be a sign to all the lost tribal members to come home again. The burning bush could suggest both Indian and Christian sacred lore. A bonfire is used to send smoke signals. Moses spoke to God in a burning bush. Alexie was raised as a Catholic and frequently mixes white and Indian cultural references in his work. The fire represents more than human forgiveness; it is the salmon's communication of divine forgiveness, now that the dams are destroyed.

Eighth Sentence

The eighth sentence promises forgiveness when the Indians have gathered around the salmon and heard three sacred secrets from it before daylight: a story to teach Indians how to pray, a story to make them laugh, and a story to make them dance. The sacred lore is now returning, bringing back Indian tradition. The salmon's stories contain wisdom, delight, and a way of connecting once more to the powers of nature through ceremony. Indian creation stories often contain characters like the salmon, representatives of the Creator (Amotkan to the Spokanes), who teach humans in the beginning how to live.

Ninth Sentence

The ninth and final sentence promises forgiveness when the speaker is dancing with his returned tribe in a powwow at the end of the world. A powwow is a gathering of Indians for socializing and celebrating or for ritual purposes. The people wear full ceremonial regalia and engage in circle dancing and chanting, sometimes for hours or days at a time. A powwow at the end of the world could suggest the Prophet or Ghost Dance, a religious rite practiced by the Spokane and other tribes in the nineteenth century, especially popular as the whites were taking over their lands. The traditional Indian view of history is cyclical, and in this ancient dance, the people participated in the destruction of the old world and beginning of a new world and in the resurrection of the dead. The speaker, through his words, has been doing just this: destroying the world of colonial domination and bringing forth a vision of new beginnings. He will not forgive until all his loved ones and ancestors have been reunited and Indian life restored, at the end of the current and unjust world.

THEMES

Colonialism

Colonialism is indicted by the poem as a cruel and racist doctrine towards American Indians. White Europeans who came to the Americas in the fifteenth century viewed the lands as vacant, because they were peopled by nomadic tribes thought to be uncivilized. The Europeans exploited the American territories, seeing them as a source of wealth. Alexie's poem, though set in the present time, looks back to the past five-hundred-year period in American Indian history when Alexie's tribe, the Spokane, was persecuted by white colonials. Native Americans still live under the heavy weight of this legacy. The colonial drive, first of the Europeans and then of the United States government in its westward expansion, all but exterminated the Indians and many animal species like the buffalo and salmon that were their food sources.

The devastating effect of white colonialism on the Spokane tribe is represented symbolically in the poem by the Grand Coulee Dam, the nuclear reactors at Hanford, the lost salmon fishing, and the speaker as one of the last of his tribe. For white Americans, the Grand Coulee Dam and the nuclear reactors were signs of technological and industrial progress. The dam provided electricity and irrigation, while the nuclear reactors produced the plutonium for a nuclear defense program during World War II and the Cold War. Both the dam and the nuclear plants had far-reaching ecological impact, however, including the depopulation of wildlife species and the poisoning of the Columbia River with nuclear waste.

For the American Indians, this white progress meant the end of their hunting grounds and salmon fishing, which provided food and were also part of their spiritual bond with the land. At the basis of the colonial doctrine were fundamental beliefs, such as the racist perception of Native Americans as savages who did not have any right to the land. Early colonials may have had some notion of coexistence, but the sheer number of whites, their superior weaponry and greed for gold, land, and other resources led to governmental policies that favored whites and attempted to get the natives out of the way.

Native American Culture

The traditional Spokane culture evoked in the poem is an alternative to colonial values. It is based on cooperation between the human sphere and the natural sphere. This view of the indigenous way of life is captured in the last half of the poem, after the speaker has symbolically destroyed the dams, cities, and reactors. Once the rivers are free and the land is free, the animals can return as well as the spirits of all the ancestors who were killed. The Native American way of life is based on the equal rights and interdependence of all creatures instead of the exploitation of nature by humans. The turn back to this balance occurs when the speaker, now alone on the reservation without his tribe, initiates a sacred ritual with the salmon who once again teaches the Indians the ancient harmony.

In native creation stories, the animal powers predate human existence and often take human form. They sacrifice themselves to keep humans alive, and the Indians reciprocate through ceremonies of thanksgiving. The powwow is the primary symbol of the Native American way of life in the poem, for it is a gathering, serving as both reunion and spiritual dance. The fact that it happens at the end of the world carries both political and religious significance. Politically, the forgiveness comes when white culture no

TOPICS FOR FURTHER STUDY

- Do research on the Spokane Indian tribe and the Spokane reservation, using both Internet and library resources. Explain the history of this tribe, mention any famous leaders or events, and summarize their cultural values. Show how Alexie incorporates this history into a short story or novel. Write this up as a research paper, or create an interactive digital timeline with links that explain the important leaders and events. Add images and video to enhance the cultural understanding.

- American Indian poets Joy Harjo and Sherman Alexie perform their poetry and use music and media in interesting ways. Give a talk (individual or group) on the similarities and differences in the poetry and style of the two, using Internet sources to show their performances on YouTube, or show film clips of their work. They have both recorded music albums. Play selections from those as well. How do they take poetry off the page and make it relevant to audiences today?

- Work with a group to find relevant Web sites on Native American life and issues today and use Delicious.com or other social bookmarking service to share results. Then select a theme for a group presentation by sharing on a large screen sample Web sites and your conclusions about contemporary Native American life.

- Watch Alexie's 1998 film *Smoke Signals*, and give a group report on the film plot, production, and use of humor to undermine stereotypes of Native Americans. The short story "This Is What It Means to Say Phoenix, Arizona," from the young-adult collection *The Lone Ranger and Tonto Fistfight in Heaven*, served as the basis for the award-winning film *Smoke Signals*, which Alexie wrote and produced. Read the short story after watching the film and compare the two. Show relevant clips and read relevant passages. Discuss with the class whether Alexie's humor works best in print or on film.

- The blues is a form of music originating with African Americans but adopted by other cultures. Give a PowerPoint presentation on the musical structure of the blues and demonstrate how it serves multicultural needs, using musical selections and lyrics from white, black, and American Indian blues singers (for instance, Robert Johnson, Sherman Alexie's *Reservations Blues: The Soundtrack* with Jim Boyd and Janis Joplin or Bob Dylan).

---

longer oppresses the Indians. Spiritually, the dance is a ceremony of cyclical renewal of nature and Indian life, even bringing back the dead.

For Native Americans, the earth is sacred and is treated as a mother. In the poem, the speaker honors the lost feminine value by invoking a Native American woman to topple the dam. Language is the essence of ritual and is used by the speaker to bring back his tribe. The repetition of phrases and long rolling sentences have a chant-like quality, making the poem into a powwow ceremony.

Survival

The poem both celebrates the survival of Indian culture and at the same time creates that survival in language. It only takes a single Indian and a single salmon meeting secretly in the bay of the reservation to bring back the whole Native American way of life and the lost tribe. One ironic reason for the speaker's survival may be his anger. He is told to forgive, to let go of anger, but he implies that the cost of the kind of forgiveness the whites would like him to give would be annihilation and forgetting Indian ways.

American Indians drumming at a powwow. (Bill Perry / Shutterstock.com)

Beginning in the nineteenth century with such novels as *The Last of the Mohicans* by James Fenimore Cooper, the romantic myth of the vanishing Indian became another way to declare the demise of the natives. Contemporary Native American writers consciously proclaim in their work that this view is false; Indians are still here, and they are survivors. Although the speaker seems to be the last, he will bring everyone back for a grand powwow.

STYLE

Ceremonial Chant

Native American ceremony is the basis of most modern Native American poetry, either directly or indirectly, because it embraces a certain perception of the world. Indian tribal ceremonies use formal structures of incantation, song, dance, prayer, visual symbols and gestures to restore wholeness to the land and community. These oral traditions had the purpose to integrate the community with the cosmic forces.

The ceremonial chant is an underlying structure in "The Powwow at the End of the World," which is constructed as though it is a ceremony to bring back the dead Indians and resurrect their world. Like ceremonies, it uses repetition to create a hypnotic sense of union with nature, each sentence beginning the same. The poem creates a circular pattern, like Indian circle dancing that maintains the eternal cycles of nature.

Native American Myth

The traditional tribal stories of creation and the interaction of gods, humans, animals, and plants are often fused with modern storytelling in Indian fiction and poetry. A myth is a story that uses symbolism as poems do. It gives meaning to the ordinary world by seeing it in an eternal dimension. The creation and resurrection myths of the Spokane inform the poem's denunciation of the white world of dams and nuclear reactors. In the modern world, a salmon is just a dumb creature used for food. In the Indian world, the salmon is a mythical or divine being who gave the Indians food and tradition, a way of life. A mythical story requires the emotional or spiritual participation of the listener rather than only intellectual understanding.

Contemporary Native American Poetry

One aim of American Indian poets in the last fifty years has been to reassert their native roots, beliefs, and customs, bringing out their unique perspective on American life. In spite of the fact that most Indian writers today are using English and are educated at universities, their poetry retains the ancient context of language in myth and magic; it is essentially lyrical, despite its modern references and topics. Although Alexie was strongly influenced by Indian writers like Louis and Simon Ortiz, Joy Harjo, Scott Momaday, Linda Hogan, and Adrian C. Louis, his poetry has gone in a satirical and political direction rather than in a lyrical direction.

Western Literature

"The Powwow at the End of the World" looks like a modern free-verse poem without end rhyme but using rhythm and line breaks. Alexie's hallmark as a poet and writer is to fuse in a satiric manner Indian tradition with western literary forms and themes. He is sometimes seen as postmodern (playful and creating hybrid forms) when he mixes pop culture, native lore, and historical details in a kind of magical realism (dream and reality together), as in certain poems from *The Summer of Black Widows* ("Owl Dancing with Fred Astaire," "Going to the Movies with Geronimo's Wife," and "After the Trial of Hamlet, Chicago, 1994").

The satire, or social criticism, in "Powwow," for instance, contrasts the destructive white practices with the nature-based Indian way of life and symbolically destroys white civilization. The angry tone also accuses anyone asking him to forget the persecution of the past as an accessory to the crime. Alexie is criticized by other Indian writers, nevertheless, for being too angry and Western in his stinging satire, for Indians excel in humor, but irony, or, saying one thing and meaning another in a scornful manner, is not favored by the Indian perspective. Alexie is a world citizen as far as literature goes, with multicultural tastes in the work of John Steinbeck, Walt Whitman, Langston Hughes, Ralph Ellison, F. Scott Fitzgerald, and Emily Dickinson. He mixes any genres he likes, such as poetry and fiction, free verse and structured forms (sonnets, sestinas, villanelles). His poems also reflect his

work in film, music, poetry slams, and stand-up comedy.

HISTORICAL CONTEXT

Native American History

NATIVE AMERICANS BEFORE COLUMBUS

When the Europeans came, they found hundreds of ethnic groups in North America, each with their own nation, language, and culture. According to some theories, the indigenous people living in the Americas had migrated some twelve thousand years ago from Europe and Asia on a land bridge across the Bering Strait. The indigenous people themselves have other versions of their origins. According to Alexie's tribe, the Spokane, Coyote from the animal people made the Spokane bodies out of the materials of the land they live on, and then Amotkan, the Creator, gave them life. The Spokane call themselves Children of the Sun.

EUROPEAN EXPLORATION AND COLONIZATION OF AMERICA

Early Spanish explorers in the fifteenth and sixteenth centuries, such as Christopher Columbus, Juan Ponce de Leon, and Hernando de Soto, brought back to Europe tales of the wealth of the Americas, prompting many European expeditions for plunder or settlement. There seemed room for all at first. Early contacts between Europeans and natives were friendly, with Native Americans helping Europeans through the hard winters by giving them food and showing them how to plant crops and survive. There is some evidence that the founders of American democracy borrowed political ideas from the tribal cultures where freedom was prized.

From the sixteenth to the nineteenth centuries, more and more Europeans came to claim American land, and the natives were seen as a threat or a problem that had to be exterminated so white settlers could civilize the continent. The indigenous people were treated as foreigners and heathens who had no legal or moral right to the land. The Europeans not only fought with the Indians with superior weapons but also took their lands by force or guile (treaties that were not honored) and decimated them with diseases such as small pox, measles, and bubonic plague, for which they had no immunity.

COMPARE
&
CONTRAST

- **1990s:** Approximately half of the American Indian population lives on reservations.

  Today: Sixty to seventy percent of American Indians live in cities.

- **1990s:** Powwows, once secret religious rites or pan-Indian celebrations, have open versions designed to draw tourists to reservations.

  Today: Fancydancing, a popular form of powwow dance, is a nationally known dance competition both on and off the reservation.

- **1990s:** Casino gaming becomes legally established on reservations as a way to combat the poverty of many Indian tribes.

  Today: Indian casinos are popular with tourists, employing many Indians, but due to their competitive nature, they attract organized crime and violence to the reservation as well.

- **1990s:** Tribal colleges open on reservations to teach accredited courses along with native culture to Indian youth who would not otherwise get a college education.

  Today: Public and private universities (such as Gonzaga University in Spokane, Washington) are partnering with tribal colleges, opening branches on their campuses, to reach Indians who live in the cities.

The Europeans brought horses, guns, and alcohol, thus changing tribal life. Although there was some fruitful trade among indigenous Americans and Europeans, as with the Spokane and French fur traders, the supposedly civilizing influence of the whites was largely destructive to the Indians.

THE WILD WEST

In the nineteenth century, as the settlers from Europe were pushing indigenous people from the east coast into the interior, the American Indians were romanticized by American writers as a noble but vanishing people (a prime example is *The Last of the Mohicans*). The Indians began to be seen not so much as subhuman heathens but as noble savages, close to nature, a melancholy and disappearing race. This sentimental view of American Indians is a stereotype satirized by Alexie in *The Lone Ranger and Tonto Fistfight in Heaven*.

When settlers wanted to move onto land that had been reserved for indigenous people, the Indians often found themselves betrayed. Treaties were broken or falsely negotiated between the U.S. government's Bureau of Indian Affairs and various tribes. Westward expansion, and the passage of the Indian Removal Act in 1830, relocating 100,000 Indians from eastern to western lands, led to Indian resistance, and the Indian Wars. Indians were portrayed as warlike in the press, but many tribes sought peace. If they fought, it was for survival.

The Spokane in Washington, Idaho, and Montana originally accepted the white men. They traded and accepted Christianity. The discovery of gold in Spokane country in the 1840s and 1850s, however, disrupted the delicate balance. The intrusion of the miners, settlers, and the railroad led to the Indians being removed to reservations. The last military defeat of the Spokane by U.S. Colonel George Wright in 1858 ended in the notorious slaughter of seven hundred Indian horses, shot and left to rot, so that the Indians could not use them. This cruel act is mentioned in many of Alexie's poems ("Sonnet: Tattoo Tears"), and Wright became a satirical character in *Reservation Blues*.

ASSIMILATION

Reservations were not the sole answer to what was known as the Indian Problem. Assimilation was a policy meant to destroy native culture. After the Civil War, boarding schools run by Christian missionaries were set up to convert and educate Indians. Children

Grand Coulee Dam is built on former American Indian lands. (*Benedictus | Shutterstock.com*)

were taken from their parents and were not allowed to speak their native language nor practice their religion. In 1894, all Indian religion was banned by the Bureau of Indian Affairs, even on the reservations, and Indians were prosecuted for singing or performing religious dances. Alexie grew up on the Spokane reservation in poverty; he witnessed the tragedy of the Midnite uranium mine where many Spokane were forced to work. The white owners took most of the profit, and the Spokane were exposed to lethal radiation doses from the open pit. When the mine was abandoned in 1981, no attempt was made to clean up the waste that continued to flow into the Spokane and Columbia Rivers.

American Indians were granted U.S. citizenship by the Indian Citizenship Act of 1924, though they were not allowed to vote. The final attempt to assimilate the native population came with the policy of termination in the 1950s and 1960s. The policy tried to take all natives off the reservation and relocate them to cities, thus disbanding their tribal groups and taking their lands for their natural resources. It meant the

government no longer recognized tribal sovereignty. With the example of the civil rights movement of the 1960s, Native American activist groups were formed and fought termination. In 1975, the Indian Self-Determination and Education Assistance Act allowed Native Americans to form their own governing bodies and to keep their reservations. In 1978, the American Indian Freedom of Religion Act was passed. The United States still does not recognize Indian nations as sovereign nations, however, and manages their lands through the Bureau of Indian Affairs.

TODAY

Although they once constituted 100 percent of the population, today American Indians are only a half of 1 percent of the United States population. Usually of mixed blood, with more than half of them living in cities, they have difficulty establishing legal identity with the government to obtain tribal rights. The high rates of alcoholism, poverty, heart disease, and drug addiction among Indians and the low rates of college attendance testify to their ongoing struggle to find a place in the modern world. Many tribes have sued the government for land compensation; the Spokane have successfully sued for the flooding of their hunting grounds by the Grand Coulee Dam. Gambling casinos, such as the Two Rivers Casino run by the Spokane, are one economic strategy for tribes to survive. A Native American Literary Renaissance in the 1970s and 1980s, of which Alexie is a beneficiary and second generation representative, proves the determined survival of American Indian culture, transformed to meet contemporary challenges.

CRITICAL OVERVIEW

Sherman Alexie's prolific and successful literary career in poetry, fiction, and screenwriting, from his debut in 1992 to the present, has met with consistent critical and popular praise. From the first review of his first book, Alexie was recognized as an important writer. In the early years, readers noted repetition of themes, characters, and motifs from one book to the next, a trait associated with the repetitive style of oral tradition. Alexie deepens and reworks his material, all the while gaining technical skill and experimenting with form. He has won support from other Native American authors, including Joy Harjo and Leslie Marmon Silko. While Alexie covers familiar Native American landscape with stories of survival and trauma, he adds an aggressive satire that is intentionally provoking.

The Summer of Black Widows (1996), which contains the poem "The Powwow at the End of the World," is one of his best collections and secured his reputation as a sustained and serious poet. The reviews are uniformly favorable. A contributor to *Publishers Weekly* admires the cultural mix in the poems, showing the complex reality of Indian life today. A *Library Journal* contributor calls the poems "intensely elegiac," giving Indian people "a sense of nobility as they struggle to maintain dignity in a world given over to hatred of the authentic."

Robert L. Berner, in *World Literature Today*, mentions that the book contains some of the most powerful contemporary statements about reservation life. He singles out "Powwow" as successful, even though he thinks that kind of angry poem rarely works. Ray Gonzalez, in the *Bloomsbury Review*, welcomes Alexie's "fresh

approach," "brutal honesty," and "uncanny control of language." In a 1997 review for *Western American Literature*, David N. Cremean admires Alexie's "quest to turn ... painful history into art" and calls him "one of the most significant Native American literary voices," citing the book's humor as one of its strengths.

In "Open Containers: Sherman Alexie's Drunken Indians," Stephen F. Evans summarizes the critical response to Alexie's poetry over the years. He praises Alexie's technical versatility in poetic genres and his improvisational comic cheek. Alexie has been criticized for his satire of reservation life by those who prefer romanticized Indians. Evans, however, considers Alexie to be a trickster figure, like Coyote, the unpredictable Indian character whom Alexie often mentions, the Creator responsible for Indian survival.

CRITICISM

Susan K. Andersen

Andersen holds a Ph.D. in literature. In the following essay, she focuses on Alexie's ability to cross borders between white and Indian cultures, for the purpose of creating greater dialogue and understanding.

Sherman Alexie's poem "The Powwow at the End of the World" takes a tribal point of view. Alexie is always influenced by his reservation background, even living the life of a successful writer and filmmaker in the city. His work is controversial, however, with both white and Indian audiences. Although he criticizes the colonial treatment of his people, he admits his success has to do with getting off the reservation and plunging into Western culture. He paints a dismal portrait of the alcoholism, poverty, violence, and hopelessness of tribal life in his novel *Reservation Blues* (1995). "Powwow" may look forward to a resurrected Indian world at the end of time, but it is, at best, an ironic vision for Indians living in twenty-first-century America, where they must find a place now. As author, performer, and filmmaker, Alexie has consciously chosen an uncharted path as an Indian without borders. He is as ready to enjoy basketball as powwows, as ready to see the humorous contradictions of indigenous life as the injustice of white prejudice. Alexie embodies the creative paradox of the post-colonial author who has to

WHAT DO I READ NEXT?

- *The Absolutely True Diary of a Part-Time Indian* by Sherman Alexie, 2007, is a young-adult novel dealing with racism, poverty, and tradition. It is semiautobiographical, about a young Indian who decides to leave the reservation for a white high school. It is a National Book Award winner.

- *Code Talker* by Joseph Bruchac (2005) is a widely recommended young-adult novel about a Navajo boy who joins the Marines in World War II and becomes one of the Code Talkers, the Indian team that invented a Navajo code the Nazis and Japanese could not crack. The code was used by the U.S. military to help win the war in the Pacific.

- Alexie's own pick for the most important book on racial stereotype in America is *The Invisible Man* by African American writer Ralph Ellison (1952). This book aptly illustrates how prejudice makes the individual invisible.

- *Native American Almanac: A Portrait of Native America Today* (1998) by Arlene Hirschfelder and Martha Kreipe de Montano presents an overview of past history and present Native American life, including facts on reservations, laws, treaties, demographics, language, education, religion, sports, and media.

- Creek poet and musician Joy Harjo's *The Woman Who Fell from the Sky* (1996) includes poems and a reinvented myth of the Iroquois creation story set in the city, along with other pieces she often performs.

- Acomo Pueblo poet Simon Ortiz's *The People Shall Continue* (1977) is a history poetically told in a distinctly American Indian voice for young readers, from creation to the present day.

forge an identity from fragments of tradition mixed with whatever is at hand in the modern world.

> AS AUTHOR, PERFORMER, AND FILMMAKER, ALEXIE HAS CONSCIOUSLY CHOSEN AN UNCHARTED PATH AS AN INDIAN WITHOUT BORDERS."

One way to read "The Powwow at the End of the World" is as a straight defense of Indian ways and a sad condemnation of the colonial legacy. In this way, the poem could be seen as a nostalgic lament for a vanished world. Because of the angry tone, however, and the second-person address to the audience, it is also a challenge to white Americans, a refusal to sweep under the rug an old blood feud. The poem came out in 1996, the same year as his novel, *Indian Killer*, one of Alexie's angriest books about racism. Many readers were disturbed by the anger in that novel, and Alexie uses the angry speaker in "Powwow" to unsettle the audience. The author said to Diane Thiel in a 2004 interview: "I think Indians have a much longer memory than white Americans," explaining why he might want to remind them of what they have forgotten. David L. Moore comments in "Sherman Alexie: Irony, Intimacy, and Agency" that the author has an "urgent project to reshape Euroamerican audiences' awareness of their liability for history."

In *The Lone Ranger and Tonto Fistfight in Heaven* (1993), Alexie made famous his formula: survival equals anger times imagination. Ron McFarland, in "Another Kind of Violence," discusses Alexie as a polemicist or political poet at war with the dominant culture. McFarland maintains that the satiric humor in Alexie's work is not an escape but a sort of catharsis, or emotional triumph over tragedy. In a 1993 interview with John and Carl Bellante, Alexie explains: "Anger in itself can be positive or destructive. That's why you need to use imagination to make it positive." In the same interview, when asked why he was angry, he admits: "I'm angry toward this patriarchal country that creates an environment totally hostile toward women." To Erik Himmelsbach in 1996 in "The Reluctant Spokesman," Alexie speaks of the tremendous Indian anger that is rarely expressed, calling it "a huge open wound."

The speaker of "Powwow," by saying that the Indian way of life will return at the end of the world, makes it ironically clear that that way of life no longer exists in the present. For better or worse, the speaker is stuck in the patriarchal world of the Grand Coulee Dam and the abandoned and leaking reactors at Hanford. He thus underscores the strain of living in two worlds, the Indian and the white, at the same time. The position is characteristic of post-colonial peoples: they cannot go back to their ethnic roots, nor can they abandon them.

In "Reservation Home Movies: Sherman Alexie's Poetry," Jennifer Gillan says contemporary Indians are "alienated from their American Indian culture as well as from America." Like the African American authors Alexie admires (Ralph Ellison, Richard Wright, and Langston Hughes), American Indian authors are forced into what black sociologist W. E. B. DuBois called a double consciousness—having to live up to the expectations of two races and two cultures at the same time. Alexie exploits this double consciousness in his satiric social criticism.

The poem "Defending Walt Whitman," from *The Summer of Black Widows*, humorously places Whitman on a basketball court watching Indian boys play basketball. Even though he does not know offense from defense, Whitman wants to be part of the game. In the poem "Tourists," Alexie envisions James Dean dancing at an Indian powwow and Marilyn Monroe welcomed by Indian women in a sweat lodge. These famous "tourists" to the reservation help white readers feel what it is to be a foreigner. James Dean, for instance, a celebrated rebel and sexy movie icon, is totally clumsy as he tries to dance in harmony with Indians, who regard him as bad news. This device of mixing cultures is not just a comedy gimmick, however; it is the way we live now in a multiethnic world. In *Reservation Blues*, black musician Robert Johnson is embraced by the Indians, and the blues he made famous is a musical form Alexie adapts as compatible to the themes and improvisational format of native culture.

Some Indian writers see the sullying and mixture of their culture with Western influences as tragic and attempt to reassert their tradition in modern art. Despite the tragic dimension of history, Alexie determines to make the best of his freedom to choose whatever forms, genres, and messages he desires, thus breaking from strict

tribal or native identity when he expresses himself as an artist. This individuality has brought him criticism from other Indians. Native critic, Elizabeth Cook-Lynn, for instance, believes Indian artists should strengthen tribal identity by the sort of lyric writing and holistic spiritual values characteristic of Scott Momaday and Leslie Marmon Silko. In "Humor Is My Green Card," an interview with Joshua B. Nelson in 2010, Alexie calls ideas like Cook-Lynn's "nostalgia" because "we're not getting it back.... Language, culture, who we were when Europeans arrived."

In his poem "Inside Dachau" from *The Summer of Black Widows*, Alexie speaks of a trip to the Nazi concentration camp, comparing the Indian and Jewish genocides. He recognizes there that every country has its sins to hide and that holocausts have been a part of human history. Still, the Indians await their own museum to their genocide, an open American admission of its own dirty past. In an interview with Duncan Campbell, "Voice of the New Tribes" (2002), Alexie expresses this desire for national confession: "The arrogance of this country to have a Holocaust museum, to point out the genocidal sins of another culture is amazing."

Alexie's anger began to soften after the terrorist attack on the Twin Towers of September 11, 2001, when he realized that it was an act of tribal people who were fundamentalists. Not wanting to identify with an Indian fundamentalist group, he understood that he belonged to many tribes, including "book nerds and basketball players," as he said to Tanita Davis and Sarah Stevenson in an interview quoted in *Conversations with Sherman Alexie*. Alexie uses humor and satire as a way to join someone else's tribe, as he explains to Nelson: "I can speak to any audience of any political persuasion because I'm funny, you know.... it's really a passport into other people's cultures. A temporary visa." Alexie's "green card" of humor allows him to cross all sorts of borders.

One constant topic in Alexie's work is basketball, one of his passions since he was a basketball star in high school. Alexie uses basketball as a cross-cultural metaphor for both competition and cooperation, as David Goldstein points out in "Sacred Hoop Dreams: Basketball in the Work of Sherman Alexie." In the poem "Why We Play Basketball," the poet says Indians can make the game into something new and find

Salmon will set the fire of forgiveness in the poem. (Sara Theophilus | Shutterstock.com)

their identity that way. In a similar way, Alexie makes western literary forms and techniques into something new to express the ironic life of an Indian in contemporary culture.

Douglas Ford, in "Sherman Alexie's Indigenous Blues," makes the case that Alexie has not really strayed from his background; he takes the indigenous oral culture and makes it into a hybrid form with the cultural material around him. Andrew Dix, in "Red, White, and Black," finds the "politics of racial and cultural hybridization" in Alexie's work to be a sort of "cosmopolitanism," which results in a "decentered, pluralist, impure" but healthy mixing of cultures.

Alexie told interviewer Ase Nygren in 2005 that his religion now is art. He feels spiritual in the presence of his own stories, including his poems, which are another form of narrative. Storytelling feels like prayer to him. He does not expect his humor to change the world but hopes it will open dialogue. Despite the past, or

even despite the problems of the present, Alexie thinks the world is getting better. He had to grow up in double consciousness, but pop culture is multicultural, a common language. He thinks his sons will be completely accepted into American life. "This country really hasn't entered puberty yet...the culture is really young...we're all struggling with our identity," he said to Jessica Chapel in "American Literature: Interview with Sherman Alexie." Alexie considers himself now as an Indian who is part of the mainstream, and as he explained to Matt Dellinger in 2009, that in itself changes the mainstream.

Source: Susan K. Andersen, Critical Essay on "The Powwow at the End of the World," in *Poetry for Students*, Gale, Cengage Learning, 2012.

Joshua B. Nelson

In the following essay, Nelson explores how Alexie uses language and writing as a way to intellectually escape poverty and entropy.

We seldom think of American Indians, like my Cherokee people for instance, as world explorers, knowing how settled we were by the 1600s, but in fact some among us knew well that we were possessed of the capacity for widespread investigation, knew that mobility ranked among our liberties, knew that if the urge struck us we could pack up and go exploring, both individually and collectively. Traveling Indians knew they could do this not least because they told themselves they could. Some of the Cherokees' earliest orature tells of our migration to the Southeast from great distances, offering precedents for the diplomatic trips to England made in the 1700s, for instance. History would soon tell us other things, though, like "this world is not yours; you are not ready for it; you can't compete in it"—and most perniciously, it would teach us to tell ourselves these things. Before long, negative associations with mobility in terms like *removal* would come to cloud all potential movements. Considering how many of these issued from colonialist campaigns, it's small wonder that there would be a reactionary circling of the wagons and in many cases an acceptance of a bounded life, which some might now call an embracing of community.

In the reservation era, the United States created rural ghettos where Indians could be contained, surveilled by the state—kept *in reserve* with all due legality and beneficence. This is the historical legacy confronted at the end of Sherman Alexie's *The Absolutely True Diary of a Part-Time Indian*, when Arnold Spirit's best friend, Rocky, muses approvingly about "old-time Indians, about how we used to be nomadic... people who move around, who keep moving." Here and throughout his poetry and prose, Alexie's metaphorical invocation of travel through time, space, and all sorts of in-between, ephemeral moments like flight and dancing reclaim the idea of exploration as resistance against boundaries physical and imaginative. Embedded in exploration, too, is a sense of return. Like exploration, return in and of Alexie's work offers less a homecoming than a report back, an example of the potential of a challenging curiosity. Critics, too, might profit by considering the benefits, problems, and necessity of forcing interpretation to confront historical and cultural circumstances as we expand, to adapt Edward Said's phrase, a traveling theory of travel.

> TIME AND AGAIN ALEXIE OFFERS METAPHORICAL ESCAPES, AS FROM PATTERNS OF SUBSTANCE ABUSE, CYCLES OF VIOLENCE, AND OTHER RECEIVED AND UNEXAMINED WAYS OF UNDERSTANDING THE WORLD. IN THIS REGARD, PERHAPS THE MOST IMPORTANT DEPARTURE OF ALL TAKEN IN ALEXIE'S WORK IS THAT OF THE WRITING ITSELF."

American Indians have a long history of coerced control over their movement. Columbus's earliest journal entries record his optimism that the indigenous people he encountered "ought to be good servants and of good skill, for I see that they repeat very quickly whatever was said to them." From the first imperial meeting, the linguistic assertion of power over the Native body—its labor, sovereignty, and mobility—has prescribed our imaginations. We might scoff at Columbus's belief that if he takes pains to make us speak we'll chirp back like well-trained parrots, but to what extent might he be right? How quickly like Caliban did we learn to curse the world we didn't understand or have cultural control over, to mimic the fear of the unknown wilds, substituting for the dark forests of the new world the cavernous avenues of the city, making of the bloodthirsty savage the money-hungry capitalist, the brutalizing teacher, or the faceless institution? These are the new monsters of the next island and the modern cannibals of the other tribe. Too often American Indian communities have taken over the policing of our restrictive borders and have narrated our own imagined reservations. The most frightening part of these ghost stories, of course, is that they're sometimes true. Folks have vanished, people have failed, and sons and daughters have left their parents.

It's also true that against such threats, community offers unparalleled support and, because of this, has come to occupy a conceptual place of privilege in Indian critical theory rivaled only by the oral tradition, which is itself after all about community. In American Indian literary criticism, shifting focus from the oral tradition to community corrected tendencies to anchor all readings in ethnology detached from context and to overextend the definition of oral tradition to encompass all the referents, background, and culture involved in the telling. For all its strength, the idea of community runs a similar risk of becoming a catch-all, magic word that when muttered at a text will supposedly unlock all its meanings, without due attention to the specifics of history and context that lend works their richness.

Failure to consider such matters closely is to allow others to do our thinking for us. Said puts it succinctly: "A breakthrough can become a trap, if it is used uncritically, repetitively, limitlessly.... Once an idea gains currency because it is clearly effective and powerful, there is every likelihood that during its peregrinations it will be reduced, codified, and institutionalized" ("Traveling Theory"). In American Indian literary theory, we have seen this happen with the major myopias on the oral tradition, mixed-blood anxiety, community, and, I hazard, we can see it now with nationalism couched as a natural political extension of community.

As Alexie's poetry and prose uncompromisingly demonstrate, communities are far from uncomplicated and are frequently themselves destructive, as with communities of substance abusers. Against such coteries and their cyclic dysfunction, we find a barely contained desire to *go* in Alexie's work. He introduces it in "Traveling," the first poem of "Distances," the first section of his first collection, *The Business of Fancydancing*, which encapsulates several persistent themes. There a vanload of mostly sleeping Spokane is returning from a basketball tournament. The speaker, listening to the joking of the two up front, remarks, "It was hunger made me move then, not a dream, and I reached down and rummaged through the cooler for something to eat, drink." Hunger of one form or another prompts all sorts of movement. They are pulled over for a DWI—driving while Indian—and a state trooper assesses their sobriety and general acquiescence to American norms. Successfully convincing him of their internal colonization, they're turned loose, only to run out of gas a short ways on. They wind up pushing the van home, slowed by and struggling against the very thing supposed to get them going. The Indian car, inevitably breaking down because no one can afford anything but emergency maintenance and sometimes not even gas money, stands in for much in the Indian world here. This is the van model in the great rez rider line, from the one-eyed Ford of the 49 song to Philbert Bono's fine war pony, "Protector," in *Powwow Highway*. This new—or more rightly, used—icon of cultural history, even as it signifies shared experience, also crucially proclaims that the preconditions of the Indian car, the setup for the punchline, are Indian *poverty* and the structures that perpetuate it, and that those are preconditions neither chosen nor acceptable. Even as we laugh at cars that only go in reverse, we should detect something very unfunny behind the lack of movement on this economic front. The speaker of "Traveling" closes the poem, "I turned back to the van, put my shoulder to the cold metal and waited for something to change."

Time and again Alexie offers metaphorical escapes, as from patterns of substance abuse, cycles of violence, and other received and unexamined ways of understanding the world. In this regard, perhaps the most important departure of all taken in Alexie's work is that of the writing itself. Departure appears in the stylistic innovations that he brings to form, which he has carried on incessantly from *Fancydancing* through the recent *War Dances* and *Face*, with his mergers of poetry and prose, realism and fantasy, his echoes of quixotic genres like mixtapes and readers' guides, his criticism of critics, and his stark refusal to write again what Momaday, Silko, or anyone else has already written. We also find it in memorable characters like Thomas Builds-the-Fire, who as the storyteller no one listens to haunts the collection *The Lone Ranger and Tonto Fistfight in Heaven* and its film adaptation, *Smoke Signals*. We might forget, though, why he was ignored and his challenge in getting heard, narrated in his early appearance in *Fancydancing*'s story "Special Delivery." We learn there how ingrained in him is the idea that his story must never change, that it must be told the same way time and again, whatever the loss of audience or relevance. This despite the fatalism of his ending: "A long time ago, my vision animal came to me.... He asked for a drink of water but I only had whiskey. He asked for deer jerky but I only had commodity cheese. He looked at me and said, '*Thomas, you don't have a dream that will ever come true.*' I've been waiting all these years for someone to tell me different." Thomas finally rejects this foregone conclusion, and only when he imagines for himself a new story does he encounter the possibility of having "a dream that could come true"; only when he connects with people, as when he offers up his vulnerability and his resources to Victor, does he earn his listeners' attention. Even the sanctified storyteller figure has to offer something in return. When he goes off the reservation, he—like other storytellers he stands in for—sees the potential return grow in proportion to the conceptual distance traveled.

Alexie frequently plays with gravity as a limit on movement, as in the closing poem of the same name in *Fancydancing*, where he intimates that what goes up must come down, and what goes out must come back. If departure takes on metaphorical possibilities, so too does return. We see proliferate and clear comings-back in "Gravity," played out by Seymour Polatkin in the film *The Business of Fancydancing*, but like the departures in stylistic innovation, the principal return we find in Alexie's work is of the work itself, the many volumes of poetry and prose becoming epistolary in their public scope. We reencounter leaving and return up through Alexie's latest poetry collection, *Face*, in which the speaker of the poem "Wheat" recalls his neighbor's fields where, "Isolated, / I often felt small and rhymeless, / But I was free to roam, / With all of my neighbors' blessing, / In any of their fields. / In this way, step by step, row by row, / I learned how to escape." The rows of grain like the lines of the poem map the terrain, chronicling the means and cause of escape, but also recording the beauty and poignancy of that which is left behind. If the speaker never sees those fields again, there is nevertheless a return, for the poem will away again to readers all around, powerfully modeling the possibility of leaving with attendant benefits and sacrifices, yes, but giving back the very idea of potential, with farther reach and longer endurance than could be accomplished working strictly at home.

To be sure, the more manifest connection between words and movement again figures as escape. "Literacy saved my ass," Alexie writes in "Tuxedo with Eagle Feathers," pointing to reading and writing as his ticket out of his reservation's stifling poverty and intellectual entropy, but intentionally or not, it's a round-trip

package. As with gravity and leaving, there are often ambivalences in escape with its implicit parallel gesture at origin, the point of departure that is not so vicious a place that it can simply be dismissed. Rather, it exerts a pull coming from the claim it establishes on the writer's and readers' sympathies, a claim repaid not by gratuitously pillorying its failings but by conscientiously identifying its deficiencies toward improving the lives of the people who stay there, or at other places of home.

Having moved through these works, I'll propose one last departure before we get too settled. Much as Alexie has changed the discourse in American Indian literature and offered innovations in style and structure to literature in general since he took up the possibility of Indians writing, and just as he refashioned it to accord with his own experience and ideas, so must we as readers, teachers, and critics meeting his work in different times and places. Around Oklahoma, several students and others with whom I've discussed Alexie's work have shied from pointed criticism of it. They note that the world of a northwestern reservation differs dramatically from their own and suggest that the lack of resemblance to their own lives poorly positions them to evaluate Alexie's representations. Others argue that while tribal lands might not exactly be reservations, places like Kenwood, Anadarko, and even Norman can be just as limiting. Whatever the restraints on its universality, Alexie's work continues to find broad audiences as readers everywhere test what is seen against both what is familiar and unfamiliar. In recognizing anomalies—places where standing interpretations do not account for experiences and ideas (theories of reification and power in Said's article; in Alexie, ideas about identity, community, and mobility)—we find unique opportunities to move conversations forward with the challenges posed by what is particular and special about our subjective positions. Said urges, "I would go as far as saying that it is the critic's job to provide resistances to theory, to open it up toward historical reality, toward society, toward human needs and interests."

Several hundred area high school students attended the talk Alexie traveled considerable distance to deliver at March's Puterbaugh Festival; many of them came quite a ways themselves. As fine as Alexie's writing is and as far as it has come, it hasn't said all there is to say about the diversity of their human needs and interests. As a teacher, just as I encourage students both to study what has been written before and to push their own thinking to write the best of what's next, surely they could expect the same of their instructors. That for me means carefully considering anomalies and testing well the theories traveling around trying to make sense of them. Leaving room for innovative ideas in our teaching and research, too, can shape another kind of return, that of intellectual respect, and even if we never depart from Tahlequah, Anadarko, or Norman, this new language of exploration just might write someone else's ticket.

Source: Joshua B. Nelson, "Fight as Flight: The Traditional Reclamation of Exploration," in *World Literature Today*, Vol. 84, No. 4, July/August 2010, pp. 44–47.

Robert L. Berner

In the following review, Berner offers a positive assessment of The Summer of Black Widows, *commenting favorably on Alexie's portrayal of the true Native American cultural experience and his use of dark satire.*

In Sherman Alexie's title poem, black widow spiders, appearing on the Spokane reservation in miraculous numbers, become a metaphor for stories. The summer is full of spiders and thus rich in stories, and even after the spiders disappear, their evidence is found in every corner of a place that remains rich in poetic possibility.

The Summer of Black Widows includes some of the most powerful poems in our literature about the experience of living on an Indian reservation surrounded by the world its tribe has lost. Consider three examples: a poem about Spokane Falls, "That Place Where Ghosts of Salmon Jump," in which the loss of the salmon to urban and industrial concrete relates to women mourning for children who cannot return home; "The Exaggeration of Despair," a catalogue of horrific cases of social and cultural disintegration; and "The Powwow at the End of the World," a denunciation of crimes against the environment and against Alexie's tribe which succeeds as a poem even though those who attempt to do this kind of thing usually fail.

Alexie shows a variety of other strengths as well. He is, for one thing, a richly comic poet—in a reference to Norman Mailer writing "yet another epic novel" he says, "Somebody needs to teach Norman about the haiku"—and he

often reveals a keen satiric sense. ("How to Write the Great American Indian Novel" is a splendid marshaling of the stereotypes which too often substitute in our culture for the reality of American Indian experience.) But as always in the greatest comic art, the humor that makes us laugh is always underlaid with a sad wisdom. For example, some of the cases of "people who die in stupid ways" (in "Elegies") are obvious (George Armstrong Custer, people who kill themselves smoking), but some are more complex (a Brinks guard dying under an avalanche of coins) and some are painfully personal: a sister who appears frequently in Alexie's poems because, too drunk to awaken, she died in a trailer fire.

Alexie's devotion to basketball, familiar to readers who have followed his career, is seen in the present collection in yet another light, united to his appreciation of Walt Whitman. The title "Defending Walt Whitman" refers not only to Alexie's defense of Whitman as a poet and personal hero but also to defensive strategies in a basketball game in which Walt is one of the players. The poem's real subject, therefore, seems to be the complexity of literary influence—that is, the need to resist it even in the act of homage.

In this, as always in the best American Indian writing, its relation to American culture as a whole is a primary subject; but Alexie also suggests that the influences are mutual, and in "Tourists" he suggests just why America needs Indian traditional tribal culture. One of the "tourists" is Marilyn Monroe, who, to become a person, something more than a beautiful piece of female flesh created by popular culture, comes to the reservation, where she is stripped by the women and led into a sweat lodge to become one with them, to be at last healed and made whole again, a person rather than a cultural artifact: "Finally, she is no more naked than anyone else."

In previous collections Alexie has earned an important position among American Indian poets, but the quality of almost all the poems in *The Summer of Black Widows* suggests that his significance now must be more broadly defined.

Source: Robert L. Berner, Review of *The Summer of Black Widows*, in *World Literature Today*, Vol. 71, No. 2, Spring 1997, p. 430.

WELL AWARE THAT HIS POEMS AND NOVELS
HAVE ANGERED INDIANS AND WHITES ALIKE, ALEXIE
ENJOYS WALKING A KIND OF CULTURAL HIGHWIRE."

Doug Marx

*In the following interview, Alexie describes his
perception of himself as an outcast among outcasts and how his experiences inform his poetry
and prose.*

Six years ago, as a 24-year-old student at
Washington State University, Sherman Alexie,
a Spokane/Coeur d' Alene Indian, set down his
career goals at the insistence of a friend: 1) to
publish ten books by age 30; 2) to see a book on
the silver screen by 35; and 3) to receive a major
literary prize by 40.

With *Indian Killer* (Forecasts, July 29), his
third prose work, a tragic thriller about the rav-
ages of cultural dilution and dissolution, out this
month from Grove/Atlantic, and *The Summer of
Black Widows*, his seventh collection of poetry,
out in October from Hanging Loose Press, the
first goal will be achieved. Three of Alexie's
books—his first short story collection, *The
Lone Ranger and Tonto Fistfight in Heaven*
(Atlantic Monthly, 1993); his novel *Reservation
Blues* (Atlantic Monthly, 1994); and *Indian
Killer*—are the subject of ongoing film negotia-
tions. As for a major literary award, if review
acclaim from such established masters as Rey-
nolds Price, Leslie Marmon Silko and Frederick
Busch, not to mention inclusion in the recent
"Best of Young American Novelists" issue of
Granta, means anything, Alexie could well win
his prize.

When asked how sudden success has
affected him, Alexie flashes a quick smile and
quips: "I like room service." The remark—even
coming from a sometime stand-up comic—is
revealing. Self-described as "mouthy, opinion-
ated and arrogant," Alexie betrays no squeam-
ishness about the mix of art and commerce. He
loves the limelight, and his readings are known
for their improvisational energy, costume
changes and singing. Six years sober after a six-
year binge that began the day he entered college,

he explains: "Today, I get high, I get drunk off of
public readings. I'm good at it. It comes from
being a debater in high school, but also, crucially, it comes from the oral tradition of my
own culture. It's in performance that the two
cultures become one." Then he laughs, adding:
"The most terrifying phrase in the world is when
an Indian man grabs a microphone and says 'I
have a few words to say.'"

Alexie has more than a few words to say. His
memory runs deep. Whether cast in poetry or
prose, his work offers a devastating and deeply
human portrait of contemporary Indian life.
Greeting *PW* in the modest Seattle apartment
where he lives with his wife of two years, Diane, a
beautiful, private woman of Hidatsa/Ho Chunk/
Potawatomi descent, Alexie proves to be affable
and generous, ready to sit down around the
kitchen table and talk about his life and art.

Tall, handsome, his long black hair tied in a
ponytail, dressed casually in a beige knit shirt
and khakis, Alexie, who played basketball in
high school, has a shooting guard's easy movements and soft touch. One would never suspect
that he was born hydrocephalic, endured a brain
operation at six months that should have left him
mentally retarded—if not dead—and for his first
seven years was beset with seizures and medi-
cated with regular doses of lithium, phenobarbi-
tal and other sedatives.

The son of Sherman Sr. and Lillian Alexie
(his father is Coeur d' Alene, his mother Spokane), Alexie was born and reared in Wellpinit,
the only town on the Spokane Indian Reservation—a place he describes as a landscape of
"HUD shacks and abandoned cars"—which
lies some 50 miles northwest of Spokane,
Wash. Alcoholism, a central concern of Alexie's
work, afflicted his family, but there was love in
the house, along with a mix of traditional and
contemporary culture. "I've come to realize my
parents did a damn good job, considering the
cards they were dealt," he says.

Then there was his maternal grandmother,
Etta Adams, who died when Alexie was eight,
and who appears as the eternal, wise and practical "Big Mom" in *Reservation Blues*. "She was
one of the great spiritual leaders of the Spokane
tribe," Alexie says, "one of the most powerful
figures to visit the Northwest, and in her last
days thousands came to pay their respects."
The need for female strength and wisdom is a
primary theme of Alexie's, sounded early on in

"Indian Boy Love Songs," four poems collected in *The Business of Fancydancing* (Hanging Loose, 1992).

Alexie began reading in earnest at an early age. Because he was unable to participate in the wild athleticism of a young male Indian's rites of passage, books became his world. "I knew what a paragraph was before I could read the words," he says, claiming that at age six, he began working his way through *The Grapes of Wrath*. Steinbeck's final image of a starving man being breast-fed is fixed in his mind: "Ah, so that's the way a story's supposed to end," he recalls telling himself. "With that kind of huge moment, which is the way the stories we tell ourselves end." Through grade and high school, he devoured every book in the school libraries, reading and re-reading Steinbeck until the copies fell apart in his hands. "I was a total geek," Alexie recalls, "which automatically made me an outcast, so in order to succeed I had to be smarter than everybody else. My sense of competitiveness came out that way. I was fierce in the classroom, I humiliated everybody and had my nose broken five times after school for being the smart kid."

PLAYING THE GOOD WHITE INDIAN

Alexie's view of Indian life acquired more complexity when, in 1981, he enrolled at an all-white high school in Reardan, a reservation border town unfriendly to Indians. With his world turned upside-down, he became the "perfect Reardan kid": an honor student and class president and the only ponytail on the crewcut Reardan Indians basketball team. "I kept my mouth shut and became a good white Indian," he acknowledges. "All those qualities that made me unpopular on the reservation made me popular at Reardan. It got to the point where I don't think they saw me as Indian."

The hard work and conformity earned Alexie a scholarship to Gonzaga University in Spokane, where he enrolled with vague intentions of becoming a doctor or lawyer—"the usual options for a bright, brown kid"—and promptly fell apart. Feeling lost, lacking a life plan, he began drinking heavily. His misery found consolation in poetry, which he began to read avidly—Keats, Yeats, Dickinson, Whitman. "I didn't see myself in them," he says, "so I felt like I was doing anthropology, like I was studying white people. Obviously, something was drawing me in that I couldn't intellectualize

or verbalize, and then I realized that the poems weren't just about white people. They were about everybody. I also realized that the poets were outcasts, too," he chuckles.

After two years, Alexie packed his bags and left Gonzaga for the University of Washington. Newly arrived in Seattle, he was robbed and soon found himself back in Wellpinit, on the verge of joining the long history of young Indians who come home to a slow death by alcohol. Waking one morning on the steps of the Assembly of God Church, hungover, his pants wet, he staggered home to mail off an application to WSU in Pullman. It was a poetry class at WSU taught by Alex Kuo that finally helped him to get his bearings as a writer, he recalls.

The boozing didn't stop, but the words poured out. Kuo, who became a father figure to Alexie, gave him a copy of the anthology *Songs of This Earth on Turtle's Back*. "In an instant I saw myself in literature," Alexie recalls. A line from an Adrian C. Louis poem called "Elegy for the Forgotten Oldsmobile" changed his life forever: "O Uncle Adrian! I'm in the reservation of my own mind." "I started crying. That was my whole life. Forget Steinbeck, forget Keats. I just kept saying that line over and over again. I sat down and started writing poems. And they came. It was scary."

Under Kuo's guidance, his first semester manuscript became his first book, *I Would Steal Horses*, which was published by Slipstream in 1992. With Native poets such as Louis and Simon Ortiz, Joy Harjo and Linda Hogan as models, he began to write his own story in his own voice. Lyrical, angry, poignant, socially engaged, the poems found their way into small literary magazines such as Brooklyn's *Hanging Loose*. Eventually, Hanging Loose Press brought out *The Business of Fancydancing*, which received a strong critical reception and has sold 11,000 copies, an astounding number for a book of poems from a small press. Serendipitously, the letter accepting the manuscript for publication arrived the day Alexie decided to quit drinking.

During his student days, and at Kuo's urging, Alexie began to experiment with prose—some of which appeared in *Fancydancing*. Other fictions were later collected in *The Lone Ranger and Tonto Fistfight in Heaven*, half of which was written in a four-month burst when agents, alert to his poetry, began calling with requests for fiction.

A friend introduced Alexie to Nancy Stauffer, who remains his agent to this day. "Nancy's really been good at helping me develop a career," he says. "We really have a plan. We're not just going book to book. First and foremost, I want to be a better writer, and I want a larger audience." In short order, Alexie found himself with a two-book, six-figure contract with Morgan Entrekin at the Atlantic Monthly Press at a time when, he says, he "didn't even have an idea for a novel."

The idea did come, in the guise of *Reservation Blues*, a novel that imagines legendary bluesman Robert Johnson arriving on a reservation seeking redemption from "a woman," in this case Big Mom. Johnson's magic guitar carries four young Indians off the reservation and into the world of rock and roll. The book explores differences between reservation and urban Indians and the effects of the church on traditional people, among other themes. It's also a bleak novel that's leavened by Alexie's signature black humor. "I'm not trying to be funny," he explains. "I don't sit down to write something funny. In my everyday life I'm funny, and when I write it comes out. Laughter is a ceremony, it's the way people cope."

There isn't much laughter in *Indian Killer*, which depicts John Smith, an Indian without a tribal affiliation. Adopted off the reservation and reared by a white couple, he becomes a suspect in a string of brutal scalpings that terrify Seattle. Tangent to Smith are a host of characters, including a racist talk-show host, a white professor of Native American studies and a defiant female Indian activist, all of whom are struggling with their senses of identity. The picture is of a man divided by culture, a culture divided by its tragic history, a city divided by race, and a nation at war with itself. And it is a vision Alexie paints with excruciating clarity.

The perception of being an outcast among outcasts contributes to Alexie's complex portrait of reservation life, a view rife with ironies and a sense of complicity that has come under fire from Indian writers for its apparent emphasis on hopelessness, alcoholism and suicide. "I write what I know," he says, "and I don't try to mythologize myself, which is what some seem to want, and which some Indian women and men writers are doing, this Earth Mother and Shaman Man

thing, trying to create these 'authentic, traditional' Indians. We don't live our lives that way."

Well aware that his poems and novels have angered Indians and whites alike, Alexie enjoys walking a kind of cultural highwire. "I use a racial criterion in my literary critiques," he says. "I have a very specific commitment to Indian people, and I'm very tribal in that sense. I want us to survive as Indians."

That said, Alexie's Indian characters are never guileless victims. Echoing Big Mom, who continually reminds her neighbors in *Reservation Blues* that their fate is in their own hands, he explains: "It's a two-way street. The system sets you up to fail, and then, somehow, you choose it."

Source: Doug Marx, "Sherman Alexie: A Reservation of the Mind," in *Publishers Weekly*, Vol. 243, No. 38, September 16, 1996, pp. 39–40.

SOURCES

Alexie, Sherman, "The Powwow at the End of the World," in *The Summer of Black Widows*, Hanging Loose Press, 1996, p. 98.

Bellante, John, and Carl Bellante, "Sherman Alexie, Literary Rebel," in *Conversations with Sherman Alexie*, edited by Nancy J. Peterson, University Press of Mississippi, 2009, p. 10; originally published in *Bloomsbury Review*, May/June 1994.

Berner, Robert. L., Review of *The Summer of Black Widows*, in *World Literature Today*, Vol. 71, No. 2, Spring 1997, p. 430.

Campbell, Duncan, "Voice of the New Tribes," in *Conversations with Sherman Alexie*, edited by Nancy J. Peterson, University Press of Mississippi, 2009, p. 117; originally published in *Guardian* (Manchester, England), January 4, 2003.

Chapel, Jessica, "American Literature: Interview with Sherman Alexie," in *Conversations with Sherman Alexie*, edited by Nancy J. Peterson, University Press of Mississippi, 2009, p. 97; originally published in *Atlantic Unbound*, June 1, 2000.

Cremean, David N., Review of *The Summer of Black Widows*, in *Western American Literature*, Vol. 32, Summer 1997, p. 182.

Davis, Tanita, and Sarah Stevenson, "Sherman Alexie," in *Conversations with Sherman Alexie*, edited by Nancy J. Peterson, University Press of Mississippi, 2009, p. 190; originally published in *Finding Wonderland*, November 7, 2007.

Dellinger, Matt, "Redeemers," in *Conversations with Sherman Alexie*, edited by Nancy J. Peterson, University

Press of Mississippi, 2009, pp. 121–27; originally published in *New Yorker*, April 21, 2003.

Dix, Andrew, "Red, White, and Black: Racial Exchanges in Fiction by Sherman Alexie," in *American Fiction of the 1990s: Reflections of History and Culture*, edited by Jay Prosser, Routledge, 2008, pp. 65, 67.

Evans, Stephen F., "Open Containers: Sherman Alexie's Drunken Indians," in *American Indian Quarterly*, Vol. 25, No. 1, Winter 2001, pp. 46–73.

Ford, Douglas, "Sherman Alexie's Indigenous Blues," in *MELUS*, Vol. 27, No. 3, 2002, p. 197.

Gillan, Jennifer, "Reservation Home Movies: Sherman Alexie's Poetry," in *American Literature*, Vol. 68, No. 1, March 1996, p. 91.

Goldstein, David, "Sacred Hoop Dreams: Basketball in the Work of Sherman Alexie," in *Ethnic Studies Review*, Vol. 32, No. 1, Summer 2009, p. 77.

Gonzalez, Ray, Review of *The Summer of Black Widows*, in *Bloomsbury Review*, January/February 1997, p. 7.

Himmelsbach, Erik, "The Reluctant Spokesman," in *Conversations with Sherman Alexie*, edited by Nancy J. Peterson, University Press of Mississippi, 2009, p. 33; originally published in *Los Angeles Times*, December 17, 1996.

McFarland, Ron, "Another Kind of Violence: Sherman Alexie's Poems," in *American Indian Quarterly*, Vol. 21, No. 2, Spring 1997, p. 251.

Moore, David L. "Sherman Alexie: Irony, Intimacy, and Agency," in *The Cambridge Companion to Native American Literature*, edited by Joy Porter and Kenneth M. Roemer, Cambridge University Press, 2005, p. 301.

Nelson, Joshua B., "Humor Is My Green Card: A Conversation with Sherman Alexie," in *World Literature Today*, Vol. 84, No. 4, July/August 2010, pp. 39–45.

Nygren, Ase, "A World of Story-Smoke: A Conversation with Sherman Alexie," in *MELUS*, Vol. 30, No. 4, 2005, p. 149.

Porter, Joy, "Historical and Cultural Contexts to Native American Literature," in *The Cambridge Companion to Native American Literature*, edited by Joy Porter and Kenneth M. Roemer, Cambridge University Press, 2005, pp. 39–68.

Ruby, Robert H., and John A. Brown, *The Spokane Indians: Children of the Sun*, University of Oklahoma Press, 1970, pp. 3–33, 51, 59, 83, 123–40.

Review of *The Summer of Black Widows*, in *Library Journal*, Vol. 121, No. 18, November 1, 1996, pp. 70, 71.

Review of *The Summer of Black Widows*, in *Publishers Weekly*, Vol. 243, No. 40, September 30, 1996, p. 82.

Thiel, Diane, "A Conversation with Sherman Alexie by Diane Thiel," in *Conversations with Sherman Alexie*, edited by Nancy J. Peterson, University Press of Mississippi, 2009, p. 138; originally published in *Crossroads: The Journal of the Poetry Society of America*, Vol. 61, 2004.

FURTHER READING

Alexie, Sherman, *Reservation Blues*, Atlantic Monthly, 1995.
Alexie's satiric view of life on the reservation is a contrast to Leslie Marmon Silko's approach in *Ceremony* and makes a good parallel read.

Francis, Lee, *Native Time: A Historical Time Line of Native America*, St. Martin's Press, 1996.
The book is organized with a narrative overview of Native American history by century, followed by a detailed timeline of important world events on the left-hand side of the page with parallel relevant Native American events on the right side, allowing the reader to integrate the two into one larger picture.

Hogan, Linda, *The Book of Medicines*, Coffee House Press, 1993.
Chickasaw poet Hogan uses the image of skin to invoke both pain and healing, reconciling Native American knowledge with contemporary life. Hogan's poetry is in the lyric vein of modern Indian poets, a contrast to Alexie's satiric and political style.

Lincoln, Kenneth, *Indi'n Humor: Bicultural Play in Native America*, Oxford, 1993.
This scholarly work on the uniqueness of American Indian humor draws on history, psychology, folklore, linguistics, anthropology, and the arts.

Silko, Leslie Marmon, *Ceremony*, Viking, 1977.
This novel is widely read and taught as an introduction to Native American culture today. It takes place on the Laguna Pueblo Reservation where Tayo, an Indian of mixed blood, returns for healing in the ancestral way after being held as a prisoner of war during World War II.

SUGGESTED SEARCH TERMS

Sherman Alexie

The Summer of Black Widows

The Powwow at the End of the World

Sherman Alexie AND YouTube

Spokane Reservation

Native American history

Native American poetry

Native American literature

Sherman Alexie AND satire

Indians AND salmon culture

Sherman Alexie AND American Indian

Sherman Alexie AND Native American

Sea Canes

DEREK WALCOTT
1976

In "Sea Canes," Nobel Prize-winning poet Derek Walcott uses his Caribbean background to illustrate the anger that people have toward death. The poem features a person coming to terms with the fact that many of his friends have died. At first the speaker is angry, but he eventually learns to see that the departed are still with him, to be found in the world that surrounds him. That world, the West Indies of Walcott's youth, is evoked in the poet's descriptions of the ocean, the moonlight, and the tall groves of sugarcane that form a barrier between the land and the sea.

Before Walcott came to international prominence, few people gave much consideration to the literature of the Caribbean. The publication of his early collection, *In a Green Night*, in 1962 changed that. By the time Walcott published *Sea Grapes*, the 1976 collection in which "Sea Canes" first appeared, he was recognized throughout the world for both his poetry and his plays, which had been performed in major theaters on Broadway and in London's West End. At a time when writers in the Caribbean were using their writings to speak out against the injustices of colonialism and the legacy left in its wake, Walcott's work was more personal and introspective, and therefore related more to the personal lives of people of all different cultures.

Almost fifty years after he first became well known, Walcott's poetry still draws international praise. "Sea Canes" is one of his most frequently

Derek Walcott (Getty Images)

anthologized poems, and it is included in his 2007 publication *Selected Poems*, published by Farrar, Straus and Giroux.

AUTHOR BIOGRAPHY

Walcott was born on January 23, 1930, in Castries, Saint Lucia, one of the Windward Islands in the West Indies. Both of his grandmothers were West Indian. His grandfather on his mother's side was Dutch, and his grandfather on his father's side was English. His father died when he was just one year old, and his mother depended on close family friends for help in raising Walcott and his twin brother, Roderick.

Walcott was raised as a Protestant—his mother ran the Methodist school in Castries, a predominantly Catholic town—but he attended the Catholic St. Mary's College on Saint Lucia, from which he graduated in 1947. He taught briefly at St. Joseph's Convent, and then in 1950, he won a Colonial Development and Welfare Scholarship to attend University College of the West Indies in Jamaica. In college, he was a very active writer. He was one of the founders of both the St. Lucia Art Guild in 1950 and the college newspaper. He was still in college when he had a play produced in London. After graduation in 1954, he moved to Trinidad, where he worked as

a theater and art critic. He studied acting in New York for a year at the Jose Quintero acting school before returning to the Caribbean. In 1958, he founded the Trinidad Theater Workshop, where many of his early plays were produced.

Walcott earned international attention in 1961 when he won the Guinness Award for Poetry. In 1962, his poetry collection *In a Green Night* brought him fame, and its republication in the United Kingdom in 1965 brought critical notice to the neglected field of Caribbean poetry. His play *Dream of a Monkey Mountain* won a 1971 Obie award when it was produced in New York.

For most of his career, Walcott was associated with Boston University, where he taught creative writing and literature. In 1981, he was given full professorship at that school. The same year, he won a prestigious John D. and Catherine T. MacArthur "Genius" award. He was awarded the Nobel Prize for Literature in 1992 and is an honorary member of the American Academy of Arts and Sciences. In 2009, he was appointed professor of poetry at the University of Essex. Walcott's 2010 collection of poetry *White Egrets* was awarded the T. S. Eliot Prize in 2011.

POEM SUMMARY

The text used for this summary is from *Sea Grapes*, Farrar, Straus and Giroux, 1976, p. 70. A version can be found on the following Web page: http://www.poetryarchive.org/poetryarchive/singlePoem.do?poemId=9185.

Lines 1–4

"Sea Canes" begins with a chilling proclamation about the many deaths in the speaker's social sphere, indicating from the start that the speaker is a person who has survived harsh times that many others could not survive. In the persona of the earth, the poem points out the basic cyclical nature of social order: friends may be lost, but others eventually come along to take their place. Although this is necessarily the way of the world, the speaker is defiant, insisting that he does not want new friends, that he wants the old ones back. (In discussing the poem, "he" may be used as a convenience, partially identifying the narrator of the poem with the poet himself, though there is no indication of the speaker's gender.) He is explicit about his old friends, stating that he even misses their faults, making it clear that his

MEDIA ADAPTATIONS

- Derek Walcott reads "Sea Canes" on the compact disc *Derek Walcott Reading from his Poems*, created by the Poetry Archive. It is available from the Poetry Bookshelf, an online arm of the Poetry Book Society, a tiny charity funded by Arts Council England.

- The same audio recording of "Sea Canes" can be heard on the Poetry Archive Web site (http://www.poetryarchive.org/poetryarchive/singlePoem.do?poemId = 9185).

- Public Broadcasting System interviewer Bill Moyers spoke with Derek Walcott about language, poetry, and politics as part of the PBS *World of Ideas* series. A video recording of that interview, volume 32 in the series, was produced in 1988 by PBS Video, under the title *Derek Walcott*. It is also available from Amazon Instant Video (http://www.amazon.com/s/ref = nb_sb_noss?url = search-alias%3Damazontv&field-keyword s = Derek + Walcott&x = 0&y = 0).

---

nostalgia for them runs deep. The emotional distress that he feels is underscored in the last words of the first stanza, which indicate both sorrow and a spontaneous outburst.

This poem begins like a dialogue between its speaker and the earth in the initial lines, but that pattern does not carry through in subsequent stanzas. The earth is not developed as a character but makes just one brief appearance.

Lines 5–7

The speaker discusses hearing his departed friends. They are talking, presumably with one another, somewhere far off. He does not hear voices, exactly, but he is reminded of the sound of their voices by the sounds of nature around him. The sound of the waves crashing against the shore, which is always present in the background in a coastal location, reminds him in some way of voices, particularly when that sound is filtered

through the thicket of sugarcane stalks that grow along the sea like gigantic blades of grass.

By the end of the second stanza, the speaker admits that his circumstances are not within his control. Though he hears his friends' voices off through the brush, he finds himself unable to move toward them or away from them. This paralysis reflects his position in the world, as he finds himself stuck in solid reality, while others who have passed beyond the line that separates life from death are no longer prisoners of their physical bodies.

Lines 8–10

The third stanza of this poem is centered on visual imagery. The speaker describes the ocean. He has already said that the stalks of cane shield him from it, so he must not be able to see it well, but the line indicates that he knows the ocean well. (If the speaker is identified with Walcott, he is describing the region in which he grew up.) He envisions the flickering swells of the waves as looking like leaves when they flicker in the moonlight. The road is white, glowing in the dimness of the night; it may be paved with crushed rock or, as is common in communities near the sea, with crushed seashells. Though these aspects provide him with ghostly, other-worldly visuals, he still is frustrated to find himself held in place by physical reality: the last line of this stanza draws attention to his awareness that the strangeness of his nighttime existence is just an illusion: he cannot really float above the situation, though he might feel as if he can.

Lines 11–13

Line 11 finishes the thought begun in line 10: the floating that the speaker feels but cannot really accomplish is similar to the flight of the owl. More significant here, though, is the way that this line refers to the earth in a disparaging, almost insulting, way. The burden of reality represented by the earth in earlier lines is described in a way that makes it seem not only cumbersome but unnecessary, a weight that the speaker would be much better off without.

In line 12, the speaker again addresses the earth, as he did in the poem's third line. In this line and the next, he compares the number of people who are buried in the earth in graves—those whom the earth has chosen to keep—with the number who are still left around. This time, the number is not a even split, as it was in the first line. As the poem has gone on, the situation has changed, indicating that time has passed, so that now the number of dead is clearly more than half.

Lines 14–16

In the fifth stanza, this poem comes around to its central idea, connecting the sea canes with the poet's friends, both those who live and those who have died. The sugarcane stalks are described in line 14 as being green, which is the color most often associated with new life, and also as being silver, which, because of its association with the hair of the elderly, is often used as a symbol for the end of life.

In line 15, the speaker indicates that his faith was protected by angels armed with spears. This image fits with the visual presence of cane stalks, which are long and thin like spears. The poet talks of his faith in the past tense, but in the next line, he points out that the lost faith is not really such a bad thing, because its loss has led to the growth of something that is stronger than faith.

Lines 17–19

The new feeling that has come to the poem's speaker has to do with both the physical world and the spiritual. The description associates it with the life of the mind, and it shines like some heavenly object and yet is down-to-earth, actually part of the earth. This new sensibility, as unstoppable as the sea wind, has taken the speaker beyond the despair that darkened the first stanzas of the poem. At the end of this stanza, the poem returns to the image of the sea canes, reminding readers of the sound that the wind makes rushing through them and the movements as the stalks sway in the wind, moving and sounding as if the field of sugarcane stalks has a life of its own. This reflects the supernatural character of the feeling of solidarity with his friends, both living and dead, that the speaker has discovered within himself.

Lines 20–21

In this couplet, the speaker refers to himself with the plural pronoun, saying "we," while previously he has said "I." He is no longer sad about the loss of his friends because the natural landscape of his homeland has given him the ability to feel that they still exist with him. The wording of line 21 resembles that of line 3, showing that the speaker has gained exactly what he wanted. In the first stanza, his insistence that his friends be returned to him unchanged seems like childish

stubbornness, but at the end of the poem, his realization that they *are* with him, unchanged, shows that he has grown in his insight.

THEMES

Nature

In "Sea Canes," Walcott uses nature to illustrate the ideas going through a man's head. At first, the abstract concept of old friends dying and new acquaintances taking their place is shown as a function of the earth. As the poem goes on, he does not just say that he remembers the voices of his departed friends; instead, he gives those voices a physical presence through the natural sounds that would surround one on a Caribbean island: the lull of ocean waves filtered through stalks of sugarcane. The images of the night blend together, so that the ripples on the ocean look like the leaves on a plant and the cane emits flashes of silver, like a fish under the surface of the water.

The middle section of the poem is so focused on images of nature that the speaker's subtle change of mind is not evident until the end, when he says that he has attained exactly what he seemed to be denied in the first stanza. The natural effects of his environment bring his loved ones to him, in a way, just as death has taken them away. The poem implies that in death, they have merged with nature and thus are still present.

Death

The tone of this poem is initially an angry one. The speaker is resentful that he has so many friends who have died. Death has separated him from particular people, presumably for eternity, and he mourns their loss. He knows that he will eventually have new friends, but because they will not be the same people as the ones he has lost, he refuses to find any consolation in that fact. The immutable fact of death has him so upset that he wants to strike out at reality, crying out to the world in his frustration. It is not until the end of the poem, when time has passed and he has cooled down, that he finds himself willing to accept death for what it is: something stronger and more eternal than he is. By the end of the poem, he has realized that his sorrow cannot affect the situation, and he finds peace with the power that death has to take the people he knows.

TOPICS FOR FURTHER STUDY

- Use online and print sources to research the basic attitudes and customs of several cultures regarding death. Use your findings to write a short essay that analyzes whether cultures are typically more angry at loss or accepting of it, covering both attitudes shown in "Sea Canes."

- Walcott is almost as well known as a playwright as he is as a poet. Expand the story of this poem into a short play, giving the earth a specific characterization and adding more characters as you think necessary. Present the play for your class or record video of it and post it to YouTube. Invite your classmates to write reviews of your production.

- Research the sociological history (that is, history of use by humans) of a plant that grows near you that could be considered as significant to your culture as sugarcane is to the people of the West Indies. Find examples of artwork, music, and literature that indicate how that plant is significant to your culture. Create a PowerPoint or SlideShare presentation to showcase your findings.

- Analyze some traditional folk music from one of the islands of the West Indies until you find a sound or instrument that could be considered inspired by the sound of sea winds through cane fields. Try to reproduce that sound, and write a song based on it.

- Walcott has pointed out in interviews that the people of the Caribbean have a unique language: it is predominantly English, but it also mixes in French, Dutch, and some African dialects. After reading about pidgin languages, read several of Walcott's poems until you find a section that you think is unusual. Write a report explaining what cultural influences might have the strongest influence on that particular section of writing.

- James Berry is a contemporary poet who grew up in Jamaica and writes for a young-adult audience. Read Berry's "Villagers' Independence," from his 1995 collection *Hot Earth Cold Earth*. Write an essay expressing your opinion about whether writing in aphonetic dialect, as Berry does, helps readers understand other cultures or confuses readers too much.

The poem's speaker does not address the reason why he is surrounded by so much death, affecting a majority of his acquaintances. In peaceful and prosperous countries, this is a situation most familiar in old age, as people approach the limits of their life spans. Walcott, coming from the island nation of Trinidad and Tobago in the years before it experienced an economic boom due to oil production, lived among poverty most of his early life, a situation in which many people die younger than they should.

Community

In this poem, the speaker is a part of a tight-knit community. Readers can see his powerful bond to his friends in his unwillingness to give them up when they die. The earth, representing the natural order of existence, tries to convince him that they will be replaced with new friends, but he retains a fierce devotion to the actual friends he has made. As the poem progresses, he hears their voices in nature, reminded of them by the sound of the sea as it filters through the patch of sugarcane.

This poem manages to convey a strong sense of community and loyalty while showing only one person. Handled in a different way, a situation like this could be used to show a person living in isolation.

The speaker does not describe his friends, but clearly he knows them very well, even appreciating and missing their flaws. Using nature imagery, Walcott shows a character who is close to a wide net of friends and who relies on them all as individuals.

Sea canes *(Tom Klima / Shutterstock.com)*

STYLE

Personification

At a few strategic points in "Sea Canes," the speaker treats the earth as if it were another human being: it speaks to him and he speaks to it. The poetic technique of giving human qualities, such as speech, to nonhuman objects, such as the earth, is called personification.

Walcott could have expressed his ideas in a realistic mode without presenting his readers with a talking planet, but the ideas are more powerful if they are presented in dialogue form. Readers generally expect poems to state things in unexpected ways that make more sense when viewed symbolically, not literally, which is the aim of personification.

Although the dialogue between the poem's speaker and the earth is quite explicit in the first stanza, the second time he addresses the earth, in stanza 4, may not be an example of personification at all. Its use of the evocative *O* is characteristic of *apostrophe*, a poetic technique in which the speaker addresses a person or object that is

not present and cannot answer. On its own, stanza 4 would count as an apostrophe, though the earlier dialogue makes it clear that the poem is showing this to be a two-way conversation.

Tercet

The technical name for a three-line stanza is tercet. It is the main structural device used in this poem: there are five tercets in the center, bracketed between a four-line stanza at the beginning and a two-line stanza at the end. Basing the poem on three-line stanzas gives Walcott the opportunity to tie his ideas together with repetitions that loop around on one another. In stanzas 2 and 3, this repetition is seen in the rhyming of the first and third lines of each stanza, and of the second lines of both stanzas with each other. In stanzas 4 and 5, the repetition is not in rhymes but in alliteration, which is the recurrence of beginning sounds of words. The strong rhyme scheme of the early tercets dissolves as the poem continues, a pattern that reflects the way the speaker's refusal to be consoled softens by the time the poem reaches the end. This flexibility of pattern is also reflected in the inclusion of non-tercet stanzas at

COMPARE
&
CONTRAST

- **1970s:** Literature classes in the United States generally teach works by American and British authors.

  Today: Multiculturalism is a familiar concept in classrooms. Students learn about other cultures by studying their poetry and fiction in literature courses.

- **1970s:** The sugarcane field is part of the Caribbean agricultural tradition, going back hundreds of years. Many subsidies exist to promote the production of sugarcane.

  Today: Sugar production has fallen, replaced in the Caribbean economy by the growth of the tourist trade. The production of sugarcane is no longer considered a cost-effective industry.

- **1970s:** Passage between the West Indies and the United States is just a matter of a boat ride. Many people would like to emigrate from the West Indies to the United States but cannot afford the fare for the trip.

  Today: Since the bombing of the World Trade Center and the Pentagon in 2001, travel to the United States has become much more difficult. Border officials are concerned about people entering the United States for malicious political reasons, while economists fear that too many people emigrating from poor nations could harm the economy.

- **1970s:** Recognizing how economic development has an impact of the calm shore lines of islands in the Caribbean, the Island Resources Foundation begins a series of resource management studies to ensure that development will have minimal impact.

  Today: Activities of environmentalists coexist with government and developer work on sustainable policies for the use of the coastal areas of the islands.

---

the beginning and the end: the pattern clearly exists throughout most of the poem, but Walcott shows that there is room for flexibility.

HISTORICAL CONTEXT

History of the West Indies

In 1976, the year that this poem was published in Walcott's collection *Sea Grapes*, the United States celebrated the two-hundredth anniversary of the signing of the Declaration of Independence. Across the West Indies, where Walcott grew up and which provided the setting for this poem, countries still struggled to establish their freedom after a long history of colonialism, cope with poverty, and discover newfound prosperity from a sudden worldwide shift in the price of oil.

Walcott lived in several Caribbean countries, including Saint Lucia, Jamaica, and Trinidad and Tobago, during his early life. With a few variations, the countries of that region share a common history. They were brought to the attention of Europeans in the late fifteenth century by Christopher Columbus, the same explorer celebrated for the discovery of the United States. By the beginning of the sixteenth century, the Spanish empire had laid claim to the entire region. Seeing it as a crucial stop on the trade route between Europe and the Americas, ships representing France, England, and eventually the Netherlands came to the region. Piracy became rampant.

The Europeans found the climate of the Caribbean islands and the nearby South American colonies ideal for growing sugar. To run the sugar plantations, they brought slave laborers from Africa. From the sixteenth to the nineteenth centuries, between eight and fifteen million Africans were brought to the region to work. In most Caribbean countries, the conditions for slaves were harsh, since laws held plantation owners accountable to no one for how they treated the

The sea is important to the meaning of the poem. (*Mariano N. Ruiz | Shutterstock.com*)

human beings they owned. The slave population quickly outnumbered the small native populations of the islands, people descended from South American Indians. Although Britain abolished slavery in the mid-1800s and France followed soon after, the emancipated people of the Caribbean still labored in conditions markedly worse than those of the Europeans who owned the land.

European colonization was a major cause for tension well into the twentieth century, as slave status was often simply replaced with the legal designation of indentured servitude. Haiti gained independence in 1804, the Dominican Republic in 1844, and Cuba in 1898, but many countries of the Caribbean did not begin seeing self-determination until Walcott's time in the second half of the twentieth century. Colonialism did not die out completely in the Caribbean until after World War II, when the British Empire found itself spent. Inspired by the successful drive for independence by India in 1947, led by Mohandas Gandhi, one colony after another began pressing for its freedom. Britain found its power overseas weakening because of the financial and military destruction of the war, and its moral right to rule faded in the postwar years. One step

taken to hold on to the Caribbean was the formation of the West Indies Federation in 1958, putting fourteen countries, including Antigua and Barbuda, the Bahamas, Barbados, Dominica, Jamaica, Saint Lucia, and others under one centralized government, answering to Great Britain. The dissolution of the West Indies Federation after four years of strife and disagreement marked the end of most British rule in the territory. Some countries, such as Anguilla and the Cayman Islands, are still British dependencies.

The Republic of Trinidad and Tobago saw its first successful oil well drilled in 1857. The country saw an economic boom when the price of oil rose in the 1970s, but other islands with insecure economies continued to rely on sugar and tobacco crops and on the increasing tourist trade.

CRITICAL OVERVIEW

Walcott is one of the world's most respected writers, having been awarded the Nobel Prize for Literature in 1992. His writing career was respected by critics all along, since the little-circulated collection *25 Poems*, which he published himself when he was just eighteen years old, in 1948. He came to international attention in the 1960s with the publication of *In a Green Night* and has been an important literary voice since then.

For audiences who did not notice his early career, the 1986 publication of *Collected Poems, 1948–1984* offered an opportunity to read poems from books that had gone out of print. Poet Joseph Brodsky probably sums up the general critical view of Walcott that year with the observation, in an essay appearing in Harold Bloom's *Derek Walcott*, that "everything this poet touches mushrooms with reverberations and perspectives, like magnetic waves whose acoustics are psychological, whose implications are echo-like." Brodsky indicates that Walcott drew his power from his background, noting, "Of course, in that realm of his, in the West Indies, there is plenty to touch—the natural kingdom alone provides a great deal of fresh material."

Rita Dove, also an esteemed poet, expresses admiration of his overall career in her essay in Bloom's *Derek Walcott*, but she ends her review of Walcott's *Collected Poems* by expressing sadness: "I find the recent work a slight diminishment of his power, the flame turned a little lower." She notes, however, that he was at a point where he was ready to start again, a view that most critics have found to be supported in the quarter-century since then.

As recently as 2011, Walcott's collection *White Egrets* won the highly prestigious T. S. Eliot Prize for Poetry.

CRITICISM

David Kelly

Kelly is a writer and instructor in literature and creative writing. In the following essay, he examines how an image such as sugarcane, which is not part of the background of poetry readers in most of the world, can be used effectively to make the message of "Sea Canes" by Derek Walcott more striking.

That readers around the globe are able to put themselves into Derek Walcott's poem "Sea Canes," a short, mannered piece from his 1976 collection *Sea Grapes*, is a testament to the poet's craft. It is a poem about mourning, rage, and

acceptance. The first line announces that the poem's speaker has seen suffering in his life; of his friends, he proclaims right from the start, half are dead and half are living. The ensuing twenty lines follow his thought process through anger and denial to understanding of his losses and, by extension, of life's overall sorrows.

This is a philosophical understanding that is common to the human experience. It could be reached by anyone, in any culture. Walcott universalizes it by using universal symbols, such as the sea, the moon, an owl, and a road stretching out ahead. There is one image, though, that stands out as being particularly, purposely narrow. It is the most important image of the poem and appears in the title, which frames the work's meaning.

Memory is a frequent theme in Walcott's writing, and it is certain that a poem about the departed is destined to be about memory. The poem distracts readers from that idea, however, by starting with an angry tone and bringing up, in the first line, a minor conceit that another writer might have used for the basis of a poem. When the poet mourns his absent friends, the earth itself speaks, offering to make more friends for him. This is a reasonable way to present what could broadly be referred to as the cycle of life, as the earth (standing for the universe, the cosmos, God, or the gods) sends more to replace what has been lost.

The idea of a dialogue with the earth is engaging, but it really turns out to be not very important to the poem. The earth speaks only once, and the poem's narrator talks to the earth just twice. This is no ongoing conversation; it is just a way for Walcott, who is as much a dramatist as a poet, to get this relationship between a man and his world across to readers in a dramatic way.

The personification of the earth is eye-catching, but what Walcott uses to drive his poem forward is more risky than that. He ties the basic universal situation to his particular part of the world, his individual experience. Cane plants grow in southern, humid climates all across the globe, but they have a special, bittersweet connection to the West Indies, where much of the population is descended from slaves brought from Africa to work the sugarcane fields. Cane is as specific and meaningful to the cultural memories of Walcott's homeland as cotton is to the descendants of Southern plantation workers.

Sugarcane is the driving force in this poem because it personalizes Walcott's message. It is

WHAT DO I READ NEXT?

- One of Walcott's most famous and often-quoted poems, "The Sea Is History," also refers to the way history is contained in nature, and can be seen as a companion piece to this poem. Published in *The Star-Apple Kingdom* in 1980, it is also available in Walcott's *Collected Poems: 1948–1984*.

- V. S. Naipaul, born in Trinidad and Tobago, is also a winner of the Nobel Prize for Literature. His 1961 novel *Miguel Street* is heavily autobiographical, taking place in Port of Spain, that country's capital city, rendering the lives of the people of Trinidad with rich detail. It is available in a 2002 edition published by Vintage.

- Of the many young-adult novels dealing with the subject of the death of someone close, Barbara Park's *Mick Harte Was Here* has earned significant praise for its realistic, unsentimental portrayal. Written from the perspective of Phoebe, a teen who has lost her younger brother in a bicycle accident, it covers the same emotions Walcott examines in this poem, but from a contemporary American perspective. It was published by Yearling in 1996.

- Many books have been published about Derek Walcott and his works. Paul Breslin's *Nobody's Nation: Reading Derek Walcott* is particularly relevant because it focuses on Walcott's life in the West Indies and his views of how that region's history has traditionally been ignored, along with his attempts to reclaim it through literature.

Breslin's book was published by the University of Chicago Press in 2001.

- Earl Lovelace, a columnist for the *Trinidad Express* newspaper, has written colorful, humorous stories about life in the Caribbean for decades. His story "The Fire Eater's Return," from Persea Press's 2003 collection *A Brief Conversion and Other Stories*, presents a good example of the kind of storytelling the people of the West Indies are inclined to see representing themselves.

- Much that is written about the life and history of the West Indies is focused on men, but recently studies have drawn attention to women's roles. Mary Johnson Osirim's essay "We Toil All the Livelong Day: Women in the English-Speaking Caribbean" provides a good look at what it is like to be a working woman in this economically oppressed area. This essay appears in *Daughters of Caliban: Caribbean Women in the Twentieth Century*, a collection published by Indiana University Press in 1997.

- There are similarities, and also differences, between the Caribbean postcolonial experience and the ways that African nations changed with independence. The most widely known book about the African experience is Chinua Achebe's novel *Things Fall Apart*, which offers an unsentimental view of Nigeria just as Europeans are entering and changing it. First published near the end of the colonial period in 1958, it is currently available in a 1996 edition published by Heinemann.

good for a poet to offer readers a universal experience, but there is some level at which a poem can be too universal, dampening its impact because it is spread too thin: a poem that is all things to all people ends up sending the message that it does not mean much to anyone in particular. By contrast, an element used in the way that sugarcane is in this poem, having no

personal significance to most readers, can tell those readers that the poet is likely reaching deeply within himself, looking for what matters deeply to him.

Readers can understand sugarcane, even if they have never experienced it themselves. They can find images in books and online; they can

The narrator laments the death of his friends. *(easys hutter | Shutterstock.com)*

study its habits, its properties, and its history. They can understand it only intellectually, though. They cannot give themselves the sort of deep-seated sense memory that comes of long-term experience. Of all of the associations Walcott is drawing on, this one is unique; it counts on all of the elements converging in just the right way: the sound of the wind off the ocean as it cuts through fields of cane. The title very specifically links the sea to the cane, showing that land-locked cane rustled by a land wind does not create the sound he has in mind. A majority of readers may have never heard that sound, and even readers who grew up in the Caribbean may not know it, but that is not necessary to know what it means to the poet.

To understand the significance of the sea canes, readers do not have to look any further than the effect expected of them. It is the effect of the wide-open world, symbolized by the wind blowing off of the ocean, being filtered through the plants that represent the writer's home terrain. This combination moves the poet and nurtures in him a new faith, the faith that those who

have died can still reach him through the objects of the physical world, which is where he ends up in the poem's final line. This faith is what he is missing when the poem starts; it grows out of the sense memory that readers can watch growing before their eyes, at the same time recalling ways their own sense memories have brought about change in themselves. Diving deeply into his sense memory and taking his readers along for the journey, Walcott shows that the line separating our idea of the past from our idea of the future is not a fixed, stable one.

The process the speaker undergoes in the poem, learning to accept the past as a living and relevant thing, presents itself in much of Walcott's writing. It shows itself in his plays and in his other poems, notably the five-part "Sainte Lucie" sequence, named after Walcott's hometown and published in the same collection as "Sea Canes." It is shown in his fascination with antiquity, such as his recasting of the story of the Odyssey through West Indian sensibilities in the 1990 epic *Omeros*. In Walcott's worldview, the past is the present and the future, the east is the west, but they all converge on the individual. There is no

> WALCOTT'S OWN WORKS ARE A
> REAFFIRMATION OF THE CARIBBEAN CULTURE
> AND IDENTITY. THE CARIBBEAN IS NOT A COPY
> OF ANYTHING, SAYS THE POET."

way for a poem to render the sound of canes rustled by a sea breeze, and even a recording would fall short of conveying the meaning that sound has to one who grew up with it, but honest poetry can show more than what it is, giving a reader a sense of what it means.

Source: David Kelly, Critical Essay on "Sea Canes," in *Poetry for Students*, Gale, Cengage Learning, 2012.

Enriqueta Cabrera

In the following essay, Cabrera calls Walcott the "voice of the Caribbean" and a "master of language."

Poet and playwright Derek Walcott received the Nobel Prize for Literature in 1992. He reached this apex of literary achievement by transmitting the Caribbean culture with strength, sensitivity, beauty, and ingenuity.

Derek Walcott was born in 1930 in Saint Lucia, then a British colony. His father died when he was very young, but he was a precocious child and his mother took great care with his education. "I knew from very early on that I was going to be a writer," he says. Eventually, he studied at both St. Mary University in Saint Lucia and the West Indies University in Jamaica.

The island of Saint Lucia, which became independent in 1979, alternated between British and French rule for centuries, producing a multilingual, multicultural place where Methodism and Catholicism coexisted and combined with religions of African influence. Walcott's own works are a reaffirmation of the Caribbean culture and identity. The Caribbean is not a copy of anything, says the poet. "It is an amalgam of everyone's experiences." It is also an amalgam of peoples—Africans, Indians, Chinese, English, Dutch, and French—in a unique environment that developed its own unique culture and identity.

Walcott recalls his first years as a writer and painter. It was an uncommon thing in the Caribbean to dedicate oneself to writing back then. There was no sophisticated audience, he says, but there was an audience that could be moved by feeling, by vitality. He recalls feeling that writers had the responsibility to move people. This passion vibrates in his poetry and his plays. It is a passion for justice, but above all, the desire to highlight the Caribbean as a culture and as a social reality.

A master of language, Walcott has been on the vanguard of his craft, opening and building a space for the Caribbean's own expression. He has written more than fifteen books of poetry and close to 30 plays. He writes in English and often introduces elements of popular language in Creole. His work is marked by the experiences of the Caribbean people and reflects their identity and their heritage.

THE POETRY AND DRAMA OF WALCOTT IS THE VOICE OF THE CARIBBEAN.

Between 1959 and 1976, Walcott directed the Trinidad Theater Workshop (called the Little Carib Theater Workshop until 1966). It was an intense and passionate time period during which he worked part-time with a troupe of actors and also held another job, since theater didn't pay him enough to live on. At that time, occasional contributions came in from the Rockefeller Foundation. Successes led the company to do presentations outside the country in Jamaica, Guyana, Toronto, Boston, and New York. Walcott eventually also became a professor of drama.

Dream on Monkey Mountain is considered Walcott's greatest work and one in which he makes a great effort to interpret the nature of the Caribbean identity. Reality and dreams are interwoven in the drama in which the main character, Makak (French patois for "ape") faces imprisonment and dreams that he is crowned king in the romantic Africa of his roots. Some say *Dream on Monkey Mountain* is influenced by Jean-Paul Sartre's theories of the black Orpheus and by the work of French sociologist Franz Fanon (*The Wretched of the Earth*). But Walcott doesn't make direct references to the classics; they are names from the Atlantic, geographic parallels, but they are not culturally integrated or articulated. What does exist in terms of reference points are fragmentary memories, associations, echoes of previous cultures. The essential is Caribbean.

Another of Walcott's great works is *Omeros*, historic reflections divided into 192 songs and written in a rhythmic verse of poetic metaphors. Joran Jmoberg describes it in the following way: "*Omeros* is . . . an epic poetic tale with a multitude of different short stories, flashbacks, conversations, monologues, episodes, descriptions, and impressions, depicting in a minute, detailed way the Caribbean world and all its everyday life, its human beings, animals, nature, waters, and woods . . . Likewise, as a background to the life of people in our time, Walcott refers to violent events in history: the siege of Troy, the extermination of the Aruac people in the Caribbean by conquistadors, the eighteenth century fights in the Caribbean between the English and the French navies, as well as the prolonged catastrophe that extinguished most native Americans. Or the cruel attacks on African villages by slave traders, the perpetual tragedy of the captives who had to leave their homes, their families, their professions, and their tools, to try to create a new identity beyond the Atlantic."

But Derek Walcott thinks it sounds "too pompous" to call *Omeros* an epic poem.

"I wanted to celebrate the island, the people there," he says. Nevertheless, the form was a challenge that he enjoyed immensely. He wanted, above all, to delight the reader.

Derek Walcott received the call telling him he had won the Nobel Prize for Literature early one morning. He remembers the shock, followed by the huge celebrations. Soon he saw the need to separate the person from the celebration and to see the prize as something more for the poetry than for the poet. The Nobel Prize is "good because of what it can do, does, or will do for Caribbean literature," he said once in a televised interview. "It was very exciting."

When Professor Kjell Espmark, member of the Swiss Academy, introduced Walcott as the Nobel Prize winner for Literature, he said; "Trying to capture Derek Walcott's oceanic work in a formula would be an absurd enterprise." He went on to quote from Walcott's *The Star-Apple Kingdom*:

> I'm just a red nigger who love the sea
> I had a sound colonial education
> I have Dutch nigger, and English in me
> And either I'm nobody, or I'm a nation.

"Theses lines call to mind how Walcott unites the white and black on his father's as well as on his mother's sides," Espmark continued, "but they also remind us of the fact that in his poetry he amalgamates material from different cultures: West Indian, African, and European."

In the same speech, Espmark also quoted from another of Walcott's autobiographical texts, *Another Life*:

> I watched the vowels curl from
> the tongue of the carpenter's plane,
> resinous, fragrant.

"Derek Walcott's extraordinary idiom is born in the meeting between European virtuosity and the sensuality of the Caribbean Adam," Espmark says.

Today, Derek Walcott is receiving ongoing recognition for his poetry and plays. He is one of the best known voices of the Caribbean and is a unique voice in poetry, drama, and criticism.

Walcott continues to write. He also teaches "Creative Writing" at Boston University and derives particular pleasure from encouraging new writers. He also continues to paint, inaugurating his first solo art exhibition in November 2005 at the June Kelly Gallery in New York City.

You published your first poem when you were fourteen, and you wrote five plays and published your first collection of poems by the time you were sixteen. How did this vocation begin?

My father was a writer. He worked in the civil service but he also wrote plays and was a very good painter and poet. He died when my twin brother and I were young. My mother was a school teacher and encouraged me a great deal. I told her fairly early on that I wanted to do what my father did. She understood me very well and she always looked for ways to motivate me. This was a determining factor. I knew very early on that I was going to be a writer, and I got to work on it very early. I also had very good teachers who encouraged me from elementary school on. Some poets are precocious, and I was one of them, but I owe a lot to my environment.

I imagine that you read a great deal as a child. Do you remember some of the authors you were reading back then?

Well, yes, I read a lot. I read at a level that was much higher than my age. I read Dickens, Walter Scott, Sabatini, and many, many poets. I read Shakespeare, also.

I understand that you also began painting when you were young.

Yes, exactly. Throughout my life, I have combined writing and painting. In fact, I had an exhibit last year. When I was young, my friends and I had an important relationship with a painter named Harold Simons. He encouraged me a lot. He was a friend and a professional painter, and we continued painting together.

They say that you experienced—and therefore reflect—the antagonism between the European Anglophone and Francophone cultures and the Caribbean culture, and between the English, French, and Creole languages. Is the search for identity at the heart of your literary work?

I suppose you could use those terms, though I don't like them because they are simplistic. I think it's not so much about resolving who I am or who I was, but about representing where I come from—who the people and landscape are in my work. It is not as much about trying to express the conflict between the European and the African as it is about trying to express the presence of something that had not been painted, pronounced, or said before.

Are identity and Nation two concepts that you link in your work?

I have never wanted to make it very political. I think what you have to understand is that there are a lot of things developing in the Caribbean that are happening at the same time. It's limiting to isolate factors, I think.

Then, perhaps what is Caribbean is not so much about a conflict as it is about a combination, an amalgam.

The conflict is there, because of history, but in terms of today's reality, it's not an active conflict, though it could be in terms of the people who are still struggling.

In relation to your autobiographical work, Another Life, some critics say that you are subconsciously programmed to "Caribbeanize" the European culture. Is there something to this, or it is just a Caribbean sensitivity that emerges from your work?

I think the people who say that are in the Caribbean, but they don't understand it. They don't understand that the Caribbean is something original in itself, not just something that has to copy the European. Maybe that's what it looks like at first glance, but the fact that we speak the same language as they do in Great Britain doesn't mean that we want to be English, and the fact that we have the same language as France doesn't mean that we are trying to be French in spirit or in time. We are not trying to copy any of the empires; we have too much of

our own culture around us. Reality is the opposite of that.

Could you talk a little bit about the nature of the Caribbean?

The first thing about the Caribbean is that it doesn't have just one essence or nature. This is the interesting thing about the Caribbean; it has different cultures simultaneously. Everything happens at the same time and doesn't develop in a linear fashion. Linear ideas can be very dangerous because they can lead to nationalism or even fascism when a single element of culture is isolated. There is too much emphasis on the African culture in the Caribbean, and there should be much more respect paid to the Indian and Chinese cultures in terms of color and origin. I say this even though it irritates some people, because there is a risk involved when we tend to leave out people, like people from the West Indies, who have contributed to our culture. We should mix these cultures. We should mix the African philosophy and culture with the Indian. It is the mixture of cultures that is the essence of the Caribbean. I think that is very exciting.

Thinking about your work in theater and poetry, which do you prefer?

You have a lot of company in theater—actor friends and many people who get involved in the production. I had a theater company almost fifty years ago. You work as a group and you share the experience with more people. It's different from poetry where you work in an isolated fashion, though I also work with lyrical poetry, hoping to involve the reader in the enjoyment.

You have had a great interest in the sea and the Homeric world that you called "an echo in the throat." Your poem, Omeros: Is it an epic poem?

I think that if we rely only on the traditional definition of epic, it is not an epic. It is not like the epic of Eneas, for example, where there is a heroic narrative, in which the primary character does something for others. The hero in my poem is a simple fisherman who doesn't conquer anything and who works with his element—the sea. That's the life of the Caribbean. That's what the poem refers to in terms of the elements that make it up. It's not about a glorious epic poem of the Caribbean.

Of course you could have some cultural references in terms of one language in particular, and if you are Octavio Paz and you are Mexican, you have to allow the presence of Cervantes. You can't deny it. You're not isolated from the culture that surrounds you. That's why I include the cultures that surround the fisherman in my book. He is an illiterate fisherman, but his natural knowledge is more than that of your average hero, or of your average heroic act.

You received the Nobel Prize in Literature in 1992. Was it a surprise? What significance does this high recognition have for you, your literature, and for the Caribbean? Also, how has your life changed since 1992?

Well, it was a pleasure to receive the Nobel Prize. It wasn't a total surprise because my name had been discussed as a possibility in the previous year also. So when it happened, it was a pleasure, a great joy, and I was very proud. And it was very good for the Caribbean and for Caribbean literature, and it helped people pay attention to the region. I was treated very well at home when I won; there were enormous celebrations. Without exaggerating and without drama, I think it was very important for the island of Saint Lucia. There have been two Nobel Prize winners in the Caribbean; Saint John Perse, the French-born writer, received the award in 1960.

What is your life like now, between Boston, New York, and Saint Lucia?

Well, I have been invited to many countries all over the world. There is a lot of curiosity about the Caribbean in different countries. I have been treated very well in my visits. I'm going to Italy. I just returned from Greece. And the invitations continue and they are truly very flattering, enriching, interesting. I am very happy to go to Italy. Where I haven't visited sufficiently is Central and South America, and I have very little knowledge of Mexico, which is something I should remedy.

Source: Enriqueta Cabrera, "Derek Walcott: The Voice of the Caribbean: Saint Lucia's Favorite Son Discusses the Emerging Identity in Literature and Prose Unique to the Islands," in *Americas*, Vol. 59, No. 3, May/June 2007, pp. 38–43.

Andrew Salkey

In the following essay, Salkey discusses recurring themes of light, harmony, and completeness in Walcott's poetry.

Rather like the generalized implication that there is a whole unified scene going for all of us in the New World, in the geographical, historical and political concept of José Martí's *nuestra*

> HIS POETIC RANGE OF EXPRESSION IS AS WIDE AS HIS HUMAN CONCERNS AND AS ALL-OF-A-PIECE AS HIS SENSE OF HARMONY AND HIS PREOCCUPATION WITH THE NATURE OF LOVE."

américa, anything anyone says about the poetry of Derek Walcott can be argued as true. His is a new voice redolent with traceries of the elitist elegance of the Old World. His poetry, or at least much of it, is also a radical truth-saying in "other words," in our time, an old report brought forward with sensitive alterations from "another country" to *nuestra américa*. And further, it is the Anglophone Caribbean bringing the salt of her history and received language to bear on the comparatively recent seasoning of our hemisphere's newness.

But more than anything else, it is Walcott's territorial and ontological promise in "Islands," from *In a Green Night*, that makes me know where I am in relation to and what I am to expect from his contribution to *nuestra américa*.

> . . . I seek
> As climate seeks its style, to write
> Verse crisp as sand, clear as sunlight,
> Cold as the curled wave, ordinary
> As a tumbler of island water. . . .

But first, how about that "island"? How about those islands which are the centrality of our Caribbean input into the hemisphere? Walcott's timely warning in that direction is one of the finest in Caribbean poetry that I know and one seldom ever reckoned with when his work is written about in the United States and Britain. His warning also comes from "islands," and I personally take it seriously; for after all, deep down we all do know that "islands can only exist / If we have loved in them." That is to say, in effect, that Walcott is our greatest living love poet and that his profoundly important contribution to *nuestra américa* is his poetry of island love, archipelago love, sea love, ocean love and his loving recollection of the formation of *nuestra américa*. It is from that view of volume after volume of his crystalline poems that I see Walcott's significance and impact in our problematical New World.

If *In a Green Night* announces his territorial and historical perspective of love, then the *Selected Poems* further enhances it and deepens his announcement into a personal declaration. *The Castaway* is another collection that carries forward the statement of New World caring in those two earlier books. Here Walcott reminds us that Crusoe is adrift on Caribbean islands, cut off from the outside world, and consequently must learn to expect little of it. Indeed, "Crusoe's Journal," one of the memorable poems in *The Castaway*, has for its epigraph a quotation from *Robinson Crusoe* which ends with Abraham's words to Dives: "Between me and thee is a great gulf fixed." In a sense *The Castaway* heralded Walcott's next book, *The Gulf*. And there is a line in "Miramar" which more than hints that "There is nowhere to go." Yet at the same time, Walcott's commitment to hope, as the first step toward gaining the necessary courage to approach and break through the inherited gloom of Caribbean underdevelopment and pessimism, urges him to complete the line as follows: "There is nowhere to go. You'd better go."

In 1969, when I read *The Gulf* in the Jonathan Cape edition, I mistook the central emphasis of the poems as suggesting that the loneliness of islands, their abject isolation, causes all islanders (hence *all* people so isolated) to strive inordinately for a protective identity, and especially for a quick, hard-edged, materialistic one at that. And, of course, there was more than enough textual evidence to endorse the mistake of that reading. Rereading *The Gulf* later on in 1975 and again in 1981 for this article, I discovered that there was just as much corroborative evidence to suggest that the metaphorical loneliness of islands (together with their "lack of identity" in the outside world's false reckoning) could also be interpreted as the inaccessible quality of love as it becomes enisled. In other words, my later readings yielded Walcott's poetic theory of isolation and namelessness as a paradigm of the death of love.

And so, even in the most literal, surface reading of *Another Life*, Walcott's autobiographical long poem of over 4,000 lines, his specific recollections of love, misconstrued and reappraised, connect fairly readily.

> Maman,
> only on Sundays was the Singer silent,
> then,
> tobacco smelt stronger, was more masculine.
> Sundays
> the parlour smelt of uncles,
> the lamppoles rang,

> the drizzle shivered its maracas,
> like mandolins the tightening wires of rain,
> then
> from striped picnic buses, *jour marron*,
> gold bangles tinkled like good-morning in Guinea
> and a whore's laughter opened like sliced fruit.

Here again, the poet speaks lovingly to his mother, his very own St. Lucian "Maman," but also to mine in Jamaica and to the mother of us all, everywhere throughout the Area, the ever-present Caribbean Sea, the old, loving shelter.

> Old house, old woman, old room
> old planes, old buckling membranes of the womb,
> translucent walls,
> breathe through your timbers; gasp
> arthritic, curling beams,
> cough in old air
> shining with motes, stair
> polished and repolished by the hands of strangers,
> die with defiance flecking your grey eyes,
> motes of a sunlit air,
> your timbers humming with constellations of
>   carcinoma,
> your bed frames glowing with radium,
> cold iron dilating the fever of your body,
> while the galvanised iron snaps in spasms of pain,
> but a house gives no outcry,
> it bears the depth of forest, of ocean and mother.
> Each consuming the other
> with memory and unuse.

And similarly in the objects of the old house, the ones handled by Maman, the same ones recollected by the poet, in pained tranquillity, those that help frame the anguished questions:

> . . . when did the tightened scream
> of that bedspring finally snap,
> when did that unsilvering mirror finally
> surrender her vanity,
> and, in turn, these objects assess us,
> that yellow paper flower with the eyes of a cat,
> that stain, familiar as warts or some birthmark,
> as the badge of some loved defect. . . .

Another Life, apart from being a "self-inquiry and cultural assessment in the context of a Caribbean life" and the dismantling and redefining of a former colonial poet's "cultural apparatus of . . . imperialist tutelage," as George Lamming, the distinguished Barbadian novelist and poet, correctly put it, is also an affecting heroic narrative of historical and contemporary defects lovingly owned up to and accepted, in spite of their harrowing memories, lingering scars and half-healed wounds. Walcott's recall of the inconsolable burden of innocence and experience of a people breaking out of the aching silence of colonial defects, cracking the solitude of underdevelopment and neo-colonialism, is the most truly remarkable personal cri de coeur so far published by any Caribbean writer I know.

When I think of the stinging truth of the following lines, I'm acutely aware of how deep Walcott has dredged our psychic loss and caused our current pain to surface—and especially so in the tellingly chosen poetic diction and metaphorical usage of his imaginative report.

> Skin wrinkles like paint,
> the forearm of a balustrade freckles,
> crows' feet radiate
> from the shut eyes of windows,
> and the door, mouth clamped, reveals nothing,
> for there is no secret,
> there is no other secret
> but a pain so alive that
> to touch every ledge of that house edges a scream
> from the burning wires, the nerves
> with their constellation of cancer,
> the beams with their star-seed of lice,
> pain shrinking every room,
> pain shining in every womb,
> while the blind, dumb
> termites, with jaws of the crabcells consume,
> in silent thunder,
> to the last of all Sundays,
> consume.

And he continues by daring us to touch those closed windows, the ledge of that house, the burning wires, those nerves, to touch the terror of death in life, if only to prove our capacity for loving a world we can't hope to move or embrace with our love.

> Finger each object, lift it
> from its place, and it screams again
> to be put down
> in its ring of dust, like the marriage finger
> frantic without its ring;
> I can no more move you from your true alignment,
> mother, than we can move objects in paintings.

Equally haunting reflections on love (ones which when lifted off the page, up to memory and recall, seem to scream to be put back instantly), together with their concomitant sense of loss and actuality of present pain, also appear in many of the poems in Walcott's latest book, *Sea Grapes*. Take this one on love turned round and badly used as a suction-trap for the unsuspecting: in part five of "Sainte Lucie," "For the Altarpiece of the Roseau Valley Church, Saint Lucia," the poet's ironic lunge at the power of the ever-loving church in underdevelopment comes first, I suspect, from his personal detestation of the betrayal of the poor and, secondly, from his quiet, political appraisal of that betrayal. In fact,

the dream-laden altarpiece sucks everything toward it, rather like a reverential art work that gobbles the faith of worshipers and distantly trusting spectators; and so the Valley Church is simply another institutional hungry maw that swallows whole the labor of the people, the goodness of the land, the dreams of the hopeful.

> This is a cursed valley,
> ask the broken mules, the swollen children,
> ask the dried women, their gap-toothed men,
> ask the parish priest, who, in the altarpiece,
> carries a replica of the church,
> ask the two who could be Eve and Adam dancing.

Of course, there's no sentimental regret here concerning the death of our own Edenic Caribbean or indeed our own Edenic New World. That is not Walcott's point at all. What I believe he truly regrets is the death of harmony, the death of love. And Walcott's is a telling, quiet regret. It matches the tone and quality of the many glimpses of love he evokes and makes poems out of in *Sea Grapes*. Both his regret and the love that it laments are understated and true, for Walcott well knows that

> Things do not explode,
> they fail, they fade,
> as sunlight fades from the flesh,
> as the foam drains quick in the sand,
> even love's lightning flash
> has no thunderous end,
> it dies with the sound
> of flowers fading like the flesh....

And, by the way, those lines from "Endings" are reflected elsewhere in *Sea Grapes*, particularly in the title poem and in others like "Sunday Lemons," "The Cloud," "Ohio Winter" and "The Wind in the Dooryard."

One or two of Walcott's myopic critics accuse him of moving narrowly from the elegiac to the barely concealed sentimental, of having two main voices only. I can't agree. His poetic range of expression is as wide as his human concerns and as all-of-a-piece as his sense of harmony and his preoccupation with the nature of love. As a matter of fact, some of Walcott's most memorable poems include cameos of irony, humor, satire, invective, vernacular wit, St. Lucian patois and classical pastiche. Yet for all that, in a poet so harmonious in sound and sense,

> ...the silence is all:
> it is deeper than the readiness,
> it is sea-deep,
> earth-deep,
> love-deep,

as he affirms in "Oddjob, a Bull Terrier." And notice where he places love! Qualitatively, it is the most profoundly silent. For Walcott, love is *the* true silence, a condition of the unspoken will to connect, an absence of utterance stronger than thunder.

> ...it becomes unutterable
> and must be said,
> in a whimper,
> in tears,
> in the drizzle that comes to our eyes
> not uttering the loved thing's name,
> the silence of the dead,
> the silence of the deepest buried love is
> the one silence,
> and whether we bear it for beast,
> for child, for woman, or friend,
> it is the one love, it is the same,
> and it is blest
> deepest by loss....

Though he writes again and again of love as lost when it is enisled, as fading into nothingness when isolated, he does imagine it nevertheless as a force, as rain which will hammer the grass blades into the ground. In "Force" he names it for what it can also be: "love is iron." And in "Winding Up": "Love is a stone / that settled on the sea-bed / under grey water."

Sea Grapes is Derek Walcott's sixth book of poems. There are other publications, brought out earlier in the Caribbean, which make rewarding reading today. I like looking back on those books and learning about his way forward from the clear trajectory of his burgeoning talent and unfolding confidence and control. He is a poet I respect and admire greatly. His work is accomplished and resonant in a concerned, people-centered way which I regard highly. And in that particular alone, *Sea Grapes*, along with *Another Life*, must be considered his most outstanding achievement so far.

Clarity and light, harmony and completeness in his finest poems are Walcott's gifts to all of us. Let him continue to reveal *nuestra américa* as he goes. Let us listen and look carefully as he redraws the old map with his songs of love and hope. I, for one, a wanderer far from home, a willful exile, a drifter-believer (the kind of runner Walcott himself has refused to become, staying rootedly in the Caribbean as he has all his writing years), will always listen to his acutely clear-sighted songs of love and hope and look at them again and again.

Source: Andrew Salkey, "Inconsolable Songs of Our America: The Poetry of Derek Walcott," in *World Literature Today*, Vol. 56, No. 1, Winter 1982, pp. 51–53.

SOURCES

Brodsky, Joseph, "The Sound of the Tide," in *Derek Walcott*, edited by Harold Bloom, Chelsea House, 2003, p. 37.

"Derek Walcott: Biography," in *Nobelprize.org*, http://nobelprize.org/nobel_prizes/literature/laureates/1992/walcott-bio.html (accessed April 15, 2011).

Dove, Rita, "Either I'm Nobody, or I'm a Nation," Review of *Collected Poems, 1948–1984*, in *Derek Walcott*, edited by Harold Bloom, Chelsea House, 2003, p. 78.

Figeuredo, D. H., and Frank Argote-Freyre, *A Brief History of the Caribbean*, Facts on File, 2008, pp. 210–16.

"Island-Focused Mission: Environmental Policy and Law," in *Island Resources Foundation*, http://www.irf.org/mission/policy/index.php (accessed June 6, 2011).

O'Brien, Sean, "Derek Walcott," in *Contemporary Writers*, British Council, http://www.contemporarywriters.com/authors/?p = authC2D9C28A0a4dc1BE88LsX2F7F 9A1 (accessed April 15, 2011).

Rogozinski, Ian, *A Brief History of the Caribbean*, rev. ed., Facts on File, 1999, pp. 278–83.

"West Indies Federation," in *Caribbean Community (CARICOM) Secretariat*, 2011, http://www.caricom.org/jsp/community/west_indies_federation.jsp?menu = community (accessed June 6, 2011).

FURTHER READING

Als, Hilton, "The Islander," in *New Yorker*, February 9, 2004, pp. 421–51.

> This extensive profile from 2004 provides some sense of Walcott's life as it has evolved after winning the Nobel Prize, touching on the scandals that have troubled his teaching career and the ways in which his view of the world has evolved.

"August Wilson and Derek Walcott: A Conversation," in *Black Renaissance/Renaissance Noire*, Vol. 9, No. 2 3, Fall/Winter 2009, pp. 24–39.

> In this interview, conducted jointly with fellow playwright August Wilson and moderated by Paul Carter Harrison, Walcott discusses language, music, and black identity, issues that are relevant to "Sea Canes" even if they are not apparent on the poem's surface.

Douillet, Catherine, "The Quest for Caribbean Identity: Postcolonial Conflicts and Cross-Cultural Fertilization in Derek Walcott's Poetry," in *AmeriQuests*, Vol. 7, No. 1, January 2010, pp. 1–14.

> This essay does not specifically mention *Sea Grapes* but it does provide readers with an overview of issues usually associated with Walcott, such as the history of his Saint Lucia home that drives his work; his concerns in the 1970s, when "Sea Canes" was written; and the many influences that have shaped Walcott's use of language.

Ismond, Patricia, *Abandoning Dead Metaphors: The Caribbean Phase of Derek Walcott's Poetry*, University of West Indies Press, 2001.

This study was written years after Walcott had left the Caribbean to teach in the United States and England. Time has given Ismond a fair critical perspective on the poet's early career, from 1948 to 1979, and she offers an exhaustive analysis of his sociological influences and poetic style.

Torres-Saillant, Silvio, *Caribbean Poetics: Toward an Aesthetic of West Indian Literature*, Peepal Tree Press, 1997, rev. ed., 2011.

In a respected, ground-breaking study, Torres-Saillant considers six decades of works written in the Caribbean region in English and identifies what is particularly Caribbean about them. The 2011 revised edition adds new insight.

SUGGESTED SEARCH TERMS

Derek Walcott

Derek Walcott AND Sea Canes

Derek Walcott AND Sea Grapes

earth AND personification

Derek Walcott AND Nobel Prize

Caribbean poetry AND Derek Walcott

West Indies poetry

Derek Walcott AND mourning

Caribbean poetry

sugarcane AND Caribbean

Seven Laments for the War-Dead

YEHUDA AMICHAI

1977

"Seven Laments for the War-Dead" is a poem by Israeli poet Yehuda Amichai, Israel's best-known poet, who has an international reputation. This poem, which was originally written in Hebrew, first appeared in an English translation in Amichai's collection *Amen* (1977), translated by Amichai and Ted Hughes, and titled "Seven Laments for the Fallen in the War." It appeared again in *The Selected Poetry of Yehuda Amichai* in 1986, in a different translation by Chana Bloch, titled "Seven Laments for the War-Dead." Bloch's translation of the poem also appears in *After the First Rain: Israeli Poems on War and Peace*, edited by Moshe Dor and Barbara Goldberg (1998). All three books are currently available, although readers should be aware that in *After the First Rain*, the poem contains a misprint (at the end of section 3, the word "hears" should be "hearts").

In "Seven Laments for the War-Dead," Amichai, who fought in several of Israel's wars, reflects on his experience of war. He recalls some of the friends he lost and offers a number of different perspectives on how people and societies mourn their dead in war. With its depth of feeling, range of allusions, and vivid imagery, "Seven Laments for the War-Dead" serves as a good introduction to Amichai's work as a whole.

Yehuda Amichai (Getty Images)

AUTHOR BIOGRAPHY

Amichai was born Ludwig Pfeuffer in Wuerzburg, Bavaria, Germany, on May 3, 1924. His father, Friedrich Moritz Pfeuffer, was a traveling salesman and store owner. In 1933, Adolf Hitler and the Nazis came to power in Germany and introduced harsh, restrictive measures against the Jews. In 1935, as Amichai and his childhood friend Ruth walked to school, they were attacked and beaten by four members of the Hitler Youth. In the same year, Amichai's father saw the bodies of two Jews from the village who had been beaten to death. He resolved to move his family to Palestine, which at the time was still under British rule. The family immigrated to Palestine in the summer of 1936 and thus escaped the Holocaust. From this point Amichai was known as Yehuda, the Jewish name he had been given at birth, and the family took the name Amichai.

Amichai fought in the British Army in North Africa during World War II and in the Israeli defense forces in the Arab-Israeli War in 1948. Amichai then became a naturalized Israeli citizen. He graduated from the Hebrew University of Jerusalem in literature and biblical studies in 1954. Later, he taught at the same university.

Amichai's first book of poetry, written in Hebrew, was published in Israel in 1955. By 1963, Amichai had published a total of four poetry collections, as well as a volume of short stories and a play. During the 1960s, his work was translated into many languages and he became one of the few poets writing in Hebrew to establish an international reputation. The first of his works to be translated into English was a 1963 novel, *Lo me-'akhshav, Lo mi-kan*, which was translated by Shlomo Katz and published as *Not of This Time, Not of This Place* by Harper in 1968.

The first volume of Amichai's poetry to appear in English was *Selected Poems* (1968), republished as *Poems* in 1969. *Selected Poems of Yehuda Amichai*, translated by Assia Gutmann, Harold Schimmel, and Ted Hughes, was published by Penguin in 1971. Other works by Amichai appearing in the 1970s included *Songs of Jerusalem and Myself* (1973), *Travels of a Latter-Day Benjamin of Tudela* (1976), and *Amen* (1977). *Amen* included "Seven Laments for the War-Dead" under the title "Seven Laments for the Fallen in the War."

By this point, Amichai was established as the foremost living Hebrew poet, and his work was translated into thirty-seven languages, including, in addition to English, French, Swedish, Chinese, and Spanish. He was awarded Israel's Prize for Poetry in 1982. Not only did he receive critical claim, he was also a very popular poet, his books becoming best sellers in Israel.

Other prominent works by Amichai in English translation include *Love Poems* (1981); *The Great Tranquility: Questions and Answers*(1983); *The Selected Poetry of Yehuda Amichai* (1986), translated by Stephen Mitchell and Chana Bloch, which includes "Seven Laments for the War-Dead"; *Even a Fist Was Once an Open Palm with Fingers: Recent Poems* (1991); *Exile at Home* (1998); and *Open Closed Open: Poems* (2000). The last is considered by many to be his greatest work.

Amichai married twice, the second time to Hanna Solokov, with whom he had three children: Ron, David, and Emanuella. He died of cancer at age seventy-six on September 25, 2000, in Jerusalem.

POEM SUMMARY

The text of used for this summary is from *The Selected Poetry of Yehuda Amichai*, edited and newly translated by Chana Bloch and Stephen

Mitchell, Harper & Row, 1986, pp. 92–96. A version of the poem can be found on the following Web page: http://www1.poemhunter.com/poem/seven-laments-for-the-war-dead/.

"Seven Laments for the War-Dead" is divided into seven sections. It can be read as one poem or as seven individual poems, since the only continuity between sections is the topic of war and its consequences.

Section 1

In the first stanza, the speaker refers to a man named Mr. Beringer, whom he encounters at Jaffa Gate, which is one of the ancient stone gates into the Old City of Jerusalem. (The Old City is a walled area within the modern city of Jerusalem.) Mr. Beringer's son was killed at the Suez Canal in Egypt during a war. The Suez Canal was completed in 1869 and provides a water route from Europe to Asia that is much quicker than the only other alternative for ships, which would involve going around the tip of southern Africa.

In the second stanza the poet comments that Mr. Beringer has become thin, and he connects this to the death of the man's son. Mr. Beringer seems almost weightless as he walks in the alleys, and the poet's heart is touched by the sight of him.

Section 2

This section consists of two short stanzas. The subject is a young man who has been killed in an unnamed war. He may or may not be the soldier mentioned in the previous section. In lines 1 and 2 of the first stanza, the poet recalls the victim as a child eating mashed potatoes. Line 3 brings home the point that the time between the victim's childhood and his death was short. He did not have time to enjoy life as an adult.

Stanza 2 contrast a living child with a dead soldier. When a child returns from playing, he must be bathed, but a dead man is bathed in a different way, by the earth and sand that form his grave, a process that will never end.

Section 3

Section 3 is longer than the first two sections, consisting of four short stanzas, varying in length from three lines to six. The first line of the first stanza refers to a Tomb of the Unknown Soldier. Many countries have such memorials to unidentified soldiers—the Tomb of the Unknown Warrior, for example, in Westminster Abbey in London—and this may be a reference to a monument set up in the midst of war by Israeli soldiers. The poet states that the memorial is now on the enemy's side, a reference to the shifting lines of battle. He also notes that the memorial will act as a landmark for soldiers in future wars.

The second stanza describes one of the several war memorials at London's Hyde Park Corner, in the southeast corner of this central London park. The memorial the poet describes in the second stanza is the Royal Artillery Memorial, a stone memorial to the casualties of the British Royal Regiment of Artillery in World War I. It was created in 1925 and shows three bronze artillery soldiers and a dead soldier, covered by a greatcoat. It also shows a howitzer, a type of short cannon. The poet sees the elements of the monument as being like a decorated cake, and in stanza 2 he likens the flag that overhangs the memorial to whipped cream being poured over the cake. The images suggest that war has been sentimentalized and glamorized. In stanza 3 he adds a corrective to this, referring to cherries on the cake that have already been devoured—by death. The cherries are a reference to all the soldiers who have died in the war the monument commemorates.

Section 4

This section begins with the poet quoting from an old textbook about birds, especially starlings, swallows, and thrushes. The book was published in Germany in 1913, and the poet notes that this was just before World War I broke out in 1914, which would prove to be a prelude to the wars in which he himself fought. In stanza 3 he recalls a friend who died in his arms in June 1948, at Ashdod. Ashdod was then an Arab village that was occupied in 1948 by Egyptian troops during the Israeli War of Independence. Israeli forces attacked and eventually took the town. The poet likens his friend to the robin, a bird that has a red breast. This is a reference to the blood that poured from the poet's mortally wounded friend.

Section 5

This section is about a soldier named Dicky, who was hit in the midsection by enemy fire and died, his belly an open wound. The poet likens him to a water tower at Yad Mordekhai, perhaps because the tower was also hit and the water flowed out. Yad Mordekhai was an Israeli kibbutz (a community that practices a communal lifestyle) that was the site of a battle between Israeli and Egyptian forces in May 1948.

In stanza 2, the poet states that the memory of Dicky standing mortally wounded, and the association of that image with the water tower, has remained with him. In the final, two-line stanza he explains that Dicky died a little way north of Yad Mordekhai, near a place called Houlayqat.

Section 6

Section 6 consists of three longer stanzas that examine the sorrow of war. In stanza 1 the poet stands casually dressed in a cemetery, probably a military one. In stanza 2 he notes that cemeteries do not cost much to keep, and nor do they require much of those who visit. People bring flowers and leave the wrappings in the small wastebaskets provided. Everyone is polite and orderly as they do what they have come to do. He notes that someone has left a plaque saying he will never forget the one who lies buried there. The poet comments there is no name on the plaque, so the person who left it remains anonymous, even more so than the dead person in the cemetery.

In stanza 3 he quotes something he reads at the cemetery, asking people to take comfort from the fact that those who died helped to build the homeland, which likely refers to the State of Israel. In the remaining lines the poet suggests that such a sentiment may not be enough to shield a person from sorrow.

Stanza 4, however, ends this section on a note of hope. In spite of all the sorrow war brings, the poet advises to make room for love, too. He likens love to leaving a light on in the room of a sleeping baby to give the child a sense of security.

Section 7

The final section of the poem is the longest, and it is divided into six stanzas. The section is set on a Memorial Day, and in the first stanza the poet suggests that this is a good time to think about all one's grief, not only the losses incurred by war.

The second stanza emphasizes hope in the sense that something good and as yet unknown may come out of all the suffering. The poet puts this sentiment in quotation marks, as if he is quoting some religious saying or proverb. He follows it by saying that continuing to indulge in suffering and grief is of no use, and then he repeats the saying he quoted earlier, with a slight change in wording and without the quotation marks.

In stanza 3, preparations are being made for a Memorial Day parade, with ropes being laid out to mark the route and keep the crowds in place. The poet is keenly aware of the presence in the parade of the dead (in people's memories) as well as the living. Children take part in the parade, dressed up brightly to mitigate the sadness of the occasion, but they are affected by it anyway.

In stanza 4, the poet describes how the flautist will still be remembering his part in the parade for many days. The second line presents an image of a dead soldier swimming and somehow mixing in with the children in the parade. Perhaps the poet means the spirit of the dead soldier; in lines 4 and 5 he seems to suggest that the dead wander, seeking life again.

Stanza 5 contains a realistic description of aspects of the parade: a flag that is blown away in the breeze; a store window full of women's dresses; all the signs written in three languages: Arabic, Hebrew, and—and here the poem departs from realism—death. It is as if nothing can alter what has prompted the parade, the deaths of many in war.

The final stanza begins with a metaphor about a dying royal animal that expires while staring at the world. The meaning of the metaphor is obscure, unless it refers to the slow demise of the British Empire, since the lion is a traditional symbol of Great Britain. In line 4, a man who has lost his son in a war walks in the street. In a simile he is compared to a woman carrying a dead fetus in the womb, the point being that he cannot escape his loss, which is too close to him. A further meaning is revealed in the final line, which repeats the saying that was stated twice in the second stanza of this final section. Underlying the tragedy of loss, some good may emerge.

THEMES

Wars

The theme of wars is both specific and general, in the sense that some of the incidents are identified clearly by time and place, with individual names,

TOPICS FOR FURTHER STUDY

- Consult the anthology *Peace and War: A Collection of Poems* (1992), an Oxford University Press book for young adults edited by Michael Harrison. Select one or two poems about war from the modern era and, in an essay, compare them to "Seven Laments for the War-Dead." Which poem do you prefer and why?

- Research the Arab-Israeli war of 1948 using online and print sources. Find out why and how many Palestinians were forced from their homes or otherwise fled the war. What happened to these people? Why over sixty years later is their fate bound up with today's dispute between Israel and the Palestinians? Create a class presentation in PowerPoint or with other visual aids to show your findings.

- Just as Amichai wrote a poem about the dead from various Israeli wars, write a poem that reflects on the U.S. war dead from the wars in Afghanistan and Iraq and perhaps also from earlier wars, such as Vietnam and the Gulf War.

- Go to UMapper.com and create a map of Israel and surrounding countries and distribute it to other students through your blog. Locate and name the major cities, countries, and regions: Jerusalem, Tel Aviv, West Bank, Gaza Strip, Jordan, Syria, Lebanon, Egypt, Sinai, Golan Heights, and the Suez Canal. Write a short paragraph to accompany the map, explaining how creating the map helped you to understand the history of and current problems in the Middle East.

---

while others, such as those contained in sections 3, 6, and 7, are more general reflections on wars and their aftermath.

The personal aspect of the poem is clear in the sections that name individuals who died in war or are related to those that did. In these sections the speaker of the poem emphasizes his own relationship with the victims. He feels their pain and continues to suffer with them. He feels compassion for the father who lost his son, for example, when he comes across him by chance at the Jaffa Gate and notices how thin he has become. He recalls his friend, although he does not name him, who died in his arms during a battle at Ashdod, in the first Arab-Israeli war. He recalls a man named Dicky, also a friend, it can be surmised, and who was killed in a battle. These examples give the poem a very personal touch. The poet himself has been affected by the war deaths he records, and he has himself been a participant in war. These personal references are interspersed with the poet's reflections on wars in general: the many dead that have been devoured in wars mentioned at the end of section 3, the dead that lie in the cemetery (section 6), and the hundreds of thousands of dead commemorated at the war memorial in London and in the Memorial Day parade. The poet does not explicitly condemn war but he feels deeply for the devastation and death it causes: the sorrow of the father who survives his son, the youth of the soldiers who are killed and the waste of human life that implies (section 2), and the loss of some of his own friends. The grief caused by these deaths lives on for a long time, the poet says. This is illustrated in the poem by the interaction between the living and the dead in the cemetery, for example, and in the Memorial Day parade. The dead still impinge upon the living; even children are affected by the losses in war, with the grief of the living entering into them (section 7, stanza 3).

Happiness

Although the poem is laden with the grief and sorrow that the poet feels for those lost in war and his anger at the mass slaughter that all wars involve, the poem also suggests taking an optimistic attitude. War is a tragedy and a cause of unmentionable suffering, yet grief and sorrow may not be as dominant or as long-lasting as might at first appear. Other emotions may be possible, even in the midst of sorrow, and the poet chooses to emphasize one in particular: happiness. This different perspective on events and emotions first appears in the second stanza of section 7. The poet emphasizes that focusing on pain and grief may be unnecessary.

Because no one knows the full extent of either the present moment or what may happen

The Jaffa Gate in Jerusalem is referenced in the first of the seven laments. (Pavel Bernshtam / Shutterstock.com)

in the future, the possibility exists that happiness may be present, either hidden from awareness now, or perhaps to manifest at some unknown point in the future. This does not seem to be a hope based on religious faith, because God is invoked only once in the entire poem and is described in terms that suggest neither power and might nor benevolence. The assertion that happiness may yet be, in spite of sorrow, is presented as a piece of gnomic wisdom—using an aphorism, or short saying, to express a great truth—placed in quotation marks to make it seem as if some sage has spoken it. It is repeated no less than three times in section 7, and the poem ends with it, giving it extra force. It seems that the poet entertains the possibility that some great unspecified happiness may yet outweigh all the suffering that wars inflict, although he offers no clue as to how that process might work, unless it is linked to the notion of love mentioned earlier in the poem, in the last stanza of section 6. In that stanza he speaks of allowing a space for love, of not being entirely swallowed up in sorrow. It is worded in the form of an instruction,

not merely a hope, as if humans are quite capable of doing it if they try.

Free Verse

Free verse, in which much modern and contemporary poetry is written, does not observe formal meter or rhythm and does not rhyme. Free verse permits the poet wide latitude in which he or she can craft the words to create the desired effect. In this poem, for example, the stanzas are of different lengths, ranging from three to nine lines each. The length of the lines also differs markedly, and the poet makes much use of short lines of one or two poetic feet at the end of the stanzas. The short line that concludes the second stanza of the second section is a good example of how four monosyllabic words arranged to form two iambic feet (an unstressed syllable followed by a stressed syllable) can be used to powerful effect, bringing home to the reader the suddenness of the death of the very youthful soldier who has been granted no time to live his adult life.

The free verse also allows for the conversational style that gives the poem its personal flavor. The speaker weaves some of the history of his country into his own memories and reflections.

Simile and Metaphor

Wars and the soldiers who fight and die in them are presented in some rich similes. A number of these occur in section 3. The monument in London is described by use of a simile: it is decorated like a cake. A simile occurs when one thing is compared to something else that is unlike it on the surface, but may have some underlying similarity in the poet's way of looking at things. In this case the poet uses the simile to offer what may be a critique of the monument, which to him seems inappropriately grand and rich. He builds on the simile in the second stanza when he refers to the sculptured flag that is part of the monument, suggesting it is like whipped cream being poured on the cake. The final stanza of that section completes the train of imagery by referring to the dead soldiers as cherries on the cake who have already been eaten—by death. This is an implied metaphor, because the soldiers are not actually mentioned, but it is clear from the

COMPARE
&
CONTRAST

- **1940s:** The nation of Israel is created in 1948. The new country fights a war of independence against several Arab nations.

  1970s: An Arab-Israeli war takes place in October 1973. Arab forces are led by Egypt and Syria. Israel is victorious. In 1979, Egypt formally signs a peace treaty with Israel, recognizing its right to exist. Israel agrees to withdraw from the Sinai, territory it had captured from Egypt during the Seven-Day War in 1967.

  Today: Israel has formal peace treaties with Egypt and Jordan, Lebanon claims parts of the Golan Heights occupied by Israel, and Israel and Syria have not formally resolved their differences and have no diplomatic ties. However, an undercurrent of unrest still resides within the region.

- **1940s:** As a consequence of the creation of the state of Israel and the subsequent Arab-Israeli War, hundreds of thousands of Palestinians are displaced, either being forcibly expelled from their homes or fleeing the war.

  1970s: The Palestinian Liberation Organization commits terrorist acts, such as airplane hijacking, in order to bring world attention to the problem of the Palestinian refugees.

  Today: The Israeli-Palestinian conflict remains unresolved, and outbreaks of violence continue. Attempts are made to create a two-state solution, which would involve the creation of a Palestinian state in the West Bank and Gaza Strip, but no agreement is reached on details.

- **1940s:** During World War II, the Axis powers invade Egypt and try to take the Suez Canal. British troops defend the canal, and after heavy fighting it is secured in 1942.

  1970s: The Suez Canal is closed by an Egyptian blockade from 1967, after the Seven-Day War, until 1975. In the Arab-Israeli war of 1973, Egyptian troops use the canal to cross into the Sinai, and Israeli forces also use it to reach Egypt.

  Today: The Suez Canal is maintained by the Suez Canal Authority of Egypt. It is one of the most heavily used shipping lanes in the world.

---

context that they are being metaphorically described as cherries.

There is a double meaning associated with the word *red*, which describes both the color of the cherries and the blood spilled by the soldiers. A similar association is presented in section 4, in which the fallen soldier is described as red-breasted; the blood that spills from his chest is what produces the comparison to the robin mentioned in the first stanza of that section.

Other notable similes include the comparison of the soldier Dicky to the water tower in section 5, and the comparison in section 7 of the world to bread and milk laid out to be eaten by a God who has no teeth.

HISTORICAL CONTEXT

The Birth of the State of Israel

The origins of the modern state of Israel go back to the late nineteenth century with the birth of the Zionist movement. Because of fierce anti-Semitism in Europe, especially Russia, in the 1880s, the Zionist movement had as its goal the establishment of a Jewish state in Palestine, the ancient home of the Jews. Jews, mostly from Russia and Eastern Europe, began to leave Europe and settle in Palestine. A major turning point came in 1917, when the British government approved the Balfour Declaration, which supported the creation of a Jewish homeland in Palestine. After World War I, the British took

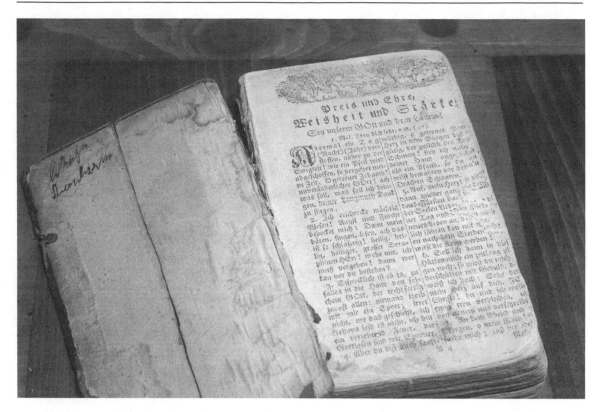

In the fourth lament, an old German book reminds the narrator of World War I and 1948. *(Kenneth Sponsler / Shutterstock.com)*

control of Palestine. In the 1920s and 1930s, thousand of new Jewish settlers arrived in Palestine. The Holocaust, in which six million Jews died at the hands of Nazi Germany, provided a new impetus for the creation of a Jewish state. In 1947, the United Nations produced a plan to partition Palestine into an Arab and a Jewish state. This plan, however, met with hostility by the Arabs. After the British pulled out, the state of Israel came into being on May 14, 1948. Egypt, Syria, Iraq, and Trans-Jordan immediately declared war on Israel and invaded the new state. The Arab armies won a lot of territory in the first weeks of the war, but the Israelis weathered the storm and took the offensive. The war ended in July 1949, when Syria signed an armistice with Israel. Israel lost 6,000 lives in the conflict, and the Egyptians lost 1,500. Other Arab casualties are unknown.

During the 1950s, immigration from around the world swelled the population of Israel. But Arab-Israeli conflict flared up again in 1956. Following sporadic attacks by Egypt and Jordan, Israeli forces attacked the Egyptians in the brief Sinai Campaign. With British and French support, the objective was for Western forces to take charge of the Suez Canal. Israel defeated the Egyptians and occupied the Sinai, but there was a quick cease-fire, and the captured territory was returned.

In June 1967, the Six-Day War occurred. Israel expected an attack by Egypt, Jordan, and Syria, and launched a preemptive attack that routed its foes in only six days. Israel captured the Sinai, the Gaza Strip (previously occupied by Egypt), and the Golan Heights (from Syria), and also occupied Arab territories on the West Bank, including parts of Jerusalem, formerly held by Jordan. Israel decided to hold on to these captured territories.

In October 1973, the fourth Arab-Israeli war was fought. This time the Arab armies of Egypt and Syria caught the Israelis by surprise, attacking them in the Sinai and Golan Heights on Yom Kippur, the holiest day in the Jewish calendar. The Egyptians had early success but were checked by Israeli counterattacks. A cease-fire brokered by the United Nations took effect within three weeks of the opening hostilities. Six years later, in 1979, Egypt and Israel signed a peace treaty. Israel withdrew from Sinai in exchange for an Egyptian commitment to normalizing relations with Israel.

CRITICAL OVERVIEW

"Seven Laments for the War Dead" has caught the attention of several critics. Edward Hirsch, in the *American Poetry Review*, observes that Amichai's poetry combines the political with the personal; a sense of history is fused with the needs and desires of the individual. Hirsch comments that "Amichai's war poems are unique in that they are informed by a strong sense of personal responsibility—the self simultaneously implicated in, and victimized by the war." Hirsch also comments directly on section 4 of "Seven Laments for the War-Dead":

> One of the remarkable and metaphysical aspects of this sly and sad poem is the way the feelings for the textbook imply, without becoming sentimental, the tender feelings for the friend. The connection is made with lightning-like precision, the name of the robin transformed and infused with new meaning as it comes to represent the dead soldier, frozen in time, red-breasted.

Mark Irwin, in the *Kenyon Review*, discusses section 5 of the poem, noting how the images and rhythm work together to create the effect on the reader:

> The juxtaposition of man with tower (living vessel with nonliving yet life-sustaining), blood with water, and mortality with steel, sears an indelible image into the mind, an image that remains standing like the ghostly outline of a water tower on the horizon.

Irwin also notes how in sections 1 and 2, the images work to raise the poem "to a mythic level."

Yair Mazor, in *World Literature Today*, argues that Amichai's war poetry succeeds in conveying emotion without slipping into sentimentality. Mazor examines section 3 of "Seven Laments for the War-Dead," contrasting the grandeur of the British war memorial in London with the makeshift Israeli one:

> The coquettish richness of the foreign memorial confronts the meekness of the Israeli monument. Whereas the latter is bleakly besieged on the enemy's side, the former is proudly located in the center of the capital,

declaring its arrogant artistry. Furthermore, the foreign memorial is made of stone, symbolically announcing that the war and its horrors are also now petrified, never to return. In contrast, the Israeli marker is described as a good target for artillerymen in future conflicts. The foreign war came to an end; the Israeli one did not and is augured to continue, as bloody as ever.

CRITICISM

Bryan Aubrey

Aubrey holds a Ph.D. in English. In the following essay, he shows how "Seven Laments for the War-Dead," by alternating between personal and impersonal views of death, works toward a solution to the sorrow experienced by the survivors.

Ben Franklin famously said that only two things were inevitable: death and taxes. He might also have included a third item—war. Not for everyone, of course, but somewhere on the planet, a war is always being fought, and people are dying in battle. The Jewish people know this as well as anyone. Six million Jews died in the Holocaust during World War II, and since the founding of the State of Israel in 1948, that nation has fought six wars against its Arab enemies: the War of Independence, 1948–1949, the Suez War of 1956, the Seven-Day War of 1967, the Yom Kippur War of 1973, and two wars against Lebanon, one in 1982 and the other in 2006. Israel has also faced continuing conflict with the Palestinians, a conflict which, as of 2011, has shown no signs of resolution. As might be expected, then, Israel's most popular poet, Yehuda Amichai, knows something about war. His public image, according to Nili Sharp Gold, in *Yehuda Amichai: The Making of Israel's National Poet*, was that of the "poet-soldier," one whose life and work was shaped by the country's wars. Indeed, Amichai served in three of those wars, as well as with the British Army's Jewish Brigade in World War II. He knows what war is all about, and his readers know this of him. His translator Chana Bloch, in the foreword to *The Selected Poems of Yehuda Amichai*, tells the story of some Israeli students who, when called up for the 1973 war, went to their rooms and packed a copy of Amichai's poems along with their other gear. Chana comments that one does not normally associate soldiering with poetry, and the story is all the more surprising

WHAT
DO I READ
NEXT?

- "Losses" is a poem by Randall Jarrell, one of the most critically acclaimed of the American poets who wrote poetry about World War II. The poem is about the young airmen who made up the U.S. bomber crews in the war, flying B-17s, B-24s, and B-29s over Europe and Japan. The title refers to the many deaths that resulted from these bombing raids, and the poem examines the attitude of the young pilots about the task they have been asked to do. It can be found in Jarrell's *Collected Poems* (1981).

- "Anthem for Doomed Youth" is a poem by Wilfred Owen, an accomplished British World War I poet. It is a lament for the many thousands of young men who are sent as cannon fodder to the front. Owen was a soldier in the British Army whose first experience of the horrors of trench warfare came early in 1917. He was awarded the Military Cross in 1918 but was killed on November 4, 1918, just seven days before the armistice. This poem can be found in *The Collected Poems of Wilfred Owen* (1965).

- *Hovering at a Low Altitude: The Collected Poetry of Dahlia Ravikovitch*, translated by Chana Bloch and Chana Kronfeld (2009), contains the work of one of Israel's most popular poets. Although she is not known primarily for war poetry, some of Ravikovitch's most powerful poetry consists of protests about the Israeli invasion of Lebanon in 1982. This event led Ravikovitch to become active in the Israeli peace movement.

- Amichai wrote poems not only of war but also of his hopes for peace. One such poem is "Wildpeace," first published in 1971. The poem can be found in the newly revised and expanded edition of *The Selected Poetry of Yehuda Amichai*, translated by Stephen Mitchell and Chana Bloch (1996). The poem does not appear in the original edition of this book.

- *A Jetblack Sunrise: Poems about War and Conflict* (2005), compiled by Jan Mark, is a poetry anthology for young adults. The anthology includes contemporary poets as well as those who wrote about World War I, World War II, and earlier wars.

- Ahron Bregman's *Israel's Wars: A History since 1947* (2010) is a concise account of all the wars Israel has been engaged in since the founding of the Israeli state. It makes compelling reading for anyone who wants to understand the turbulent history of the Middle East over the last sixty years.

- *War and the Pity of War* (1998) is a collection of historical to contemporary poetry written by well-known poets and obscure ancient poets from around the world. The young-adult collection, compiled by Neil Philip and illustrated by Michael McCurdy, represents a variety of poetry styles and covers many wars.

- *Tasting the Sky: A Palestinian Childhood* (2007) by Ibtisam Barakat is a memoir by a Palestinian woman of her experiences as a child during the Six-Day War in 1967, followed by years of living under Israeli military occupation. The author now lives in the United States.

---

given the fact that Amichai's poetry "isn't patriotic in the ordinary sense of the word, it doesn't cry death to the enemy, and it offers no simple consolation for killing and dying." And yet those young men found inspiration in his work.

Bloch's comment about Amichai's poetry might well apply to "Seven Laments for the War-Dead." The poem is not a plea for peace, and it is ambivalent (in the last stanza of section 6) about the seemingly endless sacrifices demanded

> THE POEM IS DOMINATED BY THE WAR OF
> INDEPENDENCE, AND THE INCIDENTS FROM THAT
> WAR ARE VERY PERSONAL: THE POET REMEMBERS
> THE FRIENDS HE LOST, AND HOW AND WHERE AND
> WHEN THEY DIED."

in wars to defend the existence and development of the Jewish state. The poem is dominated by the War of Independence, and the incidents from that war are very personal: the poet remembers the friends he lost, and how and where and when they died. As the poem's speaker, Amichai also visits a cemetery full of the war dead, and he observes a memorial parade. Ranging from personal history to national history, the poem on occasion elevates the casualties of war to a kind of mythical level in which (in section 2 of the poem, for example) the anonymous dead are transfigured and purified by the natural forces that work on their buried corpses. The second stanza of this section is an echo of that haunting song in William Shakespeare's *The Tempest*, sung by the spirit Ariel to a son who has lost his father in a shipwreck:

> Full fathom five thy father lies, Of his bones are coral made; Those are pearls that were his eyes; Nothing of him that doth fade, But doth suffer a sea-change Into something rich and strange. (act 1, scene 2, lines 397–402.)

Such are the blessed dead in Amichai's poem—at least in section 2. Personal grief is salved by the contemplation of something vast and universal, and also mysterious and incomprehensible. And this is the pattern of much of the poem. It deals with grief and sorrow by alternating between the personal and impersonal aspects of death, from involvement to detachment, and then, in sections 6 and 7, working toward a resolution of the feelings of loss associated with death.

The first section reflects on the personal impact of death, as experienced by the poet as he catches sight of a man who has lost his son in war. His own heart is touched at the sight of the frail father. Sections 2 and 3, however, take a more detached, impersonal view of death in war;

the poet has decided to step back and take a wider view. So many people have been killed in war. In Sections 4 and 5 there is a switch, and the poet returns to the personal. The dead soldiers in these two sections were both friends of the poet, and his grief at their loss, and the tender thoughts he has of them as he memorializes them, are plain to see. In section 6 there is yet another shift, as the poet returns to a more detached, universal view of things during a visit to a graveyard. He does not pick out any names familiar to him on the gravestones but only an anonymous note left by another visitor. This swinging back and forth from one perspective, the personal, to another, the impersonal or universal, creates a situation in which the emotions involved can be seen more clearly and the way readied for acceptance. This is not an uncommon way in which people process grief at the death of a loved one. The painful knowledge that the loved face or loved voice will never be seen or heard again is gradually assuaged by a more detached, resigned view that what has happened cannot be changed, and that even death, that great mystery, is part of the way of things and must also be accepted.

It is in section 6 that the poet starts to examine the primary emotions associated with death as a prelude to dealing with them. He wants to know exactly what it is that people experience in these situations. This section opens with a startling question and an even more startling answer. He does not know, he says, as he recalls his visit to a cemetery, whether sorrow is the right word to describe his feelings about death. As his meditation continues, he eventually finds the word to be accurate; not even the consolation that the wars help to build the State of Israel is enough to mitigate the sorrow. But then, in the last stanza of this section, comes the magic word *but*, which turns out to be the turning point of the entire sequence of poems, as the poet makes it clear that sorrow alone does not fill the entire space allocated to human emotions, even when people are grieving for the dead. There is also room for love, comfort, and security, as well as the metaphorical suggestion of a light that comes from some unknown source. It is just up to humans, the poet suggests, recognizing this possibility and acting on it. There is nothing tentative about his advice or his instruction at this point, nor in the statements that follow in section 7, the final section of the poem.

The sixth lament sounds the song of sorrow in death in referencing a cemetery. (*Aron Brand / Shutterstock.com*)

The positive affirmation that defines one of the main themes of the poem comes in the second stanza of the final section. It is all the more striking in its appearance because it follows one of the most terrible images in the entire poem: an image of the world laid out as a meal of bread and milk for God to devour. Even if this image of a devouring God represents a truth, and the poet does not deny that it may, there is no use, he says, in inner or outer protest about anything that results from it: war, death, or sorrow. Even if these are, so to speak, the "facts on the ground," the feelings associated with them can, the poet says—seeming to quote an unidentified authority—be overcome and transcended. There is another, perhaps quite unexpected reality, lurking somewhere and willing to show itself if invited: happiness. How? The poet does not say explicitly, but it is as if he is gently inviting the reader to consider an alternative possibility that might not have occurred to him or her: the

> AMICHAI HAS A PERSONA—THE SOLDIER POET, THE CYNICAL LOVER, THE TENDER TOUGH-GUY—THAT COMES THROUGH IN A CUMULATIVE WAY AND IS SUSPICIOUSLY COZY."

presence of happiness, either, one might surmise, in the midst of sorrow or as a replacement for it. This is not just a passing thought for the poet, because he returns to it with telling force right at the end of the poem. Indeed, it constitutes the last line, and like its first occurrence it follows an equally disturbing, unnatural image of a mourning father who is likened to a woman carrying a dead fetus in the womb. Such a striking image of death where one expects new life is about as nihilistic as could be imagined, and yet...following it immediately is the insistence that a tremendous happiness is concealing itself somewhere. All that remains for the suffering survivor is to get moving on this strange, high-stakes game of hide-and-seek.

Source: Bryan Aubrey, Critical Essay on "Seven Laments for the War-Dead," in *Poetry for Students*, Gale, Cengage Learning, 2012.

David R. Slavitt

In the following review, Slavitt examines Amichai's characteristic use of irony, what Slavitt calls the language of Jews.

The language of Jews, the real mother tongue, is not Yiddish or Hebrew, as it certainly is not Russian, or Polish, or English, but... irony. The complicated experiences of five millennia have elicited a series of emotional and linguistic postures by which we Jews express ourselves, and it is these double messages that American Jews have always found particularly interesting as well as demanding. Until Korea, the United States had never lost a war, and there was a sappy optimism, part positive thinking, part togetherness, part Chamber of Commerce boosterism, that seemed unrecognizable to us and, with a particular force, made us aware of our foreignness. Only the Southerners, who had lost the Civil War, had any notion of the mysterious ways of history and destiny, or understood that there can be an aristocracy of suffering. Young Jewish men and women reading William Faulkner and Eudora Welty and Flannery O'Connor were reassured by the discovery of these un-American, recognizably sane, and unimpeachably grown-up voices.

Yehuda Amichai's popularity, in Israel and here as well, owes much, I think, to his reliance on irony. His poems have that authentic ring of the words of some wise-ass uncle who is always joking around but whose jokes, we come to learn as we grow up, are more often than not in deadly earnest. Amichai's voice, even in translation from the Hebrew, has that unmistakable edge to it. He seems to make light of what is serious and terrible, but his remarks are scalpel-sharp so that the quick scratch we hardly felt is suddenly gushing with our blood.

Here, for instance, is one of his "Seven Laments for the War-Dead":

Dicky was hit.
Like the water tower at Yad Mordekhai.
Hit. A hole in the belly. Everything
came flooding out.
But he has remained standing like that
in the landscape of my memory
like the water tower at Yad Mordekhai.

He fell not far from there,
a little to the north, near Houlayquat.

This is as funny as a lament gets. The bizarre comparison between Dicky's gore pouring out of him and the water tower's water spilling down is unseemly, but then any such death is unseemly, and the only way to be faithful to it is to hold onto it, clutching its absurdity all the more tightly, holding onto its homely truth. The specificity ("not far from there, / a little to the north, near Houlayquat") hangs there, tight-lipped and eloquent. Even though Houlayquat is now Heletz, for Dicky, and for Amichai's memory of his death, time stopped.

This translation, alas, is not from the new generous selection of Amichai's verse that Benjamin and Barbara Harshav have just published (*Yehuda Amichai: A Life of Poetry*) but from a smaller volume that Harper brought out eight years ago and is still in print, *Selected Poetry of Yehuda Amichai*, edited and translated by Chana Bloch and Stephen Mitchell. The Harshav version of the same poem is rather less fortunate:

Dicky was hurt
Like the water tower in Yad Mordekhay.
Hurt. A hole in his belly. Everything
Flowed out of him.

But he remained standing like that
In the landscape of my memory.
Like the water tower in Yad Mordekhay.

He fell not far from there,
A bit to the north, near Huleikat.

Hurt? Killed is more like it. "Hit" is better because it is so much worse than "hurt" and doesn't hold out any false hopes. The tense of the Mitchell version's second stanza, suggesting that he has *even up to the present moment* remained standing is better than the imperfect which, in English, is indistinguishable from the passé simple. The Harshavs' verb implies that the action may be completed, while the whole point of the poem is its demonstration that the macabre and dreadful scene won't go away.

In one of his famous pieces, "The Real Hero," Amichai demonstrates something of the appeal he has always had for those who, like me, are more certain of their Jewishness than of their religious faith or even their politics. He tells the difficult story of Abraham's sacrifice in this way:

The real hero of the Isaac story was the ram,
who didn't know about the conspiracy between the
    others.
As if he had volunteered to die instead of Isaac.
I want to sing a song in his memory—
about his curly wool and his human eyes,
about the horns that were so silent on his living
    head,
and how they made those horns into shofars when
    he was
slaughtered
to sound their battle cries
or to blare out their obscene joy.

I want to remember the last frame
like a photo in an elegant fashion magazine:
the young man tanned and manicured in his jazzy
    suit
and beside him the angel, dressed for a party
in a long silk gown,
both of them empty-eyed, looking
at two empty places,
and behind them, like a colored backdrop, the ram,
caught in the thicket before the slaughter.
The thicket was his last friend.

The angel went home.
Isaac went home.
Abraham and God had gone long before.

But the real hero of the Isaac story
was the ram.

The subversive suggestion about how "they" made those horns into shofars for battle cries and the sounding of obscene joy is particularly welcome to me. "They" are the official spokesmen, whether governments or rabbis. In its imaginative expression, Judaism is somewhere else, and its wise guys are often closer to the complicated truth of things than its ostensible wise men.

Writing in the *Nation* some years ago, Mark Rudman called Amichai "one of the half-dozen leading poets in the world," saying that he "has found a voice that speaks across cultural boundaries and a vision so sure that he can make the conflicts of the citizen soldier in modern Israel stand for those of humankind." One of the half-dozen leading poets in the world? But it isn't hyperbole. Try to think of a sextet to outshine him. Czeslaw Milosz? Geoffrey Hill? Richard Wilbur? Derek Walcott? Zbigniew Herbert, maybe? And who else?

Here is "Huleikat—the Third Poem about Dicky" in the Harshavs' version (it is a piece Amichai wrote after the *Selected Poetry* volume):

> In the hills, even the towers of oil wells
> Are a mere memory. Here Dicky fell,
> Four years older than me, like a father to me
> In times of trouble and distress. Now I am older
>   than him
> By forty years and I remember him
> Like a young son, and I am his father, old and grieving.
>
> And you, who remember only faces,
> Do not forget the hands stretched out,
> The feet running lightly,
> The words.
> Remember: even the departure to terrible battles
> Passes by gardens and windows
> And children playing, a dog barking.
>
> Remind the fallen fruit
> Of its leaves and branches,
> Remind the sharp thorns
> How soft and green they were in springtime,
> And do not forget,
> Even a fist
> Was once an open palm and fingers.

The Biblical tonality is not an accident. Amichai is a psalmist of our time, and the Bible haunts him with its presence—inescapable and often inconvenient, like the rubble of Jerusalem in which it is all but impossible to dig without making archaeological finds. It may be interesting to scholars, but it makes life difficult for the people who are trying to put up buildings or improve roadways.

Amichai's reputation in Israel and among Jews in the United States is well established, and I confess I opened this new collection of his work with a slight narrowing of my eyes, a slightly skeptical attitude prompted by my belief that, for poets at least, too much popularity is a danger sign. Amichai has a persona—the soldier

AMICHAI HAS REDUCED POETRY TO ITS MOST POWERFUL COMMON DENOMINATOR—TRUTH."

poet, the cynical lover, the tender tough-guy—that comes through in a cumulative way and is suspiciously cozy. But one realizes that he is not at all a naif, that he is quite aware of this mask, and that he enjoys wearing it and working it for rhetorical purposes. It is not unlike Frost's pose of the craggy Vermont farmer, which he used as much as a disguise as anything else. Amichai is like Frost and Cavafy, too, perhaps, coming on in an aggressively parochial way but knowing that by the strategies of metaphor and metonymy we will refract what he is saying until it is more or less what he meant in the first place. In other words, in his poems he enlists us as his collaborators, and we have the giddy feeling of having had some small share in their creation.

Source: David R. Slavitt, "Two Jewish Ironists," in *New England Review*, Vol. 17, No. 3, Summer 1995, pp. 187–92.

Mark Irwin

In the following review, Irwin praises the poems in The Selected Poetry of Yehuda Amichai *but questions the publisher's decision to have the poems retranslated.*

Toward the end of Camus' novel *La Chute* (*The Fall*), in which the narrator Clamence rambles on in a drunken soliloquy, we are told: "Pour que la statue soit nue, les beaux discours doivent s'envoler" (For the statue to stand bare, the fine speeches must take flight). The narrator's plight, one in which speech embellished with exaggeration and lies prolongs a hypocritical life, becomes a metaphor for the predicament of language in a postmodern era. One might argue that there are two types of language: one which attempts through excess to conceal emptiness, and the other which through reduction attempts to embrace all that is absent, and which finally leads into the mysteries of silence and the most profound poetry.

In modern poetry, Yehuda Amichai has accomplished an act as significant, yet perhaps even more far-reaching, as that accomplished by William Carlos Williams. He has created a poetry whose purposeful lack of stylistic ornamentation is merely a further extension of its irony, which suggests that if language is to become truly inevitable, no artifice must stand between speaker and object. Amichai has reduced poetry to its most powerful common denominator—truth.

"Spy"

Many years ago
I was sent
to spy out the land
beyond the age of thirty.

And I stayed there
and didn't go back to my senders,
so as not to be made
to tell
about this land

and made
to lie.

Adjectiveless as it is universal, this funereal song on the loss of innocence sears into the heart. It is a faint voice, spiritually exhausted yet noble, for it is the voice of both survivor and rebel. What more could one ask in art? It stands mock-heroic and stubborn, faithlessly sustained and stripped-down as a Giacometti sculpture—a memorial to our *posteverything* era.

Amichai's work, despite its deeply biblical and historical roots, remains ultimately postmodern, for often he succeeds in expressing what escapes language, the ineffable (such as personal and political fate) through concrete images and unadorned metaphor:

Flags
make the wind.
The wind doesn't
make the wind.

The earth makes
our death.
Not us.

Your face turned west
makes the wandering in me,
not my feet.

The voice in Amichai's best work echoes the disillusioned characters created by some of this century's most significant writers: Kafka, Joyce, Beckett. It is the voice of the exile who errs endlessly and realizes the impossibility of permanence; a voice that finally accepts wandering and exile as truth.

Unfortunately, [*Selected Poetry of Yehuda Amichai*], the most comprehensive so far, does not contain the two previously quoted poems translated by Harold Schimmel. In fact, only one poem from Amichai's splendid volume

published in 1973 appears here: *Songs of Jerusalem and Myself*. My major quarrel with these poems has to do with "re-translation"—not that these translations are inadequate; in fact, many are quite good. Why, however, did Harper & Row enlist two new translators when superb versions by Yehuda Amichai, Robert Friend, Assia Gutmann, Ted Hughes, and Harold Schimmel already existed? I suspect that the answer is the attractive sales of a major poet. Compare the slang ("we even got off") and prosaic, awkward rhythms ("As far as I'm concerned, they're always") in the Mitchell version with the speed and facility of the more regularly metered lines in the Gutmann version:

"A Pity. We Were Such a Good Invention"

They amputated
your thighs off my hips.
As far as I'm concerned
they are all surgeons. All of them.

They dismantled us
each from the other.
As far as I'm concerned
they are all engineers. All of them.

A pity. We were such a good
and loving invention.
An airplane made from a man and wife.
Wings and everything.
We hovered a little above the earth.
We even flew a little.

—Translated by Assia Gutmann

"A Pity. We Were Such a Good Invention"

They amputated
your thighs from my hips.
As far as I'm concerned, they're always
doctors. All of them.
They dismantled us
from each other. As far as I'm concerned,
they're engineers.
A pity. We were such a good and loving
invention: an airplane made of a man and a woman,
wings and all:
we even got off
the ground a little.
We even flew.

—Translated by Stephen Mitchell

The tedium of the more regular rhythm is crucial here, for it mimics the collapse of humanity, in this case man and wife, through the methodical and inhumane progress of science and technology. The dissolution of marriage in society is reduced to a mechanical cross: "an airplane made from a man and wife." Eden still provides its exile in a technological era. They "even flew a little." This is the genius of simplicity. Again, consider these three lines (Mitchell translation) from another poem:

> Of three or four in a room
> there is always one who stands beside the window,
> his dark hair above his thoughts.

The third line in a previous version by Assia Gutmann reads: "Hair dark above his thoughts." The Mitchell version remains entirely literal, almost cosmetic, while the placement of the adjective "dark" after the noun allows both a literal and metaphorical range which coincides with the poem's theme of exile, wandering, and the ineffectuality of language. By not risking "drama" (a small amount) Mitchell has lost a great deal. Enough said. It only becomes embarrassing when a superb translator of Rilke inadequately renders one of Amichai's most memorable poems, "A Pity. We Were Such a Good Invention."

The notion of memorability in Amichai's poetry should be discussed, for it is the profound and elemental starkness of his images coupled with the terse incantation of his rhythms that allow his poems to sculpt their often horrid truths.

> Dicky was hit.
> Like the water tower at Yad Mordekhai.
> Hit. A hole in the belly. Everything
> came flooding out.
>
> But he has remained standing like that
> in the landscape of my memory
> like the water tower at Yad Mordekhai.
>
> ("Seven Laments for the War-Dead," trans. Chana Bloch)

The juxtaposition of man with tower (living vessel with nonliving yet life-sustaining), blood with water, and mortality with steel, sears an indelible image into the mind, an image that remains standing like the ghostly outline of a water tower on the horizon. As Ted Hughes has so aptly commented on the honed-down effect of Amichai's poems: "As they grow more open, simpler, and apparently more artless, they also grow more nakedly present, more close-up alive. They begin to impart the shock of actual events."

Heidegger defines truth as *a-letheia*, "out of forgetfulness," and he argues that pain is what flushes being out of concealment into consciousness. The often brutal truths in Amichai's poetry are distilled from experience. He carries his dead like eggs within him, and often carries them back across "the river Lethe" (forgetfulness) so that they might be born again into the light of this world where we might learn from them. The first section from the same poem illustrates this point:

> Mr. Beringer, whose son
> fell at the Canal that strangers dug
> so ships could cross the desert,
> crosses my path at Jaffa Gate.
>
> He has grown very thin, has lost
> the weight of his son.
> That's why he floats so lightly in the alleys
> and gets caught in my heart like little twigs
> that drift away.

Again, the personal loss is transposed to the universal and mythic through the uncanny senselessness of war in which a man falls by a canal originally constructed in good faith. But that canal crosses the desert (exile, estrangement) and was dug by strangers, and now, ironically, becomes the mythic vessel for transportation of the soul estranged from its body. Later, in section two, it is again an elemental simplicity coupled with the ironic notion of the earth (dirt and sand that clean) that raises the poem to a mythic level.

> A living child must be cleaned
> when he comes home from playing.
> But for a dead man
> earth and sand are clear water, in which
> his body goes on being bathed and purified
> forever.

Finally, in section seven, the poem's tragic overtone is slowly, yet hesitantly, transposed to the joy of acceptance.

> Oh sweet world, soaked like bread
> in sweet milk for the terrible
> toothless God. "Behind all this,
> some great happiness is hiding." No use
> crying inside and screaming outside.
> Behind all this, some great happiness may
> be hiding.

Let me quote sections from a more recent Amichai poem (Bloch translation) in order to give a sense of how deftly the poet moves through ranges of emotion:

> "When I Have a Stomachache"
>
> When I have a stomachache, I feel like
> the whole round globe.
> When I have a headache, laughter
> bursts out in the wrong place in my body.
> And when I cry, they're putting my father in the
>   ground
> in a grave that's too big for him, and he won't
> grow to fit it.

And later we are told:

> And if I'm the prophet Ezekiel, I see
> in the Vision of the Chariot
> only the dung-spattered feet of oxen and the muddy
>   wheels.

I'm like a porter carrying a heavy armchair
on his back to some faraway place
without knowing he can put it down and sit in it.

I'm like a rifle that's a little out of date
but very accurate: when I love,
there's a strong recoil, back to childhood, and it
hurts.

It's all here, Nietzsche's appraisal of a godless world: man, having quested absolute knowledge, is sentenced to the burden of his own exile and wandering until finally all that remains is the fragile dependence upon personal love, that god within us all.

Source: Mark Irwin, "Toward a Tragic Wisdom and Beyond," in *Kenyon Review*, Vol. 10, No. 1, Winter 1988, pp. 132–39.

SOURCES

Amichai, Yehuda, "Seven Laments for the War-Dead," in *The Selected Poetry of Yehuda Amichai*, edited and newly translated by Chana Bloch and Stephen Mitchell, Harper & Row, 1986, pp. 92–96.

Bloch, Chana, "Foreword," in *The Selected Poetry of Yehuda Amichai*, edited and newly translated by Chana Bloch and Stephen Mitchell, Harper & Row, 1986, p. xi.

Gold, Nili Scharf, *Yehuda Amichai: The Making of Israel's National Poet*, Brandeis University Press, 2008, pp. 10, 26–46.

Hirsch, Edward, "Poet at the Window," in *American Poetry Review*, May/June 1981, pp. 44–47.

Irwin, Mark, "Toward a Tragic Wisdom and Beyond," in *Kenyon Review*, Vol. 10, No. 1, Winter 1988, pp. 132–39.

"Israel," in *CIA: The World Factbook*, https://www.cia.gov/library/publications/the-world-factbook/geos/is.html (accessed March 9, 2011).

Israel, "Library of Nations" series, Time-Life Books, 1987, pp. 18–35.

Joffe, Lawrence, "Yehuda Amichai: Irreverent Poetic Conscience of Israel," in *Guardian* (London, England), September 29, 2000, http://www.guardian.co.uk/news/2000/sep/29/guardianobituaries.books?INTCMP=SRCH (accessed March 3, 2011).

Mazor, Yair, "Farewell to Arms and Sentimentality: Reflections of Israel's Wars in Yehuda Amichai's Poetry," in *World Literature Today*, Vol. 60, No. 1, Winter 1986, pp. 12–17.

Melrod, George, ed., *Israel, including the West Bank and Gaza Strip*, Houghton Mifflin, 1993, pp. 42–59.

Shakespeare, William, *The Tempest*, edited by Anne Righter, Penguin, 1974, p. 78.

"Suez Canal Authority Overview," in *Suez Canal Authority*, http://www.suezcanal.gov.eg/sc.aspx?show=2 (accessed March 9, 2011).

FURTHER READING

Abramson, Glenda, *The Writing of Yehuda Amichai: A Thematic Approach*, State University of New York Press, 1989.
    This is a critical analysis of the main themes of Amichai's poetry, emphasizing the historical background from which the work emerged.

Cohen, Joseph, *Essays on and Interviews with Yehuda Amichai, A. B. Yehoshua, T. Carmi, Aharon Applefed, and Amos Oz*, State University of New York Press, 1990.
    Amichai and other poets talk about their lives and works in this collection of interviews.

Rudman, Mark, Review of *The Selected Poetry of Yehuda Amichai*, in *Nation*, Vol. 243, No. 19, December 6, 1986, pp. 646–48.
    In this review of Amichai's poems, Rudman takes a very favorable view of Amichai as one of the leading poets in the world who speaks with a universal voice, and whose poems work well in translation. Rudman also compares Amichai's work to that of American poet James Wright (1927–80).

Schulze, Kirsten, *The Arab-Israeli Conflict*, Longman, 2008.
    This concise description of the Arab-Israeli conflict has chapters on all of Israel's wars and the Palestinian intifada, or resistance. The book also provides a detailed account of the Middle East peace process and reproductions of important historical documents.

SUGGESTED SEARCH TERMS

Yehuda Amichai AND Seven Laments for the War-Dead

Israeli poetry

Seven-Day War AND 1967

Arab-Israeli wars

Israeli War of Independence

Arab-Israeli War AND 1948

Balfour Declaration

Suez crisis AND 1956

Yom Kippur War AND 1973

Israel AND founding

Yehuda Amichai AND Israeli poetry

Yehuda Amichai AND war poetry

war poetry

Song for the Last Act

LOUISE BOGAN
1968

Louise Bogan's "Song for the Last Act" was written in 1948, according to the biography *Louise Bogan's Aesthetic of Limitations* by Gloria Bowles, though it was not published until Bogan's 1968 collection *The Blue Estuaries: Poems 1923–1968*. It is one of Bogan's best-known poems, showcasing her heart and intellect, her customary technical precision, and her free use of natural imagery. The poem combines sorrow and hope, giving readers a sense of how an artistic eye can come away from a bad situation, such as a shattered relationship, with a stronger sense of self and an appreciation for the world.

The situation described in the poem conveys the bittersweet memories a person has after a relationship is over. In each stanza, Bogan describes things she remembers about the person she was with: details that might have given her a sense that things were not well, and, finally, details that show her that the past is over and that she is ready to move on.

Though she seldom published, creating only three books of original works in a career that spanned the 1920s to the 1960s, Bogan's name is familiar to poets across the United States. She was the poetry critic for the *New Yorker* for nearly forty years, a prestigious position that put her in contact with the best writers of the twentieth century and made her the focus of generations of aspiring poets.

Louise Bogan (© *Bettmann* / *Corbis*)

The Blue Estuaries: Poems 1923–1968 has gone through several printings since its first appearance, most recently in a 1999 edition by Farrar, Straus and Giroux.

AUTHOR BIOGRAPHY

Bogan was born on August 11, 1897, in Livermore Falls, Maine. She spent her early years in turmoil. Her father, Daniel Bogan, was a clerk in the local paper mill. Her mother, Mary, displayed erratic behaviors and had a series of extramarital affairs. Bogan's parents fought constantly and moved from apartment to apartment throughout the northeast as she grew up. To cope with the anger and violence around her, Bogan began writing at a young age, first in prose and then, when she was fourteen, in verse. She attended the Girls' Latin School in Boston and enrolled in Boston University in 1915. She only stayed there for one year, though, before marrying Curt Alexander, a soldier. She moved with Alexander while he was stationed in the Panama Canal Zone, when she was four months pregnant. In October 1917, Bogan gave birth to Mathilde, her only child. The next year

she left Alexander and returned with Mathilde to Boston, where they lived with her parents. Bogan reunited with her husband briefly, but left him again. He died of pneumonia in 1920.

Bogan and her daughter lived in New York City on her war widow's pension, and she worked at the public library and at bookstores while she wrote. Five of her poems were published in the prestigious magazine *Poetry* in 1921. In 1923, her first book of poems, *Body of This Death*, was published. She met her second husband, writer Raymond Peckham Holden, in 1924. Holden was a major influence on her career, encouraging her to send her poems to Charles Scribner's Sons to be published, beginning a publishing relationship that was to last the rest of Bogan's life. Her second book, *Dark Summer*, came out in 1929. Over the next eight years she published frequently in the *New Yorker*, where she was eventually hired as the magazine's poetry critic. At the same time, she coped with paralyzing depression, and was hospitalized twice for nervous breakdowns in the 1930s.

Her marriage to Holden ended in 1937, the year that *The Sleeping Fury*, her third collection, was published. It was her last book of entirely original poems; her other three collections (*Poems and New Poems*, published in 1941; *Collected Poems, 1923–1953*, published in 1954; and *The Blue Estuaries*, published in 1968) all added a few new works to poems already in print.

She worked at the *New Yorker* for thirty-eight years, retiring in 1969, just one year before her death.

POEM SUMMARY

The text used for this summary is from *The Blue Estuaries: Poems 1923–1968*, Farrar, Straus and Giroux, 1999, pp. 119–20. A online version of the poem can be found on the following Web page: http://www.poetryarchive.org/poetryarchive/singlePoem.do?poemId = 10458.

Lines 1–8
The first stanza shows the speaker of this poem recalling another person. Bogan is unclear about whether she is actually looking at the other person, as the first-person diction of the poem would indicate, or if she is looking at a picture that was taken back when they were together. It

MEDIA ADAPTATIONS

- A audio recording of Bogan reading "Song for the Last Act" can be found at the Poetry Foundation Web site (http://www.poetry foundation.org/features/audioitem/1798).

- A audio recording of Bogan reading "Song for the Last Act," accompanied by the text of the poem, can be found at the Poetry Archive Web site (http://www.poetryarchive.org/poet ryarchive/singlePoem.do?poemId = 10458).

quickly becomes clear that their relationship had been intense for a time, and that now there is a fair amount of anger on the speaker's part. The fact that she has the other person's face memorized indicates that she has looked at it often, carefully, committing every little aspect of it to mind. That she is not interested in looking at it anymore indicates the kind of regret and hurt that comes from a broken relationship.

While avoiding the face itself, of which she feels she has seen enough, her attention is drawn to the surrounding objects. The scene is turning dark, indicating that evening is coming but, more significantly, that the relationship itself is drawing near its end. Although the fruits and flowers of the garden could be read as signs of life in another context, Bogan takes care to point out in line 7 that the summer is over, reminding readers that these plants are soon to die. The other objects in the garden indicate a cold hardness that reflects the coldness that has come over the relationship. The statues, for instance, are made of marble and lead. In the tree where apples should hang is a scythe, a tool with a large sharp blade used to mow plants down at their harvest. One of the flowers she refers to, *Lysimachia clethroides*, is called by its familiar name, shepherd's crook, implying a tool that is used to control sheep and keep them obedient to the person herding them. Overall, the imagery that comes to mind when Bogan talks about this other person is sinister and unsettling.

Line 9

Line 9 repeats the first line of the previous stanza, forcing readers to dwell on Bogan's use of the word *heart*, indicating that she knows details intimately, while also hinting at romance. This pattern is later repeated at the end of each stanza.

Lines 10–17

The second full stanza matches the first stanza's focus on visual imagery with auditory descriptions. Here, the speaker is looking at a sheet of music, conjuring the music on the page as a way of distracting herself from the memory of other person's voice. The notes on the page in front of the poet look faded; she is not able to hear the music they represent because the music is drowned out by memories of violent sounds, words that remind her of shaking and bleeding even as she tries her best to push them out of her mind.

In line 15, Bogan uses the technical term for the five lines of printed music, *staves* (the plural of *staff*). This word can also mean the band used to hold together a barrel or similar enclosure, implying confinement in place of the freedom that one would often expect to get from music. The poem goes on to focus on the silence in the music, the blank areas on the page where no music is printed, before likening the music in her mind to a powerful storm. The storm imagery turns into an image of a stream in the same way that rain water leads into a flowing stream.

In line 17, the poet combines the ideas of music, running water, and the failed relationship to show a sense of feeling pulled along by circumstances and out of control. Bogan ends this stanza with a sense of frustration, as the music that she is trying to create is interrupted by the more compelling memories of that other person's voice, which she cannot stop from ringing in her head.

Line 18

Like line 9, this line stands alone, repeating the first line of the previous stanza. As is the case with line 9, it cuts off abruptly with a verb that leads into the next line when used in the longer stanza, but that finishes as an incomplete thought when used here.

Lines 19–26

At the beginning of the third full stanza, in line 19, the poem follows the pattern established in previous stanzas, but with a twist: instead of

TOPICS FOR FURTHER STUDY

- Read the best-selling 2007 young-adult novel *The Breakup Bible*, by Melissa Kantor, about a high school girl who tries to survive the end of a romance by following the advice given in a book about breakups. Write an advice manual for Bogan that mirrors the advice given in that book, showing the specific lines from "Song for the Last Act" that inspire your advice.

- Create a questionnaire about the correlation between people in photographs and the background in the image. Give the questionnaire to at least twenty people, along with five or ten photographs of your choosing. From their responses, create a presentation that analyzes whether people generally think backgrounds are telling of a person's character or not.

- Bogan served a term as the United States Poet Laureate in the 1940s. Research the position of poet laureate and determine the qualifications and responsibilities that come with the post. Write a letter nominating yourself as poet laureate, explaining how aspects of your life fit the requirements.

- Write a poem called "Song for the First Act," using the same structure and pattern that Bogan used for this poem to show a relationship at its beginning. Present the poem to your class with an explanation of what you have done to parallel the original poem.

- The second stanza focuses on music. Find a poem that you find moving (or use this poem), and then find an instrumental song, without words, that you think captures the mood of the poem. Create a presentation using computer software such as Garageband to present the poem to the music. Analyze the musical interaction with the poem, describing which specific aspects of it make it relevant to the poem. Post the presentation and the analysis on your Web site or a social networking site and invite comments.

---

focusing on one of the senses, this stanza twists the common expression of knowing something by heart around on itself. Instead of knowing the sight of the other person's face or the sound of their voice, Bogan declares complete and intimate knowledge of what their heart is like.

This stanza continues the water imagery that ended the last stanza. Here, though, the water is not a small stream, but a large ocean. The poet stands looking through a wharf's architrave, which is the part of an arched doorway that rests on top of columns. It is a piece of traditional Greek architectural design usually associated with the temples and churches. Through this frame, she views the broad view of great ships with sails, of beach and open sky. She mentions the slaves that the ships have brought, but they are part of the broad picture, not the focal point of what she sees.

In line 23, the tension and horror of the previous stanzas is undone. Like the hook and scythe of the first long stanza and the staves of the second, there is the image of confinement in the reference to slaves, but the basic situation indicates that Bogan is ready to move on with life and consider her terrible relationship finished. The ship, which may be read as a metaphor for that relationship, has finished its journey and is anchored calmly in the harbor, so secure that its anchor chain is rusting. There is a hint of sadness in the sound of the anchor pulling against the ship's movements, which Bogan describes as a sound like weeping, and there is a reference to the end of the day in the long rays cast by the sun. But there is also a sense of peace that is not found in any of the previous stanzas.

Line 27

The last line follows the pattern of the other lines that follow long stanzas, repeating the first line of the stanza before it. The final word of the poem completes a pattern that has developed throughout the work: while the previous stanzas ended with the speaker looking and reading, in an attempt to find some understanding in what is in front of her, she ends up finally seeing, which indicates that true insight is at last achieved.

THEMES

Repression

The speaker of this poem is doing what she can to repress the memory of a failed romance. Each stanza begins with her reminding herself that she has the other person's features memorized, as if she is struggling to believe that her business with that other person is concluded. The fact that she is talking about the situation at all, though, and is so intensely aware of the physical details of their relationship, should tell readers that this situation is not as finished as she would like to pretend. There are emotional issues that are not settled between the couple in the relationship, even though the poet would like to believe that she has moved on.

One clear indicator of the fact that feelings are being repressed is the level of violence and negativity that comes through in the poem's images. Bogan starts in the second line with the fact that her image of the other person's face is framed by a backdrop that is going progressively dark. She goes on to mention images of violence, like a scythe hanging in a tree or words that draw blood, and images of repression, like viewing the music stave as a cage. She does not speak directly of the relationship that has ended, but she clearly has memories about it that she is trying to avoid.

Memory

In common discourse, knowing something by heart is used to indicate absolute, complete memorization of the subject. When Bogan uses the phrase to describe how well she knows the other person's face or voice, she is revealing that she has given her utmost attention to each, which gives readers a sense of how intense their relationship was. When she says that she knows that other person's heart as well, she is taking the situation even further, using the abstract sense of *heart* to show readers that she knows that other person thoroughly and romantically.

The poem begins with these memories and tries to replace them with new memories, indicating that she is trying to change the content of her

In the first stanza, the statues are observing the garden. *(Bertl123 | Shutterstock.com)*

heart, to revise her romantic interest. The first two stanzas show Bogan concentrating on details surrounding the other person's face and voice, in an attempt to put the memory of that person into some perspective. In the third stanza, she emphasizes that the voyage, which presumably means their relationship, is done and settled. At this point, the search for new memories to blot out memories of the bad relationship is over, and the speaker of the poem can feel at peace again.

Sorrow

Even though the poet paints the failed relationship with dismal imagery, she does not present it with an angry tone. Instead, her tone conveys weariness, as if accepting the terrible relationship as an unpleasant but unavoidable part of life. The fact that she is even looking back at it at all could be an indicator that she might even be sorry, in some small, self-destructive way, to see that this doomed relationship is over.

The poem's sorrowful undertone reaches its high point in the middle of the middle stanza, at the center of the poem. Here, Bogan discusses her attempt to use music to drown out the sound of the other person's voice. In line 14, however, she admits that she is able to focus on neither the voice nor the music printed on the page before her, but only on silence. Whatever the specifics of this situation were, they were at least the circumstances of her life: as she looks for ways to move beyond them, she fears losing them entirely. A bad life, she implies, is better than emptiness, a worldview that is certainly steeped in sorrow.

STYLE

Octave

The most common form in poetry is the four-line stanza, the quatrain. The geometric simplicity of this structure gives the poem a solid form while affording the poet great flexibility: the poem can have lines with alternating end rhymes (*abab*) or pairs of rhyming lines following one another (*aabb*).

The basic structure for "Song for the Last Act" is the octave, which is an eight-line stanza. Octaves are usually, as in the case of this poem, made from combining two quatrains: readers can see that the rhyme scheme for this poem is one set of rhymes, *aabb*, followed by another set, *cddc*. Specifically, the eight-line stanzas of Bogan's poem adhere to the standards of the Italian octave, which, as its name suggests, is formed from a pair of Italian quatrains melded together. The identifying feature of the Italian octave is the rhyme scheme: in each long stanza of "Song for the Last Act," the rhyme pattern is *abbacddc*. The Italian octave is most commonly used as the first stanza of the Italian (Petrarchan) sonnet, in which it is followed by a six-line stanza.

Repetition

In this poem, Bogan repeats the first line of each full stanza in a separate, stand-alone stanza. This method of repeating a line is common in other poetic forms, such as the villanelle, which loops the first line of one stanza into the final line of the following stanza, and the rondeau, which often repeats the first line throughout the poem, using it as a refrain. In "Song for the Last Act," no line is repeated more than once. Making readers revisit the line that starts out each stanza, forcing

them to focus on it in isolation, draws readers' attention more stringently to nuances in the line that might have been missed in the first reading. It also brings new meaning to each of the three repeated lines, since each one ends with a verb that has one meaning when it is followed by more ideas, as it is the first time the line is used, but that has a different meaning when it occurs at the end of a thought.

Rhythm

This poem is presented in iambic pentameter, which is the most common rhythm in English verse. *Iambic* refers to the basic rhythm pattern: pairs of unstressed-then-stressed syllables. *Pentameter* refers to the number of these pairs on each line: the word derives from the Greek prefix *penta*, meaning five. There are five pairs of unstressed-then-stressed syllables in each line, adding up to ten syllables per line. Sometimes, readers have to adjust their reading of the poem to fit this basic pattern, such as reading the word *insolent* as two syllables instead of the standard three, but the rare occasions where the rhythm does not exactly fit the iambic pentameter pattern are only more evidence of the pattern's powerful control over the poem's tone.

Metaphor

A metaphor is an implicit comparison, showing the similarity of two things by stating that they are the same. Unlike a simile, which says that the two things are like each other, a metaphor equates them with each other and leaves it to the reader to determine what they have in common.

The most obvious and consistent metaphor in this poem is the use of the repeated expression "by heart." It is used here to mean some form of memorization, but phrasing it this way allows Bogan to add nuances that the word "memorized" does not have, implying things about the romantic associations with hearts and implying how close that memory is, like a heart, to sustaining life.

An example of a simple metaphor is illustrated when Bogan refers to musical notes being in a cage: the lines of a staff in printed music have lines like the bars of a cage, and phrasing it this way reminds readers that printed notes are held captive in a way that audible music is not.

When the poem talks at length about a subject that can be related to another, it is an extended metaphor. The comparison between face and garden in the first stanza, for instance, contains many

COMPARE
&
CONTRAST

- **1940s:** Faces are recorded by taking film photographs on cameras. Only black-and-white film is available, and box cameras have attachments for flash bulbs. Voices are recorded on wire recording machines, which are expensive.

  1960s: Film is usually sent to a developing studio to be printed as photographs. Audio recording is seldom done by nonprofessionals, but those who do have the ability to record voices do it on reel-to-reel recorders, since cassette tapes are not yet available.

  Today: People who use smart phones can take digital audio and video recordings without any additional special equipment. Many computer software programs make it possible to create professional quality audio and video at little or no cost.

- **1940s:** Jack Kerouac coins the phrase "Beat Generation" to describe a youth movement in literature that followed the sensibilities of be-bop jazz musicians. Young poets struggle against the traditions of poetic structure.

  1960s: Poetry following a strong rhythm and rhyme scheme seems dated. Many poets work in free verse, to match the spirit of freedom sweeping across America during the radical 1960s.

  Today: The merging of words and music in hip-hop and slam poetry gives new attention to rhyme and rhythm.

- **1940s:** The publishing world is, like most businesses, dominated by men. Women write, but positions of authority are reserved for men.

  1960s: As the poetry editor for the *New Yorker*, Louise Bogan is one of the few women with a powerful voice in literary publishing.

  Today: Powerful women in the publishing business, such as *Vanity Fair/Newsweek* editor Tina Brown, are not unusual, but still are a clear minority.

small metaphors, all driving toward the same point. In the second stanza, the voice is compared to music over and over again with successive metaphors, and in the third stanza the entire relationship has points that correspond to the details Bogan gives about a docked ship.

HISTORICAL CONTEXT

Bogan and Feminism
Throughout the course of her writing career, Bogan worked to avoid categorization, usually leaving details of her life out of her poetry so that her poetry would not be considered relevant only to her specific situation. Still, she was often categorized as a woman writer. When this poem was published in 1968, the identification of her writing

with her gender was significant because the feminist movement was experiencing resurgence in America.

The struggle for gender equality has been ongoing throughout history. Early examples include nuns writing in medieval monasteries, questioning their roles as women, although their writings were not known until centuries later. In the American colonies, strange behaviors and mass hysteria raised accusations of devil worship in Salem, Massachusetts, and nearby areas in the late 1600s. Only a small minority of those accused were men, leaving the lasting impact of the famed Salem Witch Trials to be an association of women with paganism and witchcraft that is sometimes viewed as evidence of sexism inherent in traditional religions. In the nineteenth century, women were instrumental in the abolition movement opposing slavery and the temperance movement to make alcohol illegal. Both victories led to frustration, however, since women were still excluded from full participation in politics until the worldwide suffrage movement began yielding success after World War I. In the United States, women secured the right to vote with the passage of the Nineteenth Amendment in 1920.

In the 1960s, feminism took on a new meaning. The civil rights movement of the 1950s and 1960s awakened the world to social inequalities, and the public began to give attention to writers who questioned the standing social order. Women who grew up in the post-World War II generation read the works of powerful women like French philosopher Simone de Beauvoir, whose influential 1949 book *The Second Sex* laid out the case against the social roles assigned to the two genders. In the United States, feminist writers drew public attention by describing a social structure that relegated women to positions as second-class citizens. Betty Friedan, for example, provided a frank discussion of the contemporary roles of women in her best-selling book *The Feminine Mystique* in 1963, and then went on three years later to be one of the founders of the National Organization of Women (NOW), a powerful political force advocating women's rights.

In the 1960s and 1970s, the feminist movement worked with other groups that were formed to recognize the rights of historically oppressed people, such as the civil rights movement and the gay rights movement. The mutual recognition among these groups with similar goals helped them each to gain in stature and in self-assurance. During that period, the idea of raising consciousness became so prevalent as to be embraced by mainstream society. Women's studies courses appeared at universities and among book groups that were interested in finding a greater understanding the true nature of how men and women react. Books such as Marilyn French's 1977 novel *The Women's Room*, a critical look at 1950s complacency, and Erica Jong's *Fear of Flying*, a 1973 novel that took a feminist approach to sexual liberation, were read and analyzed by women who were increasingly curious about the possibilities of a world beyond sexism. Louise Bogan was frequently on reading lists for such programs, in part because of the quality of her writing but also in recognition of her powerful position in the literary world throughout much of the twentieth century.

A visualization of the ships docking is described in stanza five. (Steve Smith / Shutterstock.com)

CRITICAL OVERVIEW

Bogan's long tenure in her high-profile position as poetry editor for the *New Yorker*, one of the country's preeminent literary publications at the time when she was there, assured public attention to her works. However, the fact that she published only a few times over the course of decades helped keep her out of the public spotlight. She was considered in her lifetime to be a poet's poet: appreciated by other writers, but not widely read in English classes or discussed when important writers were discussed. As noted poet Theodore Roethke wrote in *Critical Essays on Louise Bogan*:

> The body of her complete poetic work is not great, but the 'range,' both emotional and geographical, is much wider than might be expected from a lyric poet.... Her best lyrics, unlike so much American work, have the sense of a civilization behind them—and this without the deliberate piling up of exotic details, or the taking over of a special, say Grecian, vocabulary.

Reviewing the collection that contains "Song for the Last Act," *The Blue Estuaries,* poet William Meredith, writing eight years later, echoed Roethke's surprise at the fact that Bogan's name was not better known. "Reading this book with delight," he wrote in *Prairie Schooner,* "I was struck (as Roethke must have been in 1961) by how Louise Bogan's reputation has lagged behind a career of stubborn, individual excellence. I hope *The Blue Estuaries* may set things straight."

Bogan's reputation did grow in the 1970s, after her death, when she became a staple of women's studies classes. Her identification with feminist writing became so prevalent in the following years, in fact, that readers began to forget that she was usually considered to be just a good writer during her lifetime. Reviewing Gloria Bowles's 1987 biography of the poet, Sylvan Schendler provided a list of important male authors who had written their praise of Bogan, "from Auden through Yvor Winters by way of Rolph Humphries, William Maxwell, Roethke, Tate, Wescott, Wilbur, and Edmund Wilson." The large number of male critics who clearly appreciated Bogan's work left Schendler wondering why Bowles would have written, "Because of her subject matter Louise Bogan has not been accessible to male readers and writers." To Schendler, it was clear that Bogan had always been a writer for both genders, but time had squeezed her into an exclusionary category.

"Song for the Last Act," in particular, has come to be one of Bogan's most celebrated works. Often included in anthologies, it was singled out by Paul Ramsey in a remembrance of Bogan in the *Iowa Review,* in which he called it "perhaps her greatest poem and certainly the one I find most moving." He goes on to explain that this particular poem is

> substantial to my argument.... To say that some of her lyrics will last as long as English is spoken is to say too little. For since value inheres in eternity, the worth of her poems is not finally to be measured by the length of enduring.

He names this poem and other Bogan poems, and states that to have written them "is to have wrought one of the high achievements of the human spirit, and to deserve our celebration and our love."

CRITICISM

David Kelly

Kelly is a writer and instructor in literature and creative writing. In the following essay, he discusses why the terms "masculine" and "feminine," which critics have often applied to Louise Bogan's poetry, are irrelevant at best and misleading at worst.

Reviewing *A Poet's Prose: Selected Writings of Louise Bogan* for *Poetry* magazine, Danielle Chapman wrote about a distinction that many other reviewers over the years used when discussing Louise Bogan's works. "There is something muscular, even mannish, about Bogan's prose," she wrote, "Yet she was committed to the feminine ideal." The tension between what Chapman refers to as "feminine" and "mannish," or masculine, might have come from Bogan's private life: her position as an editor for the *New Yorker* put her in the sphere of power and influence, or, to use Chapman's word, "muscle," but her writings cut close to the tender side of being human. Chapman might have been using these gender distinctions as metaphors, as they have been used since the ancient Greeks, but her language still stands out as odd from a contemporary perspective. It is difficult to not view the masculine/feminine distinction in literary criticism without considering whether using those words promotes the kind of discriminatory practices that once locked women out of careers as firefighters or executives and barred men from childcare, teaching, or nursing. The world has moved beyond gender-based language, for the most part, but literary criticism apparently has not: Chapman's review was published in 2005.

When literary critics talk about masculine traits, they generally mean writing that is logical, formal, and organized. The feminine traits referred to are the intangibles that poets always seek, the traces of the human heart: intuition and emotion. These are all aspects of good writing, and are clearly identifiable in Bogan's work, her prose as well as her verse. A good example of this is one of her most famous poems, "Song for the Last Act." In this poem, one can find all of the best that Bogan had to offer, and among these elements are those described by Chapman and others as being masculine and feminine. While masculine and feminine elements are used by all good writers, Bogan's poetry seems to particularly draw attention to the division between the two.

WHAT DO I READ NEXT?

- While Bogan never intentionally wrote a full autobiography, an account of her life from her own voice is revealed in *Journey around My Room: The Autobiography of Louise Bogan*, published in 1980 by Viking. Bogan's literary executor, Ruth Limmer, collected journal entries, memoirs, stories, poems, and correspondences to create what she calls a mosaic, rather than a chronological tale of the poet's life.

- In 1985, Alfred A. Knopf released a massive biography of Bogan called *Louise Bogan: A Portrait* by Elizabeth Frank. It has come to be considered the definitive story of Bogan's troubled but fascinating life.

- Chinese poet Li Ch'ing-Chao, writing in the ninth century CE, covered similar themes to Bogan's "Song for the Last Act" in her poem "A Song of Departure." It and its corresponding piece, "Sorrow of Departure," are presented in a modern English translation by Bogan's contemporary Kenneth Rexroth, along with co-translator King Chung, in *Li Ch'ing-Chao: Complete Poems*, published in 1980 by New Directions.

- Acclaimed writer Jennifer Echoles has fun with the idea of washing out unwanted memories after a breakup in her young-adult novel *Forget You*. The book is about a teen who is almost overwhelmed by the complexities of her life and then wakes up one morning to find that much is altered, though she does not remember how or why. The novel was published by Simon and Schuster in 2010.

- *Bailing Out: The Healthy Way to Get Out of a Bad Relationship and Survive*, by Drs. Barry Lubetkin and Elana Oumano, is one of the most read and respected recent books about how to deal with a situation like the one Bogan describes. It gives basic, practical advice for the contemporary world. It was published by Prentice Hall in 1991.

- Readers can see similar themes in Bogan's earliest published works, such as the poem "Words for Departure," found in her very first collection of poems, *Body of This Death*, which was published in 1923. This collection is available at public libraries, though it has not been reissued because of Bogan's habit of republishing poems in newer collections.

The formal traits in "Song for the Last Act" are about as tight as they can come. The entire poem is in a very tight iambic pentameter, the most common meter in the English language because it is natural to the language's ebb and flow. Therefore, the meter can be used, as Bogan does in this poem, without drawing attention to its presence. Add to that the rhyme scheme and the symmetry of the eight-line stanzas, and the result is a form as solid as the steel girders that made it possible for skyscrapers to rise up to greater heights over the course of Bogan's career, the twentieth century. It makes sense to identify such obvious, measurable characteristics as muscle, because organization is what holds the poem together, the way that muscle tissue holds a body together. The

problem with going too far in such an assessment becomes clear if the opposite case is considered. Could a free-verse poem that lacks such formal elements—Alan Ginsberg's *Howl* presents itself as the most extreme example—really be considered unmuscular or unmasculine? To define masculine writing as writing with a strong structure requires one to ignore an obvious fact: poems free of traditional structures do have structures nonetheless, each individual to the particular poem. The line that distinguishes formal writing from nonformal writing is not at all clear, making the distinction mostly irrelevant for critics. The sexism in separating masculine from nonmasculine poetry makes that language more trouble than it is worth.

The traits identified as feminine are even less worth segregating into a special category. These are, after all, the things that make life worth examining, the traits poets are fascinated with specifically because they defy measurement. To use "Song for the Last Act" again for an example: the situation, the "last act" referred to in the title, is obviously a relationship that once was intense but that has now reached its end. It may have been a romance. It may have been a personal or familial relationship ended by death, such as Bogan's difficult relationship with her mother. The specific details matter much less than the feelings that seep out between the few facts provided, which range from flowers to marble and lead, and faces to musical notes on a page. Finally, the poem uses an extended nautical metaphor that helps readers draw away from the solemnity established in the first two stanzas and prepare for what the future will hold. This is not a situation that is specific to either gender. Even the situation in a poem that does identify genders has feelings that go beyond the specifics. The situation that provides a setting for any good poem is very rarely gender-specific. The idea that awareness of the way emotions work is something that women are more likely to understand than men is an insult to humanity.

And yet, gendered language often seems prevalent when critics are trying to get a handle on what makes Bogan's work unique. This often stems from biographical elements—a tumultuous childhood that repeated itself in two messy marriages, followed by an adulthood of professional rigidity. It also draws from the context in which she came to be read, as feminist studies that evolved throughout the sixties and seventies found in her writing a comfortable fit with the experiences that women had not discussed openly in the past. These two elements, though, detour around Bogan's actual writing to connect her life before her writing with the reputation that came after she wrote. Bogan specifically avoided discussing personal details in her writings. Reviewers could find situations, like the one described in "Song for the Last Act," that could be considered indicators of Bogan's life, but these similarities are not necessarily relevant.

In her essay "Music in the Granite Hill: The Poetry of Louise Bogan," Deborah Pope quoted Llewellyn Jones as stating that Bogan presented

> a picture of the spiritual situation in America today of the young, sensitive, self-conscious woman—of such a woman in a civilization which has theoretically made room for her as a person, but practically has not quite caught up to her yet—which does not understand her.

Jones might have meant it as a compliment to how far Bogan was ahead of her time, but his inclusion of her gender weakens his premise, as if nothing so admirable could have been expected from a woman. Taking gender out of it, however, all Jones is really saying is that Bogan was someone who saw things that others were bound to see eventually, which actually is more in the spirit of admiration that Jones seemingly intended. Bogan drew attention to herself as an editor and critic, holding a powerful position while several generations of poets came and went. In the late twentieth century, the contradictions in her situation drew people toward talk of gender, just as, in an earlier time, when people were more conscious of immigration, Americans might have attributed personality traits to someone's ethnic heritage. There may be some slight truth to viewing a writer's work in terms of masculinity or femininity, but there is even more to be gained from breaking down the wall between them and finding in admirable works their overall humanity.

Source: David Kelly, Critical Essay on "Song for the Last Act," in *Poetry for Students*, Gale, Cengage Learning, 2012.

Mary Kinzie

In the following essay, Kinzie illustrates the realism that is present in Bogan's works.

The American lyric poet Louise Bogan is not usually thought of as a realist. She does not typically describe, in her poems, the interiors, with their furniture and their fabrics and their moods, or the landscapes, settled and wild, so altered by the cast of light and seasonal weathers, by gardens and blank walls, to which she devoted so much eloquent attention in her letters and journals. And yet she was profoundly affected by the atmosphere of place, connected as such an atmosphere was to the rhythms of her working, and to the lift and fall of the horizon of her energy and her hope. Rooms appealed to her—or repelled her—in proportion to their amenability to a routine of reading and work. She repeatedly defined her emotional and artistic requirements as though all need could be considered in terms of accoutrements such as books and paper and wine and cigarettes and music—and also time and calm and humor and purpose and freedom from frenzy or exigence. Frugal out of necessity, she was drawn to Edward Hopper's painting because his interiors celebrated and poured radiant light upon an extreme bareness that she, too, could imagine having chosen for herself. But she understood that, as in Hopper, the bare room overlooking the street could also be a kind of cell, a place in which one could be forced to grow old, eating less and less, haunted by the past one could no longer recover, hearing the other pensioners gossip on the stair. That such a future could be the other side of triumphantly achieved and fruitful artistic solitude is suggested by a series of undated drafts of a poem she called "Fantasy."

Fantasy

The women hang the clothes on the blocks of roofs
At the anonymous edge of the city: I dream to be
    here,
To mount this stair, put the key in the lock, to put
    down
The bundle full of tins and fruit; light the stove, pull
    the light on.

The old polished table, the desk and the books, the
    window
Facing the water; a quilt at night on the narrow bed;
The shut door; the scales on the piano.
I have fought through flood to have them; I have
    looked for them in
dreams.

I have fought for the right to smell the cooking
And hear alarm clocks go off in the winter
    mornings.
I have fought for the peace to sit alone in a room.
I can only love the dead who brought me here.

It was where I never looked.
I wanted so much beside.
It stood in the plain streets
Close to this riverside.
It was three flights up the stairs
In this cold bare room.

Finally it was there
When I came in the door
The paper bag in my arm
At last in the smell and form
At last it was my thought
And the look of the pure young dream.

In the anonymous streets
Women hang the wash.
Hidden within the flats
Nameless and without hope
I learned how the heart beat.
I can only thank the dead
Who cleverly brought me here.

Two abstract presences move in the poem. "The dead" are as peculiar to this speaker as is her "pure young dream," the latter a projection of her identity at an earlier time, toward whom the I feels bound as by a debt of obligation, no less than by the force of her identification with its emergence. That young dream reminds us of two other characters cast up by Bogan's intense personifying habit, Little Lobelia and the Sleeping Fury (both of them driven out of dreams, and marked by their weeping). The dead in "Fantasy" are also personifications, but linked more closely to other people in her life, who have compelled but disappointed her (her mother; her two husbands), than to herself. But by framing their actions as worthy of love and gratitude, Bogan the poet is working through and working out her openness to the idea that we carry with us our dead encounters (our helplessness, our suffocation by these figures), always meeting them, and propitiating them. So the fantasy of release and order and well-being in the rooms of the poem is founded on the ability to live at peace with events and correspondences that can never be changed.

In addition to fear and pity, one emotion with which Bogan as a temperament was all too intimate was scorn. Her headlong bravery, when she faced an uncomfortable choice, often drove her to take up the cudgels when she might, more sensibly, and even to better effect, have put them down. That self-goading pride sometimes found its embodiment in satire.

Letter to Mrs. Q's Sister

Adulterers' letters, unfortunately, are always the
    same.
They speak of beautiful snatched experience, usually
    in a room shaken by
trucks;
The walk later, until two in the morning; the tunnel
    to the last train;
Kisses in the shrubbery; talk by the monument;
They reach the clumsy bronze statues in the alleys of
    parks, shaded by
the late leather leaf.

So she is killed and so she is taken.
So fire mounts and air breathes again.
So tedium is relieved and courage underlined.

O what woman should weep, because of this,
Safe with her dove, her fountain, her earth, her ilex?

From the adulterous woman's point of view, love is a matter of death and fire, of flattering symmetries, decorum in gardens, and the archaic foliage of the ilex tree; from the satirist's point of view, the trysting place is shabby ("usually in a room shaken by trucks"), the sculpture in the public park clumsy, and the leaves of the trees thick and coarse as leather. For every brave instinct, one that is debased and preening. The satiric poems in Bogan's oeuvre are few—"Hypocrite Swift," "To an Artist, To Take Heart"—but always brusque, pointed, and not a little sad.

The third poem is an example of Bogan's high compressed lyric mode (the mode Bogan's biographer Elizabeth Frank calls Rilkean). The poem may well come from around 1935, about the time of her affair with Theodore Roethke, owing to its similarity to another poem, which she did publish and collect, "Song for a Lyre." The similarity is not only metrical (trimeters interleaved with dimeter lines; six-line stanzas), but also syntactic (inversion of word order, in lines 6 and 12) and grammatical ("ripple" used as a transitive verb, taking the object "stream"; "tread" as an aggressive rather than passive verb) and in manipulated level of diction (the concrete "dyke" and concise "surfeited" reciprocally counterpoint the deceptively bland "even" in "in an even sky"). In addition, the processional and logical balances of the sentences mask the desperate diminishment of the speaker's life.

> Love Severally Rhymed
>
> Fool and wise woman alike
> Ripple your stream,
> Shallow, as in a dyke,
> Running in a dream.
> Easily surfeited
> The fields your waters tread.
> In this last pang shall I
> Describe your way.
> Once, in an even sky
> I saw your day,—
> Treacherous now in love
> Like light the waters move.

Although the Yeatsian thrust of the sexual "tread" of the water across the open fields may obscure the fact, the metaphors for diminishment come from the same idea-hoard to which Bogan also turned in a late journal entry; writing about the later period of a handsome woman's life, she observes that "it is like a river which has made a broad bed for itself, but now has dwindled into a tiny stream that makes hardly any show among the wide sweep of pebbles that show the boundaries of its former strength."

Source: Mary Kinzie, "Rooms by the City: Three Undated Poems by Louise Bogan (1897–1970)," in *Tri-Quarterly*, Vol. 120, Winter 2005, pp. 80–84.

April Bernard

In the following essay, Bernard evaluates the effectiveness of Elizabeth Frank's biography of Louise Bogan in helping understand the poet.

> **HER OVERPOWERING WISH THAT BOGAN HAD BEEN MORE PRODUCTIVE, LESS TROUBLED, IS THAT OF A HAND WRINGER AT THE GRAVESIDE."**

Louise Bogan, the poet and critic who died in 1970 at the age of 72, has never suffered from too large a reputation. During her life she was probably best known as a critic: she wrote for several publications and was the *New Yorker's* poetry critic for more than 30 years, rustling a semiannual "round-up" for that magazine. Her reviews were catholic in range and stern in judgment. They lost her friends and won her as many. She had the anti-intellectualism of the autodidact, buttressed by a sympathy at all times for the "felt." To erstwhile friend Allen Tate, who had written to express his annoyance at a review, she replied: "I was reviewing a book of poetry which aroused in me respect and irritation in about equal measure. If you objected to the tone of my review, I objected, straight down to a core beyond detachment, to the tone of some of the poems."

Bogan's own poetry was read and admired—and of course also attacked—within the narrow circle of poetry's cognoscenti. Auden hailed her as one of the best poets writing, and her lyric verse won her Guggenheims, membership in the Academy of Arts and Letters, and a host of other honors from her peers. But her output was not enormous, and her poems remain difficult—chiseled, often bitter little riddles in which the poet's rational mind makes cynical (or resigned or brave) sense of the vagaries of the human heart. For all her poetry's well-tailored chic, its unmistakable power inheres in its resistance to its own good manners. But however remarkable her poetry, today not many remember, if they ever knew, who Bogan was.

Elizabeth Frank's biography contributes much to our knowledge, though rather less to our understanding, of Bogan. Her childhood, which was the source of incredible trauma, exerts a grim fascination, something like the morbid chill of a Lizzie Borden trial as told in newspaper accounts of that time. Nothing quite so sensational afflicted Bogan's small, lower-middle-class family, but her mother did take lovers, which the child was aware of, and she did muster about her a circle of furtive confidantes whom the child despised and feared. The father was foreman in innumerable paper mills; the family moved often, perhaps one step ahead of scandal, from one New England manufacturing town to another. Louise was sent to one of the best preparatory schools in Boston, Girls' Latin, and she entered Boston University in 1915. After one year, against her parents' wishes and throwing over a scholarship to Radcliffe, she married a soldier and abandoned her formal education for good.

The biography is also valuable for its chronicling of Bogan's life in literary New York, where she moved in 1920 after her first marriage ended in divorce. One of her closest friends of the 1920s and 1930s was Edmund Wilson, and she was also friendly with Margaret Mead, Eleanor Wylie, Malcolm Cowley—the whole group. (Later important associations included Theodore Roethke, Morton Zabel and John Hall Wheelock, her editor at Scribner's for many years.) Wilson was a mentor and a goad, and in later years Bogan liked to tell the story of how he had locked her in a room and forced her to write her first critical essay. She was beautiful, tall, thin and high-strung, alternately charming and abrasive, hard-working but also beset by self-doubt. She worried about her personal life, as a succession of love affairs culminated in a stormy, decadelong marriage to the writer and editor Raymond Holden. And she worried about her poetry, which emerged only slowly and painfully.

Bogan's troubles prompted her to seek psychiatric help, and on a few occasions she was hospitalized for the depression that dogged her all her life. Her emotional instability contributed in large part to the jealous rages that marred her marriage, but it is clear from Frank's portrait that Bogan's anger had a positive function as well. Two extracts from Bogan's journals: "I can feel rage, but I am never humiliated, any more." "Do not shrink from your hatreds. They may be a cover for other emotions—let that also stand. If I did not hate, if I had not hated pretense and falsehood in others, how false, how pretentious I should have been myself!" Anger and hatred provided a backbone for this vulnerable woman and fueled her relentless efforts to distinguish the true from the sham. With all her faults placed squarely before the readers of this book, Bogan emerges troubled, tormented and

cruel. (That she is also vindicated, at least in this reader's eye, is more or less in spite of the treatment she receives here.)

Where Frank's biography fails—and its failure is substantial—is in its woolly lack of purpose. This is what led, I am sure, to the meticulous over-documentation that drones through rich and bare patches alike. In a spasmodic way, Frank exerts a certain amount of "critical" authority, pausing now and again to interpret Bogan's verse, usually by means of tediously detailed correspondences between the "subject matter" of the poems and the poet's life at the time they were written. Taken too seriously, this method is perilous, especially in the case of a writer like Bogan, whose poems attempted, and often achieved, transcendence through thought imposed on feeling. Criticism that insists on linking the work to the life does an implicit disservice to such poems. There is much more to be said about Bogan's poetry, but it does not get said here.

Frank is also impeded by an unavoidable reliance on letters, diaries and memoirs. Excepting the criticism and the badinage in some letters, Bogan's prose is labored and often boring. This liability would have weighed on any biographer.

Rather like a teacher's "topic sentence" tacked to a young student's paper, this biography does claim to have a purpose. In the foreword, Frank asserts that "something stopped Louise Bogan dead in her tracks, not once but many times," and she proposes to discover "this principle of arrest." But by the end of this thoroughly long book, the search has failed on two scores: Frank never broaches a coherent answer to her question, and it becomes clear that the question of poetic "arrest" was not the right one to have posed.

Why a biography at all? So many biographies seem gratuitous, but the fault does not lie with the genre. To look at a few relatively recent examples of successful biographies, Richard Sewall's of Emily Dickinson and Walter Jackson Bate's of Samuel Johnson are enthralling because the authors were driven by a passionate engagement with their subjects. And that engagement need not be sympathetic. Lawrence Thompson's venomous, despairing portrait of Robert Frost wrestles with the poet, but always with passion. Such a book needs no excuse for having been written, even if the life explored never acquires a satisfying form and the author never unravels the puzzles left behind by the dead.

Bad biography, on the other hand, is always looking for an excuse. One prevalent type uses a life to prove a point—either Freudian or sociological. The subject is sacrificed for the greater good of theory, and the only thing to be said in favor of such exercises is that they usually remain mercifully short on documentation, since too much detail throws the game. Other sorts of weak biography may begin with good intentions—fulfillment of a dissertation, say—and even a measure of passion, but somewhere in the course of research the biographer loses the spark and comes to feel saddled by the life being chronicled; the result shows all the signs of familial exasperation. You can choose your lovers but not your relatives, and such a biographer no longer feels he has the freedom to cast his subject aside. Hence Ian Hamilton's condescension toward Robert Lowell, Diane Johnson's fatigued embarrassment with Dashiell Hammett.

Elizabeth Frank has fallen into this trap. Although she expresses admiration for Bogan, it does not seem to be particularly deep. Her overpowering wish that Bogan had been more productive, less troubled, is that of a hand wringer at the graveside. Frank writes: "The possibility, often said to be feared by people who are both creative and neurotic, that psychiatric treatment would cure their neurosis but in the process kill their creativity, may well have been, for Louise Bogan, uncannily close to the truth." If there were only one or two such passages in the book, one might discount them as a mild complaining to which the author was entitled. But they are legion. Perhaps I do Frank an injustice, but the flat, querulous tone does not suggest anything like a "felt" response to the poet or her work. *Louise Bogan: A Portrait* begins in enthusiasm for the woman and condescension for her early writing. It ends with praise for what work there was and with contempt for the woman. (The harsh way in which Frank disposes of Bogan's final days is ugly to read.) In this way, the book mirrors the habit of the world, to love the young only for what they cannot help being, and to love the old only for what they have done.

Is this book the appropriate vehicle for bringing the poet back into our gaze? How

dare anyone blame such a writer for what she did not do? Bogan's poems will survive, and *The Blue Estuaries: Poems 1923–1968*, the definitive collection of more than a hundred poems spanning her career, is still in print. Read "After the Persian," "To Be Sung on the Water," "Men Loved Wholly Beyond Wisdom," "If We Take All Gold"—read them all. Here is the final verse from "Roman Fountain": O, as with arm and hammer, Still it is good to strive To beat out the image whole, To echo the shout and stammer When full-gushed waters, alive, Strike on the fountain's bowl After the air of summer.

We must, for now, content ourselves with that, and that is much.

Source: April Bernard, Review of *Louise Bogan: A Portrait*, in *Nation*, Vol. 240, February 23, 1985, pp. 215–17.

SOURCES

Bogan, Louise, "Song for the Last Act," in *The Blue Estuaries: Poems 1923-1968*, Farrar, Straus and Giroux, 1999, pp. 199–200.

Bowles, Gloria, *Louise Bogan's Aesthetic of Limitations*, Indiana University Press, 1987, p. 128.

Chapman, Danielle, Review of *A Poet's Prose: Selected Writings of Louise Bogan*, in *Poetry*, Vol. 185, No. 3, September 2005, p. 450.

Collins, Martha, Introduction to *Critical Essays on Louise Bogan*, edited by Martha Collins, G. K. Hall, 1984, pp. 1–20.

Cott, Nancy F., *The Grounding of Modern Feminism*, Yale University Press, 1987.

Ford, Lynne E., "Feminism," in *Encyclopedia of Women and American Politics*, Facts on File, 2008.

Meredith, William, Review of *The Blue Estuaries*, in *Critical Essays on Louise Bogan*, edited by Martha Collins, G. K. Hall, 1984, p. 98.

Pope, Deborah, "Music in the Granite Hill: The Poetry of Louise Bogan," in *Critical Essays on Louise Bogan*, edited by Martha Collins, G. K. Hall, 1984, p. 149.

Ramsey, Paul, "Louise Bogan," in *Critical Essays on Louise Bogan*, edited by Martha Collins, G. K. Hall, 1984, pp. 126–27.

Roethke, Theodore, "The Poetry of Louise Bogan," in *Critical Essays on Louise Bogan*, edited by Martha Collins, G. K. Hall, 1984, p. 87.

Schendler, Sylvan, Review of *Louise Bogan's Aesthetic of Limitations*, in *American Literature*, Vol. 60, No. 2, May 1988, pp. 314–15.

Upton, Lee, *Obsession and Release: Rereading the Poetry of Louise Bogan*, Associated University Presses, 1996, pp. 19–22.

Walters, Margaret, *Feminism: A Very Short Introduction*, Oxford University Press, 2005, pp. 6–16.

FURTHER READING

Bogan, Louise, *A Poet's Prose: Selected Writings of Louise Bogan*, edited by Mary Kinzie, Swallow Press, 2005.

> This book contains examples of Bogan's many published reviews, as well as several more personal moments revealed through letters and fiction.

Dodd, Elizabeth, *The Veiled Mirror and the Woman Poet*, University of Missouri Press, 1992.

> Dodd examines the careers of Bogan, H. D., Elizabeth Bishop, and Louise Gluck through the lens of a literary technique that she identifies as "personal classicism." In the section titled "The Knife and the Perfectionist Attitude: Louise Bogan's Poetic Control," she looks at ways in which Bogan hid the details of her life within her poetry.

Knox, Clarice, *Louise Bogan: A Reference Source*, Scarecrow Press, 1990.

> This book provides a comprehensive list of writings by and about Bogan up to 1991. It is a valuable resource for researchers who are looking for specific poems, reviews, or articles.

Weston, Mildred, *"Our 30 Year Old Friendship" and Legacy*, Eastern Washington University Press, 1997.

> This book starts with a rare, brief interview with Bogan, in which she talks about her traumatic childhood and its effects on her life. A trove of Bogan's own words in her letters to Weston, a poet, follows. The last half of the book, *Legacy*, is Weston's own poetry.

SUGGESTED SEARCH TERMS

Louise Bogan

Louise Bogan AND feminism

Louise Bogan AND New Yorker

Louise Bogan AND poetry

Louise Bogan AND classical allusion

Song for the Last Act AND Modernism

Louise Bogan AND Love Poem

The Blue Estuaries: Poems 1923–1968

Louise Bogan AND poet laureate

Louise Bogan AND mental illness

Song for the Last Act AND Louise Bogan

Syrinx

AMY CLAMPITT

1994

Although she was of an older generation than most of the hippies of the 1960s, middle-aged Amy Clampitt was an enthusiastic participant in the youthful counterculture of that era, and she was one of its most eloquent literary spokeswomen. Using elegant, reasoned language, steeped in a romantic tradition based on centuries of human culture, Clampitt's poem "Syrinx" attacks, denies, and undermines human language and human culture in an essentially countercultural rebellion, even though the poet herself cannot completely throw off the shackles of culture that dictate the form of her own work. "Syrinx" devalues human language as a failed, inferior copy of the sounds of the natural world.

Paradoxically, Clampitt's attack on culture is woven from the very cultured world of her own life, seizing on material from her pastimes of birdwatching, listening to opera, and reading in ancient Greek. Clampitt's valuing nature over culture draws on a reaction to romanticism that produced a counterculture in nineteenth-century Germany. That tradition became the direct ancestor of the 1960s counterculture that Clampitt embraced.

AUTHOR BIOGRAPHY

Clampitt was born on her father's farm in New Providence, Iowa, on June 15, 1920. Growing up in a Quaker family fostered in Clampitt pacifism

and self-control that outlived her adherence to the religion. Her father and grandfather both published memoirs and had large and varied libraries in the midst of the prairie. Clampitt considered herself a writer as far back as she could recall. Largely ignored (though not neglected) by her family, Clampitt slipped away to Grinnell College, where she earned a degree in English in 1941. She moved to New York, with a fellowship at Columbia University. She soon abandoned formal education, though, and went to work as a secretary at Oxford University Press. She rose quickly to the editorial staff and won a tour of Europe in an in-house writing competition. After returning to New York, Clampitt quit her job and wrote full time, producing three novels that have never been published. She worked through the 1950s and early 1960s as the senior reference librarian at the Audubon Society. She gave up this job to become a freelance editor and eventually an editor at E. P. Dutton. She remained there until 1982, when she was finally able to make a living as a writer.

The 1950s and 1960s saw a great transformation in Clampitt's inner life. She became an Episcopalian and even considered becoming a nun until she parted ways with the church over her enthusiastic opposition to the Vietnam War. At the same time, she found her identity as a poet. She privately published a chapbook, *Multitudes, Multitudes*, in 1973. In 1978, she sold her first poem to the *New Yorker* and immediately began publishing in the *Atlantic, Kenyon Review*, and other prestigious publications.

Her first book, *The Kingfisher*, was published in 1982. With this came offers to teach and lecture, a Guggenheim fellowship, and a tremendous explosion in her poetry publication. Part of the rapid success Clampitt gained is explained by the patronage of the important critic Helen Vendler. Clampitt published five books of poetry over the next ten years, culminating in *A Silence Opens* in 1994. "Syrinx" is the first poem of that collection. She diligently worked at poetry, as her hero John Keats did, and sought to improve her talents by taking an introductory survey course in ancient Greek, an almost freakish anachronism in the postmodern 1980s; she may have had an eye toward gaining an advantage over the famously Greekless Keats.

Clampitt also published *Essays* (1991) and *A Homage to John Keats* (1984). Perhaps because critical reception of Clampitt was so polarized and because she seemed so at odds with and

disconnected from contemporary poets, Clampitt received a MacArthur Prize (a substantial cash award usually given to unrecognized artists and academics) in 1992, with which she bought her house in Lenox, Massachusetts. Shortly thereafter she was diagnosed with ovarian cancer. She died at home in Lenox on September 10, 1994.

POEM SUMMARY

The text used for this summary is from *The Collected Poems of Amy Clampitt*, Alfred A. Knopf, 1997, p. 363. A version of the poem can be found on the following Web page: http://www.amyclampitt.org/poems/syrinx.html.

"Syrinx" is divided into three sections, the first two of eighteen lines each, the final of three lines. Clampitt separates them by skipped lines. The single sentence of the first section deals directly with the subject implied by the title, the syrinx, or voice organ of birds, and the impossibility of describing the sounds it produces with human speech. The second section deals more generally with the relationship of speech to nonspeech sounds. The third section concludes the sentence that forms the second section, and it connects the poem's themes of sound and life through the commonality of breath.

Lines 1-18

Clampitt begins her poem with a series of similes, describing three things that the syrinx is like in place of describing the thing itself. The use of drawn-out, pointed similes is typical of the epic style of the ancient Greek poet Homer (in whose work Clampitt had taken a year-long introductory course of study shortly before writing "Syrinx"). The rather abrupt beginning of this long sentence, with an extended adverbial construction that is important to the idea expressed but subordinate within the grammar of the sentence, is more typical of Homeric Greek than English, although even in English the poet has far more leeway in the structure of language than is permitted in prose. This construction sets the tone of Clampitt's piece, which is highly evocative of ancient Greek literature throughout. The three things that Clampitt mentions are a foghorn, a wind chime, and the wind itself. They are like each other and like the syrinx in that they emit sounds that are not language but on which human beings impose language by attempting to write them down. The word *chime* itself is an example of what she means; it cannot be traced back through the development of English to some ordinary linguistic origin but is an attempt to write down the sound that a chime makes when struck. This technique is known as onomatopoeia.

The syrinx, Clampitt notes, is the sound-producing organ in birds, comparable to the larynx in human beings. She describes the syrinx as aeolian and as a reed, though it is neither. *Aeolian,* in this context, means a particular mode of ancient Greek music. A reed is the stalk of a plant that grows in lakes and marshes. Cut pieces of reed are used as the mouthpieces of modern wind instruments such as the clarinet or bassoon, but more particularly, a group of whole reeds cut to different lengths and tied together is a musical instrument itself, a kind of flute called the panpipe—the pipe, or flute, supposed to have been played by Pan, the Greek god of shepherds and pastures. The ancient Greek word for panpipe is syrinx, and scientific ornithologists, when they first studied bird anatomy in the seventeenth century, named the sound organ in birds after the panpipe.

Syrinx itself is another onomatopoeia, an imitation of the sound of the wind blowing over a reed. The ancient Greeks, however, could not resist making a myth to explain the origins of things, and they invented a myth of the discovery of the syrinx. The best-known version of the myth is preserved in Ovid's *Metamorphoses.* In this myth, Syrinx was the name of a nymph (nature spirit) whom the god Pan (a monster with goat's legs and horns) tried to rape. When she prayed to be protected, she was magically transformed into a bed of reeds in the water. Pan cut down the reeds and tied them together to make the musical instrument that bears his name, getting possession of her in that way. Clampitt placed small clues in the poem that are meant to evoke the memory of this sad and elegiac myth in her reader and set an emotional tone for her work: the attempt to subdue nature is exploitative and destructive.

Finally, in this first sentence, Clampitt gives a list of examples of birdcalls transcribed into human language, some of which are also the names of the birds that make them. She suggests, however, that there is no agreement on how to transcribe the calls, mentioning two common variant transcriptions of the call of the red-winged blackbird. This variation exists in many cases, and one can sometimes make a linguistic map, showing how a birdcall is transcribed differently from

village to village inside the bird's range. On the other hand, some birdcalls that she mentions, like that of the cuckoo, have had precisely the same imitation in language for more than five thousand years, going back to the proto-Indo-European ancestor of all Western languages. In the poem, this leads up to the suggestion that it is not proper to transcribe birdcalls into human writing, because they differ from language in having no meaning.

In this sentence also, Clampitt starts to point in the direction of music, which will become a more important theme in the second section of the poem. The noise of the wind is described in a way that, in a pun, evokes both musical notation, on one hand, and worry and anguish on the other. But at the same time, the wind cannot say precisely what disturbs it; it cannot be shaped as music and take a more definite form.

Lines 19-36

Clampitt begins the second section of the poem with *syntax,* a word surely chosen for its assonance, or repetition of consonants, with *syrinx.* Curiously, Clampitt explains syntax as pertaining to what words say, to their meaning, the same issue that is prominent in the first part of "Syrinx." However, that is not quite what syntax means. Syntax is the way the interconnection of words in sentences allows the reader—or the hearer in spoken rather than written language—to construe larger meanings. In English, syntax is usually expressed through word order, with the subject of the sentence first, followed by the verb, and then the direct object. The word order lets the reader know how each word functions in the sentence, but strictly speaking, syntax has nothing to do with the meaning of words themselves. However that may be, syntax, Clampitt insists, is a late development of language, or rather of sound. As a late development, syntax ought to be a higher expression than mere sound. But Clampitt is not entirely prepared to accept this and offers it merely as a commonly held opinion that, may, as an opinion, be wrong.

In contrast, Clampitt now turns to the abandonment of syntax when language, as it were, breaks under pressure. She offers the example of an opera singer producing pure vowels at the very limit of the human capacity for speech, in such a way that the meaning of the words no longer matters in comparison with the vocal artistry. Even a native speaker of the language in which the opera was written could no longer distinguish any words in what is being sung. Clampitt stresses in great detail that the ordinary quality of language is completely lost in this soaring sound. It not only has no particular meaning but cannot be described in ordinary linguistic terms. Clampitt is exaggerating, since any noise that can be made by human beings is easily describable with the International Phonetic Alphabet, which closely models the shape and movements of the organs of speech. But her point is clear enough: there is a moment when sound departs from human comprehension and control. Instead of ordinary speech, the song of the soprano is like the sounds of nature, such as those made by wind and waves.

Finally, however, the sound of the soprano, the sound of birdsong, the sound of nature, sound devoid of meaning, the sound that Clampitt is ultimately concerned with, is the *thespesiae iach* described by the Greek poet Homer. In some editions of the poem, a footnote by Clampitt is attached at this point, quoting the text of the *Odyssey* to which she is referring, to make sure the reader does not miss her meaning. In the story, Odysseus visits the land of the dead, where he must ask the ghost of the prophet Tiresias how to get home. In order to communicate with the ghosts, Odysseus performs the central ritual of ancient religion, animal sacrifice. As the ghosts, which are like shadows or twittering bats, drink the blood that he spills out on the ground from a sacrificed sheep, they take on human form and can talk as they did in life. Before they regain the power of speech, however, they make sounds that Homer describes as *thespesiae iache*, the phrase that appears in Clampitt's poem. *Iache* is a noun that means any kind of inarticulate cry; most likely it is an onomatopoeia, an imitation of human sounds that are not language. It is most frequently used of the shouts that accompanied Greek religious ritual. *Thespesiae* is an adjective meaning divine, especially in the sense of mysterious or inaccessible to human understanding. This conclusion makes it clear that Clampitt privileges the sounds of birds, the sounds of nature, and human sounds that are not speech over speech itself, in the same sense and degree that the divine is privileged over the merely human.

Lines 37-39

The poem's second sentence is concluded in the brief final section, giving a new emphasis to this passage. In these three lines, Clampitt transforms the meaning of the Homeric passage. For Homer, the ghosts were remembering how to talk as humans, regaining an ability that had been lost when they died. Clampitt, however, sees it as precisely the opposite. The ghosts are losing a sort of divine nature when they take up the physical expression of speech, supported by merely human breath.

THEMES

Animals

Clampitt was a life-long birder, though she never went to the extreme of keeping a life list or diary of all the birds she had seen, as she said in her address "Predecessors, Et Cetera," "a genuine, certified bird-watcher" would have done. When she was four or five years old, her aunt Edith told her the names of birds, creatures she found beautiful, that they saw in the woods near her home. Thereafter, she considered that kind of categorical knowledge of the natural world an ordinary part of human life.

Clampitt's interest in birding no doubt played into her long employment in the 1950s and 1960s as a librarian for the Audubon Society. As an adult, she was constantly surprised to find people who not only did not know the names of even the most common local birds but considered the matter completely unimportant. Clampitt, however, considered the control of that kind of language—the names of birds—to be indispensable to her poetic art. Her interest in bird-watching profoundly informs "Syrinx." One meaning of the title is the organ that produces song in birds. The main theme of the first section of that work concerns human efforts to transcribe birdsong through writing, into expressions that, at best, only approximate the sounds produced by birds. While Clampitt considered it a human failing not to know the conventional names of bird species, "Syrinx" proposes that humans are incapable of knowing and therefore controlling birdsong.

At the same time, Clampitt, whose poetic art was to a great degree historical, based upon her encounter with the poets of past ages, would have been aware of the long tradition of praising, if not imitating, birdsong in verse, as in Shelley's "To a Skylark." Even more to the point is the response to Shelley's poem by Gerard Manley Hopkins, "The Sea and the Skylark." Clampitt attributed her own vocation to the influence of Hopkins. Both Shelley and Hopkins establish birdsong as a symbol of a different order of

TOPICS FOR FURTHER STUDY

- Listen to a recording of Mozart's opera *Die Zauberflötte* (The Magic Flute), particularly to the Queen of the Night's aria in the second act, "Die Hölle Rache kocht im meinem Herzen!" Many recordings of the piece and video clips of filmed performances are available online. Write a short essay describing your reaction to the piece. Where does it seem to fall on a continuum between ordinary speech and the sounds of nature?

- For a period of time, keep a list of all the birds you see. Identify them using any field guide published for bird-watchers. Using your own photographs or images obtained from the Internet, make a poster or PowerPoint presentation showing the birds you saw, along with brief information about them.

- Use resources that are available to you in your library and on the Internet to research both Western opera and a non-European musical tradition, such as Chinese opera or Tuvan throat-singing. Report on the two traditions to your class, including any information you can find about how practitioners of those art forms consider them in relation to the sounds of the natural world. Create your report in a multimedia format.

- Write a poem in which you imagine how a bird might think about the relationship of nature and culture to language. Use a style similar to Clampitt's or any style that you find fitting for the observations.

- Lewis Carroll's poem "Jabberwocky," originally published in 1872 in the young-adult novel *Through the Looking Glass* (a sequel to *Alice's Adventures in Wonderland*), attempts to transcend ordinary human speech by creating an entirely new language. He is successful, since although much of the poem seems at first to be meaningless gibberish, it is able to convey a commonly perceived meaning to its audience. Write your own poem using words you invent.

---

communication from human speech, a treatment of the theme that Clampitt herself takes up in this poem.

Music

For Clampitt, birdsong and the other natural sounds she describes are bridges over the torrent of syntax to other inarticulate sounds produced by humans. One of the most important of these is music. In the second section of "Syrinx," Clampitt compares birdsong to human song, particularly to passages in opera where the sound of the singing completely swallows up the meaning of the words. She must have known the intimate connection that exists between the study of birdsong and music.

In the eighteenth century, the first scientific ornithologists realized that birdsong could be more reliably recorded in musical notation than in speech. The ultimate musical exploitation of this kind of notation was produced in the early twentieth century by Olivier Messiaen, whose *Catalogue d'Oiseaux* is a substantial set of transcribed birdsongs together with variations on each one for piano. Composers have long turned to birdsong as an inspiration. Imitated by the orchestra, it is a fairly common musical motif, occurring in, for instance, Antonio Vivaldi's *Spring* from the *Four Seasons*, in Ludwig van Beethoven's Sixth Symphony, and in Richard Wagner's opera *Siegfried*. George Frideric Handel's *The Cuckoo and the Nightingale* concerto leaves its birdsong imitation to the pipe organ. Leopold Mozart's *Toy Symphony* and Ottorino Respighi's *The Pines of Rome*, however, create a mechanical reproduction of birdsong by clockwork mechanisms. In recent performances of the Respighi piece particularly, the birdsong is increasingly supplied by digital sampling of

---

A wind chime is used as a metaphor for the bird singing. (*Arvind Balaraman | Shutterstock.com*)

that of the cuckoo, are onomatopoetic, that is, the birds are named with approximations in human speech of their characteristic call. There are many more such birds than Clampitt mentions, including the whippoorwill, the bobwhite quail, and the hoopoe. Clampitt questions, in her poem, the legitimacy of this kind of naming practice, because the human words are at best an approximation of the birdcall; more importantly, she says, the birdcall is not naturally or obviously suitable to use as the bird's name.

In the same way that human beings inevitably look for comprehensible patterns in every aspect of nature, birdsong has long been assimilated to human speech, probably as far back as prehistoric times, and the capturing of calls in language is an important part of folk culture. The white-throated sparrow, for instance, has a very distinctive call that is rendered by many different human sentences, varying from community to community, including such phrases as, "Old Sam Peabody, Peabody, Peabody" and "Sow wheat cleverly, cleverly cleverly." As Clampitt points out, the process is not very precise. However, it is precisely this uncertainty that allows for human creativity. For instance, the different regional imitations of birdsong have even been the subject of naïve poetry, such as Elizabeth van Hoevenberg's "The White-Throated Sparrow," in which several different lines of the poems consist of local approximations of that bird's song. This variety of interpretation of birdsong is at the surface of what Clampitt is referring to in "Syrinx" when she addresses the lack of human agreement in interpreting birdsong.

actual birds. More controversial are more ordinary musical passages that seem inspired by birdsong without going so far as to create an artificial birdcall. The birder Ferdinand Schuyler Mathews, for instance, sees the call of the white-throated sparrow in a famous phrase of Verdi's opera *La Traviata*. The Czech composer Leoš Janácek frequently transcribed birdsong and other sounds from nature into musical notation he later incorporated into his works, making notes in the field for that purpose.

STYLE

Onomatopoeia

Onomatopoeia is the use of a sound, imitated in ordinary language, as the name for the thing itself—a word like *crack* or *swoosh*, where human speech imitates a natural sound. "Syrinx" discusses the fact that many bird names, such as

Poetics

Clampitt came to writing poetry slowly and in an intensely private fashion. She had read poetry all her life, which is the first step in learning to write it. Once she had determined to pursue poetry rather than the novel as her form, Clampitt trained herself in a very traditional manner, writing out sonnets and imitations of Dante's cantos in a very strict form, in the same way that her hero Keats did. (These early writings were never published.) She also moved away from strict form, though, as Hopkins did.

By the time she began to publish, Clampitt was writing poems in a thoroughly modern form, dispensing with traditional poetic restrictions such as meter. Nevertheless, Clampitt's work is identifiable as poetry because of a comparatively formal structure that she imposes on

COMPARE & CONTRAST

- **1990s:** Sciences such as neurophysiology and genetics are in their infancy and suggest more than they answer about the human condition.

  Today: Advances brought about by the ever-faster pace of scientific discovery provide a wholly new understanding of human phenomena such as speech.

- **1990s:** Clampitt is criticized for her complicated syntax, unfamiliar to readers no longer educated in Latin and Greek.

  Today: The increasing use of e-mail, text messaging, and computer message boards tends to make English syntax increasingly simple and chaotic, including widespread use of abbreviations for common words.

- **1990s:** Beginning in the 1960s, the Audubon Society became concerned with the disruption in bird life cycles caused by the pesticide DDT. By the 1990s, the organization's focus broadens to general environmental issues and other causes, such as whale conservation.

  Today: The Audubon Society works against the environmental damage it perceives as caused by new techniques of drilling for natural gas, coal mining, and by movements denying the existence of global warming.

---

it and its intense use of word play. Clampitt uses traditional poetic form as a point of reference. "Syrinx" is organized into two eighteen-line sections followed by a concluding three-line section. In poetry, unlike prose, line lengths are carefully chosen, so even without a formal poetic meter, the poet controls how they are grouped on the page. Further structure is imposed on the poem by lines with parallel grammatical constructions, strikingly in the first three lines. Although there is no regular pattern of rhymes, there are some, such as the rhyme between lines 16 and 18, evoking traditional poetic forms.

Clampitt is as adept as any poet in the clever use of language. She cannot use a word like *fret* without creating a tension between its two meanings as worry and a part of a musical instrument. To cite a more substantial example, the title of the poem itself, "Syrinx," has two distinct meanings: the vocal organ of birds and the Greek name for the musical reed pipes of the god Pan, which have an entire mythological history associated with them. It might seem on first reading that Clampitt limits herself to the ornithological meaning. However, by improperly calling the bird's organ a reed, and by the use of the qualifier aeolian (which itself has double scientific and mythological meanings), she invokes the entirety of the myth in the imagination of the reader. This artful manipulation of language links older, formal poetry and modern, less structured poetry as the same form of art.

HISTORICAL CONTEXT

Bird-Watching

While human beings have, no doubt, always appreciated the beauty of birds and birdsong, the modern science of ornithology (the study of birds) and the popular movement of birding have a more definite and recent history. Until the beginning of the twentieth century, vast numbers of birds were shot in Western Europe and North America for the sake of their feathers and meat and for sport. Women's clothes were routinely decorated with feathers (sometimes whole stuffed birds), and every kind of bird flesh (such as robins) could be had in abundance in local markets. Birds such as the passenger pigeon and great auk were hunted to extinction. Revulsion at this level of casual destruction led to the founding of bird conservation societies, such as the National Audubon Society in 1905.

A foghorn is used as a metaphor for the bird singing. *(Sternstunden / Shutterstock.com)*

At the same time, bird identification, which once could be done only by shooting or trapping a specimen, became possible through the use of binoculars. Combined with the rise of the automobile, which made it possible to visit undisturbed natural areas where bird populations differed from those in cities, conditions allowed the modern pastime of bird-watching, or birding, to come into existence about the time Clampitt was born.

Clampitt was an enthusiastic birder, writing about it frequently in her letters. She also worked for most of the 1950s and 1960s as the head reference librarian of the National Audubon Society. One of her chief duties was assisting people around the country with bird identification, so her knowledge of the subject must have been immense, though she modestly downplayed this and kept up a pretense of detachment from birding, in a manner typical of her many unresolved paradoxical attitudes. In "Syrinx," Clampitt calls on her extensive knowledge and experience of bird-watching, naming the poem after an obscure feature of bird anatomy and couching much of its argument in the perennial problem of representing birdsong in writing.

Clampitt and the Counterculture

Clampitt was born in 1920, far too early to become a hippie, it might seem. But her life defied the expectations that society held for women of her generation. Born into an Iowa farming family, she never considered becoming a farm wife but instead obtained a liberal arts education and set out as quickly as possible for New York to find a career.

In some ways her experience resembled the 1956 film *The Man in the Grey Flannel Suit*, as she moved from post to post up the corporate ladder in the New York literary world, but her rungs, from secretary, to librarian, to editor, were not the ones coveted by men. Her career rather recalls the 1957 film *Desk Set*. Clampitt was a pink-collar worker trapped on the insignificant margins of a masculine world.

In the late 1960s, it was as if Clampitt came out of a cocoon and found herself finally fitting into the new world of the youth culture or the hippie movement. Until she began to publish poetry, her life was dominated by the protest movement against the Vietnam War. She was an active protester, and she wrote scathing letters to

Secretary of State Henry Kissinger. The environmental concerns of the counterculture also resonated with her love of nature and found expression in her poetry, as did the general resistance to authority, convention, and even reason itself, the main theme of "Syrinx."

Although Clampitt was often attacked by feminists, she lived out the feminist ideal of building an independent life and career. Like many in the counterculture, Clampitt disdained marriage on principle and instead lived with her companion, law professor Harold Korn, for twenty years, though she maintained her own apartment as well, as a sign of her independence. Similarly, she opposed the idea of having children on the grounds that it was incompatible with a world armed with nuclear weapons. She did finally marry Korn on June 10, 1994, a few months before her death, presumably to ease matters of inheritance and the creation of the Amy Clampitt Fund, an institution devoted to promoting poetry.

CRITICAL OVERVIEW

It is perhaps not surprising that very little criticism has been produced about a poem written as recently as 1994. Although Clampitt has been accepted into the canon of American poets, she has not as yet generated much attention from scholars. There has, for instance, been no biography of Clampitt. Knowledge about her life must be gleaned from primary sources, such as her own essays and letters (Willard Spiegelman has gathered some of them in the collection *Love, Amy*, but a larger collection will undoubtedly be published one day), and from the memoir of the poet attached by her friend and editor Mary Jo Salter to the republication of Clampitt's work, *The Collected Poems of Amy Clampitt*. The best biographical sketch of a scholarly character is that of Spiegelman, while briefer biographical and critical references can be found in reference works, such as Karen Raugust's entry in *American Women Writers*. Indeed, the greater part of Clampitt's own writing still exists as unpublished manuscripts, including many poems (with various drafts dispersed among her papers and in letters), a play about the English romantic poets, and three complete novels.

Likewise, there has not yet been a major interpretative work on her poetry. Clampitt's

critical reception was not immediately and universally positive. Editors and teachers tended to dismiss Clampitt's work on the same grounds on which she was, according to Spiegelman in his introduction to *Love, Amy*, dismissed by "certain feminist critics who scoffed at her bookish and intellectual temperament, her commitment to 'high' culture, and her exuberantly descriptive style."

According to Spiegelman, the former Poet Laureate of the United States James Dickey once derided Clampitt to her face at a party by observing that she wrote poems about flowers. However, the critic and scholar Helen Vendler, in a 1983 notice of Clampitt's first poetry collection, *The Kingfisher*, in the *New York Review of Books* (quoted by Slater), predicted that Clampitt would join the enduring poets of the ages. Vendler singled her out, in particular, for her verse's "triumph over the resistance of language." Clampitt took this praise as inspiration and indeed addresses that difficult concept in "Syrinx."

Raugust deflects common criticisms of Clampitt's poetry as being old-fashioned and elitist, with this characterization: "Its rich vocabulary includes many unfamiliar words; its syntax is complicated; and its allusions, which are central to the poems' meanings, require an educated audience."

Clampitt's friend Salter, in her introduction to *The Collected Poems of Amy Clampitt*, reads "Syrinx" as a "hint both at God's silence and at poetry's limitations." She also points out the sophisticated punning in the work as a sign of Clampitt's nearly unlimited command of poetic language. Robert Boschman, in *In the Way of Nature*, offers a slightly different reading of "Syrinx," making the most extensive critical comment on the poem published thus far. For him, "Syrinx" concerns the conflict between meaning and expression inherent in poetry, but it also deals with the archetypal and "invokes the widespread, ancient association of both wind and bird with death."

CRITICISM

Bradley A. Skeen
Skeen is a classicist. In the following essay, he situates Amy Clampitt's "Syrinx" as an emblem of the post-romantic counterculture.

WHAT DO I READ NEXT?

- Homer's *Odyssey*, which has been translated frequently (for instance, in 1961 by Robert Fitzgerald), had tremendous influence on Clampitt, not only in "Syrinx," where she quotes it, but throughout her later work. The complex architecture of her syntax that reviewers often object to was very likely based on practices she had learned from reading Homer in the original Greek.

- The 1999 *Handbook of the International Phonetic Association: A Guide to the Use of the International Phonetic Alphabet* is the standard text that describes the International Phonetic alphabet, a tool used by linguists to precisely transcribe any and every sound made in human speech.

- *Where Rivers and Mountains Sing: Sound, Music and Nomadism in Tuva and Beyond* (2006), by Theodore Levin and Valentina Süzükei, explores how the world of natural sounds—wind, water, birdsong—in Asia provides a background for the development of throat-singing among the nomadic peoples of Tuva in Mongolia. Throat singing is a technique by which the singer can simultaneously produce two notes. Limited to the folk tradition of the Tuvan people, it is perhaps the human sound furthest removed from ordinary speech, far more so than opera singing. The authors' experience presents a unique embodiment of the ideas central of "Syrinx." The book is accompanied by a DVD and music CD giving samples of what it discusses.

- Andrew Lock and Charles R. Peters's 1996 *Handbook of Human Symbolic Evolution* is a massive compendium that focuses the sciences of archaeology, psychology, neurophysiology, and many other disciplines on the problem of the evolution of the human mind and its chief instruments: language and art.

- *Backyard Birds: Peterson Field Guides for Young Naturalists*, by Karen Stray Nolting, Jonathan Latimer, and Roger Tory Peterson, is a 1999 adaptation for young-adult readers of one of the leading birding field guides. It helps its readers identify birds commonly seen in North America.

- Emiko Ohnuki-Tierney's 2002 *Kamikaze, Cherry Blossoms, and Nationalisms: The Militarization of Aesthetics in Japanese History* demonstrates another surprising development of German romanticism in the twentieth century, as the guiding philosophy of the kamikaze program in the Japanese Air Force during World War II.

- Joan Wall's *International Phonetic Alphabet for Singers: A Manual for English and Foreign Language Diction* is a 1989 textbook that describes the pronunciation used by opera singers using the International Phonetic Alphabet, a tool devised by linguists that lets any human sound be noted precisely in writing. It shows that the Latin alphabet (used in English) is far from being the last word in the transcription of speech and other sounds.

- In *The Hunting of the Snark* (1876), Lewis Carroll explores and analyzes the nature of language through the form of a fairy tale of adventure filled with humorous and nonsensical verse. The tale is available in a new 2006 edition, *The Annotated Hunting of the Snark*, which helps explain the literary, linguistic, and philosophical aspects of the story. It also contains new illustrations. This new edition makes the book much more accessible for a young-adult audience.

Clampitt is often treated as being nearly anachronistic among poets of her generation because of her indebtedness to poets of the past. Indeed, it makes more sense to consider Clampitt's work in the light of her poetic sources rather than her contemporaries, from whose world she was largely disengaged. John Keats, on whom she published a critical study, and the

"LANGUAGE IS INHERENTLY RATIONAL,
NATURE IRRATIONAL, AND THE IRRATIONAL
IS GREATER BECAUSE IT CANNOT BE CONTAINED
BY REASON."

romantic movement in general, about which she wrote an unpublished play, perhaps loomed the largest in her imagination, and a deeper understanding of "Syrinx" can be had by analyzing it in romantic terms.

Romanticism is the name now given to the leading intellectual currents of England and Germany in the late eighteenth and early nineteenth centuries. Poets and philosophers of that era lived in a world that was changing—modernizing—at an unprecedentedly rapid rate, under the impact of the Enlightenment, with its criticism of religion, monarchy, and every traditional institution of society, and the industrial revolution, which was transforming the economy and the relations between classes out of all recognition. It is not surprising then, that the romantics viewed history as a sort of argument between two impulses, the ancient or traditional, allied with human feeling, and the modern, allied with human reason. As the great historian of romantic philosophy M. H. Abrams points out in *The Mirror and the Lamp: Romantic Theory and the Critical Tradition*, poetry itself was no different and could not be allowed to be a product of human art and the advance of civilization: "It was standard procedure in [the romantic poet] Wordsworth's day, when characterizing poetry, to refer to its conjectured origin in the passionate, and therefore, naturally rhythmical and figurative, outcries of primitive men." This is an attempt to redefine poetry as part of nature rather than culture. The romantics hoped that the opposition between nature and culture would somehow be resolved, allowing the two to come together in a new and better form that would incorporate the best of both worlds, although they had no practical idea of how to bring this reconciliation about. The idea that history is a battleground between these two opposed worlds proved to be one of the most powerful ideas of the nineteenth and twentieth centuries.

Many intellectuals and many social movements have inherited from romanticism an acute awareness of the unresolved tension that exists between tradition and modernity, and they have proposed various means of resolving it. One of the most famous efforts was the communism proposed by Karl Marx, who proposed reconciling the class system into a classless society that labored equally and equally shared the benefits of labor. This, he believed, would produce the lasting utopia envisioned by the romantic philosophers, though his hopes now seem naïve.

A more common, and perhaps less obvious, reaction to the romantic problem has been the impulse to simply reject or abandon modernity and return to or restore the original tradition. An obvious problem that such attempts fail to take into account is that the past is past. The traditional world from before the Enlightenment and the Scientific Revolution no longer exists. It is, therefore, impossible to return to such a simple existence, and any effort to do so must instead result in an artificial or second-hand re-creation of the past. An example of this kind of reaction is the philosophy of traditionalism, which holds that the ideal that is to be recreated is specifically the pre-Christian (or in some versions, pre-Protestant) world. Perhaps the first traditionalist was the English philosopher Thomas Taylor (who was influential on Blake and Keats). In his autobiography, *Thomas Taylor the Platonist: Selected Writings*, he held that every social and intellectual development since ancient Greece had been a mistake that ought to be abandoned. In particular, he created a scripture consisting of the works of Plato and a few other closely related (in his view) ancient philosophical and religious texts. If anything in the modern world disagreed with these texts, it was modernity that was to be rejected. For instance, if Plato says that the sun goes around the earth, then modern science is wrong to argue that the earth goes around the sun. If Plato does not mention the existence of moons around the planet Jupiter, then when astronomers see those moons, there must be something wrong with their telescopes. Plato, who regarded his work as an ever-deepening series of penetrative questions about the nature of reality, would have been horrified to find himself treated in this dogmatic fashion, and Taylor was widely ridiculed for his position in his lifetime.

One of the most influential responses to the romantic crisis came in Germany in the form of several closely related movements referred to as the *Wandervogel* (Wandering Birds) and *Lebensreform* (Life Reform). These movements conceived of themselves as a counterculture that would lead German society back to its original, authentic nature, such as it had supposedly possessed before modern times. The manufactured mass culture produced by the budding entertainment industry was rejected in favor of folk culture. Modern medicine, with its human-designed drugs and vaccines, was rejected in favor of naturopathic medicine, which brought about cures through natural herbs and sunshine. Not scientific trials, but tradition—that is, the authority of the naturopathic practitioner—would determine whether the treatment worked or not. The most basic social conventions were to be rejected in favor of the natural, leading to movements in favor of nudism (also known as naturism), while processed foods were to be rejected in favor of natural (health) foods, and even raw foods, as if the use of fire was too civilized. Even modern housing was suspect, leading in the most extreme cases to living in caves. Reason, viewed as the corrupting influence of the modern world, was to be rejected in favor of feeling.

This movement gave birth to two unlikely offspring: the Fascists and the hippies. Fascism, especially in its German form of Nazism, which co-opted much of the *Wandervogel* program, was in many respects a product of this counterculture, above all in the rejection of intellect in favor of instinct, although the glorification of violence that animated Fascism twisted it out of all recognizable connection to the counterculture or any other tradition. At the same time, German immigrants to America kept up the countercultural movement, and in the 1940s, it came to a critical mass in the Big Sur region of California. This was a relatively pristine wilderness between the Coastal Mountain Range and the Pacific Ocean about halfway between Los Angeles and San Francisco. There a collection of artists and Bohemians flourished in small communities and in communes, and even as virtual hermits living in the wilderness, who put the counterculture into full operation, undisturbed by the outside world. New elements of Eastern mysticism, such as Buddhism and Yoga were incorporated from other immigrant communities in California. In the 1960s, this counterculture was taken up anew by disaffected American youth, who learned of the older counterculture through health food stores and other connections between Big Sur and San Francisco, creating the hippie movement.

Clampitt, though she did not make the pilgrimage to San Francisco and though she was middle-aged in the 1960s, eagerly embraced the hippie counterculture, becoming a fanatical antiwar protester. Her friend Mary Jo Slater emphasizes this fact in a memoir of the poet, pointing out almost as a literary symbol that the most prominent feature of Clampitt's home far into the 1980s was a giant psychedelic poster of Bob Dylan. Clampitt was also exposed to more orthodox forms of romanticism through her excellent liberal arts education at Grinnell College in the 1920s, as well as the intellectual leaders of the German counterculture, such as Hermann Hesse.

"Syrinx" is ultimately a poem about language, and it offers an interpretation of language based on the German romantic counterculture. Clampitt establishes a dichotomy (a set of two opposing forces) between natural sounds and human language. Human language is inferior because it cannot accurately describe, or cannot contain, the sounds of the natural world, including birdsong. By the same token, natural sounds are not limited by being bound to specific meanings. Language is inherently rational, nature irrational, and the irrational is greater because it cannot be contained by reason. She symbolizes language by syntax, its ordered structure, and conceives that this order is destroyed in human speech as art approaches the natural and becomes something greater than mere reason. Sound becomes greater as it loses meaning. She drives the point home by invoking Homeric myth. Whereas for Homer, the ghosts lapping blood from the pit below Odysseus's sacrifice *gain* the power of speech, Clampitt reinterprets the scene and makes them *lose* whatever divinity they possessed as they become limited by speech. Language and reason, as part of human culture, are inferior to the natural world, which is unbounded by reason.

Clampitt's treatment of language in "Syrinx" reveals a fundamental contradiction with her insistence that poetic tradition and the study of earlier poets are paramount. Indeed, her poetry was criticized by contemporaries for being excessively formal and learned. But this too is implicit in her countercultural approach. She acts on instinct without critical analysis. Her very being calls out that nature is superior to culture, and she does not stop to use reason to question that feeling. If she had, she could easily have consulted technical literature that suggests an entirely different interpretation of birdsong. Given her position within the Audubon society, it is hard to see how she did not know that birdsong is indeed a form of communication that conveys practical information to birds of the same species (for example, that an abundant food source is nearby or a predator is threatening) and thus is entirely analogous to human speech in the sense of conveying rational meaning. Birdsong is not innate but learned from other birds, sometimes even between species, just as human language is learned through contact with culture. Similarly, she must have known that there are far more sophisticated and accurate means of recording birdsong than merely transcribing it into the Roman alphabet (neither does she consider the opposite problem, that parrots cannot perfectly mimic human speech, nor the fact that speech can be communicated through gesture, a human practice possibly older than vocal speech). Birds cannot distinguish true birdsong from recordings (or, now, from computer-generated calls). However, those achievements of culture are ultimately irrelevant for the counterculture, which believes that feeling is more correct than knowledge.

Clampitt's approach to the problem of nature and culture in "Syrinx" is illuminated through a letter she wrote to her brother Philip on February 3, 1955. In this letter, found in her autobiography, *Love, Amy*, she mentions a letter she received from a fourteen-year-old schoolgirl in her official capacity as reference librarian at the Audubon Society. The girl wanted to know "whether or not man was descended from the ape." The answer Clampitt gave "was that we do not know." The research she did to reach this conclusion is illustrative of her approach. She skimmed through the first and last chapters of Darwin's *On the Origin of Species*. She did not think to read Darwin's work on human evolution, *The Descent of Man*, or to consult the evidence from the fossil record that had been accumulated over the past century and that forms the principal evidence in support of the proposition, and still less to take into account the then-new science of genetics. The answer that satisfied Clampitt was the one that came from instinct, and one could say that she carefully avoided carrying out a reasoned investigation that might have called her conclusion into question. For Clampitt, the product of human reason was always inferior to instinct and nature. She

A speech by Homer is referenced at the end of the poem. *(Slava Gerj | Shutterstock.com)*

must not have seriously believed that reason could answer fundamental questions. So in "Syrinx," Clampitt voices the convictions of her belief against the product of human reason, exemplifying and defending the counterculture at once. At the same time, however, Clampitt is powerless to find a means of expression that is not language—indeed, the most reasoned and traditional language.

Source: Bradley A. Skeen, Critical Essay on "Syrinx," in *Poetry for Students*, Gale, Cengage Learning, 2012.

John Taylor

In the following review, Taylor reveals the detail in Clampitt's poetry.

From her first volume, *The Kingfisher* (1983), published when she was sixty-three years old, through her fifth and last book, *A Silence Opens* (1994), Amy Clampitt (1920–94) stunned readers with her descriptions of the physical world. In her moving introduction to this splendidly produced *Collected Poems*, friend and fellow poet Mary Jo Salter rightfully points out that Clampitt's "vocabulary may well be the widest of any modern American poet, making use as it does of various sub-lexicons (botany is a favorite) . . . foreign

Languages...and...the nearly limitless aural corollaries...to the often arcane words that came naturally to her." Nearly every poem confirms this truism; here is a passage on lifting fog in "Gradual Clearing":

> then, in a lifting
> of wisps and scarves, of smoke-rings
> from about the islands, disclosing
> what had been wavering
> fishnet plisse as a smoothness
> of peau-de-soie or just-ironed
> percale, with a tatting
> of foam out where the rocks are....

Yet what motivates Clampitt's radical concern with surface detail? So witty and esoteric (yet simultaneously so tangible) are her descriptions that "sharp-eyed" would only half-qualify the Iowa-born poet and mislead. Clampitt goes to such linguistic extremes in her pursuit of "perishing residue[s] / of pure sensation" that something deeper is at stake than virtuoso word-painting. What might it be? Certainly she is sensitive to the miracle of being alive, and to an extent rivaled by only a few she creates an exuberantly baroque language to translate "the hooked-up, the humdrum, the brief, tragic / wonder of being at all." The ordinary emerges extraordinary in her poetry, as in her recollections of ringing doorbells for Eugene McCarthy, a banal night that turned into "an olfactory / adventure." "After // the mildew," she reminisces, "after / the musts and fetors / of tomcat and cockroach, / barrooms' beer-reek, / the hayfield whiff / of pot... // the ageless, / pristine, down- / to-earth aromas / of tomorrow's / bread from / Zita's Bakery."

In her best work, Clampitt not only re-actualizes sensation with striking images but also underscores its significance. In "From a Clinic Waiting Room," for example, the sunset's "tinctured / layerings vivid as delirium" are "astonishing / as merely to be living." Accenting "merely," Clampitt equates the beauties of the cosmos and our own "mere" existences, an equivalence that obtains provided we agree to delight in the shimmering appearances outside our perishable bodies. The poet even sometimes aspires to a state of "being, totally untainted by the will," as she puts it in "The Sacred Hearth Fire." But the irony of this long-poem—an inverted ars poetica in that the poet satirizes a California woman who has settled in Mykonos to make pottery—reveals that this state of pure "being" can never be attained; nor in fact is it desirable. Does not Clampitt also make "calculated object[s]"—poems—"that might be craf- // ted in a day and given to a kiln to harden"?

"The world is full of mystery," she admits, and this sentiment informs her most moving poems—which, lexically, are not necessarily the most brilliant. Not only the "wonderful," but also "the strange...are too much with us," she likewise confesses in "Nothing Stays Put." In several instances, she considers the extent to which self-scrutiny is legitimate when "all that we know, that we're / made of, is motion." Hence an intriguing wavering, in some of her work, between the corresponding Socratic injunctions (to know thyself and to examine the world) and her simultaneous wish, as when "blueberrying in August," to lose herself in the joys of living "minute to minute." Elsewhere, as she speaks to young people in a classroom, the memory of having once heard hundreds of meadowlarks singing ("a liquid millennium arising from the still / eastward-looking venue of the dark") synesthetically blends into the present, into the young faces who likewise seem "eastward-looking, bright with a mute, / estranged, ancestral puzzlement." In her best pages, Clampitt's impressionism thus also records a "puzzlement" running deeper than the senses. She also knows that delving into the bliss of sensation can allow us to "shy away from... / the dolor of the particular: // who's not speaking to whom, who's ailing / and doesn't get out any more, who's still / around and who's not."

Yet more often than not, her poetry minimizes the self's daily vicissitudes. Evoking Petrarch's Laura, in "Losing Track of Language," she admits that "whatever is left of her is language," then asks: "What is language but breath, leaves, / petals fallen or in the act of falling, pollen / of turmoil that sifts through the fingers?" At the same time, she occasionally focuses back on her "farmhouse childhood, kerosene-lit, / tatting-and-mahogany genteel," an inward-turning that contrasts with her extroverted fascination for the most minute manifestations of nature or for the oddities of foreign lands. (As a "travel poet," she ranks with the most entertaining travel writers.) Indeed, hidden beneath those natural and exotic surfaces that she paints so vividly is an Iowa childhood that remains unfulfilled, unassimilated. We may not hear or see that childhood in a given poem, but often it lurks there. Could it not be that irretrievable losses associated with her past paradoxically fuel her desire to name—and thus poetically recover—so many particulars of the present? In

"Black Buttercups," as she meditates on her exile from "the hinterland," she asks an essential question: "How is one to measure / the loss of two blue spruces, a waterfall / of bridal wreath below the porch, the bluebells / and Dutchman's-breeches ...?" There is no nostalgia in such a phrase, but rather a kind of anxiety that—because of the pain it induced—may long ago have obliged Amy Clampitt to affirm or deny, once and for all, what she was discovering elsewhere—far from Iowa. She evidently chose to affirm and, thereafter, with ever rarer glances backward, her response to this question consisted in these marvelously vivacious poems.

Source: John Taylor, Review of *The Collected Poems of Amy Clampitt*, in *Poetry*, Vol. 172, No. 4, July 1998, pp. 225–27.

Grace Schulman

In the following excerpted review, Schulman discusses the rich use of language and allusion in this volume of collected poems.

... *The Collected Poems of Amy Clampitt* is an event of another land. Clampitt published her first book of poems in 1983, when she was 63, and died three years ago leaving behind such classics as "A Procession at Candlemas," "The Burning Child," "Beethoven, Opus 111" and "The Prairie." The success of that first book, *The Kingfisher*, encouraged her to produce five volumes in eleven years, work that won her a MacArthur Fellowship and an American Academy of Arts and Letters Award in Literature. Mary Jo Salter tells us in her foreword that Clampitt, who had for years considered herself a failed novelist, resolved to make up for lost time as a successful poet.

Although new poems have surfaced since her death, this volume contains only her final choices. Happily, it arrives at a time when the early books are hard to find. It is dazzling. Like Gerard Manley Hopkins, her master, Clampitt finds miracles in common things such as "a kingfisher's burnished plunge, the color / of felicity afire." As Hopkins, in "The Windhover," cries out, "My heart in hiding / Stirred for a bird," Clampitt exclaims in her own sprung sonnet, "The Cormorant in Its Element":

Plummeting
waterward, big black feet splayed for a
landing
gear, slim head turning and turning,
vermilion
strapped, this way and that, with a

lightning glance
over the shoulder, the cormorant
astoundingly,
in one sleek involuted arabesque, a
vertical
turn on a dime, goes into that inimitable
vanishing-and-emerging-from-under-the-briny
deep act which, unlike the works of Homo
Houdini,
is performed for reasons having nothing
at all
to do with ego, guilt, ambition, or even
money.

Her language is rich with references to other languages, and with allusions to history, myth, science and world commerce. Often she finds startling ideas in her amassments of detail, as when, in "Beach Glass," she sees objects washed up on shore and imagines Chartres Cathedral.

Clampitt's triumphs are in her juxtapositions. Often social criticism lies in the contrasts between nature and human frailty, as with the cormorant and human greed. "The Reedbeds of Hackensack" contains the paradox of a "rancid asphodel" in a polluted river, and in "A Hermit Thrush," a couple uncertain of their relationship

drop everything to listen as a
hermit thrush distills its fragmentary,
hesitant, in the end
unbroken music.

More daring leaps of thought occur in major poems like "The Prairie," from *Westward*. There, Clampitt yokes Chekhov crossing the steppe and her paternal grandfather crossing the prairie, both men born in the same year. From that bond she finds new meaning in the hard American past and in her own relentless journey:

To be landless, half a nomad, nowhere
wholly
at home, is to discover, now, an epic
theme
in going back. The rootless urge that took
my father's father to Dakota, to California,
impels me there.

And in "Beethoven, Opus 111," from *The Kingfisher*, she pairs the deaf composer and her father, a Midwestern farmer. Then, contemplating Beethoven's physical limitation and his transcendent music, she writes that

dying,
for my father, came to be like that
finally—in its messages the levitation
of serenity, as though the spirit might
aspire, in its last act,
to walk on air.

In a late poem, "A Whippoorwill in the Woods," Clampitt tells of how her grandfather carried a child, her aunt, outdoors at night and said: "'That was a whippoorwill.' And she (and I) never forgot." Her achievement is like that: She captured a landscape, a bird's call, a flower growing near a gravesite, pigeons returning to a demolished building in ways never to be forgotten. In her brief career, she wrote fiercely and created poems that aspire beyond the limits of life and time.

Source: Grace Schulman, Review of *The Collected Poems of Amy Clampitt*, in *Nation*, Vol. 265, No. 14, November 3, 1997, pp. 65–67.

Robert B. Shaw

In the following review of A Silence Opens, *Shaw praises Clampitt's ability to impose an order upon the multitude of small details that leads the reader to the poem's moral message.*

Amy Clampitt's latest book [*A Silence Opens*], like her earlier ones, is at first a little intimidating in its bursts of abundance. It can seem like a cornucopia out of control. Rather than shrinking back, it is best to allow oneself to be engulfed; what seems a welter proves to have a fair amount of order after all. The plenitude in question is both in subject matter and style; geographically and philologically, the poet is well-travelled. While the multiple shifts in location throughout the book may recall Elizabeth Bishop, the style is closer to that of Bishop's mentor Marianne Moore. Like Moore, Clampitt collects curious, almost random-seeming details with magpie thoroughness, and arranges them in patterns of unexpected significance. Discursiveness can teeter on the brink of digressiveness, but both poets manage to pull firm, unbreaking threads of argument through the maze-like paths of their poems. The sentences themselves can seem maze-like: complex, even Jamesian in syntax, they overreach the bounds of tidy-looking stanzas, creating a counterpoint to these with their grammatical suspensions and dragooning of prose rhythms.

In a time when philosophy and literary criticism have tended to question the capacity of language to render either personal experience or external reality, Clampitt is bracingly unabashed in pursuing her vocation of fitting words to the world. Her enthusiasm is obvious in the authority and verve she brings to describing the localities that count most for her. The midwest prairies of her childhood, Manhattan where she has spent much of her life, the New England coast, sites in England and the Continent, all make appearances here as in her earlier volumes. There are a few new additions to the gazetteer as well. Perhaps the most imposing poem in the book concerns Virginia in the days of the first English settlements. Entitled "Matoaka" (the actual name of the princess most of us learned in school to call Pocahontas), this could be read as a darker, more skeptical rewriting of Moore's sedately enchanting travelogue "Virginia Britannia." Clampitt directs an unsparing light on "the shadowy predatory tentshow / we know as history" in this model of intricate construction. With Matoaka's own story in the foreground—her marriage to John Rolfe and voyage to England, where she soon died—the poem brilliantly captures the moment of two cultures, of the old world and the new, confronting one another:

> the gartered
> glitterings, the breathing
> propinquity of faces: through
> a pomandered fog
>
> of rooms and posturings arises,
> stunningly vivid still yet
> dim with distance, a figure
> long gone from Jamestown,
>
> an ocean's retching, heaving
> vertigo removed, and more: from
> girlhood's remembered grapevines,
> strawberries, sun-
>
> warm mulberries, leapfrog,
> cartwheels, the sound of streams,
> of names, of languages: Pamunkey,
> Chickahominy....

The subduing of nature by artifice and the greed and mendacity of colonialists (Captain John Smith and Sir Walter Raleigh serve as representative figures) are themes woven into the tapestry; so is the role of tobacco,

> the golden weed
>
> King James once railed against
> (correctly, it latterly appears)
> as noxious, till persuaded there was
> money to be made....

Throughout, the poem stresses how little can be known of this woman whose constantly changing names—Matoaka, Pocahontas, Rebecca Rolfe—symbolize her exploitative displacement. "A silence opens"—the gap in the historical record; and yet by the end of the piece Clampitt has compensated for this with her imaginative leaps of empathy:

to stroll thus
is to move nearer,

in imagination, to the nub,
the pulse, the ember of what she was—
no stranger, finally, to the mystery
of what we are.

This is surely one of her richest poems. It is well accompanied by others such as "Hispaniola," "Paumanok," and "Brought from Beyond," which similarly expose the spoliation and enslavement which are the most troubling parts of the explorers' heritage, the treasure looted for "the gilding of basilicas":

O Marco Polo and Coronado, where do
these things, these

fabrications, come from—the holy places,
ark and altarpiece, the aureoles,
the seraphim—and underneath it all
the howling?

Clampitt's ability to make a moral point briefly and tellingly may be another legacy of Marianne Moore. Both poets are adept at avoiding tedious preachiness, and both draw their moral conclusions as if inevitably from a tissue of meticulous observations.

The poems centering on the colonial past are grouped in the first section of the volume. Its further contents are more personal in focus. Many of them are fine and memorable. "Handed Down" is a much more modest piece about the New England coast than the splendid earlier elegy "What the Light Was Like"; still, it manages to be an effective dirge not merely for one drowned fisherman but for a vanishing way of life:

It's the names,
the roll call handed on and let down
in heavy seas, the visibility near zero,
the solitude total, night falling—it's the names
of the dead, kept alive, they still hold on to.

Elsewhere she lets down her own net of memory and retrieves scenes which are elemental in their clarity. "The wizened resins / of remembering turn into plunder" as she recalls huddling in her family's storm cellar in "Homeland":

Such
extravaganzas of suspense—

the brassy calm, the vapors' upthrust,
the lurid porches of foreboding
we lived among, they could be thought of

as a kind of homeland: the unease,
the dim notion of a down-to-earth
transcendence that brought us in,

that raises from the apple bin
long-dormant resonances
of an oncoming winter.

Here, as often before, she speaks as a connoisseur of what Frost liked to call "inner weather." Such exercises of memory yield insights of various kinds—moral, historical, psychological, or esthetic—and rise at moments to perceptions that can only be called religious. Again in the final poem, as in "Matoaka," "a silence opens," but it is not here the silence of unrecorded history but that of ineffable experience, the mystic's discovery of "the infinite love of God" which exists

past parentage or gender
beyond sung vocables
the slipped-between
the so infinitesimal
fault line
a limitless
interiority

This last poem is notable for its daring in pursuing such a subject, and for its humility which does not profess to understand more than mortal intelligence is equipped to.

Other intriguing or well-fashioned poems upon which I haven't room to comment include "Bayou Afternoon," "A Cadenza," "Matrix," and "The Horned Rampion." Any lapses? Well, here and there those marathon sentences seem more straggling than artfully attenuated. A few poems (I think of "Seed" in particular) are overloaded with literary allusion. A translation from Dante's *Inferno* coexists somewhat awkwardly with its surroundings. These cavillings aside, this is a book Amy Clampitt's readers should welcome wholeheartedly, with appreciation of the wholeheartedness that evidently went into the writing. For many readers her generosity of spirit has proved as I expect it will for many more in the future—to be something enlightening and wholesomely contagious.

Source: Robert B. Shaw, "High Reachers," in *Poetry*, Vol. 165, No. 3, December 1994, pp. 158–65.

SOURCES

Abrams, M. H., *The Mirror and the Lamp: Romantic Theory and the Critical Tradition*, Oxford University Press, 1953, pp. 78–84.

Ballintijn, Mechteld R., and Carel ten Cate, "Sex Differences in the Vocalizations and Syrinx of the Collared Dove (*Streptopelia decaocto*)," in *Auk*, Vol. 1114, No. 1, 1997, pp. 22–39.

Baptista, Luis Felipe, and Robin A. Keister, "Why Birdsong Is Sometimes Like Music," in *Perspectives in Biology and Medicine*, Vol. 48, No. 3, 2005, pp. 426–43.

Boschman, Robert, *In the Way of Nature: Ecology and Westward Expansion in the Poetry of Anne Bradstreet, Elizabeth Bishop and Amy Clampitt*, McFarland, 2009, pp. 191–94.

Clampitt, Amy, "Predecessors, Et Cetera," in *Predecessors, Et Cetera: Essays*, University of Michigan Press, 1991, pp. 1–5.

———, "Syrinx," in *The Collected Poems*, Alfred A. Knopf, 1997, p. 363.

Dennett, Daniel C., *Consciousness Explained*, Penguin, 1993.

Hopkins, Gerard Manley, "The Sea and the Skylark," in *Bartleby.com*, http://www.bartleby.com/122/11.html (accessed April 11, 2011); originally published in *Poems of Gerard Manley Hopkins*, Humphrey Milford, 1918.

Jensen, Kenneth K., Brenton G. Cooper, Ole N. Larsen, and Franz Goller, "Songbirds Use Pulse Tone Register in Two Voices to Generate Low-Frequency Sound," in *Proceedings: Biological Sciences*, Vol. 274, No. 1626, November 2007, pp. 2703–10.

Kennedy, Gordon, *Children of the Sun: A Pictorial Anthology from Germany to California, 1883–1949*, Nivaria, 1998.

Mathews, Ferdinand Schuyler, "White-Throated Sparrow," in *Field Book of Wild Birds and Their Music: A Description of the Character and Music of Birds, Intended to Assist in the Identification of Species Common to the Eastern United States*, G. P. Putnam's Sons, 1906. pp. 95–101.

Mosse, Georg L., *The Crisis of German Ideology: Intellectual Origins of the Third Reich*, Grosset & Dunlap, 1964.

Raugust, Karen, "Clampitt, Amy (Kathleen)," in *American Women Writers: A Critical Reference Guide from Colonial Times to the Present*, 2nd ed., edited by Taryn Benbow-Pfalzgraf, St. James Press, 2000, Vol. 1, pp. 208–209.

Salter, Mary Jo, "Foreword," in *Amy Clampitt Home Page*, http://www.amyclampitt.org/biography/salter.html (accessed March 20, 2011); originally published in *The Collected Poems of Amy Clampitt*, Alfred A. Knopf, 1997.

Spiegelman, Willard, ed., *Love, Amy: The Selected Letters of Amy Clampitt*, Columbia University Press, 2005.

Suthers, Roderick A., F. Goller, and C. Pytte, "The Neuromuscular Control of Birdsong," in *Philosophical Transactions: Biological Sciences*, Vol. 354, No. 1385, May 29, 1999, pp. 927–39.

Taylor, Thomas, *Thomas Taylor the Platonist: Selected Writings*, edited and with an introduction by Kathleen Raine and George Mills-Harper, Princeton University Press, 1969, pp. 105–21.

van Hoevenberg, Elizabeth, "The White-Throated Sparrow," in *Guide to Nature*, Vol. 8, 1915, p. 175.

Weidensaul, Scott, *Of a Feather: A Brief History of Birding*, Harcourt, 2007.

Williams, John Alexander, *Turning to Nature in Germany: Hiking, Nudism, and Conservation, 1900–1940*, Stanford University Press, 2007.

FURTHER READING

Bootzin, Robert, *The Gypsy in Me*, Golden Boots, 1993.
This is the autobiography of Gypsy Boots, whose real name was Robert Bootzin, a health-food advocate from Big Sur, who was a key figure in transmitting the hippie ideals of that community to popular culture through his numerous appearances on such television programs as *The Steve Allen Show* and *You Bet Your Life*.

Clampitt, Amy, *A Homage to John Keats*, Sarabande, 1984.
This is Clampitt's critical treatment of the romantic poet John Keats.

Clampitt, Roy J., *A Life I Did Not Plan*, Wallace-Homestead, 1966.
The autobiography of Amy Clampitt's father scarcely mentions Amy, who had largely absented herself from her father's life by moving to New York, and who, by 1966, was yet to achieved her literary fame.

Leighton, Ralph, *Tuva or Bust! Richard Feynman's Last Journey*, W. W. Norton, 2000.
In his memoir, Leighton recalls the efforts he made with his friend, the prominent physicist Richard Feynman, to reach Tuva (then inaccessible behind the Iron Curtain). Feynman, a leading figure of the counterculture, died of cancer before he could make the journey, though Leighton completed it in his memory. More than a physical place, Tuva, as Feynman conceived of it, was a sort of countercultural paradise where the human and natural worlds were perfectly integrated. In particular, Feynman, who was also an accomplished musician, studied Tuvan throat-singing, a sound unlike anything else in human speech. The Tuvan fantasy and the Tuvan journey combine to illustrate many of the main themes of "Syrinx."

SUGGESTED SEARCH TERMS

Amy Clampitt

Syrinx AND Amy Clampitt

hippie

counterculture AND Amy Clampitt

Old Sam Peabody, Peabody, Peabody

birding

ecology AND poetry

soundscape ecology

syrinx AND bird

Audubon Society AND Clampitt

Thoughts of Hanoi

NGUYEN THI VINH

1973

In her poem "Thoughts of Hanoi," Nguyen Thi Vinh laments the devastating division of Vietnam into opposing factions in the years leading up to the American War in Vietnam of the 1960s and 1970s. While the conflict would come to revolve around U.S. involvement, Nguyen's poem makes no mention of any foreign presence. Rather, reminiscing about the environs of the North Vietnamese capital of Hanoi as known years ago, the poet pleads with a brotherly relation to value their shared past and keep animosity from fully destroying their relationship.

Central to the poem is its wistful evocation of rural village life through images of active youth and complacent elders. The author Nguyen Thi Vinh is also a novelist and short-story writer. This poem first appeared in print in English in 1973 in *Voices of Modern Asia: An Anthology of Twentieth-Century Asian Literature*, compiled by Dorothy Blair Shimer. It was also included in the 1975 volume *A Thousand Years of Vietnamese Poetry*, edited by Nguyen Ngoc Bich.

AUTHOR BIOGRAPHY

Very little has been written about Nguyen Thi Vinh in English-language publications. She was born in 1924. In the early 1950s, she relocated from the north to South Vietnam and settled in Saigon (now Ho Chi Minh City). She published

the short story "Hai Chi Em" ("The Two Sisters") in 1953 and the novel *Thuong Yeu* ("Affection") in 1955.

In *An Introduction to Vietnamese Literature* (1985), a translation of a French volume, she is grouped with the novelists of her era. She was part of the Van Hoa Ngay Nay (Contemporary Culture) literary group in the 1960s. Her poem "Thoughts of Hanoi" was published in anthologies in 1973 and 1975. In 1983, she immigrated to Norway to join relatives there, and as of the first decade of the twenty-first century she was still participating in literary efforts and forums.

POEM SUMMARY

The text used for this summary is from *A Thousand Years of Vietnamese Poetry*, edited by Nguyen Ngoc Bich, translated by Nguyen Ngoc Bich with Burton Raffel and W. S. Merwin, Knopf, 1975, pp. 184–86. A version of the poem can be found on the following Web page: http://www.globaled.org/vietnamandcambodia/lessons/v_lesson_04.php.

Lines 1–13
"Thoughts of Hanoi" opens by establishing the immediate setting of a dark, cold night early in autumn, lit up now and again by flashes of lightning; it may or may not be raining. This setting evokes in the poet's mind memories of Hanoi, the capital of North Vietnam and later of unified Vietnam. Co-ngu Road was the name of a path originally constructed in the seventeenth century as a dike dividing a lake, Ho Tay, into two lakes. The road is known as perhaps the most beautiful in Hanoi.

Co-ngu Road was renamed Thanh Nien, meaning "Young People," by North Vietnam's Communist president Ho Chi Minh in 1958, so the poet's memories of the road must extend back before that point in time. Line 6 further notes that there has been a decade of division—most likely referring to the political division of North and South Vietnam, a split that was mandated by the Geneva Conference of 1954. Thus, the reader may conclude that the poem was composed or is set around 1964. The perceived date of composition is relevant because at that time, Vietnam's civil war had been under way for about five years, with American involvement still minor but soon to escalate dramatically. By 1964, Vietnam was

embroiled in a war that would prove to last a full decade longer.

Line 7 alludes to this state of ongoing war in noting that, beyond the political border, deep animosity now divides north and south. The poet seems acutely conscious of the horrors of war yet to come, voicing the desire to not just forget the past but also to obliterate the future. In line 10, the poet expresses a longing for something unspecified. In lines 11–13, the poet expresses fear, evoking the tension of lying awake through a long night in distressing circumstances.

Lines 14–22
In line 14, the poet explicitly addresses an audience or reader understood as a brother; this could refer to a literal kinship relation or a figurative relation, as felt between people of the same nationality and/or race. In that the poet is asking the brother about Hanoi, this brother would seem to be currently residing in North Vietnam. The poet wonders about specific locations in the city, such as Hang Dao, a busy commercial street with open markets selling such goods as silk and jewelry; the term *dao* refers to pink apricot blossoms, whose color is similar to that of popular dyed silk of centuries ago. The poet also asks about the temple of Ngoc Son, whose name means "Jade Mountain," which is located on a small island in Hanoi's placid Hoan Kiem Lake. The temple is dedicated to a military hero, Tran Hung Dao, who led the Vietnamese in repulsing a Mongol attack in the thirteenth century. Mention of the temple thus evokes thoughts of both a massive war effort and the tranquility of the setting of the temple itself. Lines 17–22 take the reader, along with the trains that may or may not still run, from Hanoi to the small towns on its outskirts, with the brown thatched roofs of village huts contrasting with the green of the surrounding plants.

Lines 23–39
The third stanza elaborates on the imagery of a small village by portraying local girls and boys and their daily activities. The girls are first described in terms of their appearance, with flushed cheeks, full dresses, and scarves (perhaps either colored or wrapped like a raven's curved bill). Their year-round activities include the farm work of sowing seeds and gathering crops and also making cloth. The boys are described strictly in terms of their activities. They, too, perform farm work—rice especially is cultivated by subsistence farmers throughout the lowland regions of Vietnam—and

also mind shops. At play, the boys run through the meadows, fly kites, and sing, perhaps taking turns or repeating old favorites.

Lines 40–46

The simple images of children at work and play in the third stanza, presented mostly in lines of only one, two, or three words, give that part of the poem a sense of timelessness, of eternal youth. The work being done, essential to daily life, is the work that has been done for centuries by each new generation, from youth to adulthood. The fourth stanza, in a slightly different vein, opens with an image of the expansive, eternal sky and then segues into images that expand to portray village society and community on a progressive, generational scale. The children are now learning the alphabet in school, with their education foreshadowing their future involvement in modern civilization as wage-earning adults. The later phases of the human life cycle, in turn, are highlighted in the images of elders walking to the temple, enjoying the light of the setting sun, and chewing betel leaves, which contain a mild stimulant. As the imagery cycles back to children running, the poet's line of thought is marked as cut off by the dash.

Lines 47–61

The poem now returns to the interrogative form established in the second stanza, once more addressing the brother. The poet asks whether that idyllic peace of village life has become outdated, no longer relevant or possible. The poet wonders whether the brother, too, reaches back to such a past in his mind or envisions what the future will hold. Perhaps most crucially, the poet wonders if the brother views the poet as friend or as enemy. Indeed, the poet fears a future meeting between the two, with the poet in an army marching north—that is, a South Vietnamese force—and the brother advancing south. In such circumstances, either one might end up shooting the other as part of their military duty—but the poet hopes that, beyond this duty, such killing would not be done out of hate.

Lines 62–71

In the penultimate stanza, the poet makes the most personal plea to the brother, recalling how they attended school and charted the courses of their lives together. Whatever differences there may now be, that foundation of shared youth is thought to remain strong. The last stanza opens

with the declaration that the poet and the brother are both men. Since the actual author of the poem, Vinh, is a woman, this would seem to signal that she has written the poem either from the perspective of a Vietnamese man separated from his brother in the North or, more universally, from the perspective of South Vietnam, personified as a single man, addressing North Vietnam, personified as his brother. Alternately, the wording might be intended to express the notion that the author and the brother are both adult human beings; Vietnamese women, too, were expected to participate in the war effort, so the narrator's potential marching with an army does not preclude her being a woman.

The fact of the poet's and brother's manhood comes across as somewhat tragic, especially in juxtaposition with the idyll of childhood presented in the third stanza. If the poet and brother could be concerned only with material needs—that is, the essentials of life, such as food and shelter—then they could perhaps simply attend to those needs and live in peace. However, as men, beyond such needs they have political opinions, ideas of how their nation would best function, and alliances with particular causes. Thus they have been pitted one against the other, swept up by the counteracting forces of colonialism, nationalism, Communism, and democracy—historical forces that leave the individual poet suspended with the open-ended question of why this particular fate, that of friends made enemies, should be theirs.

THEMES

Civil War

Thematically, "Thoughts of Hanoi" revolves around the tragic sense of societal division that comes about when civil war descends upon a nation. The origins of the separation of Vietnam into two states are alluded to only vaguely in the first stanza. It was the international Geneva Conference of 1954 that ended the Franco-Vietminh War, or French Indochina War, by creating the separate states of North and South Vietnam. The North would be led by Ho Chi Minh, commander of the Communist revolutionary force known as the Vietminh, while the South would be led by the former emperor Bao Dai, reinstated at the head of a democratic government.

TOPICS FOR FURTHER STUDY

- Identify a past event or period of time in your life that evokes feelings of nostalgia when you reminisce about it. Using that event or time period, write a poem similar in structure to Vinh's poem, in which you open by situating the reader in the present, transition to a number of stanzas recalling the past, and conclude by meditating on how that past might be regained and/or why it cannot be.

- From the American perspective, Ho Chi Minh, the Communist leader of the Vietminh and of North Vietnam, is often imagined as a ruthless enemy who resorted to underhanded tactics to defeat U.S. forces. To many Vietnamese, however, he is the nation's greatest revolutionary hero. Use electronic and traditional sources to write a paper examining how Ho Chi Minh rose to power in Vietnam, discussing the formative events in his political career. Focus on how he established his public persona among the Vietnamese people, including through Communist and revolu-

tionary activities, suppression of political opponents, and propaganda. In drawing a conclusion, analyze whether the ends justified his various means.

- Paint a picture or construct a collage representing the depiction of rural life in the third and fourth stanzas of "Thoughts of Hanoi."

- Read *And One for All* (1991), a work of young-adult fiction by Theresa Nelson, in which a girl named Geraldine tries to help sustain the friendship between her older brother, who wants to fight in Vietnam, and his best friend, who would rather march for peace. Write a blog post or online journal entry in which you both review the book for your peers (assessing the quality of the writing, the appeal of the plot, or the character development), and compare and contrast the circumstances of these characters with the circumstances of the poet and brother in Vinh's "Thoughts of Hanoi."

The Vietminh had been largely responsible for the successes of rallying the people around a quest for independence and defeating the occupying French forces. However, neither the French nor, in particular, the Americans, who backed them, wanted to allow a Communist government to assume control of the entire nation. Thus, they negotiated for the provisions of the Geneva Accords creating Communist North Vietnam and democratic South Vietnam. The Vietnamese people were given three hundred days to establish residence in one nation or the other according to their preference.

It was perhaps at this point in time that the narrator of Vinh's poem departed Hanoi for the South, leaving behind a "brother" whose political interests diverged from the his own. These circumstances are likely to call to the American reader's mind tales of tragic family division caused by the U.S. Civil War, when at times brothers fought

against brothers, fathers against sons. Any particular person's choice of allegiance could depend on a variety of factors, including not only political inclinations but also field of work, family circumstances, kinship connections, regional affiliations, and so forth. Many of those factors would have come into play in Vietnam.

In this poem, the narrator focuses on the emotional circumstances of this political division for individuals. The divide is first mentioned in line 6, and the ensuing line immediately characterizes that divide as one of intense animosity, of hatred, yet in terms of tone, the poem reflects no hatred whatsoever. On the contrary, after the chill and fear of the first stanza, the poet assumes a warm, conversational tone in depicting the tranquil side of life in and around Hanoi. The mention of Hang Dao evokes the bustling energy of a traditional community marketplace, while the temple on the lake is one of Hanoi's most tranquil scenes. The trains, like the marketplace, can represent communal connection—connection about which the poet is currently uncertain.

The second stanza (comprising nine lines punctuated four times by question marks) establishes a framework of uncertainty in which the idyllic imaginings of the third and fourth stanzas are set. The images of the girls and boys working and playing and the elders living out their lives in peace are thus lent a nebulous, dreamlike quality; they may or may not represent life in North Vietnam in the present. It is the state of civil war that is accountable for both the threat to these idyllic scenes and the poet's uncertainty about them. The fifth stanza, with four more question marks in the first eight lines, returns to the framework of uncertainty.

Notably, for all the uncertainty surrounding the political fates of North and South Vietnam and the potential deaths of so many Vietnamese—including the poet and the brother—what the poet seems to find most important is the uncertainty surrounding the relationship with the brother. From the middle of the fifth stanza through the closing lines, the key question is whether the poet and the brother remain friends at heart or have become enemies. The poet notes the possibility that either one might end up killing the other almost with indifference—as if the courses of their lives are simply a matter of fate, with each carrying out his fate in fulfilling his perceived duty.

What is crucial, rather, as suggested by the last two lines of the fifth stanza—perhaps the most poignant lines in the poem—is whether death will be inflicted with or without hate. The sixth stanza amounts to a plea to the brother to keep hatred out of his heart, to remember the warmth of childhood connections. The seventh stanza is a lament, as the poet acknowledges that they are children no longer. They are men, men who have been swept up in a civil war shaped by political events utterly beyond their control, thus becoming, one way or another, friends and enemies alike.

Nostalgia

At the heart of Vinh's poem is nostalgia for life before the war in the villages surrounding Hanoi. The poem opens with nighttime darkness in an uncertain locale, relieved by intermittent flashes of lightning that only serve to leave the night darker in their wake. The poet speaks of burying the past, but what is meant is the part of the past that has brought about division and animosity. From the second stanza onward, in fact, the poet directly seeks to conjure a peaceful past, as the setting shifts from the present dark, placeless void to the environs of Hanoi as the poet knew them years ago.

The metaphor comparing the jungle to the sea at the end of the second stanza evokes a scene of green palm leaves wavering in the breeze like rippling water—a transitional scene that in turn lends the wavering, ephemeral quality of recalled memory to the ensuing stanzas. By the time the girls' shining eyes appear early in the third stanza, the setting elicited in the reader's mind is almost certainly a sunny one, with no further mention of storms appearing. In this context, the farm work comes across not as laborious but as fulfilling, allowing the children fresh air and moderate exercise, meanwhile instilling them with pride, for having created nourishment for their families from the soil, and a spiritual connection to all the generations who farmed the land just so through the centuries before. (Conceptions of labor by children as being absolutely negative may come to the Western reader's mind, but arguably, farming, using one's hands and whole body to constantly perform various physical tasks, is a far more natural and healthful activity in comparison with enduring the severe restriction of movement and constant intellectual and social tension of the modern school environment.)

The mention of traditional textile work continues the imagery in a timeless vein; the images could be from ten years before the writing of the poem or from decades upon decades further in the past. Likewise, the descriptions of the boys elicit nostalgia in the reader's mind, even though the images are presented in only the most essential terms: through these nine lines, only one word, the second to last, serves as an adjective, and even that is a participle (a verb serving as an adjective). The sunny setting in the reader's mind is explicitly confirmed with the appearance of the perfectly blue sky in the fourth stanza. After the mention of the placid elders, who serve as symbols of fulfilling lives lived, the imagery cycles back—as nostalgia-fueled sentiments tend to do—returning to the children at play. While the poem then proceeds to elaborate on the division between poet and brother, the nostalgic images leave the poet and reader alike lingering in that peaceful past and wondering whether it can ever be reclaimed.

The setting of the poem is Hanoi, Vietnam.
(Luciano Mortula | Shutterstock.com)

STYLE

Free Verse

The form of "Thoughts of Hanoi" is free verse, meaning that there is no rhyme or meter (meter is the pattern of stressed and unstressed syllables in poetry). The English version of the poem is a translation of the Vietnamese original. Although some ambitious translators succeed in mimicking meter and rhyme effects through deliberate word selection, the rhyme and meter of the original poem is extremely difficult to trace.

Vietnam has a long, hallowed poetic tradition, with most poetry from before the twentieth century composed within structurally elegant metric and rhyme parameters. Especially prominent is six-eight meter, in which a given couplet (set of two lines) features a line of six syllables followed by a line of eight syllables. Vietnamese is a monosyllabic language, meaning that almost universally, each syllable equals a single word. It is also a tonal language, such that meanings of

syllables change if they are inflected differently, with two different flat, or level, tones and four different sharp tones used. Within a six-eight couplet, the even-numbered syllables alternate in having flat or sharp tones; the final syllable of the sixth line will rhyme with the sixth syllable of the eight line; and the final syllable of the eight line will rhyme with the final syllable of the six line of the ensuing couplet. Thus, using internal rhyme, connections between lines through rhyme can be continued indefinitely.

The French occupation of Indochina in part ushered Vietnamese poetry toward inclusion of free verse. The nation's new poetry movement came about in the 1930s, with the traditional poetic forms often abandoned in favor of original meters or unstructured verse. The lines in Vinh's "Thoughts of Hanoi," presumably composed in the 1960s, are short enough to suggest that they do not represent a traditional form along the lines of six-eight meter. Also, while traditional forms typically employ couplets or quatrains (set of four lines), Vinh's stanzas have odd and varying numbers of lines. Thus, the poem indeed seems, in English translation as well as in the original Vietnamese, to be pure free verse.

Pastoral Poetry

"Thoughts of Hanoi" is in part representative of a well-established pastoral tradition in Vietnamese poetry. Pastoral poetry portrays the beauty and innocence of a simple, rural life. As Kevin Bowen notes in his essay "Vietnamese Poetry: A Sense of Place," it is perhaps unsurprising that "the poetry of a people deeply uprooted by war should be a poetry of rootedness; a poetry focusing on the endurance and continuity of life in the villages, in the highlands, and along the deltas." While the war itself demanded the attention of Vietnamese poets in the 1960s, even these poets often turned their attention toward the central Vietnamese poetic themes of love and home. Vinh's poem effectively unites these two themes, as love for home is drawn on to support the poet's plea for brotherly love to endure.

Vinh does not devote many lines to depicting the natural surroundings of the Vietnamese countryside; beyond the opening lines, only the last line of the second stanza and the opening line of the fourth stanza offer descriptions of the environs (while also the evening sun appears in the fifth line of the fourth stanza). However, by virtue of the second stanza's last line, the rural setting is implicit throughout the third and fourth stanzas, providing the reader with a series of images of the people and their activities inherent to that setting. These stanzas form the core of the poem both structurally and emotionally. This pastoral core thus serves as the communal ideal that the poet reaches back toward in pleading with the brother to let love for home prevent hatred from overtaking his heart.

HISTORICAL CONTEXT

Vietnamese Independence

"Thoughts of Hanoi" focuses on the internal ruptures caused by the division of Vietnam, upon the breakup of French Indochina, into North and South Vietnam in 1954 and by the state of civil war that overtook Vietnam in the late 1950s and early 1960s. The Vietnam War is often conceived in the American imagination as one marked by political and moral uncertainty about whether the United States should have been involved and by the ultimate futility and sadness of the effort, with more than fifty-eight thousand American soldiers losing their lives and North Vietnam emerging victorious. Vinh's poem, however, makes no reference to U.S. involvement, in either personal or political terms.

While U.S. political involvement with the government of South Vietnam was part of what inspired Communist forces to launch a revolution there—the South was by then considered a "puppet state" by North Vietnam's Ho Chi Minh and those loyal to him—the war was at first largely fought among the Vietnamese. As of the spring of 1964, only some twenty thousand U.S. Army personnel were serving, primarily in advisory capacities, in South Vietnam. President Lyndon Johnson, after responding to inflammatory incidents—including a purported torpedo attack that turned out to have never occurred—with sustained air bombings, finally dispatched full battalions of troops to the South in 1965. Over one hundred and eighty thousand troops were stationed there by year's end, and within two years, over five hundred thousand U.S. troops were present. Because the American presence became so significant beginning in 1965, Vinh's failure to mention any American or foreign role in her poem seems to confirm that it was written before then, most likely in 1964, when the American personnel commitment was still minor and bore only peripheral relevance from the Vietnamese perspective.

Vietnam's complex modern history of foreign occupation extends back to the nineteenth century, when France took a militant interest in availing itself of the natural resources of the region, with help from cheap labor extorted from the native population, which it sought to convert to Christianity. The first French attack on Vietnamese territory occurred in 1858. By 1884, France had conquered the region and issued the Treaty of the Protectorate, asserting its control over Vietnam. Over the next twenty-five years, French Indochina came to include all of the Indochinese peninsula except Siam (modern Thailand).

It was during this occupation, in 1911, that the young Ho Chi Minh, born in 1890 and originally named Nguyen Sinh Cung, gained employment on an outbound ship, finding himself in France at the outbreak of World War I. He joined the French Socialist Party and was inspired by the writings of the Soviet revolutionary Vladimir Lenin, who espoused Marxist theory, purporting that in a colonized society, imbalances between workers and the owners of capital ultimately leave oppressed workers no choice but to stage revolution to gain independence. At this time Nguyen Sinh Cung began using the pseudonym Nguyen Ai Quoc, or "Nguyen the Patriot."

In 1920 he helped found the French Communist Party, and in 1923, he moved to Moscow and began working for Communist International, or Comintern, which gave him experience in Communist political efforts in both the Soviet Union and China. By 1925, he was in south China training activists in Leninist approaches through the Vietnamese Revolutionary Youth League, and by 1930, he had formed the Indochina Communist Party (ICP). Finally, in 1941, Nguyen Ai Quoc, having assumed the name Ho Chi Minh—"He Who Enlightens"—slipped back into Vietnam, and he and other ICP members formed the League for the Independence of Vietnam, known as the Vietminh, whose direct goal was to overthrow French colonial rule.

During World War II, the French, who had been cowed into submission to Nazi German occupiers at home, allowed Japanese occupiers to take advantage of the resources of Indochina rather than risk outright military defeat. Meanwhile, the Vietminh sought to strengthen its domestic organization. When Japan surrendered to the Allies in August 1945, Ho Chi Minh and

COMPARE
&
CONTRAST

- **1960s–1970s:** The Vietnamese people are at war, divided between allegiance to Hanoi, capital of the Democratic Republic of Vietnam (North Vietnam)—a Communist state—and to Saigon, capital of the Republic of Vietnam (South Vietnam), favored by Catholics and non-Communists.

  Today: The Socialist Republic of Vietnam, a unified nation since 1975, has its capital in Hanoi, while its largest city is Ho Chi Minh City (formerly Saigon). While the Communist Party runs the nation, the people are themselves largely depoliticized and interested primarily in maintaining peace in independence.

- **1960s–1970s:** With the onset of U.S. bombing raids against North Vietnam in 1965, institutions of higher education are relocated to the countryside, and the period of study is extended by one year, allowing students and professors to continue their work as well as possible under the circumstances.

  Today: With Confucian values as well as modern economic circumstances urging young Vietnamese people to gain higher degrees, university enrollment quadruples through the 1990s and continues to increase steadily. In turn, the number of higher-education institutions increases from two to three hundred through the early 2000s.

- **1960s–1970s:** As part of the campaign against North Vietnam, U.S. forces use chemical weapons like flammable napalm and Agent Orange, which kills plants that could be used by the enemy for cover but contaminates food and water sources. In all, by the war's end, some four million Vietnamese soldiers and civilians from both sides, 10 percent of the total population, are killed.

  Today: More than thirty years after the war's end, the population of Vietnam remains skewed toward youth—as of 2005, half the population was under twenty-five—and women, with elderly women outnumbering elderly men by nearly a million. Some three million Vietnamese are estimated to have been exposed to Agent Orange during the war, with one million citizens still suffering serious health problems in 2005; some one hundred and fifty thousand children survive with horrific birth defects caused by their parents' exposure to the chemical.

---

the Vietminh were poised to wrest control from the lingering Japanese in Hanoi, in the north, and declare the independence of the Democratic Republic of Vietnam (DRV). At this time the Vietminh's popular appeal was not yet widespread, but it quickly suppressed alternate factions and dominated the newly formed DRV government.

Despite these developments, French troops arrived to reclaim their nation's colony in the fall of 1945, soon occupying much of southern Vietnam. A settlement was nearly reached in 1946 in which the Republic of Vietnam would have been recognized as a free state within the French Union, but France's commissioner of Indochina preempted this by recognizing the Republic of Cochinchina, in southern Vietnam, as a free state. Thus, two distinct Vietnamese republics had been called into existence, one in the north and one in the south. Soon, Vietminh troops clashed with French naval vessels, the French retaliated, and the Franco-Vietminh War had begun. The French, strained from World War II, used limited manpower—in part relying on colonial soldiers from Africa as well as Indochina—and destructive tactics like aerial attacks with napalm that allowed civilian casualties to mount. To neutralize the French forces' material advantages, the Vietminh adapted and refined strategies of guerilla warfare, favoring surprise engagements over large-scale battles.

Stanza two describes the villages of Vietnam. *(Khoroshunova Olga | Shutterstock.com)*

In 1949, facing a stalemate, French authorities tried to create a unified Vietnam, with Saigon as the capital, naming as head of state the
former emperor Bao Dai, with whom the Vietminh were antagonistic. By this time, the Vietminh were able to attain support for the DRV
from the newly established Communist government of the People's Republic of China. In turn,
the United States recognized the southern government led by Bao Dai and lent financial support to the French effort. Meanwhile, fighting
continued, with French forces suffering substantial losses in major battles.

By 1954, after the Vietminh achieved a decisive victory at Dien Bien Phu, the French were
ready to capitulate. That year, the Geneva
Accords officially demarcated the division of Vietnam at the seventeenth parallel, in the interest of
allowing for military disengagement, with the
Vietminh regrouping in North Vietnam. In
South Vietnam at this time, Bao Dai named Ngo
Dinh Diem prime minister. Diem was an anti-
Communist Catholic who had recently resided in
the United States and did not have a political
following among the Vietnamese. Thus, South
Vietnam became more vulnerable to DRV prop-
aganda denouncing the South as a puppet state.
Elections were intended to be held in 1956 to
reunify Vietnam—but Ngo Dinh Diem and the
United States recognized that the Communist rev-
olutionary hero Ho Chi Minh would undoubtedly

have become Vietnam's president, and the elections were never held.

U.S. Involvement in Vietnam

In the several years following the division of Vietnam, Ngo Dinh Diem's government evolved
toward dictatorship, which the United States
nonetheless supported with over $200 million per
year, some 80 percent of which was used to bolster
South Vietnam's armed forces, then including
around one hundred and fifty thousand men. By
1959, North Vietnam was officially resolved to
wage long-term warfare to overthrow the repressive U.S.-backed regime in the South, and southern insurgents formed the National Liberation
Front (NLF) to fight in conjunction with the
North, using such tactics as assassination and
arson. Their attacks intensified through 1961,
reaching the vicinity of Saigon.

By 1963, open warfare was upon the region,
as South Vietnamese forces, though superior in
number and weaponry (thanks to U.S. support),
were routed by the NLF at the battle of Ap Bac,
near Saigon. That year, Diem was assassinated,
as was President John F. Kennedy, who might
have intended to withdraw U.S. troops rather
than escalate the war. As chaos descended upon
South Vietnam's government, President Lyndon
Johnson took the stance that a Communist victory would be unacceptable. Since the South was
losing ground quickly, Johnson decided, after

harassment of U.S. targets by the North Vietnamese, to push the Gulf of Tonkin Resolution through Congress in 1964, essentially enabling him to wage undeclared war. American troops poured into the region in 1965, and the war rapidly became Americanized. By this time, the evidence suggests, Vinh had composed her poem "Thoughts of Hanoi," mourning the vast tragedy unfolding in divided Vietnam. It would be another ten years and there would be several million Vietnamese casualties before North Vietnamese forces would overrun Saigon, claim victory, and unite Vietnam as a Communist nation.

CRITICAL OVERVIEW

In the absence of English-language commentary on Vinh's work, her poem is best understood within the modern Vietnamese poetic tradition, in particular among works inspired by the civil conflict that evolved into the American War in Vietnam.

In *Mountain River: Vietnamese Poetry from the Wars, 1948–1993*, Nguyen Ba Chung notes that throughout Vietnamese history, poetry has played a substantial role in defining and sustaining a national identity. This has especially been true through times of foreign occupation: Vietnam was occupied by China for seven hundred and fifty years in the first millennium, by France for the sixty years before World War II, and, in various respects in South Vietnam, by the United States for the twenty years ending in 1975. Virtually all significant Vietnamese historical figures, including politicians and military heroes, have left behind works of poetry.

In *A Thousand Years of Vietnamese Poetry*, Nguyen Ngoc Bich notes that the nation's thirty years of incessant conflict following World War II proved "strangely productive in poetry." As he asserts, "That the new poetry in Vietnam is successful—having something universal to say about war as well as about the particular Vietnamese circumstances—is a tribute to the strength and fiber of the Vietnamese, and to the genius of their literary tradition."

In *Memories of a Lost War: American Poetic Responses to the Vietnam War*, Subarno Chattarji notes in a concluding chapter on Vietnamese works that poems like Vinh's "Thoughts of Hanoi" serve to highlight "an aspect of the war often overlooked in American representations:

that it was a civil war and that families were divided by ideology or misfortune." Chattarji further notes that in such poems, "the idyllic past seems increasingly mythical, a haunting 'echo' that makes the present an unendurable nightmare." In declining to delve into the nightmarish aspects of her nation's civil conflict, Vinh presents the idyllic past as one that might someday be reclaimed.

CRITICISM

Michael Allen Holmes

Holmes is a writer and editor. In the following essay, he examines "Thoughts of Hanoi" for evidence of influence from Vietnam's three most significant religious traditions: Buddhism, Confucianism, and Taoism.

The three Eastern religious traditions of Buddhism, Confucianism, and Taoism are different schools of thought that have converged throughout eastern Asia. In Vietnam, as Nguyen Ngoc Bich notes in *A Thousand Years of Vietnamese Poetry*, there was a collective effort "to bring about religious harmony in a movement known as 'Three Religions, One Source.' Because the three religions are not considered to be mutually exclusive, this harmony spilled over into everyday life as well." The poetic tradition, Bich notes, likewise reflects this religious harmony. Vinh's poem "Thoughts of Hanoi" indeed seems to present perspectives characteristic of each of these religions.

Buddhism, Confucianism, and Taoism offer divergent perspectives on the workings of the universe but in many important ways do not directly contradict each other, as some religions do. For example, Islam, Judaism, and Christianity all disagree regarding the divinity of Jesus of Nazareth and the prophet Muhammad. The Eastern religions, however, are not centered on a divine founder but rather on a way of life in line with writings and thoughts of a respected teacher.

Buddhism is founded in the teachings of the Buddha, Siddhartha Gautama, who lived in India in the fifth century BCE, but Buddhist beliefs do not revolve around reverence toward the Buddha; rather, the mode of life he espoused—dissolving the self on the way to enlightenment—is what is essential. Similarly, while Confucius, who lived in China also around the fifth century BCE, is the founding figure of Confucianism, his ideology

WHAT DO I READ NEXT?

- Ho Chi Minh kept a diary while detained in prison in China in the 1940s, and the poems found therein (although written in Chinese) are lauded as exemplary in the Vietnamese tradition. One translation, published by Steve Bradbury in 2004, is *Poems from the Prison Diary of Ho Chi Minh.*

- While early Vietnamese poetry was composed in the traditional scholarly language of Chinese, a Vietnamese script, *chu nom*, was introduced in the late thirteenth century and first popularized as a poetic medium by the Renaissance-type genius Nguyen Trai (1380–1442). His verse is available in *Beyond the Court Gate: Selected Poems of Nguyen Trai* (2010), edited by Nguyen Do and Paul Hoover.

- *The Tale of Kieu* (1813) is Vietnam's most renowned epic poem, 3,250 lines composed in 1813 by Nguyen Du. The tale treats the union of the three religious traditions of Confucianism, Buddhism, and Taoism in Vietnam through the story of a man who is greatly troubled by the misery and strife he sees in his countrymen. An English translation was published in 1973 by Huynh Sanh Thong, subtitled *The Classic Vietnamese Verse Novel.*

- *Children of the Dragon: Selected Tales from Vietnam* (2001), a collection appropriate for young adults compiled by Sherry Garland, includes six folktales passed down through the centuries, shedding light on Vietnamese customs and values.

- Thanh T. Nguyen and the American poet Bruce Weigl have collected poems written by North Vietnamese soldiers in *Poems from Captured Documents* (1994), a bilingual edition shedding light on the humanity of America's enemy.

- David Chanoff and Doan Van Toai provide an oral history of the lives and outlooks of the Vietnamese people during the American War in *Vietnam: A Portrait of Its People at War* (2009).

- Translation and discussion of verse produced during the Spanish Civil War, fought in the late 1930s between rebelling conservative Nationalists and the more liberal Republicans, is provided by the British scholar Valentine Cunningham in *The Penguin Book of Spanish Civil War Verse* (1980).

- Yusef Komunyakaa, a famous African American poet, served in Vietnam, and his collection *Dien Cai Dau* (1988)—the phrase being Vietnamese slang for the "crazy" American soldiers—is a verse treatment of his time there. Some of the poems stem from his particular experience as an African American soldier.

- *Fallen Angels* (2008) is the story of Perry, a teenager from Harlem who volunteers to serve in Vietnam. This young-adult novel by Walter Dean Myers highlights the injustices faced by African American soldiers who fought in the Vietnam War.

---

revolves around fundamental rules of virtuous conduct, not around the practitioner's opinion of or relationship with Confucius himself. Taoism, which also originated in China some centuries before the Common Era, has several founding figures considered the authors of essential texts, but here, too, what is central is the Taoist approach to harmonizing with the way of the universe.

Of the three religious philosophies, the Confucian influence on "Thoughts of Hanoi" is perhaps the slightest. Bich concisely describes Confucianism as marked by "clear-cut imperatives of authority and 'right' action." Confucius highly stressed the importance of filial piety (a son's reverence and obedience toward his father, who in turn should treat the son kindly). Likewise, a younger brother is expected to be dutiful

> GIVEN THE GRAVE WEIGHT ATTACHED TO DESIRE IN TAOISM, THE LAST LINE OF CHAPTER 57, FRAMED AS SPOKEN BY A POETIC SAGE, MAKES A FITTING ECHO OF VINH'S POEM IN A SINGLE SENTENCE: 'I DESIRE NOT TO DESIRE, AND THE PEOPLE OF THEMSELVES ARE GENUINE AND SIMPLE, LIKE UNCARVED WOOD.'"

to an elder brother—a relationship evoked in Vinh's poem by the repeated addressing of a brother. Whether the brother is younger or older, the poet seems to consider him an equal, even if one poised in opposition, and expresses the hope that the two might continue to treat each other with the respect due a family member.

The poet's sense of duty further comes into play with regard to the possibility of military service, a potential obligation that could involve the poet killing the brother or vice versa. The poet's hope that this be done, if necessary, without hatred—that is, perhaps, humanely—reflects the injunction, as found in *The Wisdom of Confucius*, "Even in killing men, observe the rules of propriety." Regarding the images of children in the poem, Confucius was a great advocate of seeking knowledge, and thus a Confucian would surely approve of the mention of children joyfully learning the alphabet in school.

Buddhist notions are reflected in several aspects of the poem. Lines 8 and 9, in which the poet speaks of doing away with both the past and the future, call to mind the process of self-negation that a Buddhist undertakes in seeking enlightenment. To attain the peace of mind leading to enlightenment, one must gain release from all desires and attachments motivated by the ego, whether such worldly interests and connections are considered positive or negative. That is, the mind must be completely unharnessed from any limiting self-definitions and self-conceptions that have formed over the course of one's life, such as may be instilled by friends and family.

Zen Buddhism, in particular, stresses mindful and honorable living in the present, with the utmost attention paid to precisely whatever one is doing at any given moment. Thus, both sentiments about the past (like shame or pride in past acts, judgment of one's failings, or grief over the absence of a lost loved one) and sentiments about the future (like anticipation of a hoped-for event or anxiety over performance in a task) are gradually expelled from one's consciousness.

Such a state seems to be what the poet is seeking in lines 8 and 9, although pressing wartime circumstances make this difficult—as indicated in lines 51 and 52, in the fifth stanza, in which the poet admits to being caught up in grasping for the past and envisioning what the future may bring. From a Buddhist perspective, this mental churning signifies emotional agitation to be quieted; perhaps the poem was written in part to accomplish this. In specifically speaking of burning the future in the first stanza, Vinh may also be alluding to the self-immolation—sacrificing oneself by fire—undertaken by some Buddhist monks in protest against the repressive U.S.-backed government of South Vietnam in the 1960s. In such an act, one literally burns one's own future.

The descriptions of the daily activities of children in the third stanza of the poem further evoke Zen Buddhist precepts of conscious living. The images of girls and boys engaged in various forms of labor, presented mostly through gerunds (verbs used as nouns) unadorned by adjectives, convey the sense of action being performed in total absorption; the action is no more and no less than the very action itself. The elders, in turn, are able to stroll to the temple and bask in the sunshine with total mindfulness in the present. They need not dwell on the past because it is too late for them to relive their lives, and they need not concern themselves with the future because, while their own may prove short, the future that matters is personified before them in the children.

Absent from the third and fourth stanzas is any mention of the adults in between the children and the elders, reflecting the fact that men and women in the prime of life were the most likely to be swept up in matters of war. The manner in which the imagery cycles from children to elders and back to children at the end of the fourth stanza is suggestive of Buddhist conceptions of reincarnation or rebirth, whereby (put simply) one's spirit comes to inhabit another creature after one's death, with one's karma determining the dignity of that life form. That is, in terms of the poem's images, the elders are, in effect, reborn as the children running at the end of the fourth stanza.

The Vietnamese jungle (*nodff | Shutterstock.com*)

A Buddhist mindset is furthermore reflected in the poet's rejection of hatred in the fifth stanza. Part of the ideal of present mindfulness is universal compassion for all creatures; if one's soul is held open to the souls of others, one's interactions will always be infused with love.

In many respects, Taoist philosophy, like the metaphysics of Buddhist religious philosophy, can be difficult for the Western mind especially to grasp. The *Tao Te Ching*, for example, attributed to a contemporary of Confucius's known as Lao-tzu, is presented in verse rather than prose, and many of the lines and chapters seem self-contradictory or cryptic. Regarding the concept of returning to the Way—the Tao—the scholar Robert Henricks notes in his translation of the ancient work that "it seems clear that Lao-tzu wants people as adults to return to some things they all possessed more fully as children—namely genuineness, sincerity, and spontaneity."

The opening of chapter 55 of the *Tao Te Ching* reads: "One who embraces the fullness of Virtue, / Can be compared to a newborn babe." Such advocacy for a return to the innocence of childhood is conveyed in the third and fourth stanzas of Vinh's poem. The notion of a return to simple village life is analogous to a return to childhood, and so the images representing children absorbed in village life are especially well harmonized. Chapter 80 of the *Tao Te Ching* portrays the self-sufficient village community as an ideal, in which the humble farming people "will relish their food, / Regard their clothing as beautiful, / Delight in their customs, / And feel safe and secure in their homes."

The last stanza of Vinh's poem can be read as representing a significant aspect of both Buddhism and Taoism, which is the quieting of desire, the reaching of a state where one is not controlled by one's desires or, ideally, feels no desire at all. As the Vietnamese Buddhist monk Thich Nhat Hanh notes in *Zen Keys*, Buddhism recognizes three gates of personal liberation: emptiness, signlessness (or nonconceptualization), and aimlessness. Of the last, he writes, "*Aimlessness* is the attitude of someone who does not feel the need to run after anything, realize or obtain anything," an attitude often understood as "nondesire."

In the *Tao Te Ching*, Chapter 46 states, "Of crimes—none is greater than having things one desires; / Of disasters—none is greater than not knowing when one has enough. / Of defects—none brings more sorrow than the desire to attain." This chapter also asserts, "When the world lacks the Way, war horses are reared in the suburbs," thus directly equating desire with war. In the final stanza of "Thoughts of Hanoi," the poet laments that, as civilized adults, they are creatures not merely of need but also of desire. Given the grave weight attached to desire in Taoism, the last line of Chapter 57, framed as spoken by a poetic sage, makes a fitting echo of Vinh's poem in a single sentence: "I desire not to desire, and the people of themselves are genuine and simple, like uncarved wood."

Source: Michael Allen Holmes, Critical Essay on "Thoughts of Hanoi," in *Poetry for Students*, Gale, Cengage Learning, 2012.

Catherine C. Dominic

Dominic is a novelist and a freelance writer and editor. In the following essay, she explores the elegiac characteristics of "Thoughts of Hanoi," emphasizing that the poem is predominantly a lament for a past way of life, and the possible future such a way of life once contained.

Nguyen Thi Vinh's poem "Thoughts of Hanoi" frames recollections of an idealized past with ruminations on the hopelessness of the present and fears about the way the future will unfold. Vinh incorporates repeated references to time within the narrator's shifting conceptions of the nature of Vietnam in various states of existence. In this manner, the poet conveys both an enduring sense of loss and a pervasive sense of despair. The poem was most likely written during the conflict between North Vietnam and South Vietnam, a military struggle that would blossom into a full-scale war in which the United States aided South Vietnam in their resistance against the Communist North Vietnam. Although the poem does not specifically depict battles and the violence of war, it is colored by the tragedy of conflict. In many ways, "Thoughts of Hanoi" may be regarded as an elegy, a poem lamenting a keenly felt sense of loss over the death of a person, or, in this case, a loss of a way of life. (Note: As various translations of the poem divide stanzas differently, the discussion that follows will refer to portions of the poem by line number rather than by stanza.)

> IN MANY WAYS, 'THOUGHTS OF HANOI' MAY BE REGARDED AS AN ELEGY, A POEM LAMENTING A KEENLY FELT SENSE OF LOSS OVER THE DEATH OF A PERSON, OR, IN THIS CASE, A LOSS OF A WAY OF LIFE."

In the first thirteen lines, Vinh sets the tone of the poem by opening with a storm raging at night. The poet speaks of the pervasive darkness and cold of the night, and how after each flash of lightning, the night seems to congeal further as the chill sets in. Significantly, the lightning is not a source of light providing respite or comfort. Rather, it only highlights the gloom of the night, underscoring the way the darkness seems to congeal, to solidify. Vinh speaks of the separation of the north and the south in Vietnam. Such division inspires in the poet a desire to negate a past that is gone forever, and to similarly obliterate a future in which Vietnam is so divided, and so ruled by the fear and hatred of war. In speaking of the interminable nights of war, when she waited in terror for morning, the poet describes a sense of hopeless longing for a reality that no longer exists. In these lines, then, Vinh establishes the framework of her elegy by painting a picture of the present as a grim void.

In the next section of the poem, lines fourteen through twenty-two, the poet addresses a fellow countryman as a family member, asking about familiar places in Hanoi: a temple, a main street. The lines almost take the form of a letter written by the poet to a close friend or family member. The poet questions her fellow Vietnamese about the train lines that used to run from Hanoi to the smaller, nearby towns. Some of these villages are identified by name, and described in a fond manner, as the poet recalls the thatched roofs dotting a verdant landscape. This idealization of the past is common in an elegy, particularly in one with such a pastoral slant, depicting rural life in favorable terms, often romanticizing this way of living and lamenting it as a thing of the past.

Such a favorable view of the pastoral past continues in the next section of the poem, lines twenty-three through forty-six. These lines are linked with those that came directly before, when the poet, after questioning whether or not trains still ran from Hanoi to the villages, describes the contrast of the brown thatched roofs and the green meadows. Vinh focuses on the old and the young of the villages, echoing her concern with the past and the future as expressed in the opening lines of the poem. Young girls are described in terms of their health, vitality, and industriousness. They plant and harvest, spin yarn, and weave throughout the year. Similarly young boys plow, work in the fields and toil in small village shops. They run through the fields, flying kites, and singing. In these lines, Vinh recalls rural and village life as it was before the military conflicts, spoken of in the opening lines of the poem, divided her country. Vinh goes on to depict joyful children playing under a blue sky, and refers as well to their studies at school. A similarly peaceful, ideal picture of old age is presented in the poem, as elderly men walk contentedly to worship at their temple, while the grandmothers of the village enjoy the setting sun and the company of one another, while they watch the cavorting children.

In these scenes, the past is captured in an idealized manner. In looking back to the opening language and imagery of the poem, however, it is this very past that the poet spoke of burying. The present moment the poet captures in the opening lines is so hopeless and tragic, that the beauty of the past is almost too painful for the poet to endure. Not only is the past at stake in the mind of the poet, but the future is at risk of being irreparably damaged as well. In the opening lines, the poet states her desire to destroy the future in flames. The village children she so lovingly depicts in the later lines are part of the future that Vinh predicts will be unendurable. Vinh's lament, then, begins in the poem's opening lines. Both the past and the future are lost to her. In the beautiful images of a peaceful past, in the loving characterizations of the village children, Vinh carefully depicts all that can no longer be remembered without pain, all that can no longer be hoped for. This is no mere wistful nostalgia; Vinh's depiction of the past in such idealized terms emphasizes the senseless tragedy of its loss.

Vinh then, in lines forty-seven through sixty-five, returns the direct address to her Vietnamese countryman, asking him his view on the state of such a contented, peaceful rural life. She wonders if it is now a completely extinct way of life. Despite her stated desire to destroy, at least in her mind, her memory of the past and any expectations of the future, the poet asks her countryman if he too, sometimes lives in the past, sometimes wonders about the future. Vinh questions how her countryman regards her, as friend or enemy.

The future the poet now imagines is one filled with fear and violence. She constructs a scene in which she and her countryman face each other, as one marches north, and the other south. They will be forced to shoot at one another, she concludes. The poet begs of her countryman that this not be done out of hate. She begs him to remember their happy childhood, the hopes they then had for the future. The divisions revealed in the opening of the poem are mirrored here at the end, as the poet once again draws attention to the conflict between the north and the south. Just as the poet longs futilely for the past in the poem's beginning, so does she, in the closing of the poem, beg her countryman to remember during the heat of battle the comradeship of their youth. The separation of countrymen outlined in the poem's opening is protested fervently in the closing, as the poet emphatically declares the communal connections of the Vietnamese.

In the final lines of the poem, lines sixty-six through seventy-one, the poet begs her countryman to remember a sense of connection that goes deeper than material desires that motivate people. Ending the poem with a question, the poet wonders how this conflicted fate could befall them, they who should be friends, but in the present, exist as enemies.

In these last sections of the poem, then, Vinh's framework structure is made clear, and complete. The poem opened with a bleak portrait of the present state of Vietnam, and the present state of mind of the poet. The middle section of the poem portrayed the past in a glowing, idealized fashion. The final section of the poem mirrors the first, and provides the closing frame. The emphasis on the present in this last section is underscored by the poet when she asks her countryman again how things are now in Hanoi, wonders if the past gone forever, and questions whether the forecast for the future must be reshaped to correspond with the hopelessness of the present. By framing a romanticized past, a past that contained within in it the potential for a bright future, within two dismal, hopeless characterizations of the present, Vinh laments the loss of both past and future. Her elegy mourns the extinguishing of the hope that the happy, productive, content village life that once existed in Vietnam shall ever be returned to.

Source: Catherine C. Dominic, Critical Essay on "Thoughts of Hanoi," in *Poetry for Students*, Gale, Cengage Learning, 2012.

SOURCES

Anderson, David L., *The Vietnam War*, Palgrave Macmillan, 2005, pp. 21–60.

Ashwill, Mark A., with Thai Ngoc Diep, *Vietnam Today: A Guide to a Nation at a Crossroads*, Intercultural Press, 2005, pp. 27–45.

Bich, Nguyen Ngoc, ed., *A Thousand Years of Vietnamese Poetry*, translated by Nguyen Ngoc Bich with Burton Raffel and W. S. Merwin, Knopf, 1975, pp. xv–xxi, 4–5, 10–11, 20–21, 24, 39, 178.

Boudarel, Georges, and Nguyen Van Ky, *Hanoi: City of the Rising Dragon*, translated by Claire Duiker, Rowman & Littlefield, 2002, pp. vii–xiii, 115–49.

Bowen, Kevin, "Vietnamese Poetry: A Sense of Place," in *Manoa*, Vol. 7, No. 2, Winter 1995, pp. 49–50.

———, Nguyen Ba Chung, and Bruce Weigl, eds., *Mountain River: Vietnamese Poetry from the Wars, 1948–1993*, University of Massachusetts Press, 1998, pp. xi–xxiii.

Chattarji, Subarno, *Memories of a Lost War: American Poetic Responses to the Vietnam War*, Clarendon Press, 2001, pp. 201–26.

Chung, Nguyen Ba, *Mountain River: Vietnamese Poetry from the Wars, 1948–1993*, University of Massachusetts Press, 1998.

Confucius, *The Wisdom of Confucius*, Peter Pauper Press, 1963, pp. 8–47.

Durand, Maurice M., and Nguyen Tran Huan, *An Introduction to Vietnamese Literature*, translated by D. M. Hawke, Columbia University Press, 1985, pp. 134–40.

Hanh, Thich Nhat, *Zen Keys*, Doubleday, 1974, pp. 105–20.

Huan, Nguyen Tran, "The Literature of Vietnam, 1954–1973," in *Twentieth-Century Literary Criticism*, Vol. 102: *Vietnamese Literature*, edited by Linda Pavlovski, The Gale Group, 2001, pp. 337–48; originally published in *Literature & Society in Southeast Asia*, edited by Tham Seong Chee, Singapore University Press, 1981, pp. 321–45.

Jacoby, Fern J., "Thoughts of Hanoi: Nguyen Thi Vinh," in *Vietnam & Cambodia Project*, http://www.globaled.org/vietnamandcambodia/lessons/v_lesson_04.php (accessed March 18, 2011).

Lao-tzu, *Te-Tao Ching*, translated by Robert G. Henricks, Ballantine Books, 1989.

"Ngoc Son Temple," in *Asia for Visitors*, http://asiaforvisitors.com/vietnam/north/hanoi/hoankiem/ngocson.html (accessed March 18, 2011).

"The Path of Romance in Hanoi," in *Vietnam Travel Forum*, http://www.vietnamtravelforum.net/15926-path-romance-hanoi.html (accessed March 18, 2011).

"Shopper's Arcade," in *Asia Travel Blog*, http://www.asianwaytravel.com/blog/tag/hang-dao-market-hanoi/ (accessed March 18, 2011).

Taylor, Sandra C., *Vietnamese Women at War: Fighting for Ho Chi Minh and the Revolution*, University Press of Kansas, 1999, pp. 8–16.

Thong, Huynh Sanh, ed., *The Heritage of Vietnamese Poetry*, translated by Huynh Sanh Thong, Yale University Press, 1979, pp. xxv–xlv.

Vinh, Nguyen Thi, "Thoughts of Hanoi," in *A Thousand Years of Vietnamese Poetry*, edited by Nguyen Ngoc Bich, translated by Nguyen Ngoc Bich with Burton Raffel and W. S. Merwin, Knopf, 1975, pp. 184–86.

FURTHER READING

Balaban, John, *Ca Dao Vietnam: Vietnamese Folk Poetry*, Copper Canyon, 2003.

> The author, poet, and scholar John Balaban, a conscientious objector to the Vietnam War, volunteered and traveled in Vietnam during that time, in part to collect local folk poems, which he translated and offers in this bilingual volume, which also includes a discussion of the history of Vietnamese poetry.

Chomsky, Noam, *At War with Asia*, Pantheon Books, 1970.

> One of the most original and essential intellectuals in the modern United States, Chomsky drew on his own visits to Laos and North Vietnam in producing this volume of essays, published halfway through America's direct military engagement in the Vietnam War.

Harris, Ian, *Buddhism and Politics in Twentieth-Century Asia*, Continuum, 1999.

> This volume addresses the role that Buddhism has played in various historical circumstances of the modern era. Included is the essay "The Quest for Enlightenment and Cultural Identity: Buddhism in Contemporary Vietnam," by Thien Do.

Ninh, Bao, *The Sorrow of War*, translated by Frank Palmos, Secker & Warburg, 1993.

> Bao Ninh, a North Vietnamese veteran, wrote this novel relating the persistent yearning among Vietnamese to finally regain peace in their nation.

SUGGESTED SEARCH TERMS

Nguyen Thi Vinh AND Thoughts of Hanoi

Vietnam War AND poetry

North Vietnam AND poetry

South Vietnam AND poetry

Vietnam AND foreign occupation

Communism AND Vietnam

Ho Chi Minh AND poetry

Taoism AND Vietnam

Confucianism AND Vietnam

Buddhism AND Vietnam

Vietnam War AND United States

Vietnamese independence movement

The Tide Rises, the Tide Falls

HENRY WADSWORTH LONGFELLOW

1880

An American poet best known for works such as his long poem *The Song of Hiawatha* (1855), Henry Wadsworth Longfellow sought to capture Native American cultural identity in his writings. Longfellow also composed numerous brief lyrical poems, such as "The Tide Rises, the Tide Falls."

In this poem, written late in his career, Longfellow uses the imagery of the incoming and outgoing tides, along with images and language pertaining to dusk, nighttime, and dawn, to suggest the passage of time. Longfellow, through the course of the three-stanza poem, marks the progress of a nameless traveler across this coastline landscape, and through the night and morning. With this structure, the mortality of man is underscored, and it is further juxtaposed with the eternal qualities of the natural world. Longfellow further uses rhythm and repetition to complement the images of the waves on the beach and provide the poem with a traditional and familiar structure for his readers. Longfellow's incorporation of elements such as traditional structures, familiar imagery, and accessible themes, is reflective of his association with a group of poets that came to be known as the Fireside, or Schoolroom, poets. These poets, including Longfellow, John Greenleaf Whittier, and William Cullen Bryant, among others, explored the natural world, the American landscape, American history, and themes such as spirituality and mortality, in a manner that appealed

Henry Wadsworth Longfellow (*The Library of Congress*)

to many American readers. Longfellow is regarded as among the most popular American poets during this time period.

"The Tide Rises, the Tide Falls" was published in the 1880 collection of poetry by Longfellow *Ultima Thule*, published by Houghton Mifflin. The poem may also be found in such collections as *Favorite Poems of Henry Wadsworth Longfellow*, edited and introduced by Henry Seidel Canby and published in 1947 by Doubleday, and *Henry Wadsworth Longfellow: Poetry and Other Writings*, edited by J. D. McClatchy and published in 2000 by Library of America.

AUTHOR BIOGRAPHY

Longfellow was born in Portland, Maine, on February 27, 1807, to Stephen Longfellow, an attorney and congressman, and Zilpah Longfellow. The second son in a large family, Longfellow had an older brother, along with two younger

brothers and four sisters. At the age of fifteen, Longfellow entered Bowdoin College and graduated in 1825. His classmates included Nathaniel Hawthorne, who, like Longfellow, went on to become a famous writer, and Franklin Pierce, who would become the fourteenth president of the United States.

For the next several years, Longfellow prepared himself for a foreign-language teaching position at Bowdoin College by studying abroad in France, Spain, Italy, and Germany. He returned home in 1829 and secured his teaching position. In 1831, Longfellow married Mary Storer Porter, the daughter of a Portland judge. Longfellow's writings at this time included translations and scholarly essays. He published a collection of prose travel memoirs, *Outre-Mer*, in 1835, after traveling to Germany and the Scandinavian region as part of his study and preparation for a professorship at Harvard University. Later that year, Longfellow's wife died during childbirth in the Netherlands.

Following his return home, Longfellow expanded his writing career and began penning literary criticism and poetry. His *Voices of the Night*, a small poetry collection, was published in 1839. Other collections followed over the next several years. In 1843, Longfellow married Fanny Appleton, whose wealthy father offered the couple a home (formerly the headquarters of George Washington), in Cambridge, Massachusetts. The following year, the Longfellows' son Charles was born, and in 1845, another son, Ernest, was born. In 1847, a daughter, Frances, was born; she died a year later. Also in 1847, Longfellow published the long narrative poem *Evangeline*, which would become one of his best-known works. From 1850 to 1855, the Longfellows had three more daughters, Alice (1850), Edith (1853), and Anne Allegra (1855).

In 1855, Longfellow published another long poem, *The Song of Hiawatha*, a work which soon became wildly successful, and which Longfellow intended as a Native American epic. After publishing several other poetry collections, Longfellow returned to Europe in 1868. In England, he received honorary degrees from Oxford and Cambridge universities. Longfellow published *Ultima Thule*, a poetry collection including the brief lyric poem "The Tide Rises, the Tide Falls," in 1880. He died in Cambridge, Massachusetts, on March 24, 1882. His last poetry collection, *In the Harbor*, was published that same year.

POEM TEXT

The tide rises, the tide falls,
The twilight darkens, the curlew calls;
Along the sea-sands damp and brown
The traveller hastens toward the town,
    And the tide rises, the tide falls.   5

Darkness settles on roofs and walls,
But the sea, the sea in the darkness calls;
The little waves, with their soft, white hands,
Efface the footprints in the sands,
    And the tide rises, the tide falls.   10

The morning breaks; the steeds in their stalls
Stamp and neigh, as the hostler calls;
The day returns, but nevermore
Returns the traveller to the shore,
    And the tide rises, the tide falls.   15

POEM SUMMARY

The text used for this summary is from *Favorite Poems of Henry Wadsworth Longfellow*, Doubleday, 1947, pp. 37-38. Versions of the poem can be found on the following Web pages: http://www.poetry-archive.com/l/the_tide_rises_the_tide_falls.html and http://www.bartleby.com/248/208.html.

Stanza 1

"The Tide Rises, the Tide Falls" is a poem composed of three stanzas. A stanza is a unit of poetry that divides the lines of poetry into sections in the same way that paragraphs divide works of prose. In the first stanza, Longfellow establishes a rolling, wavelike rhythm in his poem, mimicking the movement of the ocean waves upon the beaches that he describes in this stanza. This is established in part through the repetition of phrases relating to the rising and falling motion of the tide, as well as the repetition of the title of the poem in the first and last lines of the first stanza, and in the last line in each subsequent stanza. In this first stanza, Longfellow marks the passage of time in the poem by noting the way twilight descends upon the ocean shore landscape. The poet makes reference to the curlew, a large bird that wades upon the wet sand of the beach. This image of the damp lip of the beach, with the waves washing over it, is repeated in the third line of the poem, when Longfellow describes the way the sands of the beach are darkened by the waves. Along this beach, a traveller, introduced in the poem's fourth line, is hurrying toward town.

Stanza 2

In the second stanza, Longfellow describes the way twilight is transformed into the dark of night. The darkness itself is depicted as a physical object. It covers the rooftops of buildings and clings to walls in an almost tangible way. Meanwhile, throughout the night, the sea, as it is described in the second line of this stanza, is beckoning. Here, Longfellow makes extensive use of personification. (Personification is the poetic attribution of human qualities to nonhuman things.) The sea is depicted as possessing the human ability to call out, although to whom it is calling remains unspecified. Similarly, just as darkness is transformed in the first line of the poem through Longfellow's language into a palpable entity, so are the ocean waves transmuted, through personification, into beings unto themselves, creatures with tiny hands that gently erase the footprints the traveler has left in the damp sand. This stanza closes with the repetition of the poem's title, emphasizing not only the rolling of the tide, but also the continued passage of time.

Stanza 3

This passage of time, to which Longfellow repeatedly directs the reader's attention, is once

again underscored in the opening lines of the third stanza, when the poet describes the breaking of dawn. The action of the poem has moved from the seaside to the town. There, the horses stomp in barnyard stalls, while their hostler, the person hired to care for the horses stabled at an inn, is beginning his day's work. Here Longfellow returns once again to the subject of the traveler, stating that the traveler has left the seashore forever, and will never return. The stanza and the poem are completed with the repetition of the poem's title. The eternity represented by the natural world, by the perpetual rise and fall of the tide, is contrasted with the traveler's finite journey along the beach, a journey that suggests the mortality of man. Not only does Longfellow allude to man's mortality in this stanza, but he also suggests that any impact a person leaves after his or her death will also, like the footprints in the sand, be erased. This lends the poem a darkness, a sense of hopelessness, that has been building through Longfellow's language and imagery throughout the poem.

THEMES

Mortality

Throughout "The Tide Rises, the Tide Falls," Longfellow repeatedly employs language and imagery that suggest not only the passing of time, but the impact of time's passage on man. Specifically, Longfellow emphasizes that man's time on earth is finite, and that man, in fact, has little lasting significance in the world. Furthermore, man's time on earth, as it is treated in the poem, occurs solely during the hours of darkness. As the poem begins, dusk is darkening the landscape, and the traveler makes his way toward town. In the darkness of night, the traveler's footsteps are eradicated by the waves. By dawn, all traces of the man's journey have been erased, and the poet emphasizes that the traveler will never again walk the beach. By asserting that the traveler will never return to the shore, although the day has been renewed, Longfellow suggests that the traveler's journey will inevitably end. As the journey itself is a metaphor for life, the end of the journey is death. While it is common in poetry for the progress of the day to be used as a metaphor marking a person's lifetime on earth (where infancy is associated with dawn, young adulthood with noontime, and old age with dusk),

Longfellow confines man's entire journey on earth to the darkness. In this way the poet provides a melancholy, bleak view of life. The erasing of the footsteps underscores the elimination of man's lasting impact on earth. In the poem's final stanza, as the new day dawns, the bustle of town life continues, as evidenced by the stirring of the horses in their stalls and the activity of the hostler. But the traveler is now absent from the poem. He has passed through the world, across the beach on his way to town, and is no longer present in the poem. The sense of hopelessness in the poem is pervasive; the journey of man is not celebrated, but shrouded in darkness and tinged with insignificance. The language and imagery used throughout the poem—the darkness in the first and second stanzas, the lonely bird in first, the act of erasure in the second, and the notable absence of the traveler in the third—emphasize this sense of despair and isolation.

Nature

In contrast to the fleeting presence of man on earth, the enduring characteristic of nature unfolds with each line of the "The Tide Rises, the Tide Falls." The rhythmic nature of the title and its repetition throughout the poem establish a sense of continuity. The rising and falling of the tide is specifically referred to four times, in precisely the same language, within the space of the three short stanzas that comprise the poem. The idea of the motion of the tide thrums throughout the work like a steady heartbeat, an assurance that while the traveler's journey begins and ends, the pulsing of the waves on the shore continues indefinitely. While the traveler hurries along the way, the natural world around him is still and steady. In the first stanza, the traveler rushes toward town. Meanwhile, the activity on the beach is calm: a curlew loiters on the damp sand of the beach, sounding his particular call. As darkness closes in on the rooftops and walls of the town's buildings, back on the beach the traveler's footsteps are inexorably being washed away by persistent tide. In the final stanza, the frenzy of the human world is suggested by the presence of the hostler and the horses. A hostler is a man hired for the express purposes of caring for the horses belonging to travelers staying at an inn. The horses, in the first two lines of the last stanza, begin to show signs of restlessness at dawn, jostling about in their stalls. This activity is once again contrasted with the stillness of the beach, now devoid of any indication that the

TOPICS FOR FURTHER STUDY

- Longfellow incorporates natural imagery into many of his works, including brief lyrics such as "The Tide Rises, the Tide Falls," using the imagery to evoke a particular emotional response to the poem's theme. The darkness of night and the perpetual motion of the waves in Longfellow's poem suggest man's mortality and despair, contrasting man's insignificance with the permanence of the natural world. Using Longfellow's work as a guide, write your own brief lyric poem in which you employ natural images that bolster the theme of your choosing. Mimic Longfellow's rhyme scheme in "The Tide Rises, the Tide Falls," or develop your own. Share your poem with the class either through a live reading or through a recording made accessible online.

- Longfellow was known for his sympathetic attitude toward Native Americans and for his desire to respect and preserve their cultures. Research the Native American populations that were indigenous to the American northeast, where Longfellow lived. Write a report or create a multimedia presentation in which you discuss the cultures of these groups and their history. Focus on the nineteenth century, but comment on the modern developments of Native American cultures in this area. Be sure to cite all of your print and online sources.

- *Night Is Gone, Day Is Still Coming: Stories and Poems by American Indian Teens and Young Adults* (2003) was edited by Annette Pina Ochoa, Betsy Franco, and Traci L. Gourdine. The book, whose title is reminiscent of some of the images and ideas in Longfellow's "The Tide Rises, the Tide Falls," contains works exploring a variety of themes. These include some of the philosophical and spiritual notions treated by Longfellow, as well as themes pertinent to Native American cultures and history. With a small group, read some of the selections in this collection. In your analysis of the works, examine the themes, language, imagery, and symbols of the Native American poems. Consider the structure of the poems. Do the young poets use stanzaic structures and establish rhyme schemes? In what ways do the works seem similar to Longfellow's poem? Create a blog in which your group members may post opinions, thoughts, and reflections, and discuss the particularities of the works.

- Although Longfellow's spiritual views are sometimes debated, he is typically associated with the Unitarian Church. Research the history of the Unitarian Church in America, focusing in particular on the church's activities in the mid- to late nineteenth century. What distinguished the Unitarian Church at that time from more traditional Christian churches? What were their beliefs about God, salvation, and sin? Did the Church pursue any political agendas at that time? Create a presentation in which these issues are explored. Comment on any prominent literary or political figures that were among the Unitarian community during this time period. Present your findings as a PowerPoint presentation, a Web page you have created for this purpose, or as a written report.

- James M. Whitfield was an African American poet who wrote during roughly the same time period as Longfellow. Using sources such as *The Works of James M. Whitfield: "America" and Other Writings by a Nineteenth-Century African American Poet*, study some of Whitfield's poems with a small group. What are Whitfield's primary concerns? How does he present the themes of American identity and culture? What can you discern of Whitfield's political beliefs from his writings? In your group, discuss the style of Whitfield's poetry and flesh out the themes and subjects of his work. Create a presentation in which you summarize these ideas for your class.

The tide (© Frank Krahmer / Corbis)

traveler had ever passed. The rhythmic movement of the tide and the gentle yet persistent sound of the waves on the shore are the final images and sounds imparted at the poem's end.

STYLE

Rhyme and Meter

Longfellow was known to experiment with different metrical forms in his poetry. Meter is a pattern of unaccented and accented syllables within a line of poetry; it is used to establish the poem's rhythm. Each unit of unaccented and accented syllables is called a foot. Some poems, like "The Tide Rises, the Tide Falls," do not make use of a standard metrical structure throughout the poem, but utilize, for some lines in the poem, a regular meter. For example, in the third and fourth lines of the first stanza, Longfellow employs a metrical pattern known as iambic tetrameter. In an iambic foot, one unaccented syllable is followed by an accented syllable. When there are four such feet in a line of verse, the pattern is known as iambic tetrameter. Longfellow's use of iambic tetrameter

in these early lines of the poem establishes the lulling rhythm that reminds the reader of the waves washing gently over the beach in the scene that Longfellow describes. This effect is also achieved through the repetition of the title of the poem in the first and last lines of the first stanza, and in the last lines of the stanzas two and three. The repetition of the end sounds of the lines of verse, or the poem's rhyme scheme, similarly creates a sense of unity and rhythm. The end rhyme of the first two lines, echoing the "falls" of the poem's title, is carried through the stanza and through the poem. Words rhyming with "falls," or the repetition of the word "falls" itself, end the first two and the last line of each stanza. The perpetual motion of the waves is thereby underscored in the recurrence of this rhyme.

Lyric

A lyric is a short verse in which the poet focuses on his or her emotions or emotional responses to a particular event. It differs from a narrative poem in which a story is being told. Longfellow was, and is, highly regarded as a lyricist, as well as the composer of fine narrative works. According

COMPARE & CONTRAST

- **1880s:** Native Americans are forced by the government to abandon their communities and cultures and to live in large group settlements known as reservations. In 1885, approximately 204,000 Native Americans live on some 171 reservations found throughout the United States.

  Today: Native Americans comprise approximately 1.5 percent of the total U.S. population, or about 4.1 million people, with only some living on reservations. There are 315 American Indian reservations and areas known as Off-Reservation Trust Lands.

- **1880s:** The popular poetry of the day incorporates themes of American culture and history, faith, mortality, and simple daily life into works with regular rhyme patterns and traditional structures. Longfellow, William Cullen Bryant, John Greenleaf Whittier, and Oliver Wendell Holmes, among others, are associated with this type of poetry and have come to be referred to as the Fireside poets.

  Today: Twenty-first century poetry features a broad array of poetic forms and is informed by a number of poetic movements, some of which are experimental in nature and eschew traditional form and structure, and others that embrace the structured lyric

  forms of the past. Some poets write in free verse (no standard stanzaic structure, rhyme scheme, or meter), while others experiment with the sound of language itself. Notable twenty-first century poets include Joshua Clover, Stacy Doris, Peter Gizzi, Myung Mi Kim, and Juliana Spahr, among others.

- **1880s:** The Unitarian Church is a small Christian sect known for its liberal beliefs. Some disagreements regarding the Christian basis of the Church arise among members resulting in some fragmentation of the Church. Prominent Unitarians include Longfellow, and other poets and writers such as Ralph Waldo Emerson and William Cullen Bryant.

  Today: Modern Unitarians, long since merged with another similar faith, Universalism, refer to themselves as Unitarian Universalists. No longer considered a Christian denomination, Unitarian Universalism is a pluralist faith that embraces a number of belief systems, and similarly welcomes atheists, agnostics, and humanists. In recent years, numbers of Unitarian Universalists have declined. In 2010, official membership in the Unitarian Universalist Association of Congregations stood at 155,748 adults.

---

to critics such as Robert A. Bain, in the 1996 *Whitman's & Dickinson's Contemporaries: An Anthology of Their Verse*, "Critics on both sides of the Atlantic praised his narrative poems, his musical lyrics," along with other genres and a variety of themes. The musicality of lyrics such as "The Tide Rises, the Tide Falls" is established through Longfellow's use of rhyme, language, and periodic inclusion of lines with a regular metrical structure, as discussed above. The emotions Longfellow conveys in his brief lyric reflect a melancholic view of man's impermanent place in his world.

HISTORICAL CONTEXT

Native Americans in the 1880s

During Longfellow's lifetime, the United States underwent drastic transformations as the American West was settled and immigrants increasingly sought new lives throughout the nation's expanding borders. These changes were disastrous for the Native American communities and cultures that were destroyed in the processes of expansion and industrialization. Longfellow was known to be sympathetic to the issues related to Native American rights, and attempted, in his *Song of*

Hiawatha (1855), to preserve some of the history and culture of the Iroquois peoples in his epic poem.

In the mid- to late 1800s, western tribes continued to be forced onto government-allotted land, or reservations. Widespread violence, sanctioned by the government but often fueled by racism, was common. Also during this time period, government funds were allocated to the "education" and "civilization" of Native American children. As Leonard Dinnerstein, Roger L. Nichols, and David M. Reimers observe in the 1996 *Natives and Strangers: A Multicultural History of Americans*, educational efforts that began in the 1870s culminated in a more sinister program. "From the late 1890s to the 1930s," the authors assert, "thousands of Indian children were legally kidnapped and forced to attend school far from home." The curriculum at such schools was focused specifically on the eradication of Native languages and cultures. The objective of such efforts, scholar Frederick E. Hoxie maintains in the preface to the 1984 work *The Campaign to Assimilate the Indians, 1880-1920*, was to create a class of people partially integrated into the dominant society. "In this way," Hoxie states, "minorities could serve the dominant culture without qualifying for social and political equality." Hoxie points out that this "more limited interpretation of Indian assimilation" was also later applied to African Americans and immigrant groups like the Japanese. Although the reservation system was already in place when Grover Cleveland became president of the United States in 1885, it was under President Cleveland's administration that many of the educational reforms were enacted. Further, President Cleveland supported and signed into a law an act (the Dawes Act of 1887) that stripped Native Americans on reservations of many of their land rights.

The Fireside poets

Longfellow was associated with a group of poets that came to be known as the Fireside poets. The group was also sometimes referred to as the Schoolroom poets. The group included Longfellow, John Greenleaf Whittier, Oliver Wendell Holmes, James Russell Lowell, and William Cullen Bryant. As a group, these poets employed conventional poetic forms and structures, often favoring regular metrical and rhyme schemes in their works. Because of these techniques, the poems had cadences that allowed for easy memorization, for recitation by schoolchildren, or

A horse greets the dawn from his stall in the stable in stanza three. *(Igor Borodin / Shutterstock.com)*

as entertainment for families gathered around their hearths. Often the works contained moral instruction as well. The poetry of this group was often regarded not only as pleasing to the ear, but accessible in terms of theme and subject matter, qualities that contributed to the popularity of the poets in the group. For the same reasons, the poetry of the Fireside poets has also sometimes been labeled as trivial or sentimental. These poets often focused on specifically American settings and subjects, as in Longfellow's long narrative poems *The Courtship of Miles Standish* (1858) and *Paul Revere's Ride* (1860), which feature New England historical themes. As the editors of *The Columbia Literary History of the United States* point out, Longfellow was "by far the most celebrated of the group" of Fireside poets. Similarly, Walter Fuller Taylor, in his 1936 *A History of American Letters*, describes the way Longfellow's "winsome simplicity in his expression aided in establishing him almost immediately as America's most popular poet—a true laureate of the fireside."

CRITICAL OVERVIEW

Although "The Tide Rises, the Tide Falls" is a much anthologized poem, individually it has received little critical analysis. Rather, it is often mentioned when grouped with Longfellow's other popular lyric poems.

For example, in the 1996 *Whitman's & Dickinson's Contemporaries: An Anthology of Their Verse*, Bain states that Longfellow's "best poems do employ metaphor and myth; the music and story of 'The Tide Rises, the Tide Falls,' 'Snow-Flakes,' 'My Lost Youth,' and more than twenty other lyrics still haunt." Steven Allaback, in the 1978 *Dictionary of Literary Biography*, Vol. 1, *The American Renaissance in New England*, uses the poem to describe Longfellow's approach to a particular theme. Allaback maintains,

> A stately poem like "The Tide Rises, the Tide Falls," written three years before his death, is a good example of Longfellow's view of life as a somewhat sad but purposeful journey which is being taken in conjunction with certain orderly natural processes.

While Longfellow's contemporary popularity is widely acknowledged, critics such as Bain point out that after World War I (1914–1918), the high esteem critics had previously had for Longfellow's work dissolved. In the aftermath of the war, Longfellow's optimism was unappreciated, and his poetry was derided for "its didacticism and shallowness," states Bain.

Other critics have similarly observed the way the criticism of the early twentieth century offered a negative revaluation of Longfellow's work. Dana Gioia, in *The Columbia History of American Poetry*, examines the way the works of Longfellow and some of his peers fell out of favor during the early years of the modernist movement at the end of the nineteenth century. (Modernism was a cultural and literary movement in which traditional modes of expression were eschewed, and new, more experimental and experiential ones were favored.) In Gioia's examination of Longfellow's poetry, the critic identifies two types of lyric: popular and literary. Classing "The Tide Rises, the Tide Falls" as written in Longfellow's popular mode, Gioia then describes the transparency of meaning available in such a poem, and discusses the way the poem "neatly balances its images" and employs a "set refrain to keep the image and the mood easily focused." Such a poem, Gioia

maintains, was geared by Longfellow toward the general, rather than the intellectual, audience.

CRITICISM

Catherine C. Dominic

Dominic is a novelist and a freelance writer and editor. In the following essay, she explores the incongruity between Longfellow's spirituality, as expressed in his poetry and letters and as attested to by those close to him, and the sense of despair, isolation, and futility that prevails in his short lyric "The Tide Rises, the Tide Falls."

Henry Wadsworth Longfellow was associated with the liberal Christian sect known as Unitarianism. His brother, Samuel Longfellow, was a Unitarian minister, and prominent Unitarian theologian William Ellery Channing was a classmate of Longfellow's father and a friend to the family. Samuel Longfellow, quoted in Edward Wagenknecht's 1955 *Longfellow: A Full-Length Portrait*, observed the way his brother's religion informed his life and work, stating

> His nature was at heart devout; his ideas of life and death, and of what lies beyond, were essentially cheerful, hopeful, optimistic. He did not care to talk much on theological points; but he believed in the supreme of good in the world and in the universe.

Many of Longfellow's works, in fact, are rooted in religious themes, and his poems are often described as pious and didactic, as Joseph E. O'Neill observes in an essay on Longfellow in the 1958 *American Classics Reconsidered: A Christian Appraisal*. Nevertheless, "The Tide Rises, the Tide Falls," written late in Longfellow's career and life, is bereft of the optimism of which his brother Samuel speaks. Also absent from the poem is a sense of peacefulness, or any reassurances about faith, God's love, salvation, or any such element that one might expect to find in a work about death by a man described as both cheerful and devout. O'Neill traces notes of sadness in poems written by Longfellow between 1840 and 1880, finding a culmination of the poet's ruminations on mortality in the lines of "The Tide Rises, the Tide Falls." O'Neill emphasizes that Longfellow, in this poem, contemplates mortality and expresses himself in a way that touches readers as "deep, universal, and true." Yet O'Neill overlooks the

WHAT DO I READ NEXT?

- Longfellow's epic poem *The Song of Hiawatha*, published in 1855, is one of his best-known works. It tells the story of a Native American hero, the founder of the Iroquois confederacy, and is written in trochaic tetrameter. It is available in a 2006 edition published by Dover.

- Charles C. Calhoun offers a highly acclaimed, modern revaluation of Longfellow's life and works in *Longfellow: A Rediscovered Life*, published in 2004 by Beacon Press.

- *The Chief American Poets: Selected Poems by Bryant, Poe, Emerson, Longfellow, Whittier, Holmes, Lowell, Whitman, and Lanier*, edited by Curtis Hidden Page, was originally published in 1923. This volume, reproduced in 2010 by Nabu Press, collects the works of several of the Fireside poets and their contemporaries.

- *Rising Voices: Writings of Young Native Americans*, edited by Arlene Hirschfelder and Beverly Singer, is a collection of Native American poetry written by and for young adults. The collection, which was published in 1993 by Ivy Books, treats such themes as identity, education, and spirituality.

- *The Colors of Nature: Culture, Identity, and the Natural World* is a collection of nature poetry written by people of color from around the world. The title is designed to demonstrate how people from all cultures, races, and ethnic backgrounds view the natural world and their own place in it. The collection, edited by Alison H. Deming and Lauret E. Savoy, was published in 2002 by Milkweed.

- Joseph A. Conforti's *Imagining New England: Explorations of Regional Identity from the Pilgrims to the Mid-Twentieth Century* includes the chapter "Old New England: Nostalgia, Reaction, and Reform in the Colonial Revival, 1870–1910," in which the author explores the dominant social and cultural peculiarities of the region Longfellow called home. The volume was published in 2000 by the University of North Carolina Press.

- Patricia Frevert's *Welcome: A Unitarian Universalist Primer* offers an introduction to the philosophy and the spirituality of modern Unitarian Universalists, allowing the student of Longfellow to understand the modern religious community that evolved from the faith that Longfellow and others practiced. This brief introduction to modern Unitarianism was published in 2008 by Skinner House Books.

---

looming sense of despair in the poem. "The Tide Rises, the Tide Falls" is not just a melancholy meditation on mortality. Rather, through its language and imagery, the poem expresses a deep sense of isolation and even hopelessness, qualities that stand in stark contrast to the religious views Longfellow was believed to have held. In W. Sloane Kennedy's *Henry W. Longfellow: Biography, Anecdote, Letters, Criticism*, published the same year as Longfellow's death (1882), Kennedy quotes "a life-long student of Longfellow," the Reverend Franklin Johnson. In discussing Longfellow's religious beliefs and spirituality, Johnson states that it is "remarkable that [Longfellow] wrote no syllable of doubt or denial; that scepticism cannot discover, from the beginning to the end of his works, a line in which to clothe itself." Yet a close reading of "The Tide Rises, the Tide Falls" reveals a steady pulse not merely of doubt, but of outright despair.

Wagenknecht's acclaimed biography underscores several salient points about Longfellow's faith. The biographer asserts that Longfellow, while subscribing to Christian beliefs as upheld by the Unitarian Church, was not particularly focused on dogma or doctrine; Wagenknecht

'THE TIDE RISES, THE TIDE FALLS' IS NOT JUST A MELANCHOLY MEDITATION ON MORTALITY. RATHER, THROUGH ITS LANGUAGE AND IMAGERY, THE POEM EXPRESSES A DEEP SENSE OF ISOLATION AND EVEN HOPELESSNESS, QUALITIES THAT STAND IN STARK CONTRAST TO THE RELIGIOUS VIEWS LONGFELLOW WAS BELIEVED TO HAVE HELD."

describes this as Longfellow's "pronounced disinclination toward theological definition and metaphysical speculation." Wagenknecht's study of Longfellow's writings suggests that Longfellow contemplated such matters of faith and theology only when deeply concerned with doubt. Such a moment of doubt seems to have occurred when Longfellow penned "The Tide Rises, the Tide Falls," a poem whose analysis is notably absent from Wagenknecht's study of Longfellow's spiritual leanings and religious beliefs. In this poem, Longfellow colors his scene darkly. His words and images conjure sentiments of isolation and futility.

Longfellow takes pains to employ the rhythm of the ocean waves as the backbone of his poem. This oceanic rhythm lulls, but the sense of calm it provides is false. The repetition of the titular line throughout each stanza of the poem, the way this line in fact frames the poem, suggests the steady persistence, and permanence, of the tide. This is further reinforced in the poem's rhyme scheme, in which the final line of each stanza repeats the rhyme of the first two lines of each stanza. This rhyme is repeated in the first, second, and fifth lines of the poem's other two stanzas as well. These sounds, all rhyming with the "falls" of the title, are soft and peaceful. Internally, however, in the space of each line, there are pauses and sudden shifts in metrical patterns that stop before they can properly get underway. In the first stanza, two of the five lines are written in iambic tetrameter (each has a pattern in which there are four units of an iambic foot—an unaccented syllable followed by an accented syllable). A third line, with the exception of one extra unaccented syllable, nearly fits

this pattern as well. Yet the song-like cadence of such lines is halted by the jarring sound of lines that begin with an accented syllable, as in the first line of the second stanza. Similarly, in the third line of that stanza, extraneous accented syllables break the softer rhythm of the iambic phrases that open the line. In the poem's final stanza, when Longfellow describes the business of the town—the activity of the hostler and the horses, the sudden bustle at dawn—the first two lines are filled with punctuation that forces mid-line pauses, and irregular jarring syntax. The effect of these disruptions to the wavelike rhythm found elsewhere into the poem is to introduce a sense of discordance into the work. The peacefulness is an illusion.

The imagery of the poem underscores this undercurrent of agitation in the poem and heightens the notion of disquiet. The curlew, the bird on the beach in the opening stanza, calls out, alone. The traveler is already gone, hurrying toward the town. Twilight is ebbing into the darkness of night. In addition to the blanket of darkness that Longfellow unfolds over his scene, the beach is described in terms of darkness as well; it is brown, rather than the gold it might have been during the sunlit portion of the day. In the second stanza, the notion of darkness is referred to twice more. It is not a mere visual effect; the term does more that simply describe the hue of the sky. Rather, Longfellow depicts the darkness as clinging to the town's buildings, to their rooftops, to their walls. At sea, darkness is omnipresent, and from within this pervasive darkness, the sea calls. The fact that darkness is given the power to touch, and is associated with the vastness of the sea, suggests the way darkness tugs at the psyche of the traveler, the reader, and the poet. As the poem proceeds, and the waves wash away the footprints in the sand, eliminating any evidence of the traveler's existence, the metaphorical nature of the traveler's journey becomes clear. His path is not simply from the beach to the town. Rather, his journey is meant to symbolize his life on earth. Yet this life, as it is depicted in the poem, is lived at night, in the dark, where despair clutches at the traveler, wherever he may be, in town or at sea.

In the unremittingly grim world Longfellow presents in the poem, the traveler himself is erased from the beach, just as his footprints—his impact or significance in the world—have already disappeared. Longfellow states that he will never again return to the shore. There is no coda, in which the poet reassures the faithful reader that while the traveler might no longer walk the earth, his spirit will live on. He is simply erased. He leaves nothing behind that will recall his one-time presence after he is gone. There is no sense of worldly immortality through action or creation. Furthermore, there is no assurance of anything to come after. The frenzied hustling in town confirms only that life will go on, but the impact of one person in the world is characterized by Longfellow in this poem as negligible. The images of isolation, such as the bird and the traveler; of despair, such as the ever-present darkness; and of meaninglessness and erasure, such as the disappearance from the shore of the traveler and his footsteps, are bleak and unrelenting.

Although Wagenknecht declares that "a steadfast faith in the immortality of the soul is the unwavering testimony of [Longfellow's] poetry from beginning to end," this faith does not find its way into "The Tide Rises, the Tide Falls." If Longfellow derived comfort from his faith as Wagenknecht suggests, the poet most likely did not do so when this poem was written. Rather, "The Tide Rises, the Tide Falls" seems better characterized as one of Longfellow's moments of doubts. Here, rather than attempting to teach a moral lesson, or demonstrating his piety, as he does in other poems, Longfellow allows his despair to gently unfold. Wagenknecht states that Longfellow "sorrowed profoundly over the great blows which life dealt to him." Wagenknecht insists that the poet met such obstacles "with courage, and without either bitterness or desperation" due to his faith in God's wisdom.

Yet poems such as "The Tide Rises, the Tide Falls" offer glimpses into the poet's fears, and reveal that at times, even with his great faith, he was not immune to "bitterness" and "desperation." While the poem gradually and quietly grows increasingly grim as the traveler's journey is recounted, the image of the sea, enveloped in darkness and calling out, may be the most moving, and the most terrifying image of the poem. Here, the desperation Longfellow explores throughout the work is made clear, and is suggestive of the deep spiritual doubts and struggles with which he may have been contending. By uniting the notion of the darkness with the vastness of the sea, Longfellow suggests the possibility of being overcome, overwhelmed, subsumed by the forces of darkness, fear, and doubt.

" HE RETURNS AGAIN TO HIS BOYHOOD IN PORTLAND, WHERE HE HAD LOVED TO LISTEN TO THE SOUND OF THE WAVES AND TO THE GENTLE RUSH OF THE TIDE COMING IN. AS HE VISUALIZED IN OLD AGE THE PHENOMENA OF WATER BEHAVIOR, IT BECAME SYMBOLIC OF LIFE."

Source: Catherine C. Dominic, Critical Essay on "The Tide Rises, the Tide Falls," in *Poetry for Students*, Gale, Cengage Learning, 2012.

Cecil B. Williams

In the following excerpt, Williams examines the scope of Longfellow's work, focusing on his simple lyrics and psalms.

I. GENERAL OBSERVATIONS ABOUT LONGFELLOW AS A POET

...We have seen that from early boyhood Longfellow wanted to be a poet and that by the time he had graduated from college the desire had intensified into a burning ambition. Just what qualifications, beyond the desire, did he have? He had a genuine poetic imagination, if not one of the most sublime; he had at an early age accumulated sufficient experience and had read enough to nourish a poetic imagination; he had an excellent ear for meter and rhyme; and, partly through translating from eighteen languages, he had become acquainted with a sufficient variety of prosodic forms to be able to choose with considerable success the one most suitable for a particular poem. His technical endowment was considerably better than average; it was, in fact, the best of any American poet of his time, and it was approached by only Bryant and Lowell. He was equipped to become a first-rate poet. Indeed, he may have been too well qualified and relied too much on mere facility. But he also had a good deal of rugged strength.

Perhaps Longfellow's natural gift for versification was too great to permit him to become a very systematic student of prosody. Indeed he seems to have been little interested in the techniques of poetry except on a pragmatic basis. He did not prepare lectures on the nature and forms of poetry as Bryant did; he did not absorb Coleridge's *Biographia Literaria* and other works of critical theory as did Poe. His Yankee thrift was apparent even here. If he had an idea for a poem, he brooded and researched until he came upon what he thought was the right form, but he exhibited little interest in prosody as such.

It appears that Longfellow's attitude toward poetic techniques was of a piece with his general approach to life; he was always more intuitive than intellectual. In his "Table Talk" he said: "I have many opinions in Art and Literature which constantly recur to me in the tender guise of a sentiment. A clever dialectician can prove to me that I am wrong. I cannot answer him. I let the waves of argument roll on: but all the lilies rise again, and are beautiful as before" (*Life*, III, 381). This no doubt partly explains his impatience and unhappiness in the presence of criticism; he seems to have anticipated William James in concluding that we cease to thrill when we dissect. He believed that "the chief end of poetry is to give delight, to build an ideal world of 'escape' from a realistic world, and, finally, to honor God" And the poet achieves poetry through sympathetic living and good intentions. Like Dorothea Brande in our own time, he believed that the writer is two persons: "the workaday man who walks, and the genius who flies." On November 14, 1845, about the time he began work on *Evangeline*, he wrote in his journal: "Felt more than ever to-day the difference between my ideal home-world of Poetry, and the outer, actual, tangible Prose world. When I go out of the precincts of my study, down the village street to college, how the scaffoldings about the Palace of Song come rattling and clattering down!" (*Life*, II, 24). He looked on the ability to write poetry as a gift, and believed that one so gifted had a duty—to God—to develop to the best of his abilities and opportunities.

His poetry displays a great variety of form, a truly remarkable versatility. First and last, he wrote iambic verse in all its usual variations of four-stress lines and in blank verse, heroic couplet, and ballad meter; he was exceptionally adept in trochaic verse in *Hiawatha* and elsewhere; he used anapestic forms in "Paul Revere's Ride" and other narrative poems; he was notably successful with the refractory dactyllic hexameter in *Evangeline* and in *The Courtship of Miles Standish*. He was highly skilled in writing the Italian or Petrarchan sonnet also, but rather oddly he apparently never attempted the English Shakespearean or Spenserian types. But he could not only handle the basic forms; he could also modify them successfully through various techniques, including occasional use of a foot other than the basic form, changing the caesura, or syncopating in the long lines by alternating heavy and light stresses. Perhaps most surprising is his occasional use of a form so free as to suggest modern "free verse."

But he was not only extraordinarily versatile in his prosody; he was equally venturesome in *types* of poetry. His works include simple homely lyrics, ballads of varying lengths, odes and elegies, epics, both religious and secular, plays, a variety of saga-type poems employing legends and other folk material, and, as already mentioned, sonnets, in which he was more successful than any other poet of his time. And all of his poetry has a certain sweetness of sound and tone peculiarly his own. His versatility extended to his imagery and diction; he had an unusual mastery of metaphor, and his large vocabulary no doubt aided his meter and rhyme, and thus the smoothness and the melody of his verse. He was, however, not so much an innovator as a refiner; he sought, and with considerable success, to do better what others had already done well. G. W. Allen's conclusion is: "Longfellow's greatest contribution . . . was not specifically any new theory or practice but a general, broad, and deep influence toward the search for new forms, based on a wide acquaintance with the chief poetic techniques of the world."

II. SIMPLE LYRICS AND PSALMS

On March 26, 1838, when he was thirty-one, Longfellow wrote in his journal: "Human life is made up mostly of a series of little disappointments and little pleasures" (*Life*, I, 282). When one leafs through his collected poems in search of the source of his fame, one is tempted to paraphrase: "Longfellow won most of his reputation through writing a series of little poems." Such a statement is not fully warranted, of course, for several of his long poems were enormously and lastingly popular; yet the number of famous short poems is indeed impressive. In the space available here, only a fraction of them, and not even all the important ones, can be discussed, but an attempt will be made to give some impression of the nature and variety of the short poems which a generation grew up on, largely through memorizing them and meeting them constantly in spelling books and readers.

One of the earliest was "Hymn to the Night," which even Poe admired, especially for its beginning: "I heard the trailing garments of the Night / Sweep through her marble halls!" Longfellow had a life-long affection for the quiet hours of night. He loved to read and write at night. He may have paid for this devotion with the eye trouble which plagued him from his early Harvard years, but even at this cost he probably would not willingly have relinquished his night vigils with the muses:

> From the cool cisterns of the midnight air
> My Spirit drank repose;
> The fountain of perpetual peace flows there,—
> From those deep cisterns flows.

Another very early poem was perhaps his most controversial one, "A Psalm of Life," already mentioned several times. Burlesqued and ridiculed in modern times, it was extravagantly praised when it was published and long afterward. However, even as early as 1886, when he wrote the biography, Samuel Longfellow felt called on to defend it: "It has perhaps grown too familiar for us to read it as it was first read. But if the ideas have become commonplace, it has well been said that it is this poem that has made them so" (*Life*, I, 271). It is a little hard today to take seriously such phrasing as "Heart within, and God o'erhead!" and the imagery can never have been fully satisfactory: for example, the juxtaposition of "dumb, driven cattle" and "hero in the strife." But the poem inspired multitudes in its own day, and even now the reader who realizes that it reflects a harassed and lovelorn young professor's reaction to Goethe and to his own deep thoughts may not find it entirely bad. To say that it is trite is only as if to say *Hamlet* is too full of familiar quotations.

Longfellow had intended "A Psalm of Life" to be merely the first of a number of psalms—philosophic comments he would make from time to time, perhaps on the model of William Blake's "Songs of Innocence" and "Songs of Experience." Apparently it was Longfellow's failure to provide this first poem with a suitable alternative title which caused it to pre-empt the title of an intended series. A few months after he wrote "A Psalm of Life," he followed it with "The Reaper and the Flowers, a Psalm of Death." This is not known, however, as "A Psalm of Death," but as "The Reaper and the Flowers." It is smoothly

flowing series of quatrains on the idea that early death for some is part of the Divine scheme; and, though it doubtless solaced many bereft parents and relatives in those days of higher infant and child mortality, it is too "sticky" for the modern taste. The same is true of "Footsteps of Angels," but this poem is more important to the student, for it directly commemorates two deaths Longfellow had recently experienced: that of his first wife at Rotterdam and that of his friend and brother-in-law George Pierce, news of which followed within a month of his wife's death. Another "Psalm" of which Longfellow himself thought highly was his "Midnight Mass for the Dying Year." The poem is interesting structurally for its introduction of a new five-line stanza form and for the use of a short final line giving the effect of a refrain; but it has little to say to a modern reader.

"The Rainy Day" is one of Longfellow's best-known short lyrics—too well known for the good of his reputation, especially such self-pitying lines as "My life is cold, and dark, and dreary" and the cheery counterpart, "Behind the clouds is the sun still shining." Longfellow could not know, conditioned as he was by the Atlantic Coast's excessive rain, how his poem would sound to other Americans in "the land of little rain"! Another sentimental poem, popular in the nineteenth century but not in the twentieth, is "Maidenhood," written in rhymed triplets, ingeniously done, but presenting a concept of feminity equally inappropriate to the nineteenth-century pioneer woman and to today's young lady with her auto driver's license at age sixteen:

> Standing with reluctant feet,
> Where the brook and river meet,
> Womanhood and childhood fleet!
> . . . . .
> Bear a lily in thy hand;
> Gates of brass cannot withstand
> One touch of that magic wand.

It is impossible today to imagine Longfellow writing the short poem "Excelsior" in the belief that it was important, or to understand his contemporaries' admiring enthusiasm for it. His editor says he was inspired to write it by finding in a scrap of newspaper the seal of the state of New York bearing the motto. He recorded finishing the poem at half-past three in the morning on September 28, 1841. He said his purpose was "to display, in a series of pictures, the life of a man of genius, resisting all temptations, laying aside all fears, heedless of all warnings, and pressing right on to accomplish his purpose" (*Poems*, 19). Written about the same time as Emerson's "Self-Reliance," it was in the *Zeitgeist*. It was a time when Americans were spurring each other on to all sorts of achievements, but probably a considerable part of the appeal of this poem, as is true of much of Longfellow's work, came from its exotic setting. I myself remember being much affected by the poem when I found it in one of my grade school readers, but more, as I recall, by its Alpine setting and the hint of thwarted romance than by the embodiment of lofty aspiration which climbs a mountain "because it is there."

It is interesting that Longfellow should have written in the same year of Tennyson's "Locksley Hall" (1842) "The Belfry of Bruges," a poem in the same trochaic eight-stress, fifteen-syllable meter. "The Belfry" and "Nuremberg," written two years later, show Longfellow capitalizing further on his knowledge of Europe and his readers' curiosity about it. Indeed these two poems are said to be "part of a plan which the poet had designed of a series of travel-sketches in verse" (*Poems*, 53). Both were very popular, presumably because of their swinging meter and the historical-traditional subject which Longfellow was able to present in a moving pageant. "Nuremberg" has the extra appeal of moving characters representing important ideals: Albrecht Dürer, "the Evangelist of Art" when "Art was still religion"; Hans Sachs, the cobbler-poet, who showed that art could be for the laboring people as well as for the intellectual aristocracy.

Two other much-read poems which form a natural pair are "The Arsenal at Springfield" and "The Old Clock on the Stairs." The chief reason for linking them is that Fanny Longfellow was at least partly responsible for Longfellow's writing both. "The Arsenal" is Longfellow's most pacifistic poem. Fanny seems to have been even more a pacifist than he was, but his lifelong belief in the biblical "faith, hope, and charity" made him readily responsive. On their wedding journey in 1843, they visited, among other places, the arsenal at Springfield, Massachusetts, with the result, Fanny said, that "I urged H. to write a peace poem." Perhaps the best stanza, expressing an oft-repeated thought, is

> Were half the power that fills the world with terror,
>   Were half the wealth bestowed on camps and
>   courts,
> Given to redeem the human mind from error,
>   There were no need of arsenals or forts.

On the same journey, the newlyweds visited the homestead of Fanny's maternal grandfather in Pittsfield, Massachusetts, and saw the old clock which inspired the poem. Longfellow's more immediate inspiration was the writings of an early French missionary, who said of eternity that it is a balance of *toujours* and *jamais*. Longfellow managed in this medium-length poem, with effective refrain of "Forever—never! / Never—forever!" to give something of the pageantry of human life marching through time.

The poems Longfellow wrote in the mid-1840's after his marriage to Fanny were naturally full of sentiment, compounded of recollected sadness and present joys. "The Day Is Done" and "The Bridge" are the best known. "The Day Is Done" was written in 1844 as the poem to *The Waif*, a volume of selections from Longfellow's poems published at Christmas time. A plea for gentle happiness, it contains this revealing stanza:

> A feeling of sadness and longing,
>   That is not akin to pain,
> And resembles sorrow only
>   As the mist resembles the rain.

Something of the Puritan distrust of happiness and of satisfaction in somber feeling came out in Longfellow from time to time; like other Puritans, he seems to have been able to achieve the paradox of being happiest when not happy.

"The Bridge" is almost Byronic in parading poetic melancholy. The poet, looking on the River Charles at midnight as he had done countless times before, sees the moon's reflection and continues to stand musing on the days past when

> I had wished that the ebbing tide
> Would bear me away on its bosom
>   O'er the ocean wild and wide!
> For my heart was hot and restless,
>   And my life was full of care,
> And the burden laid upon me
>   Seemed greater than I could bear.

He is happy now, but he still thinks of the long procession of others less fortunate: "The young heart hot and restless, / And the old subdued and slow!" The prosody of both poems is interesting. In quatrains close in form to ballad meter, Longfellow achieves remarkably smooth, melodious verse by simple variations in his meter, mainly occasional anapests and feminine endings.

In 1848 Longfellow wrote the "Hymn for My Brother's Ordination." His brother Samuel, twelve years his junior and destined to be his biographer, was being ordained in the Unitarian Church in Portland. A devoutly religious utterance, the poem was sung as part of the ordination service. It is odd that Longfellow, a flute player with an excellent ear for music, wrote so few songs and that Whittier, who was tone deaf, wrote so many.

In 1855 came the poem which many readers consider Longfellow's finest lyric, "My Lost Youth." He made frequent visits to Portland, especially until his parents died. On one of these, in 1846, he took a long walk around Munjoy's hill and to Old Fort Lawrence, listening to the sea and turning over in his mind a poem on the Old Fort (*Poems*, 193). But it was not until after he had retired from Harvard and was in an especially nostalgic mood that he wrote the lovely poem with its series of pictures of the boy and man in relation to the old seaport and with its haunting refrain, admittedly taken from an old Lapland song: "A boy's will is the wind's will, / And the thoughts of youth are long, long thoughts."

The late 1850's saw the composition of several more of the popular sentimental poems, including "Santa Filomena," "Daybreak," and "The Childrens' Hour." "Santa Filomena" was his eloquent tribute to Florence Nightingale, "Saint Nightingale," for her heroic work in the hospitals during the Crimean War:

> A Lady with a Lamp shall stand
> In the great history of the land,
>   A noble type of good,
>   Heroic womanhood.

"Daybreak," a short poem in rhyming couplets, shows the poet's delicate fancy: the wind from the sea touches enough aspects of life in rapid succession to suggest the full pageantry of human life on earth. "The Children's Hour," written in 1819, only two years before his wife's death, is a delightful picture of his three daughters and of the playful but understanding relationship between the poet-father and the little girls.

As Longfellow grew older, and particularly after he gave up his Harvard duties, he tended to devote himself more to long poems and less to short lyrics. However, he continued to turn occasionally to the shorter forms, and never lost his ability to write them. In 1864, with the Civil War nearing its end but with heavy fighting still going on, he wrote the much beloved "Christmas Bells," with its effective use of the refrain "Of

peace on earth, good-will to men!" In 1866, the war over, he wrote his best war poem, "Killed at the Ford," a lyric similar in content to Whitman's well-known "Come up from the Fields Father." This poem compares not too badly with Whitman's, though Longfellow could not match Whitman's simple and sincere pathos.

In 1873, Longfellow published *Aftermath*, a volume containing the last part of *Tales of a Wayside Inn* and miscellaneous poems. He wrote a short title poem for it which is one of his finest lyrics; it deserves quotation in its entirety:

> When the summer fields are mown,
> When the birds are fledged and flown,
> And the dry leaves strew the path;
> With the falling of the snow,
> With the cawing of the crow,
> Once again the fields we mow
> And gather in the aftermath.
> Not the sweet, new grass with flowers
> Is this harvesting of ours;
> Not the upland clover bloom;
> But the rowen mixed with weeds,
> Tangled tufts from marsh and meads,
> Where the poppy drops its seeds
> In the silence and the gloom.

The "rowen," like the "aftermath," is an after-mowing, an end-of-season crop. In this poem, Longfellow was wise enough to let the simple lyric expression stand without didactic interpretation.

In 1879, when he was seventy-two and only three years from death, he wrote the lovely "The Tide Rises, The Tide Falls," a poem reminiscent of "My Lost Youth." He returns again to his boyhood in Portland, where he had loved to listen to the sound of the waves and to the gentle rush of the tide coming in. As he visualized in old age the phenomena of water behavior, it became symbolic of life. Once again, as in the early "Psalm of Life," he uses the figure, "footprints in the sands." By now he seems not very certain that he has made lasting footprints in the sands of life, but the tone implies that it does not greatly matter. This lyric too invites full quotation:

> The tide rises, the tide falls,
> The twilight darkens, the curlew calls;
> Along the sea-sands damp and brown
> The traveller hastens toward the town,
>   And the tide rises, the tide falls.
> Darkness settles on roofs and walls,
> But the sea, the sea in the darkness calls;
> The little waves, with their soft, white hands,
> Efface the footprints in the sands,
>   And the tide rises, the tide falls.

The morning breaks; the steeds in their stalls
Stamp and neigh, as the hostler calls;
The day returns, but nevermore
Returns the traveller to the shore,
    And the tide rises, the tide falls.

It is interesting to compare this poem with Robert Frost's "Stopping by Woods on a Snowy Evening." There is a difference of only one line in the length; both feature a traveler proceeding through life. Longfellow uses sea imagery; Frost, woods and snow. Frost's lyric is the better, but Longfellow's came first and is good.

Only two weeks before his death, Longfellow wrote his last poem, "The Bells of San Blas." It is one of his finest lyrics; he had kept his poetic vision to the end. This poem can be compared with Arnold's "Dover Beach" and with other late nineteenth-century lyrics lamenting the passing of an age of religious faith. Longfellow, like Arnold, joins the lament; but unlike Arnold he accepts change with an unshaken and confident personal faith:

O Bells of San Blas, in vain
Ye call back the Past again!
The Past is deaf to your prayer;
Out of the shadows of night
The world rolls into light;
It is daybreak everywhere.

Although the short lyrics are only a small part of his total poetic production, if Longfellow had written only these, he would still have been a notable nineteenth-century American poet. . . .

Source: Cecil B. Williams, "Household Lyrics, Ballads, Odes, Elegies, Sonnets," in *Henry Wadsworth Longfellow*, Twayne Publishers, 1964, pp. 129–47.

SOURCES

Allaback, Steven, "Henry Wadsworth Longfellow," in *Dictionary of Literary Biography*, Vol. 1, *The American Renaissance in New England*, Gale Research, 1978, pp. 117–23.

Bain, Robert, ed., "Henry Wadsworth Longfellow (1807-1882)," in *Whitman's & Dickinson's Contemporaries: An Anthology of Their Verse*, Southern Illinois University, 1996, pp. 65–66.

"A Brief Guide to the Fireside poets," in *Poets.org: From the Academy of American Poets*, http://www.poets.org/viewmedia.php/prmMID/5654 (accessed April 21, 2011).

"Census 2000 Tribal Entity Counts for American Indian Reservations and Off-Reservation Trust Lands," in *U.S. Census Bureau*, http://www.census.gov/geo/www/tallies/tallyair.html (accessed April 21, 2011).

Dinnerstein, Leonard, Roger L. Nichols, and David M. Reimers, "Treatment of Indians," in *Natives and Strangers: A Multicultural History of Americans*, Oxford University Press, 1996, pp. 225–31.

Elliott, Emory, Martha Banta, Terence Martin, David Minter, Marjorie Perloff, and Daniel B. Shea, eds., "William Cullen Bryant and the Fireside Poets," in *Columbia Literary History of the United States*, Columbia University Press, 1988, pp. 278–88.

Gioia, Dana, "Longfellow in the Aftermath of Modernism," in *The Columbia History of American Poetry*, edited by Jay Parini, Columbia University Press, 1993, pp. 64–96.

"Grover Cleveland," in *American President: An Online Reference Resource*, University of Virginia's Miller Center of Public Affairs, http://millercenter.org/president/cleveland/essays/biography/4 (accessed April 21, 2011).

Harris, Mark W., "Unitarian Universalist Origins: Our Historic Faith," in *Unitarian Universalist Association of Congregations*, http://www.uua.org/publications/pamphlets/introductions/151249.shtml (accessed April 21, 2011).

Hoxie, Frederick E., Preface to *The Campaign to Assimilate the Indians, 1880-1920*, University of Nebraska Press, 1984, pp. xvii–xxiv.

Kennedy, William Sloane, "Biography," in *Henry W. Longfellow: Biography, Anecdote, Letters, Criticism*, Moses King, 1882, pp. 9–166.

Longfellow, Henry Wadsworth, "The Tide Rises, the Tide Falls," in *Favorite Poems of Henry Wadsworth Longfellow*, Doubleday, 1947, pp. 37–38.

McFarland, Ron, "A Longfellow Chronology," in *The Long Life of "Evangeline": A History of the Longfellow Poem in Print, in Adaptation and in Popular Culture*, McFarland, 2010, pp. 17–22.

Ogunwole, Stella U., "The American Indian and Alaska Native Population: 2000," in *Census 2000 Brief*, United States Census Bureau, February 2002, p. 1, http://www.census.gov/prod/2002pubs/c2kbr01-15.pdf (accessed April 20, 2011).

O'Neill, Joseph E., "Henry Wadsworth Longfellow, 1807-1882: Poet of the Feeling Heart," in *American Classics Reconsidered: A Christian Appraisal*, edited by Harold C. Gardiner, Scribner, 1958, pp. 146–75.

Rankine, Claudia, and Lisa Sewell, Introduction to *American Poets in the 21st Century: The New Poetics*, Wesleyan University Press, 2007, pp. 1–15.

Skinner, Donald E., "UUA Membership Declines for Second Year," in *Unitarian Universalist Association of Congregations*, April 12, 2010, http://www.uuworld.org/news/articles/160696.shtml (accessed April 21, 2011).

Taylor, Walter Fuller, "Henry Wadsworth Longfellow," in *A History of American Letters*, American Book, 1936, pp. 187–96.

Wagenknecht, Edward, "The Boundless Hope," in *Longfellow: A Full-Length Portrait*, Longman's, Green, 1955, pp. 289–306.

FURTHER READING

Conn, Steven, *History's Shadow: Native Americans and Historical Consciousness in the Nineteenth Century*, University of Chicago Press, 2004.

> Conn explores the attitudes and prejudices of non-Native Americans to Native Americans during the nineteenth century. The book focuses in particular on the way developments in anthropology and sociology shaped the views of the American culture at this time.

Cooke, George Willis, *Unitarianism in America: A History of its Origin and Development*, Echo Library, 2007.

> In this work, a reproduction of a volume originally published in 1902, Cooke offers a comprehensive treatment of the Unitarian faith as it originated and transformed through the late nineteenth century.

Delbanco, Andrew, ed., *Writing New England: An Anthology from the Puritans to the Present*, Belknap Press of Harvard University Press, 2001.

> In this volume, Delbanco collects a variety of writing, including prose, poetry, letters, and excerpts from longer works of fiction and history in order to present a sampling of the unique characteristics of the New England identity.

Longfellow, Henry Wadsworth, *Evangeline*, Goose Lane Editions, 2004.

> Longfellow's long narrative poem explores the mythic origins of the people of Acadia (coastal Maine).

Novak, Barbara, *Voyages of the Self: Pairs, Parallels and Patterns in American Art and Literature*, Oxford University Press, 2007.

> Novak explores the development of the American sense of identity as revealed through the art and literature of various time periods. The nineteenth century is treated in several chapters, as Novak discusses in particular the works of Henry David Thoreau, Ralph Waldo Emerson, and Walt Whitman. The creation and development of a national sense of identity during the nineteenth century is juxtaposed with prevailing American cultural views and attitudes regarding Native Americans, as well as burgeoning notions of democracy.

SUGGESTED SEARCH TERMS

Henry Longfellow AND The Tide Rises, the Tide Falls

Henry Longfellow AND Fireside Poets

Henry Longfellow AND Samuel Longfellow

Henry Longfellow AND New England

Henry Longfellow AND Native Americans

Henry Longfellow AND Unitarianism

Henry Longfellow AND Ultima Thule

Henry Longfellow AND lyric poetry

Henry Longfellow AND nature poetry

Henry Longfellow AND mortality

The Tide Rises, the Tide Falls

Glossary of Literary Terms

A

Abstract: Used as a noun, the term refers to a short summary or outline of a longer work. As an adjective applied to writing or literary works, abstract refers to words or phrases that name things not knowable through the five senses.

Accent: The emphasis or stress placed on a syllable in poetry. Traditional poetry commonly uses patterns of accented and unaccented syllables (known as feet) that create distinct rhythms. Much modern poetry uses less formal arrangements that create a sense of freedom and spontaneity.

Aestheticism: A literary and artistic movement of the nineteenth century. Followers of the movement believed that art should not be mixed with social, political, or moral teaching. The statement "art for art's sake" is a good summary of aestheticism. The movement had its roots in France, but it gained widespread importance in England in the last half of the nineteenth century, where it helped change the Victorian practice of including moral lessons in literature.

Affective Fallacy: An error in judging the merits or faults of a work of literature. The "error" results from stressing the importance of the work's effect upon the reader—that is, how it makes a reader "feel" emotionally, what it does as a literary work—instead of stressing its inner qualities as a created object, or what it "is."

Age of Johnson: The period in English literature between 1750 and 1798, named after the most prominent literary figure of the age, Samuel Johnson. Works written during this time are noted for their emphasis on "sensibility," or emotional quality. These works formed a transition between the rational works of the Age of Reason, or Neoclassical period, and the emphasis on individual feelings and responses of the Romantic period.

Age of Reason: See *Neoclassicism*

Age of Sensibility: See *Age of Johnson*

Agrarians: A group of Southern American writers of the 1930s and 1940s who fostered an economic and cultural program for the South based on agriculture, in opposition to the industrial society of the North. The term can refer to any group that promotes the value of farm life and agricultural society.

Alexandrine Meter: See *Meter*

Allegory: A narrative technique in which characters representing things or abstract ideas are used to convey a message or teach a lesson. Allegory is typically used to teach moral, ethical, or religious lessons but is sometimes used for satiric or political purposes.

Alliteration: A poetic device where the first consonant sounds or any vowel sounds in words or syllables are repeated.

Allusion: A reference to a familiar literary or historical person or event, used to make an idea more easily understood.

Amerind Literature: The writing and oral traditions of Native Americans. Native American literature was originally passed on by word of mouth, so it consisted largely of stories and events that were easily memorized. Amerind prose is often rhythmic like poetry because it was recited to the beat of a ceremonial drum.

Analogy: A comparison of two things made to explain something unfamiliar through its similarities to something familiar, or to prove one point based on the acceptedness of another. Similes and metaphors are types of analogies.

Anapest: See *Foot*

Angry Young Men: A group of British writers of the 1950s whose work expressed bitterness and disillusionment with society. Common to their work is an anti-hero who rebels against a corrupt social order and strives for personal integrity.

Anthropomorphism: The presentation of animals or objects in human shape or with human characteristics. The term is derived from the Greek word for "human form."

Antimasque: See *Masque*

Antithesis: The antithesis of something is its direct opposite. In literature, the use of antithesis as a figure of speech results in two statements that show a contrast through the balancing of two opposite ideas. Technically, it is the second portion of the statement that is defined as the "antithesis"; the first portion is the "thesis."

Apocrypha: Writings tentatively attributed to an author but not proven or universally accepted to be their works. The term was originally applied to certain books of the Bible that were not considered inspired and so were not included in the "sacred canon."

Apollonian and Dionysian: The two impulses believed to guide authors of dramatic tragedy. The Apollonian impulse is named after Apollo, the Greek god of light and beauty and the symbol of intellectual order. The Dionysian impulse is named after Dionysus, the Greek god of wine and the symbol of the unrestrained forces of nature. The Apollonian impulse is to create a rational, harmonious world, while the Dionysian is to express the irrational forces of personality.

Apostrophe: A statement, question, or request addressed to an inanimate object or concept or to a nonexistent or absent person.

Archetype: The word archetype is commonly used to describe an original pattern or model from which all other things of the same kind are made. This term was introduced to literary criticism from the psychology of Carl Jung. It expresses Jung's theory that behind every person's "unconscious," or repressed memories of the past, lies the "collective unconscious" of the human race: memories of the countless typical experiences of our ancestors. These memories are said to prompt illogical associations that trigger powerful emotions in the reader. Often, the emotional process is primitive, even primordial. Archetypes are the literary images that grow out of the "collective unconscious." They appear in literature as incidents and plots that repeat basic patterns of life. They may also appear as stereotyped characters.

Argument: The argument of a work is the author's subject matter or principal idea.

Art for Art's Sake: See *Aestheticism*

Assonance: The repetition of similar vowel sounds in poetry.

Audience: The people for whom a piece of literature is written. Authors usually write with a certain audience in mind, for example, children, members of a religious or ethnic group, or colleagues in a professional field. The term "audience" also applies to the people who gather to see or hear any performance, including plays, poetry readings, speeches, and concerts.

Automatic Writing: Writing carried out without a preconceived plan in an effort to capture every random thought. Authors who engage in automatic writing typically do not revise their work, preferring instead to preserve the revealed truth and beauty of spontaneous expression.

Avant-garde: A French term meaning "vanguard." It is used in literary criticism to describe new writing that rejects traditional approaches to literature in favor of innovations in style or content.

B

Ballad: A short poem that tells a simple story and has a repeated refrain. Ballads were originally intended to be sung. Early ballads, known as folk ballads, were passed down through generations, so their authors are often unknown. Later ballads composed by known authors are called literary ballads.

Baroque: A term used in literary criticism to describe literature that is complex or ornate in style or diction. Baroque works typically express tension, anxiety, and violent emotion. The term "Baroque Age" designates a period in Western European literature beginning in the late sixteenth century and ending about one hundred years later. Works of this period often mirror the qualities of works more generally associated with the label "baroque" and sometimes feature elaborate conceits.

Baroque Age: See *Baroque*

Baroque Period: See *Baroque*

Beat Generation: See *Beat Movement*

Beat Movement: A period featuring a group of American poets and novelists of the 1950s and 1960s—including Jack Kerouac, Allen Ginsberg, Gregory Corso, William S. Burroughs, and Lawrence Ferlinghetti—who rejected established social and literary values. Using such techniques as stream of consciousness writing and jazz-influenced free verse and focusing on unusual or abnormal states of mind—generated by religious ecstasy or the use of drugs—the Beat writers aimed to create works that were unconventional in both form and subject matter.

Beat Poets: See *Beat Movement*

Beats, The: See *Beat Movement*

Belles-lettres: A French term meaning "fine letters" or "beautiful writing." It is often used as a synonym for literature, typically referring to imaginative and artistic rather than scientific or expository writing. Current usage sometimes restricts the meaning to light or humorous writing and appreciative essays about literature.

Black Aesthetic Movement: A period of artistic and literary development among African Americans in the 1960s and early 1970s. This was the first major African-American artistic movement since the Harlem Renaissance and was closely paralleled by the civil rights and black power movements. The black aesthetic writers attempted to produce works of art that would be meaningful to the black masses. Key figures in black aesthetics included one of its founders, poet and playwright Amiri Baraka, formerly known as LeRoi Jones; poet and essayist Haki R. Madhubuti, formerly Don L. Lee; poet and playwright Sonia Sanchez; and dramatist Ed Bullins.

Black Arts Movement: See *Black Aesthetic Movement*

Black Comedy: See *Black Humor*

Black Humor: Writing that places grotesque elements side by side with humorous ones in an attempt to shock the reader, forcing him or her to laugh at the horrifying reality of a disordered world.

Black Mountain School: Black Mountain College and three of its instructors—Robert Creeley, Robert Duncan, and Charles Olson—were all influential in projective verse, so poets working in projective verse are now referred as members of the Black Mountain school.

Blank Verse: Loosely, any unrhymed poetry, but more generally, unrhymed iambic pentameter verse (composed of lines of five two-syllable feet with the first syllable accented, the second unaccented). Blank verse has been used by poets since the Renaissance for its flexibility and its graceful, dignified tone.

Bloomsbury Group: A group of English writers, artists, and intellectuals who held informal artistic and philosophical discussions in Bloomsbury, a district of London, from around 1907 to the early 1930s. The Bloomsbury Group held no uniform philosophical beliefs but did commonly express an aversion to moral prudery and a desire for greater social tolerance.

Bon Mot: A French term meaning "good word." A *bon mot* is a witty remark or clever observation.

Breath Verse: See *Projective Verse*

Burlesque: Any literary work that uses exaggeration to make its subject appear ridiculous, either by treating a trivial subject with profound seriousness or by treating a dignified subject frivolously. The word "burlesque" may also be used as an adjective, as in "burlesque show," to mean "striptease act."

C

Cadence: The natural rhythm of language caused by the alternation of accented and unaccented syllables. Much modern poetry—notably free verse—deliberately manipulates cadence to create complex rhythmic effects.

Caesura: A pause in a line of poetry, usually occurring near the middle. It typically corresponds to a break in the natural rhythm or sense of the line but is sometimes shifted to create special meanings or rhythmic effects.

Canzone: A short Italian or Provencal lyric poem, commonly about love and often set to music. The *canzone* has no set form but typically contains five or six stanzas made up of seven to twenty lines of eleven syllables each. A shorter, five- to ten-line "envoy," or concluding stanza, completes the poem.

Carpe Diem: A Latin term meaning "seize the day." This is a traditional theme of poetry, especially lyrics. A *carpe diem* poem advises the reader or the person it addresses to live for today and enjoy the pleasures of the moment.

Catharsis: The release or purging of unwanted emotions—specifically fear and pity—brought about by exposure to art. The term was first used by the Greek philosopher Aristotle in his *Poetics* to refer to the desired effect of tragedy on spectators.

Celtic Renaissance: A period of Irish literary and cultural history at the end of the nineteenth century. Followers of the movement aimed to create a romantic vision of Celtic myth and legend. The most significant works of the Celtic Renaissance typically present a dreamy, unreal world, usually in reaction against the reality of contemporary problems.

Celtic Twilight: See *Celtic Renaissance*

Character: Broadly speaking, a person in a literary work. The actions of characters are what constitute the plot of a story, novel, or poem. There are numerous types of characters, ranging from simple, stereotypical figures to intricate, multifaceted ones. In the techniques of anthropomorphism and personification, animals—and even places or things—can assume aspects of character. "Characterization" is the process by which an author creates vivid, believable characters in a work of art. This may be done in a variety of ways, including (1) direct description of the character by the narrator; (2) the direct presentation of the speech, thoughts, or actions of the character; and (3) the responses of other characters to the character. The term "character" also refers to a form originated by the ancient Greek writer Theophrastus that later became popular in the seventeenth and eighteenth centuries. It is a short essay or sketch of a person who prominently displays a specific attribute or quality, such as miserliness or ambition.

Characterization: See *Character*

Classical: In its strictest definition in literary criticism, classicism refers to works of ancient Greek or Roman literature. The term may also be used to describe a literary work of recognized importance (a "classic") from any time period or literature that exhibits the traits of classicism.

Classicism: A term used in literary criticism to describe critical doctrines that have their roots in ancient Greek and Roman literature, philosophy, and art. Works associated with classicism typically exhibit restraint on the part of the author, unity of design and purpose, clarity, simplicity, logical organization, and respect for tradition.

Colloquialism: A word, phrase, or form of pronunciation that is acceptable in casual conversation but not in formal, written communication. It is considered more acceptable than slang.

Complaint: A lyric poem, popular in the Renaissance, in which the speaker expresses sorrow about his or her condition. Typically, the speaker's sadness is caused by an unresponsive lover, but some complaints cite other sources of unhappiness, such as poverty or fate.

Conceit: A clever and fanciful metaphor, usually expressed through elaborate and extended comparison, that presents a striking parallel between two seemingly dissimilar things—for example, elaborately comparing a beautiful woman to an object like a garden or the sun. The conceit was a popular device throughout the Elizabethan Age and Baroque Age and was the principal technique of the seventeenth-century English metaphysical poets. This usage of the word conceit is unrelated to the best-known definition of conceit as an arrogant attitude or behavior.

Concrete: Concrete is the opposite of abstract, and refers to a thing that actually exists or a description that allows the reader to experience an object or concept with the senses.

Concrete Poetry: Poetry in which visual elements play a large part in the poetic effect. Punctuation marks, letters, or words are arranged on a page to form a visual design: a cross, for example, or a bumblebee.

Confessional Poetry: A form of poetry in which the poet reveals very personal, intimate, sometimes shocking information about himself or herself.

Connotation: The impression that a word gives beyond its defined meaning. Connotations may be universally understood or may be significant only to a certain group.

Consonance: Consonance occurs in poetry when words appearing at the ends of two or more verses have similar final consonant sounds but have final vowel sounds that differ, as with "stuff" and "off."

Convention: Any widely accepted literary device, style, or form.

Corrido: A Mexican ballad.

Couplet: Two lines of poetry with the same rhyme and meter, often expressing a complete and self-contained thought.

Criticism: The systematic study and evaluation of literary works, usually based on a specific method or set of principles. An important part of literary studies since ancient times, the practice of criticism has given rise to numerous theories, methods, and "schools," sometimes producing conflicting, even contradictory, interpretations of literature in general as well as of individual works. Even such basic issues as what constitutes a poem or a novel have been the subject of much criticism over the centuries.

D

Dactyl: See *Foot*

Dadaism: A protest movement in art and literature founded by Tristan Tzara in 1916. Followers of the movement expressed their outrage at the destruction brought about by World War I by revolting against numerous forms of social convention. The Dadaists presented works marked by calculated madness and flamboyant nonsense. They stressed total freedom of expression, commonly through primitive displays of emotion and illogical, often senseless, poetry. The movement ended shortly after the war, when it was replaced by surrealism.

Decadent: See *Decadents*

Decadents: The followers of a nineteenth-century literary movement that had its beginnings in French aestheticism. Decadent literature displays a fascination with perverse and morbid states; a search for novelty and sensation—the "new thrill"; a preoccupation with mysticism; and a belief in the senselessness of human existence. The movement is closely associated with the doctrine Art for Art's Sake. The term "decadence" is sometimes used to denote a decline in the quality of art or literature following a period of greatness.

Deconstruction: A method of literary criticism developed by Jacques Derrida and characterized by multiple conflicting interpretations of a given work. Deconstructionists consider the impact of the language of a work and suggest that the true meaning of the work is not necessarily the meaning that the author intended.

Deduction: The process of reaching a conclusion through reasoning from general premises to a specific premise.

Denotation: The definition of a word, apart from the impressions or feelings it creates in the reader.

Diction: The selection and arrangement of words in a literary work. Either or both may vary depending on the desired effect. There are four general types of diction: "formal," used in scholarly or lofty writing; "informal," used in relaxed but educated conversation; "colloquial," used in everyday speech; and "slang," containing newly coined words and other terms not accepted in formal usage.

Didactic: A term used to describe works of literature that aim to teach some moral, religious, political, or practical lesson. Although didactic elements are often found in artistically pleasing works, the term "didactic" usually refers to literature in which the message is more important than the form. The term may also be used to criticize a work that the critic finds "overly didactic," that is, heavy-handed in its delivery of a lesson.

Dimeter: See *Meter*

Dionysian: See *Apollonian and Dionysian*

Discordia concours: A Latin phrase meaning "discord in harmony." The term was coined by the eighteenth-century English writer Samuel Johnson to describe "a combination of dissimilar images or discovery of occult resemblances in things apparently unlike." Johnson created the expression by reversing a phrase by the Latin poet Horace.

Dissonance: A combination of harsh or jarring sounds, especially in poetry. Although such combinations may be accidental, poets sometimes intentionally make them to achieve particular effects. Dissonance is also sometimes used to refer to close but not identical rhymes. When this is the case, the word functions as a synonym for consonance.

Double Entendre: A corruption of a French phrase meaning "double meaning." The term is used to indicate a word or phrase that is deliberately ambiguous, especially when one of the meanings is risque or improper.

Draft: Any preliminary version of a written work. An author may write dozens of drafts which are revised to form the final work, or he or she may write only one, with few or no revisions.

Dramatic Monologue: See *Monologue*

Dramatic Poetry: Any lyric work that employs elements of drama such as dialogue, conflict, or characterization, but excluding works that are intended for stage presentation.

Dream Allegory: See *Dream Vision*

Dream Vision: A literary convention, chiefly of the Middle Ages. In a dream vision a story is presented as a literal dream of the narrator. This device was commonly used to teach moral and religious lessons.

E

Eclogue: In classical literature, a poem featuring rural themes and structured as a dialogue among shepherds. Eclogues often took specific poetic forms, such as elegies or love poems. Some were written as the soliloquy of a shepherd. In later centuries, "eclogue" came to refer to any poem that was in the pastoral tradition or that had a dialogue or monologue structure.

Edwardian: Describes cultural conventions identified with the period of the reign of Edward VII of England (1901-1910). Writers of the Edwardian Age typically displayed a strong reaction against the propriety and conservatism of the Victorian Age. Their work often exhibits distrust of authority in religion, politics, and art and expresses strong doubts about the soundness of conventional values.

Edwardian Age: See *Edwardian*

Electra Complex: A daughter's amorous obsession with her father.

Elegy: A lyric poem that laments the death of a person or the eventual death of all people. In a conventional elegy, set in a classical world, the poet and subject are spoken of as shepherds. In modern criticism, the word elegy is often used to refer to a poem that is melancholy or mournfully contemplative.

Elizabethan Age: A period of great economic growth, religious controversy, and nationalism closely associated with the reign of Elizabeth I of England (1558-1603). The Elizabethan Age is considered a part of the general renaissance—that is, the flowering of arts and literature—that took place in Europe during the fourteenth through sixteenth centuries. The era is considered the golden age of English literature. The most important dramas in English and a great deal of lyric poetry were produced during this period, and modern English criticism began around this time.

Empathy: A sense of shared experience, including emotional and physical feelings, with someone or something other than oneself. Empathy is often used to describe the response of a reader to a literary character.

English Sonnet: See *Sonnet*

Enjambment: The running over of the sense and structure of a line of verse or a couplet into the following verse or couplet.

Enlightenment, The: An eighteenth-century philosophical movement. It began in France but had a wide impact throughout Europe and America. Thinkers of the Enlightenment valued reason and believed that both the individual and society could achieve a state of perfection. Corresponding to this essentially humanist vision was a resistance to religious authority.

Epic: A long narrative poem about the adventures of a hero of great historic or legendary importance. The setting is vast and the action is often given cosmic significance through the intervention of supernatural forces such as gods, angels, or demons. Epics are typically written in a classical style of grand simplicity with elaborate metaphors and allusions that enhance the symbolic importance of a hero's adventures.

Epic Simile: See *Homeric Simile*

Epigram: A saying that makes the speaker's point quickly and concisely.

Epilogue: A concluding statement or section of a literary work. In dramas, particularly those of the seventeenth and eighteenth centuries, the epilogue is a closing speech, often in verse, delivered by an actor at the end of a play and spoken directly to the audience.

Epiphany: A sudden revelation of truth inspired by a seemingly trivial incident.

Epitaph: An inscription on a tomb or tombstone, or a verse written on the occasion of a person's death. Epitaphs may be serious or humorous.

Epithalamion: A song or poem written to honor and commemorate a marriage ceremony.

Epithalamium: See *Epithalamion*

Epithet: A word or phrase, often disparaging or abusive, that expresses a character trait of someone or something.

Erziehungsroman: See *Bildungsroman*

Essay: A prose composition with a focused subject of discussion. The term was coined by Michel de Montaigne to describe his 1580 collection of brief, informal reflections on himself and on various topics relating to human nature. An essay can also be a long, systematic discourse.

Existentialism: A predominantly twentieth-century philosophy concerned with the nature and perception of human existence. There are two major strains of existentialist thought: atheistic and Christian. Followers of atheistic existentialism believe that the individual is alone in a godless universe and that the basic human condition is one of suffering and loneliness. Nevertheless, because there are no fixed values, individuals can create their own characters—indeed, they can shape themselves—through the exercise of free will. The atheistic strain culminates in and is popularly associated with the works of Jean-Paul Sartre. The Christian existentialists, on the other hand, believe that only in God may people find freedom from life's anguish. The two strains hold certain beliefs in common: that existence cannot be fully understood or described through empirical effort; that anguish is a universal element of life; that individuals must bear responsibility for their actions; and that there is no common standard of behavior or perception for religious and ethical matters.

Expatriates: See *Expatriatism*

Expatriatism: The practice of leaving one's country to live for an extended period in another country.

Exposition: Writing intended to explain the nature of an idea, thing, or theme. Expository writing is often combined with description, narration, or argument. In dramatic writing, the exposition is the introductory material which presents the characters, setting, and tone of the play.

Expressionism: An indistinct literary term, originally used to describe an early twentieth-century school of German painting. The term applies to almost any mode of unconventional, highly subjective writing that distorts reality in some way.

Extended Monologue: See *Monologue*

F

Feet: See *Foot*

Feminine Rhyme: See *Rhyme*

Fiction: Any story that is the product of imagination rather than a documentation of fact. Characters and events in such narratives may be based in real life but their ultimate form and configuration is a creation of the author.

Figurative Language: A technique in writing in which the author temporarily interrupts the order, construction, or meaning of the writing for a particular effect. This interruption takes the form of one or more figures of speech such as hyperbole, irony, or simile. Figurative language is the opposite of literal language, in which every word is truthful, accurate, and free of exaggeration or embellishment.

Figures of Speech: Writing that differs from customary conventions for construction, meaning, order, or significance for the purpose of a special meaning or effect. There are two major types of figures of speech: rhetorical figures, which do not make changes in the meaning of the words, and tropes, which do.

Fin de siecle: A French term meaning "end of the century." The term is used to denote the last decade of the nineteenth century, a transition period when writers and other artists abandoned old conventions and looked for new techniques and objectives.

First Person: See *Point of View*

Folk Ballad: See *Ballad*

Folklore: Traditions and myths preserved in a culture or group of people. Typically, these are passed on by word of mouth in various forms—such as legends, songs, and proverbs—or preserved in customs and ceremonies. This term was first used by W. J. Thoms in 1846.

Folktale: A story originating in oral tradition. Folktales fall into a variety of categories, including legends, ghost stories, fairy tales, fables, and anecdotes based on historical figures and events.

Foot: The smallest unit of rhythm in a line of poetry. In English-language poetry, a foot is typically one accented syllable combined with one or two unaccented syllables.

Form: The pattern or construction of a work which identifies its genre and distinguishes it from other genres.

Formalism: In literary criticism, the belief that literature should follow prescribed rules of construction, such as those that govern the sonnet form.

Fourteener Meter: See *Meter*

Free Verse: Poetry that lacks regular metrical and rhyme patterns but that tries to capture the cadences of everyday speech. The form allows a poet to exploit a variety of rhythmical effects within a single poem.

Futurism: A flamboyant literary and artistic movement that developed in France, Italy, and Russia from 1908 through the 1920s. Futurist theater and poetry abandoned traditional literary forms. In their place, followers of the movement attempted to achieve total freedom of expression through bizarre imagery and deformed or newly invented words. The Futurists were self-consciously modern artists who attempted to incorporate the appearances and sounds of modern life into their work.

G

Genre: A category of literary work. In critical theory, genre may refer to both the content of a given work—tragedy, comedy, pastoral—and to its form, such as poetry, novel, or drama.

Genteel Tradition: A term coined by critic George Santayana to describe the literary practice of certain late nineteenth-century American writers, especially New Englanders. Followers of the Genteel Tradition emphasized conventionality in social, religious, moral, and literary standards.

Georgian Age: See *Georgian Poets*

Georgian Period: See *Georgian Poets*

Georgian Poets: A loose grouping of English poets during the years 1912-1922. The Georgians reacted against certain literary schools and practices, especially Victorian wordiness, turn-of-the-century aestheticism, and contemporary urban realism. In their place, the Georgians embraced the nineteenth-century poetic practices of William Wordsworth and the other Lake Poets.

Georgic: A poem about farming and the farmer's way of life, named from Virgil's *Georgics*.

Gilded Age: A period in American history during the 1870s characterized by political corruption and materialism. A number of important novels of social and political criticism were written during this time.

Gothic: See *Gothicism*

Gothicism: In literary criticism, works characterized by a taste for the medieval or morbidly attractive. A gothic novel prominently features elements of horror, the supernatural, gloom, and violence: clanking chains, terror, charnel houses, ghosts, medieval castles, and mysteriously slamming doors. The term "gothic novel" is also applied to novels that lack elements of the traditional Gothic setting but that create a similar atmosphere of terror or dread.

Graveyard School: A group of eighteenth-century English poets who wrote long, picturesque meditations on death. Their works were designed to cause the reader to ponder immortality.

Great Chain of Being: The belief that all things and creatures in nature are organized in a hierarchy from inanimate objects at the bottom to God at the top. This system of belief was popular in the seventeenth and eighteenth centuries.

Grotesque: In literary criticism, the subject matter of a work or a style of expression characterized by exaggeration, deformity, freakishness, and disorder. The grotesque often includes an element of comic absurdity.

H

Haiku: The shortest form of Japanese poetry, constructed in three lines of five, seven, and five syllables respectively. The message of a *haiku* poem usually centers on some aspect of spirituality and provokes an emotional response in the reader.

Half Rhyme: See *Consonance*

Harlem Renaissance: The Harlem Renaissance of the 1920s is generally considered the first significant movement of black writers and artists in the United States. During this period, new and established black writers published more fiction and poetry than ever before, the first influential black literary journals were established, and black authors and artists received their first widespread recognition and serious critical appraisal. Among the major writers associated with this period are Claude McKay, Jean Toomer, Countee Cullen, Langston Hughes, Arna Bontemps, Nella Larsen, and Zora Neale Hurston.

Hellenism: Imitation of ancient Greek thought or styles. Also, an approach to life that focuses on the growth and development of the intellect. "Hellenism" is sometimes used to refer to the belief that reason can be applied to examine all human experience.

Heptameter: See *Meter*

Hero/Heroine: The principal sympathetic character (male or female) in a literary work. Heroes and heroines typically exhibit admirable traits: idealism, courage, and integrity, for example.

Heroic Couplet: A rhyming couplet written in iambic pentameter (a verse with five iambic feet).

Heroic Line: The meter and length of a line of verse in epic or heroic poetry. This varies by language and time period.

Heroine: See *Hero/Heroine*

Hexameter: See *Meter*

Historical Criticism: The study of a work based on its impact on the world of the time period in which it was written.

Hokku: See *Haiku*

Holocaust: See *Holocaust Literature*

Holocaust Literature: Literature influenced by or written about the Holocaust of World War II. Such literature includes true stories of survival in concentration camps, escape, and life after the war, as well as fictional works and poetry.

Homeric Simile: An elaborate, detailed comparison written as a simile many lines in length.

Horatian Satire: See *Satire*

Humanism: A philosophy that places faith in the dignity of humankind and rejects the medieval perception of the individual as a weak, fallen creature. "Humanists" typically believe in the perfectibility of human nature and view reason and education as the means to that end.

Humors: Mentions of the humors refer to the ancient Greek theory that a person's health and personality were determined by the balance of four basic fluids in the body: blood, phlegm, yellow bile, and black bile. A dominance of any fluid would cause extremes in behavior. An excess of blood created a sanguine person who was joyful, aggressive, and passionate; a phlegmatic person was shy, fearful, and sluggish; too much yellow bile led to a choleric temperament characterized by impatience, anger, bitterness, and stubbornness; and excessive black bile created melancholy, a state of laziness, gluttony, and lack of motivation.

Humours: See *Humors*

Hyperbole: In literary criticism, deliberate exaggeration used to achieve an effect.

I

Iamb: See *Foot*

Idiom: A word construction or verbal expression closely associated with a given language.

Image: A concrete representation of an object or sensory experience. Typically, such a representation helps evoke the feelings associated with the object or experience itself. Images are either "literal" or "figurative." Literal images are especially concrete and involve little or no extension of the obvious meaning of the words used to express them. Figurative images do not follow the literal meaning of the words exactly. Images in literature are usually visual, but the term "image" can also refer to the representation of any sensory experience.

Imagery: The array of images in a literary work. Also, figurative language.

Imagism: An English and American poetry movement that flourished between 1908 and 1917. The Imagists used precise, clearly presented images in their works. They also used common, everyday speech and aimed for conciseness, concrete imagery, and the creation of new rhythms.

In medias res: A Latin term meaning "in the middle of things." It refers to the technique of beginning a story at its midpoint and then using various flashback devices to reveal previous action.

Induction: The process of reaching a conclusion by reasoning from specific premises to form a general premise. Also, an introductory portion of a work of literature, especially a play.

Intentional Fallacy: The belief that judgments of a literary work based solely on an author's stated or implied intentions are false and misleading. Critics who believe in the concept of the intentional fallacy typically argue that the work itself is sufficient matter for interpretation, even though they may concede that an author's statement of purpose can be useful.

Interior Monologue: A narrative technique in which characters' thoughts are revealed in a way that appears to be uncontrolled by the author. The interior monologue typically aims to reveal the inner self of a character. It portrays emotional experiences as they occur at both a conscious and unconscious level. Images are often used to represent sensations or emotions.

Internal Rhyme: Rhyme that occurs within a single line of verse.

Irish Literary Renaissance: A late nineteenth- and early twentieth-century movement in Irish literature. Members of the movement aimed to reduce the influence of British culture in Ireland and create an Irish national literature.

Irony: In literary criticism, the effect of language in which the intended meaning is the opposite of what is stated.

Italian Sonnet: See *Sonnet*

J

Jacobean Age: The period of the reign of James I of England (1603-1625). The early literature of this period reflected the worldview of the Elizabethan Age, but a darker, more cynical attitude steadily grew in the art and literature of the Jacobean Age. This was an important time for English drama and poetry.

Jargon: Language that is used or understood only by a select group of people. Jargon may refer to terminology used in a certain profession, such as computer jargon, or it may refer to any nonsensical language that is not understood by most people.

Journalism: Writing intended for publication in a newspaper or magazine, or for broadcast on a radio or television program featuring news, sports, entertainment, or other timely material.

K

Knickerbocker Group: A somewhat indistinct group of New York writers of the first half of the nineteenth century. Members of the group were linked only by location and a common theme: New York life.

Kunstlerroman: See *Bildungsroman*

L

Lais: See *Lay*

Lake Poets: See *Lake School*

Lake School: These poets all lived in the Lake District of England at the turn of the nineteenth century. As a group, they followed no single "school" of thought or literary practice, although their works were uniformly disparaged by the *Edinburgh Review*.

Lay: A song or simple narrative poem. The form originated in medieval France. Early French *lais* were often based on the Celtic legends and other tales sung by Breton minstrels—thus the name of the "Breton lay." In fourteenth-century England, the term "lay" was used to describe short narratives written in imitation of the Breton lays.

Leitmotiv: See *Motif*

Literal Language: An author uses literal language when he or she writes without exaggerating or embellishing the subject matter and without any tools of figurative language.

Literary Ballad: See *Ballad*

Literature: Literature is broadly defined as any written or spoken material, but the term most often refers to creative works.

Lost Generation: A term first used by Gertrude Stein to describe the post-World War I generation of American writers: men and women haunted by a sense of betrayal and emptiness brought about by the destructiveness of the war.

Lyric Poetry: A poem expressing the subjective feelings and personal emotions of the poet. Such poetry is melodic, since it was originally accompanied by a lyre in recitals. Most Western poetry in the twentieth century may be classified as lyrical.

M

Mannerism: Exaggerated, artificial adherence to a literary manner or style. Also, a popular style of the visual arts of late sixteenth-century Europe that was marked by elongation of the human form and by intentional spatial distortion. Literary works that are self-consciously high-toned and artistic are often said to be "mannered."

Masculine Rhyme: See *Rhyme*

Measure: The foot, verse, or time sequence used in a literary work, especially a poem. Measure is often used somewhat incorrectly as a synonym for meter.

Metaphor: A figure of speech that expresses an idea through the image of another object. Metaphors suggest the essence of the first object by identifying it with certain qualities of the second object.

Metaphysical Conceit: See *Conceit*

Metaphysical Poetry: The body of poetry produced by a group of seventeenth-century English writers called the "Metaphysical Poets." The group includes John Donne and Andrew Marvell. The Metaphysical Poets made use of everyday speech, intellectual analysis, and unique imagery. They aimed to portray the ordinary conflicts and contradictions of life. Their poems often took the form of an argument, and many of them emphasize physical and religious love as well as the fleeting nature of life. Elaborate conceits are typical in metaphysical poetry.

Metaphysical Poets: See *Metaphysical Poetry*

Meter: In literary criticism, the repetition of sound patterns that creates a rhythm in poetry. The patterns are based on the number of syllables and the presence and absence of accents. The unit of rhythm in a line is called a foot. Types of meter are classified according to the number of feet in a line. These are the standard English lines: Monometer, one foot; Dimeter, two feet; Trimeter, three feet; Tetrameter, four feet; Pentameter, five feet; Hexameter, six feet (also called the Alexandrine); Heptameter, seven feet (also called the "Fourteener" when the feet are iambic).

Modernism: Modern literary practices. Also, the principles of a literary school that lasted from roughly the beginning of the twentieth century until the end of World War II. Modernism is defined by its rejection of the literary conventions of the nineteenth century and by its opposition to conventional morality, taste, traditions, and economic values.

Monologue: A composition, written or oral, by a single individual. More specifically, a speech given by a single individual in a drama or other public entertainment. It has no set length, although it is usually several or more lines long.

Monometer: See *Meter*

Mood: The prevailing emotions of a work or of the author in his or her creation of the work. The mood of a work is not always what might be expected based on its subject matter.

Motif: A theme, character type, image, metaphor, or other verbal element that recurs throughout a single work of literature or occurs in a number of different works over a period of time.

Motiv: See *Motif*

Muckrakers: An early twentieth-century group of American writers. Typically, their works exposed the wrongdoings of big business and government in the United States.

Muses: Nine Greek mythological goddesses, the daughters of Zeus and Mnemosyne (Memory). Each muse patronized a specific area of the liberal arts and sciences. Calliope presided over epic poetry, Clio over history, Erato over love poetry, Euterpe over music or lyric poetry, Melpomene over tragedy, Polyhymnia over hymns to the gods, Terpsichore over dance, Thalia over comedy, and Urania over astronomy. Poets and writers traditionally made appeals to the Muses for inspiration in their work.

Myth: An anonymous tale emerging from the traditional beliefs of a culture or social unit. Myths use supernatural explanations for natural phenomena. They may also explain cosmic issues like creation and death. Collections of myths, known as mythologies, are common to all cultures and nations, but the best-known myths belong to the Norse, Roman, and Greek mythologies.

N

Narration: The telling of a series of events, real or invented. A narration may be either a simple narrative, in which the events are recounted chronologically, or a narrative with a plot, in which the account is given in a style reflecting the author's artistic concept of the story. Narration is sometimes used as a synonym for "storyline."

Narrative: A verse or prose accounting of an event or sequence of events, real or invented. The term is also used as an adjective in the sense "method of narration." For example, in literary criticism, the expression "narrative technique" usually refers to the way the author structures and presents his or her story.

Narrative Poetry: A nondramatic poem in which the author tells a story. Such poems may be of any length or level of complexity.

Narrator: The teller of a story. The narrator may be the author or a character in the story through whom the author speaks.

Naturalism: A literary movement of the late nineteenth and early twentieth centuries. The movement's major theorist, French novelist Emile Zola, envisioned a type of fiction that would examine human life with the objectivity of scientific inquiry. The Naturalists typically viewed human beings as either the products of "biological determinism," ruled by hereditary instincts and engaged in an endless struggle for survival, or as the products of "socioeconomic determinism," ruled by social and economic forces beyond their control. In their works, the Naturalists generally ignored the highest levels of society and focused on degradation: poverty, alcoholism, prostitution, insanity, and disease.

Negritude: A literary movement based on the concept of a shared cultural bond on the part of black Africans, wherever they may be in the world. It traces its origins to the former French colonies of Africa and the Caribbean. Negritude poets, novelists, and essayists generally stress four points in their writings: One, black alienation from traditional African culture can lead to feelings of inferiority. Two, European colonialism and Western education should be resisted. Three, black Africans should seek to affirm and define their own identity. Four, African culture can and should be reclaimed. Many Negritude writers also claim that blacks can make unique contributions to the world, based on a heightened appreciation of nature, rhythm, and human emotions—aspects of life they say are not so highly valued in the materialistic and rationalistic West.

Negro Renaissance: See *Harlem Renaissance*

Neoclassical Period: See *Neoclassicism*

Neoclassicism: In literary criticism, this term refers to the revival of the attitudes and styles of expression of classical literature. It is generally used to describe a period in European history beginning in the late seventeenth century and lasting until about 1800. In its purest form, Neoclassicism marked a return to order, proportion, restraint, logic, accuracy, and decorum. In England, where Neoclassicism perhaps was most popular, it reflected the influence of seventeenth- century French writers, especially dramatists. Neoclassical writers typically reacted against the intensity and enthusiasm of the Renaissance period. They wrote works that appealed to the intellect, using elevated language and classical literary forms such as satire and the ode. Neoclassical works were often governed by the classical goal of instruction.

Neoclassicists: See *Neoclassicism*

New Criticism: A movement in literary criticism, dating from the late 1920s, that stressed close textual analysis in the interpretation of works of literature. The New Critics saw little merit in historical and biographical analysis. Rather, they aimed to examine the text alone, free from the question of how external events—biographical or otherwise—may have helped shape it.

New Journalism: A type of writing in which the journalist presents factual information in a form usually used in fiction. New journalism emphasizes description, narration, and character development to bring readers closer to the human element of the story, and is often used in personality profiles and in-depth feature articles. It is not compatible with "straight" or "hard" newswriting, which is generally composed in a brief, fact-based style.

New Journalists: See *New Journalism*

New Negro Movement: See *Harlem Renaissance*

Noble Savage: The idea that primitive man is noble and good but becomes evil and corrupted as he becomes civilized. The concept of the noble savage originated in the Renaissance period but is more closely identified with such later writers as Jean-Jacques Rousseau and Aphra Behn.

O

Objective Correlative: An outward set of objects, a situation, or a chain of events corresponding to an inward experience and evoking this experience in the reader. The term frequently appears in modern criticism in discussions of authors' intended effects on the emotional responses of readers.

Objectivity: A quality in writing characterized by the absence of the author's opinion or feeling about the subject matter. Objectivity is an important factor in criticism.

Occasional Verse: poetry written on the occasion of a significant historical or personal event. *Vers de societe* is sometimes called occasional verse although it is of a less serious nature.

Octave: A poem or stanza composed of eight lines. The term octave most often represents the first eight lines of a Petrarchan sonnet.

Ode: Name given to an extended lyric poem characterized by exalted emotion and dignified style. An ode usually concerns a single, serious theme. Most odes, but not all, are addressed to an object or individual. Odes are distinguished from other lyric poetic forms by their complex rhythmic and stanzaic patterns.

Oedipus Complex: A son's amorous obsession with his mother. The phrase is derived from the story of the ancient Theban hero Oedipus, who unknowingly killed his father and married his mother.

Omniscience: See *Point of View*

Onomatopoeia: The use of words whose sounds express or suggest their meaning. In its simplest sense, onomatopoeia may be represented by words that mimic the sounds they denote such as "hiss" or "meow." At a more subtle level, the pattern and rhythm of sounds and rhymes of a line or poem may be onomatopoeic.

Oral Tradition: See *Oral Transmission*

Oral Transmission: A process by which songs, ballads, folklore, and other material are trans-

mitted by word of mouth. The tradition of oral transmission predates the written record systems of literate society. Oral transmission preserves material sometimes over generations, although often with variations. Memory plays a large part in the recitation and preservation of orally transmitted material.

Ottava Rima: An eight-line stanza of poetry composed in iambic pentameter (a five-foot line in which each foot consists of an unaccented syllable followed by an accented syllable), following the abababcc rhyme scheme.

Oxymoron: A phrase combining two contradictory terms. Oxymorons may be intentional or unintentional.

P

Pantheism: The idea that all things are both a manifestation or revelation of God and a part of God at the same time. Pantheism was a common attitude in the early societies of Egypt, India, and Greece—the term derives from the Greek *pan* meaning "all" and *theos* meaning "deity." It later became a significant part of the Christian faith.

Parable: A story intended to teach a moral lesson or answer an ethical question.

Paradox: A statement that appears illogical or contradictory at first, but may actually point to an underlying truth.

Parallelism: A method of comparison of two ideas in which each is developed in the same grammatical structure.

Parnassianism: A mid nineteenth-century movement in French literature. Followers of the movement stressed adherence to well-defined artistic forms as a reaction against the often chaotic expression of the artist's ego that dominated the work of the Romantics. The Parnassians also rejected the moral, ethical, and social themes exhibited in the works of French Romantics such as Victor Hugo. The aesthetic doctrines of the Parnassians strongly influenced the later symbolist and decadent movements.

Parody: In literary criticism, this term refers to an imitation of a serious literary work or the signature style of a particular author in a ridiculous manner. A typical parody adopts the style of the original and applies it to an inappropriate subject for humorous effect. Parody is a form of satire and could be considered the literary equivalent of a caricature or cartoon.

Pastoral: A term derived from the Latin word "pastor," meaning shepherd. A pastoral is a literary composition on a rural theme. The conventions of the pastoral were originated by the third-century Greek poet Theocritus, who wrote about the experiences, love affairs, and pastimes of Sicilian shepherds. In a pastoral, characters and language of a courtly nature are often placed in a simple setting. The term pastoral is also used to classify dramas, elegies, and lyrics that exhibit the use of country settings and shepherd characters.

Pathetic Fallacy: A term coined by English critic John Ruskin to identify writing that falsely endows nonhuman things with human intentions and feelings, such as "angry clouds" and "sad trees."

Pen Name: See *Pseudonym*

Pentameter: See *Meter*

Persona: A Latin term meaning "mask." *Personae* are the characters in a fictional work of literature. The *persona* generally functions as a mask through which the author tells a story in a voice other than his or her own. A *persona* is usually either a character in a story who acts as a narrator or an "implied author," a voice created by the author to act as the narrator for himself or herself.

Personae: See *Persona*

Personal Point of View: See *Point of View*

Personification: A figure of speech that gives human qualities to abstract ideas, animals, and inanimate objects.

Petrarchan Sonnet: See *Sonnet*

Phenomenology: A method of literary criticism based on the belief that things have no existence outside of human consciousness or awareness. Proponents of this theory believe that art is a process that takes place in the mind of the observer as he or she contemplates an object rather than a quality of the object itself.

Plagiarism: Claiming another person's written material as one's own. Plagiarism can take the form of direct, word-for-word copying or the theft of the substance or idea of the work.

Platonic Criticism: A form of criticism that stresses an artistic work's usefulness as an agent of social engineering rather than any quality or value of the work itself.

Platonism: The embracing of the doctrines of the philosopher Plato, popular among the poets of the Renaissance and the Romantic period. Platonism is more flexible than Aristotelian Criticism and places more emphasis on the supernatural and unknown aspects of life.

Plot: In literary criticism, this term refers to the pattern of events in a narrative or drama. In its simplest sense, the plot guides the author in composing the work and helps the reader follow the work. Typically, plots exhibit causality and unity and have a beginning, a middle, and an end. Sometimes, however, a plot may consist of a series of disconnected events, in which case it is known as an "episodic plot."

Poem: In its broadest sense, a composition utilizing rhyme, meter, concrete detail, and expressive language to create a literary experience with emotional and aesthetic appeal.

Poet: An author who writes poetry or verse. The term is also used to refer to an artist or writer who has an exceptional gift for expression, imagination, and energy in the making of art in any form.

Poete maudit: A term derived from Paul Verlaine's *Les poetes maudits* (*The Accursed Poets*), a collection of essays on the French symbolist writers Stephane Mallarme, Arthur Rimbaud, and Tristan Corbiere. In the sense intended by Verlaine, the poet is "accursed" for choosing to explore extremes of human experience outside of middle-class society.

Poetic Fallacy: See *Pathetic Fallacy*

Poetic Justice: An outcome in a literary work, not necessarily a poem, in which the good are rewarded and the evil are punished, especially in ways that particularly fit their virtues or crimes.

Poetic License: Distortions of fact and literary convention made by a writer—not always a poet—for the sake of the effect gained. Poetic license is closely related to the concept of "artistic freedom."

Poetics: This term has two closely related meanings. It denotes (1) an aesthetic theory in literary criticism about the essence of poetry or (2) rules prescribing the proper methods, content, style, or diction of poetry. The term poetics may also refer to theories about literature in general, not just poetry.

Poetry: In its broadest sense, writing that aims to present ideas and evoke an emotional experience in the reader through the use of meter, imagery, connotative and concrete words, and a carefully constructed structure based on rhythmic patterns. Poetry typically relies on words and expressions that have several layers of meaning. It also makes use of the effects of regular rhythm on the ear and may make a strong appeal to the senses through the use of imagery.

Point of View: The narrative perspective from which a literary work is presented to the reader. There are four traditional points of view. The "third person omniscient" gives the reader a "godlike" perspective, unrestricted by time or place, from which to see actions and look into the minds of characters. This allows the author to comment openly on characters and events in the work. The "third person" point of view presents the events of the story from outside of any single character's perception, much like the omniscient point of view, but the reader must understand the action as it takes place and without any special insight into characters' minds or motivations. The "first person" or "personal" point of view relates events as they are perceived by a single character. The main character "tells" the story and may offer opinions about the action and characters which differ from those of the author. Much less common than omniscient, third person, and first person is the "second person" point of view, wherein the author tells the story as if it is happening to the reader.

Polemic: A work in which the author takes a stand on a controversial subject, such as abortion or religion. Such works are often extremely argumentative or provocative.

Pornography: Writing intended to provoke feelings of lust in the reader. Such works are often condemned by critics and teachers, but those which can be shown to have literary value are viewed less harshly.

Post-Aesthetic Movement: An artistic response made by African Americans to the black aesthetic movement of the 1960s and early '70s. Writers since that time have adopted a somewhat different tone in their work, with less emphasis placed on the disparity between black and white in the United States. In the words of post-aesthetic authors such as Toni Morrison, John Edgar Wideman, and Kristin Hunter, African Americans are portrayed as looking inward for answers to their own questions, rather than always looking to the outside world.

Postmodernism: Writing from the 1960s forward characterized by experimentation and continuing to apply some of the fundamentals of modernism, which included existentialism and alienation. Postmodernists have gone a step further in the rejection of tradition begun with the modernists by also rejecting traditional forms, preferring the anti-novel over the novel and the anti-hero over the hero.

Pre-Raphaelites: A circle of writers and artists in mid nineteenth-century England. Valuing the pre-Renaissance artistic qualities of religious symbolism, lavish pictorialism, and natural sensuousness, the Pre-Raphaelites cultivated a sense of mystery and melancholy that influenced later writers associated with the Symbolist and Decadent movements.

Primitivism: The belief that primitive peoples were nobler and less flawed than civilized peoples because they had not been subjected to the tainting influence of society.

Projective Verse: A form of free verse in which the poet's breathing pattern determines the lines of the poem. Poets who advocate projective verse are against all formal structures in writing, including meter and form.

Prologue: An introductory section of a literary work. It often contains information establishing the situation of the characters or presents information about the setting, time period, or action. In drama, the prologue is spoken by a chorus or by one of the principal characters.

Prose: A literary medium that attempts to mirror the language of everyday speech. It is distinguished from poetry by its use of unmetered, unrhymed language consisting of logically related sentences. Prose is usually grouped into paragraphs that form a cohesive whole such as an essay or a novel.

Prosopopoeia: See *Personification*

Protagonist: The central character of a story who serves as a focus for its themes and incidents and as the principal rationale for its development. The protagonist is sometimes referred to in discussions of modern literature as the hero or anti-hero.

Proverb: A brief, sage saying that expresses a truth about life in a striking manner.

Pseudonym: A name assumed by a writer, most often intended to prevent his or her identification as the author of a work. Two or more authors may work together under one pseudonym, or an author may use a different name for each genre he or she publishes in. Some publishing companies maintain "house pseudonyms," under which any number of authors may write installations in a series. Some authors also choose a pseudonym over their real names the way an actor may use a stage name.

Pun: A play on words that have similar sounds but different meanings.

Pure Poetry: poetry written without instructional intent or moral purpose that aims only to please a reader by its imagery or musical flow. The term pure poetry is used as the antonym of the term "didacticism."

Q

Quatrain: A four-line stanza of a poem or an entire poem consisting of four lines.

R

Realism: A nineteenth-century European literary movement that sought to portray familiar characters, situations, and settings in a realistic manner. This was done primarily by using an objective narrative point of view and through the buildup of accurate detail. The standard for success of any realistic work depends on how faithfully it transfers common experience into fictional forms. The realistic method may be altered or extended, as in stream of consciousness writing, to record highly subjective experience.

Refrain: A phrase repeated at intervals throughout a poem. A refrain may appear at the end of each stanza or at less regular intervals. It may be altered slightly at each appearance.

Renaissance: The period in European history that marked the end of the Middle Ages. It began in Italy in the late fourteenth century. In broad terms, it is usually seen as spanning the fourteenth, fifteenth, and sixteenth centuries, although it did not reach Great Britain, for example, until the 1480s or so. The Renaissance saw an awakening in almost every sphere of human activity, especially science, philosophy, and the arts. The period is best defined by the emergence of a general philosophy that emphasized the importance of the intellect, the individual, and world affairs. It contrasts strongly with the medieval worldview, characterized by the dominant concerns of faith, the social collective, and spiritual salvation.

Repartee: Conversation featuring snappy retorts and witticisms.

Restoration: See *Restoration Age*

Restoration Age: A period in English literature beginning with the crowning of Charles II in 1660 and running to about 1700. The era, which was characterized by a reaction against Puritanism, was the first great age of the comedy of manners. The finest literature of the era is typically witty and urbane, and often lewd.

Rhetoric: In literary criticism, this term denotes the art of ethical persuasion. In its strictest sense, rhetoric adheres to various principles developed since classical times for arranging facts and ideas in a clear, persuasive, appealing manner. The term is also used to refer to effective prose in general and theories of or methods for composing effective prose.

Rhetorical Question: A question intended to provoke thought, but not an expressed answer, in the reader. It is most commonly used in oratory and other persuasive genres.

Rhyme: When used as a noun in literary criticism, this term generally refers to a poem in which words sound identical or very similar and appear in parallel positions in two or more lines. Rhymes are classified into different types according to where they fall in a line or stanza or according to the degree of similarity they exhibit in their spellings and sounds. Some major types of rhyme are "masculine" rhyme, "feminine" rhyme, and "triple" rhyme. In a masculine rhyme, the rhyming sound falls in a single accented syllable, as with "heat" and "eat." Feminine rhyme is a rhyme of two syllables, one stressed and one unstressed, as with "merry" and "tarry." Triple rhyme matches the sound of the accented syllable and the two unaccented syllables that follow: "narrative" and "declarative."

Rhyme Royal: A stanza of seven lines composed in iambic pentameter and rhymed *ababbcc*. The name is said to be a tribute to King James I of Scotland, who made much use of the form in his poetry.

Rhyme Scheme: See *Rhyme*

Rhythm: A regular pattern of sound, time intervals, or events occurring in writing, most often and most discernably in poetry. Regular, reliable rhythm is known to be soothing to humans, while interrupted, unpredictable, or rapidly changing rhythm is disturbing. These effects are known to authors, who use them to produce a desired reaction in the reader.

Rococo: A style of European architecture that flourished in the eighteenth century, especially in France. The most notable features of *rococo* are its extensive use of ornamentation and its themes of lightness, gaiety, and intimacy. In literary criticism, the term is often used disparagingly to refer to a decadent or over-ornamental style.

Romance: A broad term, usually denoting a narrative with exotic, exaggerated, often idealized characters, scenes, and themes.

Romantic Age: See *Romanticism*

Romanticism: This term has two widely accepted meanings. In historical criticism, it refers to a European intellectual and artistic movement of the late eighteenth and early nineteenth centuries that sought greater freedom of personal expression than that allowed by the strict rules of literary form and logic of the eighteenth-century neoclassicists. The Romantics preferred emotional and imaginative expression to rational analysis. They considered the individual to be at the center of all experience and so placed him or her at the center of their art. The Romantics believed that the creative imagination reveals nobler truths—unique feelings and attitudes—than those that could be discovered by logic or by scientific examination. Both the natural world and the state of childhood were important

sources for revelations of "eternal truths." "Romanticism" is also used as a general term to refer to a type of sensibility found in all periods of literary history and usually considered to be in opposition to the principles of classicism. In this sense, Romanticism signifies any work or philosophy in which the exotic or dreamlike figure strongly, or that is devoted to individualistic expression, self-analysis, or a pursuit of a higher realm of knowledge than can be discovered by human reason.

Romantics: See *Romanticism*

Russian Symbolism: A Russian poetic movement, derived from French symbolism, that flourished between 1894 and 1910. While some Russian Symbolists continued in the French tradition, stressing aestheticism and the importance of suggestion above didactic intent, others saw their craft as a form of mystical worship, and themselves as mediators between the supernatural and the mundane.

S

Satire: A work that uses ridicule, humor, and wit to criticize and provoke change in human nature and institutions. There are two major types of satire: "formal" or "direct" satire speaks directly to the reader or to a character in the work; "indirect" satire relies upon the ridiculous behavior of its characters to make its point. Formal satire is further divided into two manners: the "Horatian," which ridicules gently, and the "Juvenalian," which derides its subjects harshly and bitterly.

Scansion: The analysis or "scanning" of a poem to determine its meter and often its rhyme scheme. The most common system of scansion uses accents (slanted lines drawn above syllables) to show stressed syllables, breves (curved lines drawn above syllables) to show unstressed syllables, and vertical lines to separate each foot.

Second Person: See *Point of View*

Semiotics: The study of how literary forms and conventions affect the meaning of language.

Sestet: Any six-line poem or stanza.

Setting: The time, place, and culture in which the action of a narrative takes place. The elements of setting may include geographic location, characters' physical and mental environments, prevailing cultural attitudes, or the historical time in which the action takes place.

Shakespearean Sonnet: See *Sonnet*

Signifying Monkey: A popular trickster figure in black folklore, with hundreds of tales about this character documented since the 19th century.

Simile: A comparison, usually using "like" or "as," of two essentially dissimilar things, as in "coffee as cold as ice" or "He sounded like a broken record."

Slang: A type of informal verbal communication that is generally unacceptable for formal writing. Slang words and phrases are often colorful exaggerations used to emphasize the speaker's point; they may also be shortened versions of an often-used word or phrase.

Slant Rhyme: See *Consonance*

Slave Narrative: Autobiographical accounts of American slave life as told by escaped slaves. These works first appeared during the abolition movement of the 1830s through the 1850s.

Social Realism: See *Socialist Realism*

Socialist Realism: The Socialist Realism school of literary theory was proposed by Maxim Gorky and established as a dogma by the first Soviet Congress of Writers. It demanded adherence to a communist worldview in works of literature. Its doctrines required an objective viewpoint comprehensible to the working classes and themes of social struggle featuring strong proletarian heroes.

Soliloquy: A monologue in a drama used to give the audience information and to develop the speaker's character. It is typically a projection of the speaker's innermost thoughts. Usually delivered while the speaker is alone on stage, a soliloquy is intended to present an illusion of unspoken reflection.

Sonnet: A fourteen-line poem, usually composed in iambic pentameter, employing one of several rhyme schemes. There are three major types of sonnets, upon which all other variations of the form are based: the "Petrarchan" or "Italian" sonnet, the "Shakespearean" or "English" sonnet, and the "Spenserian" sonnet. A Petrarchan sonnet consists of an octave rhymed *abbaabba* and a "sestet" rhymed either *cdecde, cdccdc,* or *cdedce.* The octave poses a question or problem, relates a narrative, or

puts forth a proposition; the sestet presents a solution to the problem, comments upon the narrative, or applies the proposition put forth in the octave. The Shakespearean sonnet is divided into three quatrains and a couplet rhymed *abab cdcd efef gg.* The couplet provides an epigrammatic comment on the narrative or problem put forth in the quatrains. The Spenserian sonnet uses three quatrains and a couplet like the Shakespearean, but links their three rhyme schemes in this way: *abab bcbc cdcd ee.* The Spenserian sonnet develops its theme in two parts like the Petrarchan, its final six lines resolving a problem, analyzing a narrative, or applying a proposition put forth in its first eight lines.

Spenserian Sonnet: See *Sonnet*

Spenserian Stanza: A nine-line stanza having eight verses in iambic pentameter, its ninth verse in iambic hexameter, and the rhyme scheme ababbcbcc.

Spondee: In poetry meter, a foot consisting of two long or stressed syllables occurring together. This form is quite rare in English verse, and is usually composed of two monosyllabic words.

Sprung Rhythm: Versification using a specific number of accented syllables per line but disregarding the number of unaccented syllables that fall in each line, producing an irregular rhythm in the poem.

Stanza: A subdivision of a poem consisting of lines grouped together, often in recurring patterns of rhyme, line length, and meter. Stanzas may also serve as units of thought in a poem much like paragraphs in prose.

Stereotype: A stereotype was originally the name for a duplication made during the printing process; this led to its modern definition as a person or thing that is (or is assumed to be) the same as all others of its type.

Stream of Consciousness: A narrative technique for rendering the inward experience of a character. This technique is designed to give the impression of an ever-changing series of thoughts, emotions, images, and memories in the spontaneous and seemingly illogical order that they occur in life.

Structuralism: A twentieth-century movement in literary criticism that examines how literary texts arrive at their meanings, rather than the meanings themselves. There are two major types of structuralist analysis: one examines the way patterns of linguistic structures unify a specific text and emphasize certain elements of that text, and the other interprets the way literary forms and conventions affect the meaning of language itself.

Structure: The form taken by a piece of literature. The structure may be made obvious for ease of understanding, as in nonfiction works, or may obscured for artistic purposes, as in some poetry or seemingly "unstructured" prose.

Sturm und Drang: A German term meaning "storm and stress." It refers to a German literary movement of the 1770s and 1780s that reacted against the order and rationalism of the enlightenment, focusing instead on the intense experience of extraordinary individuals.

Style: A writer's distinctive manner of arranging words to suit his or her ideas and purpose in writing. The unique imprint of the author's personality upon his or her writing, style is the product of an author's way of arranging ideas and his or her use of diction, different sentence structures, rhythm, figures of speech, rhetorical principles, and other elements of composition.

Subject: The person, event, or theme at the center of a work of literature. A work may have one or more subjects of each type, with shorter works tending to have fewer and longer works tending to have more.

Subjectivity: Writing that expresses the author's personal feelings about his subject, and which may or may not include factual information about the subject.

Surrealism: A term introduced to criticism by Guillaume Apollinaire and later adopted by Andre Breton. It refers to a French literary and artistic movement founded in the 1920s. The Surrealists sought to express unconscious thoughts and feelings in their works. The best-known technique used for achieving this aim was automatic writing—transcriptions of spontaneous outpourings from the unconscious. The Surrealists proposed to unify the contrary levels of conscious and unconscious, dream and reality, objectivity and subjectivity into a new level of "super-realism."

Suspense: A literary device in which the author maintains the audience's attention through the buildup of events, the outcome of which will soon be revealed.

Syllogism: A method of presenting a logical argument. In its most basic form, the syllogism consists of a major premise, a minor premise, and a conclusion.

Symbol: Something that suggests or stands for something else without losing its original identity. In literature, symbols combine their literal meaning with the suggestion of an abstract concept. Literary symbols are of two types: those that carry complex associations of meaning no matter what their contexts, and those that derive their suggestive meaning from their functions in specific literary works.

Symbolism: This term has two widely accepted meanings. In historical criticism, it denotes an early modernist literary movement initiated in France during the nineteenth century that reacted against the prevailing standards of realism. Writers in this movement aimed to evoke, indirectly and symbolically, an order of being beyond the material world of the five senses. Poetic expression of personal emotion figured strongly in the movement, typically by means of a private set of symbols uniquely identifiable with the individual poet. The principal aim of the Symbolists was to express in words the highly complex feelings that grew out of everyday contact with the world. In a broader sense, the term "symbolism" refers to the use of one object to represent another.

Symbolist: See *Symbolism*

Symbolist Movement: See *Symbolism*

Sympathetic Fallacy: See *Affective Fallacy*

T

Tanka: A form of Japanese poetry similar to *haiku*. A *tanka* is five lines long, with the lines containing five, seven, five, seven, and seven syllables respectively.

Terza Rima: A three-line stanza form in poetry in which the rhymes are made on the last word of each line in the following manner: the first and third lines of the first stanza, then the second line of the first stanza and the first and third lines of the second stanza, and so on with the middle line of any stanza rhyming with the first and third lines of the following stanza.

Tetrameter: See *Meter*

Textual Criticism: A branch of literary criticism that seeks to establish the authoritative text of a literary work. Textual critics typically compare all known manuscripts or printings of a single work in order to assess the meanings of differences and revisions. This procedure allows them to arrive at a definitive version that (supposedly) corresponds to the author's original intention.

Theme: The main point of a work of literature. The term is used interchangeably with thesis.

Thesis: A thesis is both an essay and the point argued in the essay. Thesis novels and thesis plays share the quality of containing a thesis which is supported through the action of the story.

Third Person: See *Point of View*

Tone: The author's attitude toward his or her audience may be deduced from the tone of the work. A formal tone may create distance or convey politeness, while an informal tone may encourage a friendly, intimate, or intrusive feeling in the reader. The author's attitude toward his or her subject matter may also be deduced from the tone of the words he or she uses in discussing it.

Tragedy: A drama in prose or poetry about a noble, courageous hero of excellent character who, because of some tragic character flaw or *hamartia*, brings ruin upon him- or herself. Tragedy treats its subjects in a dignified and serious manner, using poetic language to help evoke pity and fear and bring about catharsis, a purging of these emotions. The tragic form was practiced extensively by the ancient Greeks. In the Middle Ages, when classical works were virtually unknown, tragedy came to denote any works about the fall of persons from exalted to low conditions due to any reason: fate, vice, weakness, etc. According to the classical definition of tragedy, such works present the "pathetic"—that which evokes pity—rather than the tragic. The classical form of tragedy was revived in the sixteenth century; it flourished especially on the Elizabethan stage. In modern times, dramatists have attempted to adapt the form to the needs of modern society by drawing their heroes from the ranks of ordinary men and

women and defining the nobility of these heroes in terms of spirit rather than exalted social standing.

Tragic Flaw: In a tragedy, the quality within the hero or heroine which leads to his or her downfall.

Transcendentalism: An American philosophical and religious movement, based in New England from around 1835 until the Civil War. Transcendentalism was a form of American romanticism that had its roots abroad in the works of Thomas Carlyle, Samuel Coleridge, and Johann Wolfgang von Goethe. The Transcendentalists stressed the importance of intuition and subjective experience in communication with God. They rejected religious dogma and texts in favor of mysticism and scientific naturalism. They pursued truths that lie beyond the "colorless" realms perceived by reason and the senses and were active social reformers in public education, women's rights, and the abolition of slavery.

Trickster: A character or figure common in Native American and African literature who uses his ingenuity to defeat enemies and escape difficult situations. Tricksters are most often animals, such as the spider, hare, or coyote, although they may take the form of humans as well.

Trimeter: See *Meter*

Triple Rhyme: See *Rhyme*

Trochee: See *Foot*

U

Understatement: See *Irony*

Unities: Strict rules of dramatic structure, formulated by Italian and French critics of the Renaissance and based loosely on the principles of drama discussed by Aristotle in his *Poetics*. Foremost among these rules were the three unities of action, time, and place that compelled a dramatist to: (1) construct a single plot with a beginning, middle, and end that details the causal relationships of action and character; (2) restrict the action to the events of a single day; and (3) limit the scene to a single place or city. The unities were observed faithfully by continental European writers until the Romantic Age, but they were never regularly observed in English drama. Modern dramatists are typically more concerned with a unity of impression or emotional effect than with any of the classical unities.

Urban Realism: A branch of realist writing that attempts to accurately reflect the often harsh facts of modern urban existence.

Utopia: A fictional perfect place, such as "paradise" or "heaven."

Utopian: See *Utopia*

Utopianism: See *Utopia*

V

Verisimilitude: Literally, the appearance of truth. In literary criticism, the term refers to aspects of a work of literature that seem true to the reader.

Vers de societe: See *Occasional Verse*

Vers libre: See *Free Verse*

Verse: A line of metered language, a line of a poem, or any work written in verse.

Versification: The writing of verse. Versification may also refer to the meter, rhyme, and other mechanical components of a poem.

Victorian: Refers broadly to the reign of Queen Victoria of England (1837-1901) and to anything with qualities typical of that era. For example, the qualities of smug narrowmindedness, bourgeois materialism, faith in social progress, and priggish morality are often considered Victorian. This stereotype is contradicted by such dramatic intellectual developments as the theories of Charles Darwin, Karl Marx, and Sigmund Freud (which stirred strong debates in England) and the critical attitudes of serious Victorian writers like Charles Dickens and George Eliot. In literature, the Victorian Period was the great age of the English novel, and the latter part of the era saw the rise of movements such as decadence and symbolism.

Victorian Age: See *Victorian*

Victorian Period: See *Victorian*

W

Weltanschauung: A German term referring to a person's worldview or philosophy.

Weltschmerz: A German term meaning "world pain." It describes a sense of anguish about the nature of existence, usually associated with a melancholy, pessimistic attitude.

Z

Zarzuela: A type of Spanish operetta.

Zeitgeist: A German term meaning "spirit of the time." It refers to the moral and intellectual trends of a given era.

Cumulative Author/Title Index

Cumulative Author/Title Index

Cumulative Nationality/Ethnicity Index

Marlowe, Christopher
The Passionate Shepherd to His Love: V22
Marvell, Andrew
To His Coy Mistress: V5
Masefield, John
Cargoes: V5
Maxwell, Glyn
The Nerve: V23
Milton, John
[On His Blindness] Sonnet 16: V3
On His Having Arrived at the Age of Twenty-Three: V17
When I Consider (Sonnet XIX): V37
Noyes, Alfred
The Highwayman: V4
Owen, Wilfred
Anthem for Doomed Youth: V37
Dulce et Decorum Est: V10
Pope, Alexander
The Rape of the Lock: V12
Raine, Craig
A Martian Sends a Postcard Home: V7
Raleigh, Walter, Sir
The Nymph's Reply to the Shepherd: V14
Rossetti, Christina
A Birthday: V10
Goblin Market: V27
Remember: V14
Up-Hill: V34
Sassoon, Siegfried
"Blighters": V28
Service, Robert W.
The Cremation of Sam McGee: V10
Shakespeare, William
Seven Ages of Man: V35
Sonnet 18: V2
Sonnet 19: V9
Sonnet 29: V8
Sonnet 30: V4
Sonnet 55: V5
Sonnet 116: V3
Sonnet 130: V1
Shelley, Percy Bysshe
Ode to the West Wind: V2
Ozymandias: V27
Song to the Men of England: V36
To a Sky-Lark: V32
Sidney, Philip
Ye Goatherd Gods: V30
Ozymandias: V27
Smith, Stevie
Not Waving but Drowning: V3
Spender, Stephen
An Elementary School Classroom in a Slum: V23
What I Expected: V36

Spenser, Edmund
Sonnet 75: V32
Swift, Jonathan
A Description of the Morning: V37
A Satirical Elegy on the Death of a Late Famous General: V27
Taylor, Edward
Huswifery: V31
Taylor, Henry
Landscape with Tractor: V10
Tennyson, Alfred, Lord
The Charge of the Light Brigade: V1
The Eagle: V11
The Lady of Shalott: V15
Proem: V19
Tears, Idle Tears: V4
Ulysses: V2
Williams, William Carlos
Overture to a Dance of Locomotives: V11
Queen-Ann's-Lace: V6
The Red Wheelbarrow: V1
This Is Just to Say: V34
Wordsworth, William
I Wandered Lonely as a Cloud: V33
Lines Composed a Few Miles above Tintern Abbey: V2
The World Is Too Much with Us: V38
Wyatt, Thomas
Whoso List to Hunt: V25

French

Apollinaire, Guillaume
Always: V24
Baudelaire, Charles
Hymn to Beauty: V21
Invitation to the Voyage: V38
Malroux, Claire
Morning Walk: V21
Rimbaud, Arthur
The Drunken Boat: V28

German

Amichai, Yehuda
Not like a Cypress: V24
Seven Laments for the War-Dead: V39
Blumenthal, Michael
Inventors: V7
Erdrich, Louise
Bidwell Ghost: V14
Heine, Heinrich
The Lorelei: V37
Mueller, Lisel
Blood Oranges: V13
The Exhibit: V9
Rilke, Rainer Maria
Archaic Torso of Apollo: V27
Childhood: V19

Roethke, Theodore
My Papa's Waltz: V3
The Waking: V34
Sachs, Nelly
But Perhaps God Needs the Longing: V20
Sajé, Natasha
The Art of the Novel: V23

Ghanaian

Du Bois, W. E. B.
The Song of the Smoke: V13

Greek

Cavafy, C. P.
Ithaka: V19
Sappho
Fragment 16: V38
Fragment 2: V31
Hymn to Aphrodite: V20

Hispanic American

Alvarez, Julia
Exile: V39
Castillo, Ana
While I Was Gone a War Began: V21
Cervantes, Lorna Dee
Freeway 280: V30
Cruz, Victor Hernandez
Business: V16
Espada, Martín
Colibrí: V16
Mora, Pat
Elena: V33
Uncoiling: V35
Ortiz Cofer, Judith
The Latin Deli: An Ars Poetica: V37
Walcott, Derek
Sea Canes: V39
Williams, William Carlos
Overture to a Dance of Locomotives: V11
Queen-Ann's-Lace: V6
The Red Wheelbarrow: V1
This Is Just to Say: V34

Indian

Divakaruni, Chitra Banerjee
My Mother Combs My Hair: V34
Mirabai
All I Was Doing Was Breathing: V24
Ramanujan, A. K.
Waterfalls in a Bank: V27
Shahid Ali, Agha
Country Without a Post Office: V18

Subject/Theme Index

Cumulative Index of
First Lines

Gray mist wolf (Four Mountain Wolves) V9:131

Grown too big for his skin, (Fable for When There's No Way Out) V38:42

H

"Had he and I but met (The Man He Killed) V3:167

Had we but world enough, and time (To His Coy Mistress) V5:276

Hail to thee, blithe Spirit! (To a Sky-Lark) V32:251

Half a league, half a league (The Charge of the Light Brigade) V1:2

Having a Coke with You (Having a Coke with You) V12:105

He clasps the crag with crooked hands (The Eagle) V11:30

He was found by the Bureau of Statistics to be (The Unknown Citizen) V3:302

He was seen, surrounded by rifles, (The Crime Was in Granada) V23:55–56

Hear the sledges with the bells— (The Bells) V3:46

Heart, you bully, you punk, I'm wrecked, I'm shocked (One Is One) V24:158

Her body is not so white as (Queen-Ann's-Lace) V6:179

Her eyes the glow-worm lend thee; (The Night Piece: To Julia) V29:206

Her eyes were coins of porter and her West (A Farewell to English) V10:126

Here, above, (The Man-Moth) V27:135

Here, she said, *put this on your head.* (Flounder) V39:58

Here they are. The soft eyes open (The Heaven of Animals) V6:75

His Grace! impossible! what dead! (A Satirical Elegy on the Death of a Late Famous General) V27:216

His speed and strength, which is the strength of ten (His Speed and Strength) V19:96

Hog Butcher for the World (Chicago) V3:61

Hold fast to dreams (Dream Variations) V15:42

Hope is a tattered flag and a dream out of time. (Hope is a Tattered Flag) V12:120

"Hope" is the thing with feathers— ("Hope" Is the Thing with Feathers) V3:123

How do I love thee? Let me count the ways (Sonnet 43) V2:236

How is your life with the other one, (An Attempt at Jealousy) V29:23

How shall we adorn (Angle of Geese) V2:2

How soon hath Time, the subtle thief of youth, (On His Having Arrived at the Age of Twenty-Three) V17:159

How would it be if you took yourself off (Landscape with Tractor) V10:182

Hunger crawls into you (Hunger in New York City) V4:79

I

I am fourteen (Hanging Fire) V32:93

I am not a painter, I am a poet (Why I Am Not a Painter) V8:258

I am not with those who abandoned their land (I Am Not One of Those Who Left the Land) V36:91

I am silver and exact. I have no preconceptions (Mirror) V1:116

I am the Smoke King (The Song of the Smoke) V13:196

I am trying to pry open your casket (Dear Reader) V10:85

I became a creature of light (The Mystery) V15:137

I Built My Hut beside a Traveled Road (I Built My Hut beside a Traveled Road) V36:119

I cannot love the Brothers Wright (Reactionary Essay on Applied Science) V9:199

I caught a tremendous fish (The Fish) V31:44

I died for Beauty—but was scarce (I Died for Beauty) V28:174

I don't mean to make you cry. (Monologue for an Onion) V24:120–121

I don't want my daughter (Fear) V37:71

I do not know what it means that (The Lorelei) V37:145

I felt a Funeral, in my Brain, (I felt a Funeral in my Brain) V13:137

I gave birth to life. (Maternity) V21:142–143

I have been one acquainted with the night. (Acquainted with the Night) V35:3

I have eaten (This Is Just to Say) V34:240

I have just come down from my father (The Hospital Window) V11:58

I have met them at close of day (Easter 1916) V5:91

I have sown beside all waters in my day. (A Black Man Talks of Reaping) V32:20

I haven't the heart to say (To an Unknown Poet) V18:221

I hear America singing, the varied carols I hear (I Hear America Singing) V3:152

I heard a Fly buzz—when I died— (I Heard a Fly Buzz— When I Died—) V5:140

I know that I shall meet my fate (An Irish Airman Foresees His Death) V1:76

I know what the caged bird feels, alas! (Sympathy) V33:203

I leant upon a coppice gate (The Darkling Thrush) V18:74

I lie down on my side in the moist grass (Omen) v22:107

I looked in my heart while the wild swans went over. (Wild Swans) V17:221

I love to go out in late September (Blackberry Eating) V35:23

I met a traveller from an antique land (Ozymandias) V27:173

I prove a theorem and the house expands: (Geometry) V15:68

I saw that a star had broken its rope (Witness) V26:285

I see them standing at the formal gates of their colleges, (I go Back to May 1937) V17:112

I shall die, but that is all that I shall do for Death. (Conscientious Objector) V34:46

I shook your hand before I went. (Mastectomy) V26:122

I sit in one of the dives (September 1, 1939) V27:234

I sit in the top of the wood, my eyes closed (Hawk Roosting) V4:55

I thought, as I wiped my eyes on the corner of my apron: (An Ancient Gesture) V31:3

I thought wearing an evergreen dress (Pine) V23:223–224

I, too, sing America. (I, Too) V30:99

I wandered lonely as a cloud (I Wandered Lonely as a Cloud) V33:71

I was angry with my friend; (A Poison Tree) V24:195–196

My father stands in the warm evening (Starlight) V8:213

My friend, are you sleeping? (Two Eclipses) V33:220

my grandmother (Grandmother) V34:95

My grandmothers were strong. (Lineage) V31:145–46

My heart aches, and a drowsy numbness pains (Ode to a Nightingale) V3:228

My heart is like a singing bird (A Birthday) V10:33

My life closed twice before its close— (My Life Closed Twice Before Its Close) V8:127

My long two-pointed ladder's sticking through a tree (After Apple Picking) V32:3

My mistress' eyes are nothing like the sun (Sonnet 130) V1:247

My one and only! (Letter to My Wife) V38:114

My uncle in East Germany (The Exhibit) V9:107

N

Nature's first green is gold (Nothing Gold Can Stay) V3:203

No easy thing to bear, the weight of sweetness (The Weight of Sweetness) V11:230

No monument stands over Babii Yar. (Babii Yar) V29:38

Nobody heard him, the dead man (Not Waving but Drowning) V3:216

Not like a cypress, (Not like a Cypress) V24:135

Not like the brazen giant of Greek fame, (The New Colossus) V37:238

Not marble nor the gilded monuments (Sonnet 55) V5:246

Not the memorized phone numbers. (What Belongs to Us) V15:196

Now as I was young and easy under the apple boughs (Fern Hill) V3:92

Now as I watch the progress of the plague (The Missing) V9:158

Now hardly here and there a Hackney-Coach (A Description of the Morning) V37:48

Now I rest my head on the satyr's carved chest, (The Satyr's Heart) V22:187

Now one might catch it see it (Fading Light) V21:49

O

O Captain! my Captain, our fearful trip is done (O Captain! My Captain!) V2:146

O Lord our Lord, how excellent is thy name in all the earth! who hast set thy glory above the heavens (Psalm 8) V9:182

O my Luve's like a red, red rose (A Red, Red Rose) V8:152

O what can ail thee, knight-at-arms, (La Belle Dame sans Merci) V17:18

"O where ha' you been, Lord Randal, my son? (Lord Randal) V6:105

O wild West Wind, thou breath of Autumn's being (Ode to the West Wind) V2:163

Oh, but it is dirty! (Filling Station) V12:57

old age sticks (old age sticks) V3:246

On a shore washed by desolate waves, *he* stood, (The Bronze Horseman) V28:27

On either side the river lie (The Lady of Shalott) V15:95

On the seashore of endless worlds children meet. The infinite (60) V18:3

Once some people were visiting Chekhov (Chocolates) V11:17

Once upon a midnight dreary, while I pondered, weak and weary (The Raven) V1:200

One day I'll lift the telephone (Elegy for My Father, Who Is Not Dead) V14:154

One day I wrote her name upon the strand, (Sonnet 75) V32:215

One foot down, then hop! It's hot (Harlem Hopscotch) V2:93

one shoe on the roadway presents (A Piéd) V3:16

Our vision is our voice (An Anthem) V26:34

Out of the hills of Habersham, (Song of the Chattahoochee) V14:283

Out walking in the frozen swamp one gray day (The Wood-Pile) V6:251

Oysters we ate (Oysters) V4:91

P

Pentagon code (Smart and Final Iris) V15:183

Poised between going on and back, pulled (The Base Stealer) V12:30

Q

Quinquireme of Nineveh from distant Ophir (Cargoes) V5:44

Quite difficult, belief. (Chorale) V25:51

R

Recognition in the body (In Particular) V20:125

Red men embraced my body's whiteness (Birch Canoe) V5:31

Remember me when I am gone away (Remember) V14:255

Remember the sky you were born under, (Remember) V32:185

Riches I hold in light esteem, (Old Stoic) V33:143

S

Season of mists and mellow fruitfulness, (To Autumn) V36:295–296

Shall I compare thee to a Summer's day? (Sonnet 18) V2:222

She came every morning to draw water (A Drink of Water) V8:66

She reads, of course, what he's doing, shaking Nixon's hand, (The Women Who Loved Elvis All Their Lives) V28:273

She sang beyond the genius of the sea. (The Idea of Order at Key West) V13:164

She walks in beauty, like the night (She Walks in Beauty) V14:268

She was my grandfather's second wife. Coming late (My Grandmother's Plot in the Family Cemetery) V27:154

Side by side, their faces blurred, (An Arundel Tomb) V12:17

since feeling is first (since feeling is first) V34:172

Since the professional wars— (Midnight) V2:130

Since then, I work at night. (Ten Years after Your Deliberate Drowning) V21:240

S'io credesse che mia risposta fosse (The Love Song of J. Alfred Prufrock) V1:97

Sky black (Duration) V18:93

Sleepless as Prospero back in his bedroom (Darwin in 1881) V13:83

so much depends (The Red Wheelbarrow) V1:219

So the man spread his blanket on the field (A Tall Man Executes a Jig) V12:228

What passing-bells for these who die as cattle? (Anthem for Doomed Youth) V37:3

What thoughts I have of you tonight, Walt Whitman, for I walked down the sidestreets under the trees with a headache self-conscious looking at the full moon (A Supermarket in California) V5:261

Whatever it is, it must have (American Poetry) V7:2

When Abraham Lincoln was shoveled into the tombs, he forgot the copperheads, and the assassin . . . in the dust, in the cool tombs (Cool Tombs) V6:45

When despair for the world grows in me (The Peace of Wild Things) V30:159

When he spoke of where he came from, (Grudnow) V32:73

When I consider how my light is spent ([On His Blindness] Sonnet 16) V3:262

When I consider how my light is spent (When I Consider (Sonnet XIX) V37:302

When I die, I want your hands on my eyes: (Sonnet LXXXIX) V35:259

When I go away from you (The Taxi) V30:211–212

When I have fears that I may cease to be (When I Have Fears that I May Cease to Be) V2:295

When I heard the learn'd astronomer, (When I Heard the Learn'd Astronomer) V22:244

When I see a couple of kids (High Windows) V3:108

When I see birches bend to left and right (Birches) V13:14

When I was a child (Autobiographia Literaria) V34:2

When I was born, you waited (Having it Out with Melancholy) V17:98

When I was one-and-twenty (When I Was One-and-Twenty) V4:268

When I watch you (Miss Rosie) V1:133

When Love with confinéd wings (To Althea, From Prison) V34:254

When the mountains of Puerto Rico (We Live by What We See at Night) V13:240

When the world was created wasn't it like this? (Anniversary) V15:2

When they said *Carrickfergus* I could hear (The Singer's House) V17:205

When we two parted (When We Two Parted) V29:297

When you consider the radiance, that it does not withhold (The City Limits) V19:78

When you look through the window in Sag Harbor and see (View) V25:246–247

When, in disgrace with Fortune and men's eyes (Sonnet 29) V8:198

Whenever Richard Cory went down town (Richard Cory) V4:116

Where dips the rocky highland (The Stolen Child) V34:216

While I was gone a war began. (While I Was Gone a War Began) V21:253–254

While my hair was still cut straight across my forehead (The River-Merchant's Wife: A Letter) V8:164

While the long grain is softening (Early in the Morning) V17:75

While this America settles in the mould of its vulgarity, heavily thickening to empire (Shine, Perishing Republic) V4:161

While you are preparing for sleep, brushing your teeth, (The Afterlife) V18:39

Who has ever stopped to think of the divinity of Lamont Cranston? (In Memory of Radio) V9:144

Whose woods these are I think I know (Stopping by Woods on a Snowy Evening) V1:272

Whoso list to hunt: I know where is an hind. (Whoso List to Hunt) V25:286

Why should I let the toad *work* (Toads) V4:244

With thorns, she scratches (Uncoiling) V35:277

Y

You are small and intense (To a Child Running With Out-stretched Arms in Canyon de Chelly) V11:173

You can't hear? Everything here is changing. (The River Mumma Wants Out) V25:191

You do not have to be good. (Wild Geese) V15:207

You should lie down now and remember the forest, (The Forest) V22:36–37

You stood thigh-deep in water and green light glanced (Lake) V23:158

You were never told, Mother, how old Illya was drunk (The Czar's Last Christmas Letter) V12:44

Cumulative Index of Last Lines

A

... a capital T in the endless mass of the text. (Answers to Letters) V21:30–31

a fleck of foam. (Accounting) V21:2–3

A heart that will one day beat you to death. (Monologue for an Onion) V24:120–121

A heart whose love is innocent! (She Walks in Beauty) V14:268

a man then suddenly stops running (Island of Three Marias) V11:80

A perfect evening! (Temple Bells Die Out) V18:210

a space in the lives of their friends (Beware: Do Not Read This Poem) V6:3

A sudden blow: the great wings beating still (Leda and the Swan) V13:181

A terrible beauty is born (Easter 1916) V5:91

About him, and lies down to pleasant dreams. (Thanatopsis) V30:232–233

About my big, new, automatically defrosting refrigerator with the built-in electric eye (Reactionary Essay on Applied Science) V9:199

about the tall mounds of termites. (Song of a Citizen) V16:126

Across the expedient and wicked stones (Auto Wreck) V3:31

affirming its brilliant and dizzying love. (Lepidopterology) V23:171

Ah, dear father, graybeard, lonely old courage-teacher, what America did you have when Charon quit poling his ferry and you got out on a smoking bank and stood watching the boat disappear on the black waters of Lethe? (A Supermarket in California) V5:261

All deaths have a lingering echo (All) V38:17

All losses are restored and sorrows end (Sonnet 30) V4:192

Amen. Amen (The Creation) V1:20

Anasazi (Anasazi) V9:3

and a vase of wild flowers. (The War Correspondent) V26:239

and all beyond saving by children (Ethics) V8:88

and all the richer for it. (Mind) V17:146

And all we need of hell (My Life Closed Twice Before Its Close) V8:127

And, being heard, doesn't vanish in the dark. (Variations on Nothing) V20:234

and changed, back to the class ("Trouble with Math in a One-Room Country School") V9:238

and chant him a blessing, a sutra. (What For) V33:267

And covered up—our names— (I Died for Beauty) V28:174

And dances with the daffodils. (I Wandered Lonely as a Cloud) V33:71

And death i think is no parenthesis (since feeling is first) V34:172

And Death shall be no more: Death, thou shalt die (Holy Sonnet 10) V2:103

and destruction. (Allegory) V23:2–3

And drunk the milk of Paradise (Kubla Khan) V5:172

And each slow dusk a drawing-down of blinds. (Anthem for Doomed Youth) V37:3

and fear lit by the breadth of such calmly turns to praise. (The City Limits) V19:78

And Finished knowing—then— (I Felt a Funeral in My Brain) V13:137

And gallop terribly against each other's bodies (Autumn Begins in Martins Ferry, Ohio) V8:17

And gathering swallows twitter in the skies. (To Autumn) V36:295–296

and go back. (For the White poets who would be Indian) V13:112

And handled with a Chain— (Much Madness is Divinest Sense) V16:86

And has not begun to grow a manly smile. (Deep Woods) V14:139

And his own Word (The Phoenix) V10:226

And I am Nicholas. (The Czar's Last Christmas Letter) V12:45

And I let the fish go. (The Fish) V31:44

And I was unaware. (The Darkling Thrush) V18:74

And in the suburbs Can't sat down and cried. (Kilroy) V14:213

And it's been years. (Anniversary) V15:3

and joy may come, and make its test of us. (One Is One) V24:158

And kept on drinking. (Miniver Cheevy) V35:127

And laid my hand upon thy mane— as I do here. (Childe Harold's Pilgrimage, Canto IV, stanzas 178–184) V35:47

and leaving essence to the inner eye. (Memory) V21:156

And life for me ain't been no crystal stair (Mother to Son) V3:179

And like a thunderbolt he falls (The Eagle) V11:30

And makes me end where I begun (A Valediction: Forbidding Mourning) V11:202

And 'midst the stars inscribe Belinda's name. (The Rape of the Lock) V12:209

And miles to go before I sleep (Stopping by Woods on a Snowy Evening) V1:272

and my father saying things. (My Father's Song) V16:102

And no birds sing. (La Belle Dame sans Merci) V17:18

And not waving but drowning (Not Waving but Drowning) V3:216

And oh, 'tis true, 'tis true (When I Was One-and-Twenty) V4:268

And reach for your scalping knife. (For Jean Vincent D'abbadie, Baron St.-Castin) V12:78

and retreating, always retreating, behind it (Brazil, January 1, 1502) V6:16

And School-Boys lag with Satchels in their Hands. (A Description of the Morning) V37:49

And settled upon his eyes in a black soot ("More Light! More Light!") V6:120

And shuts his eyes. (Darwin in 1881) V13: 84

and so cold (This Is Just to Say) V34:241

And so live ever—or else swoon to death (Bright Star! Would I Were Steadfast as Thou Art) V9:44

and strange and loud was the dingoes' cry (Drought Year) V8:78

and stride out. (Courage) V14:126

and sweat and fat and greed. (Anorexic) V12:3

And that has made all the difference (The Road Not Taken) V2:195

And the deep river ran on (As I Walked Out One Evening) V4:16

And the midnight message of Paul Revere (Paul Revere's Ride) V2:180

And the mome raths outgrabe (Jabberwocky) V11:91

And the Salvation Army singing God loves us. . . . (Hope is a Tattered Flag) V12:120

And therewith ends my story. (The Bridegroom) V34:28

and these the last verses that I write for her (Tonight I Can Write) V11:187

And the tide rises, the tide falls, (The Tide Rises, the Tide Falls) V39:280

and thickly wooded country; the moon. (The Art of the Novel) V23:29

And those roads in South Dakota that feel around in the darkness . . . (Come with Me) V6:31

and to know she will stay in the field till you die? (Landscape with Tractor) V10:183

and two blankets embroidered with smallpox (Meeting the British) V7:138

and waving, shouting, *Welcome back*. (Elegy for My Father, Who Is Not Dead) V14:154

And—which is more—you'll be a Man, my son! (If) V22:54–55

and whose skin is made dusky by stars. (September) V23:258–259

And wild for to hold, though I seem tame.' (Whoso List to Hunt) V25:286

And would suffice (Fire and Ice) V7:57

And yet God has not said a word! (Porphyria's Lover) V15:151

and you spread un the thin halo of night mist. (Ways to Live) V16:229

and your dreams, my Telemachus, are blameless. (Odysseus to Telemachus) V35:147

And Zero at the Bone— (A Narrow Fellow in the Grass) V11:127

(answer with a tower of birds) (Duration) V18:93

Around us already perhaps future moons, suns and stars blaze in a fiery wreath. (But Perhaps God Needs the Longing) V20:41

aspired to become lighter than air (Blood Oranges) V13:34

As any She belied with false compare (Sonnet 130) V1:248

As ever in my great Task-Master's eye. (On His Having Arrived at the Age of Twenty-Three) V17:160

As far as Cho-fu-Sa (The River-Merchant's Wife: A Letter) V8:165

as it has disappeared. (The Wings) V28:244

As the contagion of those molten eyes (For An Assyrian Frieze) V9:120

As they lean over the beans in their rented back room that is full of beads and receipts and dolls and clothes, tobacco crumbs, vases and fringes (The Bean Eaters) V2:16

as we crossed the field, I told her. (The Centaur) V30:20

As what he loves may never like too much. (On My First Son) V33:166

at home in the fish's fallen heaven (Birch Canoe) V5:31

away, pedaling hard, rocket and pilot. (His Speed and Strength) V19:96

B

Back to the play of constant give and change (The Missing) V9:158

Beautiful & dangerous. (Slam, Dunk, & Hook) V30:176–177

Before it was quite unsheathed from reality (Hurt Hawks) V3:138

before we're even able to name them. (Station) V21:226–227

behind us and all our shining ambivalent love airborne there before us. (Our Side) V24:177

Black like me. (Dream Variations) V15:42

Bless me (Hunger in New York City) V4:79

bombs scandalizing the sanctity of night. (While I Was Gone a War Began) V21:253–254

But, baby, where are you?" (Ballad of Birmingham) V5:17

But be (Ars Poetica) V5:3

But for centuries we have longed for it. (Everything Is Plundered) V32:34

but it works every time (Siren Song) V7:196

but the truth is, it is, lost to us now. (The Forest) V22:36–37

But there is no joy in Mudville— mighty Casey has "Struck Out." (Casey at the Bat) V5:58

But we hold our course, and the wind is with us. (On Freedom's Ground) V12:187

by a beeswax candle pooling beside their dinnerware. (Portrait of a Couple at Century's End) V24:214–215

by good fortune (The Horizons of Rooms) V15:80

C

Calls through the valleys of Hall. (Song of the Chattahoochee) V14:284

chickens (The Red Wheelbarrow) V1:219

clear water dashes (Onomatopoeia) V6:133

Columbia. (Kindness) V24:84–85

Come, my *Corinna*, come, let's goe a Maying. (Corinna's Going A-Maying) V39:6

come to life and burn? (Bidwell Ghost) V14:2

comfortless, so let evening come. (Let Evening Come) V39:116

Comin' for to carry me home (Swing Low Sweet Chariot) V1:284

cool as from underground springs and pure enough to drink. (The Man-Moth) V27:135

crossed the water. (All It Takes) V23:15

D

Dare frame thy fearful symmetry? (The Tyger) V2:263

"Dead," was all he answered (The Death of the Hired Man) V4:44

deep in the deepest one, tributaries burn. (For Jennifer, 6, on the Teton) V17:86

Delicate, delicate, delicate, delicate—now! (The Base Stealer) V12:30

Die soon (We Real Cool) V6:242

Do what you are going to do, I will tell about it. (I go Back to May 1937) V17:113

down from the sky (Russian Letter) V26:181

Down in the flood of remembrance, I weep like a child for the past (Piano) V6:145

Downward to darkness, on extended wings. (Sunday Morning) V16:190

drinking all night in the kitchen. (The Dead) V35:69

Driving around, I will waste more time. (Driving to Town Late to Mail a Letter) V17:63

dry wells that fill so easily now (The Exhibit) V9:107

dust rises in many myriads of grains. (Not like a Cypress) V24:135

dusty as miners, into the restored volumes. (Bonnard's Garden) V25:33

E

endless worlds is the great meeting of children. (60) V18:3

Enjoy such liberty. (To Althea, From Prison) V34:255

Eternal, unchanging creator of earth. Amen (The Seafarer) V8:178

Eternity of your arms around my neck. (Death Sentences) V22:23

even as it vanishes—were not our life. (The Litany) V24:101–102

ever finds anything more of immortality. (Jade Flower Palace) V32:145

every branch traced with the ghost writing of snow. (The Afterlife) V18:39

F

fall upon us, the dwellers in shadow (In the Land of Shinar) V7:84

Fallen cold and dead (O Captain! My Captain!) V2:147

False, ere I come, to two, or three. (Song) V35:237

father. (Grape Sherbet) V37:110

filled, never. (The Greatest Grandeur) V18:119

Firewood, iron-ware, and cheap tin trays (Cargoes) V5:44

Fled is that music:—Do I wake or sleep? (Ode to a Nightingale) V3:229

For I'm sick at the heart, and I fain wad lie down." (Lord Randal) V6:105

For nothing now can ever come to any good. (Funeral Blues) V10:139

For the coming winter (Winter) V35:297

For the love of God they buried his cold corpse. (The Bronze Horseman) V28:31

For the world's more full of weeping than he can understand. (The Stolen Child) V34:217

forget me as fast as you can. (Last Request) V14:231

4:25:9 (400Meter Freestyle) V38:3

from one kiss (A Rebirth) V21:193–194

G

garish for a while and burned. (One of the Smallest) V26:142

going where? Where? (Childhood) V19:29

H

Had anything been wrong, we should certainly have heard (The Unknown Citizen) V3:303

Had somewhere to get to and sailed calmly on (Mus,e des Beaux Arts) V1:148

half eaten by the moon. (Dear Reader) V10:85

hand over hungry hand. (Climbing) V14:113

Happen on a red tongue (Small Town with One Road) V7:207

hard as mine with another man? (An Attempt at Jealousy) V29:24

Has no more need of, and I have (The Courage that My Mother Had) V3:80

Has set me softly down beside you. The Poem is you (Paradoxes and Oxymorons) V11:162

Hath melted like snow in the glance of the Lord! (The Destruction of Sennacherib) V1:39

He rose the morrow morn (The Rime of the Ancient Mariner) V4:132

He says again, "Good fences make good neighbors." (Mending Wall) V5:232

He writes down something that he crosses out. (The Boy) V19:14

here; passion will save you. (Air for Mercury) V20:2–3

History theirs whose languages is the sun. (An Elementary School Classroom in a Slum) V23:88–89

How at my sheet goes the same crooked worm (The Force That Through the Green Fuse Drives the Flower) V8:101

How can I turn from Africa and live? (A Far Cry from Africa) V6:61

How sad then is even the marvelous! (An African Elegy) V13:4

I

I am a true Russian! (Babii Yar) V29:38

I am black. (The Song of the Smoke) V13:197

I am going to keep things like this (Hawk Roosting) V4:55

I am not brave at all (Strong Men, Riding Horses) V4:209

I could not see to see— (I Heard a Fly Buzz—When I Died—) V5:140

I cremated Sam McGee (The Cremation of Sam McGee) V10:76

I didn't want to put them down. (And What If I Spoke of Despair) V19:2

I have been one acquainted with the night. (Acquainted with the Night) V35:3

I have just come down from my father (The Hospital Window) V11:58

I hear it in the deep heart's core. (The Lake Isle of Innisfree) V15:121

I know why the caged bird sings! (Sympathy) V33:203

I lift my lamp beside the golden door!" (The New Colossus) V37:239

I never writ, nor no man ever loved (Sonnet 116) V3:288

I rest in the grace of the world, and am free. (The Peace of Wild Things) V30:159

I romp with joy in the bookish dark (Eating Poetry) V9:61

I see Mike's painting, called SARDINES (Why I Am Not a Painter) V8:259

I shall but love thee better after death (Sonnet 43) V2:236

I should be glad of another death (Journey of the Magi) V7:110

I stand up (Miss Rosie) V1:133

I stood there, fifteen (Fifteen) V2:78

I take it you are he? (Incident in a Rose Garden) V14:191

I, too, am America. (I, Too) V30:99

I turned aside and bowed my head and wept (The Tropics in New York) V4:255

I would like to tell, but lack the words. (I Built My Hut beside a Traveled Road) V36:119

If Winter comes, can Spring be far behind? (Ode to the West Wind) V2:163

I'll be gone from here. (The Cobweb) V17:51

I'll dig with it (Digging) V5:71

Imagine! (Autobiographia Literaria) V34:2

In a convulsive misery (The Milkfish Gatherers) V11:112

In an empty sky (Two Bodies) V38:251

In balance with this life, this death (An Irish Airman Foresees His Death) V1:76

in earth's gasp, ocean's yawn. (Lake) V23:158

In Flanders fields (In Flanders Fields) V5:155

In ghostlier demarcations, keener sounds. (The Idea of Order at Key West) V13:164

In hearts at peace, under an English heaven (The Soldier) V7:218

In her tomb by the side of the sea (Annabel Lee) V9:14

in the family of things. (Wild Geese) V15:208

in the grit gray light of day. (Daylights) V13:102

In the rear-view mirrors of the passing cars (The War Against the Trees) V11:216

In these Chicago avenues. (A Thirst Against) V20:205

in this bastion of culture. (To an Unknown Poet) V18:221

in your unsteady, opening hand. (What the Poets Could Have Been) V26:262

iness (l(a) V1:85

Into blossom (A Blessing) V7:24

Is Come, my love is come to me. (A Birthday) V10:34

is love—that's all. (Two Poems for T.) V20:218

is safe is what you said. (Practice) V23:240

is still warm (Lament for the Dorsets) V5:191

It asked a crumb—of Me ("Hope" Is the Thing with Feathers) V3:123

It had no mirrors. I no longer needed mirrors. (I, I, I) V26:97

It is our god. (Fiddler Crab) V23:111–112

it is the bell to awaken God that we've heard ringing. (The Garden Shukkei-en) V18:107

it over my face and mouth. (An Anthem) V26:34

It rains as I write this. Mad heart, be brave. (The Country Without a Post Office) V18:64

It takes life to love life. (Lucinda Matlock) V37:172

It was your resting place." (Ah, Are You Digging on My Grave?) V4:2

it's always ourselves we find in the sea (maggie & milly & molly & may) V12:150

its bright, unequivocal eye. (Having it Out with Melancholy) V17:99

It's the fall through wind lifting white leaves. (Rapture) V21:181

its youth. The sea grows old in it. (The Fish) V14:172

J

Judge tenderly—of Me (This Is My Letter to the World) V4:233

Just imagine it (Inventors) V7:97

K

kisses you (Grandmother) V34:95

L

Laughing the stormy, husky, brawling laughter of Youth, half-naked, sweating, proud to be Hog Butcher, Tool Maker, Stacker of Wheat, Player with Railroads and Freight Handler to the Nation (Chicago) V3:61

Learn to labor and to wait (A Psalm of Life) V7:165

Leashed in my throat (Midnight) V2:131

Leaving thine outgrown shell by life's un-resting sea (The Chambered Nautilus) V24:52–53

Let my people go (Go Down, Moses) V11:43

Let the water come. (America, America) V29:4

life, our life and its forgetting. (For a New Citizen of These United States) V15:55

Life to Victory (Always) V24:15

like a bird in the sky … (Ego-Tripping) V28:113

like a shadow or a friend. *Colombia.* (Kindness) V24:84–85

Like Stone— (The Soul Selects Her Own Society) V1:259

Little Lamb, God bless thee. (The Lamb) V12:135

Our love shall live, and later life renew." (Sonnet 75) V32:215

outside. (it was New York and beautifully, snowing . . . i was sitting in mcsorley's) V13:152

owing old (old age sticks) V3:246

P

patient in mind remembers the time. (Fading Light) V21:49

Penelope, who really cried. (An Ancient Gesture) V31:3

Perhaps he will fall. (Wilderness Gothic) V12:242

Petals on a wet, black bough (In a Station of the Metro) V2:116

Plaiting a dark red love-knot into her long black hair (The Highwayman) V4:68

Powerless, I drown. (Maternity) V21:142–143

Práise him. (Pied Beauty) V26:161

Pro patria mori. (Dulce et Decorum Est) V10:110

Q

Quietly shining to the quiet Moon. (Frost at Midnight) V39:75

R

Rage, rage against the dying of the light (Do Not Go Gentle into that Good Night) V1:51

Raise it again, man. We still believe what we hear. (The Singer's House) V17:206

Remember. (Remember) V32:185

Remember the Giver fading off the lip (A Drink of Water) V8:66

Ride me. (Witness) V26:285

rise & walk away like a panther. (Ode to a Drum) V20:172–173

Rises toward her day after day, like a terrible fish (Mirror) V1:116

S

Sans teeth, sans eyes, sans taste, sans everything. (Seven Ages of Man) V35:213

Shall be lifted—nevermore! (The Raven) V1:202

shall be lost. (All Shall Be Restored) V36:2

Shall you be overcome. (Conscientious Objector) V34:46

Shantih shantih shantih (The Waste Land) V20:248–252

share my shivering bed. (Chorale) V25:51

she'd miss me. (In Response to Executive Order 9066: All Americans of Japanese Descent Must Report to Relocation Centers) V32:129

Show an affirming flame. (September 1, 1939) V27:235

Shuddering with rain, coming down around me. (Omen) V22:107

Simply melted into the perfect light. (Perfect Light) V19:187

Singing of him what they could understand (Beowulf) V11:3

Singing with open mouths their strong melodious songs (I Hear America Singing) V3:152

Sister, one of those who never married. (My Grandmother's Plot in the Family Cemetery) V27:155

Sleep, fly, rest: even the sea dies! (Lament for Ignacio Sánchez Mejías) V31:128–30

slides by on grease (For the Union Dead) V7:67

Slouches towards Bethlehem to be born? (The Second Coming) V7:179

so like the smaller stars we rowed among. (The Lotus Flowers) V33:108

So long lives this, and this gives life to thee (Sonnet 18) V2:222

So prick my skin. (Pine) V23:223–224

so that everything can learn the reason for my song. (Sonnet LXXXIX) V35:260

Somebody loves us all. (Filling Station) V12:57

Speak through my words and my blood. (The Heights of Macchu Picchu) V28:141

spill darker kissmarks on that dark. (Ten Years after Your Deliberate Drowning) V21:240

Stand still, yet we will make him run (To His Coy Mistress) V5:277

startled into eternity (Four Mountain Wolves) V9:132

Still clinging to your shirt (My Papa's Waltz) V3:192

Stood up, coiled above his head, transforming all. (A Tall Man Executes a Jig) V12:229

strangers ask. *Originally?* And I hesitate. (Originally) V25:146–147

Surely goodness and mercy shall follow me all the days of my life: and I will dwell in the house of the Lord for ever (Psalm 23) V4:103

switch sides with every jump. (Flounder) V39:59

syllables of an old order. (A Grafted Tongue) V12:93

T

Take any streetful of people buying clothes and groceries, cheering a hero or throwing confetti and blowing tin horns . . . tell me if the lovers are losers . . . tell me if any get more than the lovers . . . in the dust . . . in the cool tombs (Cool Tombs) V6:46

Than from everything else life promised that you could do? (Paradiso) V20:190–191

Than that you should remember and be sad. (Remember) V14:255

that does not see you. You must change your life. (Archaic Torso of Apollo) V27:3

that might have been sweet in Grudnow. (Grudnow) V32:74

That then I scorn to change my state with Kings (Sonnet 29) V8:198

that there is more to know, that one day you will know it. (Knowledge) V25:113

That when we live no more, we may live ever (To My Dear and Loving Husband) V6:228

That's the word. (Black Zodiac) V10:47

The benediction of the air. (Snow-Bound) V36:248–254

the bigger it gets. (Smart and Final Iris) V15:183

The bosom of his Father and his God (Elegy Written in a Country Churchyard) V9:74

the bow toward torrents of *veyz mir.* (Three To's and an Oi) V24:264

The crime was in Granada, his Granada. (The Crime Was in Granada) V23:55–56

The dance is sure (Overture to a Dance of Locomotives) V11:143

The eyes turn topaz. (Hugh Selwyn Mauberley) V16:30

the flames? (Another Night in the Ruins) V26:13

The frolic architecture of the snow. (The Snow-Storm) V34:196

The garland briefer than a girl's (To an Athlete Dying Young) V7:230

The Grasshopper's among some grassy hills. (On the Grasshopper and the Cricket) V32:161

The guidon flags flutter gayly in the wind. (Cavalry Crossing a Ford) V13:50

The hands gripped hard on the desert (At the Bomb Testing Site) V8:3

The holy melodies of love arise. (The Arsenal at Springfield) V17:3

the knife at the throat, the death in the metronome (Music Lessons) V8:117

The Lady of Shalott." (The Lady of Shalott) V15:97

The lightning and the gale! (Old Ironsides) V9:172

The lone and level sands stretch far away. (Ozymandias) V27:173

the long, perfect loveliness of sow (Saint Francis and the Sow) V9:222

The Lord survives the rainbow of His will (The Quaker Graveyard in Nantucket) V6:159

The man I was when I was part of it (Beware of Ruins) V8:43

the quilts sing on (My Mother Pieced Quilts) V12:169

The red rose and the brier (Barbara Allan) V7:11

The self-same Power that brought me there brought you. (The Rhodora) V17:191

The shaft we raise to them and thee (Concord Hymn) V4:30

the skin of another, what I have made is a curse. (Curse) V26:75

The sky became a still and woven blue. (Merlin Enthralled) V16:73

The song of the Lorelei. (The Lorelei) V37:146

The spirit of this place (To a Child Running With Outstretched Arms in Canyon de Chelly) V11:173

The town again, trailing your legs and crying! (Wild Swans) V17:221

the unremitting space of your rebellion (Lost Sister) V5:217

The woman won (Oysters) V4:91

The world should listen then—as I am listening now. (To a Sky-Lark) V32:252

their dinnerware. (Portrait of a Couple at Century's End) V24:214–215

their guts or their brains? (Southbound on the Freeway) V16:158

Then chiefly lives. (Virtue) V25:263

There are blows in life, so hard ... I just don't know! (The Black Heralds) V26:47

There is the trap that catches noblest spirits, that caught— they say— God, when he walked on earth (Shine, Perishing Republic) V4:162

there was light (Vancouver Lights) V8:246

They also serve who only stand and wait." ([On His Blindness] Sonnet 16) V3:262

They also serve who only stand and wait." (When I Consider (Sonnet XIX)) V37:302

They are going to some point true and unproven. (Geometry) V15:68

They have not sown, and feed on bitter fruit. (A Black Man Talks of Reaping) V32:21

They rise, they walk again (The Heaven of Animals) V6:76

They say a child with two mouths is no good. (Pantoun for Chinese Women) V29:242

They think I lost. I think I won (Harlem Hopscotch) V2:93

They'd eaten every one." (The Walrus and the Carpenter) V30:258–259

This is my page for English B (Theme for English B) V6:194

This Love (In Memory of Radio) V9:145

Tho' it were ten thousand mile! (A Red, Red Rose) V8:152

Though I sang in my chains like the sea (Fern Hill) V3:92

Till human voices wake us, and we drown (The Love Song of J. Alfred Prufrock) V1:99

Till Love and Fame to nothingness do sink (When I Have Fears that I May Cease to Be) V2:295

Till the gossamer thread you fling catch somewhere, O my soul. (A Noiseless Patient Spider) V31:190–91

To an admiring Bog! (I'm Nobody! Who Are You?) V35:83

To be a queen! (Fear) V37:71

To every woman a happy ending (Barbie Doll) V9:33

to float in the space between. (The Idea of Ancestry) V36:138

to glow at midnight. (The Blue Rim of Memory) V17:39

to its owner or what horror has befallen the other shoe (A Piéd) V3:16

To live with thee and be thy love. (The Nymph's Reply to the Shepherd) V14:241

To mock the riddled corpses round Bapaume. ("Blighters") V28:3

To strengthen whilst one stands." (Goblin Market) V27:96

To strive, to seek, to find, and not to yield (Ulysses) V2:279

To the moaning and the groaning of the bells (The Bells) V3:47

To the temple, singing. (In the Suburbs) V14:201

To wound myself upon the sharp edges of the night? (The Taxi) V30:211–212

too. (Birdfoot's Grampa) V36:21

torn from a wedding brocade. (My Mother Combs My Hair) V34:133

Turned to that dirt from whence he sprung. (A Satirical Elegy on the Death of a Late Famous General) V27:216

U

Undeniable selves, into your days, and beyond. (The Continuous Life) V18:51

under each man's eyelid. (Camouflaging the Chimera) V37:21

unexpectedly. (Fragment 16) V38:62

until at last I lift you up and wrap you within me. (It's like This) V23:138–139

Until Eternity. (The Bustle in a House) V10:62

unusual conservation (Chocolates) V11:17

Uttering cries that are almost human (American Poetry) V7:2

W

War is kind (War Is Kind) V9:253

watching to see how it's done. (I Stop Writing the Poem) V16:58

water. (Poem in Which My Legs Are Accepted) V29:262

We are satisfied, if you are; but why did I die? (Losses) V31:167–68

we tread upon, forgetting. Truth be told. (Native Guard) V29:185

Went home and put a bullet through his head (Richard Cory) V4:117

Were not the one dead, turned to their affairs. (Out, Out—) V10:213

Were toward Eternity— (Because I Could Not Stop for Death) V2:27

What will survive of us is love. (An Arundel Tomb) V12:18

When I died they washed me out of the turret with a hose (The Death of the Ball Turret Gunner) V2:41

When locked up, bear down. (Fable for When There's No Way Out) V38:43

When the plunging hoofs were gone. (The Listeners) V39:136

when they untie them in the evening. (Early in the Morning) V17:75

when you are at a party. (Social Life) V19:251

When you have both (Toads) V4:244

Where deep in the night I hear a voice (Butcher Shop) V7:43

Where ignorant armies clash by night (Dover Beach) V2:52

Which Claus of Innsbruck cast in bronze for me! (My Last Duchess) V1:166

Which for all you know is the life you've chosen. (The God Who Loves You) V20:88

which is not going to go wasted on me which is why I'm telling you

about it (Having a Coke with You) V12:106

which only looks like an *l*, and is silent. (Trompe l'Oeil) V22:216

whirring into her raw skin like stars (Uncoiling) V35:277

white ash amid funereal cypresses (Helen) V6:92

Who are you and what is your purpose? (The Mystery) V15:138

Why am I not as they? (Lineage) V31:145–46

Wi' the Scots lords at his feit (Sir Patrick Spens) V4:177

Will always be ready to bless the day (Morning Walk) V21:167

will be easy, my rancor less bitter . . . (On the Threshold) V22:128

Will hear of as a god." (How we Heard the Name) V10:167

Wind, like the dodo's (Bedtime Story) V8:33

windowpanes. (View) V25:246–247

With courage to endure! (Old Stoic) V33:144

With gold unfading, WASHINGTON! be thine. (To His Excellency General Washington) V13:213

with my eyes closed. (We Live by What We See at Night) V13:240

With silence and tears. (When We Two Parted) V29:297

with the door closed. (Hanging Fire) V32:93

With the slow smokeless burning of decay (The Wood-Pile) V6:252

With what they had to go on. (The Conquerors) V13:67

Without cease or doubt sew the sweet sad earth. (The Satyr's Heart) V22:187

Would scarcely know that we were gone. (There Will Come Soft Rains) V14:301

Wrapped in a larger. (Words are the Diminution of All Things) V35:316

Y

Ye know on earth, and all ye need to know (Ode on a Grecian Urn) V1:180

Yea, beds for all who come. (Up-Hill) V34:280

You live in this, and dwell in lovers' eyes (Sonnet 55) V5:246

You may for ever tarry. (To the Virgins, to Make Much of Time) V13:226

you who raised me? (The Gold Lily) V5:127

You're all that I can call my own. (Woman Work) V33:289

you'll have understood by then what these Ithakas mean. (Ithaka) V19:114